Tutorial

ADVANCED
COMPUTER ARCHITECTURE

Dharma P. Agrawal

IEEE Computer Society Order Number 667
Library of Congress Number 86-80958
IEEE Catalog Number EH0246-9
ISBN 0-8186-0667-3

 IEEE COMPUTER SOCIETY   THE INSTITUTE OF ELECTRICAL AND ELECTRONICS ENGINEERS, INC.   COMPUTER SOCIETY PRESS

IEEE

Published by IEEE Computer Society Press
1730 Massachusetts Avenue, N.W.
Washington, D.C. 20036-1903

COVER DESIGNED BY JACK I. BALLESTERO

IEEE Computer Society Order Number 667
Library of Congress Number 86-80958
IEEE Catalog Number EH0246-9
ISBN 0-8186-0667-3 (Paper)
ISBN 0-8186-4667-5 (Microfiche)

Order from: IEEE Computer Society
Post Office Box 80452
Worldway Postal Center
Los Angeles, CA 90080

IEEE Service Center
44 Hoes Lane
Piscataway, NJ 08854

 THE INSTITUTE OF ELECTRICAL AND ELECTRONICS ENGINEERS, INC.

Preface

Since computer architecture is considered to be an area that bridges the gap between digital hardware and computer software, substantial work has been done to provide a good interface between the two disciplines. Current research activities in computer architecture have been greatly influenced by recent advances in VLSI technology and by demand for increased computational power. In fact, national and international interest is currently focused on the development of a high-performance system that could provide a quantum increase in computational speed over conventional systems. With several issues involved, an appropriate selection or combination of various factors might provide much needed speed enhancement. Many of these concepts are based on parallel and concurrent processing techniques. A thorough investigation is needed before defining architecture of future systems. This tutorial is an outcome of such a need.

This tutorial emphasizes the importance of a close interaction between hardware and software and the impact of parallel and distributed processing and VLSI technology on the architecture has been clearly shown. The tutorial is organized into 10 chapters, each consisting of one to five papers. Introductory remarks and additional references are given at the beginning of each chapter. Various chapters are organized in such a way that there is continuity and a smooth transition from one subject to another. Additional references are appended at the end of each chapter so that interested readers could have easy access to relevant publications.

Chapter 1 provides an introduction and a review of classification schemes for computer architectures. Detailed technical descriptions of architectures for important existing machines are given in Chapter 2, while some of the proposed machine architectures have been included in Chapter 3. Design of arithmetic units and various performance enhancement techniques in performing arithmetic functions, including microprogramming, constitute Chapter 4.

In a parallel processing environment, interconnection networks are crucial for interprocessor communication. Thus, different strategies have to be employed for multiprocessor- and multicomputer-based systems. One type of network utilizes multiple programmable stages of smaller switches, while others need dedicated links between a pair of computers. These two broad categories of networks are described in Chapters 5 and 7, respectively.

Other related design issues, software partitioning techniques, scheduling of processes to processors, and the performance of two different types of network-based systems, are included in Chapters 6 and 8.

The effect of VLSI is seen in various fields and some of the VLSI-based regular structures and their impact on architecture are described in Chapter 9.

Strategies for defining architectures for specialized applications are discussed in Chapter 10.

I would like to thank various individuals for making this task possible. The IEEE-CS Press Editorial Board and other IEEE-CS Press staff have always provided the needed help and valuable guidance. My sincere thanks go to Dr. N.A. Masnari, our department chairman, for his constant encouragement. Imad Mahgoub helped me in collecting references and reprints of the papers.

I also thank Melanie Gay for her secretarial help and Sharon Nesbitt in revising the introductory material for each chapter. Finally, I am indebted to all of the students in my ECE 691 class who gave me enough feedback and inspiration to produce this tutorial text. I am also grateful to the IEEE Computer Society for providing the opportunity to prepare this tutorial, which, I hope, will be useful to the general community in the architecture area, including supercomputers.

Tutorial Text on Advanced Computer Architecture

Objectives:

Computer architecture is expected to cover the gap between digital hardware and computer software. This tutorial will emphasize the importance of such a close interaction, and the impact of parallel/distributed processing and VLSI technology will be clearly shown. Other important issues include examination of tradeoffs in the design of supercomputers and potential advantages of unique architectural concepts. Strategies for evaluating system performance will also be covered.

Audience:

This tutorial is meant for system designers, application engineers, scientists, researchers, and students who would like to know more about new emerging architectures and who would like to realize the impact of VLSI technology and parallel/distributed processing techniques. Some background in computer organization/architecture will be assumed.

Table of Contents

Chapter 1: Introduction

Computer architecture is an area that interacts closely with both digital hardware and computer software. The necessity of such a close interaction has always been emphasized. The introduction of several processing units in a single system adds to the importance of computer architecture, which is accentuated when different control mechanisms, data storage schemes, and other techniques are used for improved performance, which leads to increased use of concurrent execution of instructions and processing of multiple data streams, which in turn has an impact on computer architecture.

Several alternative methods of organization with varying degrees of complexity and capabilities encourage the need for classifying computer systems.[1-5] A brief history and evolution of various architectures has been covered recently.[6] Different attributes and strategies are used in characterizing various architectures. Flynn's classification[1] is based on the way an instruction stream is executed on a data stream; the multiplicity of such streams leads to the following four schemes:

SISD: Single instruction stream: Single data stream

SIMD: Single instruction stream: Multiple data stream

MISD: Multiple instruction stream: Single data stream

MIMD: Multiple instruction stream: Multiple data stream

Various extensions to these have been made to allow distinction between real implementations. Handler[5] compares several alternative ways of describing the architecture and introduces a more comprehensive scheme. A comparison of two-processor schemes is provided by Mehra et al.[7] while a survey of parallel machine organizations is given by Kuck.[8] A taxonomy of computer architecture, based on the data type[9] and also other parameters[10-12] of architecture has been discussed. Hufnagel[13] and Thurber[14-15] offer comparisons of selected arrays and parallel architectures.

An alternative taxonomy[16] is based on the characteristics of various parallel computing modules and categorizes different architectures as microprogrammed versus other designs, pipelined uniprocessors, array processors, nonhomogeneous (multifunction) multiprocessors, and homogeneous multiprocessors. Some of the other considerations in such a categorization are synchronous versus asynchronous nature of systems, memory architecture (shared or private memory and loosely- or tightly-coupled hierarchy), memory hierarchy (number of levels, relative speed and cost, data transfer efficiencies/inefficiencies between various levels), virtual memory (size, placement, and coherency of multiple caches), and memory and/or processor interconnection topology (static or dynamic, shared bus, cross bar, multistage networks, multiple buses or hypercube structures, etc.). Some of the software considerations include the scheduling strategy, degree of parallelism, granularity of computation, synchronization primitives, fixed or roving supervisor, input-output handling techniques, etc.

The advances in VLSI technology, increased use of special-purpose architectures, and a better understanding of artificial intelligence have led to new and exciting projects. An enhanced system availability through extensive parallelism has led to two important measures of MIPS (millions of instructions per second) and MFLOPS (millions of floating point operations per second). Emphasis has also been given to reduced cost per computation and guaranteed allocation of system bandwidth by appropriate load balancing. Attempts also have been made to define the architecture for the next generation of computers. Details of several fifth-generation computer systems and supercomputers are described.[17-26]

In organizing this tutorial, we have carefully considered the continuity of the subject matter and concentrated on just a few topics in each chapter. Thus, we were forced to take into account only a few classification parameters. In particular, Chapters 5 through 8 consist of papers dealing only with static versus dynamic networks and multiprocessors with shared versus private memories. An attempt has also been made to include a case study paper in each chapter.

One paper is included in Chapter 1 to characterize the classification of various architectures.

References

1 M.J. Flynn, "Some Computer Organizations and Their Effectiveness," *IEEE Trans. Computers*, Vol. C-21, No. 9, Sept. 1972, pp. 948-960.

2 P.H. Enslow (ed.), *Multiprocessors and Parallel Processing*, Wiley-Interscience, New York, N.Y., 1974.

3 T. Feng, "Some Characteristics of Associative/Parallel Processing," *Proc. 1972 Sagamore Computer Conf.*, IEEE Computer Society, Washington, D.C., 1972, pp. 5-16.

4 P.H. Enslow, "Multiprocessor Organization," *Computing Surveys*, Vol. 9, No. 1, March 1977, pp. 103-129.

5 W. Händler, "The Impact of Classification Schemes on Computer Architecture," *Proc. 1977 Int'l. Conf. Parallel Processing*, IEEE Computer Society, Washington, D.C., 1977, pp. 7-15.

6 J.L. Baet, "Computer Architecture," *Computer*, Vol. 17, No. 10, Oct. 1984, pp. 77-87.

7 S.K. Mehra, J.W. Wong, and J.C. Majithia, "A Comparative Study of Some Two-Processor Organizations," *IEEE Trans. Computers*, Vol. C-29, No. 1, Jan. 1980, pp. 44-49.

8 D.J. Kuck, "A Survey of Parallel Machine Organization and Programming," *ACM Computing Surveys*, Vol. 9, No. 1, March 1977, pp. 29-59.

9 W.K. Giloi, "Towards a Taxonomy of Computer Architecture Based on the Machine Data Type View," *Proc. 10th Ann. Int'l. Symp. Computer Architecture*, IEEE Computer Society, Washington, D.C., 1983, pp. 6-15.

10 R. Lee, "Empirical Results on the Speed, Efficiency, Redundancy and Quality of Parallel Computations," *Proc. 1980 Int'l. Conf. Parallel Processing*, IEEE Computer Society, Washington, D.C., 1980, pp. 91-96.

11 A. Tanenbaum, "Implication of Structured Programming for Computer Architecture, *Comm. of ACM*, Vol. 21, No. 3, March 1978, pp. 237-246.

12 K. Krishna and K. Kriishnamohan "Architectural Quality," *ACM Computer Architecture News*, Vol. 12, No. 1, March 1984, pp. 64-72.

13 S. Hufnagel, "Comparison of Selected Array Processor Architecture," *Computer Design*, Vol. 18, No. 3, March 1979, pp. 151-158.

14 K.J. Thurber, "Parallel Processor Architectures, Part I: General Purpose Systems," *Computer Design*, Vol. 18, No. 1, Jan. 1979, pp. 89-97.

15 K.J. Thurber, "Parallel Processor Architectures, Part II: Special Purpose Systems," *Computer Design*, Vol. 18, No. 2, Feb. 1979, pp. 103-114.

16 D.P. Rodgers, "Improvements in Multiprocessor System Design," *Proc. 12th Int'l. Symp. Computer Architecture*, IEEE Computer Society, Washington, D.C., 1985, pp. 225-231.

17 T. Moto-Oko, "Overview to the Fifth Generation Computer System Project," *Proc. 10th Ann. Symp. Computer Architecture*, IEEE Computer Society, Washington, D.C., 1983, pp. 417-422.

18 N.R. Lincoln, "Supercomputers - Colossal Computations + Enormous Expectations + Renowned Risk," *Computer*, Vol. 16, No. 5, May 1983, pp. 38-47.

19 P.C. Treleaven and I.G. Lima, "Future Computers: Logic, Dataflow, . . . , Control Flow?" *Computer*, Vol. 17, No. 3, March 1984, pp. 47-48.

20 C. Norrie, "Supercomputers for Superproblems: An Architectural Introduction," *Computer*, Vol. 17, No. 3, March 1984, pp. 67-74.

21 E.E. Swartzlander, Jr. and B.K. Gilbert, "Super-Systems: Technology and Architecture," *IEEE Trans. Computers*, Vol. C-31, No. 5, May 1982, pp. 399-409.

22 J.O. Ullman, "Flux, Sorting and Supercomputer Organization for AI Applications," *Journal of Parallel and Distributed Computing*, Vol. 1, No. 2, Nov. 1984, pp. 133-151.

23 R.W. Hockney, "Characterizing Computers and Optimizing the FACR (L) Poisson-Solver on Parallel Unicomputers," *IEEE Trans. Computers*, Vol. C-32, No. 10, Oct. 1983, pp. 933-941.

24 G. Rodrigue, E.O. Giroux, and M. Pratt, "A Multicriteria Approach to Supersystem Architecture Definition," *IEEE Trans. Computers*, Vol. C-31, No. 5, May 1982, pp. 410-418.

25 J.P. Ignizio, D.F. Palmer, and C.M. Murphy, "A Multicriteria Approach to Supersystem Definition," *IEEE Trans. Computers*, Vol. C-31, No. 5, May 1982, pp. 410-418.

26 J.P. Riganati and P.B. Schneck, "Supercomputing," *Computer*, Vol. 17, No. 10, Oct. 1984, pp. 97-113.

THE IMPACT OF CLASSIFICATION SCHEMES ON COMPUTER ARCHITECTURE

Wolfgang Händler*

Universidade Estadual de Campinas
Instituto de Matemática, Estatística e Ciência da Computação
Campinas S.P., Brasil

1. Remarks on
Classification Schemes and Formal Systems

Classification schemes, languages, and formal systems of all kinds have a considerable influence on our thinking. Structures which are inherently the subject-matter of a language as well as of classification schemes form the basic material of what can be expressed in a language or can be comprehended from its position in a classification scheme. The same statement seems to be valid for formal systems in a more specific sense. Thus the tool can be used in the application area for which it was created.

For example the Ricci-Calculus performs this role only in the area for which it was created, certain areas of physics and partial differential equations. Outside this area problems arise for which it is not suitable.

B. Whorf has said that language guides thought [11] and that therefore language sometimes prevents the appropriate solution of a problem being found. We must admit that in many cases a language (it can be referred to as a calculus or notation) can be a barrier rather than an aid in solving a problem. It is also true that a classification scheme can be a barrier, although it can provide an insight into the relationships between the elements of some group.

If such a classification scheme is to be applied to animals and plants, then the elements are existing objects and the scheme cannot completely fail, although the discovery of a new species can present difficulties in fitting it into an existing classification scheme. Such a scheme can be called a taxonomy, since all the species are considered to be descended from a single species, in accordance with the biological theory of evolution.

It seems more difficult to create a classification scheme, or even a taxonomy, for some area of contemporary technology. It is necessary to project future advances as well as placing existing examples in it.

---

*On sabbatical leave from: Institut für Mathematische Maschinen und Datenverarbeitung (III), University of Erlangen-Nuremberg, Martensstr. 3, D-8520 Erlangen, Fed. Republic of Germany.

The aim of this paper is to show that some existing schemes may fail to indicate the right direction for the development of computer architecture, as compared with a new and promising classification scheme introduced in [3], [4]. We would, however, not claim that the proposed classification scheme will cover all computer structures which will arise in the future. We do show that the proposed scheme does cover several very interesting structures which cannot be placed at an appropriate point in the scheme of Flynn [1] and Feng [2].

The justification of the proposed scheme is that it should be useful in classifying structures and concepts which will emerge in the next years, and be of use to the designers of these structures. A further justification of the scheme is that the elements of the classification scheme can be composed and decomposed by operations which are suitable for the purposes of the computer architect.

2. Contemporary Classification Schemes

Existing classification schemes differ in the information on which they are based. For instance M. Flynn [1] bases his scheme on a 'data stream' and an 'instruction stream'. By combining these simple concepts he can classify many of the new computer structures. In contrast, Feng [2] emphasises the number of bits which are processed simultaneously. These schemes are outlined in sections 2.1 and 2.2 in order to contrast them with the scheme outlined in chapter 3. In section 2.3 the definitions of multiprocessing proposed by the American National Standards Institute [5] and by Enslow [6] are discussed.

2.1 Flynn's Classification

Flynn proposed in 1966 a classification based on the instruction streams and data streams. In the conventional Princeton type computer a single data stream is processed by a single instruction stream. This is described as SISD (single instruction single data).

In an array computer such as ILLIAC IV, a single instruction stream processes many data streams. Such a computer is known as SIMD (single instruction multiple data). In ILLIAC IV 64 copies

Reprinted from *Proceedings of the 1977 International Conference on Parallel Processing*, 1977, pages 7-15. Copyright © 1977 by The Institute of Electrical and Electronics Engineers, Inc.

of the same instruction are executed simultaneously by 64 arithmetic units. The Goodyear STARAN is also a SIMD computer. It differs from ILLIAC IV in many respects, in particular in being an associative array processor.

MISD is an abbreviation for multiple instruction single data. Some authors include various types of pipeline computers in this class though it is doubtful whether this is appropriate, and it is unsatisfactory because it does not distinguish between the three kinds of pipelining (see section 3.3 below).

MIMD is an abbreviation for multiple instruction multiple data. Here multiple processors are working on multiple data streams. The simplest case is where each processor is executing its own program on its own data. The processors can be connected via a bus system or can access multi-port memory. The classification does not contain any information about the type of connection used.

Flynn's classification is illustrated by fig. 1, where many contemporary computers can be classified by assigning them to one of the four vertices of a graph. However, the classification does not fully satisfy the needs of computer architects because it is not fine enough and because the interpretation of the class MISD is not clear (cf. [7]). In the literature many authors restrict themselves to the classes SISD, SIMD, and MIMD. A further difficulty occurs if a computer contains both parallelism and pipelining.

2.2 Feng's classification

Feng [2] classifies according to the wordlength, i.e. the number of bits which are processed in parallel in a word, and the number of words which are processed in parallel. A computer structure is represented by a point in a plane (fig.2) where the abscissa is the wordlength (normally 12, 16, 24, 32, 48, 60 or 64), and the ordinate is the number of words processed in parallel. The latter can be determined by the number of processors. For example C.mmp which contains 16 PDP-11's with wordlength 16 bits is represented by (16,16). The ordinate can also be determined by the number of arithmetic and logical units in an array processor. Thus ILLIAC IV is represented by (64,64).

Thus Feng's classification does not allow to distinguish between multiprocessors like C.mmp and array processors. This caused Enslow [7] to represent C.mmp in "gang" mode by (16,256). But C.mmp in gang mode can be regarded as similar to ILLIAC IV, with 16 ALU's executing a single program, which would give the point (16,16) which is the same as when gang mode is not used. The classification also does not distinguish between autonomous processors which execute programs and ALU's which execute operations, i.e. it does not distinguish between processing levels.

The TIASC (Texas Instruments Advanced Scientific Computer) is represented as (64,2048). The number 2048 os obtained from the 4 pipelines each consisting of 8 stages with 64 bits. However the

number 2048 can be obtained in many ways, e.g. 8 pipelines, 8 stages, 32 bits. Thus the classification cannot represent a multiple pipeline structure like the TIASC accurately.

It is also not possible to represent the pipeline structure at the program level of PEPE. PEPE is characterized as (32,16), and the fact that each set of data (up to 288, each representing a flying object) is processed successively in three different ways is not represented. This is performed in three separate series of ALU's, and we can regard this as a three stage macropipeline (cf. section 3.3).

The lack of a rigorous definition of pipelining in the context of Feng's classification scheme leads to difficulties in classifying structures containing both pipelining and parallelism. Thus the scheme is not entirely satisfactory for the computer architect either.

2.3 Definition of Multiprocessing

Similarly to classification schemes, if definitions are too narrow, some viable computer structures may be excluded from consideration.

The American National Standards Institute [5] defines a multiprocessor as:

"A computer employing two or more processing units under integrated control." Manufacturers of systems containing two to four processors did not find themselves in conflict with this definition. The definition did not exclude future developments in computer architecture, but does not seem to have had any impact on contemporary architecture. Subsequently Enslow suggested a more detailed definition in his excellent book [6] which included

1. two or more processors, having access to a common memory, whereby private memory is not excluded,

2. shared I/O,

3. a single integrated operating system,

4. hardware and software interactions at all levels,

5. the execution of a job must be possible on different processors,

6. hardware interrupts.

We will concentrate on the first characteristic:

A common memory is mandatory. Such a structure is shown in fig. 3. It is easily seen that as the number of processors increases the congestion in the access to the common memory will also increase. Thus Enslow's definition seems to exclude systems containing very large numbers of processors. Microprocessors costing a few dollars are now available, so that systems containing thousands of processors are now possible. Some of the more progressive projects of computer architecture such as PRIME [9] are also excluded. On the other hand some structures which satisfy Enslow's definition are subject to severe limitations on their expandibility and application due to their use of an expensive crossbar switch [10].

Thus Enslow's definition does not either satisfy the requirements of contemporary computer architecture.

2.4 The Influence of Classification Schemes and Definitions

We have tried to show in the previous sections that definitions and classification schemes have their limitations and can prove a hindrance beyond a certain point. The computer architect should recognize when this point has been reached, and consider whether an entirely new classification scheme or definition is needed, which will ideally include all existing structures within a particular area and also all structures which will be considered in this area in the future. There is no doubt that one should consider very carefully the consequences of introducing a new classification, because of its possible educational and normative effects.

3. The Erlangen Classification Scheme

3.1 Introduction

The Erlangen classification scheme (ECS) was developed mainly in order to avoid the drawbacks of existing classification schemes, as outlined in section 2.

The basic requirements are

1. the objects to be classified should not be unnecessarily restricted. Any kind of computer system - in particular parallel processors, array processors, multiprocessors, pipeline processors must be classifiable in the scheme;

2. the classification must be sufficiently fine to express those differences between the objects considered important;

3. the classification must be unambiguous.

The classification scheme developed was also found to be a useful technique in computer architecture, in the sense that:

4. Composed computer configurations can be described by using operators which are applied to primitive elements of the scheme.

5. It can be used in evaluating architectural configurations, in particular with reference to cost.

6. It provides a measure for the flexibility of a system.

7. It provides a starting point for scheduling

of flexible structures.

The objects of the classification are not necessarily computers only. This will be amplified below. The flexibility mentioned in 6. above is connected with the fact that a computer can be represented by more than one point in the classification. The various points which represent a computer will be referred to as modes. The more modes a computer has, the more choice of mode it has for a particular application, and so the greater is its flexibility.

The classification scheme can be used for algorithms as well as for computers, and demonstrates the inherent partitioning of the algorithm into parallel sections and pipeline stages. The classification of algorithms must then be related to the classification of the computers on which they are to be run. In general, jobs must be investigated to identify the classes of the algorithms contained, and matched to the classes of the computers on which they are to be run. A more detailed discussion of this question will be given in another paper.

3.2 Parallelism

Our classification aims at characterizing the parallelism and pipelining present in a computer system. The connections between the processors and the memory blocks are not included in the classification. It is assumed that the connections can carry the expected traffic and provide the required availability. In such a case the performance of the system is mainly determined by the processors, including their capability to transfer information.

The classification is based on the distinction between three processing levels:

1. Program control unit - Using a program counter and some other registers, and, in most cases, a microprogram device, the PCU interprets a program instruction by instruction.

2. Arithmetic and logical unit - The ALU uses the output signals of a microprogram device to execute sequences of microinstructions according to the interpretation process performed by the PCU.

3. Elementary logic circuit - Each of the microoperations which make up the microoperation set initiates an elementary switching process. The logic circuits belonging to one bit position of all the microoperations are called an ELC.

A computer configuration can include a number of PCU's. Each PCU can control a number of ALU's all of which perform the same operation at any given time. Finally, each ALU contains a number of ELC's, each dedicated to one bit position. The number of ECL's is commonly known as the wordlength.

If we disregard pipelining for the moment, the number of PCU's, ALU's per PCU, and ELC's per

ALU form a triple, written

$$t \text{ (computer type)} = (k, d, w).$$

We give some examples of the triple, where we assume that the reader is familiar with at least some of the computers:

$t(\text{MINIMA}) = (1,1,1)$

The "classical" serial computer. Some early European computers were of this form.

$t(\text{IBM701}) = (1,1,36)$

An example of the early "parallel" (on the 3rd level) Princeton computers.

$t(\text{SOLOMON}) = (1,1024,1)$

The historical concept of an array processor.

$t(\text{ILLIAC IV}) = (1,64,64)$

The famous array processor developed at the University of Illinois (without PDP 10).

$t(\text{STARAN}) = (1,8192,1)$

The well-known associative array processor (without host and sequential control processor) fully extended (32 frames of 256 bits each).

$t(\text{C.mmp}) = (16,1,16)$

The Carnegie-Mellon University mulit-mini project using 16 PDP-11's.

$t(\text{PRIME}) = (5,1,16)$

The University of California, Berkeley, project in which time-sharing is replaced by multi-processing.

The different systems exhibit different kinds of parallelism, which is uniquely attached to one of the three levels. The numbers which make up the triple show this directly.

At first sight, the triples are able to classify all viable structures, particularly in regard to parallelism. But although parallelism is the most important phenomenon in contemporary computer architecture, pipelining must also be considered. The examples above exhibit parallelism but not pipelining. In the next section the classification is extended to include pipelining.

3.3 Pipelining

Pipelining can also be implemented at the three levels described in section 3.2, i.e. 1. PCU, 2. ALU, and 3. ELC.

For example level 3 pipelining is the well-known pipelining of the arithmetic unit used in the CD STAR-100 and the TIASC. The STAR-100 uses a four stage pipeline and the TIASC an eight stage pipeline.

An arithmetical pipeline can be regarded as a "vertical" replication of ECL's, compared with the "horizontal" replication used in a parallel ECL. It is therefore reasonable to multiply the number of ECL's, w, by the number of stages in the pipeline, w', to characterize the ALU. For the TIASC we have then

$$t(\text{TIASC}) = (1,4,64 \times 8).$$

The multiplication sign will be used at all levels to separate the number representing the degree of parallelism from the number representing the number of stages in the pipeline.

The next higher level of pipelining is instruction pipelining. This involves the existence of a number of function units which can operate simultaneously to process a single instruction stream. It is based on the inspection of instructions prior to execution to identify those instructions which can be executed simultaneously without conflict. This is done by a scoreboard, in the terminology of Control Data. These instructions are executed as soon as a suitable function unit is free. This technique is referred to as "instruction lookahead", "instruction pipelining", or "parallelism of function units".

A classical example of this kind is the CD 6600 computer. Disregarding for the moment the input-output section (i.e. the peripheral processors), the internal structure of CD 6600 with 10 function units becomes:

$$t(\text{CD 6600 central proc.}) = (1,1 \times 10,60).$$

The 10 units in this case are highly specialized (e.g. floating point multiplication, integer addition, incrementation, etc.) and therefore a gain of a factor of 10 cannot be achieved. The real factor depends on the special program actually running. An average of 2.6 is a typical figure according to information available from Control Data. A combination of several function units of the same type seems to be quite reasonable regarding the better utilization of equipment on the one hand and the now available large-scale integration technology on the other hand. These latter considerations nevertheless are not directly a subject of this paper.

Finally, we have to consider the pipelining concept of level 1, which is so far not very known. This concept can be called "macro-pipelining"[12]. Assuming that a data set has to be processed by two different tasks sequentially, then it can be performed in two different processors, each one processing one task. The data stream then passes the first processor (1. task), is stored in a memory block, which the second processor also has access to, and will then pass the second processor (2. task). Since both processors can work at the same time (on different data), the effective processing speed can be in an ideal case doubled in comparison with the use of only one processor.

In such a way stepping from processor to processor data are 'refined' [12] on one hand or are 'integrated' [13, 8] in the case of ordinary differential equations on the other hand.

The PEPE array (without the host installation) then is characterized as

t(PEPE) = (1×3,288,32) (3-fold macropipelining).

Summarizing now, the triple has been extended to a sixtuple to incorporate pipelining. Nevertheless, we keep calling it a triple because the three levels of consideration (as introduced in 3.2) suggest that we think in three terms, which have to be extended in some cases by an additional term, attached to the other value (of the same level) by using the sign ×.

The triple now reads as follows:

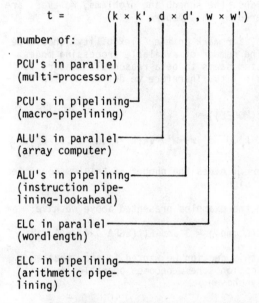

t =   (k × k', d × d', w × w')

number of:

PCU's in parallel
(multi-processor)

PCU's in pipelining
(macro-pipelining)

ALU's in parallel
(array computer)

ALU's in pipelining
(instruction pipe-
lining-lookahead)

ELC in parallel
(wordlength)

ELC in pipelining
(arithmetic pipe-
lining)

All entities are independent of one another. All combinations therefore can appear.

Regarding the 'completeness' we claimed in section 3.1, we would have to prove that, apart from the three levels mentioned in section 3.2, no essential other level can be defined, and that there are also no phenomena apart from parallelism and pipelining. This is not pointed out in detail here, because this paper centers on another point, the impact of classification schemes on computer architecture. But there is some evidence regarding the completeness of our classification. While there are some modifications in details, how the level 2 pipelining is designed, there are no doubts about the other levels. With respect to parallelism and pipelining there is an exclusive duality as is known from other fields of science where parallelism and serialism also appear.

Regarding the triple notation, we introduced the following simplifications:

k=1, or k'=1, or d=1 etc. mean, respectively, the simple cases, in which no parallelism or pipelining appear;

we write then

(1×k',d×d',w×w') = (×k', d×d', w×w')
$$\qquad\qquad\qquad\qquad\qquad \text{if } k' \neq 1$$

(k×1,d×d',w×w') = (k,d×d', w×w')

(k×k',1×d',w×w') = (k×k',×d',w×w')
$$\qquad\qquad\qquad\qquad\qquad \text{if } d' \neq 1$$

(k×k',d×1,w×w') = (k×k',d,w×w')

(k×k',d×d',1×w') = (k×k',d×d',×w')
$$\qquad\qquad\qquad\qquad\qquad \text{if } w' \neq 1$$

(k×k',d×d',w×1) = (k×k',d×d',w)

If there is any form of pipelining then the character × is preserved in the corresponding level. In the case of no pipelining the triple degenerates to

t(MODEL) = (k,d,w).

This convention contributes to the clearness considerably as well as to the transparency of notation. Therefore we will use this convention in the following.

3.4 Operations on Triples

As a triple characterizes a computer structure of a certain homogeneity, a combination of triples connected by an operator can denote

a) a more complex computer structure
   (as given e.g. by a special I/O section
   of processors or by a special host,
   which are connected to a specific computer configuration);

b) a selection of operation modes of a
   structure, which can be used alternatively, fitting to different needs,
   according to the algorithmic nature
   of different applications.

It should be noted in connexion with b) that for any application there can exist a number of algorithms, each one fitting a different computer structure. E.g. one algorithm which is a solution to a given problem can be highly suited for execution on a conventional Princeton type computer, while another may be better suited for a parallel or pipelining computer.

The forementioned computer CD 6600 would read its complete structure, using a multiplication sign ×:

t(CD 6600) = (10,1,12) × (1,×10,60).

The first term on the right hand side of "="

denotes the existence of ten processors of a simple structure with a wordlength of 12 bits. The second term is the characterization of the nucleus of the CD 6600, as it was given earlier. The multiplication sign visualizes the fact that all algorithms (programs) must be forwarded through the peripheral processors first, in order to be processed then in the central processor $(1,\times10,60)$.

Another example of contemporary computer architecture is PEPE (Parallel Element Processor Ensemble). Its host is one CD 7600 with the characteristic

$$t(CD\ 7600) = (15,1,12) \times (1,\times9,60).$$

PEPE then becomes

$$t(PEPE) = (15,1,12) \times (1,\times9,60) \times (\times3,288,32)$$

where the last term $(\times3,288,32)$ corresponds to the actual PEPE structure. As, in this example, a certain flow of information penetrates the three structures, the sign $\times$ is used between the corresponding terms.

The structures characterized by the primitive terms in these examples are very different. Therefore a further condensation of the presentation is not suggested. A further decomposition can be indicated, e.g. by the use of other operators, for instance in the special case of a CD 7600 by

$$(15,1,12) \times (1,\times9,60) =$$

$$\underbrace{[(1,1,12) + (1,1,12)+\ldots+(1,1,12)]}_{15\ times}\times(1,\times9,60),$$

where $\underbrace{(n,d,w) = (1,d,w)+(1,d,w)+\ldots(1,d,w)}_{n\ times}.$

We note that the operators $\times$ and $+$ again reflect parallelism and pipelining in a certain sense. The last example shows 15 equal processors allocated in parallel. A given job (or task) will be forwarded to the central processor. It may also be necessary to allocate processors serially, if there are different tasks to be performed one after another. This is supported by the use of functionally dedicated processors, specialized to the respective task.

The last operator we have proposed so far is the 'alternative' operator v, which is to be understood as an 'exclusive or'. For the C.mmp project which can be used in three different kinds of operation modes, an expression becomes:

$$t(C.mmp) = (16,1,16) \text{ v } (\times16,1,16) \text{ v } (1,16,16).$$

Similarly, the EGPA project (4×4 array of processors, 32 bits each, described e.g. in [13]) reads

$$t(EGPA\ 4\times4) = (16,1,32) \text{ v } (\times16,1,32) \text{ v }$$

$$(1,16,32) \text{ v } (1,512,1).$$

The last term of this expression denotes the operation mode "vertical processing" in which the 16 processors are used, each as if it consisted of 32 one-bit processors working in parallel. 16 processors then result in an ensemble consisting of 16×32 one-bit processors. Information then is oriented to one-bit vertical streams (items) and the machine-word of the memory becomes what is called a 'bit-slice' in associative processors.

The operator v visualizes alternatives regarding the processing modes which can basically be used. An extended operator $+$ can be used for a further partitioning of a system in which the ensemble is working. Scheduling algorithms have to be developed which have to centre on the best utilization of the system with respect to a given set of jobs. The scheduling problems, however, are not covered by this paper.

Yet, a remark on the 'flexibility' should be added. The number of available processing modes of a system seems to be a reasonable measure for its flexibility. Therefore we define (F=Flexibility):

$$F(t(MODEL)) =$$

$$\left| (k_1 \times k_1', d_1 \times d_1', w_1 \times w_1') \text{ v } (k_1 \times k_1', d_2 \times d_2', w_2 \times w_2') \text{v} \ldots \right|$$

where $||$ gives the number of triples connected by the v sign.

For the examples presented above we have:

$$F(t(C.mmp)) = 3 \text{ and } F(t(EGPA\ 4\times4))= 4.$$

In this section we wanted to show that a classification scheme becomes operable if it is carefully chosen.

Nevertheless, it is not the aim of this paper to introduce ECS[a] completely. We have used it as a further example of the discussion about the 'impact of classification schemes on computer architecture'.

4. Summary and Outlook

Some things which can be done with ECS (chapter 3), cannot be done with any of the systems mentioned earlier (chapter 2). Although we do not claim that ECS is the only possible classification scheme, we have found it useful for evaluating computer structures, throughput, flexibility etc.

In this respect ECS seems, as briefly presented here, to be an approach which can become a viable design tool. It classifies enough objects and it does not limit too seriously the set of objects.

---

[a] A rigid and more formal presentation of ECS is under preparation.

The only limitation we perceive so far is the inherently binary nature of the definition of w (wordlength). If a computer is based on another modulo-number system, then we would have to slightly modify the ECS as presented.

If, for historical reasons, we have to, for example, include the old mechanical calculating machines of Ch. Babbage, then it would be necessary to extend ECS. Also excluded from ECS are computers of the analogue type. But this limitation seems to be quite natural in that analogue data processing is quite different.

The only criticism which at this time can be made within the aims of this paper could center on the number of levels we introduced in chapter 3. There we defined a triple according to three processing levels. If perhaps in a later step of evolution a level above the program interpretation level will be created, then we would have to extend the triple to a quadruple.

But just this step to achieve a new level of computer structure is a real evolution step we are searching for at present. It was exactly for this that the classification scheme has been developed as a tool. About such an evolutionary step a decision cannot be made in advance. It is rather the ECS classification scheme and the operations defined on the elements (triples) which seem to be the appropriate starting point for investigations of that kind. We hope that ECS will not limit too narrowly a future development, for it includes all structures which so far have been proved as viable examples of computer architecture.

Acknowledgement

The assistance of Mr. R. K. Bell and Dr. V. Sigmund in the preparation of this paper is gratefully acknowledged.

References

[1] M. Flynn, "Very high computing systems", Proc. of the IEEE 54 (1966), 1901-1909.

[2] T. Feng, "Some characteristics of associative/parallel processing", Proc. of the 1972 Sagamore Comp. Conf., Syracuse University, 1972, 5-16.

[3] W. Händler, "On classification schemes for computers in the post-von-Neumann era", in: D. Siefkes (ed.), GI-4.Jahrestagung, Berlin, Okt. 1974, Lecture Notes in Computer Science 24, Springer, Berlin (1975), 439-452.

[4] W. Händler, "Zur Genealogie, Struktur und Klassifizierung von Rechnern", Parallelismus in der Informatik, Arbeitsberichte des IMMD, Universität Erlangen-Nürnberg, 9 (1976)/8, 1-30.

[5] "Vocabulary for Information Processing", American National Standard, X.3.12-1970.

[6] Ph. E. Enslow, Multiprocessor and Parallel Processing, John Wiley and Sons, New York, 1974.

[7] P. H. Enslow, "Multiprocessors and other parallel systems - an introduction and overview", W. Händler (ed.), Computer Architecture, Workshop of the GI, Erlangen, May 1975, Springer Verlag Berlin (1976), 133-198.

[8] W. Händler, "Aspects of Parallelism in Computer Architecture", Proc. of the IMACS (AICA)-GI-Symposium on Parallel Computers, Parallel Mathematics, Munich (March 1977), North Holland Amsterdam, to appear.

[9] H.B. Baskin, Borgerson and Roberts, "PRIME - a modular architecture for terminal-oriented systems", SJCC 1972, pp. 431-437.

[10] W.A. Wulf, C.G. Bell, "C.mmp - A Multi-Mini-Processor", AFIPS Conf. Proc. FJCC 1972 41, pp. 765-777.

[11] B. Whorf, "Language, Thought and Reality", M.I.T. Press, Cambridge, Massachusetts, 1963.

[12] W. Händler, "The concept of macro-pipelining with high availability", Elektronische Rechenanlagen 15 (1973), pp. 269-274.

[13] W. Händler, F. Hofmann, H.J. Schneider, "A General Purpose Array with a Broad Spectrum of Applications", W. Händler (ed.), Computer Architecture, cf. [7].

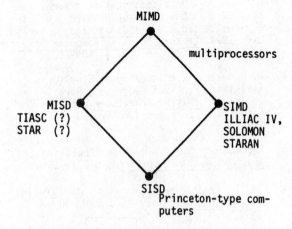

Fig. 1: M. Flynn's classification with some examples

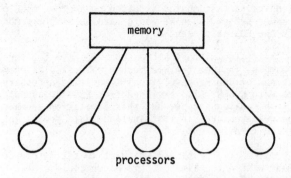

Fig. 3: P.E. Enslow's definition of a multiprocessor leads to "one common memory block" (private memory blocks, owned by a processor exclusively, are not excluded by the definition).

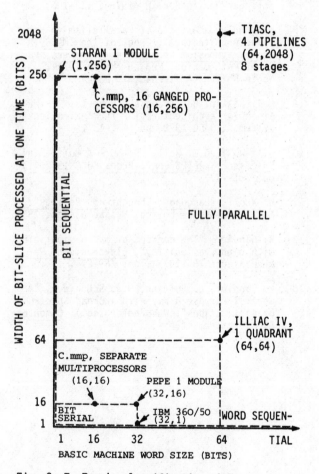

Fig. 2: T. Feng's classification with some examples

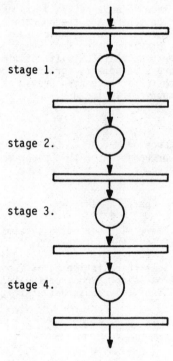

Execution of one instruction in 4 stages
$w'=4$

Fig. 4: Arithmetic pipelining (level 3 pipelining)

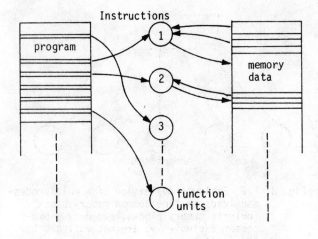

Fig. 5: Instruction-pipelining (level 2 pipelining)

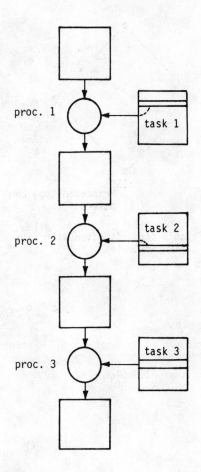

Fig. 6: Macropipelining (level 1 pipelining)

Chapter 2: Some Existing Architectures

The literature is replete with numerous architectures, but most of them remain just paper designs. This chapter covers some of the schemes that have been implemented.

Some of the projects, although close to being completed, were later abandoned because of various reasons. The Illiac IV[1] could be considered one of the initial important projects. Even though it is no longer in operation, it spurred the need for organized research activities, and many projects are attributed to the inspiration received from the results of research on Illiac-IV. Some of the other early designs include Texas Instruments' Advanced Scientific Computer[2], Carnegie-Mellon's Cm*[3], and IBM's 370[4]. Each one of these could be said to possess some specific characteristics, and pros and cons could be easily identified.

However, the design and use of these machines have enabled us to learn many useful lessons, that have everlasting influence on future design philosophies. Use of interleaving, pipelining, and multiple functional units has been extensively explored in the design of the first successful commercial vector computer CRAY-1[5] (and its variant[6]). Vectorization of loops and introduction of chaining concepts have further enhanced its capability and usefulness.

Many other issues have also been addressed[7-8]. Other vector computers are also described in[9-10]. A single instruction stream/multiple data stream (SIMD) type computer employing a large number of VLSI-based simple processors has been developed by the Goodyear Aerospace Corporation for NASA's application[11-16].

The flexibility in adjusting the word length makes MPP suitable for a variety of image processing algorithms wherein word length requirement in representing pixel intensity is application dependent. Its suitability for numerical[16] calculations has also been considered. Several new concepts including the use of prime numbers of memory modules and skewed storage of array data have been advocated in the design of the Burroughs Scientific Processor[17-19]. The machines in the MIMD (multiple instruction stream multiple data stream) category are the shared resource MIMD computer[20] and the HEP[21]. Denelcor HEP, the first commercially available MIMD computer, executes multiple pipelines of instructions in various processors. Another MIMD computer, known as Flex/32[22], has been designed to support different processor types and achieves interprocesser communication through a VME bus connection. The Flex/32 also employs extended concurrent C and concurrent FORTRAN 77 that allow concurrent high-level programming. The Texas Reconfiguration Array Computer[23] is the first system to use a multistage network in the form of the Banyan network, which provides a programmable data path between the processors and the shared memory modules. In this project, it has been observed that the complexity of switches requires larger PC-board area than the processors or memory modules themselves.

The advances in VLSI technology are reflected by the Inmos single-chip design[24] which contains four on-chip OMA channels and adequate memory storage; several such chips could be configured in several different topologies including mesh, tree, binary-cube, etc. Other multiprocessor organizations and highly parallel schemes are described elsewhere[25-29].

Five papers are included in this chapter to provide a general idea and wider representation of existing architectures.

References

1   W.K. Bouknigt et al., "The ILLIAC System," *Proc. IEEE*, Vol. 60, No. 4, April 1972, pp. 369-379.

2   Texas Instruments, Inc., "Description of the ASC System: Parts 1 to 5," *Manual Nos. 934662 and 934666*, Texas Instruments, 1971.

3   R.J. Swan, A. Bechtholsheim, K.W. Lai, and J.K. Ousterhout, "The Implementation of the Cm* Multimicroprocessor," *Proc. AFIPS 1977 Nat. Computer Conf.*, Vol. 46, AFIPS Press, Reston, Va., 1977, pp. 645-655.

4   A. Padegs, "System/370 Extended Architecture: Design Consideration," *IBM Journal of Research and Development*, Vol. 27, No. 2, March 1983, pp. 198-205.

5   R.M. Russell, "The CRAY-1 Computer Systems," *Comm. of the ACM*, Vol. 21, No. 1, Jan. 1978, pp. 63-72.

6   J.L. Larson, "Multitasking on the Cray X-Mp-2 Multiprocessor," *Computer*, Vol. 17, No. 7, July 1984, pp. 62-69.

7   T. Cheung and J.E. Smith, "An Analysis of the Cray X-MP Memory System," *Proc. 1984 Int'l. Conf. Parallel Processing*, IEEE Computer Society, Washington, D.C., 1984, pp. 499-505.

8   V.P. Srini and J.F. Asenjo, "Analysis of Cray-1S Architecture," *Proc. 10th Ann. Int'l. Symp. Computer Architecture*, IEEE Computer Society, Washington, D.C., 1983, pp. 194-206.

9 E.W. Kozdrowicki and D.J. Theis, "Second Generation of Vector Supercomputers," *Computer*, Vol. 13, No. 11, Nov. 1980, pp. 71-83.

10 C. Worth and E. Alan, "An Approach to Scientific Array Processing: The Architectural Design of the AP-120B/FPS-164 Family," *Computer*, Vol. 14, No. 9, Sept. 1981, pp. 18-27.

11 K.E. Batcher, "Design of a Massively Parallel Processor," *IEEE Trans. Computers*, Vol. C-29, No. 9, Sept. 1980, pp. 836-840.

12 J.T. Burkley, "MPP VLSI Multiprocessor Integrated Circuit Design," *Proc. 1982 Int'l. Conf. Parallel Processing*, IEEE Computer Society, Washington, D.C., 1982, pp. 268-270.

13 K.E. Batcher, "MPP Staging Memory," *Proc. 1984 Int'l. Conf. Parallel Processing*, IEEE Computer Society, Washington, D.C., 1984, pp. 496-498.

14 J.T. Burkley, "MPP VLSI Multiprocessor Integrated Circuit Design," *Proc. 1982 Int'l. Conf. Parallel Processing*, IEEE Computer Society, Washington, D.C., 1982, pp. 268-270.

15 J.L. Potter, "Image Processing on the Massively Parallel Processor," *Computer*, Vol. 16, No. 1, Jan. 1983, pp. 62-67.

16 E.J. Gallopoulos and S.D. McEwan, "Numerical Experiments with the Massively Parallel Processor," *Proc. 1983 Int'l. Conf. Parallel Processing*, IEEE Computer Society, Washington, D.C., 1983, pp. 29-35.

17 R.A. Stokes, "Burroughs Scientific Processor," in *High Speed Computer and Algorithm Organizations*, Academic Press, Orlando, Fl., 1977, pp. 85-89.

18 S.E. Lundstrom and G.H. Barnes, "A Controllable MIMD Architecture," *Proc. 1980 Int'l. Conf. Parallel Processing*, IEEE Computer Society, Washington, D.C., 1980, pp. 19-27.

19 D.J. Kuck and R.A. Stokes, "The Burroughs Scientific Processor (BSP)," *IEEE Trans. Computers*, Vol. C-31, No. 5, May 1982, pp. 363-376.

20 B.J. Smith, "A Pipelined, Shared Resource MIMD Computer," *Proc. 1978 Int'l. Conf. Parallel Processing*, IEEE Computer Society, Washington, D.C., 1978, pp. 6-8.

21 H.F. Jordan, "Performance Measurements on HEP—A Pipelined MIMD Computer," *Proc. 10th Ann. Int'l. Symp. Computer Architecture*, IEEE Computer Society, Washington, D.C., 1983, pp. 207-212.

22 N. Matelan, "The Flex/32 Multicomputer," *Proc. 12th Int'l. Symp. Computer Architecture*, IEEE Computer Society, Washington, D.C., 1985, pp. 209-213.

23 J.C. Browne, "TRAC: An Environment for Parallel Computing," *Proc. COMPCON*, IEEE Computer Society, Washington, D.C., Spring 1984, pp. 294-298.

24 I. Barron. P. Cavill, D. May, and P. Wilson, "Transputer Does 10 or More MIPS Even When Not Used in Parallel," *Electronics*, Nov. 1983, pp. 109-115.

25 C. Maples, D. Weaver, W. Rathbun, and D. Logan, "The Operation and Utilization of the MIDAS Multiprocessor Architecture," *Proc. 1984 Int'l. Conf. Parallel Processing*, IEEE Computer Society, Washington, D.C., 1984, pp. 197-206.

26 D. Logan, C. Maples, D. Weaver, and W. Rathbun, "Adapting Scientific Programs to the MIDAS Multiprocessor Systems," *Proc. 1984 Int'l. Conf. Parallel Processing*, IEEE Computer Society, Washington, D.C., 1984, pp. 15-24.

27 H. Nishimura, H. Ohno, T. Kawata, I. Shirakawa, and K. Omura, "Links-1: A Parallel Pipelined Multimicro computer System for Image Creation," *Proc. 10th Ann. Int'l. Symp. Computer Architecture*, IEEE Computer Society, Washington, D.C., 1983, pp. 387-394.

28 T. Hoshino, et al., "Highly Parallel Processor Array Pax for Wide Scientific Applications," *Proc. 1983 Int'l. Conf. Parallel Processing*, IEEE Computer Society, Washington, D.C. 1983, pp. 95-103.

29 T. Ericsson and P. Danielsson, "LIPP—A SIMD Multiprocessor Architecture for Image Processing," *Proc. 10th Ann. Int'l. Symp. Computer Architecture*, IEEE Computer Society, Washington, D.C., 1983, pp. 395-400.

"The CRAY-1 Computer System" by R.M. Russell from *Communications of the ACM*, Volume 21, Number 1, January 1978, pages 63-72. Copyright 1978, Association for Computing Machinery, Inc., reprinted by permission.

Computer Systems   G. Bell, S. H. Fuller, and D. Siewiorek, Editors

The CRAY-1 Computer System

Richard M. Russell
Cray Research, Inc.

This paper describes the CRAY-1, discusses the evolution of its architecture, and gives an account of some of the problems that were overcome during its manufacture.

The CRAY-1 is the only computer to have been built to date that satisfies ERDA's Class VI requirement (a computer capable of processing from 20 to 60 million floating point operations per second) [1].

The CRAY-1's Fortran compiler (CFT) is designed to give the scientific user immediate access to the benefits of the CRAY-1's vector processing architecture. An optimizing compiler, CFT, "vectorizes" innermost DO loops. Compatible with the ANSI 1966 Fortran Standard and with many commonly supported Fortran extensions, CFT does not require any source program modifications or the use of additional nonstandard Fortran statements to achieve vectorization. Thus the user's investment of hundreds of man months of effort to develop Fortran programs for other contemporary computers is protected.

Key Words and Phrases: architecture, computer systems

CR Categories: 1.2, 6.2, 6.3

Introduction

Vector processors are not yet commonplace machines in the larger-scale computer market. At the time of this writing we know of only 12 non-CRAY-1 vector processor installations worldwide. Of these 12, the most powerful processor is the ILLIAC IV (1 installation), the most populous is the Texas Instruments Advanced Scientific Computer (7 installations) and the most publicized is Control Data's STAR 100

Author's address: Cray Research Inc., Suite 213, 7850 Metro Parkway, Minneapolis, MN 55420.

(4 installations). In its report on the CRAY-1, Auerbach Computer Technology Reports published a comparison of the CRAY-1, the ASC, and the STAR 100 [2]. The CRAY-1 is shown to be a more powerful computer than any of its main competitors and is estimated to be the equivalent of five IBM 370/195s.

Independent benchmark studies have shown the CRAY-1 fully capable of supporting computational rates of 138 million floating-point operations per second (MFLOPS) for sustained periods and even higher rates of 250 MFLOPS in short bursts [3, 4]. Such comparatively high performance results from the CRAY-1 internal architecture, which is designed to accommodate the computational needs of carrying out many calculations in discrete steps, with each step producing interim results used in subsequent steps. Through a technique called "chaining," the CRAY-1 vector functional units, in combination with scalar and vector registers, generate interim results and use them again immediately without additional memory references, which slow down the computational process in other contemporary computer systems.

Other features enhancing the CRAY-1's computational capabilities are: its small size, which reduces distances electrical signals must travel within the computer's framework and allows a 12.5 nanosecond clock period (the CRAY-1 is the world's fastest scalar processor); a one million word semiconductor memory equipped with error detection and correction logic (SECDED); its 64-bit word size; and its optimizing Fortran compiler.

Architecture

The CRAY-1 has been called "the world's most expensive love-seat" [5]. Certainly, most people's first reaction to the CRAY-1 is that it is so small. But in computer design it is a truism that smaller means faster. The greater the separation of components, the longer the time taken for a signal to pass between them. A cylindrical shape was chosen for the CRAY-1 in order to keep wiring distances small.

Figure 1 shows the physical dimensions of the machine. The mainframe is composed of 12 wedgelike columns arranged in a 270° arc. This leaves room for a reasonably trim individual to gain access to the interior of the machine. Note that the love-seat disguises the power supplies and some plumbing for the Freon cooling system. The photographs (Figure 2 and 3) show the interior of a working CRAY-1 and an exterior view of a column with one module in place. Figure 4 is a photograph of the interior of a single module.

An Analysis of the Architecture

Table I details important characteristics of the CRAY-1 Computer System. The CRAY-1 is equipped with 12 i/o channels, 16 memory banks, 12 functional

Fig. 1. Physical organization of mainframe.

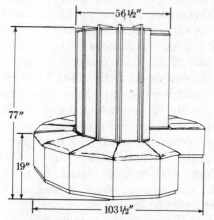

— Dimensions
  Base–103¼ inches diameter by 19 inches high
  Columns—56½ inches diameter by 77 inches high including height of base
— 24 chassis
— 1662 modules; 113 module types
— Each module contains up to 288 IC packages per module
— Power consumption approximately 115 kw input for maximum memory size
— Freon cooled with Freon/water heat exchange
— Three memory options
— Weight 10,500 lbs (maximum memory size)
— Three basic chip types
  5/4 NAND gates
  Memory chips
  Register chips

Fig. 2. The CRAY-1 Computer.

Fig. 3. CRAY-1 modules in place.

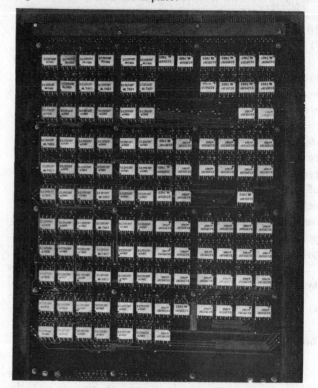

units, and more than 4k bytes of register storage. Access to memory is shared by the i/o channels and high-speed registers. The most striking features of the CRAY-1 are: only four chip types, main memory speed, cooling system, and computation section.

Four Chip Types

Only four chip types are used to build the CRAY-1. These are 16 × 4 bit bipolar register chips (6 nanosecond cycle time), 1024 × 1 bit bipolar memory chips (50 nanosecond cycle time), and bipolar logic chips with subnanosecond propagation times. The logic chips are all simple low- or high-speed gates with both a 5 wide and a 4 wide gate (5/4 NAND). Emitter-coupled logic circuit (ECL) technology is used throughout the CRAY-1.

The printed circuit board used in the CRAY-1 is a 5-layer board with the two outer surfaces used for signal runs and the three inner layers for −5.2V, −2.0V, and ground power supplies. The boards are six inches wide, 8 inches lon., and fit into the chassis as shown in Figure 3.

All integrated circuit devices used in the CRAY-1 are packaged in 16-pin hermetically sealed flat packs supplied by both Fairchild and Motorola. This type of package was chosen for its reliability and compactness. Compactness is of special importance; as many as 288 packages may be added to a board to fabricate a module (there are 113 module types), and as many as 72 modules may be inserted into a 28-inch-high chassis.

Such component densities evitably lead to a mammoth cooling problem (to be described).

Main Memory Speed

CRAY-1 memory is organized in 16 banks, 72 modules per bank. Each module contributes 1 bit to a 64-bit word. The other 8 bits are used to store an 8-bit check byte required for single-bit error correction, double-bit error detection (SECDED). Data words are stored in 1-bank increments throughout memory. This organization allows 16-way interleaving of memory accesses and prevents bank conflicts except in the case

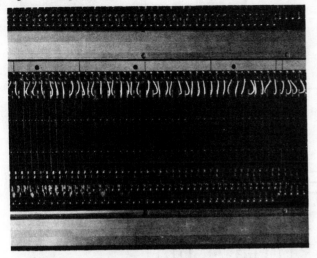

Fig. 4. A single module.

Table I. CRAY-1 CPU characteristics summary

Computation Section
  Scalar and vector processing modes
  12.5 nanosecond clock period operation
  64-bit word size
  Integer and floating-point arithmetic
  Twelve fully segmented functional units
  Eight 24-bit address (A) registers
  Sixty-four 24-bit intermediate address (B) registers
  Eight 64-bit scalar (S) registers
  Sixty-four 64-bit intermediate scalar (T) registers
  Eight 64-element vector (V) registers (64-bits per element)
  Vector length and vector mask registers
  One 64-bit real time clock (RT) register
  Four instruction buffers of sixty-four 16-bit parcels each
  128 basic instructions
  Prioritized interrupt control
Memory Section
  1,048,576 64-bit words (plus 8 check bits per word)
  16 independent banks of 65,536 words each
  4 clock period bank cycle time
  1 word per clock period transfer rate for B, T, and V registers
  1 word per 2 clock periods transfer rate for A and S registers
  4 words per clock period transfer rate to instruction buffers (up to
    16 instructions per clock period)
i/o Section
  24 i/o channels organized into four 6-channel groups
  Each channel group contains either 6 input or 6 output channels
  Each channel group served by memory every 4 clock periods
  Channel priority within each channel group
  16 data bits, 3 control bits per channel, and 4 parity bits
  Maximum channel rate of one 64-bit word every 100 nanoseconds
  Maximum data streaming rate of 500,000 64-bit words/second
  Channel error detection

of memory accesses that step through memory with either an 8 or 16-word increment.

Cooling System

The CRAY-1 generates about four times as much heat per cubic inch as the 7600. To cool the CRAY-1 a new cooling technology was developed, also based on Freon, but employing available metal conductors in a new way. Within each chassis vertical aluminum/stainless steel cooling bars line each column wall. The

Freon refrigerant is passed through a stainless steel tube within the aluminum casing. When modules are in place, heat is dissipated through the inner copper heat transfer plate in the module to the column walls and thence into the cooling bars. The modules are mated with the cold bar by using stainless steel pins to pinch the copper plate against the aluminum outer casing of the bar.

To assure component reliability, the cooling system was designed to provide a maximum case temperature of 130°F (54°C). To meet this goal, the following temperature differentials are observed:

Temperature at center of module	130°F (54°C)
Temperature at edge of module	118°F (48°C)
Cold plate temperature at wedge	78°F (25°C)
Cold bar temperature	70°F (21°C)
Refrigerant tube temperature	70°F (21°C)

Functional Units

There are 12 functional units, organized in four groups: address, scalar, vector, and floating point. Each functional unit is pipelined into single clock segments. Functional unit time is shown in Table II. Note that all of the functional units can operate concurrently so that in addition to the benefits of pipelining (each functional unit can be driven at a result rate of 1 per clock period) we also have parallelism across the units too. Note the absence of a divide unit in the CRAY-1. In order to have a completely segmented divide operation the CRAY-1 performs floating-point division by the method of reciprocal approximation. This technique has been used before (e.g. IBM System/360 Model 91).

Registers

Figure 5 shows the CRAY-1 registers in relationship to the functional units, instruction buffers, i/o channel control registers, and memory. The basic set of programmable registers are as follows:

  8 24-bit address (A) registers
  64 24-bit address-save (B) registers
  8 64-bit scalar (S) registers
  64 64-bit scalar-save (T) registers
  8 64-word (4096-bit) vector (V) registers

Expressed in 8-bit bytes rather than 64-bit words, that's a total of 4,888 bytes of high-speed (6ns) register storage.

The functional units take input operands from and store result operands only to A, S, and V registers. Thus the large amount of register storage is a crucial factor in the CRAY-1's architecture. Chaining could not take place if vector register space were not available for the storage of final or intermediate results. The B and T registers greatly assist scalar performance. Temporary scalar values can be stored from and reloaded to the A and S register in two clock periods. Figure 5 shows the CRAY-1's register paths in detail. The speed of the cFT Fortran IV compiler would be

Fig. 5. Block diagram of registers.

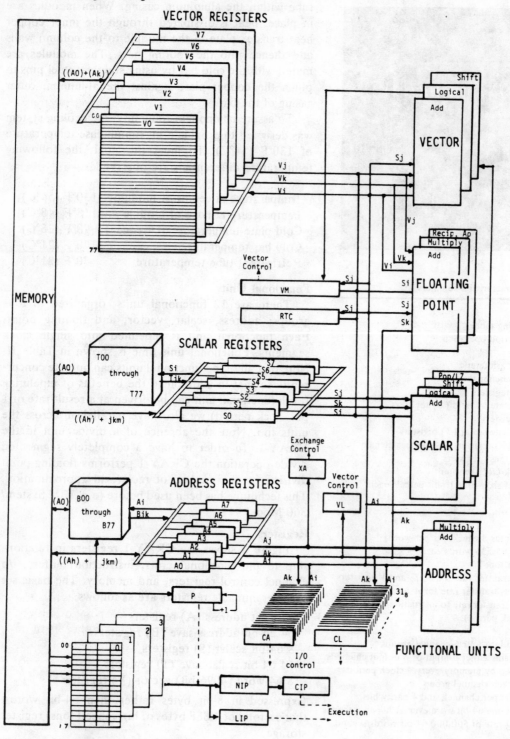

VECTOR REGISTERS

INSTRUCTION BUFFERS

seriously impaired if it were unable to keep the many Pass 1 and Pass 2 tables it needs in register space. Without the register storage provided by the B, T, and V registers, the CRAY-1's bandwidth of only 80 million words/second would be a serious impediment to performance.

Instruction Formats

Instructions are expressed in either one or two 16-bit parcels. Below is the general form of a CRAY-1 instruction. Two-parcel instructions may overlap memory-word boundaries, as follows:

Fields	g	h	i	j	k	m
	0–3	4–6	7–9	10–12	13–15	16–31
Bit positions	(4)	(3)	(3)	(3)	(3)	(16)

Parcel 1	Parcel 2

The computation section processes instructions at a maximum rate of one parcel per clock period.

Table II. CRAY-1 functional units

	Register usage	Functional unit time (clock periods)
Address function units		
address add unit	A	2
address multiply unit	A	6
Scalar functional units		
scalar add unit	S	3
scalar shift unit	S	2 or 3 if double-word shift
scalar logical unit	S	1
population/leading zero count unit	S	3
Vector functional units		
vector add unit	V	3
vector shift unit	V	4
vector logical unit	V	2
Floating-point functional units		
floating-point add unit	S and V	6
floating-point multiply unit	S and V	7
reciprocal approximation unit	S and V	14

For arithmetic and logical instructions, a 7-bit operation code (gh) is followed by three 3-bit register designators. The first field, i, designates the result register. The j and k fields designate the two operand registers or are combined to designate a B or T register.

The shift and mask instructions consist of a 7-bit operation code (gh) followed by a 3-bit i field and a 6-bit jk field. The i field designates the operand register. The jk combined field specifies a shift or mask count.

Immediate operand, read and store memory, and branch instructions require the two-parcel instruction word format. The immediate operand and the read and store memory instructions combine the j, k, and m fields to define a 22-bit quantity or memory address. In addition, the read and store memory instructions use the h field to specify an operating register for indexing. The branch instructions combine the i, j, k, and m fields into a 24-bit memory address field. This allows branching to any one of the four parcel positions in any 64-bit word, whether in memory or in an instruction buffer.

Operating Registers

Five types of registers — three primary (A, S, and V) and two intermediate (B and T) — are provided in the CRAY-1.

A registers — eight 24-bit A registers serve a variety of applications. They are primarily used as address registers for memory references and as index registers, but also are used to provide values for shift counts, loop control, and channel i/o operations. In address applications, they are used to index the base address for scalar memory references and for providing both a base address and an index address for vector memory references.

The 24-bit integer functional units modify values (such as program addresses) by adding, subtracting, and multiplying A register quantities. The results of these operations are returned to A registers.

Data can be transferred directly from memory to A registers or can be placed in B registers as an intermediate step. This allows buffering of the data between A registers and memory. Data can also be transferred between A and S registers and from an A register to the vector length registers. The eight A registers are individually designated by the symbols A0, A1, A2, A3, A4, A5, A6, and A7.

B registers — there are sixty-four 24-bit B registers, which are used as auxiliary storage for the A registers. The transfer of an operand between an A and a B register requires only one clock period. Typically, B registers contain addresses and counters that are referenced over a longer period than would permit their being retained in A registers. A block of data in B registers may be transferred to or from memory at the rate of one clock period per register. Thus, it is feasible to store the contents of these registers in memory prior to calling a subroutine requiring their use. The sixty-four B registers are individually designated by the symbols B0, B1, B2, . . . , and B77$_8$.

S registers — eight 64-bit S registers are the principle data handling registers for scalar operations. The S registers serve as both source and destination registers for scalar arithmetic and logical instructions. Scalar quantities involved in vector operations are held in S registers. Logical, shift, fixed-point, and floating-point operations may be performed on S register data. The eight S registers are individually designated by the symbols S0, S1, S2, S3, S4, S5, S6, and S7.

T registers — sixty-four 64-bit T registers are used as auxiliary storage for the S registers. The transfer of an operand between S and T registers requires one clock period. Typically, T registers contain operands that are referenced over a longer period than would permit their being retained in S registers. T registers allow intermediate results of complex computations to be held in intermediate access storage rather than in memory. A block of data in T registers may be transferred to or from memory at the rate of one word per clock period. The sixty-four T registers are individually designated by the symbols T0, T1, T2, . . . , and T77$_8$.

V registers — eight 64-element V registers provide operands to and receive results from the functional units at a one clock period rate. Each element of a V register holds a 64-bit quantity. When associated data is grouped into successive elements of a V register, the register may be considered to contain a vector. Examples of vector quantities are rows and columns of a matrix, or similarly related elements of a table. Computational efficiency is achieved by processing each element of the vector identically. Vector merge and test instructions are provided in the CRAY-1 to allow operations to be performed on individual elements designated by the content of the vector mask (VM) register. The number of vector register elements to be processed is contained in the vector length (VL) register. The eight V registers are individually designated by the symbols V0, V1, V2, V3, V4, V5, B6, and V7.

Supporting Registers

The CPU contains a variety of additional registers that support the control of program execution. These are the vector length (VL) and vector mask (VM) registers, the program counter (P), the base address (BA) and limit address (LA) registers, the exchange address (XA) register, the flag (F) register, and the mode (M) register.

VL *register* — the 64-bit vector mask (VM) register controls vector element designation in vector merge and test instructions. Each bit of the VM register corresponds to a vector register element. In the vector test instruction, the VM register content is defined by testing each element of a V register for a specific condition.

P *register* — the 24-bit P register specifies the memory register parcel address of the current program instruction. The high order 22 bits specify a memory address and the low order two bits indicate a parcel number. This parcel address is advanced by one as each instruction parcel in a nonbranching sequence is executed and is replaced whenever program branching occurs.

BA *registers* — the 18-bit base address (BA) register contains the upper 18 bits of a 22-bit memory address. The lower four bits of this address are considered zeros. Just prior to initial or continued execution of a program, a process known as the "exchange sequence" stores into the BA register the upper 18 bits of the lowest memory address to be referenced during program execution. As the program executes, the address portion of each instruction referencing memory has its content added to that of the BA register. The sum then serves as the absolute address used for the memory reference and ensures that memory addresses lower than the contents of the BA register are not accessed. Programs must, therefore, have all instructions referencing memory do so with their address portions containing relative addresses. This process supports program loading and memory protection operations and does not, in producing an absolute address, affect the content of the instruction buffer, BA, or memory.

LA *register* — the 18-bit limit address (LA) register contains the upper 18 bits of a 22-bit memory address. The lower 4 bits of this address are considered zeros. Just prior to initial or continued execution of a program, the "exchange sequence" process stores into the LA register the upper 18 bits of that absolute address one greater than allowed to be referenced by the program. When program execution begins, each instruction referencing a memory location has the absolute address for that reference (determined by summing its address portion with the BA register contents) checked against the LA register content. If the absolute address equals or exceeds the LA register content, an out-of-range error condition is flagged and program execution terminates. This process supports the memory protection operation.

XA *register* — the 8-bit exchange address (XA) register contains the upper eight bits of a 12-bit memory address. The lower four bits of the address are considered zeros. Because only twelve bits are used, with the lower four bits always being zeros, exchange addresses can reference only every 16th memory address beginning with address 0000 and concluding with address 4080. Each of these addresses designates the first word of a 16-word set. Thus, 256 sets (of 16 memory words each) can be specified. Prior to initiation or continuation of a program's execution, the XA register contains the first memory address of a particular 16-word set or exchange package. The exchange package contains certain operating and support registers' contents as required for operations following an interrupt. The XA register supports the exchange sequence operation and the contents of XA are stored in an exchange package whenever an exchange sequence occurs.

F *register* — the 9-bit F register contains flags that, whenever set, indicate interrupt conditions causing initiation of an exchange sequence. The interrupt conditions are: normal exit, error exit, i/o interrupt, uncorrected memory error, program range error, operand range error, floating-point overflow, real-time clock interrupt, and console interrupt.

M *register* — the M (mode) register is a three-bit register that contains part of the exchange package for a currently active program. The three bits are selectively set during an exchange sequence. Bit 37, the floating-point error mode flag, can be set or cleared during the execution interval for a program through use of the 0021 and 0022 instructions. The other two bits (bits 38 and 39) are not altered during the execution interval for the exchange package and can only be altered when the exchange package is inactive in storage. Bits are assigned as follows in word two of the exchange package.

Bit 37 — Floating-point error mode flag. When this bit is set, interrupts on floating-point errors are enabled.

Bit 38 — Uncorrectable memory error mode flag. When this bit is set, interrupts on uncorrectable memory parity errors are enabled.

Bit 39 — Monitor mode flag. When this bit is set, all interrupts other than parity errors are inhibited.

Integer Arithmetic

All integer arithmetic is performed in 24-bit or 64-bit 2's complement form.

Floating-Point Arithmetic

Floating-point numbers are represented in signed magnitude form. The format is a packed signed binary fraction and a biased binary integer exponent. The fraction is a 49-bit signed magnitude value. The exponent is 15-bit biased. The unbiased exponent range is:

$$2^{-20000_8} \text{ to } 2^{+17777_8},$$

or approximately

$$10^{-2500} \text{ to } 10^{+2500}$$

An exponent equal to or greater than 2^{+20000_8} is recognized by the floating-point functional units as an overflow condition, and causes an interrupt if floating point interrupts are enabled.

Chaining

The chaining technique takes advantage of the parallel operation of functional units. Parallel vector operations may be processed in two ways: (a) using different functional units and V registers, and (b) chaining; that is, using the result stream to one vector register simultaneously as the operand set for another operation in a different functional unit.

Parallel operations on vectors allow the generation of two or more results per clock period. A vector operation either uses two vector registers as sources of operands or uses one scalar register and one vector register as sources of operands. Vectors exceeding 64 elements are processed in 64-element segments.

Basically, chaining is a phenomenon that occurs when results issuing from one functional unit (at a rate of one/clock period) are immediately fed into another functional unit and so on. In other words, intermediate results do not have to be stored to memory and can be used even before the vector operation that created them runs to completion.

Chaining has been compared to the technique of "data forwarding" used in the IBM 360/195. Like data forwarding, chaining takes place automatically. Data forwarding consists of hardware facilities within the 195 floating-point processor communicating automatically by transferring "name tags," or internal codes between themselves [6]. Unlike the CRAY-1, the user has no access to the 195's data-forwarding buffers. And, of course, the 195 can only forward scalar values, not entire vectors.

Interrupts and Exchange Sequence

Interrupts are handled cleanly by the CRAY-1 hardware. Instruction issue is terminated by the hardware upon detection of an interrupt condition. All memory bank activity is allowed to complete as are any vector instructions that are in execution, and then an exchange sequence is activated. The Cray Operating System (cos) is always one partner of any exchange sequence. The cause of an interrupt is analyzed during an exchange sequence and all interrupts are processed until none remain.

Only the address and scalar registers are maintained in a program's exchange package (Fig. 6). The user's B, T, and V registers are saved by the operating system in the user's Job Table Area.

Fig. 6. Exchange package.

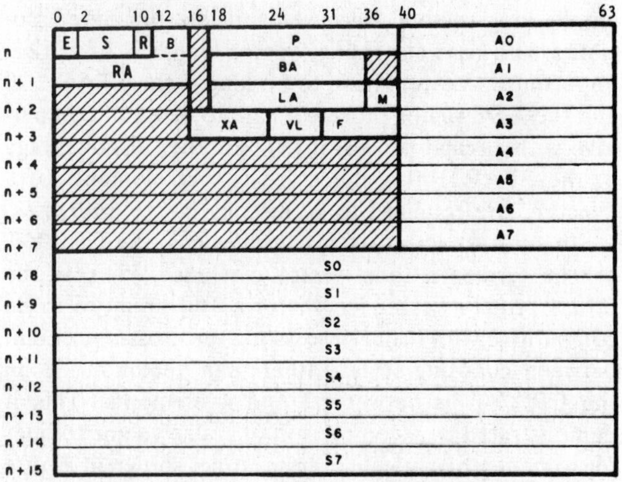

	M - Modes[†]		Registers	
36	Interrupt on correctable memory error	S	Syndrome bits	
37	Interrupt on floating point	RAB	Read address for error (where B is bank)	
38	Interrupt on uncorrectable memory error	P	Program address	
39	Monitor mode	BA	Base address	
		LA	Limit address	
	F - Flags[†]	XA	Exchange address	
31	Console interrupt	VL	Vector length	
32	RTC interrupt			
33	Floating point error		E - Error type (bits 0,1)	
34	Operand range	10	Uncorrectable memory	
35	Program range	01	Correctable memory	
36	Memory error			
37	I/O interrupt		R - Read mode (bits 10,11)	
38	Error exit	00	Scalar	
39	Normal exit	01	I/O	
		10	Vector	
		11	Fetch	

[†]Bit position from left of word

The CRAY-1's exchange sequence will be familiar to those who have had experience with the CDC 7600 and Cyber machines. One major benefit of the exchange sequence is the ease with which user jobs can be relocated in memory by the operating system. On the CRAY-1, dynamic relocation of a user job is facilitated by a base register that is transparent to the user.

Evolution of the CRAY-1

The CRAY-1 stems from a highly successful line of computers which S. Cray either designed or was associated with. Mr. Cray was one of the founders of Control Data Corporation. While at CDC, Mr. Cray was the principal architect of the CDC 1604, 6600, and 7600 computer systems. While there are many similarities with these earlier machines, two things stand out about the CRAY-1; first it is a vector machine, secondly, it utilizes semiconductor memories and integrated circuits rather than magnetic cores and discrete components. We classify the CRAY-1 as a second generation vector processor. The CDC STAR 100A and the Texas Instruments ASC are first-generation vector processors.

21

Both the STAR 100 and the ASC are designed to handle long vectors. Because of the startup time associated with data streaming, vector length is of critical importance. Vectors have to be long if the STAR 100 and the ASC vector processors are to be at all competitive with a scalar processor [3]. Another disadvantage of the STAR 100 architecture is that elements of a "vector" are required to be in consecutive addresses.

In contrast with these earlier designs, the CRAY-1 can be termed a short vector machine. Whereas the others require vector lengths of a 100 or more to be competitive with scalar processors, the cross-over point between choosing scalar rather than vector mode on the CRAY-1 is between 2 and 4 elements. This is demonstrated by a comparison of scalar/vector timings for some mathematical library routines shown in Figure 1 [7].

Also, the CRAY-1's addressing scheme allows complete flexibility. When accessing a vector, the user simply specifies the starting location and an increment. Arrays can be accessed by column, row, or diagonal; they can be stepped through with nonunary increments; and, there are no restrictions on addressing, except that the increment must be a constant.

Vector Startup Times

To be efficient at processing short vectors, vector startup times must be small. On the CRAY-1, vector instructions may issue at a rate of one instruction parcel per clock period. All vector instructions are one parcel instructions (parcel size = 16 bits). Vector instructions place a reservation on whichever functional unit they use, including memory, and on the input operand registers. In some cases, issue of a vector instruction may be delayed by a time (in clock periods) equal to vector length of the preceding vector operation + 4.

Functional unit times are shown in Table II. Vector operations that depend on the result of a previous vector operation can usually "chain" with them and are delayed for a maximum "chain slot" time in clock periods of functional unit time + 2.

Once issued, a vector instruction produces its first result after a delay in clock periods equal to functional unit time. Subsequent results continue to be produced at a rate of 1 per clock period. Results must be stored in a vector register. A separate instruction is required to store the final result vector to memory. Vector register capacity is 64-elements. Vectors longer than 64 are processed in 64-element segments.

Some sample timings for both scalar and vector are shown in Table III [8]. Note that there is no vector ASIN routine and so a reference to ASIN within a vectorized loop generates repetitive calls to the scalar ASIN routine. This involves a performance degradation but does allow the rest of the loop to vectorize (in a case where there are more statements than in this example). Simple loops 14, 15, and 16 show the

Table III.

Execution time in clock periods per result for various simple DO loops of the form
DO 10 I = 1.N
10 A(I) = B(I)

Loop Body	$N = 1$	10	100	1000	1000 Scalar
1. $A(I) = 1.$	41.0	5.5	2.6	2.5	22.5
2. $A(I) = B(I)$	44.0	5.8	2.7	2.5	31.0
3. $A(I) = B(I) + 10.$	55.0	6.9	2.9	2.6	37.0
4. $A(I) = B(I) + C(I)$	59.0	8.2	3.9	3.7	41.0
5. $A(I) = B(I)*10.$	56.0	7.0	2.9	2.6	38.0
6. $A(I) = B(I)*C(I)$	60.0	8.3	4.0	3.7	42.0
7. $A(I) = B(I)/10.$	94.0	10.8	4.1	3.7	52.0
8. $A(I) = B(I)/C(I)$	89.0	13.3	7.6	7.2	60.0
9. $A(I) = SIN(B(I))$	462.0	61.0	33.3	31.4	198.1
10. $A(I) = ASIN(B(I))$	430.0	209.5	189.5	188.3	169.1
11. $A(I) = ABS(B(I))$	61.0	7.5	2.9	2.6	
12. $A(I) = AMAX1(B(I), C(I))$	80.0	11.2	5.2	4.8	
13. $\begin{cases} C(I) = A(I) \\ A(I) = B(I) \\ B(I) = CCI \end{cases}$	90.0	12.7	6.3	5.8	47.0
14. $A(I) = B(I)*C(I) + D(I)*E(I)$	110.0	16.0	7.7	7.1	57.0
15. $A(I) = B(I)*C(I) + (D(I)*E(I))$	113.0	14.7	6.6	6.0	63.0
16. $A(I) = B(I)*C(I) + D(I)$	95.0	12.7	5.5	5.0	52.0

Fig. 7. Scalar/vector timing.

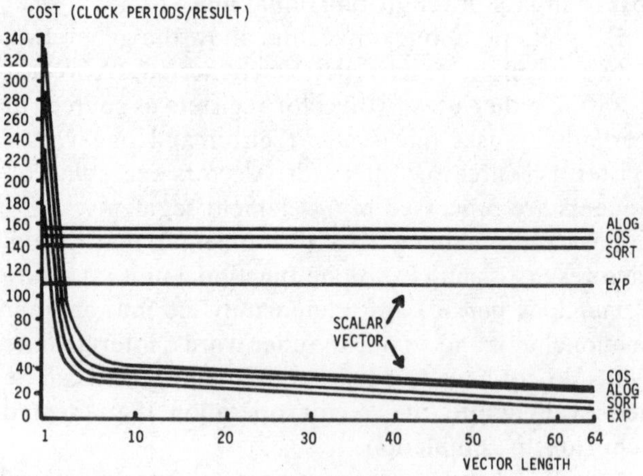

influence of chaining. For a long vector, the number of clock periods per result is approximately the number of memory references + 1. In loop 14, an extra clock period is consumed because the present CFT compiler will load all four operands before doing computation. This problem is overcome in loop 15 by helping the compiler with an extra set of parentheses.

Software

At the time of this writing, first releases of the CRAY Operating System (COS) and CRAY Fortran Compiler (CFT) have been delivered to user sites. COS is a batch operating system capable of supporting up to 63 jobs in a multiprogramming environment. COS is designed to be the recipient of job requests and data files from front-end computers. Output from jobs is normally staged back to the front-ends upon job completion.

CFT is an optimizing Fortran compiler designed to compile ANSI 66 Fortran IV to take best advantage of the CRAY-1's vector processing architecture. In its present form, CFT will not attempt to vectorize certain

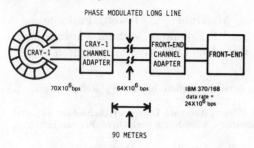

Fig. 8. Front-end system interface.

PHASE MODULATED LONG LINE

CRAY-1 — CRAY-1 CHANNEL ADAPTER — FRONT-END CHANNEL ADAPTER — FRONT-END

70X10⁶bps   64X10⁶ bps   IBM 370/168 data rate = 24X10⁶ bps

90 METERS

loops which, due to dependence conditions, appear at first sight, unvectorizable.

However, future versions of CFT will be designed to eliminate as many dependency conditions as possible increasing the amount of vectorizable code. Basically, to be vectorizable, a DO loop should manipulate arrays and store the results of computations in arrays. Loops that contain branches such as GO TO's, IF's, or CALL statements are not currently vectorized. Loops may contain function references if the function is known to the compiler to have a vector version. Most of the mathematical functions in the CRAY library are vectorizable. By using the vector mask and vector merge features of the CRAY-1, future versions of the compiler will be able to vectorize loops containing IF and GO TO statements.

Early experience with CFT has shown that most Fortran loops will not run as fast as optimally hand-coded machine language equivalents. Future versions of CFT will show improved loop timings due mainly to improved instruction scheduling.

Other CRAY-1 software includes Cray Assembler Language (CAL) which is a powerful macro assembler, an overlay loader, a full range of utilities including a text editor, and some debug aids.

Front-End Computer Interface

The CRAY-1 was not designed for stand-alone operation. At the very minimum a minicomputer is required to act as a conduit between the CRAY-1 and the everyday world. Cray Research software development is currently being done using a Data General Eclipse computer in this category. The Cray Research "A" processor, a 16-bit, 80 MIPS minicomputer is scheduled to replace the Eclipse in early 1978. Front-end computers can be attached to any of the CRAY-1's 12 i/o channels.

The physical connection between a front-end computer and the CRAY-1 is shown in Figure 8. In this example an IBM 370/168 is assumed in the front-end role. Note that each computer requires a channel adapter between its own channel and a Cray Research phase-modulated long line. The link can only be driven at the speed of its slowest component. In this example it is the IBM block multiplexer channel speed of 3 megabytes/second. The discipline of the link is governed by the Cray Link Interface Protocol.

CRAY-1 Development Problems

Two of the most significant problems [9] encountered on the way to the CRAY-1 were building the first cold bar and designing circuits with a completely balanced dynamic load.

Building the Cold Bar

It took a year and a half of trial and error before the first good cold bar was built. The work was done by a small Minnesota company. A major problem was the discovery, quite early, that aluminum castings are porous. If there is a crack in the stainless steel tubing at the bond between the tubing and the elbow then the Freon leaks through the aluminum casing. The loss of the Freon is not itself a problem, but mixed with the Freon is a little oil, and the oil can cause problems if it is deposited on the modules. Aluminum also tends to get bubbles in it when it is cast, requiring a long process of temperature cycling, preheating of the stainless steel tube, and so on.

Designing the Circuits

CRAY-1 modules are 6 inches wide. The distance across the board is about a nanosecond which is just about the edge time of the electrical signals. Unless due precautions are taken, when electric signals run around a board, standing waves can be induced in the ground plane. Part of the solution is to make all signal paths in the machine the same length. This is done by padding out paths with foil runs and integrated circuit packages. All told, between 10 and 20 per cent of the IC packages in the machine are there simply to pad out a signal line. The other part of the solution was to use only simple gates and make sure that both sides of every gate are always terminated. This means that there is no dynamic component presented to the power supply. This is the principal reason why simple gates are used in the CRAY-1. If a more complex integrated circuit package is used, it is impossible to terminate both sides of every gate. So all of the CRAY-1's circuits are perfectly balanced. Five layer boards have one ground layer, two voltage layers, and then the two logic layers on the outside. Twisted pairs which interconnect the modules are balanced and there are equal and opposite signals on both sides of the pairs. The final result is that there is just a purely resistive load to the power supply!

Summary

The design of the CRAY-1 stems from user experience with first generation vector processors and is to some extent, evolved from the 7600 [2]. The CRAY-1 is particularly effective at processing short vectors. Its architecture exhibits a balanced approach to both scalar and vector processing. In [1], the conclusion is drawn that the CRAY-1 in scalar mode is more than twice as fast as the CDC 7600. Such good scalar performance is required in what is often an unvectorizable world.

At the time of this writing, Cray Research has shipped CRAY-1 systems to three customers (Los Alamos Scientific Laboratory, National Center for Atmospheric Research, and the European Center for Medium Range Weather Forecasts) and has contracts to supply three more systems, two to the Department of Defense, and one to United Computing Systems (UCS). Production plans already anticipate shipping one CRAY-1 per quarter. As the population of CRAY-1 computers expands, it will become clear that the CRAY-1 has made a significant step on the way to the general-purpose computers in the future.

Received February 1977; revised September 1977

Acknowledgments. Acknowledgments are due to my colleagues at Cray Research. G. Grenander, R. Hendrickson, M. Huber, C. Jewett, P. Johnson, A. La Bounty, and J. Robidoux, without whose contributions, this paper could not have been written.

References
1. CRAY-1 Final Evaluation by T. W. Keller, LASL, LA-6456-MS.
2. CRAY-1 Report, Auerbach Computer Technology Report, Auerbach Publisher's, 6560 North Park Drive, Pennsauken, N. J. 08109.
3. Preliminary Report on Results of Matrix Benchmarks on Vector Processors: Calahan, Joy, Orbits, System Engineering Laboratory, University of Michigan, Ann Arbor, Michigan 48109.
4. Computer Architecture Issues in Large-Scale Systems, 9th Asilomar Conference, Naval Postgraduate School, Monterey, California.
5. Computer World, August 1976.
6. The IBM 360/195 by Jesse O'Murphy and Robert M. Wade, Datamation, April 1970.
7. Work done by Paul Johnson, Cray Research.
8. Work done by Richard Hendrickson, Cray Research.
9. The section on CRAY-1 development problems is based on remarks made by Seymour Cray in a speech to prospective CRAY-1 users in 1975.

Design of a Massively Parallel Processor

KENNETH E. BATCHER

Abstract—The massively parallel processor (MPP) system is designed to process satellite imagery at high rates. A large number (16 384) of processing elements (PE's) are configured in a square array. For optimum performance on operands of arbitrary length, processing is performed in a bit-serial manner. On 8-bit integer data, addition can occur at 6553 million operations per second (MOPS) and multiplication at 1861 MOPS. On 32-bit floating-point data, addition can occur at 430 MOPS and multiplication at 216 MOPS.

Index Terms—Array processing, bit-slice processing, computer architecture, image processing, parallel processing, satellite imagery.

INTRODUCTION

In this decade, NASA will orbit imaging sensors that can generate data at rates up to 10^{13} bits per day. A variety of image processing tasks such as geometric correction, correlation, image registration, feature selection, multispectral classification, and area measurement are required to extract useful information from this mass of data. The expected workload is between 10^9 and 10^{10} operations per second.

In 1971 NASA Goddard Space Flight Center initiated a program to develop ultra high-speed image processing systems capable of processing this workload. These systems use thousands of processing elements (PE's) operating simultaneously (massive parallelism) to achieve their speed. They exploit the fact that the typical satellite image contains millions of picture elements (pixels) that can generally be processed at the same time.

In December 1979 NASA Goddard awarded a contract to Goodyear Aerospace to construct a massively parallel processor (MPP) to be delivered in the first quarter of 1982. The basic elements of the MPP architecture were developed at NASA Goddard. This correspondence presents the design of the MPP system. The major components are shown in Fig. 1. The array unit (ARU) processes arrays of data at high speed and is controlled by the array control unit (ACU), which also performs scalar arithmetic. The program and data management unit (PDMU) controls the overall flow of data and programs through the system and handles certain ancillary tasks such as program development and diagnostics. The staging memories buffer and reorder data between the ARU, PDMU, and external (host) computer.

Manuscript received August 6, 1979; revised April 9, 1980. This work was partially funded by NASA Goddard Space Flight Center under Contracts NAS5-25392 and NAS5-25942.

The author is with the Digital Technology Department, Goodyear Aerospace Corporation, Akron, OH 44315.

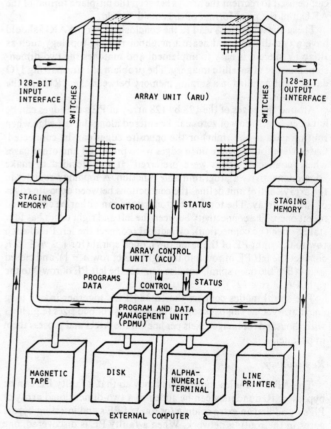

Fig. 1. Block diagram of the massively parallel processor (MPP).

Reprinted from *IEEE Transactions on Computers*, Volume C-29, Number 9, September 1980, pages 836-840. Copyright © 1980 by The Institute of Electrical and Electronics Engineers, Inc.

ARRAY UNIT

Logically, the array unit (ARU) contains 16 384 processing elements (PE's) organized as a 128 by 128 square. Physically, the ARU has an extra 128 by 4 rectangle of PE's that is used to reconfigure the ARU when a PE fault is detected. The PE's are bit-serial processors for efficiently processing operands of any length. The basic clock rate is 10 MHz. With 16 384 PE's operating in parallel, the ARU has a very high processing speed (see Table I). Despite the bit-serial nature of the PE's, even the floating-point speeds compare favorably with several fast number crunchers.

Routing Topology

Each PE in the 128 by 128 square communicates with its nearest neighbor; up, down, right, and left—a topology similar to Illiac IV and some other array processors. Alternative routing topologies such as the flip network [1] or one of its equivalents [2] were investigated. They have the ability to shift data over many PE's in one step and allow data to be accessed in many different directions [3]. Certain paths in the alternative topologies have long runs that complicate their layout and limit their cycle rate. When the number of PE's interconnected is only 256 as in the STARAN* computer, this is no problem; when 16 384 PE's are interconnected, it is a severe problem.

Most of the expected workload does not use the routing flexibility of the alternative topologies. The ability to access data in different directions is important when arrays of data are input and output; it can be used to reorient the arrays between the bit-plane format of the ARU and the pixel format of the outside world.

These considerations lead to the conclusion that the ARU should have a two-dimensional nearest neighbor routing topology such as Illiac IV since it is easy to implement and matches the two-dimensional nature of satellite imagery. The problem of reformatting I/O data is best handled in a staging memory between the ARU and the outside world.

Around the edges of the 128 by 128 array of PE's the edges can be left open (e.g., a row of zeros can be entered along the left edge when routing data to the right) or the opposite edges can be connected. Cases were found where open edges were preferred and other cases where connected edges were preferred. It was decided to make edge-connectivity a programmable function. A topology-register in the array control unit defines the connections between opposite edges of the PE array. The top and bottom edges can either be connected or left open. The connectivity between the left and right edges has four states: open (no connection), cylindrical (connect the left PE of each row to the right PE of the same row), open spiral (for $1 \leq n \leq 127$, connect the left PE of row n to the right PE of row $n - 1$), and closed spiral (like the open spiral, but also connect the left PE of row 0 to the right PE of row 127).

The spiral modes connect the 16 384 PE's together in one long linear array. One can pack several linear arrays of odd sizes (e.g., lines with thousands of image pixels per line) in the ARU and process them in parallel.

Redundancy

The ARU includes some redundancy so that a faulty PE can be bypassed. Redundancy can be added to a two-dimensional array of PE's by adding an extra column (or row) of PE's and inserting bypass gates in the routing network. When a faulty PE is discovered, one disables the whole column containing the faulty PE and joins the columns on either side of it with the bypass gates.

* Registered service mark of the Goodyear Aerospace Corporation, Akron, OH 44315.

TABLE I
SPEED OF TYPICAL OPERATIONS

Operations	Execution Speed*
Addition of Arrays	
8-bit integers (9-bit sum)	6553
12-bit integers (13-bit sum)	4428
32-bit floating-point numbers	430
Multiplication of Arrays (Element-by-Element)	
8-bit integers (16-bit product)	1861
12-bit integers (24-bit product)	910
32-bit floating-point numbers	216
Multiplication of Array by Scalar	
8-bit integers (16-bit product)	2340
12-bit integers (24-bit product)	1260
32-bit floating-point numbers	373

*Million Operations per Second

The PE's in the ARU are implemented with two-row by four-column VLSI chips, thus, it is more convenient to add four redundant columns of PE's and bypass four columns at a time. The PE array has 128 rows and 132 columns. It is divided into 33 groups, with each group containing 128 rows and four columns of PE's. Each group has an independent group-disable control line from the ACU. When a group is disabled, all its outputs are disabled and the groups on either side of it are joined together with 128 bypass gates in the routing network.

When there is no faulty PE, an arbitrary group is disabled so that the size of the logical array is always 128 by 128. Application programs are not aware of which group is disabled and need not be modified when the disabled group is changed. They always use the logical address of a PE to access PE dependent data. The logical address of a PE is a pair of 7-bit numbers X and Y showing its position in the logical array of enabled PE's. A simple routine executed in 27 μs will load the memory of each PE with its logical address.

When a faulty PE is discovered, its data cannot be trusted so the normal error recovery procedure is to reconfigure the ARU to disable the column containing the fault and then to restart the application program from the last checkpoint or from the beginning.

Bit-Serial Processing

The data arrays being processed have a wide range of element lengths. A spectral band of an input pixel may have a resolution of 6 to 12 bits. Intermediate results can have any length from 6 to more than 30 bits. Single-bit flag arrays are generated when pixels are classified. Some computations may be performed in floating point. Thus, the PE's should be able to process operands of any length efficiently.

Conventional computers typically use bit-parallel arithmetic units with certain fixed-word lengths such as 8, 16, or 32 bits. Operands of odd lengths are extended to fit the standard word sizes of the machine. Some of the hardware in the memory and the arithmetic unit is wasted storing and processing the extensions.

Bit-serial processors process operands bit by bit and can handle operands of any length without any wasted hardware. Their slower speed can be counteracted by using a multitude of them and processing many operands in parallel.

There is a wide variety of operand lengths and a prevalence of low-precision operands in the expected workload. Thus, bit-serial processors are more efficient in the use of hardware than bit-parallel processors.

Processing Elements

The initial MPP design had PE's using downshifting binary counters for arithmetic [4], [6], [7]. The PE design was modified to use a full adder and shift register combination for arithmetic. The modified design performs the basic arithmetic operations faster. Each of the PE's has six 1-bit registers (A, B, C, G, P, and S), a shift register with a programmable length, a random-access memory, a data bus (D), a full adder, and some combinatorial logic (see Fig. 2). The basic cycle time of the PE is 100 ns.

Logic and Routing: The P-register is used for logic and routing operations. A logic operation combines the state of the P-register and the state of the data bus (D) to form the new state of the P-register. All 16 Boolean functions of the two variables P and D are implemented. A routing operation shifts the state of the P-register into the P-register of a neighboring PE (up, down, right, or left).

Arithmetic: The full adder, shift register, and registers A, B, and C are used for bit-serial arithmetic operations. To add two operands, the bits of one operand are put into the A-register, one at a time, least significant bit (LSB) first; corresponding bits of the other operand are put into the P-register; the full adder adds the bits in A and P to the carry bits in the C-register to form the sum and carry bits; each carry bit is stored in C to be added in the next cycle; and each sum bit is stored in B. The sum formed in B can be stored in the random-access memory and/or in the shift register. Two's complement subtraction is performed by adding the one's complement of the operand in P to the operand in A and setting the initial carry bit in C to 1 instead of 0.

Multiplication is a series of addition steps where the partial product is recirculated through the shift register and registers A and B. Appropriate multiples of the multiplicand are formed in P and added to the partial product as it recirculates. Division is performed with a nonrestoring division algorithm. The partial dividend is recirculated through the shift register and registers A and B while the divisor or its complement is formed in P and added to it.

Floating-point addition compares exponents; places the fraction of the operand with the least exponent in the shift register; shifts it to the right to align it with the other fraction; adds the other fraction to the shift register; and normalizes the sum. Floating-point multiplication is a multiplication of the fractions, a normalization of the product, and an addition of the exponents.

Masking: The G-register can hold a mask bit that can control the activity of the PE. Unmasked logic, routing, and arithmetic operations are performed in all PE's. Masked operations are only performed in those PE's where the G-register equals 1.

Several operations may be combined in one 100 ns instruction. Logic and routing operations are masked independently of arithmetic operations so one can combine a masked routing operation with an unmasked arithmetic operation or vice versa. This feature proves to be quite useful in a number of algorithms.

Storage: The random-access memory stores 1024 bits per PE. Standard RAM integrated circuits are used to make it easy to expand storage as advances occur in solid-state memory technology. The ACU generates 16-bit addresses so ARU storage can be expanded to 65 536 bits per PE. Thus, the initial complement of 2 Mbytes of ARU storage can be expanded sixty-fourfold if technology allows it.

Parity error detection is used to find memory faults. A parity bit is added to the eight data bits of each 2 by 4 subarray of PE's. Parity bits are generated and stored for each memory write cycle and checked when the memories are read. A parity error sets an error

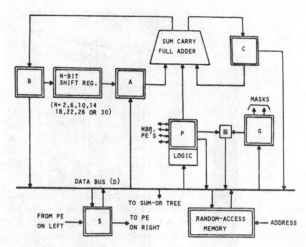

Fig. 2.   One processing element

flip-flop associated with the 2 by 4 subarray. A tree of logic elements gives the ACU an inclusive-or of all error flip-flops (after some delay). By operating the group-disable control lines, the ACU can locate the group containing the error and disable it.

Sum-Or Tree: The data bus states of all enabled PE's are combined in a tree of inclusive-or elements called the sum-or tree. The output of this tree is fed to the ACU and used in certain operations such as finding the maximum or minimum value of an array in the ARU.

Input/Output: The S-register is used to input and output ARU data. While the PE's are processing data in the random-access memories, columns of input data are shifted into the left side of the ARU (Fig. 1) and through the S-registers (Fig. 2) until a plane of 16 384 bits is loaded. The input plane is then stored in the random-access memories in one 100 ns cycle by interrupting the processing momentarily in all PE's and moving the S-register values to the memory elements. Planes of data are output by moving them from the memory elements to the S-registers and then shifting them out column by column through the right side of the ARU. The shift rate is 10 MHz; thus, up to 160 Mbytes/s can be transferred through the ARU I/O ports. Processing is interrupted for 100 ns for each bit plane of 16 384 bits transferred—less than 1 percent of the time.

Packaging

Standard 4- by 1024-bit RAM elements are used for the PE memories. All other components of a 2 by 4 subarray of PE's are packaged on a custom VLSI CMOS/SOS chip. The VLSI chip also contains the parity tree and the bypass gates for the subarray.

Each $8\frac{1}{2}$ in by 14 in printed circuit board contains 192 PE's in a 16 by 12 array. A board contains 24 VLSI chips, 54 memory elements, and some support circuitry. Eleven boards make up an array slice of 16 by 132 PE's.

Eight array slices (88 boards) make up the ARU. Eight other boards contain the topology switches, control fan out, and other support circuitry. The 96 boards of the ARU are packaged in one cabinet (the leftmost cabinet in Fig. 3). Forced-air cooling is used.

ARRAY CONTROL UNIT

Like the control units of other parallel processors, the array control unit (ACU) performs scalar arithmetic and controls the PE's. It has three sections that operate in parallel (see Fig. 4): PE control, I/O control, and main control. PE control performs all array arithmetic of the application program. I/O control manages the flow of data in and out of the ARU. Main control performs all scalar arithmetic of

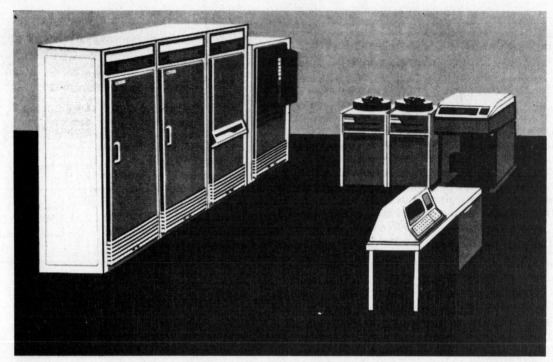

Fig. 3. MPP physical configuration.

the application program. This arrangement allows array arithmetic, scalar arithmetic, and input/output to be overlapped for minimum execution time.

PE Control

PE control generates all ARU control signals except those associated with I/O. It contains a 64-bit common register to hold scalars and eight 16-bit index registers to hold the addresses of bit planes in the PE memory elements, to count loop executions, and to hold the index of a bit in the common register. PE control reads 64-bit-wide microinstructions from PE control memory. Most instructions are read and executed in 100 ns. One instruction can perform several PE operations, manipulate any number of index registers, and branch conditionally. This reduces overhead significantly so that little, if any, PE processing power is wasted.

PE control memory contains a number of system routines and user-written routines to operate on arrays of data in the ARU. The routines include both array-to-array and scalar-to-array arithmetic operations. A queue between PE control and main control queues up to 7 calls to the PE control routines. Each call contains up to 8 initial index-register values and up to 64 bits of scalar information. Some routines extract scalar information from the ARU (such as a maximum value) and return it to main control.

I/O Control

I/O control shifts the ARU S-registers, manages the flow of information in and out of the ARU ports, and interrupts PE control momentarily to transfer data between the S-registers and buffer areas in the PE memory elements. Once initiated by main control or the PDMU, I/O control can chain through a number of I/O commands. It reads the commands from main control memory.

Main Control

Main control is a fast scalar processor. It reads and executes the application program in the main control memory. It performs all

scalar arithmetic itself and places all array arithmetic operations on the PE control call queue. It contains 16 general-purpose registers, three registers to control the ARU group-disable lines, 13 registers associated with the call queue, 12 registers to receive scalars from PE control, and six registers to monitor and control the status of PE control, I/O control, and the ARU.

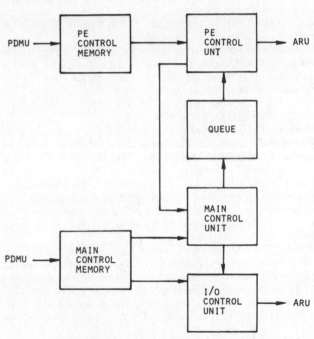

Fig. 4. Block diagram of array control unit (ACU).

PROGRAM AND DATA MANAGEMENT UNIT

The program and data management unit (PDMU) controls the overall flow of programs and data in the system (Fig. 1). Control is from an alphanumeric terminal. The PDMU is a minicomputer (DEC PDP-11) with custom interfaces to the ACU control memories and registers and to the staging memories. The operating system is DEC's RSX-11M real-time multiprogramming system.

The PDMU also executes the MPP program-development software package. The package includes a PE control assembler to develop array processing routines for PE control, a main assembler to develop application programs executing in main control, a linker to form load modules for the ACU, and a control and debug module that loads programs into the ACU, controls their execution, and facilitates debugging. This package is written in Fortran for easy movement to the host computer.

STAGING MEMORIES

The staging memories reside between the wide I/O ports of the ARU and the PDMU. They also have a port to an external (host) computer. Besides acting as buffers for ARU data being input and output, the memories reorder arrays of data.

Satellite imagery is normally stored in pixel order in the PDMU and other conventional computers. That is, line 1 pixel 1 followed by line 1 pixel 2, etc., followed by the pixels of line 2, line 3, etc. The imagery might be band-interleaved (all spectral bands of a pixel stored together) or band-sequential (band 1 of all pixels followed by band 2 of all pixels, etc.).

Arrays of data are transferred through the ARU ports in bit-sequential order. That is, the most (or least) significant bit of 16 384 elements followed by the next bit of 16 384 elements, etc. Reordering is required to fit the normal order of satellite imagery in the PDMU or the host. Thus the staging memories are given a reordering capability.

The staging memories are packaged together in a large multidimensional-access (MDA) or corner-turning memory. Items of data flow through a substager which is a smaller MDA memory. Input data items from the ARU, PDMU, or host are reformatted in the substager into patches which are sent to the large staging memory. Output data patches from the large staging memory are reformatted in the substager for transmission to the ARU, PDMU, or host.

The large staging memory uses 1280 dynamic RAM integrated-circuits for data storage and 384 RAM's for error-correcting-code (ECC) storage. (A 6-bit ECC is added to each 20-bit word.) Initially, the boards will be populated with 16K bit RAM's for a capacity of 2.5 Mbytes. Later, as memory technology advances, the 16K bit RAM's can be replaced with 64K bit RAM's or 256K bit RAM's to increase the capacity of 10 Mbytes or 40 Mbytes.

The substager can access the main stager at a 320 Mbyte per second rate (thirty-two 20-bit words every 250 ns). The accesses can be spread across the main stager in a variety of ways. Patches of data in various orientations can be read or written conveniently.

The substager has a smaller memory with 1-bit words. It assembles input data into patches for the main staging memory and disassembles patches of data from the main staging memory for output.

The main staging memory and the substager are controlled by a control unit that can be programmed to input and output imagery in a wide variety of formats.

HOST INTERFACE

The MPP to be delivered to NASA will use a DEC VAX-11/780 for a host computer. The staging memories of the MPP are connected to a DR-780 high-speed user interface of the VAX-11/780. Imagery can be transferred over this path at the rate of the DR-780 (at least 6 Mbytes/s). To allow control of the MPP by the host, the custom interface of the MPP is switched from the PDMU to the host. The switching is simplified by the fact that both the PDMU (a DEC PDP-11) and the host (a DEC VAX-11/780) have a DEC UNIBUS. The transfer of system software to the host is simplified by writing much of it in Fortran and using the compatibility mode of VAX to execute those portions written in PDP-11 code.

CONCLUSIONS

The massively parallel processor is designed to process satellite imagery at high rates. Its high-processing speed, large memory capacity, and I/O reformatting capabilities should make it useful in other applications. Preliminary studies indicate that the MPP can support such diverse application areas as general image processing, weather simulation, aerodynamic studies, radar processing, reactor diffusion analysis, and computer-image generation.

The modular structure of the MPP allows it to be scaled up or down for different applications. The number of processing elements in the ARU can be adjusted to support different processing rates. The sizes of the ARU and staging memories are also adjustable. Host computers other than the VAX-11/780 can be accommodated. The PDMU functions can be absorbed by the host or alternatively, the PDMU can act as the host (since the PDMU is in the PDP-11 and VAX family, a wide variety of PDMU capacities and configurations are feasible).

As part of their ongoing program to develop space-borne image processors, NASA Opaque Goddard is pursuing the design of a miniaturized version of the MPP [5].

REFERENCES

[1] K. E. Batcher, "The flip network in STARAN," in *1976 Proc. Int. Conf. Parallel Processing,* pp. 65–71.
[2] H. J. Siegel and S. D. Smith, "Study of multistage SIMD interconnection networks," in *Proc. 5th Annu. Symp. Comput. Architecture,* Apr. 1978, pp. 223–229.
[3] K. E. Batcher, "The multi-dimensional-access memory in STARAN," *IEEE Trans. Comput.,* vol. C-26, pp. 174–177, Feb. 1977.
[4] L-W Fung, *A Massively Parallel Processing Computer; High-Speed Computer and Algorithm Organization,* D. J. Kuck *et al.,* Ed. New York: Academic, 1977, pp. 203–204.
[5] D. H. Schaefer, "Massively parallel information processing systems for space applications," presented at AIAA Comput. Aerospace Conf. II, Oct. 1979.
[6] L. W. Fung, "MPPC: A massively parallel processing computer," Goddard Space Flight Center, Greenbelt, MD, GSFC Image Systems Section Rep., Sept. 1976.
[7] Request for Proposal, RFP GSFC-5-45191/254 (Appendix A).

A CONTROLLABLE MIMD ARCHITECTURE[a]

by
Stephen F. Lundstrom
George H. Barnes
Burroughs Corporation
Paoli, PA 19301

Abstract -- A MIMD architecture targeted at 1000 Mflop/sec has been described to NASA. This system is targeted to be the Flow Model Processor (FMP) in the Numerical Aerodynamic Simulator. This paper describes the strategies adopted for making a many-processor multiprocessor controllable and efficient, primarily by decisions that are made at compile time. Hardware features include the division of memory into space private to each processor and space shared by all, and a hardware synchronization of all processors. The connection network, connecting 512 processors to 521 memory modules, is an essential element.

Two main constructs are needed in the language to control the architecture. First, an expression that a number of instances of a given section of code can be executed concurrently, and second, a determination as to whether variables are local to the instance or global to the entire program.

Performance validations used whole programs, not kernels. Simulation and analysis combine to demonstrate achievement of the goal of 1000 Mflop/sec on suitable programs and good performance on others.

Introduction

Present generation very-high-speed computers generally exploit vector algorithms for their highest performance. A study for NASA Ames Research Center was conducted to determine the feasibility of a "Flow Model Processor" (FMP) which could achieve a sustained computational rate of one billion floating point operations per second on complete aerodynamics flow programs [1]. It concluded that the dependence on vector operations for high throughput was no longer necessary.

Given that device technology has been fully utilized, parallelism can be used to achieve performance beyond that possible with a uniprocessor. Historically, two approaches have been used to achieve parallelism: a pipeline

where parallelism is achieved by each stage of the pipeline operating on a different step of successive operation, or an array of identical execution units each simultaneously evaluating the same instruction on different data. References [2,3,4, and 5] have recent examples of both. In either case the result is a vector machine where the data comes from orderly addresses in memory and the same instruction acts on each data element.

The Flow Model Processor makes use of the parallelism of a MIMD (multiple instruction stream, multiple data stream) architecture. The architecture includes specific features so that a single program can be issued to all the processors and result in cooperative execution on a single application for a single user.

This paper describes motivations behind the design and some of the strategies used to ensure controllability. The architecture described here avoids or sidesteps the limitation observed in some MIMD architectures which are unable to utilize more than a few processors effectively. The result is an architecture that is somewhat specialized to a class of applications (although much less specialized than a vector machine would be). This architecture exploits any concurrency inherent in the problem, whether or not that concurrency can be described as vector operations.

The problem was approached by first studying the aerodynamic applications [6]. These applications have a large numerical component, much inherent concurrency, and simple control structures. Due to the wide variation in the amount of computation that may concurrently proceed between times at which synchronization is required, efficient implementation of the synchronization function is required. Due to the many different natural modes of accessing data, a large memory equally accessible to all processors is required. Due to the practical limitation on the speed attainable in a large common memory, and due to the need for speed, an architecture is required which allows many memory accesses to be from memory local to each processor.

Software strategy is based on the premise that source text submitted to the compiler should

---

[a]This work was done for NASA under Contract NAS2-9897 and reported to them in [1].

result in a single program being compiled for all processors in the array which will then execute it cooperatively. This premise is also advocated in [7]. From another point of view, the compiler emits a single program which is to be executed independently by each of the processors in the array. Included by this program are instructions which cause the processors to cooperate by sharing data and by synchronizing their actions appropriately when needed.

A second element of the strategy is to make certain decisions at compile time instead of run time. These decisions can then be supported by efficient hardware mechanisms, not by system software.

The functional constructs on which a language for this architecture is to be based can be compared to discussions previously found in the literature. A general discussion of parallel languages is found in [8]. Some proposed parallel languages are directed at the vector type of architecture, as in [9,10,11,12], others are not [13,14,15]. Some workers have proposed that the requisite parallelism can be found by starting from algorithms expressed in serial form [16,17] so that standard Fortran can be mapped onto various parallel architectures without language extensions. In the present case the architecture is such that the operations which can be done independently of each other and in parallel are whole sections of code, not restricted to single operations.

We believe that the architecture proposed here has several advantages over other parallel architectures previously proposed and that the simulations and performance validations reported below uphold this view. While no single feature of this architecture is by itself new, we believe the combination of features is. Some previously proposed architectures have all memory shared among all processors, [18, 19, 20, 21] but without processor private memory for data. In some cases, a central control processor is involved with the control of interconnections between processors, or from processors to memory [22]. N such centralized control is required here during execution of user programs. To our knowledge, fast hardware synchronization as seen here has not been proposed for MIMD architectures, although any SIMD machine, such as in [3], will be synchronized.

The development of the system concepts evolved from the applications to system architecture (involving both hardware and software) to a more detailed definition of both the hardware and software. In order to simplify the introduction of the software concepts, they will be preceded by a short summary of the hardware architecture. Following the software concept summary, a more detailed description of some parts of the hardware will be provided.

Hardware Overview

The block diagram of the proposed multiprocessor is shown in Figure 1. Salient features of this hardware are:

* A prime number of memory modules to reduce memory access conflicts.
* Separation of the memory space seen from each processor into a private part, and a section shared among all processors.
* A connection network whereby all processors can simultaneously request access to various memory modules.
* Hardware synchronization, a P-way AND of the signal from each processor that marks its having gotten to a specific point in the program.

Each of the 512 processors has its own program counter, its own local memory for program and data, and its own connection to a shared memory. The shared memory is built of many (521) independently accessible modules. In order to provide connectivity between the processors and the memory modules, a connection network which has a complexity of $O(P \log(P))$, instead of the $O(P^2)$ complexity expected for a fully general cross-point network, was chosen. This choice satisfies both the economic requirements and the bandwidth requirements of the system. For discussion of the connection network, see [23].

Software

The expense involved in application software development and maintenance over the life of a system now often exceeds the total costs of operations support and acquisition/ amortization of the computational equipment especially in development environments. The development of any new capabilities for such environments must, therefore, carefully consider both efficient utilization of the computational facility and the efficiency with which application development can proceed. In the past, unfortunately, the emphasis has been almost entirely on efficient hardware utilization. The provision of capabilities to embed assembly or machine code within high-level languages such as FORTRAN are an example of this approach. One recently introduced extended FORTRAN supports both development, with application-oriented vector forms, and efficient hardware utilization [12].

The major concern during the study was the feasibility of a hardware system with the required sustained performance. Automatic conversion of standard FORTRAN was not required. Rather, the project emphasized the definition of FORTRAN extensions that provided efficient control of the hardware capabilities ease in application definition.

Language Overview

The basic language construct chosen for this

MIMD system was one of computational processes that proceed concurrently between appropriate synchronization points. This type of construct is clearly compatible with a MIMD system. Such a construct is also convenient for application descriptions in that it is more general than the vector forms currently in use. The concurrent processes may include boundary value computations and central value computations simultaneously. Thus, each program for the FMP has a structure of pieces of normal serial code, which describe the details of what must be done at a given time, or at a given element of some index set, embedded in a control structure that expresses the location of concurrency and where the synchronization must occur.

Three extensions to standard FORTRAN are proposed. The primary extension is the construct described above which allows the definition of the inherent concurrency in a process. This construct is called "DOALL". The second extension is a construct to allow the definition of index sets, called "DOMAIN"s. The third extension is a means for identifying the data or variable dependencies between the instances of various processes and for differentiating which variables or data are independent of the global process structure and are therefore local to a particular instance.

Domains

A means for describing index sets to the compiler is needed. In FMP FORTRAN such sets are called DOMAINs. A DOMAIN has an associated name and can be interpreted as a one or multi-dimensional index set. For example, the declaration
DOMAIN/EYEJAY/: I=1, IMAX; J=1, JMAX
declares that there are IMAX*JMAX elements, each consisting of one pair of values of I and J, with values in the range shown. Standard set operators are allowed. For example, if one has also declared
DOMAIN/KAY/: K=1,KMAX
then the cartesian product
DOMAIN/IJK/: EYEJAY .X. KAY
defines a three-dimensional domain with extents in each dimension of IMAX, JMAX, and KMAX.

In the aero flow applications, only rectangular domains such as the example "IJK" were seen. Extensions to the domain concept will be needed for other applications. Simple modifications to domains can be implemented by conditional statements within the doall program segment.

In addition to their use in specifying the index sets for doalls as explained in the next section, domains can substitute for the iteration index sets in do loops, and for dimensionality in the declaration of arrays.

One convenient use of the DOMAIN construct is for the description of the geometry (or computational limits) of the problem. By naming the controlling index set, and referring to the index set by name throughout the rest of the program, changes relating to geometry need be made in only one place in the program.

DOALL Construct

The DOALL construct is the FMP FORTRAN extension for describing the inherent concurrency in a process. Figure 2 shows the conceptual flow of execution in this construct. Once the construct is entered, all individual parts may proceed simultaneously dependent on the availability of resources. Control is not allowed to pass beyond the construct until all individual parts (called instances) have completed whatever computation they are to do.

The doall construct consists of a "DOALL" header, followed by a doall program segment followed by a doall terminating delimiter. The header will contain a specification of a domain, perhaps by name. If the domain in the header is the domain "EYEJAY" as declared in the example of the previous section, and IMAX = 100 and JMAX = 50, then there are 5000 intances of the doall program segment to be executed. Each instance of the doall program segment can execute independently of, and without any interaction with, every other instance of the doall program segment. Within each instance, there may not be any references to computations within any other instance, but no restrictions on references to "old" values exist. The computation within each instance may be conditional on location in the model, on data, or on any other condition.

Hardware Support of the DOALL Construct

An issue is the mapping of the DOALL construct onto real processor resources. A DOALL construct execution begins when processors 0 through 511 pick up instance numbers 0 through 511. For a DOALL with I and J for instance variables as in the example above, each processor computes I and J values from the instance number by solving the equation
$$\text{instance number} = J*IMAX + I$$
Specifically, I is instance number modulo IMAX and J is instance number DIV IMAX. When each processor has finished its instance of the DOALL program segments, it increments instance number by 512, computes new I and J values, and proceeds to iterate thus until the I and J values computed are outside the domain. Once the processor has completed all assigned instances, it drops down to a "WAIT" instruction. When all processors get to "WAIT", a 512-way AND of the WAITing state is used to create a "go" signal which causes all processors to step to the next construct or instruction. Thus, an essential feature to make the DOALL construct work is a fast hardware

synchronization operation. DOALL program segments can be as short as a single statement. A single-statement DOALL with regular subscripting on variables exactly corresponds to a vector operation in a vector machine and hence this MIMD architecture includes vector computations as a subset of its capabilities.

Waiting implies processor idle time. In the aerodynamic flow and weather codes which were analyzed during the study, the amount of processing per processor was nearly equal for all processors, and hence processor efficiency was high, the first processor to finish being only slightly ahead of the last.

Memory Allocation

System control is simplified by making decisions at compile time rather than having them made by system software art run time. The distinction between the various sorts of memory is made in the compiler with help from programmer declarations.

The potential four types of memory allocation are:

1. A variable or array element is visible to any part of the program, can be accessed from within any instance of a doall program segment, or from any serial section of code between doall program segments.

2. A variable is a temporary variable which need not remain defined after the end of the instance in which it is used.

3. A variable is so frequently accessed that each processor deserves to have its own local copy.

4. A one-to-one relationship between the elements of an array and the elements of a domain holds. Within the instances of a doall program segment over that domain, elements of that array are accessed in correspondence to the relationship.

The exact form of the declarations for helping the compiler make appropriate assignments of different data to different types of space is still under discussion. It is clear that some analysis on the compiler's part is possible; an array which is subscripted with the instance variables inside a doall must be either type 1 or type 4, for example. If the language is to be an extended Fortran, each common area must contain variables of only one category.

The sets of memory declarations suggested to date contain some common features. First, there is a declaration to the effect that a variable is shared (type 1). Second, there is a declaration (or default) that a variable is temporary to the instance (type 2). Third, there is a means for declaring that a set of variables is of type 4. This last is the "INALL" declaration. The INALL declaration couples a variable or array with the dimensionality and index set of a domain. For example, the declaration

INALL/EYEJAY/ C1, C2, A(5)

declares that there is an element of C1, an element of C2 and five elements of A associated with each element of the domain "EYEJAY". When there is a doall construct over the domain "EYEJAY (I,J)" then these variables can be used with the doall program segment and each instance will have its own copy. Referring to a variable such as C2 either without subscripts, or with "centered subscripts" i.e., "C2(I,J)", is permissible and functionally identical. Outside of doalls over "EYEJAY", these three identifiers will identify arrays which have dimensionality C1(IMAX,JMAX), C2(IMAX,JMAX), and A(IMAX, JMAX,5) respectively.

Given that there are two kinds of memory space, memory private to each processor and memory shared by all processors, variables of type 2 and type 3 will be found in processor private memory, and type 1 would be in shared memory. If a variable of type 4 is only accessed within doalls over the appropriate domain, and always on centered subscripts, it can be held in the private memories of the processor that will compute the instances that are in one-to-one correspondence with the appropriate array elements.

Parallel Functions

Some common parallel operations and first-order linear recurrences would be supported by new intrinsics.

Parallel sum. Consider a variable defined within each instance at the end of a doall. The parallel sum of all those variables is created, which will then be accessible after the end of the doall. 512 such variables can be summed in 9 steps using interprocessor communication. Similar parallel functions are parallel AND, parallel OR, and MAXIMUM across all instances.

First-order linear recurrence. Given quantities $B(I)$ and $C(I)$ in each instance of a doall whose index set is I=1, IMAX, form the sequence $A(I) = A(I-1)*B(I) + C(I)$. $A(0)$ is given as an initial value. As with the parallel sum, this function can be implemented in N steps when $IMAX = 2^N$. [24]

Other Software Issues

Although the mechanisms shown demonstrate that one can design a langauge to enhance control of the MIMD machine by imposing structure and regularity on the MIMD interprocessor interactions at compile time, there are certain issues which have to be resolved before fixing on a final design for the language.

One issue is a trade between making memory allocation decisions based on programmer declarations and making allocation decisions by compiler analysis. Many users of high-throughput machines insist on being able to control every detail of machine action, out of fear that the vendor's compiler will be inefficient if left to its own devices.

Using Fortran as a starting point raises an issue that might not arise with some other starting point because of the requirement in Fortran for separate compilation. At compile time the compiler must distinguish between a subroutine called within a doall program segment where each instace of the doall calls its own copy, and a subroutine called outside the doall which runs on the array as a whole. The simplest solution would be to distinguish between the two kinds of subroutine by a difference in the SUBROUTINE statements.

"Every instance of the doall program segment must be independent of and free from any side effects that would interfere with any other instance of the same doall program segment". This over-simplified statement is true at the first level of understanding of the working of the machine. However, steps taken to enforce this rule are subject to a trade between authoritarian and libertarian schools of programming. There is no hardware limitation on the processors fetching or storing any variable in shared memory at any point in the program. Since the relative timing between actions that occur in different instances of the doall is not controlled, this allows for data accesses and definitions to occur in an uncontrolled order. Hence there is a question about the enforcement of data precedence. Absolute enforcement by the compiler, so that code which is emitted is guaranteed to be free of data precedence violations, may be undesirable. First, such a compiler will be unable to detect all cases in which the instances are independent of each other and as a result will forbid certain useful functions. Second, for some applications [25] a change in the sequence of performing the computations will change the result to another, different, but still acceptable result. One does not wish to forbid such programs. However, if the compiler made no check, gave the user no help, unnecessary errors might be committed. The following rule is observed to cover all cases that arise in the aero flow and weather codes, and appears simple to implement. "If an array element in shared memory is used on the right side of an assignment statement within a doall program segment then any assignment to that array in the same doall program segment must be on centered subscripts and will be held in a "new" copy of the array. The "new" copy will replace the old copy of the array at the time of synchronization at the end of the doall."

Hardware Details

Instead of implementation details, discussion below will concentrate on how hardware features support the langauge extensions.

Processor

Analysis of the aerodynamic flow and global weather model programs (provided by NASA Ames during the NASF Feasibility Study as samples of typical application programs) showed that up to several thousand processors could efficiently work in parallel. In these cases, the actual number of processors supplied is irrelevant over a large range; only total throughput matters. The design intent was to supply a processor that had maximum throughput at minimum cost. The trade-off evaluation was based on assumptions of the technology suitable for 1983 delivery and on the desire to limit complexity to control project risk. The result was 512 processors, each having capability of about 3Mflop/sec.

Each processor has independent integer and floating-point execution units with limited instruction look-ahead. To hide access time of the shared memory, each processor has a one-slot queue, called the "CN Buffer", which manages accesses to the shared memory while other processor operations go on concurrently. A processor-local memory of about 32K words is appropriate to the applications studied.

Shared Memory

In reference (1), the shared memory is called "Extended Memory" (EM). It consists of a prime number of memory modules (521) in order to reduce conflicts for the case that the pattern of accesses from the processors forms a regular pattern [26,27].

All processors independently compute accesses in shared memory, and independently access memory. Given that processor no. i is to access shared memory address A(i) the processor will compute address-within-module given by

$$L(i) = A(i) \text{ DIV } 512$$

and module number

$$M(i) = A(i) \text{ modulo } 521$$

When the addresses being accessed by the processors form a vector with constant stride the formula for the A(i) is

$$A(i)=A(0)+p*i$$

Here the M(i) fall into 512 different memory modules because p and the number of memory modules are relatively prime. This is the basis for claiming that a prime number of memory modules makes certain kinds of accessing "conflict-free".

Features for Fault Tolerance

Because of the flexibility of the connection network, a simple method of providing spare processors and memory modules is planned. Each

CN buffer contains a "replacement unit directory" to redirect connections around spare units. Single error correction, double error detection (SECDED) code covers all memory and transfers through the connection network. The connection network, being duplexed, has a simplex mode of operation as backup.

Staging Memory

Staging memory is called "Data Base Memory" in (1) where a size of 128 Mwd is assumed. Later discussions have centered on a size of 256 Mwd. Transfer rates must be on the order of 50 Mwd per second to and from shared memory. Access time requirements make disk undesirable. If staging memory were to be built of semiconductor components, then 256k-bit chips would be desirable.

The design and control of the staging memory has no surprises. The structure is one of a dual port memory. One port responds to requests from the coordinator for high-speed transfers between staging memory and Extended Memory. The other port is externally controlled and provides the high-speed data path to the rest of the system.

Connection Network

The connection network is used like a dial-up network, with any processor requesting connection to any memory module at any time, with the concommittant "message" being an address plus one word of data either stored to or fetched from the memory module involved. All processors could request simultaneously. Blockage must be low enough that the average added delay due to blockage is small compared to the time due to cable delays, access time of the memory module and memory conflicts. In addition processors must be treated "fairly". In the intended applications all processors have an equal amount of work to do. If any processor had a low probability of making its connections through the connection network, then that slower processor would tend to be the last processor arriving at the synchronization points, thereby slowing up the whole system.

The chosen configuration (Figure 3) is called the "baseline" network by Wu and Feng 28]. We first derived it as an isomorphism to the Omega network of Lawrie [29]. A parallel paper [22] discusses the design and validation of the connection network showing that it indeed performs as desired.

The time it takes to make a connection from any one of the 512 processors to any one of the 521 memory modules is estimated at 120 ns., barring conflicts or blockage. The throughput analysis of the FMP assumed a path width of 11 bits. During throughput analysis of the FMP, a particular distribution of shared memory conflicts and of blockage in the connection

network was assumed. After the simulations to evaluate performance were nearly finished, simulation of the connection network [23] showed that the assumed delays were in fact correct.

Synchronization

Synchronization is mechanized by the WAIT instruction. A processor continues to execute WAIT until a "go" signal is received. The "go" signal is the 512-way AND of a signal emitted by each waiting processor. Synchronization ensures that no processor tries to fetch new data until that data has in fact been produced, perhaps by the slowest processor, in the preceding DOALL construct.

Figure 4 shows a mechanism whereby the 512-input AND gate is implemented as a tree-form cascade of 8-input AND gates (Figure 4 is actually drawn for a 27-input AND gate implemented as a cascade of 3-input AND gates; the number of levels in the tree comes out the same in either case). The root node of the tree reflects the "GO" signal back to all processors when the "AND" output is true at the root node. Note that the spare processors must always appear to be waiting even when being serviced or checked off-line from the primary problem.

The total delay from the last processor accessing a WAIT instruction until the "go" signal reaches all processors has been estimated at 160 ns.

Performance Validation

NASA had supplied two complete three-dimensional aerodynamic flow codes, solutions of the time-averaged Navier Stokes equations, and some weather codes. Three of these programs were completely analyzed. The method of analysis was to determine the calling sequence, the path of execution through the entire program, with notations as to how often each section of the code was called. Appropriate DO loops were converted into concurrent "DOALL" constructs in which DO iterations are converted into DOALL instances. Representative sections of the programs were exercised in simulation to determine running time. Other sections had their running estimated based on how their parameters were related to the parameters of the simulated sections. The most significant parameter was the number of floating point operations per reference to the shared memory. The running time and number of floating point operations in each section are each summed to give the running time for the whole program and the number of floating point operations for the whole program. The quotient of these two totals is then the throughput for the entire program in terms of floating point operations per second. Details are in [1] in Appendix A.

The results of this analysis are summarized in Table I. In brief, performance met the target of 1.0 Gflop/sec for favorable aerodynamic applications, and varied from 0.5 Gflop/sec on up for other suitable applications. The chemistry and radiation portions of the global circulation model were not vectorized, but consisted of a doall with one instance at each point on the globe; the doall program segment having much data dependent branching within it.

Conclusion

A generalization of vector architectures for high-throughput numerical computing has been presented. The lack of any need to vectorize the application should make it more widely applicable than are the current generation of vector machines. Validation using actual application programs supports the expectation of high throughput.

The three programming constructs are the parallel execution of many instances of the same code, the use of named index sets, and the concept of two types of memory, one private to a single instance, the other shared across the entire program.

Acknowledgements

In any project of this size, many people contribute. The authors have singled out, for special acknowledgement of their contributions, Howard Pearlmutter and Philip E. Shafer.

References

[1] Final Report, Numerical Aerodynamic Simulation Facility Feasibility Study, Contract No. NAS2-9897 Burroughs Corporation, Paoli, PA, for NASA Ames, March 1979.

[2] R. M. Russell, "The Cray-1 Computer System", Communications of the ACM, Volume 21, No. 1 January 1978, pp. 63-72.

[3] P. M. Flanders, D. J. Hunt, S. F. Reddaway, D. Parkinson, "Efficient High Speed Computing with the Distributed Array Processor", in High Speed Computer and Algorithm Organization, ed. D. J. Kuck, et al, Academic Press, 1977, pp. 85-89 (SIMD).

[4] R. A. Stokes, "Burroughs Scientific Processor", in High Speed Computer and Algorithm Organization, ed., D. J. Kuck et al, Academic Press, 1977 pp. 85-89.

[5] L. Fung, "A Massively Parallel Processing Computer", in High Speed Computer and Algorithm Organization, ed., D. J. Kuck et al, Academic Press 1977, pp. 203-204 (MPP).

[6] D. R. Chapman, "Computational Aerodynamics Development and Outlook", Dryden Lectureship in Research, 17th Aerospace Sciences Meeting 1979 NASA Technical Report 79-0129.

[7] T. Christopher, O. El-Dessouki, M. Evens, P. Greene, A. Hazra, W. Huen, A. Rastogi, R. Robinson, and W. Wojciechowski, "Uniprogramming a Network Computer", 1978 International Conference on Parallel Processing IEEE, Computer Society, Long Beach CA, 1978, pp. 312-138.

[8] D. J. Kuck, "A Survey of Parallel Machine Organization and Programming", Computing Survey, Volume 9, No. 1 (March 1977), pp. 29-60.

[9] D. H. Lawrie, T. Layman, D. Baer, J. M. Randal, "Glypnir - A Programming Language for Illiac IV", Communications of the ACM, Volume 18, No. 3, March 1975, pp. 157-164.

[10] E. W. Davis "STARAN Parallel Processor System Software", AFIPS National Computer Conference, 1974, pp. 17-22.

[11] J. R. Dingledine, H. G. Martin, and W. M. Patterson, "Operating System and Support Software for PEPE", Sagamore Conference on Parallel Processing, Proceedings, 1973 IEEE, pg. 170-178 (claims to describe PFOR).

[12] Burroughs Corporation, Burroughs Scientific Processor (BSP) Fortran Reference Manual, Ref. No. 1118338, February 1980, Paoli, PA.

[13] J. B. Dennis, D. P. Misunas, and C. K. Leung, "A Highly Parallel Processor Using a Data Flow Machine Language", Computation Structures Group Memo. 134, MIT, January 1977.

[14] P. Brinch-Hansen, "The Programming Language Concurrent Pascal", IEEE Transactions on Software Engineering, June, 1975, pp. 199-207.

[15] J. P. Anderson, "Program Structure for Parallel Processing", Communications of the ACM, Volume 8, No. 13 (December 1965), pp. 431-155. (Very early discussion of "conventional" multiprocessors).

[16] D. J. Kuck, P. P. Budnick, S. C. Chen, E. W. Davis, Jr., J. C. Han, P. W. Kraska, D. H. Lawrie, Y. Muraoka, R. E. Strebendt, and R. A. Towle, "Measurements of Parallelism in Ordinary Fortran Programs", IEEE Computer, Vol. 7, No. 1, pp. 37-46, Jan, 1974.

[17] Leslie Lamport, "Parallel Execution of DO Loops", Communications of the ACM, Volume 17, No. 2, February 1974, pp. 83-93.

[18] R. J. Swan, S. H. Fuller, D. P. Siewiorek, "Cm*, a Modular, Multiprocessor", in "Collection

of Papers on Cm*", Technical Report, Computer Science Dept., Carnegie-Mellon University, February, 1977.

[19] W. A. Wulf, C. G. Bell, "C.mmp - A Multi-mini-processor", AFIPS Conference Proceedings Vol. 14, Part II, FJCC 1972, pp. 765-777.

[20] H. J. Siegel, P. T. Mueller, Jr., and H. E. Smalley, Jr., "Control of a Partitionable Multi-microprocessor System", Proceedings of the 1978 International Conference on Parallel Processing, IEEE Computer Society, 1978.

[21] Burton J. Smith, "A Pipelined, Shared Resource MIND Computer", Proceedings of the 1978 International Conference on Parallel Processing, IEEE Computer Society, 1978.

[22] R. Kober, C. H. Kunzia, "SMS - A Multi-processor Architecture for High Speed Numerical Calculations", Proceedings of the 1978 Inter-atnional Conference on Parallel Processing, IEEE Computer Society, 19781.

[23] G. H. Barnes, "Design and Validation of a Connection Network for Many-processor Multi-processor Systems", this conference.

[24] S. C. Chen, D. J. Kuck, "Time and Parallel Processor Bounds for Linear Recurrence System", IEEE Transactions on Computers, Volume C-24, No. 7, July 1975, pp. 701-717.

[25] Gerald M. Baudet "Asynchronous Iterative Methods for Multiprocessors", Journal of the ACM, Volume 25, No. 2, April 1978, pp. 226-244.

[26] P. Budnick and D. J. Kuck, "The Organization and Use of Parallel Memories", IEEE Transactions on Computers, December 1971.

[27] Roger C. Swanson, "Interconnection for Parallel Memories to Unscramble p-ordered Vectors, IEEE Transactions on Computers, November 1974.

[28] C. Wu and T. Feng, "Routing Techniques for a Class of Multistage Interconnection Networks", Proceedings of the 1978 International Conference on Parallel Processing, IEEE Computer Society, 1978.

[29] D. H. Lawrie, "Access and Alignment of Data in an Array Processor", IEEE Transactions on Computers, C-24 (1975), pp. 1145-1155.

Table I

Performance Summary

Case	Grid Size	No. Time Step	Thru put; Gf/s	Run Time min.
Implicit	100x 50x200	100	1.01	6
Explicit	100x100x100	100	0.89	9
Weather	89x144x 9	1008	0.53	4.5
FFT	512 to 4096	-	0.45-0.7	-

Implicit = Implicit Aero Flow Code
Explicit = Mixed Explicit/Implicit Aero Flow Code
Weather = Global Circulation Model
FFT   = Fast Fourier Transform

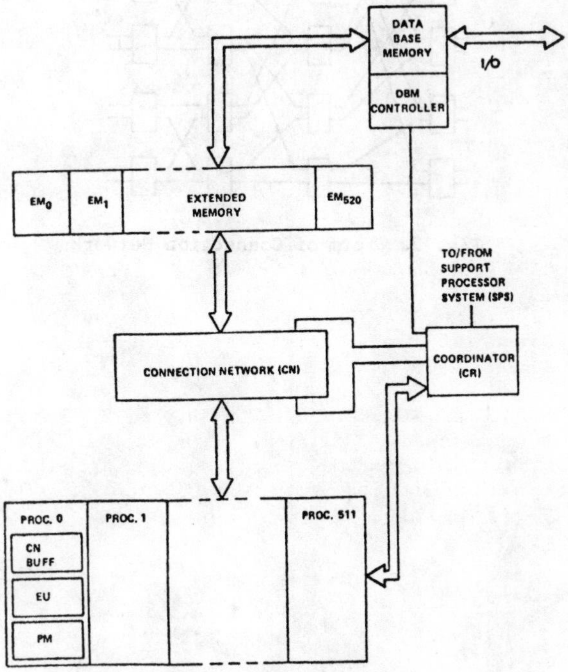

Fig. 1. Block Diagram

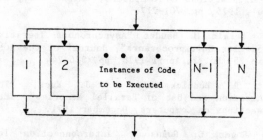

Fig. 2. Flowchart, Concurrent Construct

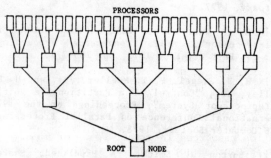

Fig. 4. Tree Form of AND Implementation

Fig. 3. Form of Connection Network

A PIPELINED, SHARED RESOUCE MIMD COMPUTER

Burton J. Smith
Denelcor, Inc.
Denver, Colorado 80205

Abstract -- The HEP computer system currently
being implemented by Denelcor, Inc., under contract to the U.S. Army Ballistics Research Laboratory is an MIMD machine of the shared resource
type as defined by Flynn. In this type of organization, skeleton processors compete for
execution resources in either space or time.
In the HEP processor, spatial switching occurs
between two queues of processes; one of these
controls program memory, register memory, and
the functional units while the other controls
data memory. Multiple processors and data
memories may be interconnected via a pipelined
switch, and any register memory or data memory
location may be used to synchronize two processes on a producer-consumer basis.

Overview

The HEP computer system currently being implemented by Denelcor, Inc., under contract to
the U.S. Army Ballistics Research Laboratory is
an MIMD machine of the shared resource type as
defined by Flynn [1]. In this type of organization, skeleton processors compete for execution
resources in either space or time. For example,
the set of peripheral processors of the CDC 6600
[5] may be viewed as an MIMD machine implemented
via the time-multiplexing of ten process states
to one functional unit.

In a HEP processor, two queues are used to
time-multiplex the process states. One of these
provides input to a pipeline which fetches a three
address instruction, decodes it, obtains the two
operands, and sends the information to one of
several pipelined function units where the operation is completed. In case the operation is a
data memory access, the process state enters a
second queue. This queue provides input to a
pipelined switch which interconnects several data
memory modules with several processors. When the
memory access is complete, the process state is
returned to the first queue. The processor organization is shown in Figure 1, and the over-all
system layout appears in Figure 2.

Each processor of HEP can support up to 128
processes, and nominally begins execution of a
new instruction (on behalf of some process) every
100 nanoseconds. The time required to completely
execute an instruction is 800 ns, so that if at
least eight totally independent processes, i.e.
processes that do not share data, are executing
in one processor the instruction execution rate
is 10^7 instructions per second per processor. The
first HEP system will have four processors and
128K words of data memory.

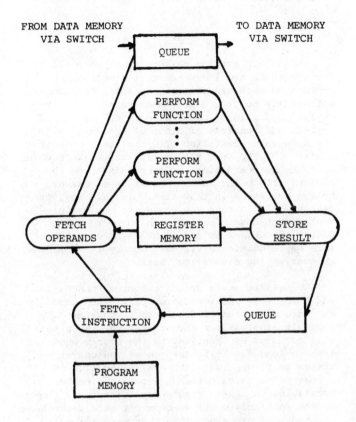

Figure 1. Processor Organization

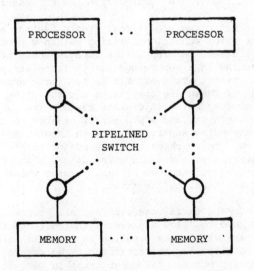

Figure 2. Overall System Layout

EH0246-9/86/0000/0039$01.00 © 1978 IEEE

HEP instructions and data words are 64 bits wide. The floating point format is sign magnitude with a hexadecimal, seven-bit, excess-64 exponent. All functional units can support one instruction execution every 100 nanoseconds except the divider, which can support this rate momentarily but is slower on the average.

Tasks

Since HEP attains maximum speed when all of its processes are independent, a simple set of protection mechanisms is incorporated to allow potentially hostile users to execute simultaneously. A domain of protection in HEP is called a task, and consists of a set of processes with the same task identifier (TID) in their process state. The TID specifies a task status word which contains base and limit addresses defining the regions within the various memories accessible by the processes in that task. In this way, processes within a task may cooperate but are prevented from communicating with those in other tasks. Processes in different tasks or processors may communicate via data memory if they have an overlapping allocation there.

Processes are a scarce resource in HEP; in addition, the synchronization primitives used in HEP make processes difficult to virtualize. As a result, the maximum number of processes a task will use must be specified to the system when the task is loaded. It is the job of the operating system to insure that its total allocation of processes to tasks does not exceed the number available, so that a create fault (too many processes) can only occur when one or more tasks have created more processes than they were allocated. In this event, the offending task or tasks (not necessarily the task that actually caused the create fault) are removed from the processor.

Protection violations, create faults, and other error conditions arising within a process cause traps. A trap is the creation of a process executing in a supervisor task. There are a total of sixteen tasks available in each processor; eight of these are user tasks and the other eight are corresponding supervisor tasks. When any process in it, and a process is created in the corresponding supervisor task to handle the condition. This scheme is not used for create fault, however; a create fault suspends execution of all processes (regardless of task) except those actually handling the fault.

Create fault occurs before all processes have been used to allow any create instructions in progress within the pipeline to complete normally and to allow for the creation of the create fault handler process. All other traps in HEP are precise in the sense that no subsequent instructions will be executed from the offending task, a useful feature when one is trying to debug a concurrent algorithm.

Synchronization

The synchronization of processes in HEP is made simple by virtue of the fact that any register or data memory location can be used to synchronize two processes in a producer-consumer fashion. This requires three states in general: a reserved state to provide for mutual exclusion, a full state, and an empty state. The execution of an instruction tests the states of locations and modifies them in an indivisible manner; typically, an instruction tests its sources full and its destination empty. If any of these tests fails, the instruction is reattempted by the process on its next turn for servicing. If all tests succeed, the instruction is executed; the process sets both sources empty and the destination reserved. The operands from the sources are sent to the function unit, and the program counter in the process state is incremented. When the function unit eventually writes a result in the destination location that was specified in the instruction it sets the destination full. Provisions are made to test a destination full rather than empty, to preserve the state of a source, or to totally override the state of a source or destination with the proviso that a reserved state may not be overridden except by certain privileged instructions. Input-output synchronization is handled naturally by mapping I/O device registers into the data memory address space; an interrupt handler is just a process that is attempting to read an input location or write an output location. I/O device addresses are not relocated by the data memory base address and all I/O-addressed operations are privileged.

Switch

The switch that interconnects processors and data memories to allow memory sharing consists of a number of nodes connected via ports. Each node has three ports, and can simultaneously send and receive a message on each port. The messages contain the address of the recipient, the address of the originator, the operation to be performed by the recipient, and a priority. Each switch node receives a message on each of its three ports every 100 nanoseconds and attempts to re-transmit each message on a port that will reduce the distance of that message from its recipient; a table mapping the recipient address into the number of a port that reduces distance is stored in each node for this purpose. If conflict for a port occurs, the node routes one of the contending messages correctly and the rest incorrectly. To help insure fairness, an incorrectly routed message has its priority incremented as it passes through the node, and preference is given in conflict situations to the message(s) with the highest priority.

The time required to complete a memory operation via the switch includes two message transmission times, one in each direction, since the success or failure of the operation (based on the state of the memory location, i.e. <u>full</u> or <u>empty</u>) must be reported back to the processor so that it can decide whether to reattempt the operation or not. The propagation delay through a node and its associated wiring is 50 nanoseconds. Since a message is distributed among two (or three) nodes at any instant, the switch must be two-colorable to avoid conflicts between the beginning of some message and the middle part of another. When the switch fills up due to a high conflict rate, misrouted massages begin to "leak" from the switch. Every originator is obliged to reinsert a leaking message into the switch in preference to inserting a new message. Special measures are taken when the priority value reaches its maximum in any message to avoid indefinite delays for such messages; a preferable scheme would have been to let priority be established by time of message creation except for the large number of bits required to specify it.

FORTRAN Extensions

Two extensions have been made to FORTRAN to allow the programmer to incorporate parallelism into his programs. First, subroutines whose names begin with "$" may execute in parallel with their callers, either by being CREATEd instead of CALLed or by executing a RESUME prior to a RETURN. Second, variables and arrays whose names begin with "$" may be used to transmit data between two processes via the <u>full-empty</u> discipline. A simple program to add the elements of an array $A is shown in Figure 3. The subroutines $INPUT and $OUTPUT perform obvious functions, and the subroutine $ADD does the work of adding up the elements. There are a total of 14 processes executing as a result of running the program.

```
C       ADD UP THE ELEMENTS OF
C       THE ARRAY $A
        REAL $A(1000),$S(10),$SUM
        INTEGER I
        CREATE $INPUT($A,1000)
        DO 10 I=1,10
        CREATE $ADD($A(100*I-99),$S(I),100)
   10 CONTINUE
        CREATE $ADD($S,$SUM,10)
        CREATE $OUTPUT($SUM,1)
        END

C       NOELTS ELEMENTS OF $V
C       ARE ADDED AND PLACED IN $ANS
        SUBROUTINE $ADD($V,$ANS,NOELTS)
        REAL $V(1),$ANS,TEMP
        INTEGER J, NOELTS
        TEMP=0.0
        DO 20 J=1,NOELTS
        TEMP=TEMP+$V(J)
   20 CONTINUE
        $ANS=TEMP
        RETURN
        END
```

Figure 3. HEP FORTRAN Example

Applications

As a parallel computer, HEP has an advantage over SIMD machines and more loosely coupled MIMD machines in two application areas. The first of these involves the solution of large systems of ordinary differential equations in simulating continuous systems. In this application, vector operations are difficult to apply because of the precedence constraints in the equations, and loosely coupled MIMD organizations are hard to use because a good partition of the problem to share workload and minimize communication is hard to find. Scheduling becomes relatively easier as the number of processes increases [3], and is quite simple when one has one process per instruction as in a data flow architecture [4].

A second type of application for which HEP seems to be well suited is the solution of partial differential equations for which the adjacencies of the discrete objects in the model change rapidly. Free surface and particle electrodynamics problems have this characteristic. The difficulty here is one of constantly having to rearrange the model within the computer to suit the connectivity implied by the architecture. Tightly coupled MIMD architectures have little implied connectivity. Associative SIMD architectures of the right kind may perform well on these problems, however.

Conclusion

The HEP system described above represents a compromise between the very tightly coupled data flow architectures and more loosely coupled multicomputer systems [2]. As a result, it has some of the advantages of each approach: It is relatively easy to implement parallel algorithms because any memory location can be used to synchronize two processes, and yet it is relatively inexpensive to implement large quantities of memory. In addition, the protection facilities make it possible to utilize the machine either as a multiprogrammed computer or as an MIMD computer.

References

[1] Flynn,M.J. "Some Computer Organizations and Their Effectiveness", IEEE-C21 (Sept. 1972).

[2] Jordan,H.F. "A Special Purpose Architecture for Finite Element Analysis", International Conference on Parallel Processing (1978).

[3] Lord,R.E. "Scheduling Recurrence Equations for Parallel Computation", Ph.D. Thesis, Dept. of Computer Science, Wash. State Univ. (1976).

[4] Rumbaugh,J. "A Data Flow Multiprocessor", IEEE-C26, p. 138 (Feb. 1977).

[5] Thornton,J.E. "Parallel Operation in the Control Data 6600", Proc. FJCC vol 26, part 2, p. 33 (1964).

THE FLEX/32 MULTICOMPUTER

Nicholas Matelan

Flexible Computer Corporation
1801 Royal Lane, Suite #810
Dallas, TX 75229

ABSTRACT

The FLEX/32 MultiComputer is a directly programmable general purpose, Multiple Instruction Stream/Multiple Data Stream (MIMD) computing environment. It is a collection of computers that share high-speed memory and synchronization and messaging hardware. The FLEX/32 can expand in power with minimal software modification and its hardware can be configured and reconfigured easily. It is a generic "multicomputing environment" for cooperating multiple processors. The FLEX/32 can support a number of different processor types by providing consistent storage and input/output facilities to its differing processors accessable through standard VMEbus connections.

The FLEX/32 supports the full UNIX* System V Operating System and languages associated with it, plus the extended ConCurrent C** and ConCurrent FORTRAN** 77 languages that allow programming of concurrent software at a high level.

INTRODUCTION

The FLEX/32 is a MultiComputing Environment (figure 1); that is, it is an environment that supports multiple computers working on one or more tasks together or independently under coordinated software. These computers need not be the same. Therefore, the environment is heterogeneous in nature. The computers (which are FLEX/32 modules) supported in this environment can differ in power, in the amount of memory supported, and in their basic orientations. Some of these computers could contain processors dedicated to control, while others might be used for array processing and floating point operations, for example.

A new computer, with its new processor and instruction set, can be adapted to the environment according to the FLEX Integration Model. Such new computer modules can be used, side by side, with all previously available computer modules. Once the adaptation has been made, the generic software and input/output capabilities of the environment are fully available to the new processor. Such software includes the UNIX* System V Operating

*UNIX is a trademark of AT&T Bell Laboratories
**ConCurrent C and ConCurrent FORTRAN are trademarks of Flexible Computer Corporation

FIGURE 1   THE FLEX/32 MULTICOMPUTER

System, and other special tools needed for developing concurrent programs.

Input/Output is performed via a set of standard VMEbuses. These buses support interfaces to peripheral equipment that may be purchased from any of the 100 or more current providers of VMEbus interfaces or from Flexible Computer Corporation, giving a truly open architecture.

A final, but no less significant, feature of the environment is its SelfTest System. Built-in

Reprinted from *Proceedings of the 12th International Symposium on Computer Architecture*, 1985, pages 209-213. Copyright © 1985 by The Institute of Electrical and Electronics Engineers, Inc.

to the environment and distributed throughout its modules (computers, memory and peripheral interfaces) are test circuits dedicated to determining the health and performance of the environment as a whole. This system allows not only such features as automatic shutdown and restart in response to power failures, but also fault isolation and repair verification, and performance analysis based on information collected during the run-time execution of programs.

THE FLEX/32

The FLEX/32 is an MIMD (Multiple Instruction Stream/Multiple Data Stream) Multiprocessor System. Its architecture is generically represented in figure 2.

The components of the FLEX/32 hardware are divided into the Card Level, the Backplane Level, and the Unit Level. There are three classes of cards in a FLEX/32 System. These are Universal Cards, Common Communication Cards, and Peripheral Cards.

Universal Cards support local bus activities such as computation, memory storage, array processing, and other such activities. Common Communication Cards allow access to, arbitration of, and control over the common buses and their shared resources, such as the common memory. Peripheral Interface Cards are standard single, dual, or triple Eurocard interfaces available from commercial manufacturers. These cards are interconnected via a backplane supporting the Local Bus, Common Bus, and SelfTest Buses.

The Local Bus is a standard, asynchronous VMEbus with extensions for control internal to the FLEX/32 cabinet. The Common Bus is a synchronous version of the Local Bus. The Common Communication Cards house a high-speed shared memory. The SelfTest Bus is an RS422´bus supporting the SDLC protocol. All external communications are through bus interfaces on Universal Cards to standard VMEbuses (no extensions). Peripheral buses are attached to standard VMEbus Interface Cards.

Cards are housed in two types of units. One unit is the MultiComputer Unit, or MU. It is the MU that houses both Universal Cards and Common Communication Cards. All Interface Cards to peripheral equipment are housed in a second type of unit called a Peripheral Control Unit or PCU. Cables between the two units allow computers attached to local buses to control their various I/O devices.

The MultiComputer Unit can support up to ten local buses and two common buses. There can be twenty universal cards in a MultiComputer Unit, two per local bus. The MultiComputer Unit supports up to ten communication cards, one for each local bus, allowing any processor attached to any local bus to communicate with any other processor, either through a shared memory associated with a common communication card or through the direct

interprocessor messaging capability. Furthermore, a common lock capability allows a processor to define a critical region in the shared memory and to own that region for operations without affecting traffic on the common bus.

The initial Universal Cards offered by Flexible Computer Corporation are the Computer 1 Card and the Mass Memory Card. The C1C (Computer 1 Card) is based on the National 32032 processor. Other cards, such as the C2C, are based on other processor types. Each Computer Card includes its processor with attached floating point coprocessor and 128K bytes of ROM, one to four megabytes of memory protected by error correction and detection logic, and a VMEbus port that can be configured to either 32 or 16-bits of data. The processor can access its bus interfaces and its memory on this card without affecting the operation of its local bus. It should be noted that all FLEX/32 processor types can be mixed and matched in each FLEX/32 MultiComputer Unit, running at the same time under the same software.

The Memory Card supports from 1 to 8 megabytes of random access memory protected by error correction and detection logic. It also contains a VMEbus interface.

The MultiComputer Unit can be configured in a number of ways. For example, a unit can be configured with twenty computer cards giving a machine with twenty processors, twenty megabytes of memory, and twenty VMEbus interfaces. This system could also be configured to support up to 20 megabytes of fast common memory. Another system could be configured with one computer card, and the remainder of the MU filled with memory. This would give a system with one processor and twenty VMEbus interfaces plus 153 megabytes of memory. A more usual card complement would be four or five computer cards with an extra mass memory card giving processors with 9 megabytes of memory each, and perhaps a few single processing cards without extra memory. Future computer card types will include floating point capability in the 4 to 6 megaflops (millions of floating point operations per second) range.

VMEbus interfaces can be simply connected together giving extra shared paths than those associated with the common buses. Interprocess communications over these paths can be made using read/modify/write interprocess communication instructions between Local Memories. The same connections can be used to connect multiple MultiComputer Units together forming much larger systems. Four of these VMEbuses, for example, could be used to connect to neighbors north and south, and east and west. Such a method could be used to define planes of MultiComputer Units, connected in rings, stars or other configurations. For example, six interconnections could be used to define hypercube elements of MultiComputer Units yielding a large number of computers (dozens to thousands) that could be applied to the same or separate tasks.

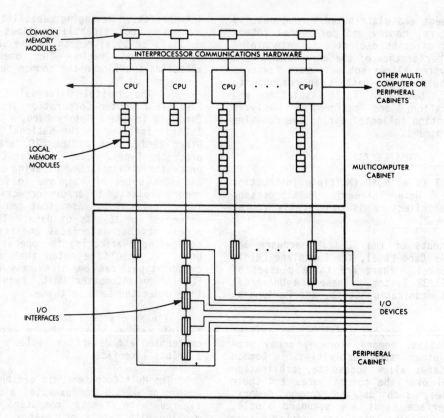

COMMON MEMORY MODULES

INTERPROCESSOR COMMUNICATIONS HARDWARE

CPU   CPU   CPU   . . .   CPU

OTHER MULTI-COMPUTER OR PERIPHERAL CABINETS

LOCAL MEMORY MODULES

MULTICOMPUTER CABINET

I/O INTERFACES

I/O DEVICES

PERIPHERAL CABINET

FIGURE 2
THE FLEX/32 GENERIC ARCHITECTURE AND PACKAGING

THE PROGRAMMING AND OPERATING ENVIRONMENTS

Three different operating environments are provided with the FLEX/32 MultiComputer (figure 3). They are:

o UNIX System V - sequential or concurrent operating environment;

o Concurrency Simulator under UNIX System V-simulated MMOS concurrent operating environment used for code development;

o Multicomputing Multitasking Operating System (MMOS)- concurrent operating environment.

The first environment is the UNIX System V Operating System itself. UNIX supports both sequential and concurrent processing. The second environment provides for execution of processes within a simulated MMOS concurrent environment under UNIX System V. The third environment (MMOS), allows execution under a Concurrent Executive; it is a true parallel computer, concurrent operating environment allowing fully stand-alone, non-UNIX execution.

These three environments allow a phased migration from sequential programs to fully concurrent applications. This is especially impor-

tant in developing concurrent programs for execution in a multicomputing environment where many system developers and programmers are developing code.

Flexible Computer provides the full UNIX System V Operating System supported on each computer within the MultiComputing Environment. UNIX includes support software such as SCCS (Source Code Control System) and its associated editors and language processors, such as FORTRAN 77, RATFOR, SNOBOL, and Assembly Language. It provides development and debugging tools and file management capabilities within the most portable operating system presently available. In addition, concurrent execution of processes can be simulated using the "shared memory" software capability of UNIX System V, or truly executed simultaneously.

For development of concurrent applications, Flexible Computer has also extended the C and FORTRAN languages to produce the new languages ConCurrent C[1] and ConCurrent FORTRAN. These languages are standard C and FORTRAN with an extra set of statements that allow direct specification of concurrent programs for execution in the FLEX/32 environment.

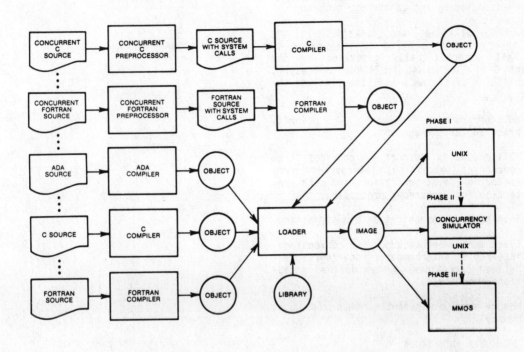

FIGURE 3   MULTICOMPUTING ENVIRONMENT DEVELOPMENT TOOLS

Multicomputing Environment Development Tools

The FLEX/32 provides extensions to the UNIX System V interprocess communications (IPC) that support applications in a multiprocessing environment. The three IPC components are: semaphores, shared memory, and messaging. These components are extended in the following ways:

o To support semaphores shared by multiple computers, Common Bus semaphores are implemented by using the conditional critical region concept with semaphore data structures stored in Common Memory. Synchronization is implemented in one of two ways: by polling for change of status or by interprocess messages activated on a change of status.

o Shared memory is provided by placing shared memory data structures in Common Memory. Processes can place a section of Common Memory in their virtual address space by using an extension of the system calls to attach and detach shared memory.

o Flexible's extensions to messaging system calls, and the placement of message data structures in Common Memory, allow messages to be sent from a process in one computer to another process in another computer. The messaging driver uses special FLEX/32 hardware to synchronize

access to the message queues and to retrieve messages from queues. Message arrival is signalled to waiting receivers either by polling for new messages or by interprocess messages.

A number of "session level" services are supported by using FLEX/32 MultiComputer primitives. These services include:

1. Remote line printer queuing - allows multiple computers to share line printers.

2. Remote mail - permits electronic mail to be sent from one computer to another computer.

3. Remote process execution - allows processes to create (open) other processes on other computers.

4. File transfer - permits the sending and receiving of files from one computer to another computer.

Multicomputing Multitasking Operating System

The Multicomputing Multitasking Operating System (MMOS) is a real-time operating system that contains utilities and library routines to provide concurrent processing run-time support. At load time these routines satisfy system calls that are generated during ConCurrent C or ConCurrent FORTRAN precompilation. These system calls perform run-time activities, such as synchronization and timing directed by the concurrent programs.

The MMOS utilities are contained in the System Library and are called by the Loader to resolve all external calls generated by the ConCurrent C or ConCurrent FORTRAN preprocessor. The capabilities of the MMOS utilities include the following:

o Multiprogramming support - priority oriented task management.

o Multicomputing support - provides true concurrent processing, interprocess communication, synchronization, and data protection for concurrent processing.

o Interprocess communication and signalling.

o Event management to supervise conventional interrupts, intercomputer interrupts, user defined exceptions, system defined exceptions, and timers.

o Memory pool management (Common and Local Memory).

o MMOS/UNIX interfaces.

Any program can run under UNIX or MMOS with no changes.

CONCLUSION

Multiple processor architectures can offer not only aggregated power, but also flexibility in both logical and physical configuration. The FLEX/32 is such an architecture. Its physical regularity, software and expansion capability make it suitable for a wide range of applications.

REFERENCES

1. Naeini, Ray: The ConCurrent C Programming Language, Electronics, vol. 57, no. 13, June 28, 1984.

Chapter 3: Proposed Novel Architectures

Several novel architectural features have been proposed[1-6], and many of them have been implemented. One of the major innovative ideas that has induced enormous interest is the data flow architecture, which is based on the concept of flow of data, thereby eliminating the need for a program counter. As the data flow explores all the inherent parallelism, it has far reaching impact on the way systems are designed and/or are programmed. Several alternative data flow schemes, emphasizing different aspects, have been proposed in the literature[9-22]. The instruction set design and data flow within a task have been considered[23-29]. The design for signal processing applications is described by Sawkar et al.[30] and by Hogenauer et al.[31]. The execution of data-flow program and language issues is discussed in[32-37], while allocation of data and mapping of algorithms onto architecture are taken up in[38-41]. An extensive overview of data flow and similar architectures are provided[41-43]. Some of the limitations and problems associated with routing of data in data flow machines are addressed by Gajski et al.[44]. Two alternative schemes that address some of these issues are described by Requa and McGraw[45], Fostel[46], and Charlesworth[47].

Substantial progress has been made in defining architectures for array and vector processing[45-50]. The advances in VLSI technology have specifically enhanced the feasibility of including thousands of processors, and off-chip time delays have encouraged the use of a large number of simple processors on a single VLSI chip[48,51]. Several on-chip and off-chip switches have been introduced in designing programmable and dynamic architectures[54-58]. Haynes et al.[59] and Hoshino et al.[60] review highly parallel schemes. Many other important projects have been persued. Some of the supercomputers and fifth-generation computer system projects are described[72-83].

Relative advantages of SIMD, multiple SIMD, and MIMD machines are not clear, and pros and cons of employing one or the other and their suitability for various applications are still open questions. In view of this, various architectures for MIMD computations and partitionable SIMD/MIMD machines[87-96] have been covered.

Four papers are included in this chapter, which basically covers several of the novel architectures described in the literature and currently being examined and followed by various researchers.

References

1 R.W. Doran, "The Amdahl 470 V/8 and the IBM 3033: A Comparison of Processor Designs," *Computer*, Vol. 15, No. 4, April 1982, pp. 27-36.

2 D.J. Kuck and R.A. Stokes, "The Burroughs Scientific Processor (BSP)," *IEEE Trans. Computers*, Vol. C-31, No. 5, May 1982, pp. 363-376.

3 L.H. Holley et al., "VM/370 Asymmetric Multiprocessing," *IBM Systems Journal*, Vol. 18, No. 1, 1979, pp. 47-70.

4 K. Miura and K. Uchida, "FACOM Vector Processor VP-100/VP-200," *Proc. NATO Advanced Research Workshop on High-Speed Computing*, Springer-Verlag, New York, N.Y., 1983.

5 R. Bonami, J.M. Cotton, and J.N. Denenberg, "ITT 1240 Digital Exchange Architecture," *Electrical Communication, ITT Tech. Journal*, Vol. 56, No. 213, 1981, pp. 126-134,

6 J.B. Dennis, "The Varieties of Data Flow Computers," *Proc. 1st Int'l. Conf. Distributed Computing Systems*, IEEE Computer Society, Washington, D.C., 1979, pp. 430-439.

7 J. Rumbaugh, "A Data Flow Multiprocessor," *IEEE Trans. Computers*, Vol. C-26, No. 2, Feb. 1977, pp. 138-146.

8 J.B. Dennis, "Data Flow Supercomputers," *Computer*, Vol. 13, No. 11, Nov. 1980, pp. 48-56.

9 J.B. Dennis, G.A. Boughton, and C.K. Leung, "Building Blocks for Data Flow Prototypes," *Proc. 7th Ann. Symp. Computer Architecture*, IEEE Computer Society, Washington, D.C., May 1980, pp. 193-200.

10 J. Gurd and I. Watson, "Data Driven System for High Speed Parallel Computing—Part 1: Structuring Software for Parallel Execution," *Computer Design*, Vol. 19, No. 6, June 1980, pp. 90-100; "Data Driven System for High Speed Parallel Computing—Part 2: Hardware Design," *Computer Design*, Vol. 9, No. 7, July 1980, pp. 97-106.

11 J.L. Gaudiot and M.D. Ercegovac, "A Scheme for Handling Arrays in Dataflow Systems," *Proc. 3rd Int'l. Conf. Distributed Computing Systems*, IEEE Computer Society, Washington, D.C., 1982, pp. 724-729.

12 G.S. Miranker, "Implementation of Procedures on a Class of Data Flow Processors," *Proc. 1977 Int'l. Conf. Parallel Processing*, IEEE Computer Society, Washington, D.C., 1977, pp. 77-86.

13 R.W. Marczyski and J. Milewski, "A Data Driven System Based on a Microprogrammed Processor Module," *Proc. 10th Ann. Symp. Computer Architecture*, IEEE Computer Society, Washington, D.C., 1983, pp. 98-107.

14 D. Conte, N. Hifdi, and J.C. Syre, "The Data Driven LAV Multiprocessor System: Results and Perspectives," *Proc. IFIP Congress*, IFIPS Press, North Holland, Amsterdam, The Netherlands.

15 J.B. Dennis and G.C. Rong, "Maximum Pipelining of Array Operations on Static Data Flow Machine" *Proc. 1983 Int'l. Conf. Parallel Processing,* IEEE Computer Society, Washington, D.C., 1983, pp. 331-334.

16 K. Hiraki, T. Shimada, and K. Nishida, "A Hardware Design of the Sigma-1, A Data Flow Computer for Scientific Computations," *Proc. 1984 Int'l. Conf. Parallel Processing*, IEEE Computer Society, Washington, D.C., 1984, pp. 524-531.

17 W.M. Leler, "A Small, High-Speed Data Flow Processor," *Proc. 1983 Int'l. Conf. Parallel Processing*, IEEE Computer Society, Washington, D.C., 1983, pp. 341-343.

18 N. Takahashi and M. Amamiya, "A Data Flow Processor Array System: Design and Analysis," *Proc. 10th Ann. Symp. Computer Architecture*, IEEE Computer Society, Washington, D.C., 1983, pp. 243-250.

19 K.W. Todd, "Function Sharing in a Static Data Flow Machine," *Proc. 1982 Int'l. Conf. on Parallel Processing*, IEEE Computer Society, Washington, D.C., 1982, pp. 137-139.

20 M. Tokoro, J.R. Jaganathan, and H. Unahara, "On the Working Set Concept for Data-Flow Machines," *Proc. 10th Ann. Symp. Computer Architecture*, IEEE Computer Society, Washington, D.C., 1983, pp. 90-97.

21 A. Omondi and D. Klappholz, "Data Driven Computation on Process-Based MIMD Machines," *Proc. 1984 Int'l. Conf. Parallel Processing*, IEEE Computer Society, Washington, D.C., I984, pp. 535-538.

22 I. Watson and J. Gurd, "A Practical Data Flow Computer," *Computer*, Vol. 15, No. 2, Feb. 1982, pp. 51-57.

23 B.R. Preiss and V.C. Homacher, "Data Flow on a Queue Machine," *Proc. 12th Int'l. Symp. Computer Architecture*, IEEE Computer Society, Washington, D.C., 1985, pp. 342-351.

24 R. Vedder and D. Finn, "The Hughes Data Flow Multiprocesor: Architecture for Efficient Signal and Data Processing," *Proc. 12th Int'l. Symp. Computer Architecture*, IEEE Computer Society, Washington, D.C., 1985, pp. 324-332.

25 R. Vedder, M. Campbell, and G. Tucker, "The Hughes Data Flow Multiprocessor," *Proc. 5th Int'l. Conf. Distributed Computing Systems*, IEEE Computer Society, Washington, D.C., 1985, pp. 2-9.

26 M. Kishi, H. Yasijara, and Y. Kawamura, "DDDP: A Distributed Data Driven Processor," *Proc. 10th Ann. Symp. Computer Architecture*, IEEE Computer Society, Washington, D.C., 1983, pp. 236-242.

27 J.C. Syre et al., "The Data Driven LAU Multiprocessor System," *Information Processing 80*, edited by Lavington, North-Holland, New York, N.Y., 1980.

28 F.J. Burkowski, "Instruction Set Design Issues Relating to a Static Data Flow Computer," *Proc. 9th Ann. Symp. Computer Architecture*, IEEE Computer Society, Washington, D.C., 1982, pp. 101-111.

29 R. Jaganathan and E.A. Ashcroft, "Easyflow: A Hybrid Model for Parallel Processing," *Proc. 1984 Int'l. Conf. Parallel Processing*, IEEE Computer Society, Washington, D.C., 1984, pp. 514-523.

30 P.S. Sawkar, T.J. Forquer, and R.P. Perry, "Programmable Modular Signal Processor—A Data Flow Computer for Real-Time Signal Processing," *Proc. 1983 Int'l. Conf. Parallel Processing,* IEEE Computer Society, Washington, D.C., 1983, pp. 344-349.

31 E.B. Hogenauer, R.F. Newbold, and Y.J. Inn, "DDSP: A Data Flow Computer for Signal Processing," *Proc. 1982 Int'l. Conf. Parallel Processing,* IEEE Computer Society, Washington, D.C., 1982, pp. 126-133.

32 J. Dennis and R. Gao, "Maximum Pipelining of Array Operations on Static Dataflow Machine," *Proc. 1983 Int'l. Conf. Parallel Processing,* IEEE Computer Society, Washington, D.C., 1983, pp. 23-26.

33 L. Bic, "Execution of Logic Programs on a Dataflow Architecture," *Proc. 11th Ann. Int'l. Symp. Computer Architecture*, IEEE Computer Society, Washington, D.C., 1984, pp. 290-296.

34 W.B. Ackerman, "Data Flow Languages," *Computer*, Vol. 15, No. 2, Feb. 1982, pp. 15-25.

35 A.L. Davis and R.M. Keller, "Data Flow Program Graphs," *Computer*, Vol. 15, No. 2, Feb. 1982, p. 26.

36 L.J. Caluwaerts, J. Debacker, and J. Peperstraete, "Implementing Streams on a Data Flow Computer System with Paged Memory," *Proc. 10th Ann. Int'l. Symp. Computer Architecture*, IEEE Computer Society, Washington, D.C., 1983, pp. 76-83.

37 V.K. Arvind and K. Pingali, "A Data Flow Architecture with Tagged Tokens," *Laboratory for Computer Science, Technical Memo 174*, MIT, Cambridge, Mass., Sept. 1980.

38 L.Y. Ho and K.B. Irani, "An Algorithm for Processor Allocation in a Data Flow Multiprocessing Environment," *Proc. 1983 Int'l. Conf. Parallel Processing,* IEEE Computer Society, Washington, D.C., 1983, pp. 338-340.

39 S. Masahiro and T. Murata, "A Data Flow Computer Architecture with Program and Token Memories," *IEEE Trans. Computers,* Vol. C-31, No. 9, Sept. 1982, pp. 820-824.

40 G.-G. Rong, "Pipelined Mapping of Homogeneous Data Flow Programs," *Proc. 1984 Int'l. Conf. Parallel Processing,* IEEE Computer Society, Washington, D.C., 1984, pp. 47-58.

41 T. Agerwala and V.K. Arvind, Guest Editors, Special Issue: "Data Flow Systems," *Computer,* Vol. 5, No. 2, Feb. 1982, pp. 104-114.

42 V.K. Arvind and R.A. Iannucci, "A Critique of Multiprocessing von Neumann Style," *Proc. 10th Ann. Symp. Computer Architecture,* IEEE Computer Society, Washington, D.C., June 1983, pp. 426-436.

43 P.C. Treleaven and I.G. Lima, "Future Computers: Logic, Data Flow . . . , Control Flow?" *Computer,* Vol. 17, No. 3, March 1984, pp. 47-58.

44 D.D. Gajski, D.A. Padua, D.J. Kuck, and R.H. Kuhn, "A Second Opinion on Dataflow Machines and Languages," *Computer,* Vol. 15, No. 2, Feb. 1982, pp. 58-70.

45 J.E. Requa and, J.R. McGraw, "The Piecewise Data Flow Architecture Control Flow and Register Management," *Proc. 10th Ann. Symp. Computer Architecture,* IEEE Computer Society, Washington, D.C., 1983, pp. 84-89.

46 G.N. Fostel, "Summary of a Hybrid Data Flow System," *Proc. 1982 Int'l. Conf. Parallel Processing,* IEEE Computer Society, Washington, D.C., 1982, pp. 134-136.

47 A.E. Charlesworth, "An Approach to Scientific Processing: The Architectural Design of the AP-120B/FBS-164 Family," *Computer,* Vol. 14, No. 12, Dec. 1981, pp. 12-30.

48 R.A. Wagner, "The Boolean Vector Machine," *Proc. 10th Ann. Symp. Computer Architecture,* IEEE Computer Society, Washington, D.C., 1983, pp. 59-66.

49 E.U. Cohler and J.E. Storer, "Functionally Parallel Architecture for Array Processors," *Computer,* Vol 14, No. 9, Sept. 1981, pp. 41-44.

50 D. Kuck et al., "The Structure of an Advanced Vectorizer for Pipelined Processors," *Proc. COMPSAC 1980,* IEEE Computer Society, Washington, D.C., 1980, pp. 709-715.

51 Goodyear Aerospace Co., "Massively Parallel Processor (MPP)," *Tech. Report GER-16684.*

52 *E.W. Kozdrowicki and D.J. Theis, "Second-Generation of Vector Supercomputers," Computer,* Vol. 13, No. 11, Nov. 1980, pp. 71-83.

53 I. Koren and G.M. Silberman, "A Direct Mapping of Algorithms into VLSI Processing Arrays Based on the Data Flow Approach," *Proc. 1983 Int'l. Conf. Parallel Processing,* IEEE Computer Society, Washington, D.C., 1983, pp. 335-337.

54 G.J. Lipovski and A. Tripathi, "A Reconfigurable Varistructured Array Processor," *Proc. 1977 Intl. Conf. Parallel Processing,* IEEE Computer Society, Washington, D.C., 1977, pp. 488-514.

55 W.-H. Lee and M. Malek, "A Partitionable and Reconfigurable Multicomputer Array," *Proc. 1985 Int'l. Conf. Parallel Processing,* IEEE Computer Society, Washington, D.C., 1983, pp. 506-510.

56 S.P. Kartashev and S.I. Kartashev, "Distribution of Programs for a System with Dynamic Architecture," *IEEE Trans. Computers,* Vol. C-31, No. 6, June 1982, pp. 488-514.

57 S.Y. Kung, K.S. Arun, R.-J. Galezer, and D.V. Bhaskar Rao, "Wavefront Array Processor: Language, Architecture and Applications," *IEEE Trans. Computers,* Vol. C-31, No. 11, Nov. 1982, pp. 1054-1066.

58 A. Kapauan, J.T. Field, D.B. Gannon, and L. Snyder, "The Pringle Parallel Computer," *Proc. 11th Int'l. Symp. Computer Architecture,* IEEE Computer Society, Washington, D.C., 1984, pp. 12-20.

59 L.S. Haynes et al., "A Survey of Highly Parallel Computing," *Computer,* Vol. 15, No. 1, Jan. 1982, pp. 9-26.

60 T. Hoshino et al., "Highly Parallel Processor Array 'PAX' for Wide Scientific Applications," *Proc. 1983 Int'l. Conf. Parallel Processing,* IEEE Computer Society, Washington, D.C., 1983, pp. 95-105.

61 L.C. Widdoes, Jr., "The S-1 Project: Developing High-Performance Digital Computers," *Digest of Papers: IEEE COMPCON,* IEEE Computer Society, Washington, D.C., Spring 1980, pp. 282-291.

62 C.E. McDowell, "A Simple Architecture for Low Level Parallelism," *Proc. 1983 Int'l. Conf. Parallel Processing,* IEEE Computer Society, Washington, D.C., 1983, pp. 472-477.

63 K.N. Karna, "Review of the Logical Design of Multiple Microprocessor Systems," *Computer,* Vol. 15, No. 2, Feb. 1982, pp. 134-135.

64 A.R. Pleszkun and E.S. Davidson, "Structured Memory Access Architecture," *Proc. 1983 Int'l. Conf. Parallel Processing,* IEEE Computer Society, Washington, D.C., 1983, pp. 461-471.

65 T. Yoshiyasu, "A Novel Approach to Parallel Processing Cryptosystem," *Proc. 1982 Int'l. Conf. Parallel Processing,* IEEE Computer Society, Washington, D.C., 1982, pp. 313-315.

66 G. Fritsch, W. Kleinoeder, C.U. Linster, and J. Volkert, "EMSY 85—The Erlanger Multiprocessor System for a Broad Spectrum of Applications," *Proc. 1983*

Int'l. Conf. Parallel Processing, IEEE Computer Society, Washington, D.C., Aug. 1983, pp. 325-333.

67 H. Hayashi, A. Hattori, and H. Akimoto, "ALPHA: A High-Performance LISP Machine Equipped with a New Stack Structure and Garbage Collection System," *Proc. 10th Ann. Symp. Computer Architecture*, IEEE Computer Society, Washington, D.C., 1983, pp. 342-348.

68 Lawrence Livermore Laboratory, "The S-1 Project: Ann. Reports," Vol. 1 Architecture, Vol. 2 Hardware, and Vol. 3 Software, *UCID-18619*, University of California, Livermore, Calif., 1979.

69 K.A. Al-Ayat, "The Intel 8089: An Integrated I/O Processor," *Computer*, Vol. 12, No. 6, June 1979, pp. 67-68.

70 C. Maples, "Performance of a Modular Interactive Data Analysis System (MIDAS)," *Proc. 1983 Int'l. Conf. Parallel Processing*, IEEE Computer Society, Washington, D.C., 1983, pp. 514-519.

71 L. Stringa, "EMMA: An Industrial Experience on Large Multiprocessing Architecture," *Computer*, Vol. 14, No. 11, Nov. 1981, pp. 53-67.

72 N. Dimopoulos, "The Homogeneous Multiprocessor Architecture—Structure and Performance Analysis," *Proc. 1983 Int'l. Conf. Parallel Processing*, IEEE Computer Society, Washington, D.C., 1983, pp. 326-333.

73 P.E. Danielsson and S. Leviadi, "Computer Architecture for Pictorial Information Systems," *Computer*, Vol. 14, No. 1, Nov. 1981, pp. 53-67.

74 F.-Y. Villemin, "SERFRE: A General Purpose Multiprocessor Reduction Machine," *Proc. 1982 Int'l. Conf. Parallel Processing*, IEEE Computer Society, Washington, D.C., 1982, pp. 140-141.

75 N.R. Lincoln, "Supercomputers = Colossal Computations + Enormous Expectations + Renowned Risk," *Computer*, Vol. 16, No. 5, May 1983, pp. 38-47.

76 C. Norrie, "Supercomputers for Superproblems: An Architectural Introduction," *Computer*, Vol. 17, No.3, March 1984, pp. 62-74.

77 S. Fernbach, "Applications of Supercomputers in the US: Today and Tomorrow," *Proc. Symp. Supercomputer Architecture*, Oct. 1981, pp. 33-79.

78 ETA Systems, "The New Force in Supercomputing," *Announcement Note, ETA Systems, Inc.*, St. Paul, Minn., Dec. 1983.

79 M. Ginsberg, "Some Observations on Supercomputer Computational Environments." *Proc. 10th IMACS World Congress on System Simulation and Scientific Computation*, 1983.

80 R. Sugarman, "Superpower Computers," *IEEE Spectrum*, Vol. 17, No. 4, April 1980, pp. 28-34.

81 D. Fuss and C.G. Tull, "Centralized Supercomputer Support for Magnetic Fusion Energy Research," *Proc. IEEE*, Vol. 72, No. 1, Jan. 1984, pp. 332-341.

82 N.R. Lincoln, "Technology and Design Tradeoffs in the Creation of a Modern Supercomputer," *IEEE Trans. Computers*, Vol. C-31, No. 5, May 1982, pp. 349-362.

83 M.-O. Tohru, "Overview to the Fifth Generation Computer System Project." *Proc. 10th Ann. Int'l. Symp. Computer Architecture*, IEEE Computer Society, Washington, D.C., 1983, pp. 417-422.

84 H. Kashiwagi and K. Miura, "Japanese Superspeed Computer Project," *Proc. Advances in Reactor Computation*, American Nuclear Society, Salt Lake City, Utah, March 1983.

85 M.-O. Tohru, "Overview of the Fifth Generation Computer System Project," *Proc. 10th Ann. Symp. Computer Architecture*, June 1983, pp. 417-422.

86 M.-O. Tohru and H.S. Stone, "Fifth-Generation Computer Systems: A Japanese Project," *Computer*, Vol. 17, No. 3, March 1984, pp. 6-13.

87 B.W. Arden and R. Ginosar, "MP/C: A Multiprocessor/Computer Architecture," *IEEE Trans. Computers*, Vol. C-31, No. 5, May 1982, pp. 444-473.

88 R.E. Buehrer et al., "The ETH-Multiprocessor EMPRESS: A Dynamically Configurable MIMD System," *IEEE Trans. Computers*, Vol. C-31, No. 11, Nov. 1982, pp. 1035-1044.

89 B.J. Smith, "A Pipelined Shared Resources MIMD Computer," *Proc. 1978 Int'l. Conf. Parallel Processing*, IEEE Computer Society, Washington, D.C., 1978, pp. 6-8.

90 B.J. Smith, "Architecture and Application of the HEP Multiprocessor Computer System," *Real Time Signal Processing IV*, Vol. 298, Aug. 1981.

91 J. Sasidhar and K.G. Shin, "Design of a General-Purpose Multiprocessor with Hierarchical Structure," *Proc. 1981 Int'l. Conf. Parallel Processing*, IEEE Computer Society, Washington, D.C., 1981, pp. 141-150.

92 K.G. Shin, Y.H. Lee, and J. Sasidhar, "Design of HM³P—A Hierarchical Multimicroprocessor for General-Purpose Applications," *IEEE Trans. Computers*, Vol. C-31, No. 11, Nov. 1982, pp. 1045-1053.

93 A. Gottlieb and J.T. Schwartz, "Networks and Algorithms for Very Large-Scale Parallel Computation," *Computer*, Vol. 15, No. 1, Jan. 1982, pp. 27-36.

94 A. Gottlieb, R.C. Grishman, C.P. Kruskal, K.P. McAuliffe, L. Rudolph, and M. Snir, "The NYU Ultracomputer—Designing and MIMD Shared Memory Parallel Computer," *IEEE Trans. Computers*, Vol. C-32, No. 2, Feb. 1983. pp. 175-189.

95 H.J. Siegel, L.J. Siegel, F.C. Kemmerer, P.T. Mueller, Jr., H.E. Smalley, Jr., and S.D. Smith, "PASM: A Partitionable SIMD/MIMD System for Image Processing and Pattern Recognition," *IEEE Trans. Computers*, Vol. C-20, No. 12, Dec. 1981, pp. 934-947.

96 F.A. Briggs, K.-S. Fu, K. Hwang, and B.W. Wah, "PUMPS Architecture for Pattern Analysis and Image Data Base Management," *IEEE Trans. Computers*, Vol. 15, No. 10, Oct. 1982, pp. 969-983.

Reprinted from *Proceedings of the First International Conference on Distributed Computing Systems*, October 1979, pages 430–439. Copyright © 1979 by The Institute of Electrical and Electronics Engineers, Inc.

THE VARIETIES OF DATA FLOW COMPUTERS[1]

Jack B. Dennis
Laboratory for Computer Science
Massachusetts Institute of Technology
Cambridge, Massachusetts 02139

Abstract -- Architectures of computer systems based on data flow concepts are attracting increasing attention as an alternative to conventional sequential processors. This paper discusses and contrasts several approaches to data flow computation representative of current work on experimental prototype machines.

Introduction

The architects of future computer systems face three challenges -- an architectural concept that successfully addresses these challenges will prove a major breakthrough toward computer systems that have high performance and contribute to easing the software problem.

1. Achieve high performance at minimal hardware cost.

This has always been an objective of computer architecture. Of course, the nature of the architecture required changes as one traverses the range of scale from microprocessing to super-computer, and as applications and technology evolve.

2. Utilize effectively the capabilities of LSI technology.

Using LSI devices effectively in medium to large scale computers is a generally recognized problem without generally accepted solutions. Architectures are needed which use large numbers each of a few part types which have a high logic-to-pin ratio. The most popular suggestion having these characteristics is a large number of interconnected microcomputers; however sufficiently good schemes for interconnecting and programming them have not been forthcoming.

3. Programmability

Any radical departure from conventional architectures based on sequential program execution must address the problem that the existing body of software methodology and tools may not be applicable. The architects of supercomputers and multiprocessor systems have not addressed this challenge, trusting that the "software problem" can be successfully attacked by the "software people." This is fallacious.

A good way to ensure that a radical architecture is programmable is to make the computer system a *language-based* design. This means the system is designed as a hardware interpreter for a specific *base language* in terms of which programs to be run on the system must be expressed [10]. However, much of the work on language-based architecture has not been fruitful because the languages chosen (Fortran and Algol, for example) embody some of the principal limitations of conventional machines (global memory), and lack generality (no provision for expressing concurrency).

Computer designs based on principles of data flow are attracting increasing interest as an alternative to architectures derived from conventional notions of sequential program execution. These new designs offer a possible solution to the problem of efficiently exploiting concurrency of computation on a large scale, and they are compatible with modern concepts of program structure and therefore should not suffer so much from the difficulties of programming that plague other approaches to highly parallel computation: array and vector processors, and shared-memory multprocessor systems.

Fundamentally, the data flow concept is a different way of looking at instruction execution in machine level programs -- an alternative to the Von Neuman idea of sequential instruction execution. In a data flow computer, an instruction is ready for execution when its operands have arrived -- there is no concept of "control flow," and data flow computers do not have program location counters. A consequence of data-activated instruction execution is that many innstructions of a data flow program may be available for execution at once. Thus highly concurrent computation is a natural accompaniment of the data flow idea.

The idea of data driven computation is old [21, 22], but it is only in recent years that architectural schemes have been developed that can support an interestingly general level of user language, and are attractive in terms of anticipated performance and practicality of construction. Work on data

1. This research was supported by the Lawrence Livermore Laboratory of the University of California under contract 8545403.

driven concepts of program structure and on the design of practical data driven computers is now in progress in at least a dozen laboratories in the United States and Europe. Several processors using data-driven instruction execution have been built, and more hardware projects are being planned.

Most of this work on architectural concepts for data flow computation is based on a program representation known as *data flow program graphs* (Dennis [11]), which evolved from work of Rodriguez [19], Adams [3] and Karp and Miller [16]. In fact, data flow computers are a form of language-based architecture in which program graphs are the base language. As shown in Fig. 1, data flow program graphs serve as a formally specified interface between system architecture on one hand and user programming language on the other. The architect's task is to define and realize a computer system that faithfully implements the formal behavior of program graphs, while the language implementer's task is to translate source language programs into their equivalent as program graphs.

The techniques used to translate source language programs into data flow graphs [7] are similar to the methods used in conventional optimizing compilers to analyze the paths of data dependency in source programs. High level programming languages for data flow computation should be designed so it is easy for the translator to identify data dependence and generate program graphs that expose parallelism. The primary sources of difficulty are unrestricted transfer of control, and the "side effects" resulting from assignment to a global variable or to input arguments of a procedure. Removal of these sources of difficulty not only makes concurrency easy to identify, but programs have better structure -- they are more modular, and are easier to understand and verify.

These implications of data flow for language designers are discussed by Ackerman [1]. Moreover, new programming languages have been designed specifically for data flow computations: ID developed at Irvine [4] and VAL designed at MIT [2, 18].

This paper presents a sample from the variety of architectural schemes devised to support computations expressed as data flow program graphs. We explain data flow graphs by means of examples, and show how they are represented as collections of *activity templates*. Then we describe the basic instruction handling mechanism using activity templates that is characteristic of most current projects to build prototype data flow systems. We discuss the reasons for the different hardware organizations used by various projects, in particular, the different approaches to communicating information between parts of a data flow computer.

Data Flow Programs

A data flow program graph is made up of actors connected by arcs. One kind of actor is the operator shown in Fig. 2

Language

Data Flow Program Graphs

Architecture

Fig. 1. Program graphs as a base language.

which is drawn as a circle with a function symbol written inside -- in this case + -- indicating addition. An operator also has input arcs and output arcs which carry *tokens* bearing values. The arcs define paths over which values from one actor are conveyed by tokens to other actors.

Tokens are placed on and removed from the arcs of a program graph according to *firing rules*, which are illustrated for an operator in Fig. 3. To be *enabled*, tokens must be present on each input arc, and there must be no token on any output arc of the actor. Any enabled actor may be *fired*; in the case of an operator, this means removing one token from each input arc, applying the specified function to the values associated with those tokens, and placing tokens labelled with the result value on the output arcs.

Operators may be connected as shown in Fig. 4 to form program graphs. Here, presenting tokens bearing values for x and y at the two inputs will enable computation of the value

$$z = (x + y) * (x - y)$$

by the program graph, placing a token carrying the result value on output arc z.

To understand the working of data flow computers, it is useful to introduce another representation for data flow

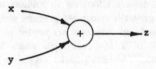

Fig. 2. Data flow actor.

(a) before   (b) after

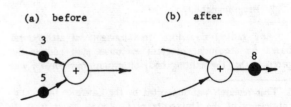

Fig. 3. Firing rule.

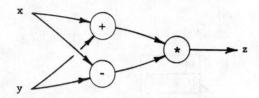

Fig. 4. Interconnection of operators.

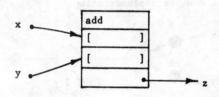

Fig. 5. An activity template.

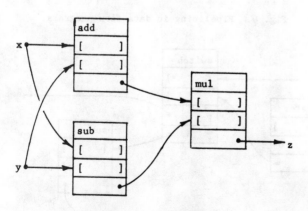

Fig. 6. Configuration of activity templates for the program graph of Fig. 4.

programs -- one that is much closer to the machine language used in prototype data flow computers. In this scheme, a data flow program is a collection of *activity templates*, each corresponding to one or more actors of a data flow program graph. An activity template corresponding to the plus operator (Fig. 2) is shown in Fig. 5. There are four fields for (1) an operation code specifying the operations to be performed; (2) two *receivers*, which are places waiting to be filled in with operand values; and (3) destination fields (in this case one), which specify what is to be done with the result of performing the operation on the operands.

An *instruction* of a data flow program is the fixed portion of an activity template and consists of the operation code and the destinations.

> instruction:
> <opcode, destinations>

Fig. 6 shows how activity templates are joined to represent a program graph, specifically the composition of operators in Fig. 4. Each destination field specifies a target receiver by giving the *address* of some activity template and an *input* integer specifying which receiver of the template is the target.

> destination:
> <address, input>

Program structures for conditionals and iteration are illustrated in Fig. 7 and Fig. 8. These make use of two new data flow actors, *switch* and *merge*, which control the routing of data values. The switch actor sends a data input to its T or F output according as a boolean control input is **true** or **false**. The merge actor forwards a data value from its T or F input according to its boolean input value.

The conditional program graph and implementation in Fig. 7 represent computation of

$$y := (if \ x > 3 \ then \ x + 2 \ else \ x - 1) * 4$$

and the program graph and implementation in Fig. 8 represent the iterative computation

$$while \ x > 0 \ do \ x := x - 3$$

Execution of a machine program consisting of activity templates is viewed as follows: When a template is activated by the presence of an operand value in each receiver, the contents of the template from an *operation packet* of the form

> operation packet:
> <opcode, operands, destinations>

Such a packet specifies one *result packet* having the form

> result packet:
> <value, destination>

for each destination field of the template. Generation of a

53

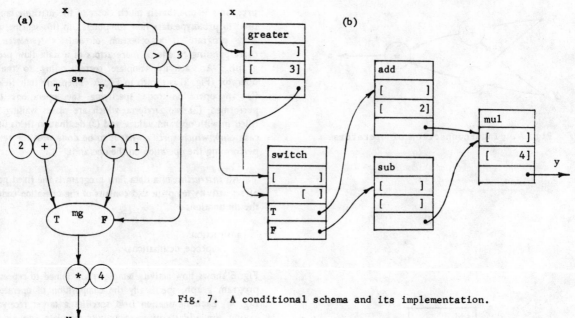

Fig. 7. A conditional schema and its implementation.

result packet, in turn, causes the value to be placed in the receiver designated by its destination field.

Note that this view of data flow computation does not explicitly honor the rule of program graphs that tokens must be absent from the output arcs of an actor for it to fire. Yet there are situations where it is attractive to use a program graph in pipelined fashion, as illustrated in Fig. 9a. To faithfully represent this computation the *add* instruction must not be reactivated until its previous result has been used by the *multiply* instruction. This constraint is enforced through use of *acknowledge signals* which are generated by specially marked destinations (※) in an activity template, and in general are sent to the templates that supply operand values to the activity template in question (Fig. 9b). The enabling rule now

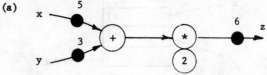

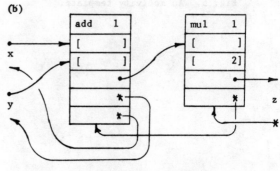

Fig. 9. Pipelining in data flow programs.

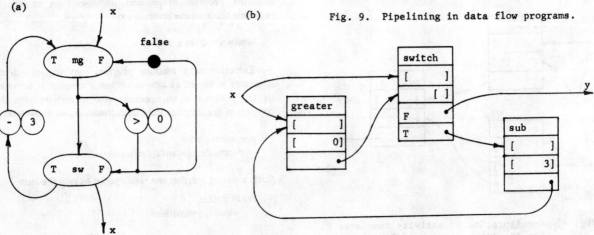

Fig. 8. An iterative schema and its implementation.

requires that all receivers contain values, and the required number of acknowledge signals have been received. This number (if nonzero) is written adjacent to the opcode of an activity template.

The Basic Mechanism

The basic instruction execution mechanism used in a number of current data flow projects is illustrated in Fig. 10. The data flow program describing the computation to be performed is held as a collection of activity templates in the *Activity Store*. Each activity template has a unique address which is entered in the *Instruction Queue* unit (A FIFO buffer store) when the instruction is ready for execution.

The *Fetch* unit takes an instruction address from the Instruction Queue and reads the activity template from the activity store, forms it into an operation packet, and passes it on to the *Operation Unit*. The Operation Unit performs the operation specified by the operation code on the operand values, generating one result packet for each destination field of the operation packet. The *Update* unit receives result packets and enters the values they carry into operand fields of activity templates as specified by their destination fields. The Update unit also tests whether all operand and acknowledge packets required to activate the destination instruction have been received, and, if so, enters the instruction address in the Instruction Queue.

During program execution, the number of entries in the Instruction Queue measures the degree of concurrency present in the program. The basic mechanism of Figure 10 can exploit this potential to a limited but significant degree: once the Fetch unit has sent an operation packet off to the Operation Unit, it may immediately read another entry from the Instruction Queue without waiting for the instruction previously fetched to be completely processed. Thus a continuous stream of operation packets may flow from the Fetch Unit to the Operation Unit so long as the Instruction Queue is not empty.

This mechanism is aptly called a "circular pipeline" -- activity controlled by the flow of information packets traverses the ring of units leftwise. A number of packets may be flowing simultaneously in different parts of the ring on behalf of different instructions in concurrent execution. Thus the ring operates as a "pipeline" system with all of its units actively processing packets at once. The degree of concurrency possible is limited by the nummber of units on the ring and the degree of pipelining within each unit. Additional concurrency may be exploited by splitting any unit in the ring into several units which can be allocated to concurrent activities. Ultimately, the level of concurrency is limited by the capacity of the data paths connecting the units of the ring.

This basic mechanism is essentially that implemented in a prototype data flow processing element built by a group at the Texas Instruments Company [8]. The same mechanism, elaborated to handle data flow procedures, was described earlier by Rumbaugh [20], and a new project at Manchester University (see below) uses a different variation of the same scheme.

Data Flow Multiprocessor

The level of concurrency exploited may be increased enormously by connecting together many processing elements of the form we have described to form a *data flow multiprocessor* system. Figure 11a shows many processing elements connected through a communication system, and Fig. 11b shows how each processing element relates to the communication system. The data flow program is divided into parts which are distributed over the processing elements. The activity stores of the processing elements collectively realize a single large address space, so the address field of a destination may select uniquely any activity template in the system. Each processing element sends a result packet through the communication network if its destination address specifies a nonlocal activity template, and to its own Update unit otherwise.

The communication network is responsible for delivering each result packet received to the processing element that holds the target activity template. Such a network, in which each packet arriving at an input port is transmitted to the output specified by information contained in the packet, is called a *routing network*.

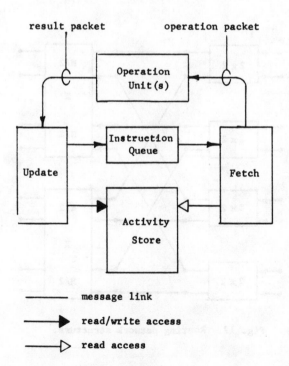

result packet   operation packet

Fig. 10. Basic instruction execution mechanism.

———— message link

———▶ read/write access

———▷ read access

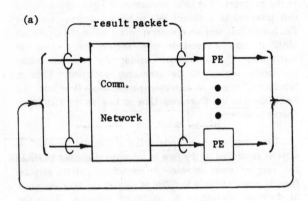

(a)

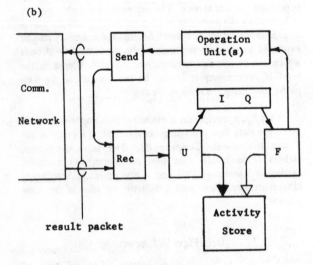

(b)

Fig. 11. Data flow multiprocessor.

have been proposed. The ring form of communication network has been used in many computer networks and has been used by Texas Instruments to couple four processing elements in their prototype data flow computer. The ring has the drawback that delay grows linearly with size, and there is a fixed bound on capacity.

Several groups have proposed tree-structured networks for communicating among processing elements [9, 15, 17]. Here, the drawback is that the traffic density at the root node may be unsatisfactorily high. Advantages of the tree are that the worst case distince between leaves grows only as $\log_2 N$ (for a binary tree), and that many pairs of nodes are connected by short paths.

The packet routing network shown in Fig. 12 is a structure currently attracting much attention. A routing network with N input and N output ports may be assembled from $(N/2) \log(N)$ units each of which is a 2 x 2 router. A 2 x 2 router receives packets at two input ports and transmits each received packet at one of its output ports according to an address bit contained in the packet. Packets are handled first come, first served, and both output ports may be active concurrently. Delay through an N x N network increases as $\log_2 N$ and capacity rises nearly linearly with N. This form of routing network is described in [23], and several related structures have been analyzed for capacity and delay [6].

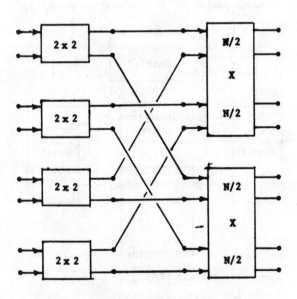

Fig. 12. Routing network structure.

The characteristics required of a routing network for a data flow multiprocessor differ in two important ways from the properties demanded of a processor/memory switch for a conventional multiprocessor system. First, information flow in a routing network is in one direction -- an immediate reply from the target unit to the originating unit is not required. Second, since each processing element holds many enabled instructions ready for processing, some delay can be tolerated in transmission of result packets without slowing down the overall rate of computation.

The "cross bar switch" used in conventional multiprocessor systems meets requirements for immediate respoonse and small delay by providing for signal paths from any input to any output that are established on request and maintained until a reply completes a processor/memory transaction. This arrangement is needlessly expensive for a data flow multiprocessor and a number of alternative network structures

Token Labelling

An experimental data flow computer being constructed at Manchester University, England [24], uses an elaboration of the basic mechanism designed so more than one instance of an instruction may be active at a time. This feature provides for overlapped execution of successive cycles of an iteration, and makes possible a natural machine level implementation of procedure application.

The Manchester processing element design is sketched in Fig. 13. In place of the Activity Store there is an *Instruction Store* and a *Matching Store*. Since more than one instance of execution of an instruction is allowed, the result packet format is extended to include a *label* field used to distinguish instances of the target instruction. No longer can arrived operand values be held in a single activity template for an instruction. Rather, instructions are divided into just two classics -- those that require only one operand, and those that require two operands -- and result packets include an indicator *count* of how many operands the target instruction requires. For single operand instructions, the one result packet is sent directly to the Instruction Store, where the instruction is fetched and an operation packet constructed. For two-operand instructions, the first result packet to arrive at the Matching Store is held until the second result packet arrives. Then information from the two result packets is combined and sent on to the Instruction Store where an operation packet is constructed. The matching store is an associative memory that uses the address and label fields of a result packet as its search key.

The MIT Architecture

In a data flow multiprocessor (Fig. 11) we noted the problem of partitioning the instructions of a program among the processing elements so as to concentrate communication among instructions held in the same processing element. This is advantageous because the time to transport a result packet to a nonlocal processor through the routing network will be longer (perhaps much longer) than the time to forward a result locally.

At MIT, an architecture has been proposed [12, 13] in response to an opposing view: Each instruction is equally accessible to result packets generated by any other instruction, independent of where they reside in the machine. The structure of this machine is shown in Fig. 14. The heart of this architecture is a large set of Instruction Cells, each of which holds one activity template of a data flow program. Result packets arrive at Instruction Cells from the Distribution Network. Each Instruction Cell sends an operation packet to the Arbitration Network when all operands and signals have been received. The function of the Operation Section is to execute instructions and to forward result packets to target instructions by way of the Distribution Network.

As drawn in Fig. 14, this design is impractical if the Instruction Cells are fabricated as individual physical units since the number of devices and interconnections would be

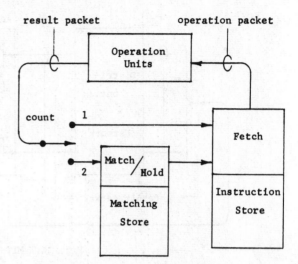

operation packet:

    <opcode, operands, destination>

result packet:

    <value, label, destination>

destination:

    <address, input, count>

Fig. 13. Data flow processor with labels.

enormous. A more attractive structure is obtained if the Instruction Cells are grouped into blocks and each block realized as a single device. Such an Instruction Cell Block has a single input port for result packets, and a single output port for operation packets. Thus one Cell Block unit replaces many Instruction Cells together with the associated portion of the Distribution Network.

Moreover, to further reduce the number of interconnections between Cell Blocks and other units, a byte-serial format for result and operation packets is chosen.

The resulting structure is shown in Fig. 15. Here, several Cell Blocks are served by a shared group of functional units P_i, ..., P_k. The Arbitration Network in each section of the machine passes each operation packet to the appropriate functional unit according to its opcode.

The number of functional unit types in such a machine is likely to be small (four, for example), or just one universal functional unit type might be provided in which case the arbitration network becomes trivial.

The relationship between the MIT architecture and the basic mechanism described earlier becomes clear when one

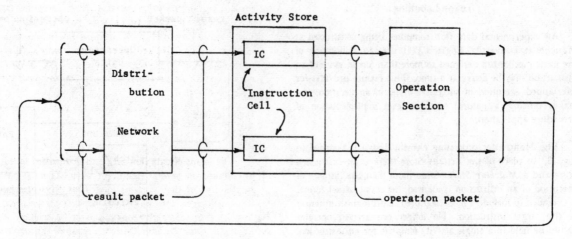

Fig. 14. MIT data flow processor.

considers how a Cell Block unit would be constructed. As shown in Fig. 16 a Cell Block would include storage for activity templates, a buffer store for addresses of enabled instructions and control units to receive result packets and transmit operation packets that are functionally equivalent to the Fetch and Update units of the basic mechanism. The Cell Block differs from the basic data flow processing element in that the Cell Block contains no functional units, and there is no shortcut for result packets destined for successor instructions held in the same Cell Block.

Discussion

In the Cell Block machine, communication of a result packet from one instruction to its successor is equally easy (or equally difficult depending on your point of view) regardless of how the two instructions are placed within the entire activity store of the machine. Thus the programmer need not be concerned that his program might run slowly due to an unfortunate distribution of instructions in the activity store address space. In fact, a random allocation of instructions may prove to be adequate.

In the data flow multiprocessor, communication between two instructions is much quicker if these instructions are allocated to the same processing element. Thus a program may run much faster if its instructions are clustered so as to minimize communication traffic between clusters, and each cluster is allocated to one processing element. Since it may be handling significantly less packet traffic, the communication network of the data flow multiprocessor will be simpler and

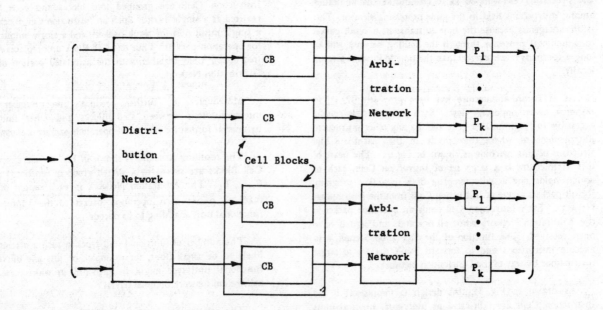

Fig. 15. Practical form of the MIT architecture.

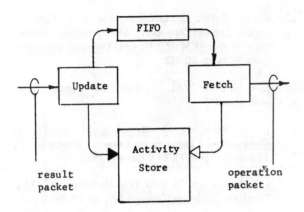

Fig. 16. Cell Block implementation.

less expensive than the Distribution Network of the MIT machine. Whether the cost reduction justifies the additional programming effort is a matter of debate, and depends on the area of application, the technology of fabrication and the time frame under consideration.

Although the routing networks in the two forms of data flow processor have a much more favorable growth of logic complexity (N log N) with increasing size than the switching networks of conventional multiprocessor systems, their growth is still more than linear. Moreover, closer examination reveals that in all suggested physical structures for N x N routing networks, the complexity as measured by total *wire length* grows as $O(N^2)$. This fact shows that interconnection complexity still places limits on the size of practical multi-unit systems which support universal intercommunication. If we need yet larger systems, it appears we must settle for arrangements of units that only support immediate communication with neighbors. It is not at all clear how such a system could support a general approach to program construction. A variety of views are currently held as to the circumstances which would favor construction of machines having only local interconnections. A view implicit in most proposals for distributed computing systems is that the programmer (or, alternatively, a *very* smart compiler) will plan how the computation should be distributed so as to optimize resource utilization. A corollary of this view is that programming such systems will be at least as difficult as programming a conventional single processor system; that is, this form of distributed architecture makes no contribution to ameliorating the software problem.

Another view is that the system itself should dynamically allocate its resources among portions of the computation to be performed so that in each interval of computation, only local interactions are required. This view is consistent with current advanced thinking about programming languages and methodology. For this to be possible, very flexible mechanisms must be built into the hardware to support dynamic reallocation of processing and memory resources without

imposition on the programmer. Systems proposed from this viewpoint include the Irvine data flow architeture [5], the Utah project toward a demand driven implementation of applicative Lisp [17], and an operational concept of data flow program execution developed by Weng [14, 25]. Whether these proposals can be developed into practical computer systems is an open question.

Extensions

The forms of data flow architecture discussed in this paper are limited in several significant ways. There is no specific mechanism in these systems to provide efficient support for data structures, and only the Manchester University machine incorporates even rudimentary support for multiple instances of instruction execution such as required for implementing concurrent or recursive procedure activations. Moreover, in each of these systems, all instructions are held in the same level of storage and there is no provision for "caching" instructions, so programs beyond some limiting size become impractical due to their need to occupy relatively fast storage.

A variety of proposals have been made of approaches to overcome these limitations of current prototype construction projects, but none have yet reached the stage that even experimental construction of a machine is warranted. It will be fascinating to see how these concepts evolve over the coming decade.

References

[1] W. B. Ackerman, "Data Flow Languages," Proc. of the ACM 1979 National Computer Conference (June 1979), pp. 1087-1095.

[2] W. B. Ackerman and J. B. Dennis, VAL -- A Value Oriented Algorithmic Language, Preliminary Reference Manual, Laboratory for Computer Science, M.I.T., Technical Report TR-218 (June 1979), 80 pp.

[3] D. A. Adams, A Computation Model With Data Flow Sequencing, Computer Science Dept., School of Humanities and Sciences, Stanford University, Technical Report CS 117 (December 1968).

[4] Arvind, K. P. Gostelow, and W. Plouffe, An Asynchronous Programming Language and Computing Machine, Dept. of Information and Computer Science, University of California, Irvine, Technical Report 114a (December 1978), 97 pp.

[5] Arvind, and K. P. Gostelow, "A Computer Capable of Exchanging Processors for Time," Information Processing 77, North Holland (1977), pp. 849-854.

[6] G. A. Boughton, Routing Networks in Packet Communication Architectures, Dept. of Electrical Engineering and Computer Science, M.I.T., S.M. Thesis (June 1978).

[7] J. D. Brock and L. B. Montz, "Translation and Optimization of Data Flow Programs," Proceedings of the 1979 International Conference on Parallel Processing (August 1979).

[8] M. Cornish, Private communication, Texas Instruments Corp., Austin, Texas.

[9] A. Davis, "A Data Flow Evaluation System Based on the Concept of Recursive Locality," Proc. of the ACM 1979 National Computer Conference (June 1979), pp. 1079-1086.

[10] J. B. Dennis, "On the Design and Specification of a Common Base Language," Proc. of Symposium on Computers and Automata, Polytechnic Press, Polytechnic Institute of Brooklyn (1971).

[11] J. B. Dennis, "First Version of a Data Flow Procedure Language," Lecture Notes in Computer Science, 19, Springer-Verlag (1974), pp. 362-376.

[12] J. B. Dennis, and D. P. Misunas, A Preliminary Architecture for a Basic Data-Flow Processor, Laboratory for Computer Science, M.I.T., CSG Memo 102 (August 1974), 27 pp.

[13] J. B. Dennis, C. K. C. Leung, and D. P. Misunas, A Highly Parallel Processor Using a Data Flow Machine Language, Laboratory for Computer Science, M.I.T., CSG Memo 134-1 (June 1979), 33 pp.

[14] J. B. Dennis, and K. Weng, "An Abstract Implementation for Concurrent Computation With Streams," Proceedings of the 1979 International Conference on Parallel Processing (August 1979).

[15] A. Despain and D. Patterson, "X-Tree: A Tree Structured Multi-Processor Computer Architecture," Proceedings of the 5th Annual Symposium on Computer Architecture (April 1978), pp 144-150.

[16] R. M. Karp, and R. E. Miller, "Properties of a Model for Parallel Computations: Determinacy, Termination, Queueing," SIAM J. of Applied Mathematics (November 1966), pp. 1390-1411.

[17] R. M. Keller, G. Lindstrom, and S. S. Patil, "A Loosely-Coupled Applicative Multi-processing System," Proc. of the ACM 1979 National Computer Conference (June 1979), pp. 613-622.

[18] J. R. McGraw, "VAL -- A Data Flow Language," these proceedings.

[19] J. E. Rodriguez, A Graph Model for Parallel Computation, Laboratory for Computer Science, M.I.T., Technical Report TR-64 (September 1969).

[20] J. E. Rumbaugh, "A Data Flow Multiprocessor," IEEE Trans. on Computers (February 1977), pp. 138-146.

[21] R. R. Seeber and A. B. Lindquist, "Associative Logic for Highly Parallel Systems," Proc. of the AFIPS Conference (1963), pp. 489-493.

[22] R. M. Shapiro, H. Saint and D. L. Presberg, Representation of Algorithms as Cyclic Partial Orderings, Applied Data Research, Wakefield, Mass., Report CA-7112-2711 (December 1971).

[23] A. R. Tripathi and G. J. Lipovski, "Packet Switching in Banyan Networks," Proceedings of the 6th Annual Symposium on Computer Architecture (April 1979), pp. 160-167.

[24] I. Watson and J. Gurd, "A Prototype Data Flow Computer With Token Labelling," Proc. of the ACM 1979 National Computer Conference (June 1979), pp. 623-628.

[25] K. Weng, An Abstract Implementation for a Generalized Data Flow Language, Laboratory for Computer Science, M.I.T., Technical Report, forthcoming.

A HARDWARE DESIGN OF THE SIGMA-1, A DATA FLOW COMPUTER FOR SCIENTIFIC COMPUTATIONS

Kei Hiraki, Toshio Shimada, and Kenji Nishida

Computer Systems Division
Electrotechnical Laboratory

1-1-4 Umezono, Sakura-mura Niihari-gun,
Ibaraki, 305 Japan

Abstract -- A detailed description of the architecture of the SIGMA-1, a high speed data flow computer, is presented. The system is designed to attain 100 MFLOPS when executing scientific programs in a 256 PE machine. The construction of the matching memory, efficiency in the execution of programs including sequential parts, structure management and interruption problems of an actual data flow computer are discussed. Solutions for these problems are proposed.

1. Introduction

Data flow architecture is accepted as the architecture for future computers because it can exploit potentially all the parallelism in a program. In order to show the capability of a data flow computer for high speed computation there are many problems to be solved. In the design of an actual data flow computer the main problems are:

 i. construction of a large and fast matching memory at a reasonable cost,

 ii. construction and management of a structure memory,

 iii. network construction,

 iv. interruption, error and exception handling,

 v. limitation of the length of the context that consists of I (iteration counter), LN (link number that indicates the entry of the link register), D (displacement of the operation), and FLG (flag that indicates the operation of the matching unit and the input port of the packet),

 vi. inefficiency due to insufficient parallelism.

Many studies of data flow computers have been performed using software simulators [1,2,3], but very few actual data flow computers have been built [4,5]. Since the size and kind of programs which can be executed in the simulators are severely restricted, the above problems are not readily apparent.

The object of SIGMA-1, an experimental data flow computer, is to show the feasibility of the data flow computer in scientific and numerical computations. For this purpose not only the logical correctness of the architecture, but also the balance of speed and the amount of the hardware between its components must be considered in the design.

The final goal is to construct a 100 MFLOPS data flow computer [6] for the execution of practical scientific programs. This paper describes the hardware design of the SIGMA-1 and discusses the solution to the above problems.

2. Basic architecture.

The SIGMA-1 is constructed using 256 processing elements (PE) which are divided into 32 groups connected by a multi-level network as shown in Figure 1. Each PE in the SIGMA-1 is pipelined to increase performance.

In Figure 2, the M, or matching, unit triggers the execution of two operand operations. The F unit fetches the instruction addressed by the context field of the input packet. These two units form the first pipeline stage in the PE. The D unit produces output packets using the results of the E unit (execution unit) together with the instructions fetched by the F unit. The S unit is a structure memory which consists of a structure memory and a waiting queue. These units will be discussed in more detail.

The first problem exists in the trade-off between the number of pipeline stages (the total execution time for a datum, or the total pipeline delay) and the time slice of the pipeline (throughput). When the parallelism in the program to be executed is much larger than N * M, where N is the number of PEs in the system and M the number of pipeline stages in a PE, the throughput is the most important factor for the computing speed. Consequently, a PE with many pipeline stages (small time slice) is suitable. Although a PE with a smaller number of pipeline stages gives less throughput, a system with a smaller number of pipeline stages gives the same performance when the number of PE increases. When the parallelism in the program is smaller than N * M, especially in a sequential program, only the total pipeline delay affects the system performance. In this case, a PE with smaller pipeline stages is suitable. The system performance cannot increase even when the number of PEs increases. Since one

Reprinted from *Proceedings of the 1984 International Conference on Parallel Processing*, 1984, pages 524-531. Copyright © 1984 by The Institute of Electrical and Electronics Engineers, Inc.

61

of the objectives of the SIGMA-1 is to execute a program which cannot be executed efficiently in a conventional vector computer, the total pipeline delay is more important than the throughput of the system. Hence the SIGMA-1 uses only two pipeline stages as shown in Figure 2. In the same way, a multi-level network is better than a single-level network because the total pipeline delay of a multi-level network is shorter than that of a single level network when the destination PE is near to the source PE. Owing to the short pipeline architecture and the multi-level network, a PE in the SIGMA-1 executes an instruction in three clock cycles in the completely sequential program (c.f. Figure 10).

The second problem is to select the packet format. From the software point of view, a longer packet is better, since each packet must carry its context . On the other hand, shorter packets are better from the hardware point of view, because a short packet reduces the amount of hardware and network connections. If the length of the context is too short, however, overflow in the I or LN field becomes a serious problem. Furthermore, the length of the context depends on the length of the packet. For example, the "SPECIAL" type packet used for interruption which is described in the next section carries two context fields on the packet. Consequently, the length of the context must be less than half of the packet length. We chose eighty eight bits for the length of a packet in the SIGMA-1.

3. Data, packet and instruction format.

The SIGMA-1 uses fixed size packets for communication between PEs, structure memory access, I/O communication, hardware initialization and hardware maintenance. The eighty eight bit packet is divided into two forty bits words and an eight bit PE field. The types of packets used are (1) "USER" packets to communicate between PEs during the execution of a program (Figure 3), (2) "SYS" packets for subroutine calls and returns, (3) "SPECIAL" packets for interrupt handling and system management, (4) "STRUCT" packets for structure operations and (5) "MAINT" packets for system initialization and maintenance.

A USER packet consists of a key field and a data field. The key field contains the context of the packet and the data field contains the operand for the operation. The sub-fields in the key field are (1) PE (the destination PE number), (2) TYP (packet type), (3) I (iteration counter), (4) LN (the subroutine identifier), (5) D (instruction location in the subroutine), and (6) FLG (the matching unit operation and the input port).

The FLG field determines the firing rule in the matching unit. It is used for handling loop invariant variables, detecting and deleting packets in the matching unit, and handling interruptions.

Data objects in the SIGMA-1 are 40-bits long, including an 8 bit tag. In the prototype, both

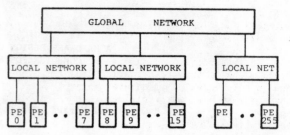

Figure 1. Global Architecture of the SIGMA-1.

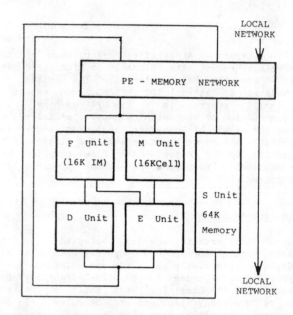

Figure 2. Block Diagram of a Processing Element.

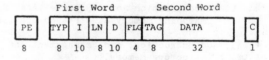

PE: Destination PE number
TYP: Packet Type
I: Iteration Number
LN: Link Number (Entry for LINK REGISTER)
D: Displacement (Offset from the TOP)
C: Cancel Flag

Figure 3. Format of the USER type packet.

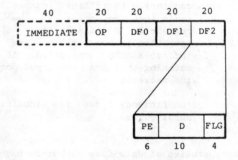

Figure 4. Format of the Instruction.

integers and floating point numbers are restricted to single precision.

An instruction consists of an operation field, one to three destination fields (Figure 4) and in some cases an immediate operand. When the instruction has a single destination field, the instruction is a single word (40 bits), otherwise the instruction is two words (80 bits). An immediate operand requires one additional word.

4. Matching unit.

The performance of the matching unit is an important factor in determining performance of data flow computers. Among matching methods already proposed[7,8,9,10], a chained hashing hardware is used for upgrading the performance of the matching unit in the SIGMA-1.

Figure 5 shows a block diagram of the M unit. HAG is the hashing address generator which generates the address for the first probe. The function in the HAG affects the performance of the hashing table to a considerable degree since a bad function produces many collisions. However, a good function with small, fast hardware is yet to be found. Two stages of EXOR gates are used for the hashing function in the M unit.

The key, pointer, flags (the top, bottom and empty flags that indicate the top and bottom cell of the collision list and the empty cell respectively) and data memory are 16K packets deep fast static memory, with lengths of 32, 14, 3 and 40 bits respectively. A separate bit table is used as the empty flag table to improve the insertion speed. The MAR is the address register which holds the next probe address, the HAR is the current probe address register for checking the result, and the PAR is the previous address register for the pointer handling operations in insertion and deletion. The memory read registers, EMPR, FLR, PRR, KRR and DRR can get the new read value at every clock cycle. The KEQ is a equality comparator for key matching. The PEQ is a equality comparator for relocating a conflict cell in insertion.

Examples of insertion and deletion are performed as follows. In insertion, the first probe address is generated by the HAG. The memories are read in the first cycle. The latched data are checked in the second cycle. Suppose that the probed cell is empty, that is, no collision exists. The input packet is written into the key memory and the data memory with the top and bottom flags. Then the insertion terminates. In deletion, the first and second cycles are the same as insertion. In order to increase the operating speed of the hashing memory, the read operation to the memory and the analysis of the probed cell are performed in parallel. The probed value in the second cycle is checked in the third cycle. Suppose that the value in the KRR matches to the value in KEY in the third cycle, i.e. the operation is fired. Then the values on the DRR and DATA are sent to the E unit as operands of the instruction. The address of the previous list element is held in the PAR. In the fourth cycle, the pointer field of the cell pointed by the PAR is replaced by the PRR value and the empty flag of the matched cell is set in the fifth cycle. Thus on average the first packet of the two input operation can be inserted within four clock cycles and the second can fire the operation within 2.6 clock cycles after arrival, unless the matching memory is not full (the load factor is less than 0.7).

Parallel open hashing hardware [8] is much slower than chained hashing because the performance of the matching memory must be measured by the average number of memory accesses in insertion and deletion instead of the average number of memory accesses in successful search or unsuccessful search.

The full associative memory is also not suitable for the matching memory because it needs a lot of VLSI hardware [9]. The matching unit overflow is another serious problem. The chained hashing hardware can handle the overflow easily. When an overflow occurs, the bottom element of the chained list will change to the overflow flag, and the packet that caused the overflow is sent to another PE by the interruption mechanism.

5. Structure memory

The implementation of structures is one of the most serious problems in the design of the data flow computer. If the structures are implemented in the matching unit as scalar variables, there are no problems of allocation, read/write synchronization or structure release. The matching memory consumes, however, much memory compared to the separate array memory due to the loss for the key memory. The collection of garbage cells due to the structure synchronization is also a serious problem that usually decreases the efficiency of the program.

Structure memory can be separated from the matching unit. In this case the structure memory consists of an ordinary memory with a waiting queue. However, such a scheme has many defects, e.g. overhead time due to the memory allocation, initialization and garbage collection. In the following discussion we assume that the size of the array is S, each memory cell is read only once after the write operation, and the number of garbage cells are much less than S. In order to use the structure memory, we must follow the steps listed below:

(1) SRE (Search Empty Region) Search the contiguous empty region to allocate a new array.

(2) ALC (Allocate Structure) Turn off all the empty bits in the array. Reset all the P (presence) flags and W (wait) flags in the array.

(3) WA (Write Array) Write to a cell in

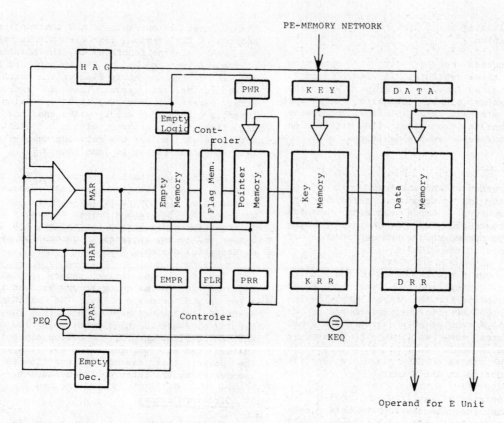

Figure 5. Block Diagram of the M Unit.

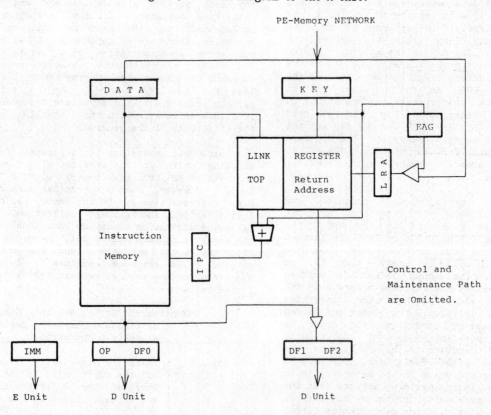

Figure 6. Block Diagram of the F unit.

64

the array. Set P bit and reset W bit in that cell. If there are any read requests in the waiting queue, return the write value to these requests.

(4) RA   (Read Array) Read a cell in the array. If that cell is not yet written, the request is inserted into the waiting queue, bit W is set.

(5) SRW   (Search Waiting Cell) Search the cell where the read requests wait for the arrival of the write data.

(6) RWQ   (Read Waiting Queue) Read the request in the waiting queue.

(7) DALC (Deallocate the Array) Set all the empty bit in the array.

If these operations are performed on the structure with three flag bits in each cell (W,P,E), it takes 5 * S memory accesses for using an array (accesses are for allocation and initialization, write, read, search garbage cell, and deallocation). Furthermore, some allocation program must be executed for searching and allocating an array. If the array is not large, the overhead time for allocation cannot be ignored. Hence the structure memory in a data flow computer is much slower than the main storage in a conventional computer unless it is equipped with special hardware for the above operations.

The S unit of the SIGMA-1 provides three hierarchical bit tables for increasing the speed of these operations. Figure 7 shows the block diagram of the S unit and Figure 8 shows the construction of the hierarchical bit table. For example, the first level bit table is the P bit table. We can access N bits in a column at a time. Note that in the Figure 8, N is four, although N is sixteen in the S unit. Each column (four bit) in the first level corresponds to two bits (El and Fl) in the second level bit table. If all the bits in the column are zero, set the El bit. If all the bits are one, set the Fl bit. The second column is the example of the latter and the third is the former in the figure. We can also access 2N bits in a column at a time in the second level. The third level is constructed in the same way. This procedure is repeated until the last level has only one column. For example, when the size of the column is sixteen, six level tables are sufficient for the 16M bits table.

For example, when a search bit request arrives to the bit table, all the tables are read in parallel. When a bit (0 or 1 according to the request) is found in the first level, return the position. When the bit is not found in the first level but is found in the second level, the first level table is again read by the address calculated from the second level table. Thus at most log N read operations are performed. The speeds of the operations are listed in Table 1.

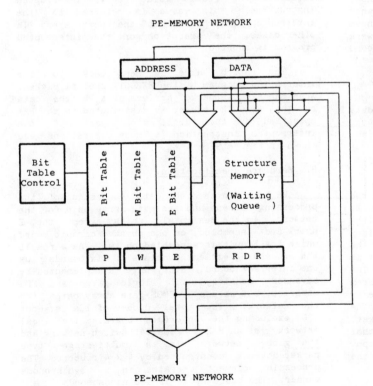

Figure 7. Block Diagram of the S unit.

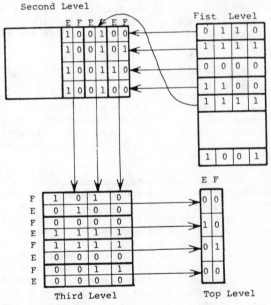

N = 4.

Figure 8. Hierarchical bit table.

Detailed algorithms are described in [11]. Thus $2 * S + 3 * \log S$ accesses are needed for the array in the SIGMA-1. This is more than twice as fast as an implementation using the simple bit table.

6. Other units.

The F unit consists of a link register and an instruction memory. The link register contains the top address and the size of the instruction block, the return address from the subroutine and two flags (empty and unloaded). The instruction memory is a 16K word memory which stores the instructions and immediate operands. The construction of the F unit is shown in Figure 8.

The E unit is an execution unit which performs arithmetic and logical operations, floating point operations, structure addressing operations and other operations common to conventional computers. It also performs the interrupt handling operation described later. The whole E unit is controlled by the horizontal micro program, the size and width of which are 1K and 60 bits respectively.

The D unit is the output unit to the network. It generates output packets from the instruction and the E unit output. Since a packet is divided into two contiguous words, the D unit sends the first half of the packet in parallel with the E unit operation. The simultaneous operation in the D unit and the E unit reduces the total pipeline delay by 50 % in many instructions such as ADD, but the packet cancel mechanism is necessary when an error occurs in the E unit. The packet whose first half has already been sent to the network can be cancelled by the cancel bit in the second half of the packet.

7. Interruption

Interruption is the basic mechanism in a data flow computer for communicating between a user program and the system management program. However, there have been few studies of interruptions in data flow computers. We propose an interrupt mechanism.

The interrupt mechanism consists of (1) the invocation of the interrupt handling process, (2) the argument passing mechanism from the interrupted instruction to the interrupt handling process, (3) the mechanism for resuming the interrupted program. In the SIGMA-1, the first is performed by the subroutine call mechanism. The SYS type packet is sent to the PE where the system manager exists. Then the argument is transfered to the system manager through the M unit. The last is carried out by the EXECUTE special packet. This packet enters into the instruction that causes the interruption and distributes the output packets according to the destination fields of the instruction.

In the SIGMA-1, we determine several causes of interruption such as arithmetic faults, data type error, overflow in the context field(I or LN), and instruction loading errors for dynamic loading. In order to explain the operations in interruption, we assume that an arithmetic fault occurs during the execution of the ADD instruction.

The execution of the instruction is cancelled after occurrence of interruption. Then the two operands that caused the interruption are inserted into the matching unit in the same PE as the ERROR level packets with the same positional informations (PE, LN, D, I). Since the firing rule for the ERROR level packet is different from that of the normal packets the ERROR level packets are stored in the M unit until the SALV special packet picks them up. Then a SYS packet informs the system and/or group manager of the occurrence of the arithmetic fault. The operation of the interrupted instruction terminates after sending these packets. The SYS packet invokes the interrupt handling process.

The first task of the interrupt handling process is to extract input arguments from the ERROR level packet in the PE. These operations are carried out by the SALV special packet. The SALV packet is sent to the PE where the interruption occurred. The the SALV packet extracts the ERROR level packet from the M unit, changes the destination part of the packet to the destination operand given by the SALV packet and sends the packet to the interrupt handling process. The interrupt handling process may calculate the result value for the interrupted instruction. This value is returned to the interrupted instruction in the next step. In other cases, the execution of the interrupted program is aborted.

The return value is sent back to the interrupted program by the EXECUTE special packet. When the EXECUTE packet arrives at a PE, the data on the EXECUTE packet is distributed to the PEs specified by the destination part of the interrupted instruction. These operations are shown in Figure 9.

8. Hardware specification.

We have finished the detailed design of the processing element and the gate array chip for the network. In the design all units except the E unit are assembled on one printed circuit board while the E unit is assembled on two. As a result the processing element consists of six boards plus one interface board. Every unit is implemented by advanced Schottky TTL logic gates and MOS memories, but we use BI-CMOS gate array chips for the network. The total number of ICs is about 1500 excluding the interface board. The local network is an 8 X 8 cross bar switch network and the global network is a multi-stage type packet-network constructed by 4 X 4 routers. The processing element operates in a synchronous manner. The basic cycle is 100 nanoseconds.

The processing element fetchs the first 40

bits (a context field) of a packet at the first cycle, dispatches it to the F, M or S unit depending on the type of the packet, and receives the next 40 bits (data field) at the second cycle. The F unit processes the context part of the packet by the end of the second cycle. When the instruction is unary, the input data passes through the matching unit and enters the E unit at the second cycle. The second stage (the D and E units) begins execution at the third cycle. When the instruction is binary, the M unit processes it in three cycles, but the data are sent to the E unit at the second cycle. Both the F and M units can begin the next operation at the fourth or sometimes at the third cycle.

The E unit begins the operation at the third cycle and takes one cycle for an integer arithmetic operation and three cycles for a floating arithmetic operation other than the division operation. The D unit starts sending the first half of the packet one cycle before the E unit terminates the operation and the D unit sends the second half just after the E unit finishes. Figure 10 shows the timing diagram for unary integer instructions and binary floating point instructions.

The E unit determines the maximum pipeline delay three cycles in this case. Hence the processing element is a 3 MFLOPS machine.

9. Concluding remarks

The features of the SIGMA-1 are summarized as:

. average speed 100 MFLOPS,
. short pipeline architecture and multi-level networking,
. interrupt mechanism,
. sticky packet for loop invariant variables,
. matching memory by chained hashing hardware, and
. special hardware for the structure management.

This year we construct a single PE prototype by commercial ICs. In a few years, we will re-design the PE by LSI technology for reducing the size of the PE and construct a 256 PE system.

Acknowledgement

The authors wish to thank Dr. T.Yuba, Mr. Y.Yamaguchi and Mr. K.Toda for stimulating discussions. The authors are also grateful to Dr. H.Kashiwagi for continuous encouragement. This research is supported by the High-Speed Computing System for Scientific and Technological Use Project of the MITI, Japan.

References

[1]   N. Takahashi and M. Amamiya, "A Data Flow Processor Array System: Design and Analysis," Proc. 10th Ann. Symp. Computer Architecture, June 1983.

[2]   K. P. Gostelow and R. E. Thomas, "Performance of a simulated Dataflow Computer," IEEE Trans. Computers, Vol. C-29, No. 10, Oct. 1980, pp.905-919.

[3]   Y. Yamaguchi, K. Toda, and T. Yuba, "A Performance Evaluation of a Lisp-based Data-driven Machine (EM-3)" Proc. 10th Ann. Symp. Computer Architecture, pp. 363-369, June 1983.

[4]   J. R. Gurd and I. Watson, "Data Driven System for High Speed Parallel Computer -- Part 2: Hardware Design, " Computer Design, July, 1980, pp. 97-106.

[5]   M. Kishi,H.Yasuhara, and Y. Kawamura, "DDDP: A Distributed Data Driven Processor", Proc. 10th Ann. Symp. ComputerArchitecture, pp. 236-242, June 1983.

[6]   T. Shimada, K. Hiraki, and K. Nishida, "An Architecture Of a Data Flow Computer and its evaluation" COMPCON '84 Spring.

[7]   K. Hiraki, K. Nishida, and T. Shimada, "Evaluation of Associative Memory Using Parallel Chained Hashing", To appear on IEEE Trans. Computers.

[8]   T. Ida and E. Goto, "Performance of a Parallel Hash Hardware with Key Deletion," Proc. IFIP Congress 77, Aug. 1977, pp. 643-647.

[9]   K. Nishida, K. Hiraki, T. Shimada, "Empirical study of LSI Matching Unit for Data-flow Computer," Papers of Tech. Group on Comp., EC83-24, IECE Japan Sep. 1983, pp. 31-38, in Japanese.

[10] J. da Silva, I. Watson, "Pseudo-associative store with hardware hashing," IEE PROC. Vol. 130, Pt.E, No.1, Jan. 1983, pp19-24.

[11] K. Hiraki, "Hierarchical Bit Table Algorithms," Sigma-Memo 8, Electrotechnical Laboratory, Jan. 1984.

Operation	Simple bit table	Hierarchical bit table
Search the first 1 / 0	O(N)	O(1)
Search contiguous M bits	O(N)	O(1)
Get size of Contiguous M bits	M	log M
Set a bit	1	N ------- N - 1
Set contiguous M bits	M	log M
Amount of bit table	N	N + 2/C

N : Size of the table
M : Size of the region
C : Size of the column

Table 1

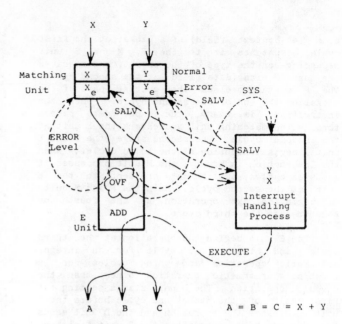

Figure 9. Interrupt Mechanism.

$A = B = C = X + Y$

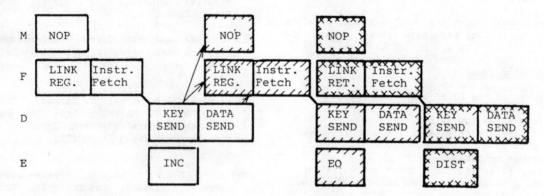

The second instruction uses the result of the
first instruction.

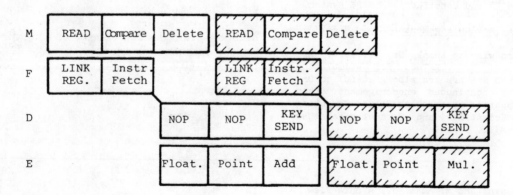

Figure 10 Timing diagram of a PE.

Cedar—A Large Scale Multiprocessor

Daniel Gajski, David Kuck, Duncan Lawrie, and Ahmed Sameh

Laboratory for Advanced Supercomputers
Department of Computer Science
University of Illinois at Urbana-Champaign

Abstract

This paper presents an overview of Cedar, a large scale multiprocessor being designed at the University of Illinois. This machine is designed to accommodate several thousand high performance processors which are capable of working together on a single job, or they can be partitioned into groups of processors where each group of one or more processors can work on separate jobs. Various aspects of the machine are described including the control methodology, communication network, optimizing compiler, and plans for construction.

1. Motivation

The primary goal of the Cedar project is to demonstrate that supercomputers of the future can exhibit general-purpose behavior and be easy to use. The Cedar project is based on five key developments which have reached fruition in the past year and taken together offer a comprehensive solution to these problems.

(1) **The development of VLSI components makes large memories and small, fast processors available at low cost.** Thus, highly parallel (e.g., 1024 processors) systems are not ruled out by cost or physical volume considerations as they have been in the past. Particularly important are the 32-bit 2.5 megaflop chips or chip-sets developed in the past year [WaMc82]. Thus, basic hardware building blocks will be available off-the-shelf in the next few years.

(2) Given the hardware components for a highly parallel system, accessing a parallel shared memory and moving data between memories and processors has been a traditional architectural stumbling block. Many systems have been built that have severe constraints in the memory (e.g., access to columns only) or interconnection network (e.g., nearest neighbors only). **Based on many years of work, it is possible to have a shared memory and switch design which will provide high bandwidth over a wide range of computations and applications areas.**

(3) Compilation for parallel, pipeline, and multiprocessor systems has been another serious traditional problem. **The Parafrase project has demonstrated that by restructuring ordinary programs these supercomputer architectures can be exploited effectively.** It has also been shown that Parafrase can restructure programs to effectively exploit various levels of a memory hierarchy. An important consequence is that a compiler can be used to manage caches in a multiprocessor and thus avoid cache coherency problems.

(4) The control of a highly parallel system is another problem of long-standing concern and controversy. It is probably the most controversial of the five topics listed here, mainly because it seems to be the least amenable to rigorous analysis. From an abstract viewpoint, the traditional dataflow approach seems best because control is distributed out to the level of operations on scalar operands. In practice, it seems that dealing with this low level of granularity has many weaknesses. **By using a hierarchy of control, we have found that dataflow principles can be used at a high level (macro-dataflow), thus avoiding some of the problems with traditional dataflow methods.** We have also demonstrated that a compiler can restructure programs written in ordinary programming languages to run well on such a system.

(5) Algorithms for systems with concurrency have been studied for a number of years. Many successes have been achieved in exploiting the array parallelism of various pipeline and parallel machines. But there have been a number of difficulties as well. It has long been realized that some of these difficulties should be surmountable using a multiprocessor because the parallelism in such a machine is not as rigid as in array-type machines. **Recent work in**

This work was supported in part by the National Science Foundation under Grants No. US NSF MCS81-00512 and US NSF MCS80-01561, the US Department of Energy under Contract No. US DOE DE AC02-81ER10822, and by the Department of Computer Science at the University of Illinois

numerical algorithms seems to indicate great promise in exploiting multiprocessors without the penalty of high synchronization overheads which has proved fatal in some earlier studies. Furthermore, nonnumerical algorithms have been developed at a rapidly increasing rate in the past few years. These can generally use a multiprocessor more efficiently than a vector machine, particularly in cases where the data is less well structured. Our group has been active in developing both numerical and nonnumerical algorithms.

To reach the goal stated in the opening paragraph, we believe that a two-phase approach is necessary. The first phase is to demonstrate a working prototype system, complete with software and algorithms. The second phase would include the participation of an industrial partner (one or more) to produce a large scale version of the prototype system called the production system. Thus, the prototype design must include details of scaling the prototype up to a larger, faster production system.

Our goal for the *prototype* is to achieve Cray-1 speeds for programs written in high level languages and automatically restructured via a preprocessing compiler. We would expect to achieve ten to twenty megaflops for a much wider class of computations than can be handled by the Cray-1 or Cyber 205. This assumes a four cluster, 32-processor prototype where each processor delivers 2.5 megaflops.

The *production* system will use processors that deliver over 10 megaflops, so a 1024 processor system should realistically deliver (through a compiler) several gigaflops by the late 1980s. Actual speeds might be higher if (as we expect) our ideas scale up to more processors, if higher speed VLSI technology is available, and if better algorithms and compilers emerge to exploit the system.

An integral part of the design for the prototype and final system is to allow multiprogramming. Thus, the machine may be subdivided and used to run a number of jobs, with clusters of eight processors, or even a single processor being used for the smallest jobs.

2. The Cedar Architecture

In order to integrate the discussion, we show in Fig. 1 an overall system diagram. More details of our preliminary view of the system are discussed in [GLPV83].

2.1. Processor Cluster. A Processor Cluster (PC) is the smallest execution unit in the Cedar machine. A chunk of program called a Compound Function can be assigned to one or more PCs.

A PC consists of n processors, n local memories, and a high speed switching network that allows each processor access to any of the local memories. Each processor

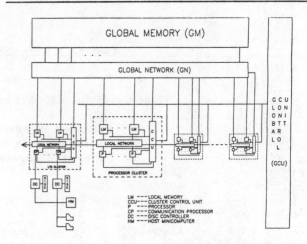

Figure 1. Overall system diagram.

can also access its own local memory directly without going through the switch. In this way, extra delay is incurred only when the data is not in its own local memory. Furthermore, each processor can directly access global memory for data that is not in local memory. Our compiler is targeted at exploiting this hierarchy of memory access speeds.

Each processor consists of a floating-point arithmetic unit, address generation unit, and Processor Control Unit (PCU), with program memory. There are no programmer accessible data registers in the processor. However, the local memory is dynamically partitionable into pseudo-vector registers of different sizes, and so it serves really as a large set of general-purpose registers. There are two reasons for this type of cluster organization. Firstly, it simplifies the compiler design. Secondly, there is no need for general-purpose registers since off-the-shelf floating-point arithmetic is an order of magnitude slower than medium size static memories (500 ns vs. 50 ns). Each local memory has its own global memory access unit that allows movement of data between global and local memories to proceed concurrently with the computation.

The entire PC is controlled by the Cluster Control Unit (CCU), which mostly serves as a synchronization unit that starts all processors when the data is moved from global memory to local memory and signals the Global Control Unit (GCU) when a compound function execution is finished.

In this paper we discuss two different machine sizes: the prototype and production machine. The prototype machine is a 4 cluster (8 processors per cluster) machine built for the purpose of debugging architectural and software concepts and justifying performance estimates for a broadly chosen set of applications. An architecturally and technologically upward scalable production machine is a 64-128 cluster (8-16 processors per cluster)

70

high performance supercomputer.

To obtain short design time, we will use for the prototype machine off-the-shelf components, standard memory chips, and gate arrays, while the production machine will use custom VLSI parts and high density packaging technology.

Communication between disks, etc., and global memory will be through a special I/O cluster. An I/O cluster is equivalent to a PC except for the processors themselves. Instead of the usual processors, the I/O cluster will have communication processors. These in turn will connect to Extended Storage (solid state disks) which serves as a buffer between Cedar and the support machines (e.g., VAX) which will provide access to disks, terminals, etc.

2.2. Global Network

Large scale multiprocessors require access to a shared memory system and convenient interprocessor communication. Early parallel computers tended to be mesh-connected—that is, access to neighboring processors and memories was fast, but more global communication/access took proportionally more time. Vast amounts of manpower were expended devising special algorithms which could execute in this type of environment. (Pipeline processors are not immune to this problem—the performance degradation due to non-unit vector strides or irregular addressing patterns are generally recognized problems.)

Our network is based on an extension of the omega network [Lawr75] and is similar in concept to the omega network designed for the Burroughs FMP machine [Burr79], [BaLu81]. That network was nominally 1024x1024, and was a circuit-switching network where the data path at each node was 11 bits wide. They estimated that the minimum time required to set up a connection would be 120 ns.

Our initial design differs in several respects from the FMP design. It is based on the use of 8x8 switches located on 160 pin boards, rather than 2x2 switches. Taking into account expected delays due to conflicts, time multiplexing of 120-bit packets, memory access, and return transmission, we estimate an expected delay time of less than 2 μs/1024 words between processor and memory. (Using the same techniques we can design networks to provide average global memory access in as little as 500 ns, but these designs would require as many as 8 boards per processor.)

An example of one of these networks connecting 16 processors to 8 memories is shown in Fig. 2. This example uses 4x4 switches, but illustrates the principles we will use in constructing the 1024 port global network. We have discovered ways to add redundancy in larger networks that allow us to use this redundancy both for conflict avoidance and fault tolerance [Padm83]. Notice that unlike the omega network, this network allows more than one path between any processor port and any output port. This path redundancy provides both fault

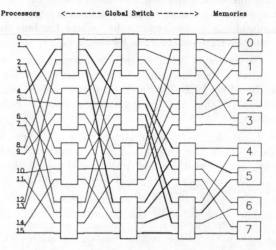

Figure 2. Example of a global network connecting 16 processors with eight memories. Notice the redundant paths from processor 4 to memory 5.

tolerance and conflict avoidance. Thus, from every switch (except the last) there are at least two valid paths. If either of these is either blocked by another message or by a failure, a connection can still be made via an alternate path. (A total blockage can exist if *all* alternate paths are blocked by conflicts with other messages and/or faults. However, analytic and simulation results indicate that the probability of conflicts is significantly lower with the redundant paths than without them, and that the probability of there being enough faults to block a message is so small that the mean time between fault-blocked-messages is on the order of one year even for the production machine.) The control logic which allows this conflict/fault avoidance is distributed throughout the network and is not very different from the classical omega control algorithm.

2.3. Memory System

The overall memory system has a great deal of structure to it, but the user need not concern himself with anything but the global shared memory. However, the fast local memories present in the design can be used to mask the approximately 2 μs access time to global memory. Each cluster of eight processors contains eight, 16K local memories A given processor can access its own local memory module directly, or any local memory in its cluster through the cluster network.

User transparent access to these local memories will be provided in several ways. First, program code can be moved from global to local memories in large blocks by the cluster and global control units. Time required for these transfers will be masked by computation. Second, the optimizing compiler will generate code to cause movement of blocks of certain data between global and local memory. Third, automatic caching hardware (using the local memories) will be available for certain data where the compiler cannot determine *a priori* the details of the access patterns but where freedom from cache coherency problems can be certified.

All levels of memory include operand level synchronization facilities (similar to the full/empty bit of the Denelcor HEP [Smit82]), and the global shared memory includes the (programmer) option of virtual memory.

Figure 3 shows a programmers' view of the memory system. Both the cluster and local memories include cache space (which is physically implemented in the local 16K memories) for global memory accesses. This cache is different from most cache memory schemes in that not all global memory accesses are cached–only those predetermined by the programmer or compiler. In this way, we avoid the cache consistency problems which plague most multiprocessor cache designs. Thus, only read-only data (or data that is determined by the compiler to be read-only during a short phase of a program) or data that is only written by a single processor (private data) is cached.

Thus a user need only be concerned with a single uniform globally shared memory, and he could quickly design a program to execute from this memory. When he is satisfied with his results, he can use the optimizing compiler to improve his performance by making better use of the entire memory hierarchy and by utilizing more

GLOBAL SHARED MEMORY	GLOBAL SHARED VIRTUAL MEMORY	CLUSTER SHARED MEMORY	CLUSTER SHARED CACHE	LOCAL MEMORY	LOCAL CACHE

Figure 3. Programmers' view of the memory system.

parallelism.

2.4. Global Control Unit. The execution of a program is limited by the parallelism exhibited by the control mechanism. In a von Neumann machine, the parallelism is limited by a serial control mechanism in which each statement is executed separately in the order specified by the program.

The execution speed can be increased by using parallel control flow or dataflow mechanisms [TrBH82]. Each of these mechanisms tries to execute all independent operations in parallel, where the operation is a typical arithmetic operation (e.g., addition, multiplication, etc.) or control operation (e.g., decision). However, the number of resources (e.g., operational units) in the machine is limited and sometimes not all independent

operations can be executed in parallel. Therefore, the resources must be allocated and deallocated in the order specified by the computation. The price paid for parallelism is in the form of extra time or hardware needed to allocate operational units to instructions and keeping track of the execution order, the process we call scheduling. Proposed dataflow architectures are very inefficient on regular structures because of this fine granularity of their operations. When data is structured (vectors, matrices, records), the control and dataflow is very regular and predictable and there is no need to pay high overhead for scheduling.

In our system, we adapt to the granularity of the data structure. We treat large structures (arrays) as one object. We reduce scheduling overhead by combining together as many scalar operations as possible, and executing them as one object[Corn81]. In our machine, each Processor Cluster (PC) can be considered as an execution unit of a macro-dataflow machine. Each PC executes a chunk of the original program called a compound function (CF).

From the GCU point of view, a program is a directed graph called a flow graph. The nodes of this graph are compound functions and the arcs define the execution order for the compound functions of a program.

The nodes in our graph can be divided into two groups: Computational (CPF) and Control (CTF). All CTFs are executed in the GCU, and all the CPFs are done by clusters. All CPFs have one predecessor and one successor. CTFs are used to specify multiple control paths, conditional or unconditional.

The compound function graph is executed by the GCU. Each node requires two different types of action:

(1) Computation of the original part of the program specified in the CF which may be done by the GCU itself or allocated to PCs. The latter case is for CPFs, and it requires their scheduling and preparation. The CTFs either do not have this part at all, or perform computation related to control.

(2) Graph update after the executable part of a node is done (if it had one). Successors of each node are updated and checked for readiness. The updating consists of recording that the predecessor node was executed. A node is ready when all its predecessors in the graph are done. When a node is finished, the predecessor information is reinitialized for the next execution of the node (if it is a cycle, for instance).

The second problem of dataflow architectures is storage allocation, deallocation and movement of data, resulting in slow data access. In our machine, data is stored permanently in global memory and it can be shared there by all PCs. The data is moved into the assigned PC before the execution of a CF and later stored back to global memory. In this way, the movement of data is minimized while the order and locality of data is preserved. **Thus, the macro-dataflow architecture combines the control mechanism of** dataflow **architectures and storage management of the von Neumann machine.**

3. Software

The primary language for Cedar will be Fortran (although we expect several other languages to become available as well). In Fortran, users will have a choice of writing programs directly in an extended Fortran (based on the ANSI 8X standard), or of using their old programs as is. The powerful restructuring capabilities of Parafrase [KuPa79] will usually be brought to bear on programs written in serial Fortran and may also (though not necessarily) be applied to programs written in extended (parallel) Fortran. Since the Parafrase system operates in a source-to-source manner, the user who used Parafrase can then choose to maintain his original code or the new, restructured version (thus obviating the need for further restructuring. [KPSW82])

The compiler will provide the Cedar system with code that may be regarded as a dependence graph containing several types of nodes called compound functions (CFs). This macro-dataflow graph is presented to the global control unit (GCU) which oversees its execution. Some CFs are control functions executed in the GCU itself, while other nodes are computational and are passed down to clusters of processors [GaKP81].

Four important kinds of parallelism may be distinguished in the Cedar macro-dataflow code. The first is parallelism between CFs themselves. This includes executing some CFs on the GCU and some in processor clusters, as well as executing several CFs at once in different processor clusters.

The second kind of parallelism is in the loop control of the computational CFs. For example, all iterations of a loop may be executable at once and so each iteration can be assigned to a different processor. Of course, the GCU may fold a computation onto a limited number of processors and each processor will then do a number of iterations ([KuPa79], [PaKL80]).

Third, is a kind of pipelining effect achieved by moving data from global to local memories before it is needed for the computation of a CF. We can prefetch data for iteration $i+1$ while computing iteration i, for example, or we can prefetch larger blocks. Experimental evidence shows that this approach will be effective in exploiting the local memories in clusters. This software cache management only works effectively for data that can be guaranteed (by the compiler) to be written at most once in a given phase of a computation. Otherwise, cache coherency problems can develop, and our solution to this is to force any nonsafe code to execute directly from the global shared memory. This will cause some speed decrease (by a constant factor) and should be a rather rare event in any case. The global memory has of course only one copy of the data, and hardware will ensure that the correct value is stored.

The fourth kind of parallelism will be exploited mainly for phases of computations in which there is less parallelism than processors. This involves spreading expressions across more than one processor for execution. For example, if a loop of 50 iterations could be run as 50 independent iterations, but our machine had 100 processors available, two processors could be used for each iteration. This code spreading is entirely within individual compound functions and may involve executing independent assignment statements in distinct processors or even spreading single expressions over two or more processors. Experiments to date show that spreading can be very effective in some cases but it is not a first priority technique.

Some standard operating system functions will be handled by our hardware, e.g., task scheduling in the GCU. The I/O clusters will handle some of the activities that are traditionally at the interface between the compiler, OS, and I/O channels. In particular, we plan to have the I/O clusters execute I/O statements and do format conversions. They will also handle page faults between the global memory and disk system. We also plan to attach front-end processors to the I/O clusters.

A front-end processor will provide various user services. We would expect it to be a network node in any installation and in the Department of Computer Science at the University of Illinois we will attach it to a VAX/Ethernet network within the department. The point is that users should be able to access the system through an interface with which they are familiar and happy (VMS, UNIX, NOS, or whatever). Thus, a user would submit a job through a front-end processor which sends it to an I/O cluster, which in turn can initiate I/O directly or begin execution through the GCU. Results will be returned through the I/O cluster to the front-end processor for output, graphics display, etc. In this way, we hope to make the architectural details of the Cedar system as invisible to the user as possible.

4. Summary

The Cedar architecture nicely integrates the five key developments sketched in the introduction. We believe that the Cedar system will deliver high performance over a much wider range of applications and algorithms than today's supercomputers can handle. Because the Cedar clock speed is slow relative to such systems, the complexities of building and manufacturing this system are substantially reduced. Due to the ever-decreasing costs of integrated circuits and the relative ease with which the Cedar design can be partitioned, we feel that the monetary cost per megaflop will be much lower than could be achieved by attempting to push today's pipelined supercomputers to higher speeds.

REFERENCES

[BaLu81] G. H. Barnes and S. T. Lundstrom, "Design and Validation of a Connection Network for Many-Processor Multiprocessor Systems," *IEEE Computer*, Vol. 14, No. 12, pp. 31-41, Dec., 1981.

[Burr79] Burroughs Corporation, "Numerical Aerodynamic Simulation Facility Feasibility Study," Mar., 1979.

[Corn81] Cornish, M., "Lecture Notes in Dataflow Computer Architecture," MIT, 1981.

[GaKP81] D. D. Gajski, D. J. Kuck, and D. A. Padua, "Dependence Driven Computation," *Proc. of the COMPCON 81 Spring Computer Conf., San Francisco, CA*, pp. 168-172, Feb., 1981.

[GLPV83] D. D. Gajski, D. H. Lawrie, J-K. Peir, A. Veidenbaum, and P-C. Yew, "Second Preliminary Specification of Cedar," Cedar document no. 8, Univ. of Ill. at Urb.-Champ., Dept. of Comput. Sci., Feb., 1983.

[KPSW82] D. Kuck, D. Padua, A. Sameh, and M. Wolfe, "Languages and High-Performance Computations," Invited paper, *Proc. of the IFIP Working Conf. on The Relationship Between Numerical Computation and Programming Languages*, Boulder, CO, pp. 205-221, Aug., 1982 (North-Holland).

[KuPa79] D. J. Kuck and D. A. Padua, "High-Speed Multiprocessors and Their Compilers," *Proc. of the 1979 Int'l. Conf. on Parallel Processing*, pp. 5-16, Aug., 1979.

[Lawr75] D. H. Lawrie, "Access and Alignment of Data in an Array Processor," *IEEE Trans. on Computers*, Vol. C-24, No. 12, pp. 1145-1155, Dec., 1975.

[Padm83] K. Padmanabhan, PhD Thesis, University of Illinois, in preparation, 1983.

[PaKL80] D. A. Padua, D. J. Kuck, and D. H. Lawrie, "High-Speed Multiprocessors and Compilation Techniques," *IEEE Trans. on Computers*, Vol. C-29, No. 9, pp. 763-776, Sept., 1980.

[Smit82] B. S. Smith, "Architecture and Applications of the HEP Multiprocessor Computer System," *Proc. of the International Society for Optical Engineering*, Vol. 298, pp. 241-248, 1982.

[TrBH82] P. C. Treleaven, D. R. Brownbridge, and R. P. Hopkins, "Data-Driven and Demand-Driven Computer Architectures," *Comput. Surveys*, Vol. 14, No. 1, pp. 93-143, Mar., 1982.

[WaMc82] F. Ware and W. McAllister, "C-MOS Chip Set Streamlines Floating-Point Processing," *Electronics*, pp. 149-152, Feb. 10, 1982.

SIMD AND MSIMD VARIANTS OF THE

NON-VON SUPERCOMPUTER[1]

David Elliot Shaw

Department of Computer Science
Columbia University

ABSTRACT

Each member of the NON-VON family of
supercomputers employs massive parallelism to
obtain substantial performance improvements in a
wide range of applications. The NON-VON 1 and
NON-VON 3 machines, which are in various stages of
construction at Columbia University, function for
the most part as single instruction stream,
multiple data stream (SIMD) [2] machines. We have
recently begun to design an enhanced version of
the machine, called NON-VON 4, which would be
capable of functioning as an ensemble of one or
more independent SIMD machines communicating
through a high bandwidth interconnection network.
This paper reviews the essential architectural
features of the NON-VON family, and highlights the
principal differences between NON-VON 4 and its
SIMD predecessors.

1. OVERVIEW

NON-VON [3], [4] is a family of massively parallel
supercomputers characterized by an extensive
intermingling of processing and memory resources
at various levels. The machines are intended to
support the extremely rapid execution of many
large scale data manipulation tasks, including
relational database operations and other functions
relevant to commercial data processing.

All members of the family incorporate a primary
processing subsystem (PPS), which comprises a
large number (as many as a million) of very
simple, highly area-efficient small processing
elements (SPE's), each associated with a small (64
bytes) local random access memory. The PPS is
currently being implemented using custom nMOS VLSI
circuits, each of which is to contain eight
processing elements (at 1983 device dimensions).
While this extremely fine granularity offers the

potential for unprecedented computational
concurrency, it also results in a local memory
that is far too small to store meaningful
programs. NON-VON's SPE's are thus forced to
"import" their programs from one or more
(depending on the version) external instruction
sources.

The design of each member of the NON-VON family
also includes a secondary processing system (SPS)
based on a bank of "intelligent" disk drives,
connected with the PPS through a high-bandwidth
parallel interface. Because of funding
limitations, we have not yet been able to
undertake the implementation of an SPS for any
version of the NON-VON machine. If implemented
using contemporary technology, however, the
machine might incorporate a reasonably large
number of Winchester disk drives, each of moderate
size. A small amount of processing hardware would
be associated with each disk head. This hardware
would allow records to be inspected "on the fly",
to determine whether a given record is relevant to
the operation at hand before transferring it to
the PPS. The hardware would support certain other
operations, such as hashing, that play a key role
in many disk-based NON-VON operations.

While the components we have just described are
incorporated in all members of the NON-VON family,
there are certain essential differences between
the three versions now being designed or
constructed at Columbia. Specifically, NON-VON 1
and 3 include a single control processor, which is
used to broadcast instructions for execution by
the PE's in the PPS. With the exception of
certain input/output operations discussed in Shaw
[1982], these machines thus function in an
instruction-synchronous (SIMD) mode, with all
SPE's simultaneously executing a single
instruction "in lock step".

NON-VON 4, on the other hand, would include a

[1]This research was supported in part by the
Defense Advanced Research Projects Agency
under contract N00039-80-G-0132.

certain input/output operations discussed in Shaw [1982], these machines thus function in an instruction-synchronous (SIMD) mode, with all SPE's simultaneously executing a single instruction "in lock step".

NON-VON 4, on the other hand, would include a number of large processing elements (LPE's), each capable of serving as a control processor for some portion of the PPS. This should give NON-VON 4 the capacity for multiple instruction stream, multiple data stream (MIMD) and multiple SIMD (MSIMD) operations, multi-tasking and multi-user applications, and such problems as physical simulation for which the top of the NON-VON 3 tree would otherwise represent a significant communication bottleneck.

Additional enhancements anticipated for NON-VON 4 derive from the fact that a significant amount of storage (in the form of commercially available dynamic RAM chips) would be associated with each LPE. In addition to its use as storage for an individual LPE, this RAM should prove useful as swapping storage for the local RAM's incorporated in the SPE's with which it is associated. Finally, we hope to realize an additional multiplicative factor in total throughput in NON-VON 4 by reducing the effective instruction cycle time (which is equal to the time required for parallel inter-SPE communication) far below the estimated two microseconds projected for NON-VON 1 and 3 using a number of engineering techniques that are beyond the scope of this paper.

2.   EVOLUTION OF THE NON-VON ARCHITECTURE

In order to minimize the risk involved in developing a highly unconventional supercomputer, we have adopted a three-stage, partially overlapped development strategy. We have begun by implementing and testing a relatively simple machine which nonetheless incorporates what we regard as the most essential elements of a full-scale NON-VON supercomputer. Architectural enhancements are to be added in stages, yielding incremental increases in power and generality without the introduction of an unmanageable increase in conceptual or engineering complexity at any single stage.

2.1. NON-VON 1

The first version we are actually implementing, which we now call NON-VON 1, is based on a custom nMOS VLSI chip that we have recently fabricated through the MOSIS "silicon brokerage" system. The chip is now undergoing extensive testing at Columbia, and has passed all tests successfully as of the time of this writing. Each chip contains a single SPE, including its own small local RAM. These single-SPE chips are to be interconnected to form the PPS, which is configured as a binary

tree, with a single control processor attached to the root. A degenerate PPS consisting of three SPE chips has recently been constructed and, in preliminary tests, has performed according to specification. At least one additional fabrication run is anticipated prior to the fabrication of production quantities of parts in order to make improve certain electrical characteristics of the chip.

Because only a single control processor will be incorporated in the NON-VON 1 prototype, the machine will be limited to SIMD applications, in which the control processor sends instructions to be executed concurrently by all processing elements. Although a complete system would also include an SPS based on a number of "intelligent" disk drives, we will not be developing a working SPS within the scope of our current research contract, as noted above. In short, NON-VON 1 will be limited to the execution of SIMD algorithms in which the argument and result data does not exceed the capacity of the PPS.

Unlike more recent versions of the architecture, NON-VON 1 performs all arithmetic and logical operations in a bit-serial fashion and is rather limited its choice of operands for most instructions. Because only one SPE is embedded on each chip, a relatively low priority was placed on the minimization of silicon area; detailed measurements of the NON-VON 1 layout have, however, formed the basis for the highly efficient floor plans now under development for use in later versions.

A large part of the evolution from NON-VON 1 to its successors was attributable to our experiences in developing software for the machine. NON-VON 1 was simulated at no less than five levels of detail (from the functional to circuit levels) in the course of its construction. The most useful from the viewpoint of architectural evolution was based on an instruction-level simulator implemented in LISP, which was used by several dozen researchers and students to design and test parallel implementations of a number of algorithms. This activity helped us to measure the frequency of execution of various NON-VON 1 instructions, to identify commonly instruction sequences, and to identify functional weaknesses in the instruction set. Our findings had a major influence on the design of later versions of the processing element.

2.2. NON-VON 2

For the sake of completeness, it is probably worth mentioning at this point that the name NON-VON 2 was assigned to an interesting architectural exercise that we do not currently plan to carry beyond the "paper-and-pencil" stage, although its central ideas may well influence future NON-VON designs.

2.3. NON-VON 3

The machine we have come to call NON-VON 3, on the other hand, forms the basis for much of our current work. Like NON-VON 1, our NON-VON 3 prototype will include no disk drives and only a single control processor, and will thus capable of executing only SIMD algorithms in which the data do not exceed the capacity of the PPS. The machine will be similar in most respects to the original NON-VON 1 design, but will incorporate a number of improvements suggested by the results of our initial experiments in chip design and software development. In particular, the NON-VON 3 SPE will feature:

1. An area-efficient eight-bit ALU to replace the one-bit ALU incorporated in the prototype NON-VON 1 SPE chip.

2. Fewer local registers, based on NON-VON 1 area measurements and software simulation results.

3. A far better floor plan, formulated using precise measurements taken from the prototype chip.

4. A generalization of certain NON-VON 1 instructions to support the more efficient execution of many common instruction sequences.

The NON-VON 3 instruction set is nearly identical to, and with few exceptions, more general than the one employed in NON-VON 1. Some of the additions in fact correspond to commonly used macros in our existing NON-VON 1 software. Before adopting this instruction set, however, we were careful to insure that all existing NON-VON 1 software could be simply and mechanically translated into NON-VON 3 instructions, so that none of our work to date would be lost. Translated programs would take advantage of some, but not all of NON-VON 3's enhancements. In the future, of course, NON-VON 3 software will be written using NON-VON 3 instructions, allowing the exploitation of all of these features.

The development of NON-VON 3 has been greatly accelerated by the availability of a highly automated system for the specification, design, layout and testing of VLSI-based processing elements that we implemented for use in designing NON-VON 3. Within this semi-automatic development environment, changes in the instruction set may be realized in hardware in a fraction of the time that would otherwise be required, facilitating extensive experimentation and "fine tuning" of the floor plan.

2.4. NON-VON 4

The NON-VON 1 and 3 machines should serve to validate many of our most important architectural ideas, yielding major performance improvements on a number of problems amenable to SIMD execution. The more sophisticated NON-VON 4 architecture, though, is intended to provide for the highly efficient execution of a much wider range of computational tasks than NON-VON 1 and 3. At present, NON-VON 4 is in the earliest stages of preliminary design. It must thus be emphasized that much of the material we will be presenting must be regarded as tentative, and that many of our ideas have yet to be validated.

3. Organization of NON-VON 4

In the NON-VON 4 machine, each node above a certain fixed level in the PPS tree would be connected to its own LPE. (In a machine containing 256K SPE's, for example, somewhere between 511 and 1K-1 such LPE's might be provided.) Each LPE would include an off-the-shelf microprocessor (a Motorola 68000 or National Semiconductor 16032, for example), a reasonable amount (say, between 256 KBytes and 1 Megabyte), and a modest amount of custom hardware for interfacing with the rest of the machine.

The set of LPE's would be mutually interconnected through a high-bandwidth multistage interconnection network. While the details of this network have not yet been specified, we have recently begun to investigate the possibility of using a "folded" 2-log-n-stage banyan network operating on a circuit-switched basis. Our idea (which, it must be emphasized, is quite tentative) would be to incorporate logic within the individual switches that would support the rapid, parallel identification of some unblocked path through the network whenever any such path exists. This technique is closely related to the broadcasting and resolving functions used in the NON-VON PPS [Shaw, 1982].

Although we have no supporting data at present, we believe that the circuitry for such a network might be simple enough to allow the construction of a moderately high-order switch (that is, one with a number of independent input and output paths) using a single high-speed bipolar gate array chip. Since each switch chip would, in essence, function as a full crossbar switch, the use of higher-order switches would reduce the number of network paths subject to contention. Additional performance advantages should result from the the reduced number of chip-to-chip delays in a network built with higher-order chips, which would in general have fewer stages. Another potentially attractive feature of this "broadcast circuit switch" approach is the fact that later stages in the network are automatically bypassed (and hence relieved of congestion) in cases where the source and destination LPE's are "close" (in a particular sense defined in terms of their addresses).

Some subset of the LPE's (perhaps one-eighth to one-quarter in a realistic system) would be equipped with Winchester disk drives of moderate capacity, but having the kind of specialized "intelligent head unit" hardware described above.

4. Operation of NON-VON 4

It will not be possible in the limited space remaining in this paper to describe all aspects of NON-VON 4 that distinguish its behavior from that of the SIMD NON-VON machines. A simple example chosen from one of the machine's original domains of intended application, however, will serve to illustrate the manner in which the SPS/LPE network complex would often be used. Our example is the relational join operation [1], which takes two relations (tables) as arguments and produces a new table as output. Each tuple (row) in the result relation is formed by concatenating two tuples, one from each argument relation, that have the same value for the corresponding attribute (column).

On a von Neumann machine, this operation is typically executed by sorting the two argument relations on their respective join attributes (the columns on which the comparison is to be made), then performing a "merge-like" operation to produce the result tuples; the running time of the algorithm is typically dominated by the O (n log n) time required for sorting. The SIMD NON-VON machines reduce this time to linear, and provide a significant savings in absolute running time, given certain assumptions about the input data. In NON-VON 4, however, these assumptions are weakened in practically important ways, and the time required to join large relations is reduced far below those of all database machines (actual and "paper") to which we have compared it.

In "internal" cases, where the data does not exceed the capacity of the PPS, the NON-VON algorithm [3] (for both SIMD and MIMD machines) involves the broadcasting of each join value through the PPS and the associative identification of all matching tuples in the other relation. In the "external" case, however, where the argument relations exceed the capacity of the PPS, the argument relations must be divided into key-disjoint partitions, which have the property that no join value appears in more than one partition.

An external algorithm executing in linear time, but under fairly restrictive assumptions, has been presented [3] for the SIMD NON-VON machines. In NON-VON 4, however, key-disjoint partitioning may be accomplished by storing the argument relations "spread across" the various disk heads in the SPS, hashing each join value passing under each head, and dynamically routing the tuples through the LPE network to a different disk head depending on its hashed join value. This process produces k different key-disjoint partition files, where k is the number of disk heads involved, and requires time proportional to the capacity of the full file divided by k.

We are presently investigating the use of an "internal analog" of the above hash partitioning algorithm to produce the join results after external hash partitioning is complete. The essential idea is to hash the join values of all tuples in the PPS (in constant time), and then to migrate each tuple through the LPE network to a PPS subtree determined by the resulting hash value. Each subtree would then apply the internal SIMD join algorithm in parallel, resulting in a speedup proportional to the number of subtrees employed. It should be noted, however, we have not yet completed the detailed statistical analysis necessary to balance the degree of speedup with the cost of overflow and recovery within the subtrees.

References

[1] E. F. Codd, "Relational Completeness of Data Base Sublanguages", in R. Rustin (ed.), Courant Computer Science Symposium 6: Data Base Systems, Prentice-Hall, Inc., 1972.

[2] M. Flynn, "Some Computer Organizations and their Effectiveness", in IEEE Transactions on Computers, vol. C-21, pp. 948-960, September, 1972.

[3] D. E. Shaw, "A Hierarchical Associative Architecture for the Parallel Evaluation of Relational Algebraic Database Primitives", Stanford Computer Science Department Report STAN-CS-79-778, October, 1979.

[4] D. E. Shaw, "The NON-VON Supercomputer", Columbia Computer Science Department Report, August, 1982.

Chapter 4: Arithmetic System Design

Since the advent of computers, much effort has been expended in search of fast arithmetic techniques. A long delay in propagating the carry in parallel adders forced researchers to look into new ways of speeding up the process. Two new techniques, the conditional sum[1] and the carry lookahead[2], were introduced. The carry lookahead, however, became more popular because of its modularity and, as seen from recent publications[3-6] is still of current interest. Some of the other factors in implementing binary parallel adders include the number of connections[7] and the regularity of the layout[8]. A multifunctional arithmetic array that has an almost regular connection pattern and can perform all the four basic operations has been described by Agrawal[9]. Other authors have described division, floating-point operation, logarithm and exponential computation[10-14].

The impact of VLSI has influenced the design of arithmetic units as well. The pin limitation encourages the use of bit serial arithmetic, and several recent papers[15-21] describe the advances in this area. Design for the RISC IBM 3081 processor unit is shown in various papers[22-23], and Aberth[24] describes the design for processor-precise computation. Direct implementation of FP and residue-based functions are also given by two papers[25-26]. The error analysis and finite precision arithmetic are covered in various papers[27-33], and the use of residue codes is illustrated[34-35]. A basis for quantitative comparison of number systems is introduced bv Ong and Atkins[36]. The effect of pipelining on the performance of arithmetic arrays[37] and detection of circuit errors in ALUs[38-39] is addressed. Units for arithmetic expressions, for the solution of differential equations, and for matrix operations is also dealt with[40-47].

It is worth mentioning that the selection of an appropriate instruction set has a major impact on the way a processing unit is designed and the way associated control synchronization signals are generated[48-50]. Having complex machine language instructions does not necessarily guarantee improvement in execution speed for typical application programs[51-59]. Thus, it is imperative to have an appropriate instruction set. Research efforts[60-68] been directed toward designing systems that can directly execute high level language instructions.

Designing a processor with a family of languages in mind started with the Burroughs B1700 computers. This was achieved by having specific microprograms for each high level language. Since then, several researchers have done extensive investigation in this area. Some recent publications[60-68] include defining microprograms for a family of languages and devising architectural description languages for verifying computers and for comparing their performance. More than one level of microprograms is also advocated[81-84]. The capability of incorporating user micropro-grammability has been advocated in several proposed machines, and a very long instruction word machine has also been proposed. Other language issues[85-97] are also considered.

Four papers are included in this chapter to cover various aspects of arithmetic unit design and microprogramming.[2]

References

1 J. Sklansky, "Conditional-Sum Addition Logic," *IRE Trans. Electronic Computers*, Vol. EC-9, No. 6, June 1960, pp. 226-231.

2 O.L. MacSorley, "High Speed Arithmetic in Binary Computers," *Proc. IRE*, Vol. 49, No. 1, Jan. 1961, pp. 67-91.

3 L. Bhuyan and D.P. Agrawal, "On the Generalized Binary System," *IEEE Trans. Computers*, Vol. C-31, No. 4, April 1982, pp. 870-882.

4 L.H. Chi and S. Muroga, "Logic Networks of Carry-Save Adders," *IEEE Trans. Computers*, Vol. C-31, No. 9, Sept. 1982, pp. 870-882.

5 R. Kallman, "A Faster 8-Bit Carry Circuit," *IEEE Trans. Computers*, Vol. C-32, No. 12, Dec. 1983, pp. 1209-1211.

6 T. Rhyner "Limitations on Carry Lookahead Networks," *IEEE Trans. Computers*, Vol. C-33, No. 4, April 1984, pp. 373-374.

7 A. Sakurai and S. Muroga, "Parallel Binary Adders with a Minimum Number of Connections," *IEEE Trans. Computers*, Vol. C-32, No. 10, Oct. 1983, pp. 969-976.

8 R.P. Brent and H.T. Kung, "A Regular Layout for Parallel Adders," *IEEE Trans. Computers*, Vol. C-31, No. 3, March 1982, pp. 260-264.

9 D.P. Agrawal, "High-Speed Arithmetic Arrays," *IEEE Trans. Computers*, Vol. C-28, No. 3, March 1979, pp. 215-224.

10 A. Feldstein and R. Goodman, "Loss of Significance in Floating Point Subtraction and Addition (Corresp.)," *IEEE Trans. Computers*, Vol. C-31, No. 4, April 1982, pp. 328-335.

11 S. Halász, "Usual Division Wrong" *Computer*, Vol. 14, No. 10, Oct. 1981, p. 10.

12 J.H.P. Zurawski, "Design of High-Speed Digital Divider Units," *IEEE Trans. Computers*, Vol. C-30, No. 9, Sept. 1981, pp. 691-699.

13 A.H. Karp, "Exponential and Logarithm by Sequential Squaring," *IEEE Trans. Computers*, Vol. C-33, No. 5, May 1984, pp. 462-464.

EH0246-9/86/0000/0079$01.00 © 1986 IEEE

14 E.E. Swartzlander, Jr., D.V.S. Chandra, H.T. Nagle, Jr., and S.A. Starks, "Sign/Logarithm Arithmetic for FFT Implementation." *IEEE Trans. Computers*, Vol. C-32, No. 6, June 1983, pp. 526-534.

15 K.E. Batcher, "Bit-Serial Processing Systems," *IEEE Trans. Computer*, Vol. C-31, No. 5, May 1982, pp. 377-384.

16 B.G. Mackey and M.J. Irwin, "A Digit On-Line Arithmetic Simulator," *Proc. 1982 Int'l. Conf. Parallel Processing*, IEEE Computer Society, Washington, D.C., 1982, pp. 304-306.

17 D.S. Raghavendra and M.D. Ercegovac, "A Simulator for On-Line Arithmetic," *Proc. Fifth Symp. Computer Arithmetic*, IEEE Computer Society, Washington, D.C., May 1981, pp. 92-98.

18 H.J. Sips, "Comments on: An O (n) Parallel Multiplier with Bit-Sequential Input and Output," *IEEE Trans. Computers*, Vol. C-31, No. 4, April 1982, pp. 325-327.

19 R.M. Owens, "Techniques to Reduce the Inherent Limitations of Fully Digit On-Line Arithmetic (Corresp.)," *IEEE Trans. Computers*, Vol. C-32, No. 4, April 1983, pp. 406-411.

20 M.J. Irwin and R.M. Owens, "Fully Digit On-Line Networks," *IEEE Trans. Computers*, Vol. C-34, No. 4, April 1983, pp. 402-406.

21 H.J. Sips, "Bit Sequential Arithmetic for Parallel Processors," *IEEE Trans. Computers*, Vol. C-33, No. 1, Jan. 1984, pp. 7-20.

22 R.N. Crustafson and F.J. Sparcio, "IBM 3081 Processor Unit: Design Considerations and Design," *IBM Journal of Research and Development*, Vol. 26, No. 1, Jan. 1982, pp. 12-21.

23 J. Reilly, A. Sutton, R. Nasser, and R. Griscom, "Processor Controller for the IBM 3081," *IBM Journal of Research and Development*, Vol. 26, No. 1, Jan. 1982, pp. 22-29.

24 D. Aberth, "Precise Scientific Computation with a Microprocessor," *IEEE Trans. Computers*, Vol. C-33, No. 8, Aug. 1984, pp. 685-690.

25 M. Castan and E.I. Organick, "u3L: An HLL-RISC Processor for Parallel Execution of FP-Language Programs," *Proc. 9th Ann. Symp. Computer Architecture*, IEEE Computer Society, Washington, D.C., 1982, pp. 238-247.

26 C.A. Papachristou, "Direct Implementation of Discrete and Residue Based Functions Via Optimal Encoding: A Programmable Array Logic Approach (Corresp.)," *IEEE Trans. Computers*, Vol. C-32, No. 10, Oct. 1983, pp. 961-968.

27 C. Halatsis, N. Gaitanis, and M. Sigala, "Error-Correcting Codes in Binary Coded Radix-r Arithmetic (Corresp.)," *IEEE Trans. Computers,* Vol. C-32, No. 3, March 1983, pp. 326-328.

28 P. Kornerup and D.W. Matula, "Finite Precision Rational Arithmetic: An Arithmetic Unit," *IEEE Trans. Computers*, Vol. C-32, No. 4, April 1983, pp. 378-388.

29 E.V. Krishnamurthy and Venu K. Murthy, "Fast Iterative Division of P-adic Numbers (Corresp.)," *IEEE Trans. Computers*, Vol. C-32, No. 4, April 1983, pp. 396-398.

30 D.C. Watanuki, "Error Analysis of Certain Floating-Point On-Line Algorithms," *IEEE Trans. Computers*, Vol. C-32, No. 4, April 1983, pp. 352-358.

31 N. Gaitanis and C. Halatsis, "Near-Perfect Codes for Binary-Coded Radix-y Arithmetic Units (Corresp.)," *IEEE Trans. Computers*, Vol. C-32, No. 5, May 1983, pp. 494-497.

32 E.V. Krishnamurthy, "On the Conversion of Hensel Codes to Farey Rationals," *IEEE Trans. Computers*, Vol. C-32, No. 4, April 1983, pp. 331-337.

33 A. Froment, "Error Free Computation: A Direct Method to Convert Finite-Segment P-adic Numbers into Rational Numbers," *IEEE Trans. Computers*, Vol. 32, No. 4, April 1983, pp. 337-343.

34 R.M. Owens, "Error Analysis of Unnormalized Arithmetic," *Dept. of Computer Science*, Pennsylvania State Univ., College Park, Penn., Aug. 1981.

35 N.-K. Tsao, "A Simple Approach to the Error Free Analysis of Division-Free Numerical Algorithms," *IEEE Trans. Computers*, Vol. C-32, No. 4, April 1983, pp. 343-351.

36 S. Ong and D.E. Atkins, "A Basis for the Quantitative Comparison of Computer Number Systems," *IEEE Trans. Computers*, Vol. C-32, No. 4, April 1983, pp. 359-369.

37 J.R. Jump and S.R. Ahuja, "Effective Pipelining of Digital Systems," *IEEE Trans. Computers*, Vol. C-27, No. 9, Sept. 1978, pp. 855-865.

38 J.H. Patel and L.Y. Fung, "Concurrent Error Detection in ALU's by Recomputing with Shifted Operands," *IEEE Trans. Computers*, Vol. C-31, No. 7, July 1982, pp. 589-595.

39 J.H. Patel and L.Y. Fung, "Concurrent Error Detection in Multiply and Divide Arrays (Corresp.)" *IEEE Trans. Computers*, Vol. C-32, No. 4, April 1983, pp. 417-422.

40 R. Brent, "The Parallel Evaluation of General Arithmetic Expressions," *Journal of the ACM*, Vol. 21, No. 2, April 1974, pp. 201-206.

41 F. Baccelli and T. Fleury, "On Parsing Arithmetic Expressions in a Multiprocessing Environment," *Acta Informatica*, Vol. 17, 1982, pp. 287-321.

42 K. Hwang and Y.C. Cheng, "Partitioned Matrix Algorithm for VLSI Arithmetic Systems," *IEEE Trans. Computers*, Vol. C-31, No. 12, Dec. 1982, pp. 1215-1224.

43 A.R. Bazelow and J. Raamot, "On the Ordinary Differential Equations Using Integer Arithmetic," *IEEE*

Trans. Computers, Vol. C-32, No. 2, Feb. 1983, pp. 204-207.

44 P. Chow, Z.G. Vranesic, and J.L. Yen, "A Pipelined Distributed Arithmetic PFFT Processor," *IEEE Trans. Computers*, Vol. C-32, No. 12, Dec. 1983, pp. 1128-1136.

45 H.J. Sips, "A Bit-Sequential Multi-Operand Inner Product Processor," *Proc. 1982 Int'l. Conf. Parallel Processing*, IEEE Computer Society, Washington, D.C., 1982, pp. 301-303.

46 J. Vanaken and G. Zick, "The Expression Processor: A Pipelined Multiprocessor Architecture," *IEEE Trans. Computers*, Vol. C-30, No. 8, Aug. 1981, pp. 525-536.

47 K. Hwang, "VLSI Computer Arithmetic for Real-Time Image Processing," *VLSI Electronics: Microstructure Science*, edited by Einpruch, Vol. 7, Academic Press, Orlando, Fla., 1984.

48 W.J. Kaminsky and E.S. Davidson, "Developing a Multiple-Instruction-Stream Single-Chip Processor," *Computer*, Vol. 12, No. 12, Dec. 1979, pp. 66-76.

49 T.G. Rausher and P.N. Adams, "Microprogramming: A Tutorial and Survey of Recent Development," *IEEE Trans. Computers*, Vol. C-29, No. 1, Jan. 1980, pp. 2-20.

50 P.J. Denning, "Working Sets—Past and Present," *IEEE Trans. Software Engineering*, Vol. SE-6, No.1, Jan. 1980, pp. 64-84.

51 R.D. Ditzel and D.A. Patterson, "The Case for the Reduced Instruction Set Computer," *Computer Architecture News*, Vol. 8, No. 6, Oct. 1980, pp. 25-33.

52 D.A Patterson, "A RISCy Approach to VLSI," *Computer Architecture News*, Vol. 10, No. 1, March 1982, pp. 28-32.

53 D.A. Patterson and R.S. Pispho, "RISC Assessment: A High-Level Language Experiment," *Proc. 9th Ann. Symp. Computer Architecture*, IEEE Computer Society, Washington, D.C., 1982, pp. 1-5.

54 H. Cragon, P. Goldberg, D. Patterson, J. Rattner, D. Earnest, P. Denning, and K. Kavi, (Moderator), "Innovative Architecture and Commercial Computers," *T.R. 81-3-2*, Panel Discussion, Computer Science Department, The University of Southwestern Louisiana, T.R. 81-3-2, 1981.

55 C.A. Hoare, "Hints on Programming Language Design," *Proc. 4th Int'l. Conf. Computer Software and Applications*, IEEE Computer Society, Washington, D.C., 1980, pp. 43-53.

56 H. El Halabi and D.P. Agrawal, "Microinsructions as the Image Architecture and Its Impact on Software Metrics," *Proc. COMPCON Spring 1983*, IEEE Computer Society, Washington, D.C., 1983, pp. 99-103.

57 P.J. Denning, "Computer Architecture: Some Old Ideas That Have Not Quite Made It Yet," *Comm. of the ACM*, Vol. 24, No. 9, Sept. 1981, pp. 553-554.

58 S. Isoda, Y. Kobayashi, and T. Ishida, "Global Compaction of Horizontal Microprograms Based on the Generalized Dependency Graph," *IEEE Trans. Computers*, Vol. C-32, No. 10, Oct. 1983, pp. 922-933.

59 P. Bose and E.S. Davidson, "Design of Instruction Set Architectures for Support of High-Level Languages," *Proc. 11th Ann. Int'l. Symp. Computer Architecture*, IEEE Computer Society, Washington, D.C., 1984, pp. 198-207.

60 Y. Chu, "Architecture of a Hardware Data Interpreter," *IEEE Trans. Computers*, Vol. C-28, No. 2, Feb. 1979, pp. 101-109.

61 N.R. Harris, "A Directly Executable Language Suitable for a Bit Slice Microprocessor Implementation," *Proc. Int'l. Workshop High-Level Language Computer Architecture*, University of Maryland, College Park, Md., 1980, pp. 40-43.

62 S. Dasgupta, "Some Aspects of High Level Microprogramming," *ACM Computing Surveys*, Vol. 12, No. 3, Sept. 1980, pp. 295-321.

63 Y. Chu and M. Abrams, "Programming Languages and Direct-Execution Computer Architecture," *Computer*, Vol. 14, No. 7, July, 1981, pp 22-40.

64 M.J. Flynn and L.W. Hoevel, "Execution Architecture: The Deltran Experiment," *IEEE Trans. Computer*, Vol. C-32, No. 2, Feb. 1983, pp. 156-175.

65 L. Lopriore, "Capability Based Tagged Architectures," *IEEE Trans. Computers*, Vol. C-33, No. 9, Sept. 1984, pp. 786-803.

66 D.R. Ditzel and D.A. Patterson, "Retrospective on High-Level Language Computer Architecture," *Proc. 7th Ann. Symp. Computer Architecture*, IEEE Computer Society, Washington, D.C., 1980, pp. 97-104.

67 Y. Chu and Marc Abrams, "Programming Languages and Direct-Execution Computer Architecture, *Computer*, Vol. 14, No. 7, July 1981, pp. 22-32.

68 Y. Chu, "High-Level Computer Architecture," *Computer*, Vol. 14, No. 7, July 1981, pp. 7-8.

69 H.A. El-Halabi, "Microinstructions of the Image Architecture in a Multi-Language Environment," Ph.D Thesis, Wayne State University, Detroit, Mich., 1983.

70 H. Hagiwara et al., "A Dynamically Microprogrammable Computer with Low-Level Parallelism," *IEEE Trans. Computers*, Vol. C-29, No. 7, July 1980, pp. 577-595.

71 M. Sint, "A Survey of High-Level Microprogramming Languages," *Proc. 13th Ann. Microprogramming Workshop*, IEEE Computer Society, Washington, D.C., 1980, pp. 141-153.

72 S. Dasgupta, "S*A: A Language for Describing Computer Architectures," *Proc. 5th Int'l. Conf. Computer Hardware Description Languages, and Their Applications*, North-Holland Publishing Company, Amsterdam, The Netherlands, 1981.

73 S. Dasgupta and M. Clafsson, "Towards a Family of Languages for the Design and Implementation of Machine Architectures," *Proc. 9th Ann. Symp. Computer Architecture*, IEEE Computer Society, Washington, D.C., April 1982, pp. 158-170.

74 D.A. Patterson, "An Experiment in High-Level Language Microprogramming and Verification," *Comm. of the ACM*, Vol. 24, No. 10, Oct. 1981, pp. 699-709.

75 S. Dasgupta, "On the Verification of Computer Architectures Using an Architecture Description Language," *Proc. 10th Ann. Int'l. Symp. Computer Architecture*, IEEE Computer Society, Washington, D.C., 1983, pp. 32-38.

76 F. Andre, J.P. Banatre, H. Leroy, G. Paget, F. Ployette, and J.P. Routeau, "KENSUR: An Architecture Oriented Towards Programming Languages Translation," *Proc. 7th Ann. Symp. Computer Architecture*, IEEE Computer Society, Washington, D.C., 1980, pp. 17-22.

77 W.A. Wulf, "Trends in the Design and Implementation of Programming Languages," *Computer*, Vol. 13, No. 1, Jan. 1980, pp. 14-25.

78 D.A. Fisher, "DoD's Common Programming Language Effort," *Computer*, Vol. 11, No. 3, March 1978, pp. 24-33.

79 T. Baba et al., "Hierarchical Micro-Architecture of a Two-Level Microprogrammed Multiprocessor Computer," *Proc. 1983 Int'l. Conf. Parallel Processing*, IEEE Computer Society, Washington, D.C., 1983, pp. 478-485.

80 S. Tomita, K. Shibayama, T. Kitamura, T. Nakata, and H. Hagiwara, "A User Microprogrammable Local Host Computer with Low-Level Parallelism," *Proc. 10th Ann. Int'l. Symp. Computer Architecture*, IEEE Computer Society, Washington, D.C., 1983, pp. 151-157.

81 E.E. Klingman, "Hierarchical Coding of Microcomputers for High-Level Architecture," *IEEE Micro*, Vol. 1, No. 1, Feb. 1981, pp. 53-57.

82 J.A. Fenner, J.A. Schmidt, H.A. Halabi, and D.P. Agrawal, "MASCO: An Academic Exercise in Computer Design Using Microprogramming," *Proc. 17th Ann. Microprogramming Workshop*, IEEE Computer Society, Washington, D.C., 1984, pp. 21-30.

83 R.G. Wedig and M.J. Flynn, "Concurrency Detection in Language-Oriented Processing Systems," *Proc. 2nd Int'l. Conf. Distributed Computing Systems*, IEEE Computer Society, Washington, D.C., 1982, pp. 805-810.

84 Z. Segall, A. Singh, R.T. Snodgrass, A.K. Jones, and D.P. Siewiorek, "An Integrated Instrumentation Environment for Multiprocessors," *IEEE Trans. Computers*, Vol. C-32, No. 1, Jan. 1983, pp. 4-14.

85 B. Brodie, "Precompilation of Fortran Programs to Facilitate Array Processing," *Computer*, Vol. 14, No. 9, Sept. 1981, pp. 46-51.

86 M.L. Powell, "MODULA-2: Good News and Bad News," *Proc. COMPCON Spring 1984*, IEEE Computer Society, Washington, D.C., 1984, pp. 438-440.

87 J.C. Browne et al., "A Language for Specification and Programming of Reconfigurable Parallel Computation Structures," *Proc. 1982 Int'l. Conf. Parallel Processing*, IEEE Computer Society, Washington, D.C., 1982, pp. 142-149.

88 G.J. Andrews and J. R. McGraw, "Language Features for Parallel Processing and Resource Control," *Proc. Conf. Design and Implementation of Programming Languages*, 1976.

89 G.R. Andrews, "Parallel Programs: Proofs, Principles and Practice," *Comm. of the ACM*, Vol. 24, No. 3, March 1981, pp. 140-146.

90 H.S. Stone, "Computer Research in Japan," *Computer*, Vol. 17, No. 3, March 1984, pp. 26-32.

91 P. Wegner, *Programming with Ada: An Introduction by Means of Graduated Examples*, Prentice Hall, Englewood Cliffs, N.J., 1980.

92 S. Crespi-Reghizzi, P. Corti, and A. Dapra, "A Survey of Microprocessor Languages," *Computer*, Vol. 13, No. 1, Jan. 1980, pp. 48-66.

93 W.A. Wulf, "Compilers and Computer Architecture," *Computer*, Vol. 14, No. 7, July 1981, pp. 41-47.

94 J. Backus, "Function-Level Computing," *IEEE Spectrum*, Vol. 19, No. 8, Aug. 1982, pp. 22-27.

95 H. Arvind and J.D. Brock, "Resource Managers in Functional Programming," *Journal of Parallel and Distributed Computing*, Vol. 1, No. 1, Aug. 1984, pp. 5-21.

96 A. Nicolau and J.A. Fisher, "Measuring the Parallelism Available for Very Long Instruction Word Architectures," *IEEE Trans. Computers*, Vol. C-33, No. 11, Nov. 1984, pp. 968-976.

97 J.A. Fisher, "Very Long Instruction Word Architectures and the ELI-512," *Proc. 10th Ann. Symp. Computer Architecture*, IEEE Computer Society, Washington, D.C., pp. 140-149.

High-Speed Arithmetic Arrays

DHARMA P. AGRAWAL, MEMBER, IEEE

Abstract—High-speed multifunction arithmetic arrays for multiplication, division, square and square-root operations are presented in this paper. These arrays seem attractive due to their versatility and speed. A recently described quotient-bit evaluation technique that uses the carry-save method in a nonuniform division array is extended here for the restoring-division process. This array includes the multiplication process as well, and the division time approaches that of multiplication. The design objective of multifunctional arithmetic arrays precludes consideration of other high-speed division techniques. A further extension of the restoring division process is shown to make the design of an array for square/square-root operation straightforward. The two underlying arrays can be coalesced to perform any one of the four operations. Possible methods of merging the arrays, with their relative merits, are also discussed. For illustration purposes, complete internal details of such a generalized pipelined array for 4-bit operation is included in this paper. Due consideration is also given to the possibility of large-scale integration of the different arrays illustrated in this paper.

Index Terms—Arrays, carry-look-ahead, carry-save, division, high-speed arithmetic, multifunction, multiplication, pipelining, sign detection, square, square-root.

I. INTRODUCTION

SINCE THE inception of computers, much effort has been expended in search of fast arithmetic techniques. The ripple carry adder, which uses a minimum number of gates, forces a long delay in producing the sum as the carry must be propagated through the entire number. The breakthrough came with the introduction of the conditional sum adders [1] and the carry look-ahead adders [2]. These are the two most economical fast adders. The conditional sum method is an ideal means to meet the challenge of using circuits with small fan-in and fan-out when superspeed circuits are used [3]. But as carry-look-ahead circuits are modular in nature, virtually all commercial MSI and LSI adder structures use it for high performance.

In digital design techniques, much attention has also been paid to network design in the form of a repeated pattern of identical circuits. The composite network so designed is called an iterative or cellular array. This design idea has become particularly attractive since it is suitable for large-scale integration. A large number of papers have appeared dealing with the design of cellular arrays for various arithmetic operations such as multiplication, division, square

Manuscript received March 1, 1977; revised February 11, 1978. This work was supported in part by the National Science Foundation under Grant ENG 76-11237. A preliminary version of this paper was presented at the 3rd Symposium on Computer Arithmetic, Southern Methodist University, Dallas, TX, November 1975.

The author was with the Department of Computer Science, Southern Methodist University, Dallas, TX 75275. He is now with the Department of Electrical and Computer Engineering, Wayne State University, Detroit, MI 48202.

and square-root. These arrays are normally designed from either a regular or semiregular structure point of view and utilize arithmetic cells, performing two or more functions such as addition, subtraction, and transfer (no arithmetic). The complexity of these arithmetic cells and their corresponding arrays vary greatly. These basic arrays, however, are relatively slow, particularly for division and square-rooting. To speed up the division process, the carry-save addition technique of designing high-speed multiplier arrays [4] has been recently employed in an adequately fast-divider array [5]. Such a divider array is nonuniform since, in each row of the array, carry-look-ahead circuitry has to be added for computing the sign bit. However, this seems to be the best possible solution from the speed point of view.

In this paper, the carry-save technique, carry-look-ahead circuitry for sign-bit computation in each row, and carry-look-ahead adders for the addition of the final two summands are employed to design faster arithmetic arrays. The speed up techniques utilized here reduce the division and square-root time to approximately that of the multiplication operation. But they make the array depart from strict uniformity. To increase the utilization of the array hardware, application of pipelining [6], [7] is also examined in detail.

II. MULTIPLIER ARRAY

Various cellular multiplier arrays based on different algorithms have been described in the literature. For example, the application of Booth's algorithm [8] for multiplication leads to such an array. This array is not suitable for its extension as a multifunction array (see Section IV). Similarly, the signed-digit system [9] and another recently described complex arithmetic subunit for multipliers [10] also are not at all suitable in this respect because of their dedicated design for high performance but unifunction arithmetic. The usual method of multiplication utilizes "shift" and "add" processes, wherein the multiplier bits are scanned either from right-to-left or from left-to-right. Multiplier arrays for either of the two scanning methods have a great deal of similarity and for the sake of completeness, an array for the second method is shown in Fig. 1(b). This array is formed with the basic cell of Fig. 1(a), which is characterized by the following input–output relations:

$$s = a \oplus c_1 \oplus [bp] \tag{1a}$$

and

$$c_2 = ac_1 + [a + c_1]bp \tag{1b}$$

where b, p, a, s, c_1, and c_2 are the multiplicand, multiplier,

Reprinted from *IEEE Transactions on Computers*, Volume C-28, Number 3, March 1979, pages 215-224. Copyright © 1979 by The Institute of Electrical and Electronics Engineers, Inc.

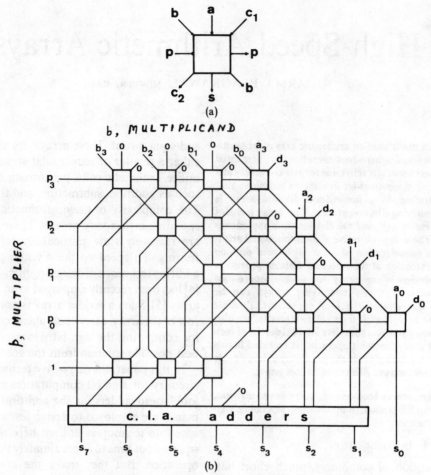

Fig. 1. (a) Arithmetic cell. (b) Right-shift multiplier array $s = a + bp + d$.

previous sum, present sum, carry-in, and carry-out, respectively. In Fig. 1(b), the cells are connected in a carry-save mode and the final two partial sums are added by fast carry-look-ahead (CLA) adders. In multiplying two "n" bit numbers, the time delay T_m for the multiplier can be given as

$$T_m = (n + 1)T + T_{\text{CLA}} \qquad (2)$$

where T is the delay in each arithmetic cell and T_{CLA} represents the delay in the CLA adders. The structure of Fig. 1(b) is directly adoptable for performing division, as the division operation requires arithmetic to be started from the most significant bit (MSB). The selection of a carry-save iterative array is justified by the fact that this is more efficient [7] as compared to other multipliers.

III. DIVIDER ARRAY

Several well-known techniques for the division operation exist in the literature [3]. Arrays for the division operation can be classified into two categories: 1) restoring [11]–[13] and 2) nonrestoring [13]–[15]. The speed of these two types of arrays is almost equal while only the restoring technique gives a true remainder. But, when the cells are connected in a carry-save mode, the time delay to obtain the individual sum-bit in the cell is more for the restoring case. In either of the two methods, subtraction is performed directly or implemented by adding the 2's complement of the divisor. The functional requirements of the different division techniques are depicted in Table I. Now the question of

TABLE I
FUNCTIONAL REQUIREMENTS OF DIFFERENT DIVISION TECHNIQUES

	Technique	Direct Subtract	2's complement addition
1.	Restoring	Subtract-transfer	Add transfer
2.	Nonrestoring	Add-subtract	Add-add (without 2's complement)

preference needs consideration. When an array is to be designed explicitly for the division operation only, any one of these four possibilities can be taken up for the basic cell design. But when the same array is to do multiplication, the restoring and 2's complement addition technique has to be preferred. This type of cell requires inclusion of only two functions of "add"–"transfer," while other combinations necessitate one additional function (as multiplication needs "add"–"transfer" functions). An added advantage of this selection is that the sign-bit detection logic is needed only for addition; while more complex circuits are essential for all other combinations.

One such array structure is shown in Fig. 2(b). This array utilizes the basic cell of Fig. 2(a). In this cell, the signal "b_i" is added to the summation of "a_i" and "c_i" only when the signal "q_j" is "1." But "c_i" is always included while computing the expected carry-out "e_{i+1}" and the two carry-look-ahead terms "G_{i+1}" and "P_{i+1}." Boolean expressions for the cell can be given as

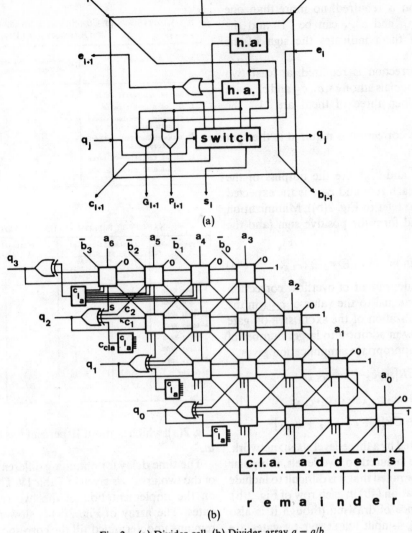

(a)

(b)

Fig. 2. (a) Divider cell. (b) Divider array $q = a/b$.

$$s_i = (a_i \oplus c_i) \oplus (q_j b_i) \qquad (3a)$$

$$c_{i+1} = a_i c_i + (a_i + c_i) q_j b_i \qquad (3b)$$

$$e_{i+1} = a_i c_i + (a_i + c_i) b_i \qquad (3c)$$

$$G_{i+1} = (a_i \oplus b_i \oplus c_i) e_i \qquad (3d)$$

and

$$P_{i+1} = a_i \oplus b_i \oplus c_i + e_i. \qquad (3e)$$

The carry-look-ahead circuits, shown in Fig. 2(b) as a block marked with CLA, can be normally implemented with two-level NAND networks. However, due to fan-in consideration, multilevel carry-look-ahead circuits might have to be utilized for long word lengths.

The array of Fig. 2(b) divides "a" (having 7 bit word length) by "b" (4 bits) and the quotient bits are obtained at the "q" terminals. In accordance with the principle of the restoring method, the quotient bit is taken as "1" only when the 2's complement addition of the divisor "b" yields a positive remainder and is indicated by a carry overflow from the most significant bit position. Otherwise, it is taken as "0" and the original value of the remainder is restored. The array

of Fig. 2(b) utilizes carry-save which produces two partial sums in each row of the array. Hence, the restoration is accomplished in a slightly modified form compared to the usual array. When restore or "no arithmetic" is desired, the summation of the two partial remainders from the antecedent step (without adding 2's complement of the divisor) is allowed to be transmitted as inputs to the next row. The 2's complement addition is achieved by adding the complement of all individual divisor bits and forcing the carry-in input "e_i" of the right-most cell to "1." If the quotient bit thus obtained is one, this carry-in "1" is accounted for by adding it along with the succeeding row.

Another significant difference in this array is in the logic for sign-detection. Here, as the carry-save furnishes two remainders, the test for positive sign in the usual arrays [6], [16] by "carry-overflow" from MSB position is not at all adequate. Also, in the previous row, if the quotient digit is "1" and the carry-overflow has not taken place (rather, is still present in the previous remainder which is now available in the form of two partial sums), a correction factor has to be considered while evaluating the sign of the remainders presently under consideration. The truth table for this can be prepared by following the underlying observations:

1) When no correction is required, no more than one variable among s, c_1, c_2, and c_{CLA} can be "1" and the presence of any *one* of them indicates the sign of the remainders to be positive.

2) When overflow correction is required, at least two signals and at most three signals among s, c_1, c_2, and c_{CLA} are in the state "1" and when three of them are "1," the remainders are positive.

3) When $c_{CLA} = 1$, the correction is required in the next step.

The signals "s," "c_1," and "c_2" are the outputs of the extreme leftmost cell of each row and c_{CLA} is the expected carry-out of the row (also refer to Fig. 2(b)). Minimization gives the following closed form for positive sign (and the quotient bit q) as

$$q \equiv \text{positive sign} = s \oplus c_1 \oplus c_2 \oplus c_{CLA}. \quad (4a)$$

The expression (4a) is independent of overflow correction CR. But the correction is equal to the value of c_{CLA} in the previous row and the realization of the EXCLUSIVE-OR gate requires longer time delay in addition to larger number of components. Hence, an appropriate simplification gives

$$\begin{aligned}
\text{positive sign} = CR[&sc_1c_2 + sc_1c_{CLA} \\
&+ sc_2c_{CLA} + c_1c_2c_{CLA}] \quad (4b) \\
&+ \overline{CR}[s + c_1 + c_2 + c_{CLA}]
\end{aligned}$$

and this can be implemented by a three-level NAND network. In fact, this delay can be reduced to two levels, if bipolar circuits are used. It may be noted that it is difficult to include the logic realization of relation (4b) in each row of Fig. 2(b). Hence, for the convenience of drawing (though it is also valid as defined by (4a)), 4-input EXCLUSIVE-OR gates are shown in all diagrams in this paper.

The array of Fig. 2(b) can be easily extended for longer word lengths. The time delay for such an array is proportional to the number of quotient bits to be evaluated and for "n" bits, the expression can be given as

$$T_d = n(T + T_s + T_{CLA}) \quad (5)$$

where T is the delay in each cell, T_s is the delay in each sign detection logic shown by EXCLUSIVE-OR gate and T_{CLA} is the delay in carry-look-ahead circuits. This value of T_d is comparable with the delay in the multiplier array (see expression 2). Thus, the extra cost of carry-look-ahead circuits for sign-bit detection is justifiable. We will now compare the nonrestoring array of Cappa *et al.* [5] and the restoring array of Fig. 2(b) on qualitative and quantitative basis.

The array proposed here does not require the cell for the sign-bit, but the look-ahead circuits are required for an additional bit position. Table II gives the component requirements of the two designs and Table III shows the number of NAND/NOR gates needed for the arithmetic cells. When these two cells are implemented with MOS technology, the cell of Cappa *et al.* requires 22 resistors and 68 transistors, while 24 resistors and 55 MOS transistors are needed for the cell of

TABLE II
COMPARISON OF COMPONENT REQUIREMENTS FOR "n" BITS OF QUOTIENT AND DIVISOR

Item	Non-restoring array of Cappa et. al.	Restoring array proposed here in Fib. 2.b
1. No. of arithmetic cells	n^2	n^2
2. No. of sign-bit cells	n	-
3. Sign-bit carry-look-ahead circuit for no. of bits	$n-1$	n
4. Gates needed for quotient bits computation		
i no. of Exclusive-OR gates	n	-
ii no. of NAND gates	-	$9n$

TABLE III
NAND/NOR IMPLEMENTATION OF ARITHMETIC CELLS

Type of gate	Arithmetic cell of Cappa et. al.		Arithmetic cell of Fig. 2.a		Modified cell of Fig. 3	
	No. of Gates	Total Circuit Inputs	No. of Gates	Total Circuit Inputs	No. of Gates	Total Circuit Inputs
8-input NAND	1	8	-	-	1	8
6-input NAND	-	-	-	-	1	6
5-input NAND	1	5	-	-	-	-
4-input NAND	8	32	1	4	10	40
3-input NAND	4	12	11	33	10	30
2-input NAND	2	4	5	10	5	10
2-input NOR	1	2	1	2	1	2
Inverter	5	5	6	6	5	5
TOTAL	22	68	24	55	33	101

Fig. 2(a), which is about 10 percent less than that of Cappa *et al.*

The time delay for obtaining different signals in each row of the two arrays is given in Table IV. These values are based on the implementation of the two cells with NAND/NOR gates. The array of Fig. 2(b) is slower, as the restoration remains undetermined till the corresponding quotient bit is being computed. This time delay can, however, be reduced if the restoring process is included in the cell of the following row. This necessitates certain alterations and the modified arithmetic cell is shown in Fig. 3. The Boolean relations for this cell, in a simplified form, can be given as

$$\bar{s}'_i = q_{j+1}\overline{(a_i \oplus c_i)} + \bar{q}_{j+1}\overline{(a'_i \oplus c'_i)} \quad (6a)$$

$$\begin{aligned}
\bar{s}_i = {}& q_{j+1}\overline{(a_i \oplus c_i)} + \bar{q}_{j+1}\overline{(a'_i \oplus c'_i)}\bar{b}_i \\
&+ q_{j+1}(a_i \oplus c_i) + \bar{q}_{j+1}(a'_i \oplus c'_i)b_i, \quad (6b)
\end{aligned}$$

$$\bar{c}'_{i+1} = (\bar{a}_i + \bar{c}_i)q_{j+1} + (\bar{a}'_i + \bar{c}'_i)\bar{q}_{j+1} \quad (6c)$$

$$\begin{aligned}
\bar{c}_{i+1} = {}& q_{j+1}(\bar{a}_i\bar{b}_i + \bar{b}_i\bar{c}_i + \bar{a}_i\bar{c}_i) \\
&+ \bar{q}_{j+1}(\bar{a}'_i\bar{b}_i + \bar{b}_i\bar{c}'_i + \bar{a}'_i\bar{c}'_i) \quad (6d)
\end{aligned}$$

and

$$\bar{e}_{i+1} = \bar{c}_{i+1}. \quad (6e)$$

As is clear from relations (6) and is indicated in Tables III and IV, these expressions are more complex than those given by (3) and hence requires 65 percent more components.

It is also worth mentioning here that the array of Fig. 2(b) (and of Cappa *et al.*) can be used to obtain the division of sum of two 6-bit numbers, i.e., $q = (a + c)/b$ can be performed by applying proper values of "c" inputs along with

TABLE IV
COMPARISON OF DELAYS IN OBTAINING DIFFERENT SIGNALS OF EACH ROW

Delay in terms of No. of gates	Array of Cappa et.al.	Array of Fib. 2.b	Modified array using cell of Fig. 3
(i) for G and P terms	4	4	4
(ii) in sign-bit carry-look-ahead circuits	2	2	2
(iii) in sign-bit detection	3	2	2
(iv) for quotient-bit evaluation	9	8	8
(v) for carry term(s)	3	10	4
(vi) for sum term(s)	4	11	4
(vii) total delay in each row	9	11	8

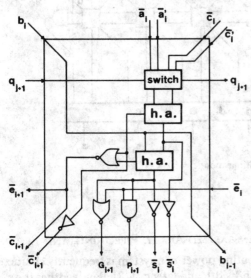

Fig. 3. Modified divider cell.

"a" input bits. The main advantage of the restoring array is in its straightforward extension for multiplication and this is considered in the next section.

IV. MULTIPLIER/DIVIDER ARRAY

Most multiplier/divider arrays described in the literature [6], [7], [16] are designed from a fully iterative point of view. The division speed-up technique of Cappa *et al.* has been discussed in Section III, and any attempt to include the multiplication operation in their array results in the necessity of an additional control line in each arithmetic cell. However, the restoring array described here and in Section III, can easily incorporate the multiplication operation. This modified form is shown in Fig. 4. The selection of multiplication or division is controlled by the "x" line ($x = 0$ for multiplication and $x = 1$ for division). Suitable modifications are also made to perform 2's complement addition in the division operation. According to the value of "x," multiplexer switches transmit either the multiplier inputs "p" or the quotient signals "q." The time delay for obtaining "n" quotient bits or multiplying "n" bits by "n" bits, can be given as

$$T_{md} = (n + 1)T + n(T_s + T_{CLA} + T_x) + T_{ex} + T_{lsa} \quad (7)$$

where T_x, T_{ex}, and T_{lsa} are the delays in each multiplexer, EXCLUSIVE-OR gate and the last stage CLA adders, respectively.

Considering the hardware requirement, speed of operation, suitability to large-scale integration, and its multifunction characteristics, this multiplier/divider array seems to be a practical, attractive design. To include square-root functions, this array is further modified and is discussed in Section V.

V. ARRAY FOR SQUARE-ROOTING AND SQUARE

The process of square-rooting is similar to that of division, except that in the division operation the subtrahend remains the same, while in square-rooting, the successive subtrahend changes. This change occurs in the restoring method in a particular fashion [6], and can be easily derived as briefly shown now. Let the square-root of a "$2n$" bit number "a" be "r" and given as

$$\sqrt{a} = r_{n-1} r_{n-2} \cdots r_2 r_1 r_0. \quad (8)$$

Hence, if r_{n-1} is "1," "a" must be at least equal to square of "n" bit number $(1\,0\,0\,\cdots\,0\,0)$, i.e., greater than "$2n$" bit number given by $(0\,1\,0\,0\,\cdots\,0\,0)$. Hence, the very first subtrahend is "01" and this is to be subtracted from two most significant bits of "a." In a similar way, the successive subtrahends for lower significant bits can also be obtained as is shown in [6].

Both restoring and nonrestoring arrays for square-rooting have been described in the literature. The interconnection patterns for these arrays are not regular because of the changes in successive subtrahends. An additional control signal, employed to change the subtrahend bits in the desired manner, has been shown to make the design of a fully-iterative array feasible [6]. In his near-iterative square-rooting array, Majithia [17] obtained the square by adding the subtrahends. In this paper, a fully iterative array structure for square and square-rooting is designed. This array is shown to have an additional significant speedup feature of carry-save and sign-bit carry-look-ahead techniques which is accomplished in exactly the same way as is done in Section IV. Another characteristic of vital importance is the iterative interconnection of the cells in the array which leads to its possible extension for multiplication and division operations (see Section VI).

The basic cell used in the proposed array is shown in Fig. 5(a). This cell is almost similar to the divider cell of Fig. 2(a) with two more lines, "d" and "h," added for the desired successive changes in the subtrahend. Also, to achieve 2's complement addition, the EXCLUSIVE-OR gate is brought to the cell-level at its "b" input (rather than putting it at the top of the array, as done in multiplier/divider array of Fig. 4). Logic equations for the cell of Fig. 5(a) can be given as

$$s_i = a_i \oplus c_i \oplus [r_j(b_i \oplus x)] \quad (9a)$$

$$c_{i+1} = a_i c_i + (a_i + c_i) r_j (b_i \oplus x) \quad (9b)$$

$$e_{i+1} = a_i c_i + (a_i + c_i)(b_i \oplus x) \quad (9c)$$

$$G_{i+1} = (a_i \oplus b_i \oplus c_i \oplus x) e_i \quad (9d)$$

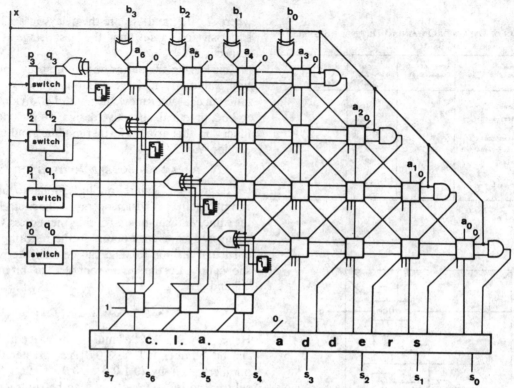

Fig. 4. Multiplier/divider array: $x = 0$ for multiplication; $s = bp$. $x = 1$ for division; $q = a/b$.

$$P_{i+1} = a_i \oplus b_i \oplus c_i \oplus x + e_i \qquad (9e)$$

$$g_{i-1} = d_i(b_i + r_j) \qquad (9f)$$

$$h_{i-1} = b_i + d_i r_j. \qquad (9g)$$

Here, "b" is the subtrahend and the next level subtrahend is denoted by "g." It has been shown in [6] that the changes in successive subtrahends can be achieved by selecting specific values of the variables "b" and "d." The cell of Fig. 5(a) performs three functions: addition, complement addition, and transfer (or restore).

As already pointed out for the square operation [17], the usual subtrahend of the square-rooting process is generated and LOGICAL-AND is performed between this subtrahend and the corresponding square bit. Finally, the result of such an AND operation is added to the partial square already computed. The array for obtaining the square-root of 8-bits or the square of 4-bit numbers is shown in Fig. 5(b). The basic concept of this array is similar to that of multiplier/divider array of Fig. 4 and hence a detailed explanation will not be given. The number of cells in each row of Fig. 5(b) increases as the word length of successive subtrahends in this process changes. The control line "x" is made "1" for square-rooting and "0" for square. The arithmetic cell of Fig. 5(a) needs more gates than that of Fig. 2(a). But the array of Fig. 5(b) remains equally fast and the time delay for square and square-rooting operations can be seen to be equal to the delay in performing multiplication and division operations in the array of Fig. 4.

VI. GENERALIZED ARRAY, PIPELINING, AND EFFICIENCY

Computing power of a system is frequently characterized by its bandwidth and latency [18]. Bandwidth is the number of tasks that can be performed in a unit time interval and latency is the length of time required to perform a single task. For a system that operates on only one task at a time, latency is the inverse of bandwidth. Pipelining is a technique to provide increases in bandwidth by allowing simultaneous execution of many tasks [6], [7]. The key to pipelining a system is the use of temporary storage or latch circuits between successive stages of the system. The bandwidth of a pipelined unit is the inverse of the latency per stage and not the latency of the entire unit. But this is true only on a throughput basis, i.e., with every clock-pulse, the operands are furnished and fed to the system for processing.

Recently Deverell [7] has given a detailed consideration of the effect of pipelining various multipliers and multiplier-divider arrays. In fact, most of the arrays described in the literature can be pipelined and their effective efficiencies can be increased. As the efficiency also depends on the rate of availability of operands, a system with multifunction capability and comparable delay time will be, in general, more efficient. Hence, to obtain an increase in the versatility, a significant step was taken by Kamal *et al.* [6]. They designed the array from the fully iterative structure point of view. It is shown in the following that a further enhancement in operating speed can be achieved by employing carry-save and sign-bit carry-look-ahead techniques.

Designing a single pipelined array for all the four opera-

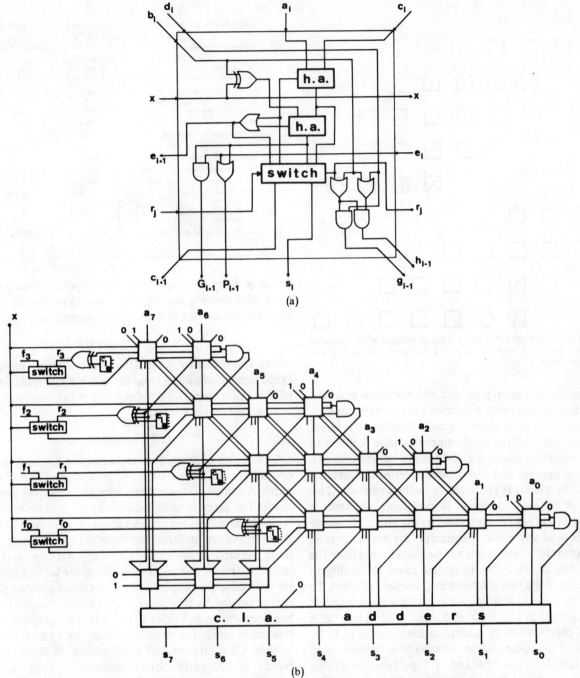

Fig. 5. (a) Cell for square root and square. (b) Array for square root and square: $x = 0$ for square; $s = (f)^2$. $x = 1$ for square root; $r = \sqrt{a}$.

tions (multiplication, division, square, and square-rooting) needs mixing of the arrays shown in Figs. 4 and 5(b). The square-root cell shown in Fig. 5(a) is more general and is thus selected for the combined unit. The process of square-rooting requires the change of subtrahends in a particular fashion and a direct overlapping of the two arrays is not feasible. One solution is to use the square-root array and keep the initiation of multiplication-division operations postponed [6] until the number of cells in a row at least equals the word length of the multiplicand/subtrahend. Such a solution allows the array of Fig. 5(b) to multiply 3 bits by 3 bits; or to divide 5 bits by 3 bits. Normally, we perform the four functions on the same word length. This

requires placing additional cells at the end of the array of Fig. 5(b) and is indicated by back-slash in Fig. 6(a). An alternative is to add cells on the left-hand side of the array so that the word length is adequately increased. This permits activation of multiplication/division process right from the first row. This design cell pattern is shown in Fig. 6(b). Among these two designs, few cells are redundant for each arithmetic operation. Table V shows the relative merits of the two design versions.

It is evident from Table V that both methods utilize an equal number of cells and the second design contains a smaller number of rows with longer word length. So the look-ahead circuit for the second option is more complex.

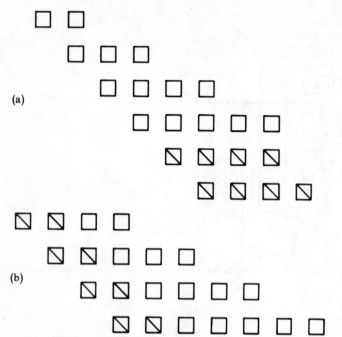

(a)

(b)

Fig. 6. (a) Arithmetic cell pattern for a 4-bit generalized array with additional cells indicated by back slash. (b) Another solution for 4-bit generalized array.

Both these designs, when pipelined, can operate at approximately the same frequency and hence have the same latency. The first contains more steps and so its bandwidth is larger than the second. But the total computing time required to make the results available (i.e., the time in between the two operands is applied and the computation of the result is completed by the array) is larger in the first solution. This means that the second design is preferable whenever a recursive relation is to be computed by the array. Moreover it does not need any initial alignment of the operands as all the four arithmetic operations can be started right from the very first row of the array. In certain cases, an intelligent combination of the two solutions may be more efficient. To illustrate the midway solution, an array for a word length of 4 is diagrammed in Fig. 7. An additional control line "y" is added to decide whether multiplication/division is to be done ($y = 0$); or square/square-rooting is to be performed ($y = 1$). Suitable values of "b" and "d" inputs are also written at the top of the array. One important point worth mentioning is that while performing division, the rightmost cell is not the cell for the least significant bit and normally "1" is forced as a carry-in to LSB position while performing 2's complement addition. It can be seen from studying the figure that this addition is automatically achieved in the array. Also, after the irregularity has occurred in the structure of the array (such as the 5th row of Fig. 7), the look-ahead terms for the missing cells are to be considered for the division operation. These terms can be obtained by performing LOGICAL-AND with the quotient bit and the look-ahead terms just before the presence of irregularity.

For longer word length, carry-look-ahead circuits become much more complex and fan-in constraint forces the adoption of a multilevel carry-look-ahead network. This problem can be partly resolved (up to word length of 16 for a

TABLE V
COMPARISON OF TWO DESIGNS SHOWN IN FIG. 6(a) AND (b)
FOR EVEN VALUES OF "n"

Item	First design illustrated in Fig. 6.a	Second design illustrated in Fig. 6.b
1. No. of arithmetic cells	$n(3n-1)/2$	$n(3n-1)/2$
2. Additional cells needed for the final step addition	$(n-1)$	$(n-1)$
3. No. of rows	$(2n-2)$	n
4. No. of cells in the first row	2	n
5. No. of cells in the last row	n	$(2n-1)$
6. Maximum no. of cells in a row	$(n+1)$	$(2n-1)$
7. Start of square and square-root	1st row	1st row
8. End of square and square-root	nth row	nth row
9. Start of multiplication and division	$(n-1)$th row	1st row
10. End of multiplication and division	$(2n-2)$th row	nth row
11. No. of columns of arithmetic cells	$(3n-3)$	$(3n-2)$

fan-in of 8) by dividing the carry-look-ahead adders in two parts and moving the right-half portion upwards by one row. The time delay in each row of the cells can be given as

$$T_c = T + T_s + T_{CLA} + T_l \qquad (10)$$

where T_l is the delay in the latch circuit. Hence, considering throughput computing time for one bit manipulation, the effective processing time for any one of the four operations can be said to be T_c only.

VII. LSI CONSIDERATION

The design of array-like structures for all the four basic operations has been considered in Sections II to VI of this paper. All these arrays utilize arithmetic cells in a carry-save mode. The carry-look-ahead circuits for sign bit and carry-look-ahead adders for final addition of two operands make these arrays nonuniform. But these arrays are faster and/or more versatile than all existing fully iterative and near-iterative arrays. The pipelining technique further increases their effective efficiencies. The approximate number of transistors needed by these arrays with and without pipelining has been shown in Tables VI and VII. These entries include transistor count for arithmetic cells, EXCLUSIVE-OR gates, latches, CLA circuits and CLA adders. With the present trends in integrated circuit technology, their hardware implementation would not seem to be impossible. The transistor count is based on the application of n-channel MOS gates with a maximum of 9 MOS transistors for an 8-input NAND gate. The arithmetic cells have also been considered to have utilized a minimum number of transistors [41 for the cell of Fig. 2(a) and 50 for the cell of Fig. 5(a)].

From Table VII it is evident that a generalized and fully pipelined array requires slightly less hardware than two separate arrays (one multiplier/divider and another square-root/square). This is due to the fact that only "$2n$" cells are effectively utilized for any one of the four operations while latch circuit overhead becomes prohibitively large and the replication of partially pipelined arrays can be more effective [19]. Hence, for the computers having distributed arithmetic units or having multiple arithmetic units, it is advisable to

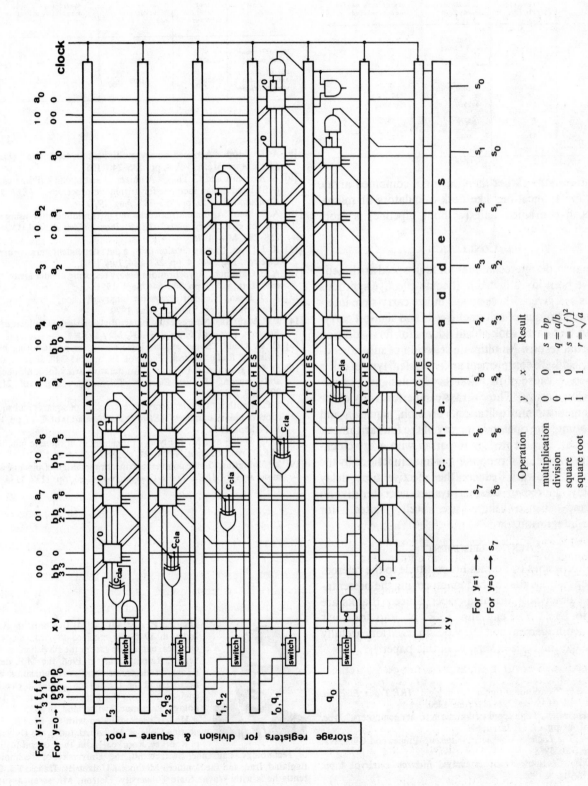

Fig. 7. Generalized pipeline array for 4-bit wordlength.

Operation	y	x	Result
multiplication	0	0	$s = bp$
division	0	1	$q = a/b$
square	1	0	$s = (f)^2$
square root	1	1	$r = \sqrt{a}$

TABLE VI
TRANSISTOR REQUIREMENTS OF MULTIPLIER-DIVIDER ARRAY-LIKE STRUCTURE

No. of bits	Total no. of arithmetic cells	No. of M.O.S. transistors needed	No. of M.O.S. transistors needed when pipelined
2	6	400	600
3	14	800	1150
4	25	1350	2200
5	39	1850	3175
6	56	2550	4400
7	76	3375	5825
8	99	4025	7175

TABLE VII
TRANSISTOR REQUIREMENTS OF DIFFERENT ARRAY-LIKE STRUCTURES FOR 4 BITS

	Multiplier-divider array-like structure	Square-root-array-like structure	Multiplier-divider-square-root – square array-like structure
No. of transistor needed	1325	1375	2000
No. of transistor needed when pipelined	2200	2200	3800

have separate units rather than having a combined array. However, for applications like desk-calculators or microprocessors, a combined unit (without pipeline) is more useful.

VIII. CONCLUSION

In this paper, design techniques for high-speed arithmetic arrays have been investigated and some effective synthesis procedures are given. These arrays utilize carry-save interconnection technique of arithmetic cells and sign-bit carry-look-ahead and carry-look-ahead adders for final addition of two partial results. An ultimate selection of subtrahend-controlled "add–2's complement and–transfer" type of cell is justified here because of its suitability for designing generalized pipelined arrays. These arrays can perform any of the four arithmetics: multiplication, division, square, and square-rooting. The operands for any of the four arithmetic operations can be accepted by the array with every clock-pulse and thus pipelined processing of multifunctions by the same digital hardware reduces the effective time delay considerably. Moreover these arrays are near iterative in nature and hence they are well suited for large-scale-integration.

ACKNOWLEDGMENT

The author wishes to express his gratitude to the referees for their suggestions that helped in improving the presentation of this practically oriented paper. Sincere thanks are also due to Drs.T-Y. Feng and T. R. N. Rao for their constant encouragement and Dr. V. K. Agarwal for carefully going through the revised version of this paper.

REFERENCES

[1] J. Sklansky, "Conditional-sum addition logic," *IRE Trans. Electron. Comput.*, vol. EC-9, pp. 226–231, June 1960.

[2] O. L. MacSorley, "High speed arithmetic in binary computers," *Proc. IRE*, vol. 49, pp. 67–91, Jan. 1961.

[3] I. Flores, *The Logic of Computer Arithmetic*. Englewood Cliffs, NJ: Prentice Hall, 1963.

[4] K. J. Dean, "Versatile multiplier arrays," *Electron. Lett.*, vol. 4, pp. 333–334, Aug. 9, 1968.

[5] M. Cappa and V. C. Hamacher, "An augmented iterative array for high-speed binary division," *IEEE Trans. Comput.*, vol. C-22, pp. 172–175, Feb. 1973.

[6] A. K. Kamal, H. Singh, and D. P. Agrawal, "A generalized pipeline array," *IEEE Trans. Comput.*, vol. C-23, pp. 533–536, May 1974.

[7] J. Deverell, "Pipeline iterative arithmetic arrays," *IEEE Trans. Comput.*, vol. C-24, pp. 317–322, Mar. 1975.

[8] A. D. Booth, "A signed binary multiplication technique," *Quart. J. Mech. Appl. Math.*, vol. 4, pp. 236–240, 1951.

[9] A. Avizienis and C. Tung, "A universal arithmetic building element (ABE) and design methods for arithmetic processors," *IEEE Trans. Comput.*, vol. C-19, pp. 733–745, Aug. 1970.

[10] A. R. Meo, "Arithmetic networks and their minimization using a new line of elementary units," *IEEE Trans. Comput.*, vol. C-24, pp. 258–280, Mar. 1975.

[11] K. J. Dean, "Binary division using a data dependent iterative arrays," *Electron. Lett.*, vol. 4, pp. 283–284, July 1968.

[12] A. B. Gardiner, "Asynchronous binary restoring divider array," *Electron. Lett.*, vol. 7, pp. 542–544, Sept. 1971.

[13] K. J. Dean, "Cellular arrays for binary division," *Proc. Inst. Elec. Eng.*, vol. 117, pp. 917–920, May 1970.

[14] J. C. Majithia, "Nonrestoring binary division using a cellular array," *Electron. Lett.*, vol. 6, pp. 303–304, May 1970.

[15] H. H. Guild, "Some cellular logic arrays for nonrestoring binary division," *Radio Electron. Eng.*, vol. 39, pp. 345–348, June 1970.

[16] D. P. Agrawal and H. Singh, "An iterative array for multiplication and division," *J. Inst. Electron. Telecommun. Eng.*, vol. 21, pp. 207–209, Feb. 1975.

[17] J. C. Majithia, "Cellular array for extraction of squares and square-roots of binary numbers," *IEEE Trans. Comput.*, vol. C-21, pp. 1023–1024, Sept. 1972.

[18] T. G. Hallin and M. J. Flynn, "Pipelining of arithmetic functions," *IEEE Trans. Comput.*, vol. C-21, pp. 880–888, Aug. 1972.

[19] J. C. Majithia, "Some comments concerning design of pipeline arithmetic arrays," *IEEE Trans. Comput.*, vol. C-25, pp. 1132–1134, Dec. 1976.

Dharma P. Agrawal (M'74) was born in Balod, India, in 1945. He received the B.E. degree in electrical engineering from the Ravishankar University, Raipur, India, in 1966, the M.E. degree (Hons) in electronics and communication engineering, and the D.Sc. Tech. degree in electrical engineering from the Federal Institute of Technology, Lausanne, Switzerland, in 1975.

He has been affiliated with the M.N.R. Engineering College, Allahabad, India, the University of Roorkee, Roorkee, India, the Federal Institute of Technology, Lausanne, Switzerland, the University of Technology, Baghdad, Iraq, and the Southern Methodist University, Dallas, TX. Currently he is with Wayne State University, Detroit, MI, as an Assistant Professor in the Department of Electrical and Computer Engineering. He has taught courses in the area of computer engineering and has several publications in both European and American journals. He has also acted as a referee for various technical journals and conferences. His current fields of interest are microcomputer systems, computer architecture, parallel processing, and fault-tolerant computing.

Dr. Agrawal is a member of the Association for Computing Machinery.

Reprinted from *IEEE Transactions on Computers*, Volume C-33, Number 1,
January 1984, pages 7-20. Copyright © 1984 by The Institute of Electrical
and Electronics Engineers, Inc.

Bit-Sequential Arithmetic for Parallel Processors

HENK J. SIPS

Abstract—A bit-sequential processing element with $O(n)$ complexity is described, where n is the wordlength of the operands. The operations performed by the element are $A * B + C * D$, A/B, and $\sqrt{A}$. The operands are fixed point or floating point numbers with variable precision. The concept of semi-on-line algorithms is introduced. A processing element that uses semi-on-line algorithms produces a result δ clock cycles after the absorption of the n-bit operands, where δ is small compared to n. In the paper the processing element and the algorithms are described. A performance comparison between the bit-sequential processing element and conventional pipelined arithmetic units is given.

Index Terms—Cost-effectiveness, floating point arithmetic, large scale integration, on-line algorithms, parallelism, pipelining.

I. INTRODUCTION

IN demanding numerical computations such as arise in weather forecasting, signal processing, theoretical physics, simulation, etc., the use of parallel computers is necessary to increase the problem throughput. There are a number of ways to speed up computation. One is the use of multiple pipelined arithmetical units, such as in the Cray-1 and the Cyber 205 [1], [2], in which the operation to be performed is divided in a number of segments with equal processing times. An example is the floating point addition where the segments can consist of exponent comparison, exponent subtraction, fraction alignment, fraction addition and postnormalization. Pipelining gives no advantage for the first operation, since the total processing time is equal to the sum of the processing times of the segments, but each subsequent operation is carried out in the time required to process a single segment. This approach requires that the problem can be formulated in a pipelined way, i.e., that there should exist no dependency between the operands being operated upon simultaneously in the pipeline. Many problems can be formulated in this way. The number of segments in a pipeline is dependent on the segmentation algorithm. Given a certain number of segments, the effectiveness of a pipeline is dependent on the vector length of the operands.

There is, however, a large class of problems for which pipelining is difficult to apply. An example is simulation of systems [19]. A system can often be described by a set of differential or difference equations and the solution is found by solving (mostly) nonlinear recurrence systems. The data dependency is high and often conditional looping occurs, i.e., data dependent decisions determine the data flow. Pipelining of the operands gives little speed up. Only for linear recurrence sys-

Manuscript received August 17, 1982; revised August 2, 1983.
The author is with the Department of Applied Physics, Delft University of Technology, Lorentzweg 1 2628CJ Delft, Holland.

tems can pipelined machines be successfully used by introducing some redundancy [4].

The alternative to a pipelined architecture is a parallel architecture consisting of a number of processing elements and a given interconnection structure. According to Flynn [5], the parallel architectures can be classified as Single Instruction-Multiple Data (SIMD) or Multiple Instruction-Multiple Data (MIMD) processors. In both types, a large number of processors must be incorporated in order to achieve a speed comparable to that of a pipelined architecture. A parallel processor consisting of a large number of processing elements (PE's) needs an interconnection network of considerable complexity. This interconnection network is an important cost factor in parallel processors of this kind.

To diminish the switching complexity (number of switches), and often also processing element complexity, the use of bit-sequential processing elements can be attractive and have in fact been used in a number of parallel processor designs. An early example is the SOLOMON-1 [6], and current examples are the ICL DAP [7] and the MPP [8].

Because the operands in bit-sequential processing are transported bit by bit, the data transportation time can degrade the overall system performance quite seriously compared with bit-parallel designs.

This paper shows a way to avoid data transport delay by simultaneously performing the arithmetical operation on the operands and the data transport of the operands. For this purpose the concept of semi-on-line algorithms is introduced in Section II, together with outlines of semi-on-line algorithms for the inner product, division and square root. Section III describes a PE implementation of the algorithms. Cost-efficiency of the PE is considered in Section IV in comparison with a full bit-parallel pipelined PE. The applicability of the PE is dealt with in Section V.

II. SEMI-ON-LINE ALGORITHMS

Bit-sequential processing reduces the speed of the arithmetic operations compared with bit-parallel processing, provided the implementation uses the same technology. On the other hand, bit-sequential designs are simpler than bit-parallel designs, so a high speed technology bit-sequential implementation may compete with a low speed technology (but more dense) bit-parallel implementation.

To improve the system speed of bit-sequential processors several *on-line* algorithms have been developed. On-line algorithms are defined [13] by the property that to generate the jth bit (or digit) of the result, it is necessary and sufficient to have the operands available up to the $(j + \delta)$th bit (or digit), where δ is a small positive constant. The factor δ is called the on-line delay. On-line algorithms speed up the computation of arithmetic expressions by overlapping the operations.

On-line algorithms can be defined with the most significant bit (MSB), or least significant bit (LSB) first. For convenience we use the "bit" terminology, but of course the discussion also applies to general radix-r digits. We shall refer to the MSB on-line algorithms as MOL algorithms, and to the LSB on-line algorithms as LOL algorithms. The properties of the basic arithmetical operations, addition, subtraction, multiplication, and division are considered now when using on-line algorithms.

The LOL algorithm for addition and subtraction is the most obvious algorithm due to the natural carry propagation from the lower-order bits to the higher-order bits. LOL algorithms for multiplication have been developed by Atrubin [9], Knuth [10], and Chen [11]. Knuth showed that it is possible to multiply two n-bit numbers with $n/2$ automata. Chen's multiplier uses $2n$ simple $(5, 3)$ counters to multiply two n-bit numbers (a $(5, 3)$ counter adds 5 inputs of equal weight and produces a 3 bit result). This can be reduced by a different arrangement to n-counters [12]. An important disadvantage of the LOL multiplication algorithm is that the most significant half of the $2n$ bit product starts to become visable after n time steps. So if we want to calculate $a * b + c * d$ to n-bits precision in a fractional system, the first bit of the n-bit result is available after $n + \delta$ time steps. The speed in overlapped operations is seriously reduced by this property.

Unlike the basic arithmetic functions, addition, subtraction, and multiplication, the division function is the most difficult to implement. LOL division with a nonredundant number system is impossible. The knowledge of the least significant digits of the divisor and the dividend do not determine the least signficant digit of either the quotient or the remainder of a division operation. For example $138/23 = 6$ and $138/33 = 4.18$, so the knowledge of 8 and 3 tells us nothing about the least significant digit of the result. Of course, to circumvent this, division can also be accomplished by applying iterative techniques using multiplication [15], [16].

For MOL algorithms the use of redundant number representations is mandatory. If a nonredundant number system is used, there is in both addition and subtraction a delay of $\delta = n$ due to carry propagation. Trivedi et al. [13] have developed a MOL algorithm for multiplication and two MOL algorithms for division using a redundant number system. The first division algorithm accepts operands in nonredundant form and gives a redundant result, while the second division algorithm accepts redundant operands and gives a redundant result. The first algorithm is not suitable for solving recurrence systems as each iteration a conversion is needed between the redundant and nonredundant number system. The second division algorithm has a more serious disadvantage; it does not work for radix-2 numbers. Besides these two disadvantages specific for the algorithms of Trivedi et al., in general one may note two other disadvantages in using redundant number systems for on-line processing. The first disadvantage is that the hardware becomes more complex. Secondly and more important, redundant number systems increase the wordsize. This reduces

the speed in bit-sequential processing at least with a factor 2/3 when a $+1, 0, -1$ digit set is used in a radix 2 system. The point here is that redundant number systems may be used in bit-parallel computations, but their use in bit-sequential processing reduces speed.

Current on-line algorithms have been designed for fixed point numbers only, with the exception of the square root operation [3]. In order to be fully acceptable as an arithmetic tool the algorithms must be able to handle floating point operands. In on-line processing the floating point operation gives rise to trouble in the addition of two operands. The normalization procedure required after the addition disturbs the on-line behavior. The number of shifts necessary for normalization of the fractional part of the result is only known after the complete processing of the fractional parts of the input operands.

Another important characteristic of on-line algorithms is that they are only effective if long expressions are evaluated. This is illustrated in Fig. 1. In Fig. 1(a) the result y has an effective delay of 2δ and can be used for further evaluation. If, however, a recurrent equation is solved such as in Fig. 1(b), the result must be delayed by $n - 2\delta$ time steps, where n is the wordlength of the operands. Thus, for expressions which can be evaluated in one on-line operation cycle and for recurrence equations, the speed cannot be faster than the speed in which the bits of the operands can be applied to the PE. The conclusion may be drawn that on-line algorithms are less attractive as they appear at first sight.

In this paper we introduce the concept of *semi-on-line* algorithms. Semi-on-line algorithms are less restrictive in a computational sense than on-line algorithms and have the same performance for expressions which can be evaluated in one operation cycle and for recurrence equations.

We define *semi-on-line* agorithms by the property that δ clock cycles after the absorption of the last bits of the operands, the first bit of the result is available, with δ is a small positive constant (3 or 4). Of course normal bit-parallel operations also have this property if an appropriate δ is chosen. To exclude this case, we demand that $\delta < \delta_p$, where δ_p is the time to complete a full bit-parallel operation. The definition can be further tightened by the demand that the implementation is of $O(n)$ complexity, where n is the wordlength of the operands. The operation time of a bit-sequential PE using semi-on-line algorithms is $n + \delta$ clock cycles. The δ clock cycles in which no operand transport takes place can be used to pass on operand status information (such as underflow and overflow), or parity information.

Semi-on-line algorithms (SOL) can be called *forward* or *backward*. A forward SOL algorithm processes on the bits while they are absorbed by the PE. In the next cycle the result is outputted bit by bit and the next input operands are processed at the same time. In a backward SOL algorithm this is reversed: processing starts when the last bit of the input operands has been absorbed.

In the following paragraphs SOL algorithms for the inner product, division and square root are outlined. The algorithms operate with fixed point or floating point numbers with variable precision. The floating point number A is represented by the

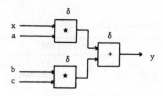

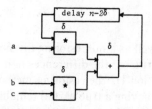

Fig. 1.   (a) Implementation of $y = x \cdot a + b \cdot c$. (b) Implementation of $x_{i+1} = x_i \cdot a + b \cdot c$.

pair

$$A(e) = -a_l(e) \cdot 2^l + \sum_{i=0}^{l-1} a_i(e) \cdot 2^i$$

$$A(m) = (-1)^{a_0(m)} \cdot \sum_{i=1}^{k} a_i(m) \cdot 2^{-i}$$

or $\qquad A(m) = -a_0(m) + \sum_{i=1}^{k} a_i(m) \cdot 2^{-i}$ (1)

where $A(e)$ is the l-bit exponent in two's complement form and $A(m)$ is the k-bit mantissa (exclusive sign bit) either in sign-magnitude or two's complement form. The two's complement form can only be used for the inner product algorithm. Semi-on-line division and square root require a sign-magnitude mantissa (see Sections II-B and II-C).

A. The Inner Product

An important operation occurring frequently in matrix operations, correlation and convolution functions, simulation etc. is the inner product $a * b + c * d$. In order to be able to execute the addition the exponents must be known first. So the obvious choice is to enter the exponents first in bit-sequential form to the PE. To determine the preshift of one of the mantissas, the difference DF must be calculated according to

$$DF = A(e) + B(e) - C(e) - D(e). \qquad (2)$$

DF can be ≥ 0 or < 0. If DF is ≥ 0 the operands c and d have to be preshifted with a factor 2^{-DF}. If DF is < 0, the operands a and b have to be preshifted with a factor 2^{DF}.

In many floating point number representations the exponent is chosen in biased form. This is done in order to be able to do a fast comparison of the exponents without involving the sign of the exponents. In our case this is not useful as the exponents are compared while the mantissas are not known yet and a 4 operand operation has to be performed. The choice here is an exponent in two's complement form. There is still the choice whether the LSB or the MSB of the exponent is evaluated first. The LOL algorithm for addition is the simplest one, as the carry propagation is limited to the next bit.

In the algorithm to be outlined below, the addition and the multiplication of the operands are performed at the same time.

Here again we have the choice of taking a LSB first or MSB first algorithm. For reasons explained later in the discussion of the division and square root operation, the MSB first algorithm has been chosen. The algorithm is best explained by assuming that the mantissas are unsigned numbers. The algorithm is based on the well known technique of incremental multiplication [13] and is the MSB first version of the algorithm described in [11]. Let

$$A_j(m) = \sum_{i=1}^{j} a_i(m) \cdot 2^{-i}$$

$$B_j(m) = \sum_{i=1}^{j} b_i(m) \cdot 2^{-i}. \qquad (3)$$

$A_j(m)$, $B_j(m)$ are the mantissas of A and B up to the jth bit. From (3) it follows

$$A_j(m) = A_{j-1}(m) + a_j(m) \cdot 2^{-j}$$
$$B_j(m) = B_{j-1}(m) + b_j(m) \cdot 2^{-j}. \qquad (4)$$

It then follows that

$$A_j(m) \cdot B_j(m) = A_{j-1}(m) \cdot B_{j-1}(m)$$
$$+ A_{j-1}(m) \cdot b_j(m) \cdot 2^{-j} + B_j(m) \cdot a_j(m) \cdot 2^{-j}. \qquad (5)$$

Suppose

$$P_j(ab) = A_j(m) \cdot B_j(m) \cdot 2^j, \qquad P_0 = 0. \qquad (6)$$

We then obtain the recurrent equation

$$P_j(ab) = 2 \cdot P_{j-1}(ab)$$
$$+ A_{j-1}(m) \cdot b_j(m) + B_j(m) \cdot a_j(m). \qquad (7)$$

The same procedure can be followed for C and D. If $A(e) + B(e) > C(e) + D(e)$ then

$$P_j(cd) = 2 \cdot P_{j-1}(cd) + C_{j-1}(m) \cdot d_j(m) \cdot 2^{-DF}$$
$$+ D_j(m) \cdot c_j(m) \cdot 2^{-DF}. \qquad (8)$$

Now, (7) and (8) can be combined. Let

$$P_j(ab + cd) = P_j(ab) + P_j(cd). \qquad (9)$$

We then obtain

$$P_j(ab + cd) = 2 \cdot P_{j-1}(ab + cd) + A_{j-1}(m) \cdot b_j(m)$$
$$+ B_j(m) \cdot a_j(m) + C_{j-1}(m) \cdot d_j(m)$$
$$\cdot 2^{-DF} + D_j(m) \cdot c_j(m) \cdot 2^{-DF}. \qquad (10)$$

The first bit to be entered after the exponent must contain information about the signs of the operands, as at each recursion step of equation (10) it must be known whether or not the partial operands $A_{j-1}(m) \cdot b_j(m)$, $B_j(m) \cdot a_j(m)$, etc. have a positive or negative weight. If the mantissa is a sign-magnitude number, the sign bit has to be entered before the magnitude bits. The signs of the product pair (A, B) determine whether $A_{j-1}(m) \cdot b_j(m) + B_j(m) \cdot a_j(m)$ in (10) is weighted in total as a positive or negative number. The same holds for the product pair (C, D).

When the mantissa is represented as a two's complement number all bits except the first (MSB) bit are treated as if they were positive. From definition (1) it follows that the MSB bit in a two's complement mantissa can be treated the same as the other bits in the mantissa except that the first bit has a negative weight.

Defined in this way, the inner product algorithm is clearly a forward SOL algorithm. The total format of the floating point number representation is shown in Fig. 2.

Precision: If A, B, C and D have mantissas of length k, a full precision multiplication and addition requires $2k + 1$ bits if no prealigning of the mantissa is needed. The question arises how many extra bits β are needed to retain precision when $A(m) * B(m)$ or $C(m) * D(m)$ have to be aligned by the factor DF. In that case the evaluation of (10) requires a $2k + \beta + 1$ bits full addition. Suppose for simplicity that $A(e) + B(e) > C(e) + D(e)$ and C and D are chopped at p bits. If the absolute error in $A(m)$, $B(m)$, $C(m)$, and $D(m)$ is ± 0.5 LSB, the absolute error in $A(m) * B(m)$ and $C(m) * D(m)$ (unnormalized) is given by

$$2^{-k-1} \leqslant |\Delta ab| \leqslant 2^{-k}$$
$$2^{-p-1} \leqslant |\Delta cd| \leqslant 2^{-p}. \qquad (11)$$

Now, $C(m) * D(m)$ is preshifted with a factor DF, so

$$2^{-p-1-DF} \leqslant |\Delta cd| \leqslant 2^{-p-DF}. \qquad (12)$$

The total error is now

$$2^{-k-1}(1 + 2^{k-p-DF}) \leqslant |\Delta(ab + cd)|$$
$$\leqslant 2^{-k}(1 + 2^{k-p-DF}) \qquad (13)$$

if $p = k$ (13) becomes

$$2^{-k-1}(1 + 2^{-DF}) \leqslant |\Delta(ab + cd)| \leqslant 2^{-k}(1 + 2^{-DF}). \qquad (14)$$

By defining

$$\beta = -k + p + DF \qquad (15)$$

(13) becomes

$$2^{-k-1}(1 + 2^{-\beta}) \leqslant |\Delta(ab + cd)| \leqslant 2^{-k}(1 + 2^{-\beta}). \qquad (16)$$

If $\beta = 3$ or $\beta = 4$ then the total error is acceptably small.

B. Division

In bit-parallel arithmetic division has never been a very attractive operation. The reason is that the speed of multiplication relative to division can be increased drastically by all sorts of techniques like bit-scanning. The SOL inner product algorithm has an operation speed which is linearly dependent on the number of bits of the operands. The division algorithm outlined below, has the same operational speed as the inner product algorithm. In contrast to the inner product algorithm, the division algorithm is a backward SOL algorithm. The operands must be completely available in order to produce the first bit of the result. Let

$$Q = N/D \qquad (17)$$

with Q, N and D floating point numbers. The exponents must be subtracted first. The mantissa of Q satisfies

$$2^{-1} < Q(m) < 2. \qquad (18)$$

So, if $q_1 = 1$, the exponent $Q(e)$ must be incremented by one.

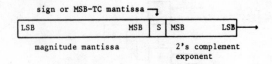

Fig. 2. Floating point format.

A restoring as well as a nonrestoring division method can be used [17]. Apart from the differences in implementation as outlined in Section III the restoring method has the advantage of always having a true partial remainder. The nonrestoring algorithm can be described as follows:

step 1 [initialize] $R_0 \leftarrow 2^{-1} \cdot N(m), j \leftarrow 0, q_0 \leftarrow 1$
step 2 [recursion] if $q_j = 0$ do $R_{j+1} = 2 \cdot R_j + D$ (19a)
  if $q_j = 1$ do $R_{j+1} = 2 \cdot R_j - D$
step 3 [test] if $R_{j+1} < 0$ then $q_{j+1} = 0$
  if $R_{j+1} \geqslant 0$ then $q_{j+1} = 1$
  if $j < k - 1$ then $j \leftarrow j + 1$ goto
  step 2.

During each iteration a full addition or subtraction is needed. The restoring algorithm can be expressed by the recursion formula

$$R_{j+1} = 2 \cdot R_j - q_{j+1} \cdot D. \qquad (19b)$$

Here only subtractions are necessary. As follows directly from the division algorithm the mantissa of the result is in sign-magnitude form. Because the result bits must be transported to other PE's before the complete division operation is finished, no conversion to two's complement notation can take place.

C. Square Root

The square root algorithm is very much like the algorithm for division. The main difference is that in each cycle the successive subtrahends change. This implies some added complexity in the realization hardware. The square root algorithm is also a backward SOL algorithm. Let

$$Q = \sqrt{A} \qquad (20)$$

where Q and A are floating point numbers. Here also the mantissa of Q is a sign-magnitude number. If $A(e)$ is uneven the mantissa $A(m)$ must be shifted one place to the right, and the exponent $A(e)$ must be incremented. The exponent of Q is then equal to $2^{-1} \cdot A(e)$. If $A(e)$ is even then $Q(e) = 2^{-1} \cdot A(e)$. The mantissa of Q has the following property:

$$2^{-2} \leq A(m) \leq 2^0 \Rightarrow 2^{-1} < Q(m) < 2^0. \qquad (21)$$

So, no postnormalization is required. The algorithm is the normal paper and pencil method [17]. The first subtrahend $D_0 = (0.01)_2$ is subtracted from $A(m)$. If the remainder $R_1 \geqslant 0$ then $q_1 = 1$ and in the next cycle $D_1 = (0.q_1\bar{q}_1 1)_2$ is subtracted from $2 \cdot R_1$. If $R_1 < 0$ then $D_1 = (0.q_1\bar{q}_1 1)_2$ is added to the remainder $2 \cdot R_1$ in the next cycle. Again nonrestoring as well as restoring algorithms can be applied. The nonrestoring algorithm works as follows:

step 1 [initialize] $j \leftarrow 0, R_0 \leftarrow 2^{-1} \cdot A(m), q_0 \leftarrow 1$

step 2 [recursion]
$$D_j = \sum_{v=1}^{j} q_v \cdot 2^{-v} + 2^{-j-2} + \overline{q}_j$$
$$\cdot 2^{-j-1}$$

step 3 [test]
$$\text{if } q_j = 1 \text{ then } R_{j+1} = 2 \cdot R_j - D_j \quad (22a)$$
$$\text{if } q_j = 0 \text{ then } R_{j+1} = 2 \cdot R_j + D_j$$
$$\text{if } R_{j+1} < 0 \text{ then } q_{j+1} = 0$$
$$\text{if } R_{j+1} \geq 0 \text{ then } q_{j+1} = 1$$
$$\text{if } j < k - 1 \text{ then } j \leftarrow j + 1 \text{ goto}$$
step 2.

As can be seen in this algorithm the forming of the subtrahend D_j is more complicated than in the case of the division algorithm. The restoring algorithm can be expressed by the recursion formula

$$R_{j+1} = 2 \cdot R_j - q_{j+1} \cdot D_j. \quad (22b)$$

The term $\overline{q}_j \cdot 2^{-j-1}$ in D_j must in this case be omitted.

III. Implementation of the Bit-Sequential PE

In this section we deal with the question how the algorithms described in Section II can be implemented effectively. Implementation of the inner product has been described by Swartzlander et al. [20], who describe a quasi-serial implementation. The disadvantage of their scheme is that the implementation is for fixed point numbers only, and requires additional modifications to allow overlapped computation [21]. Furthermore, their implementation does not include division.

In the computation of the inner product using floating point numbers, the following steps can be distinguished: exponent handling, mantissa alignment, mantissa calculation and postnormalization.

Exponent Handling: The handling of the exponent of the operands is simple. The alignment factor DF, as well as the exponents of the product pairs $A * B$ and $C * D$, can be calculated using three one bit full adders.

Mantissa Calculation: After the alignment of the mantissas (see next paragraph) the five terms of equation (10) have to be added. The operation is performed in three steps as follows:

1) compression of the terms in (10) into a sum and a carry vector,
2) addition of the sum and carry vector,
3) accumulation of the result in an up/down counter.

The steps 1)–3) are performed in a pipelined way. This pipeline causes most of the semi-on-line delay δ. For the implementation of step 1) a five operand carry save adder array is used, which is shown in Fig. 3. The cells of the array consist of full adders. The array produces a sum and a carry vector. Note that in Fig. 3 the two top rows can be deleted. The A and B operands can be directly connected to the full adders of row 3. The cells of row 1 and row 2 are included as additional logic must be included in each cell to generate the operands according to (10).

For the addition in step 1) the operands must be in two's complement form. If the operands are sign-magnitude num-

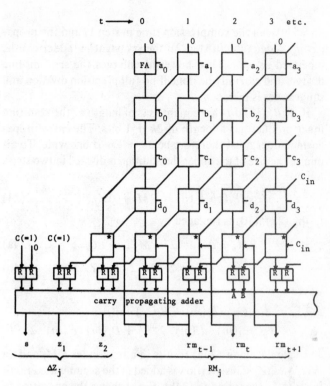

Fig. 3. Operand compression and propagation.

bers they must be converted to two's complement numbers. When both operands of a product pair are sign-magnitude numbers and have the same sign, they are already in the correct form. When the operands have opposite signs, the weight of the product pair will be negative. The complementing of the operands can be done by complementing the individual bits of the operands and putting a 1 on the spare carry inputs on the right-hand side of the array. The sign bits on the sign-magnitude format are not involved in the computation of the partial operands. The combination of the sign bits of a product pair only determines the positive or negative weight of the product pair.

When both operands are two's complement numbers the operands are already in the desired form. Only the MSB bit must be interpreted as a negative weighting factor.

For the addition of the partial operands the method described in [18] is used, in which a 1 is added to the sign bit position of each operand. Assume a binary point just right to the MSB bit of the operand. Adding a 1 to the sign-bit position increases each operand value by 1, therefore for four operands participating in the addition, the total of 4 has to be subtracted from the sum of the operands. The correction factor C in two's complement form is given by $(1100)_2$ (Fig. 3).

The partial sum $2 \cdot P_{j-1}$, generated in the preceding time step, is added to the compressed sum of the A, B, C and D partial operands in an extra row of full adders (marked with a * in Fig. 3). The partial sum is not included in the correction factor, because for this operand the extended wordlength must be used.

In step 2) the carry and sum vector are propagated in a carry propagating adder. For fast propagation a full carry look-ahead adder (FCLA) must be used. To achieve a better balance between the compression time in step 1) and the propagating adder time in step 2), the propagating adder can be pipelined as well. This, however, enlarges the semi-on-line delay δ and can only be done if no full precision division and square root is included.

If A, B, C and D have mantissas of length k, the resulting inner product has a length of $2k + 1$ bits. The carry propagating adder must therefore be $2k + 1 + \beta$ bits wide. To diminish the size of the adder the addition is divided in two steps. Let

$$P_j(ab + cd) = RM_j + \Delta Z_j. \qquad (23)$$

Using (23), (10) is replaced by

$$RM_j + \Delta Z_j = 2 \cdot RM_{j-1} + PO_{j-1} \qquad (24a)$$

$$RE_j = 2 \cdot RE_{j-1} + \Delta Z_{j-1} \qquad (24b)$$

where

$$PO_{j-1} = A_{j-1}(m) \cdot b_j(m) + B_j(m) \cdot a_j(m)$$
$$+ C_{j-1}(m) \cdot d_j(m) \cdot 2^{-DF} + D_j(m) \cdot c_j(m) \cdot 2^{-DF}.$$

The calculation of (24a) results in a remainder RM_j and an overflow ΔZ_j. This overflow is added to the accumulated result [as step 3] according to (24b). Fig. 4 shows the operation of (24). The overflow ΔZ_j consists of two bits z_1 and z_2 and a sign bit s. Equation (24b) can be implemented by means of a left shifting up/down counter (RE-counter). The final result is formed after $k + \delta$ clock cycles by the concatenation of RE and RM. The overflow bit z_2 is appended at each step to the LSB bit of the RE-counter. The addition of the bits s and z_1 to RE_{j-1} results in an increment, decrement or no operation of the counter. Suppose for convenience that there exists a binary point just right to the bit z_2. The operation by ΔZ_j on the RE-counter can only be applied if the following condition is met:

$$-2 \leqslant \Delta Z_j \leqslant 3. \qquad (25)$$

($\Delta Z_j = -3$ and $\Delta Z_j = -4$ result in an addition of -2 to the RE-counter and are therefore illegal.)

We have to determine the length of $RM_j + \Delta Z_j$ for which the condition (25) holds. Suppose RM_j is q bits longer than the mantissas of the partial operands A, B, C, and D. RM_j can be considered as a positive number satisfying

$$0 \leqslant RM_j < 1. \qquad (26)$$

The sum of the mantissas of the partial operands, PO_j, satisfies

$$-2^{2-q} < PO_j < 2^{2-q}. \qquad (27)$$

Combining (26) and (27) results in

$$-2^{2-q} < 2 \cdot RM_j + PO_j < 2 + 2^{2-q}. \qquad (28)$$

It follows from (26), (24a) and (28) for ΔZ_j

$$-2^{2-q} \leqslant \Delta Z_j \leqslant 1 + 2^{2-q}. \qquad (29)$$

The condition (25) is satisfied for $q = 1$. For mantissas of k bits long, the carry propagating adder forming $RM_j + \Delta Z_j$ must have a length of $k + 3 + \beta$ bits and the RE-counter must have a length of $k - 1$ bits.

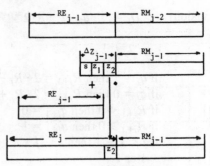

Fig. 4. Evaluation of P_j.

Mantissa Generation and Alignment: The carry save adder array description in Fig. 3 does not include the control mechanism needed to generate the partial operands according to (10). The aim must be to design a cell which is simple of structure and has a minimum number of connections to the outside world. From (10) it can be seen that for each time step a new bit is appended to the operands. Whether or not the operand participates in the addition of that time step is dependent on the new bit of the corresponding other operand. The minimum needed is a full adder, one storage cell to hold the operand and a few gates. Fig. 5 shows the basic cell layout. The operand line (here the B operand is chosen) is a line along all cells where the operand is to be stored, which is a row of the array. The control lines $\sigma_t(ab)$ are the decoded outputs of a counter (t is the column number of the carry save adder array). They successively activate each column. The line $\sigma_t(ab)$ loads successively each new bit of the operand in the next column. The line a_j qualifies the operand B_j. The treatment of the A operand is a little different because of the difference in the j index (A_{j-1}). Therefore the new bit a_j must be suppressed. This is indicated by the line $\sigma_{t+1}(ab)$. The complement line determines whether the operand is $\geqslant 0$ ($com = 0$ and $c_{in} = 0$), or < 0 ($com = 1$ and $c_{in} = 1$).

The structure of the sign cell is a little different from the other cells in the array. The output is always inverted according to the described multioperand addition algorithm. To accomplish the inversion the AND gate in Fig. 5 is replaced by a NAND gate in the sign cell. When operating on sign-magnitude numbers, the sign bit is not involved in the computation of (10), therefore the a_j line is not present in the sign cell. For two's complement numbers the sign bit is involved in the computation of (10) and the a_j line is present here. The cells of the product pair (C,D) are constructed likewise.

The alignment factor DF preloads one of the two counters (determined by the sign of DF), which determine the $\sigma_t(ab)$ and $\sigma_t(cd)$ control lines. In this way the alignment of the mantissas is achieved automatically.

Postnormalization: After the computation the result has to be normalized. This can be done in parallel by inspecting the contents of the RE-counter after the last step. An alternative way is to inspect the quantity ΔZ_j each time step and keep track of the number of leading zeros if the partial result is $\geqslant 0$, or the number of leading ones if the partial result is < 0. This implies that something must be known about the number stored in the RE-counter. This state of the RE-counter is called the *mode* M_i. The addition of ΔZ_j to the RE-counter

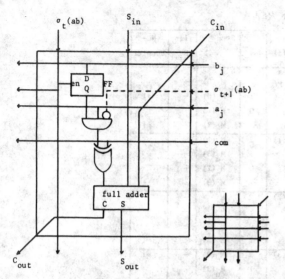

Fig. 5.   Cell layout.

causes a state transition $M_i \rightarrow M_j$. If the number of possible states M_i is small, a finite state machine can keep track of the number of leading zeros or ones.

The simplest choice is to allow at most one *closed* field of 1's if $RE_j \geq 0$, or 0's if $RE_j < 0$. We define three mode types: $M_p(i)$, $M_n(i)$, and M_s (assume a binary point just right to the LSB of RE_j).

1) $M_p(i)$: $RE_j = 2^l - 2^s$
$$\text{if } RE_j \geq 0, l \geq s, \qquad l, s = 0, 1, 2, \cdots$$

2) $M_n(i)$: $RE_j = -2^l + 2^s - 1$
$$\text{if } RE_j < 0, l \geq s, \qquad l, s = 0, 1, 2, \cdots \quad (30)$$

3) M_s: no more changes in leading 0's or 1's irrespective of ΔZ_j's in the steps $j + 1, j + 2, \cdots$, etc.

Fig. 6 shows the representations of RE_j. The quantity AD is defined as the number that can be added to RE_j in the steps $j + 1, j + 2, \cdots$, etc.,

$$AD = \sum_{r=0}^{L} \Delta Z_{j+r} \cdot 2^{-r} \qquad L \gg k \qquad (31)$$

(the binary point remains fixed at RE_j). Combining (29) and (31) gives

$$-2^{3-q} < AD < 2 + 2^{3-q}. \qquad (32)$$

If RE_j is ≥ 0 and in the mode M_s, it contains more than one field of 1's. The value of $RE_j = (00101)_2$ is the most sensitive one to changes, and results from applying $\Delta Z_{j-1} = (001)_2$ to $RE_{j-1} = (0010)_2$ (allowed according to 30.1). The contents of RE_j can only be definitive in the mode M_s if $-2 \leq AD < 6$. If $RE_j < 0$ and in the mode M_s, it contains more than one field of 0's. In this case the value of $RE_j = (11010)_2$ is the most sensitive one to changes, and results from applying $\Delta Z_{j-1} = (000)_2$ to $RE_j = (1101)_2$. The contents of RE_j can only be definitive in the mode M_s if $-4 \leq AD < 4$. Therefore, AD must satisfy

$$-2 \leq AD < 4. \qquad (33)$$

From (33) it follows that for $q = 2$ the condition (32) is satisfied. This implies that the length of the carry propagating adder must be increased by one bit ($k + 4 + \beta$ bits) and the length of the RE-counter must be decreased by one bit ($k - 2$ bits). If follows from (29) for ΔZ_j

$$-1 \leq \Delta Z_j \leq 2. \qquad (34)$$

The determination of the modes $M_p(i)$ and $M_n(i)$ can be done in the following ways:

a) $RE_j \geq 0$. There are no more changes in the number of leading 0's if

$$\text{ent } \lfloor \log_2 \{2(2^l - 2^s)\} \rfloor$$
$$= \text{ent } \lfloor \log_2 \{2(2^l - 2^s) + AD\} \rfloor \quad (35)$$

where ent $\lfloor x \rfloor$ the largest integer not larger than x. The combination of (35) and (33) leads to the condition

$$1 \leq s < l - 1. \qquad (36)$$

The number of leading 0's can change if RE_j has one of the following mode representations:

$M_p(0)$: $l = 0, s = 0$,   e.g., $RE_j = (00000)_2$

$M_p(1)$: $l = 1, s = 0$,   e.g., $RE_j = (00001)_2$

$M_p(2)$: $l \geq 2, s = 0$,   e.g., $RE_j = (01111)_2$ (37)

$M_p(3)$: $l = s + 1, s \geq 1$,   e.g., $RE_j = (01000)_2$.

b) $RE_j < 0$. There are no more changes in the number of leading 1's if

$$\text{ent } \lfloor \log_2 OC\{2(2^s - 2^l - 1)\} \rfloor =$$
$$\text{ent } \lfloor \log_2 OC\{2(2^s - 2^l - 1) + AD\} \rfloor \quad (38)$$

where OC is the one's complement function.

Combining (38) and (33) leads to the condition

$$1 \leq s < l - 1. \qquad (39)$$

The number of leading 1's can change if RE_j has one of the following mode representations:

$M_n(0)$: $l = 0, s = 0$,   e.g., $RE_j = (11111)_2$

$M_n(1)$: $l = 1, s = 0$,   e.g., $RE_j = (11110)_2$

$M_n(2)$: $l \geq 2, s = 0$,   e.g., $RE_j = (11000)_2$ (40)

$M_n(3)$: $l = s + 1, s \geq 1$,   e.g., $RE_j = (10111)_2$.

It has to be shown now that if RE_{j-1} is in one of the modes defined in (30), applying ΔZ_{j-1} to RE_{j-1} according to (24b) results in a mode defined by (30):

1) $M_p(0)$: $RE_{j-1} = 0$ and $\Delta Z_{j-1} = (-1, 0, 1, 2)$ results in $RE_j = (-1, 0, 1, 2)$
      which are representations of $M = \{M_n(0), M_p(0), M_p(1), M_p(3)\}$

2) $M_p(1)$: $RE_{j-1} = 1$ and $\Delta Z_{j-1} = (-1, 0, 1, 2)$ results in $RE_j = (1, 2, 3, 4)$
      which are representations of $M = \{M_p(1), M_p(3), M_p(2), M_p(3)\}$

TABLE I
OPERATIONS ON RE_j

step j $M_p(i)$	ΔZ_{j-1}	step j+1 M	sign RE_{j+1}	NC-counter	step j $M_n(i)$	ΔZ_{j-1}	Step j+1 M	sign RE_{j+1}	NC-counter
$M_p(0)$	-1	$M_n(0)$	-	+1	$M_n(0)$	2	$M_p(0)$	+	+1
	0	$M_p(0)$	+	+1		1	$M_n(0)$	-	+1
	1	$M_p(1)$	+			0	$M_n(1)$	-	
	2	$M_p(3)$	+	-1		-1	$M_n(3)$	-	-1
$M_p(1)$	-1	$M_p(1)$	+	+1	$M_n(1)$	2	$M_n(1)$	-	+1
	0	$M_p(3)$	+			1	$M_n(3)$	-	
	1	$M_p(2)$	+			0	$M_n(2)$	-	
	2	$M_p(3)$	+	-1		-1	$M_n(3)$	-	-1
$M_p(2)$	-1	M_s	+		$M_n(2)$	2	M_s	-	
	0	M_s	+			1	M_s	-	
	1	$M_p(2)$	+			0	$M_n(2)$	-	
	2	$M_p(3)$	+	-1		-1	$M_n(3)$	-	-1
$M_p(3)$	-1	$M_p(2)$	+	+1	$M_n(3)$	2	$M_n(2)$	-	+1
	0	$M_p(3)$	+			1	$M_n(3)$	-	
	1	M_s	+			0	M_s	-	
	2	M_s	+			-1	M_s	-	

3) $M_p(2)$: $RE_{j-1} = 2^l - 1$ $(l \geqslant 2)$

$\Delta Z_{j-1} = (1, 2)$ results in $RE_j = (2^{l+1} - 1, 2^{l+1}) \Rightarrow M = \{M_p(2), M_p(3)\}$,

$\Delta Z_{j-1} = -1$ results in $RE_j = 2^{l+1} - 3$, therefore the first bit with a "1" value is located in position ent $\lfloor \log_2 (RE_j) \rfloor = l$. From (33) follows for the next and following steps, that the first bit with a "1" value is located in position ent $\lfloor \log_2(2 \cdot RE_j + AD) \rfloor = l + 1$. Therefore there can be no more changes in the number of leading 0's: $M = M_s$,

$\Delta Z_{j-1} = 0$ results in $RE_j = 2^{l+1} - 2 \Rightarrow$ ent $\lfloor \log_2(RE_j) \rfloor = l$, from (33) follows ent $\lfloor \log_2(2 \cdot RE_j + AD) \rfloor = l + 1 \Rightarrow M = M_s$.

4) $M_p(3)$: $RE_{j-1} = 2^{l-1}$ $(l \geqslant 2)$

$\Delta Z_{j-1} = (-1, 0)$ results in $RE_j = (2^l - 1, 2^l) \Rightarrow M = \{M_p(2), M_p(3)\}$,

$\Delta Z_{j-1} = 1$ results in $RE_j = 2^l + 1 \Rightarrow$ ent $\lfloor \log_2 (RE_j) \rfloor = l$, from (33) follows ent $\lfloor \log_2(2 \cdot RE_j + AD) \rfloor = l + 1 \Rightarrow M = M_s$,

$\Delta Z_{j-1} = 2$ results in $RE_j = 2^l + 2 \Rightarrow$ ent $\lfloor \log_2(RE_j) \rfloor = l$, from (33) follows ent $\lfloor \log_2(2 \cdot RE_j + AD) \rfloor = l + 1 \Rightarrow M = M_s$.

The same procedure can be applied to the modes $M_n(i)$. The results are tabulated in Table I. In Table I, column 5, the amount in which the number of leading 0's or 1's change in each step is given. These changes are simply increments or decrements and can be stored in a normalize up/down counter, denoted as NC-counter. The mantissa of the result lies in the interval $(-2, 2)$. Therefore at most one shift to the right is possible. The NC-counter is initially set to -1. After $k + \delta$ steps the required number of postnormalization shifts is known, as well as the sign of the mantissa. If $NC = -1$ the mantissa must be shifted one place to the right, if $NC = p$ $(p > 0)$ the mantissa must be shifted p places to the left. A possible implementation of the counting control mechanism is depicted in Fig. 7.

Division and Square Root: For the implementation of the division and square root algorithms the full adder cell, marked in Fig. 3 with an asterisk (*), has to be slightly changed. This change for the nonrestoring algorithm is outlined in Fig. 8. A mode signal L_1 determines whether the cell is switched as a normal full adder or a special function cell for square root and division. In the latter case, the outputs of the carry propagating adder are directly connected to the sum output of the cell. If a division is implemented the I_2 inputs of the cell contain the divisor D. By previously loading the dividend N into the carry propagating adder, (19) can easily be solved.

The most critical part in the square root operation is the generation of the $q_j \bar{q}_j$ bits in D_j in (22a). The equation for D_j can be rewritten in the form

$$D_j = D_j(1) + D_j(2)$$
$$D_j(1) = \sum_{v=1}^{j-1} q_v \cdot 2^{-v} \tag{41}$$
$$D_j(2) = q_j \cdot 2^{-j} + \bar{q}_j \cdot 2^{-j-1} + 2^{-j-2}.$$

The generation of $D_j(1)$ is non-time-critical since it only contains the generated q's up to step $j - 1$. The second term is time critical and is directly generated in the cell of Fig. 8(c). The ϵ_t lines are control lines, which like the $\sigma_t(ab)$ lines, successively activate each column in the carry save adder array. The lines ϵ_{t-1} and ϵ_{t-2} can easily be supplied by neighboring cells.

With the nonrestoring algorithms the carry propagating adder has to be able to perform addition as well as subtraction as determined by q_j. If a restoring algorithm is chosen only addition is necessary (provided the D term is supplied as a negative number). The cell structure of Fig. 8(c) has to be changed as is shown in Fig. 9. The choice between the nonrestoring and the restoring method is implementation dependent.

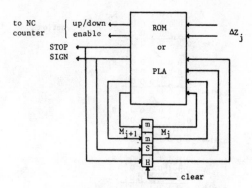

Fig. 7.   Implementation counter control.

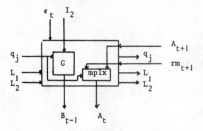

Fig. 9.   Modified FA cell for restoring square root and division.

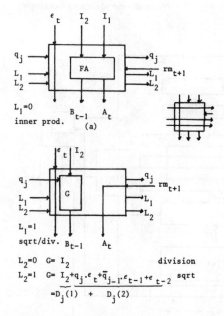

Fig. 8.   Modified FA cell for nonrestoring square root and division. (a) Connections for the inner product. (b) Connections for square root and division.

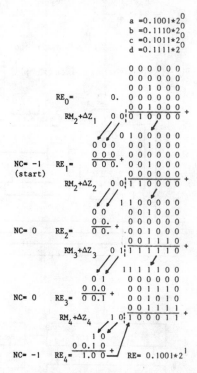

Fig. 10.   Multiplication and addition example.

In some high speed arithmetic designs [22] besides the square root operation also the square operation is included. In this design the square of a number can be formed using the multiplication algorithm. Examples of the inner product, division and square root operation are shown in Figs. 10, 11, and 12.

Implementation: A complete implementation of the PE is shown in Fig. 13. For the inner product operation, the serial adders S_1 and S_2 calculate the exponent of $A * B$ and $C * D$. These exponents are loaded into the shift registers R_1 and R_2. At the same time S_3 computes the difference DF which is placed in R_3. If $DF \geq 0$ the alignment factor DF is loaded in the counter R_6 and R_5 is set to the default start value of non-preshifted mantissa. If $DF < 0$ the complemented value of DF is loaded in R_5 with R_6 set to the default start value. Each time step when a new mantissa bit is entered into the PE, the R_5 and R_6 counters are incremented. The contents of these counters are used to generate the σ_t control signals (see Fig. 5). The operation of the carry save adder array, the carry propagating adder and the up/down result counter (R_7) is already described in detail.

After the completion of the operations on the last bits of the mantissas of the input operands, the NC-counter R_8 contains the number of required postnormalization shifts. The value of R_8 can directly be added to R_1 or R_2 in S_4, and the exponent of the result can be placed bit by bit on the output line.

The mantissa of the result is accumulated in R_7 in two's complement form. If the mantissa of the result must be in sign-magnitude representation, a conversion is necessary. This can be done in various ways. One solution is to modify the counter R_7 slightly, so that both the result and the inverse of the result are available. After the last operation on the mantissa an extra decrement operation is performed if the result is negative. This operation also affects the NC-counter contents. The magnitude of the mantissa is then available on the inverse outputs of the result counter.

The final result is placed in the result register R_4, since the R_7 counter must be available for the next operation. The NC-counter also determines where the first significant bit of the mantissa is located in R_7. By copying R_8 in R_9, a multiplexer can be set to get the proper bits out of the shiftregister R_4 (R_8 is also needed in the next operation cycle). While the exponent is outputted, the contents of R_4 can be preshifted as determined by the two lower-order bits of R_9. The multiplexer complexity can then be reduced by a factor of 4. The restriction here is that the exponent size must be a multiple of 4 bits.

N = 0.1101
D = 0.1001

```
        0 1 1 0 1 0 0    R₀ = N
        0 1 0 0 1 0 0    I₂ = D
q₁=1←  1 0 0 1 0 0 0 0   -

        0 1 0 0 0 0 0
        0 1 0 0 1 0 0    R₁
q₂=0← 0 1 1 1 1 1 0 0    -

        1 1 1 1 0 0 0    R₂
        0 1 0 0 1 0 0    +
q₃=1← 1 0 0 1 1 1 0 0

        0 1 1 1 0 0 0    R₃
        0 1 0 0 1 0 0    -
q₄=1← 1 0 0 1 0 1 0 0
```

Q = 1.011   Remainder = 0.00010100

Fig. 11.   Nonrestoring division example.

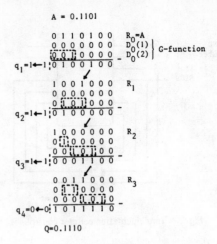

Q=0.1110

Fig. 12.   Nonrestoring square root example.

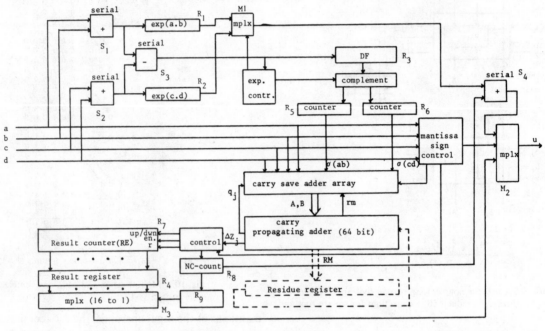

Fig. 13.   PE implementation.

The division and square root operations are performed the other way around. The input operands are only accumulated, while the actual operation is performed on the operands which were entered in the previous operation cycle. This requires no extra accumulation registers; as for division, only one register is needed to hold the divisor. Two of the other three input registers can be used to accumulate the new divisor and dividend. For the square root operation only one accumulating register is needed. Some control circuitry must be added to handle the exponents as described in Section II-B and II-C. This will require minor modifications of the PE outlined in Fig. 13.

Residue Register: For certain applications the inclusion of a residue register can be an improvement with respect to precision. Since the least significant half of the resutl is retained in the carry propagating adder, it can be stored in a residue register (see Fig. 13). In the next cycle the contents of the residue register is fed back into the carry propagating adder. The operation performed is given by

$$U + R_i \leftarrow A * B + C * D + R_{i-1}. \qquad (42)$$

If 64 bit floating point arithmetic is used, this will not be necessary for most applications. But since the speed of the operations in the PE is linearly dependent on the number of bits of the operands, in some applications the use of a residue register allows shorter wordlengths to be used, while retaining the required precision.

Generalized Inner Product: The algorithm for the two term inner product can be easily extended to the general inner product of the form

$$P = \sum_{r=1}^{N} A^r \cdot B^r. \qquad (43)$$

Equation (10) then becomes

$$P_j = 2 \cdot P_{j-1} + \sum_{r=1}^{N} A_{j-1}^r(m) \cdot b_j^r(m) + B_j^r(m) \cdot a_j^r(m). \qquad (44)$$

The consequence for fixed point numbers is that the carry save adder array must be extended with two rows of cells for every extra product pair. The complexity of the processing element is then $O(N*n)$. For large values of N, pipelining of the carry save adder array may be necessary. This enlarges the semi-on-line delay δ.

For floating point numbers there is a difficulty in the calculation of the alignment factors of the mantissas. For N product pair there are $1/2(N^2 - N)$ differences to be calculated. This means that the number of differences has a quadratic property with respect to the number of product pairs and therefore the required hardware for exponent calculation will be quite substantial for large value of N.

IV. EFFICIENCY OF THE PE

In this section the speed and cost-effectiveness of the proposed PE are compared with more parallel implementations. The speed of the bit-sequential SOL-PE is compared with a full bit-parallel PE implementation (FP-PE) (including the data transportation from PE to PE) and an internally bit-parallel PE implementation with restrictions in the number of bits transported from PE to PE (RP-PE).

It is always difficult to make a universal valid comparison because many costs are hidden (complex control logic) or not known (technology or implementation dependent). The derived results should be interpreted as a rough approximation. For the comparison only the inner product operation is considered. In Jump *et al.* [23] the effectiveness of pipelined arithmetic is considered. Although the results of this work are not directly applicable to our case, the same name conventions for parameters will be used.

The parameters have the following definitions:

τ_s : system clock
τ_d : data transportation time
τ_p : processing time
$\tau(M)$: time per operation when M operations are performed
τ : time per operation when $M \rightarrow \infty$
δ : semi-on-line delay
$\eta(M)$: cost per operation when M operations are performed
η : cost per operation when $M \rightarrow \infty$
M : average number of operations
n : wordlength of the operands
z : number of pipeline stages
t : number of system clocks per pipeline stage
μ : data transport utilization factor.

To consider the configurations the model depicted in Fig. 14 is taken. The transportation time of the data between two PE's is τ_d, the processing time of the operands within a PE is τ_p, and the PE's have an internal system clock τ_s.

First of all, the scalar and vector performance of the FP-PE is considered. Since all bits of the operands are transported in parallel between the PE's (a direct interconnection is assumed) the transport can be as fast as the system clock, thus $\tau_d = \tau_s$. The PE has an internal pipeline of z stages with a duration of t system clocks cycles per stage. One operation takes the following amount of time:

$$\tau(1) = (1 + z \cdot t)\tau_s. \quad (45)$$

If $t = 1$ we call the system *balanced* with respect to the utilization of the data transport system. We can define a data

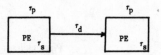

Fig. 14. Performance evaluation model.

transport *utilization factor:*

$$\mu = 1/t. \quad (46)$$

After the first operation the next $M - 1$ operations have an effective processing time of $t \cdot \tau_s$. For M operations the average processing time becomes

$$\tau(M) = \left\{ \frac{t(M - 1 + z) + 1}{M} \right\} \cdot \tau_s \quad (47)$$

and

$$\tau = \lim_{M \to \infty} \tau(M) = t \cdot \tau_s.$$

In the second case (RP-PE), the data transport is restricted to n_0-bits at a time, making the data transport time $\tau_d = (n/n_0) \cdot \tau_s$. The process delay for one operation is given by

$$\tau(1) = \left(\frac{n}{n_0} + z \cdot t \right) \tau_s. \quad (48)$$

When M operations are performed the average process time becomes

$$\tau(M) = \left\{ \frac{t(M - 1 + z) + \dfrac{n}{n_0}}{M} \right\} \cdot \tau_s \quad (49)$$

and

$$\tau = \lim_{M \to \infty} \tau(M) = t \cdot \tau_s$$

and

$$\mu = \frac{n}{n_0 \cdot t}.$$

It clearly makes no sense to take the pipeline delay smaller than the minimum time to transfer the operands, so (49) is only valid for

$$t \geqslant \frac{n}{n_0} \quad (50)$$

which restricts the possible speed for large values of M.

As a third case the proposed SOL-PE is considered. The result is available δ clock cycles after the absorption of the operands. There is no difference between scalar and vector performance. The process delay time is given by

$$\tau(M) = \tau = (n + \delta) \cdot \tau_s. \quad (51)$$

The data transport utilization factor is given by

$$\mu = \frac{n}{n + \delta}. \quad (52)$$

In Table II the differences in processing speed between the considered PE implementations are summarized. In the second column some characteristic values of the parameters are

TABLE II
PROCESSING DELAY, $\tau_s = 20$ ns, $\delta = 3$, $n = 32$, $z_1 = 14$, $t_1 = 1$, $z_2 = (1,2)$, $t_2 = (32, 8)$, $n/n_0 = (32, 8)$, $t_2 \geqq n/n_0$

Implementation	Scalar (M=1)		Vector (M=10)		Vector (M→∞)		μ	
FP-PE	$(1+z_1 \cdot t_1)\tau_s$	300	$\left[\frac{t_1(M-1+z_1)+1}{M}\right]\tau_s$	48	$t_1 \cdot \tau_s$	20	$\frac{1}{t_1}$	1
RP-PE	$(\frac{n}{n_0}+z_2 \cdot t_2)\tau_s$	1280 480	$\left[\frac{t_2(M-1+z_2)+\frac{n}{n_0}}{M}\right]\tau_s$	700 192	$t_2 \cdot \tau_s$	640 160	$\frac{n/n_0}{t_2}$	1
SOL-PE	$(n+\delta)\tau_s$	700	$(n+\delta)\tau_s$	700	$(n+\delta)\tau_s$	700	$\frac{n}{n+\delta}$	0.92

substituted. They have been chosen as realistically as possible. For instance $z_1 = 14$ is the number of clock cycles in which the CRAY-1 performs the two term inner product algorithm [1]. In the case of the RP-PE two examples are considered. The first example is a complete bit-sequential solution and the second example is a 4-bits at a time solution. The value of z_2 is chosen such that $t_2 \cdot z_2$ approaches z_1 as close as possible. The examples are optimized with respect to the data transport utilization factor μ. The clock cycle of $\tau_s = 20$ ns is based on ECL technology with a gate delay of 700 ps. The most critical part of the SOL-PE is the carry propagating adder. If the carry span is 4 bits and only 2 input NOR and NAND gates are used, the delay of a full carry look-ahead addition of two 64 bit operands is approximately 13 ns [17]. With a carry span of 8 bits this is reduced to 8.4 ns. A SOL-PE operating at the speed of $\tau_s = 20$ ns is therefore fairly realistic.

From Table II we can see that the FP-PE is twice as fast as the SOL-PE. For vectors of length $M = 20$ this factor is approximately 15, and for $M \to \infty$ this is 35. In the case of a complete bit-sequential RP-PE, Table II shows that the performance of the RP-PE is equal to or worse (in the scalar case) than the SOL-PE. If a RP-PE with 4-bit parallel transport is considered the performance improves, but in the vector case the performance is still seriously degraded by the restrictions in the data transport system.

Another way of looking at the performance of the SOL-PE is to estimate its maximum performance in MFLOPS (million floating point operations per second). If $\tau_s = 20$ ns and the inner product is considered as 3 floating point operations, the maximum speed per PE is 4.3 MFLOPS (32 bit numbers). If the same configuration as the MPP [8] is taken, the maximum speed is 70400 MFLOPS or 70.4 GFLOPS. Of course this assumes full utilization of each PE in the array. The speed of a MPP element is 0.0048 MFLOPS for the inner product operation. Since the MPP-PE operates at a clock cycle of 100 ns, this should be multiplied with a factor of 5 to get comparable speed with the SOL-PE. This results in 0.024 MFLOPS per MPP-PE if a 20 ns clock cycle is used. Theoretically, this would make the proposed SOL-PE a factor 178 faster than the MPP-PE. Of course the internal hardware of the SOL-PE is more complex than the internal hardware of the MPP-PE.

Another important measure in the cost-effectiveness analysis is the cost per operation η. The cost of the system is obtained by summing the costs of all the hardware components. Hence, the cost per operation is given by

$$\eta(M) = K \cdot \tau(M) \tag{53}$$

in which K is the total cost of the hardware. The total cost K consists of the following components:

$$K = K_v + K_a + K_i \tag{54}$$

where K_v is the cost of the two multiplications, K_a is the cost of the addition and K_i is the cost of the chosen interconnection system.

An interesting parameter is $\gamma = K_p/K_{sol}$ where K_p is the cost of a FP-PE or RP-PE implementation and K_{sol} is the cost of a SOL-PE implementation. An accurate estimation of γ is hard to make because many costs are technology and implementation dependent. Besides the number of gates the required gate-interconnections are important since in some designs more than 60 percent of the chip area consists of interconnections. If the gate count grows with N^2 in some circuitry the number of interconnections or the chip area occupied by the interconnections tend to grow faster than N^2 due to fanning problems and longer wires [24]. The ability to bit-slice the design may also be an important cost factor.

The cost in cells of a multiplier when using iterative arrays is $O(n^2)$ [17], [23]. The outlined SOL-PE is of order $O(n)$. The cost K_i is linearly dependent on the number of bits transported in parallel, counting the number of wires and the number of cells. To get a rough approximation of γ, the assumption is made that the cost of the multiplication is dominant over the cost of the addition ($K_v \gg K_a$). Furthermore it is assumed that the cost to multiply one-bit operands is A_1 for the FP-PE, and A_2 for the SOL-PE. The cost of a one-bit interconnection network is B. In the case of the FP-PE the total cost is $K_p = 2n^2A_1 + (n/n_0)B$ since two multiplications have to be performed. The cost of a SOL-PE is $K_{sol} = nA_2 + B$. Now γ becomes

$$\gamma = \frac{2n^2A_1 + (n/n_0)B}{nA_2 + B}. \tag{55}$$

When the interconnection costs are dominant $\gamma_1 = n/n_0$ ($B \gg A$). When the PE costs are dominant ($A \gg B$), three scenarios are considered; $A_1 = A_2$ ($\gamma_2 = 2n$), $A_2 = 2A_1$ ($\gamma_3 = n$), and $A_2 = 3A_1$ ($\gamma_4 = (2/3)n$). The cost A_2 is in general somewhat larger than the cost A_1, due to the cost of the extra control logic in the SOL-PE.

In Table III the values of η belonging to the examples in Table II are given. For the RP-PE implementation $n/n_0 = 8$ is taken. Table III shows that certainly for $\eta(1)$ and $\eta(10)$ the SOL-PE is more cost-effective than the FP-PE or the RP-PPE (K_{sol} is taken equal to 1).

TABLE III
COST PER OPERATION ($K_{sol} = 1$)

	$\eta(1)$				$\eta(10)$				$\eta(\infty)$			
	γ_1	γ_2	γ_3	γ_4	γ_1	γ_2	γ_3	γ_4	γ_1	γ_2	γ_3	γ_4
FP-PE	9600	19200	9600	6400	1536	3072	1536	1024	640	1280	640	427
RP-PE	3850	30720	15360	10240	1556	12288	6144	4096	1280	10240	5120	3413
SOL-PE	700	700	700	700	700	700	700	700	700	700	700	700

$\gamma_1 = n/n_0$, $\gamma_2 = 2n$, $\gamma_3 = n$, $\gamma_4 = (2/3)n$, for RP-PE $n/n_0 = 8$

The purpose of these calculations is to show that the SOL-PE design is quite competitive compared to the FP-PE and RP-PE. This even without taking into account other important design criteria such as simplicity, reliability, modularity, ease of implementation, etc., where the bit-sequential design is superior to the bit-parallel designs.

The SOL-PE is especially suited for LSI/VLSI implementation. Internally, the adder array and the propagating adder can be sliced in 4-bit slices with an IC pin count of approximately 40 pins. In VLSI the complete SOL-PE can be placed on one chip with a very low pin count since all the variables are bit-sequential.

V. APPLICABILITY OF THE SOL-PE

The proposed SOL-PE can serve as a direct replacement for the processing elements in processor arrays like the MPP or the ICL-DAP [7], [8]. The bit-sequential nature of the SOL-PE makes it extremely well suited for tree types of architectures like the expression processor proposed by Van Aken *et al.* [25]. The SOL-PE would also perform quite well as the inner product element in the systolic array processor [14].

The main motivation for developing the SOL-PE concepts is simulation of systems. As outlined in Section I the traditional pipelined computers are not suited for simulation of systems. At Delft University of Technology work is in progress to define and construct a parallel processor for simulation of systems [27]. In order to experiment with parallel algorithms and parallel data structures an experimental parallel processor was constructed [26]. This experimental parallel processor consists of eight fully interconnected PE's. The PE's in this design are microprocessor based, as speed was not the ultimate goal of the design. Experience with the system has proved that the concept of modules (in which a number of PE's are fully interconnected), with restricted intermodular interconnections, is very adequate in simulation of systems. Restrictions in the intermodular connections will not cause a serious constraint in the applicability of such a parallel processor in simulation of systems, as in practice a system to be simulated consists of subsystems in a hierarchically ordered structure and consequently, for large systems the structure matrix will be a sparse band matrix. By using bit-sequential processors a sufficient number of PE's can be placed within a module, keeping the cost of the interconnection system at a moderate level.

In applications where reliability and redundancy are important design criteria (such as in avionics), the proposed SOL-PE could be of importance because of its potential speed and reduced demand for interconnections.

VI. CONCLUSIONS

In this paper the design of a bit-sequential PE using semi-on-line algorithms was outlined. It was shown that in certain application areas the performance of the proposed PE is much better than the more traditional pipelined architectures. The SOL-PE is also a good candidate for future processor arrays. Another property of the PE is that the basic algorithms have the same operation time and that this operation time is linearly dependent on the number of bits of the operands. The hardware was shown of $O(n)$ complexity.

For recurrent expressions the speed of the bit-sequential PE is optimal with respect to the data transport and processor utilization. Further research is needed in the area of controlling a large number of relatively simple PE's. A large control structure per PE may outbalance the system and degrade the overall performance.

REFERENCES

[1] *Cray-1 Computer System*, Cray Research Inc. Reference Manual.
[2] "CDC Cyber 200–Model 205," Control Data Corporation, Tech. Rep., Nov. 1980.
[3] V. G. Oklobdzya and M. D. Ercegovac, "An on-line square root algorithm," *IEEE Trans. Comput.*, vol. C-31, Jan. 1982.
[4] D. D. Gajski, "An algorithm for solving linear recurrence systems on parallel and pipelined machines," *IEEE Trans. Comput.*, vol. C-30, Mar. 1981.
[5] M. J. Flynn, "Some computer organizations and their effectiveness," *IEEE Trans. Comput.*, vol. C-21, Sept. 1972.
[6] D. L. Slotnick, W. C. Borck, and R. C. McReynolds, "The Solomon computer," *Fall Joint Comput. Conf.*, 1962.
[7] P. M. Flanders, D. J. Hunt, S. F. Reddaway, and D. Parkinson, "Efficient high speed computing with the distributed array processor," in *High Speed Computer and Algorithm Organization.* New York: Academic, 1977.
[8] K. E. Batcher, "Bit-serial parallel processing systems," *IEEE Trans. Comput.*, vol. C-31, May 1982.
[9] A. J. Atrubin, "A one-dimensional real-time iterative multiplier," *IEEE Trans. Electron. Comput.* vol. EC-14, June 1965.
[10] D. E. Knuth, *The Art of Computer Programming, Seminumerical Algorithms, Vol. 2.* Reading, MA: Addison-Wesley, 1971, Sec. 4.3.3.
[11] I. N. Chen and R. Willoner, "An $O(n)$ parallel multiplier with bit-sequential input and output," *IEEE Trans. Comput.*, vol. C-28, Oct. 1979.
[12] H. J. Sips, "Comments on $O(n)$ parallel multiplier with bit-sequential input and output," *IEEE Trans. Comput.*, vol. C-31, Apr. 1982.
[13] K. S. Trivedi and M. D. Ercegovac, "On-line algorithms for division and multiplication," *IEEE Trans. Comput.*, vol. C-26, July 1977.
[14] R. W. Priester, H. J. Whitehouse, K. Brombley, and J. B. Clary, "Signal processing with systolic arrays," in *Proc. 1981 Conf. Parallel Process.*, Bellaire, MI.
[15] M. J. Flynn, "On division by functional iteration," *IEEE Trans. Comput.*, vol. C-19, 1970.
[16] D. Ferrari, "A division method using a parallel multiplier," *IEEE Trans. Electron. Comput.*, vol. EC-16, 1967.

[17] K. Hwang, *Computer Arithmetic; Principles, Architecture and Design.* New York: Wiley, 1979.

[18] D. P. Agrawal and T. N. Rao, "On multioperand addition of signed binary numbers," *IEEE Trans. Comput.*, vol. C-27, Nov. 1978.

[19] W. J. Karplus and D. Cohen, "Architectural and software issues in the design and application of peripheral array processors," *Computer*, vol. 14, Sept. 1981.

[20] E. Swartzlander, B. Gilbert, and I. Reed, "Inner product computers," *IEEE Trans. Comput.*, vol. C-27, Jan. 1978.

[21] J. Blankenbaker, "Comments on 'Inner product computers,' " *IEEE Trans. Comput.*, vol. C-28, Dec. 1979.

[22] D. P. Agrawal, "High speed arithmetic arrays," *IEEE Trans. Comput.*, vol. C-28, Mar. 1979.

[23] J. Jump and S. R. Ahuja, "Effective pipelining of digital systems," *IEEE Trans. Comput.*, vol. C-27, Sept. 1978.

[24] M. A. Franklin, "VLSI performance comparison of banyan and crossbar communication networks," *IEEE Trans. Comput.*, Apr. 1981.

[25] J. Van Aken and G. Zick, "The expression processor: A pipelined multiprocessor architecture," *IEEE Trans. Comput.*, vol. C-30, Aug. 1981.

[26] J. H. M. Andriessen, H. J. Sips, and H. de Swaan Arons, "An experimental study of parallel data processing structures," in *Proc. 9th IMACS Congress Simulation Syst.*, 1979, Sorrento, Italy.

[27] L. Dekker, E. J. H. Kerckhoffs, G. C. Vansteenkiste, and J. C. Zuidervaart, "Outline of a future simulator," in *Proc. 9th IMACS Congress Simulation Syst.*, 1979, Sorrento, Italy.

Henk J. Sips was born in Amsterdam, Holland on October 14, 1950. He received the M.S. degree in electrical engineering from Delft University of Technology, Delft, Holland, in 1976.

Since 1976, he has been with the Department of Applied Physics, Delft University of Technology, where he is currently an Assistant Professor. His research interests include simulation of systems, computer architecture, parallel processing, and VLSI design.

Mr. Sips is a member of the Society for Computer Simulation (SCS) and the IEEE Computer Society.

Reprinted from *IEEE Transactions on Computers*, Volume C-30, Number 8, August 1981, pages 525-536. Copyright © 1981 by The Institute of Electrical and Electronics Engineers, Inc.

The Expression Processor: A Pipelined, Multiple-Processor Architecture

JERRY R. VANAKEN, MEMBER, IEEE, AND GREGORY L. ZICK, MEMBER, IEEE

Abstract—A new multiple-processor architecture is described that can exploit the instruction-level concurrency in numerical processing tasks. The expression processor contains multiple processing elements (PE's), which can be configured either as an SIMD [8] array or as an expression tree pipeline. An expression tree is the parse tree constructed by a compiler from an arithmetic or logical expression. The expression tree pipeline, or "X-pipe," is a binary-tree network of PE's upon which expression trees are executed intact. A series of expression trees can be executed in pipelined fashion for enhanced concurrency. With this capability, the expression processor can exploit the concurrency in vector merges and scalar tasks, as well as conventional vector tasks. The architecture is designed for low-cost implementation using large-scale integrated (LSI) components.

Index Terms—Arithmetic expression, binary-tree network, multiple-processor architecture, overlap and pipelining, parallelism.

INTRODUCTION

THIS paper introduces the *expression processor*, a new concept in LSI-compatible multiple-processor architecture. The expression processor is a low-cost machine capable of exploiting the potential concurrency in both vector and scalar processing applications. Its low cost is achieved by implementing substantial portions of the machine logic as densely-integrated, single-chip circuits.

Unlike some large-scale architectures, the expression processor is intended to speed up the execution of a single, large task, rather than be multiplexed among a number of smaller tasks. Moreover, the program concurrency exploited by the expression processor is low-level parallelism existing between individual instructions, as opposed to high-level parallelism existing between two or more communicating sequential processes. In this respect, the expression processor can be compared with previous machines such as the CDC 6600, IBM 360/91, Illiac IV, TI ASC, CDC STAR-100, and CRAY-1 [3], [6], [14]. As with these predecessors, conditional branching and list processing erode machine concurrency. The software strategy is to develop algorithms which reduce the number of conditional branches and to vectorize computations where possible. The expression processor design is therefore more conservative in regard to its handling of the branching problem [15] than the approach proposed by data-flow advocates, who hope to demonstrate that this problem can be overcome by discarding altogether the notion of a program counter [7], [9].

The expression processor consists of a number of processing elements (PE's) and a large resister space for high-speed access of vector and scalar data. It interfaces to a main memory containing data and program code.

The PE's in the expression processor can be configured in two ways: either as an SIMD array, similar to the Illiac IV, or as an expression tree pipeline. The expression tree pipeline, abbreviated as "X-pipe" for convenience, is a binary-tree network of PE's upon which expression trees (the parse trees for arithmetic and logical expressions) are executed intact [19]. The operation of an X-pipe of seven PE's evaluating the expression tree for $(7 * 8 + 6/2) - (3 * 4 + 5 + 1)$ is illustrated in Fig. 1. The PE's are data-driven, and a series of such expression trees can be executed in overlapped or pipelined fashion for greater concurrency.

A number of features have been adopted from previous vector and scalar architectures. The CRAY-1 in particular has served as a useful model in terms of its combined vector and scalar processing capabilities, and its large resister space for vector data, which reduces the start-up time for vector operations.

The concept of expression tree pipelining, central to the expression processor architecture, was the basis of an earlier architecture, the *tree processor*, proposed by Kuck and Muraoka in 1968 [11], and described in 1971 by Swanson [18]. Despite the underlying similarity in concept with the expression processor, the tree processor is in many ways a pre-LSI architecture. The PE's in the tree processor are internally pipelined. Widespread use is made of general-purpose alignment networks, and this results in a correspondingly complex control system to keep track of data.

The expression processor is a direct descendant of the tree processor, but its design reflects a greater emphasis on limiting the complexity of the interconnection topology and distributing control functions in a modular fashion. This emphasis follows from the recognition that while memories and processors are declining in cost due to LSI technology, random control logic and alignment networks remain expensive due to the difficulty of integrating them. The irregularity of random logic is at odds with the economics of LSI, although gate arrays and other forms of semicustom logic are helping to alleviate this problem to some degree. Alignment networks pose difficulties due to the large number of pinouts required. A crossbar switching

Manuscript received October 5, 1979; revised October 17, 1980 and March 9, 1981.

J. R. VanAken is with the MOS Microcomputer Department, Texas Instruments, Inc., Houston, TX 77036.

G. L. Zick is with the Department of Electrical Engineering, University of Washington, Seattle, WA 98195.

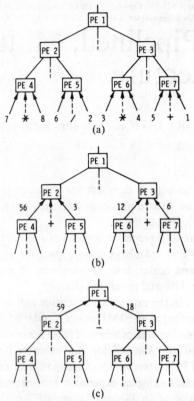

Fig. 1. *X*-pipe evaluation of an arithmetic expression.

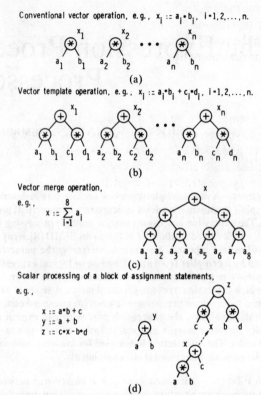

Fig. 2. Types of vector and scalar concurrency in the expression processor.

network [13] connecting *n* processors to *n* memories, for example, requires (in excess of) $n^2 w$ gates, where *w* is the width of each data path in bits. The number of pinouts required for such a network is (in excess of) $2nw$, yielding a gate to pinout ratio of only $n/2$.

The philosophy behind the expression processor can be stated as follows. The primary machine resources are the PE's and memory. A certain amount of support hardware, or "logical glue," is needed to bind the PE's and memory together to form a working processing system. The job of the architect is to reduce the complexity and cost of this "glue," while providing a versatile and efficient architecture that can make effective use of the PE's and memory over a wide range of processing applications. The versatility of the resulting architecture is exhibited in the description of the processing capabilities of the expression processor presented in the next section.

NUMERICAL PROCESSING CAPABILITIES

The expression processor is capable of exploiting the concurrency in several types of vector and scalar processing tasks, as indicated in Fig. 2.

A conventional vector operation is illustrated in Fig. 2(a) with the example

$$x(i) := a(i) * b(i), \qquad i = 1, 2, \cdots, n.$$

Given a sufficiently large *n*, this is the type of task which can be performed efficiently on a vector (or array) processor such as the Illiac IV, CDC STAR-100, or TI ASC. The Illiac IV can exploit the parallelism inherent in this task by distributing the *n* multiply operations among its 64 PE's. The expression

processor operates in similar fashion to achieve high PE utilization when the vector length *n* is large.

A vector operation such as

$$x(i) := a(i) * b(i) + c(i) * d(i), \qquad i = 1, 2, \cdots, n$$

will be referred to as a vector template operation. The expression tree for $(a * b + c * d)$ can be thought of as the template for the computation, which is executed *n* times, once for each value of index *i*. This is indicated in Fig. 2(b). For large *n*, the most efficient strategy is to decompose the vector template computation into a series of conventional vector operations similar to Fig. 2(a). First, two temporary vectors, say *q* and *r*, are computed

$$q(i) := a(i) * b(i), \quad r(i) := c(i) * d(i),$$
$$i = 1, 2, \cdots, n.$$

The vector *x* is formed by adding together the corresponding elements of *q* and *r*. For small *n*, however, decomposition may be an inefficient strategy. Given $n = 4$, for example, the Illiac IV keeps only four of its 64 PE's busy, while the remaining 60 stand idle. The expression processor, on the other hand, is capable of executing the expression tree templates intact, as in Fig. 2(b), rather than in decomposed form. This allows advantage to be taken of the fact that the two multiplies in each copy of the template $(a * b + c * d)$ can be computed in parallel on two different PE's. Executing vector template computations in this fashion can increase PE utilization significantly when the vector length is small compared to the number of PE's.

During a vector merge operation, the elements of a vector are merged together to produce a single element. Examples of vector merges are adding or multiplying the elements of a vector together or finding the maximum or minimum value among the vector elements. Fig. 2(c) presents the expression tree for the summation

$$x := \sum_{i=1}^{8} a(i)$$

as an example of a vector merge operation. Although techniques have been devised for performing vector merges on the Illiac IV and CRAY-1, these are awkward to implement and do not execute as efficiently as conventional vector operations. The binary-tree structure of the expression processor's X-pipe, however, is exceptionally well suited to performing vector merges. In multiplying two 8×8 matrices, for example, a series of 64 summations is generated, each having an expression tree similar to that of Fig. 2(c). By pipelining these expression trees one after the other through the X-pipe, high utilization of the PE's is achieved.

Scalar processing is illustrated in Fig. 2(d) using as an example the block of assignment statements [12]

$s1$	$x := a * b + c$
$s2$	$y := a + b$
$s3$	$z := c * x - b * d.$

Statements $s1$ and $s2$ can be computed in parallel, but $s3$ is data dependent upon $s1$. The parallel arithmetic units in scalar machines such as the CDC 6600 and IBM 360/91 are able to exploit the parallelism in scalar problems, while detecting and resolving all data dependencies through their lookahead control logic [10]. The expression processor is similarly able to exploit the concurrency in scalar tasks, although it utilizes a different set of mechanisms for doing so. Most data dependencies, i.e., those occurring between the individual data operations within each expression, can be satisfied within the binary-tree structure of the X-pipe. The potential concurrency between operations is thereby exploited without the intervention of external control mechanisms. A data dependency existing between one expression and another is resolved by means of a straightforward logical interlock external to the X-pipe, to be described later. Our studies [20] indicate that an X-pipe of 15 or 31 PE's can exploit at least 80 percent of the potential concurrency in typical scalar tasks.

While scalar tasks typically contain less potential concurrency than vector operations, several studies [1], [5], [16] have demonstrated the importance of providing both scalar and vector processing power in the same machine. Vector-oriented numerical algorithms typically contain some amount of scalar processing. Performance gains made during vector processing can be substantially eroded during scalar processing if the architecture is weak in this area. The classic example of this problem is the Illiac IV, which during scalar processing utilizes only one of its 64 PE's. The expression processor fares better in this regard because it distributes processing among the various PE's in the X-pipe for greater hardware concurrency.

As an illustration of the effect of scalar processing upon overall performance, say that a portion of a program representing 90 percent of the serial execution time of the program can be vectorized to run 20 times faster than serial, while the remaining 10 percent is scalar and runs at serial speed. The overall speed up of the program with respect to its serial execution time is $1/(0.1 + 0.9/20) = 6.90$. If the scalar portion of the program is now speeded up by a mere factor of two, the overall speed up increases to $1/(0.1/2 + 0.9/20) = 10.53$, a net performance improvement of over 50 percent.

The above remarks concerning the importance of scalar concurrency to overall performance apply as well to vector template concurrency when the vector length is small. In fact, each of the four types of machine concurrency illustrated in Fig. 2 complements the other types and makes the expression processor an efficient architecture over a wide range of processing applications.

CONFIGURABILITY

An expression processor containing 32 PE's and eight register modules will be described in this paper, although smaller configurations are introduced to simplify particular examples. The 32 PE's are configured either as an SIMD array for conventional vector operations or as an X-pipe for vector template operations, vector merges, and scalar tasks. Data are buffered in a large, high-bandwidth register space implemented as a set of eight fast random-access memory (RAM) modules that operate in parallel. Parallel data paths between the PE's and registers can transmit up to eight words per register cycle.[1]

When configured as an SIMD array, as in Fig. 3(a), eight register cycles are required to route a pair of operands to each of the 32 PE's, and another four cycles are required to route the 32 results back to the registers. The bandwidths of the PE's and register modules are balanced for long vector operations if each PE requires $8 + 4 = 12$ register cycles to process a pair of operands. Were the PE's substantially faster or slower than this, the ratio of the number of PE's to register modules could be altered accordingly.

The X-pipe configuration is represented in Fig. 3(b) as a triangle, and in more detail in Fig. 4. PE number 0 is not included in Fig. 4 and is used only in the SIMD array configuration. Operand data can be input to the X-pipe from the registers at a rate of eight words per cycle, using the same data paths as for the SIMD configuration. However, all results from the X-pipe are output from PE 1, the root node of the PE tree, in serial fashion. As each result emerges, it is collected into an eight-word result buffer, shown in Fig. 3(b). When full, the eight words in the buffer are written in parallel to the eight register modules.

The fact that results emerge in serial fashion from the X-pipe means that the rate at which it can output data is lower than the rate at which it can input data. The X-pipe output is built to operate in this way primarily to simplify the hardware, but this arrangement can be rationalized by observing that the X-pipe bandwidth requirements are in fact substantially lower for output data than for input data. In Fig. 2(b) and (c), each

---

[1] A register cycle is the cycle time required to transmit a datum from one register to another. In the particular case discussed here, a register cycle corresponds to the cycle time of the RAM used for the registers.

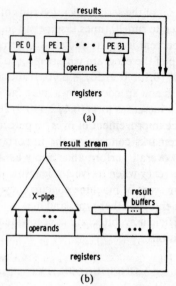

(a)

(b)

Fig. 3. The PE's may be configured either as (a) an SIMD array or (b) an expression tree pipeline.

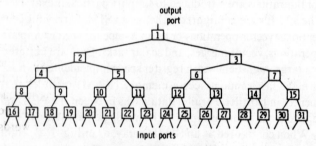

Fig. 4. An X-pipe of 31 PE's.

set of four or eight operands generates only a single result. The data reduction that takes place within the X-pipe tends to alleviate the potential bottleneck at the output. Scalar tasks typically contain less inherent concurrency than vector tasks, and their bandwidth requirements are correspondingly lower for input data as well as output data.

OVERVIEW OF ARCHITECTURE

A block diagram of the expression processor architecture is presented in Fig. 5 with the PE's shown configured as an X-pipe. Operand values are routed to the various input ports of the X-pipe via a set of eight operand corridors. Each of the eight operand corridors fans out to eight PE input ports. A single result stream is shown leaving the X-pipe to be collected in the result buffers. Not shown are the eight result corridors used to route result data in parallel from the PE's to the registers during SIMD configurations.

A large register space of 1024 or more words is provided for high-speed data storage and retrieval. The eight parallel register modules are numbered 0 through 7, with the least significant three bits of each register address identifying the module containing the register.

A general-purpose alignment network is used to route operands from the register modules to the operand corridors. If implemented as a crossbar switch, the alignment network requires $8 \times 8 \times w$ switching elements, where w is the data path width. This can be reduced to $6 \times 8 \times w$ switches if an addi-

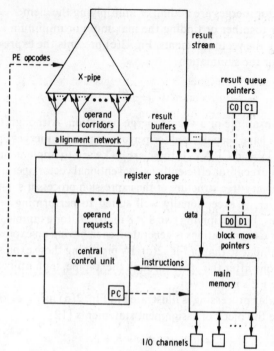

Fig. 5. An overview of the expression processor.

tional propagation time of two gate delays can be tolerated [13]. The cost of the alignment network is justified by the need to move operand data rapidly (in parallel) from the registers to the X-pipe inputs.

The PE configuration always receives its operands from the registers (via the operand corridors) and deposits results back into the registers. Rather than allow the PE's to exchange data directly with main memory, the registers act as intermediary. Block transfers of data take place between the registers and main memory. (A block length of one can be specified, although this is less efficient.) This is similar to the CRAY-1, whose large register space can be regarded as a programmable (i.e., not transparent to the programmer, but explicitly manipulated) cache serving to buffer data between memory and the functional units. The CRAY-1 contains eight scalar and eight vector registers. Each vector register can hold a vector of up to 64 words in length. Longer vectors must be partitioned, leaving a discontinuity at every 64th element. In contrast, the expression processor's register space is not partitioned at the hardware level. A vector can therefore be as large as the register space permits, and the user can designate any portion of the register space to contain scalar or vector data.

Also shown in Fig. 5 are two pairs of address pointers $C0$-$C1$ and $D0$-$D1$, which are used during data transfers to and from the registers. Each pair of pointers manages a queue of contiguous register locations. The $D0$-$D1$ pointers are responsible for handling block transfers of data between the registers and main memory. At the beginning of the block transfer, $D0$ is set to point to the first element in the block and $D1$ to the last. As each element is read from (or written to) main memory, it is written to (or read from) the register location pointed to by $D0$ and $D0$ is incremented by one. This process continues until finally $(D0) = (D1) + 1$,[2] at which point the block transfer is

<hr>

[2] Enclosing $D0$ in parentheses means that the *contents* of $D0$ are being referred to.

complete. The $C0$-$C1$ pointers queue the results from the X-pipe as they are generated. They operate in a manner similar to the $D0$-$D1$ pointers.

The main memory contains both data and program code. A set of I/O channels, shown interfaced to the main memory in Fig. 5, permits communication with external processors, mass storage, and high-speed I/O devices. One or more external processors is used to interface the expression processor with the outside world and to perform such functions as editing, compilation, and file handling.

The central control unit shown in Fig. 5 manages the program counter (PC), interprets instructions, and updates register address pointers $C0$-$C1$ and $D0$-$D1$. It also initiates scalar and vector tasks by supplying the opcodes needed to program the PE's and generating the requests for register data to be input to the PE's as operands. A conditional branch capability permits the decision to update the PC to be based upon the value of a Boolean result produced by the X-pipe. A natural division of control functions occurs between the X-pipe and central control unit, with the former executing all arithmetic and logical operations and the latter performing global coordination and program control.

The expression processor can be compared to a conventional Von Neumann machine, with the X-pipe (or SIMD array) taking the place of the arithmetic-logical unit (ALU). Whereas the control unit in a conventional processor may initiate ALU operations at the level of individual shifts and adds, the central control unit of the expression processor initiates processing tasks at the level of whole vector or scalar tasks. Only within the PE configuration are these composite operations decomposed into individual arithmetic-logical operations.

Successively accessed vector elements in register space are always written to or read from contiguous register addresses, but an arbitrary address increment may be specified between vector elements read from or written to main memory. This allows permutations of vector elements (e.g., perfect shuffle [17]) to be performed during block transfers between the registers and main memory. The potential also exists for using the alignment network located between the register modules and the operand corridors to perform certain types of data permutations at register speeds.

Like the registers, main memory is composed of a number of parallel modules. Hence, an alignment network may be required at the processor-memory interface, although multiplexing can be used to reduce the size of this network if the bandwidth of the memory interface bus is sufficiently high compared to the bandwidth of an individual memory module.

EXPRESSION TREE PIPELINE

Selected portions of the expression processor architecture will be examined in greater depth. In particular, the operation of the X-pipe, the I/O structure of the PE's, and the data routing system will be described.

All PE's in the expression processor are identical and have arithmetic and logical processing capabilities. Arithmetic functions minimally include integer and floating-point addition, multiplication, and division. In the X-pipe configuration, each expression tree is mapped node-for-node directly onto the PE tree to be executed. The flow of data during execution is from the bottom up. In order to satisfy data dependencies between consecutive levels of an expression tree, the lower level must be evaluated before the next higher level can be evaluated, and so on.

Fig. 1 demonstrates the evaluation of the expression tree for $(7 * 8 + 6/2) - (3 * 4 + 5 + 1)$ on an X-pipe of seven PE's (for simplicity). The calculation of $7 * 8$, $6/2$, $3 * 4$, and $5 + 1$ are performed by PE's 4–7 in (a). Next, PE's 2 and 3 evaluate $56 + 3$ and $12 + 6$ in (b). In (c) PE 1 calculates 59-18, and the result is then output (not shown).

Fig. 6(a) depicts this computation as a wave front propagating through consecutive levels of the X-pipe (represented as a triangle). This immediately leads to another observation. By allowing wave fronts, each representing an expression being evaluated, to propagate through the X-pipe one after the other, a pipeline is formed. This is indicated in Fig. 6(b).

Each PE in the X-pipe of Fig. 1 has left and right input ports for operands and an output port for results. Data paths are represented as solid lines with the output port of one PE connecting to the input port of the PE above. The broken lines represent the paths through which opcodes are issued to the PE from the central control unit. Opcodes may be queued until the PE is ready to interpret them. Similarly, timing irregularities in the flow of incoming and outgoing data may be smoothed over by placing a FIFO buffer, two to four words deep, in each data path.

Each PE is data-driven. The PE is intelligent enough not to attempt to read from an empty input port or write to an output port that is full. The execution of the opcode currently being interpreted is delayed until the required operands are present at the input ports. This is necessary since the execution times of operations such as addition and multiplication will differ in general. While operands must arrive at a PE input port in a designated order, they may do so at unpredictable times.

With each PE operating in the manner described above, the wave fronts shown in Fig. 6(b) will never pass each other while traversing the pipeline. This means that results leave the X-pipe in precisely the same order in which the original expressions enter the X-pipe. This deterministic ordering simplifies the mechanisms needed to keep track of individual results and resolve data dependencies between expressions during scalar processing.

TRANSMIT-OP'S AND PARTITIONING

Given an X-pipe containing some fixed number of PE's, expression trees constructed during compilation of typical programs will frequently fail to conform precisely to the shape of the X-pipe. This section presents methods for executing expression trees larger or smaller than the X-pipe.

A transmit operator is defined to permit execution of expression trees that are smaller than the X-pipe. The transmit-op $\Phi_{i,j}$ is a specialized opcode that tells the PE to pass data from either of its two data input ports to its output port. Indices i and j specify the number of operands to be transferred from

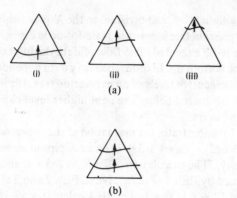

(a)

(b)

Fig. 6. The evaluation of an expression is represented in (a) as a wave front propagating through the X-pipe, and in (b) the pipelining of expressions is indicated.

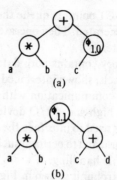

(a)

(b)

Fig. 7. An expression tree containing transmit-op $\Phi_{1,0}$ is shown in (a), and in (b) $\Phi_{1,1}$ permits two independent operations to proceed in parallel.

each port. First, the PE transfers i operands from the left input port to the output port, and then it transfers j operands from the right input port to the output port.

For example, to evaluate the expression $a * b + c$ on an X-pipe of three PE's (for simplicity), the expression tree can be extended using an $\Phi_{1,0}$ operator in the manner indicated in Fig. 7(a). Similarly, the scalar operations

$$x := a * b$$

$$y := c + d$$

can be performed in parallel on the three-PE X-pipe using the transmit-op $\Phi_{1,1}$, as shown in Fig. 7(b). Following the definition of the transmit-op above, the results emerge from PE 1 in the order x, y.

An expression tree that is larger than the X-pipe must be partitioned into two or more smaller trees prior to execution. For example, the computation

$$x := (a * b + c * d) * q + r * s$$

can be partitioned as

$$tmp := a * b + c * d$$

$$x := tmp * q + r * s.$$

Each of these expressions is now small enough to be executed on the three-PE X-pipe. The data dependency is preserved by introducing temporary variable tmp.

DISTRIBUTED MAPPING

The general technique of mapping two or more small expression trees onto different areas of a comparatively large X-pipe to achieve greater concurrency will be referred to as distributed mapping. Fig. 7(b) presents a simple example of this technique. The expression processor implementation of distributed mapping differs for scalar and vector tasks. The mapping for scalar tasks is performed by the compiler prior to execution, whereas the mapping for vector tasks is performed during run time by the machine control logic.

During compilation of a scalar task, each expression is parsed into tree form, tree-height reduction [2], [12] is performed where possible, and the expression trees are mapped onto the compiler's internal representation of the target X-pipe

configuration. In the resulting machine code each opcode and operand is accompanied by routing information that directs it to the proper PE.

During compilation of vector tasks, the vector length and start address of each vector is encoded. For a vector template operation, the expression tree template is encoded also. For a vector merge operation the operator type (e.g., addition operator if summation) is encoded. Vector computations differ from scalar computations in that the information encoded at compile time is used at run time to dynamically construct the individual expression trees that are mapped onto the X-pipe for execution. The control logic required to perform this mapping makes use of the regular structure of the vector tasks.

Distributed mapping for vector tasks is demonstrated in Fig. 8 using the example vector template computation

$$x(i) := a(i) * b(i) + c(i) - d(i), \qquad i = 1, 2, \cdots, n.$$

If executed on an X-pipe of seven or more nodes, distributed mapping is required to utilize the PE's efficiently. Given the 31-PE X-pipe of Fig. 4, "composite" trees $T2$, $T3$, and $T4$ of Fig. 8 are constructed using the expression tree for $a * b + c - d$ as template. Each composite tree is formed by consolidating several copies of the template into a single executable expression tree, using transmit-ops to hold the pieces together. The root node of each composite tree coincides with PE 1 when mapped onto the X-pipe. Operands $a(1)$, $b(1)$, $c(1)$, and $d(1)$ are input to PE's 4 and 5 from the operand corridors, operands $a(2)$, $b(2)$, $c(2)$, and $d(2)$ are input to PE's 6 and 7, and so on. Composite tree Ti, $i = 2, 3, 4$, contains 2^{i-1} copies of the template. A $T1$ is not included for reasons explained later in this section.

During execution the composite trees are executed in the order $T2$, $T3$, $T4$. These trees can be pipelined through the X-pipe in the same manner as any expression trees. Tree $T2$ is first initiated into the X-pipe to generate results $x(1)$ and $x(2)$. Tree $T3$ follows in pipeline fashion to generate $x(3)$ through $x(6)$. Tree $T4$ follows next to generate $x(7)$ through $x(14)$. If $n > 14$ another tree similar to $T2$ follows $T4$ to generate $x(15)$ and $x(16)$, and so on. In other words, the sequence

$$T2, T3, T4, T2, \cdots$$

is executed until all $x(i)$, $i = 1, 2, \cdots, n$, are generated.

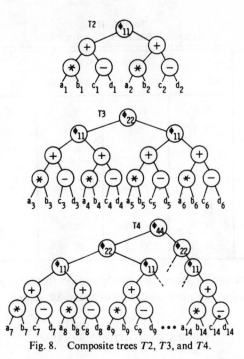

Fig. 8.   Composite trees $T2$, $T3$, and $T4$.

The root nodes of $T2$, $T3$, and $T4$ contain opcodes $\Phi_{1,1}$, $\Phi_{2,2}$, and $\Phi_{4,4}$, respectively. Hence, PE 1 executes the opcode sequence

$$\Phi_{1,1}, \Phi_{2,2}, \Phi_{4,4}, \Phi_{1,1}, \cdots.$$

PE 2 executes

$$+, \Phi_{1,1}, \Phi_{2,2}, +, \cdots$$

and so on for the other PE's. At the start of the vector template computation, the central control unit issues to each PE its set of opcodes. Each PE proceeds to cycle through its opcodes in an infinite loop until it receives a signal indicating the end of the vector. The end-of-vector signal is introduced first to the PE's on the bottom level of the tree (PE's 16–31). These PE's pass the end-of-vector signal to the PE's on the next higher level (PE's 8–15), the process repeating until the signal has propagated to PE 1. The end-of-vector signal forms a wavefront, similar to Fig. 6(a), separating the end of one vector operation from the start of the next. With this wavefront serving to define the boundary between one task and the next, there is no necessity to flush the pipeline between tasks.

No tree $T1$ is included in Fig. 8 for reasons having to do with the width of the operand corridors, which transmit up to eight words in parallel. Including $T1$ would require that a set of four operands be sent to the inputs of PE's 2 and 3, only half filling the corridors. This would complicate the the generation of vector operand addresses, described in the next section. Adding $T1$ to the distributed mapping sequence would also create a potential bottleneck at the output of PE 1 since this PE would be required to perform add operations in addition to its job of passing along the results generated by the other PE's in the X-pipe.

Some improvement in performance may be achieved by recognizing that with $T1$ eliminated from the distributed mapping, which now contains only $T2$, $T3$, and $T4$, the bottleneck in the X-pipe may occur at some PE other than PE 1.

It may occur at PE 4, for instance, which is required to perform additions, multiplications, and transmit-ops. Excluding $T3$ or even $T2$ from the distributed mapping may therefore result in the most efficient PE utilization, as determined by the relative execution times of the various arithmetic operations and transmit-ops. The structure of the expression processor permits any of these distributed mappings to be selected by the programmer.

PE STRUCTURE

In this section the I/O structure of each PE is examined. All 32 PE's are identical and have the structure indicated in Fig. 9. The block designated "ALU and PE control" contains all the logic needed to interpret opcodes, perform arithmetic and logical operations, and control the input and output ports of the PE. Control and access of these I/O ports is through the PE bus.

When the PE's are configured as an X-pipe, the links through which PE n communicates with the other PE's are provided by the ports marked FATHER, LSON, and RSON. The FATHER port is used to queue result data being output from PE n to the PE occupying the next higher level in the tree, PE number $\lfloor n/2 \rfloor$.[3] The FATHER port of PE 1 serves as the output of the X-pipe.

PE number n, $n = 1, 2, \cdots, 15$, reads its operands from PE's $2n$ and $2n + 1$, the PE's occupying the next lower level in the X-pipe, through its LSON and RSON ports, respectively. These two ports are in fact the FATHER ports of PE's $2n$ and $2n + 1$. PE n is connected to these ports by means of the cable shown in Fig. 9. By placing PE's $2n$ and $2n + 1$ on the same printed-circuit board, only a single cable is required. All 32 PE's in the system reside in pairs upon 16 such boards, all identical, although PE's 0 and 16–31 have no LSON or RSON connections.

The LOPD, ROPD, and RESULT ports in Fig. 9 are used to connect each PE n, $n = 0, 1, \cdots, 31$, to two operand corridors and one result corridor. The expression processor contains eight operand corridors, numbered 0–7, and eight result corridors, numbered in similar fashion. Each operand corridor contains slots for eight PE inputs and each result corridor has slots for four PE outputs. The RESULT port of PE n occupies slot number $\lfloor n/8 \rfloor$ on result corridor number $n \bmod 8$. The LOPD and ROPD (left operand and right operand) ports receive data from operand corridors $2(n \bmod 4)$ and $2(n \bmod 4) + 1$, respectively. The LOPD and ROPD ports of PE n occupy slot $\lfloor n/4 \rfloor$ on each of their respective operand corridors.

The rules governing the I/O connections of each PE are summarized in Table I. A list of the operand corridor connections is presented in Table II. Each pair of operand corridors provides data to the LSON (even corridor number) and RSON (odd corridor number) ports of eight PE's. For example, the leftmost column of Table II indicates that corridor 0 provides operands to the LSON ports of PE's 0, 4, $\cdots$, 28; corridor 1 provides operands to the RSON ports of these PE's.

[3] Writing $\lfloor x \rfloor$ means the largest integer value that is less than or equal to x.

113

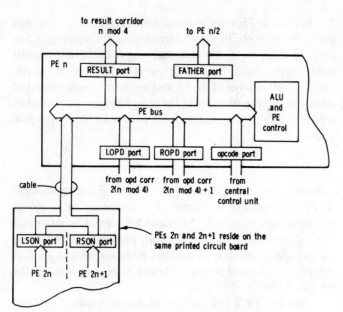

to result corridor
n mod 4

to PE n/2

Fig. 9.   PE structure.

TABLE I
I/O CONNECTION RULES FOR PE NUMBER N

(1) $n = 0,1,\ldots,31$

LOPD port occupies slot $\lfloor n/4 \rfloor$ of operand corridor
number $2(n \bmod 4)$.

ROPD port occupies slot $\lfloor n/4 \rfloor$ of operand corridor
number $2(n \bmod 4) + 1$.

RESULT port occupies slot $\lfloor n/8 \rfloor$ of result corridor
number $n \bmod 8$.

(2) $n = 1,2,\ldots,15$

LSON port is FATHER port of PE $2n$.

RSON port is FATHER port of PE $2n+1$.

(3) $n = 2,3,\ldots,31$

FATHER port connects to PE $\lfloor n/2 \rfloor$ as LSON port
(n even) or RSON port (n odd).

(4) $n = 1$

FATHER port serves as output of X-pipe.

A slot address appears to the left of each row. The input ports of PE's 0, 1, 2, and 3 occupy slot number 0 on their respective corridors, and so on.

An opcode port, also shown in Fig. 9, is used to queue opcodes issued to PE n from the central control unit. Each opcode contains two single-bit control fields that specify which data I/O ports are to be used for the operation. The first control bit specifies whether the operands are to be input from the LSON and RSON ports or from the LOPD and ROPD ports. The second control bit specifies whether the result is to be transmitted to the FATHER port or RESULT port.

The process of reconfiguring the PE's to form either an X-pipe or SIMD array can now be explained. This reconfiguration does not take place under any centralized control, but is entirely determined within each PE by the input and output paths specified by the two I/O control bits in each opcode. Hence, there is no waiting time for the X-pipe to flush itself

TABLE II
OPERAND CORRIDOR CONNECTIONS

SLOT (TAG)	OPERAND CORRIDORS							
	000	001	010	011	100	101	110	111
000	PE 0		PE 1		PE 2		PE 3	
001	PE 4		PE 5		PE 6		PE 7	
010	PE 8		PE 9		PE 10		PE 11	
011	PE 12		PE 13		PE 14		PE 15	
100	PE 16		PE 17		PE 18		PE 19	
101	PE 20		PE 21		PE 22		PE 23	
110	PE 24		PE 25		PE 26		PE 27	
111	PE 28		PE 29		PE 30		PE 31	

before changing from one configuration to the other—the opcodes for the next configuration can be issued immediately.

OPERAND ROUTING SYSTEM

Execution of each of the four types of operation indicated in Fig. 2 is accomplished within the expression processor by routing opcodes and operands to the PE's in some designated order. The routing of operands to PE's is felt to be the more interesting problem and will be described here. For details on the issuing of opcodes to PE's, the reader is referred to [20].

Fig. 10 is a block diagram of the operand routing system. At the top are eight operand request buffers, numbered 0–7, and at the bottom are the operand corridors. The requests for the operand values to be routed to a slot on operand corridor n, $n = 0, 1, \cdots, 7$, are placed in request buffer n. The requests are filtered through two blocks of arbitration logic prior to being serviced. The upper arbitration block resolves access conflicts between two or more operand requests addressing the same register module. An alignment network follows to direct operand requests to the designated register modules. Each request is accompanied by the three-bit address n of the target operand corridor. A second arbitration block is encountered before the requests reach the register modules. This block resolves priorities between the operand requests and other types of pending register accesses, such as the storing of results generated by the PE's or block transfers of data to or from main memory. For simplicity, the data paths for these other types of access are not shown in Fig. 10. Once the operand requests are allowed to proceed, they are issued in parallel to the register modules and the operands are fetched. The alignment network below the register modules routes each operand to its target operand corridor, and from there to one of the slots 0–7 along the corridor.

Each request issued from an operand request buffer n is accompanied by a three-bit destination tag, in addition to the three-bit operand corridor number mentioned above. When the operand arrives at the intermediate operand buffer at the top of operand corridor n, the tag is used to direct it to one of the slots on the corridor. For example, a tag value of 7 on operand corridor 1 directs the operand to slot 7, the ROPD port of PE 28.

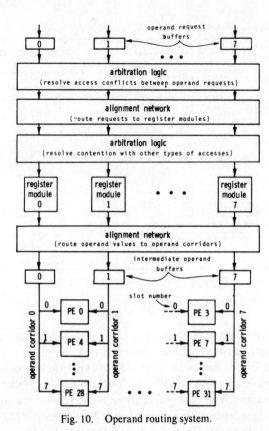

Fig. 10. Operand routing system.

	OPERAND CORRIDORS							
TAG	000	001	010	011	100	101	110	111
001	a_1	b_1	c_1	d_1	a_2	b_2	c_2	d_2
010	a_3	b_3	c_3	d_3	a_4	b_4	c_4	d_4
011	a_5	b_5	c_5	d_5	a_6	b_6	c_6	d_6
100	a_7	b_7	c_7	d_7	a_8	b_8	c_8	d_8
101	a_9	b_9	c_9	d_9	a_{10}	b_{10}	c_{10}	d_{10}
110	a_{11}	b_{11}	c_{11}	d_{11}	a_{12}	b_{12}	c_{12}	d_{12}
111	a_{13}	b_{13}	c_{13}	d_{13}	a_{14}	b_{14}	c_{14}	d_{14}

TABLE III
OPERAND ROUTING FOR A VECTOR TEMPLATE OPERATION

THE ROUTING OF VECTOR OPERANDS

Using the operand routing system described above, the generation of operand requests during vector operations is straightforward. The examples presented in this section illustrate how the operand routing system in Fig. 10 conveniently supports all types of vector operation shown in Fig. 2. The requests issued to the eight operand request buffers during a vector operation of any type are generated by a set of eight address counters programmed to count in increments of 1, 2, 4, or 8.

Consider again the vector template computation

$$x(i) := a(i) * b(i) + c(i) - d(i), \qquad i = 1, 2, \cdots, n$$

and the routing of operands for the composite trees of Fig. 8. Comparing with Fig. 4, the LOPD and ROPD ports of PE's 4–7 are to receive operands $a(1), b(1), \cdots, d(2)$; PE's 8–15 are to receive $a(3), b(3), \cdots, d(6)$; and PE's 16–31 are to receive $a(7), b(7), \cdots, d(14)$. The sequence of operands routed along each operand corridor is shown in Table III, along with the three-bit operand corridor number and three-bit destination tag (target slot number). In the leftmost column, operands $a(1), a(3), a(5), \cdots$ are routed along operand corridor 0. The sequence of addresses placed in operand request buffer 0 is generated by a counter which is initially set to the address of $a(1)$, and incremented by two to generate each new request. The requests for the operands in the other columns are generated in similar fashion. Each operand is tagged individually during routing, but since the operands in each row of Table III have identical destination tags, the tags are shown once to the left of each row. The reader can verify from Fig. 8 and Table II that each operand is routed correctly. Different distributed mappings may be implemented by modifying the sequence of tags. For example, omitting 010 and 011 from the sequence of tags eliminates composite tree $T3$.

A larger template can also be accommodated by the operand routing system. For example, given the vector template computation

$$x(i) := a(i) * b(i) + c(i) * d(i) + e(i) - f(i) + s(i)/d(i),$$
$$i = 1, 2, \cdots, n$$

the template contains seven operators and eight operands, and is similar in shape to the expression tree of Fig. 2(c). Without presenting the details, a set of three composite trees are constructed similar to Fig. 8 and the successive operands routed along each operand corridor are separated by an address increment of one. Using all three composite trees, the destination tag sequence is the same as in Table III. Templates larger than this, however, are not accommodated by the routing system and must be partitioned into two or more smaller templates prior to execution.

The routing of operands for a vector merge operation is similar. Consider the execution of the summation

$$x := \sum_{i=1}^{32} a(i).$$

The expression tree is four times as broad at the base as that shown in Fig. 2(c). Operands $a(1)$ and $a(2)$ are input to PE 16, $a(3)$ and $a(4)$ to PE 17, $\cdots$, and $a(31)$ and $a(32)$ to PE 31. The operand routing for this vector merge operation is shown in Table IV. A uniform address increment of 8 is used to generate the requests for successively-accessed operands in each column.

Table V displays the operand routing for a conventional vector operation executed in SIMD fashion. The example

$$x(i) := a(i) * b(i), \qquad i = 1, 2, \cdots, 32$$

is used. Each PE n, $n = 0, 1, \cdots, 31$, receives the operands $a(n + 1)$ and $b(n + 1)$. A uniform address increment of 4 is used to generate the requests for successively-accessed operands in each column.

For a discussion of techniques for eliminating register access conflicts during parallel operand fetches and methods for dealing with templates containing both vector and scalar operands, the reader is again referred to [20].

TABLE IV
OPERAND ROUTING FOR A VECTOR MERGE OPERATION

	OPERAND CORRIDORS							
TAG	000	001	010	011	100	101	110	111
100	a_1	a_2	a_3	a_4	a_5	a_6	a_7	a_8
101	a_9	a_{10}	a_{11}	a_{12}	a_{13}	a_{14}	a_{15}	a_{16}
110	a_{17}	a_{18}	a_{19}	a_{20}	a_{21}	a_{22}	a_{23}	a_{24}
111	a_{25}	a_{26}	a_{27}	a_{28}	a_{29}	a_{30}	a_{31}	a_{32}

TABLE V
OPERAND ROUTING FOR A CONVENTIONAL VECTOR OPERATION

	OPERAND CORRIDORS							
TAG	000	001	010	011	100	101	110	111
000	a_1	b_1	a_2	b_2	a_3	b_3	a_4	b_4
001	a_5	b_5	a_6	b_6	a_7	b_7	a_8	b_8
010	a_9	b_9	a_{10}	b_{10}	a_{11}	b_{11}	a_{12}	b_{12}
011	a_{13}	b_{13}	a_{14}	b_{14}	a_{15}	b_{15}	a_{16}	b_{16}
100	a_{17}	b_{17}	a_{18}	b_{18}	a_{19}	b_{19}	a_{20}	b_{20}
101	a_{21}	b_{21}	a_{22}	b_{22}	a_{23}	b_{23}	a_{24}	b_{24}
110	a_{25}	b_{25}	a_{26}	b_{26}	a_{27}	b_{27}	a_{28}	b_{28}
111	a_{29}	b_{29}	a_{30}	b_{30}	a_{31}	b_{31}	a_{32}	b_{32}

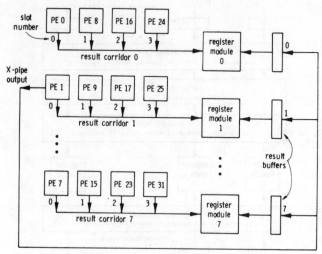

Fig. 11. Result routing system.

RESULT ROUTING SYSTEM

The result corridors and result buffers are shown in Fig. 11.

During X-pipe operations, the FATHER port of PE 1 serves as the output of the X-pipe. As the results emerge one-by-one from the X-pipe, they are placed in the result buffers. When the buffers are full, they are written in parallel to the eight register modules. Each result buffer n, $n = 0, 1, \cdots, 7$, writes directly to module n. This parallel write places (up to) eight new values in eight contiguous locations in the result queue managed by pointers $C0$ and $C1$, and $C0$ is updated. Each series of eight contiguous register addresses is distributed among all eight register modules and no access conflicts occur during this write.

A higher bandwidth system is used for routing results produced during conventional vector operations, for which the PE's are configured as an SIMD array. As indicated on the left side of Fig. 11, eight result corridors are provided for this purpose, and each receives data from four PE's. The RESULT port of PE n is connected to slot number $\lfloor n/8 \rfloor$ of result corridor number $n \bmod 8$, and this result corridor writes directly to register module $n \bmod 8$. The results produced by PE's 0, 8, 16, and 24 are always written to register module 0; the results from PE's 1, 9, 17, and 25 are written to module 1, and so on. During a conventional vector operation, the first parallel write involves the eight results from the slots with address 0 (PE's 0–7), the second write involves the eight results from the slots with address 1 (PE's 8–15), and so on. If PE 0 computes the first element, the result vector will start at an address having the least-significant three bits 000.

SCALAR PROCESSING

The importance of scalar processing power in a vector machine such as the expression processor has been discussed. In this section the mechanisms needed to exploit scalar concurrency while ensuring that the resolution of data dependencies are presented. The binary-tree structure of the X-pipe allows most dependencies–those occurring within individual expressions–to be satisfied without the intervention of an external control mechanism. However, frequently a result generated during the evaluation of one expression is needed later in the evaluation of another expression in the same block of assignment statements. In this case, a logical interlock external to the X-pipe is required to ensure that no attempt is made to read the earlier result from a location into which it has not yet been written.

Operand routing during scalar processing is performed by the same system used to route vector operands, shown in Fig. 10. In the program code generated by the compiler for a scalar task, each operand address is accompanied by two routing parameters: the operand corridor number and destination tag. At run time the central control unit issues each address-tag pair to the request buffer opposite the specified operand corridor.

The distributed mapping of the expression trees generated from a block of assignment statements is similar in principle to that described for vector template operations, despite the fact that the distributed mapping for a scalar task is performed at compile time rather than run time. The composite tree for the scalar task in Fig. 2(d) is shown in Fig. 12. (For tasks containing more expressions, additional composite trees could be constructed.) The root node of the composite tree maps onto PE 1. When the tree of Fig. 12 is executed, the results emerge from the X-pipe in the order x, y, z. Since z is data dependent upon x, the multiplication $c * x$ must be deferred until the value of x has been updated.

Scalar control in the expression processor makes use of the fact that the ordering of tasks in the task stream entering the X-pipe remains unaltered during traversal of the pipeline. The results emerge in an order that can be determined at compile time. (This last statement applies only to individual blocks of

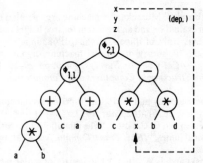

Fig. 12. Distributed mapping for a scalar task.

assignment statements within the program that contain no conditional branches or similar sources of unpredictable behavior [12].) This ordering is preserved by queueing each result as it leaves the X-pipe so that a particular result is identified by its position in the queue. (The tree processor [18] does not preserve this ordering and its results must be tagged and kept track of individually.) This result queue is implemented as a set of contiguous register addresses with hardware support in the form of the pointers $C0$ and $C1$.

Assume that the result queue for the scalar task shown in Fig. 12 is designated to begin at register 0. Pointers $C0$ and $C1$ are initially set to point to registers 0 and 2, respectively. As each result leaves the X-pipe it is queued into the register location pointed to by $C0$, and $C0$ is incremented by one. Hence, results x, y, and z are stored into registers 0, 1, and 2. (For the moment we will ignore the result buffers shown in Fig. 5 and assume that each result is written directly to its result queue location as soon as it leaves the X-pipe.) Some care is required to ensure that register 0, reserved for x, is not read until it has been updated. The logical interlock works by inhibiting reads of the register addresses ($C0$) to ($C1$), referred to as C-space. A request for an operand in C-space is forced to wait. As soon as the value of x is stored into register 0 (pointed to by $C0$), $C0$ is incremented. At this instant register 0 is no longer in C-space and may be read for use in the calculation of z.

This scheme does not interfere with the reading of data from valid locations, and the hardware required for implementation is relatively simple, consisting of a counter and address-comparison logic. In fact, the interlock is somewhat more complex than this due to the fact that data may reside in the result buffers of Fig. 11 for some arbitrary period of time before being written to the result queue in register space. The interlock must therefore be modified so that while a request is being screened through the C-space interlock, a parallel check is made to determine if the requested operand resides in one of the result buffers. If so, the datum can be read directly from the result buffer and routed to the appropriate X-pipe input.

Two further aspects of scalar processing on the expression processor will be mentioned briefly. First, the latest value of a variable x may have to be moved from its result queue location to another designated register in order to avoid subsequent ambiguity with regard to which of several possible result queues contains the latest value of x. Such ambiguity could arise if variable x appears to the left of two or more assignment statements in a program, with one or more of these assignment statements enclosed in an IF-statement. Second, the same result queue locations can be utilized by successive iterations of a FOR-loop, or even nested FOR-loops, provided that during each iteration the C-space interlock is not enforced during reads of data generated during the previous iteration. The contents of the result queue are initialized prior to beginning the first iteration. The details of these techniques are presented in [20].

PROGRAMMABILITY

An important issue that must be addressed in regard to any new multiple-processor architecture is its programmability. Specifically, the compiler for a high-level language should be able to produce efficient machine code. Given a highly concurrent machine, a compiler must do two things. First, it must detect the potential parallelism in the program. Second, it must map detected parallelism onto the structure of the target machine. In regard to the first, the expression processor, while containing a number of individual PE's, is designed to appear to the programmer (or compiler) as a single, large processor having vector and scalar processing capabilities. A great deal of effort has already been expended to develop algorithms and compiler techniques for existing machines having similar capabilities, and much of this body of knowledge can be applied directly to the expression processor. A survey of these techniques is presented by Kuck [12].

Concerning the mappings of detected parallelism onto the machine structure, the expression processor differs in certain respects from previous architectures, particularly in its use of expression tree pipelining. Techniques for constructing expression trees and performing tree-height reduction are well known, however [2], [12]. Without going into detail, the mapping of expression trees onto the X-pipe is felt to be comparable in difficulty with mapping polish notation onto a stack machine.

One interesting problem that merits further investigation is the management of the large register space during subroutine calls. This problem is not unlike that encountered with the CRAY-1, and the techniques developed for this machine [4] can probably be adapted to the expression processor as well.

CONCLUSION

The modularity of the expression processor simplifies the designer's job. If a machine contains n identical modules, then once the first module is designed, all are designed. Modularity reduces the inventory of part numbers and helps decrease the costs of fabrication, testing, and maintenance. This modularity is seen in the identical structure of the PE's (Fig. 9) and in the regularity of the data routing system (Figs. 10 and 11).

Any control function that can be distributed among a number of identical modules is a control function that does not have to be implemented in random logic in a central control unit. The expression processor is largely a data-driven machine. While it does have a central control unit to perform global coordination, this unit initiates requests for register data and issues opcodes to PE's without concern for the subsequent timing of the operations it has set in motion. By giving the central control unit fewer responsibilities, it becomes less complex, less time-critical, and less costly to build.

The expression processor represents a compromise between complexity and versatility. For the sake of hardware simplicity, the PE's operate in only two configurations–as an SIMD array or as an X-pipe–but these configurations are versatile enough to permit the expression processor to exploit the concurrency in all four types of operation shown in Fig. 2. The interconnection topology is regular in structure and the package count is small enough that the machine can be made relatively compact. Compactness helps to alleviate transmission line problems, and this is one reason why high-performance computers are destined to rely increasingly on LSI technology. Most of the interconnection complexity is located in the interface between the PE's and register modules. The portions of this interface requiring the highest package counts are the alignment network for operand data, and the four data I/O buffers contained in each PE module, repeated 32 times within the machine.

During large vector problems the PE's are used with high efficiency. For example, in multiplying an $m \times 32$ matrix and a $32 \times n$ matrix, mn inner products must be calculated, each requiring 32 multiplies and a 32-term summation. The multiplies can be performed as a series of conventional vector operations with the 32 PE's configured as an SIMD array; the summations are pipelined one after the other through a 31-PE X-pipe configuration. Nearly total utilization of PE's is achieved during both phases. This also suggests an effective means for partitioning larger matrices for multiplication.

The cost of processors and memory continues to decrease due to LSI, and lately, VLSI technology. Meanwhile, the cost of random logic and alignment networks remains high due to their incompatibility with LSI. The expression processor represents an attempt to design a highly concurrent machine based upon the hardware economics of the LSI and VLSI eras.

REFERENCES

[1] G. M. Amdahl, "Validity of the single-processor approach to achieving large-scale computing requirements," *Comput. Design*, vol. 6, pp. 39–40, Dec. 1967.
[2] J. L. Baer and D. P. Bovet, "Compilations of arithmetic expressions for parallel computations," in *Proc. IFIP Congress*, Amsterdam, The Netherlands: North-Holland, 1968, pp. 340–346.
[3] G. H. Barnes *et al.*, "The Illiac IV computer," *IEEE Trans. Comput.*, vol. C-17, pp. 746–757, Aug. 1968.
[4] F. Baskett and T. W. Keller, "An evaluation of the Cray-1 computer," in *High Speed Computer and Algorithm Organization*, D. J. Kuck et al., Eds. New York: Academic, 1978, pp. 71–84.
[5] T. C. Chen, "Parallelism, pipelining and computer efficiency," *Comput. Design*, vol. 10, pp. 69–76, Jan. 1971.
[6] Cray Research, Inc., *Cray-1 Computer System: Hardware Reference Manual*, no. 2240004, 1977.
[7] J. B. Dennis, "First version of a data flow procedure language," in *Lecture Notes in Computer Science*, vol. 19. New York: Springer, 1974, pp. 362–376.
[8] M. J. Flynn, "Some computer organizations and their effectiveness," *IEEE Trans. Comput.*, vol. C-21, pp. 948–960, Sept. 1972.
[9] J. Gurd and I. Watson, "Data driven system for high speed parallel computing—Part 2: Hardware design," *Comput. Design*, pp. 97–106, July 1980.
[10] R. M. Keller, "Look-ahead processors," *Comput. Surveys*, vol. 7, pp. 177–195, Dec. 1975.
[11] D. J. Kuck and Y. Muraoka, "A machine organization for arithmetic expression evaluation and an algorithm for tree height reduction," Dep. Comput. Sci., Univ. of Illinois, Urbana, 1968, unpublished.
[12] D. J. Kuck, "A survey of parallel machine organization and programming," *ACM Comput. Surveys*, vol. 9, pp. 29–59, Mar. 1977.
[13] ——, *The Structure of Computers and Computations*. New York: Wiley, 1978.
[14] C. V. Ramamoorthy and H. F. Li, "Pipeline architecture," *Comput. Surveys*, vol. 9, pp. 61–102, Mar. 1977.
[15] E. M. Riseman and C. C. Foster, "The inhibition of potential parallelism by conditional jumps," *IEEE Trans. Comput.*, vol. C-21, pp. 1405–1415, Dec. 1972.
[16] L. Rudsinski and J. Worlton, "The impact of scalar performance on vector and parallel processors," in *High Speed Computer and Algorithm Organization*, D. J. Kuck et al., Ed. New York: Academic, 1978, pp. 451–452.
[17] H. S. Stone, "Parallel processing with the perfect shuffle," *IEEE Trans. Comput.*, vol. C-20, pp. 153–161, Feb. 1971.
[18] L. A. Swanson, "Simulation of a tree processor," M.S. thesis, Dep. Comput. Sci., Univ. of Illinois, Urbana, Jan. 1972, pp. 1–40.
[19] J. R. VanAken and G. L. Zick, "The X-pipe: A pipeline for expression trees," in *Proc. 1978 Int. Conf. on Parallel Processing*, pp. 238–245.
[20] J. R. VanAken, "The megaprocessor: A multiple-processor architecture based upon expression tree pipelining," Ph.D. dissertation, Dep. Elec. Eng., Univ. of Washington, Seattle, May 1979, pp. 1–253.

Jerry R. VanAken (S'75–M'79) was born in 1948 in Los Angeles, CA. He received the B.S.E.E., M.S.E.E., and Ph.D. degrees in 1974, 1975, and 1979, respectively, all from the University of Washington, Seattle.

From 1975 to 1976 he worked as an Applications Programmer for Fluke Manufacturing in Seattle. In 1978 he was an Assistant Lecturer in the Department of Electrical Engineering at the University of Washington. Since 1979 he has been a Computer Systems Engineer at Texas Instruments, Houston, TX. His research interests include multiprocessor architecture and microcomputer systems.

Dr. VanAken is a member of Tau Beta Pi.

Gregory L. Zick (S'69–M'75), was born in Chicago, IL, on August 11, 1948. He received the B.S. degree in electrical engineering from the University of Illinois, Urbana, in 1970 and the M.S. and Ph.D. degrees in biomedical engineering from the University of Michigan, Ann Arbor in 1972 and 1974, respectively.

From 1970 to 1974 he was the recipient of an NIH Traineeship for the study of biomedical engineering. He has done research and served as a Consultant to industry in the areas of medical instrumentation and real-time computer systems. Currently, he is an Associate Professor in the Department of Electrical Engineering at the University of Washington, Seattle. His current research interests are software engineering and new system I/O architectures.

Towards a Family of Languages for
The Design and Implementation of Machine Architectures (*)

Subrata Dasgupta and Marius Olafsson

Department of Computing Science
The University of Alberta
Edmonton, Alberta T6G 2H1 Canada

Abstract

In recent years, increases in complexity of hardware/ firmware systems, and the concern for systems reliability have resulted in growing interest in methodologies and tools for the design, description and verification of computer systems. A vital component of any such design methodology is the language used for representing the design. In the case of particularly complex systems the design process may involve a succession of stages each of which represents the system at a particular level of abstraction. In such situations several languages may be required, each suited to a particular level of abstraction.

We present here, one such *family of languages*, consisting at present of two members, S*A, an architectural description language, and S*, a high level microprogramming language schema. These closely related ("kin") languages may be used collaboratively for the systematic, top-down development of an architecture, down to the microcode level. The resulting descriptions of the architecture provide, in addition, a complete unified document of the multilevel design process.

1. Introduction

Although hardware description languages have been in existence since the 1960's [1,6] their use has not been particularly widespread. This situation appears to be changing rather rapidly at the present time and one may identify several reasons for this:

(a)   As a result of development in LSI and VLSI technologies, processor chips of unprecedented *circuit complexity* are now becoming available. The design, modeling and implementation of such LSI- and VLSI-based processors demand highly structured and rigorous methodologies. [11]

(b)   With the large scale availability of cheap microprocessors, the feasibility of cost-effective distributed systems, networks, and multiprocessors is now widely recognized. Thus computer systems of unprecedented *organizational complexity* are currently being designed and studied. The need for structuring both the design process and the design description seems imperative if we are to produce well behaved, well-structured, understandable and intellectually managable systems.

(c)   In the last decade many microprogrammable systems with writable control stores became available [18] which allow the "user" to alter or redefine the outer architecture of the system through emulation. However, the potential for such user redefinition of architecture has been, in the main, unrealized largely due to the paucity of firmware design tools. [4]

(*) This work was supported by Grant No. A4989 from the Natural Sciences and Engineering Research Council Canada.

In general, then, advances in technology and the resulting (potential or actual) increase in hardware/firmware system complexity demand more disciplined methods for their design. At the same time, concern for systems reliability has brought about an interest in design processes that are, in some sense, conducive to reliable designs. A vital component of any design methodology is the language used for representing the design. In the case of particularly complex systems the design process may involve a succession of stages each of which represents the system at a particular level of abstraction. In such situations several languages may be required, each suited to the particular level of abstraction (similar to pseudo-language/ implementation language levels in software design).

This paper is concerned with the elaboration of the above idea. More specifically, we shall present here a particular *family of languages* (consisting at present of two members) that may be applied to the design and implementation of computer architectures. We envisage the eventual use of this language family within a (possibly semi-automatic) *design environment*.

The advantages that we claim for such a family of languages are many:

(a)   By expressing an architecture in a formal language, the design may be formally verified with respect to an initial set of specifications.

(b)   The different members of the family would be used for the various stages or levels of the design process. By designing the languages so that they are relatively close to one another (i.e. bear "kinship") the transformation from one level to the next becomes relatively painless and mentally managable. Furthermore all stages of the design may be documented within a unified framework, and the high-level modularity of the design should carry over to the actual implementation language.

(c)   Rather than define a single, huge description language capable of representing all levels of the design abstraction, a language family may comprise of two or more closely, compact related languages, one for each of the principal levels of the design process. One thus obtains the distribution of complexity necessary for a structured, top-down design.

The rest of this paper is organized along the following lines: in Section 2 we identify three distinct *levels of architecture*. This helps to provide the framework and motivation for the proposed language family which we call the S* family (denoted by the symbol [S*]). In section 3 the general features of [S*] are introduced. We discuss briefly the *microprogramming language schema* S* (from which the family derives its name). Since S* has been extensively described elsewhere [3,4,8,9] we shall discuss it only in the context of the language family. Section 4 describes the second (and as of now the only other) member of [S*], S*A, a general purpose language for the specification of *architectures* [5,6]. We discuss the main characteristics of S*A, and for the sake of readability we introduce the language here informally using reasonably small examples. A more rigorous and complete definition of S*A is available in [13].

Reprinted from *Proceedings of the 9th Annual Symposium on Computer Architecture*, 1982, pages 158-167. Copyright © 1982 by The Institute of Electrical and Electronics Engineers, Inc.

Our purpose is to demonstrate how the kinship of S*A and S* helps in transforming an *architectural design* into a *microprogrammed implementation* on a given machine. In section 5 we discuss an example of such a transformation.

2. Levels of Architecture

As Simon [19] has pointed out, complex systems are characteristically hierarchic; they are also rich in the variety of levels at which they may be described meaningfully.

In the context of computer systems these observations seem specially valid. Consider for example, the levels of description for a typical hardware system (Fig. 1). At the highest level we may identify the system's outer architecture or *exo-architecture* by which we mean the *logical structure and capabilities of the system* as visible to the machine-language programmer or the compiler writer.

Exo-architecture may be thought of as an abstraction of the *endo-architecture*. The latter includes the *functional capabilities of the physical components*, their *interconnections*, the nature of the *information flow between components*, and the *means whereby this flow is controlled*. The abstraction occurs in the sense that many of the functional components, internal storage elements, data paths and details of the instruction cycle – typical aspects of endo-architecture – are suppressed at the exo-architectural level.

The endo-architecture may itself have been realized by means of microprogramming. Thus, there exists a lower level of machine description, the *micro-architecture* – the architecture of the machine as seen from the perspective of the microprogrammer. Micro-architecture becomes specially relevant in the case of dynamically microprogrammable computers [18].

All three architectural levels are exhibited by the running example we use in this paper: a "language-directed" machine called the QM-C [14] designed to support the compilation and execution of the C programming language [7]. Its exo-architecture consists of the syntax and semantics of an instruction set that is "C-oriented". The machine's endo-architecture characterizes, in addition to the instruction set, the structure of instruction fetch, decode, and execute cycle (including its pipelined nature), the interrupt structure, the functional properties of various units, and the data path structure. Finally, QM-C's endo-architecture was realized by emulating the image machine (as defined by the exo-architecture) on the Nanodata QM-1 [12] at the nanocode level. Thus the micro-architecture in this case, is represented by nano-level architecture for the QM-1 host. Quite naturally, given the nature of the emulation, the QM-C endo-architecture reflects many properties of the QM-1 micro (i.e. nano) architecture.

3. The S* Family

At present [S*] consists of two "kin" languages, S* and S*A. Their characteristics are compared and summarized in the leftmost three columns of Table I. As described in earlier publications [3,4], S* is a microprogramming language schema in that its syntax and semantics are only partially defined. For a given micro-architecture M1 a particular language S*(M1) is obtained by filling in the specification of S* on the basis of the idiosyncratic properties of M1. S* is then said to be *instantiated* into a particular language S*(M1).

The fully defined entities in S* (see Table I) include: a set of primitive and structured data types; constructs for declaring microprogrammable data objects; and a set of composite statements including *parallel* statements. Elementary statements are only partially defined in S* since their form and meaning may vary from one microarchitecture to another. Thus, given two instantiated languages S*(M1) and S*(M2) for two machines M1 and M2 respectively, the only substantial distinction should be at the level of elementary statements. As noted in [4] the idea of such schemata appears to represent the best we can achieve in terms of *machine independent* microprogramming languages.

Referring to Fig. 1, an instantiated language S*(M1) represents a "higher level" specification of the host micro-architecture, M1. Microprograms written in this language would be compiled into object microcode for loading into the control store of M1. However, as Fig. 1 also suggests, such a microprogram provides a means of implementing a target architecture. *In the methodology proposed here, the architect/designer begins with a specification and a design of either the exo- or the endo-architecture in S*A, and constructs a microprogrammed implementation of the architecture on a given host machine M1, using S*(M1).* Because of the kinship between S*A and S* (and therefore between S*A and the instantiated language S*(M1)), transformation from design to implementation can be controlled and made intellectually managable. Furthermore, as previously mentioned, the entire design and implementation can be represented, documented and communicated in a unified way. This is the motivation behind this work.

For the purpose of describing both exo- and endo-architecture, S*A has been developed [5]. While the important features of S*A are described in the next section, we note the following points here:
(a) S*A and S* share almost the same set of data types, data declaration facilities, and execution and control statements (see Table I). However S*A is a fully defined language while S* is a schema that must be instantiated before use.
(b) S* contains constructs that may be used for the specification of clock related operations that are so critical in the microprogramming domain. Since such low-level timing issues are conventionally suppressed or hidden at the endo-/exo-architectural levels these constructs are absent in S*A.

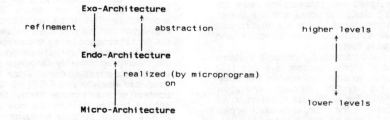

Fig. 1

120

Characteristics	S*A	S*	S*(QM-1)
Primitive data types	bit	bit	bit
Structured data types	seq, array, tuple stack, assoc array	seq, array, tuple stack, assoc array	seq, array, tuple
Synchronizing Primitives	yes	yes	no
Constant Declaratives	yes	yes	yes
Pseudo Variables	no	yes	yes
Channels	yes	no	no
Basic executional statement	assignment statement	assignment statement schema	machine specific assignment statement
Control Statemets	if..fi, while..do, repeat..until, case, call, act, return, exit, goto	if..fi, while..do, repeat..until, case, call, return, goto	if..fi, while..do, repeat..until, case, call, act, return, goto
Parallel Statements	yes	yes	yes
Machine-timing related constructs	None	cocycle..coend, stcycle..stend, region..endreg	cocycle..coend, stcycle..stend, region..endreg
Modularization concepts	system, mechanism, procedure	program, procedure	program, procedure, macro

Table I

(c) In our view, the main purpose of machine "architecture" is that it allows us to abstract from the physical machine structure. We may, in fact, view an architecture as a set of logical information processing systems (e.g. systems for addressing, memory protection, instruction pipelining, etc.) which we call *architectural systems*. We need a means of designing and analysing such systems *in isolation* if necessary. Thus, in the design of S*A, particular attention has been given to the problem of *modularizing* architectural descriptions. The principal constructs in S*A for this purpose are the *system* and the *mechanism*. These are absent in S*.

(d) Finally, we note that the present composition of [S*] constrains us to designing and implementing architectures on microprogrammable machines. The impact of other implementation techniques (e.g. bit–slice logic) are presently being investigated. We surmise that other kin languages may be added to [S*] to reflect the specifics of different implementation styles.

4. Characteristics of S*A
The modularization constructs available in S*A allow an architecture to be described as a collection of entities called *systems*, which may, in turn, be composed of simpler systems. However the most elementary system is composed of one or more basic modules called *mechanisms*.

The purpose of the mechanism construct has been discussed elsewhere [5]. We recapitulate briefly, these objectives:
(a) It facilitates segmentation of design for the purpose of enhancing understandability.
(b) It allows the description of architecture modules that function as critical regions [2].
(c) Mechanisms make possible the specification of architectural *data abstractions*.
(d) They facilitate *information hiding* [16].

4.1 Mechanisms and Systems
Basically, an S*A mechanism consists of a set of *global* and *private state variable declarations*, *public procedures* (that can be invoked from other mechanisms), and *private procedures*.

A procedure in S*A is a description of the data flow sequence that is necessary for realizing a particular hardware function. The underlying *data path structure* implied by a procedure cannot, however, be explicitly described in S*A.

A mechanism is *active* whenever one of its procedures is being "executed". A procedure is considered to be active from the time it begins execution to the time it either returns control or simply terminates. Mechanisms may be activated by *initialization statements* or by calls on its public procedures from (public) procedures inside other mechanisms. Public procedures inside the same mechanism cannot call one another.

Private procedures can only be invoked from procedures inside their own mechanism. Thus, mechanisms can only interact with one another through their respective public procedures.

Mechanisms satisfy the following *mutual exclusion rule*: a public procedure cannot be called when the mechanism is already active. Finally, mechanisms are organized into larger entities called *systems*.

Example 1: The overall composition of the QM-C system is shown as Fig. 2. The system is partitioned into four simpler systems named INSTRUCTION__CYCLE, MEMORY, INTERRUPT and NANO__ARCHITECTURE respectively. INSTRUCTION__CYCLE consists of two mechanisms INSTRUCTION__FETCH and INSTRUCTION__DECODE, and a subsystem named INSTRUCTION__EXEC. The remaining principal subsystems of QM-C are composed of sets of mechanisms. Note that the ordering of the systems or mechanisms within an enclosing system has no significance.

```
sys QM_C:

    sys INSTRUCTION_CYCLE:

        mech INSTRUCTION_FETCH;   ...   endmech;
        mech INSTRUCTION_DECODE;  ...   endmech;

        sys INSTRUCTION_EXEC:

            mech FETCH_OPRND;     ...   endmech;
            mech EXECUTE;         ...   endmech;
            mech DEPOSIT_OPRND;   ...   endmech;

        endsys;

    endsys;

    sys MEMORY:

        mech MAIN_MEM;    ...   endmech;
        mech AUX_MEM;     ...   endmech;

    endsys;

    sys INTERRUPT:

        mech INT_HANDLERS;   ...   endmech;
        mech STATE_CHANGE;   ...   endmech;

    endsys;

    sys NANO_ARCHITECTURE:

        mech EXEC_PRIM;   ...   endmech;
        mech IO_PRIM;     ...   endmech;
        mech MEM_PRIM;    ...   endmech;

    endsys;

endsys;
```

Fig. 2

Example 2: A portion of the INSTRUCTION_CYCLE
system is shown as Fig. 3. It contains a set of data type and
data object declarations relevant to this and subsequent
examples. The INSTRUCTION_FETCH mechanism shown
contains a single global procedure which activates the main
memory mechanism to prefetch an instruction and the
INSTRUCTION_DECODE mechanism to decode the
previously fetched instruction.

4.2 Data Types and Data Objects
Many of the data types available in the S* family appear in
Fig. 3. While references [3,4] discuss these in detail, their
salient characteristics may be reviewed here.

The only primitive data type in [S*] is the **bit**,
consisting of the values 0,1 . Bits may be structured into
ordered *sequences* or into higher ordered structures such
as "arrays", "stacks", tuples" or "associative arrays".

Elements of type **array** are accessed by indexing
the array name with an integer constant or with the name
of some other data object. The **tuple** (which is similar to
the Pascal record) denotes an ordered collection of
components (called *fields*) which may themselves (as Fig. 3
shows) be structured. Thus given the global tuple variable
"local_store" one may refer to its i'th element as
local_store[i], or to the j'th "index" register as
local_store.index[j]. Note that elements of an array may
themselves be structured. Other data types in [S*] (not
shown here) are **stack** and **assoc array**. [3,4,13]

Using the type declaration facility, a structured data
type may be declared and named, e.g. the data type
"Is_register" in Fig. 3. Global (**glovar**) and private (**privar**)
variables may subsequently be defined as instances of such
named types.

An important characteristic of declarations in [S*] is
the facility to specify alternate data structures for
variables. Thus, the **glovar** "local_store" is declared both
as **array** and a **tuple**; the tuple field "local_store.inst_reg"
(say) can be further defined in terms of alternate
structures, as shown in Fig. 6. The advantage this offers is
that the architect/designer may reference the most
appropriate representation as and when required.

The **with** clause in the **array** declaration of
"local_store" specifies *pointers*. Thus, only these particular
pointers (fmod, etc.) may be used as index variables for
referencing elements of local store *as an array*.

4.3 Invocation of Procedures and Mechanisms
Procedures are "quasi-sequential" in that, while they consist
of a sequence of executional statements, some of the
statements may in turn be composed of more elementary
statements executing *concurrently* in a simple, synchronous
fashion. Such synchronous concurrency is represented by
the I__I symbol. A statement S1 I__I S2 specifies that S1
and S2 begin execution together; the next statement in
sequence begins execution only when both S1 and S2 have
terminated. An example of the concurrent statement is
shown in Fig. 3.

As mentioned above, a public procedure may invoke
public procedures in other mechanisms. It can do so by
means of the **call** and **act** statements. Given a mechanism X
containing a (public) procedure a, the statement "call X.a"
appearing in some other procedure b inside mechanism Y,
causes X.a to be activated. The procedure b remains
suspended at the point of call until execution of X.a
terminates, at which point control returns to Y.b. Thus, **call**
is similar to a conventional subroutine call.

The **act** statement also causes the activation of the
named procedure. However, the activating procedure *is not
suspended at that point, but continues on to its next
sequential statement*. Thus, **act** enables one form of
inter-mechanism parallelism to be effected.

4.4 Other Features of [S*]
For reasons of space we are unable to discuss in this
paper all the aspects of [S*] summarized in Table I.
Particular mention must be made, however, of the two
synchronizing operations **sig** and **await** which allows
asynchronous concurrent systems to be described.
Examples of such systems are given in [5]. Also available in
S*A (but not in S*) is the concept of a *channel* which is a
special class of data objects that provides a means of
representing *data communications* between mechanisms.
Informally, the S*A channel may be regarded as an
abstraction of communication paths (e.g. buses), much as
the **line** variable is in the I/O descriptive language SLIDE
[15]. The syntax of the channel declaration is of the form:

        chan 'identifier': 'type'

where 'type' is either the symbol **bit**, a sequence, or a tuple.
In S*A the main distinction between channels and variables

are: (i) variables are abstractions of memory elements while
channels represent communication paths; (ii) variables may
be private or global to a mechanism while channels are
always global; (iii) state transitions in channel bits are
testable conditions; and finally (iv) a channel can only be of
type **bit**, **seq** or, less commonly, **tuple**.

5. The Use of the [S*] Family: An Example
In this section we present an example showing how [S*]
was used to design an emulator for the C oriented machine
QM-C [14] on the Nanodata QM-1 [12]. The emulator is
intended to run at the nano-architectural level of the
QM-1, with the object code of a C program residing in
control store. (Fig. 4)

```
sys INSTRUCTION_CYCLE;

    type     ls_register    = seq [ 17..0 ] bit;
    type     f_register     = seq [ 5..0 ] bit;
    type     bus            = seq [ 17..0 ] bit;
    .
    .
    glovar   main_store_output : bus;
    glovar   local_store : array [ 0..31 ] of ls_register
                           with    fmod, fcod, faod, feod, fair, fail, gspec
                         : tuple
                           general_purpose   : array [ 0..23 ] of ls_register
                           index             : array [ 0..3 ] of ls_register
                                                 with   fmpc
                           general_purpose2  : array [ 0..2 ] of ls_register
                           inst_reg          : ls_register
                           endtup;
    glovar   f_store      : array [ 0..31 ] of f_register
                          : tuple
                            fmix, fmod, fcia, fail, fcid, fair : f_register
                            fcod, faod, fsid, fsod, feid, feod : f_register
                            feia, feoa, fact, fusr, fmpc, fidx : f_register
                            fist, fiph,                        : f_register
                            backup            : array [ 0..11 ] of f_register
                            endtup;
    .
    .
    const   n_pc   : dec(6) 25;
    const   n_sp   : dec(6) 28;
    const   n_fp   : dec(6) 24;
    const   n_eb   : dec(6) 26;
    .
    .
    .
    mech INSTRUCTION_FETCH;
    /*
     *   Context of Activation :   at end of each instruction execution,
     *   and interrupt handlers.
     *
     *   Decoding of a previously fetched instruction (say i) is initated
     *   in parallel with the fetching of the new instruction (i+1).
     *
     */
       proc NEXT;

          act MAIN_MEM.READ_P1 ☐ act INSTRUCTION_DECODE.SELECT_NEXT;

       endproc;
    endmech;
    .

endsys;
```

Fig. 3

Since S* is a schema the development of the emulator requires an instantiation of S* with respect to the "nano-architecture" of the QM-1. Such an instantiation already exists and the resulting language, S*(QM-1), is described in [8,9]. The rightmost column of Table I lists its principal features. (The development of S*(QM-1) was a separate and relatively independent project undertaken to study the feasibility of using S* in the development of a high level microprogramming language for a "real", complex machine such as the QM-1).

The general methodology for the design of the QM-C architecture and its emulator is shown in Fig. 5. At the time of writing, the parser and scanner phases of the compiler have been completed while the code generation and compaction phases are still under development [10,17].

The QM-C exo-architecture is characterized by the machine's instruction set, and the types and representations of data objects. We consider here, a very small part of this architecture, viz, the specification of the CALL instruction; as may be expected, its overall objective is to perform the necessary tasks of saving the contents of the QM-C registers and allocating space on a stack prior to transferring control to the called procedure. In the context of the overall description of the QM-C, CALL is defined as one of the global procedures inside the EXECUTE mechanism which in turn is part of the INSTRUCTION__EXEC system (Fig. 2). The data objects (variables and constants) used by CALL are defined as *synonyms* of previously defined global variables (Fig 3) and are shown in Fig 6.

These declarations illustrate an important facility in [S*], that of declaring synonyms. In designing architectures and microprograms, there frequently arises the need for associating with the same physical object (memory element) either alternate data structures (types), or names or both. In S*A, given a global or private variable declaration, the designer may provide such alternative types and names through the synonym declaration, with the syntax:

syn 'synonym identifier': 'type' = 'object identifier'
where 'synonym identifier' is the new name (synonym), 'type' (which is an optional clause) is the associated data type, and 'object identifier' is the identifier of a previously declared data object (or part thereof), or another synonym. Clearly the type associated with the synonym must be consistent with the type of the object referenced on the right hand side of the declaration. In the most general form, a single synonym declaration may define several, alternate synonyms (with associated types) for the same data object. (Fig. 6)

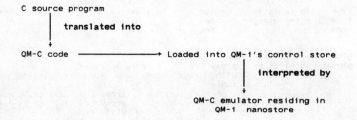

```
C source program
        |
        | translated into
        v
QM-C code  ────────────────────►  Loaded into QM-1's control store
                                                    |
                                                    | interpreted by
                                                    v
                                          QM-C emulator residing in
                                             QM-1  nanostore
```

Fig. 4

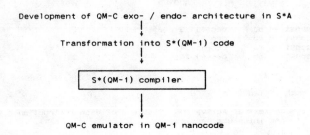

```
Development of QM-C exo- / endo- architecture in S*A
                            |
                            v
            Transformation into S*(QM-1) code
                            |
                            v
                ┌───────────────────────┐
                │   S*(QM-1) compiler    │
                └───────────────────────┘
                            |
                            v
            QM-C emulator in QM-1 nanocode
```

Fig. 5

```
syn  main_output = control_store_output;               /* Main memory output bus  */

syn  reg  : array [ 0..31 ] of ls_register             /* QM-C register file */
            with  dest, source, addr, alt_source,
                  inst_reg.ab.a, inst_reg.ab.b
          : tuple
                        : array [ 0..11 ] of ls_register  /* Not used by QM-C  */
               temp     : array [ 0..3 ] of ls_register   /* Tempraries        */
               var      : array [ 0..7 ] of ls_register   /* Variable reg.     */
               index    : array [ 0..3 ] of ls_register
                          with mm_index_select
                        : tuple
                               fp  :  ls_register        /* Frame pointer     */
                               pc  :  ls_register        /* Program counter   */
                               eb  :  ls_register        /* External base     */
                               ax  :  ls_register        /* Aux mem index     */
                          endtup
               sp       : ls_register                    /* Stack pointer     */
               scr1     : ls_register                    /* Nano scratch reg #1 */
               scr2     : ls_register                    /* Nano scratch reg #2 */
               inst_reg : tuple                          /* Instruction register */
                               opcode : seq [ 6..0 ] bit

                               ab     : tuple
                                           a : seq [ 4..0 ] bit
                                           b : seq [ 5..0 ] bit
                                        endtup
                          endtup
                        : tuple                          /* 6 // 18 interface    */
                               c  :  f_register
                               a  :  f_register
                               b  :  f_register
                          endtup
             endtup = local_store;

syn  mm_addr_select : seq [ 5..0 ] bit      /* Selects main memory address source */
                    = f_store.fcia[ 5..0 ];
syn  mm_index_select: seq [ 1..0 ] bit      /* Selects  address+offset source */
                    = f_store.fmpc[ 1..0 ];
syn  mm_data_select : seq [ 5..0 ] bit      /* Selects mm data source  */
                    = f_store.fcid[ 5..0 ];
```

Fig. 6

124

The scope of a synonym declaration is the mechanism or system containing it. For example, the name "pc" in Fig. 6, can be used freely (as can the identifier "local__store.index[1]") inside INSTRUCTION__CYCLE system.

At the time a CALL instruction is executed, the *stack* (held in QM-C's main memory) is as shown in Fig. 7, and the first word of the procedure being CALLed is a "mask" whose format is given in Fig 8. In addition, the following "pre-conditions" are assumed to hold: (i) fp points to the start of the activation record for the calling procedure; (ii) pc points to the CALL instruction in memory; (iii) eb denotes the base address for the entire C object program; (iv) inst__reg contains the operand of the CALL instruction (it points to a word in memory relative to the base address specified in eb, that holds the aforementioned mask).

Given these conditions, the sequence of actions resulting from the CALL instruction – i.e its *architecture* – is given by the S*A procedure in Fig. 9. This procedure includes calls to three (of eleven) public procedures within the mechanism MAIN__MEM, and to the INSTRUCTION__FETCH mechanism (see Fig. 2).

The next stage is to transform or translate this *architecture description* into a *microprogram*. Because of the kinship between S*A and S* (and therefore between S*A and S*(QM-1)), the microprogram will be very similar to the architectural description with the following important differences:

1. The constructs **mech** and **sys** which are used in S*A for global structuring of architectural descriptions are too "high level" for specifications in microprograms. Furthermore, in S*(QM-1), procedures are functionally distinguished as implementing subroutines, interrupts and instructions. Thus, the transformation from S*A to S*(QM-1) requires reorganizing the original description from the **sys/mech/proc** hierarchy to a set of **proc**'s and **macro**'s in S*(QM-1).

2. Generally speaking, the data objects specified in an S*A description are precisely those that contribute to the particular exo-/endo-architecture being designed. These data objects may be global or local to particular mechanisms. In S* (and its instantiations), data objects are global to all procedures, and represent actual memory resources in the host machine. Thus, in transforming from S*A to S*(QM-1), appropriate mappings of data objects must be performed. This task is greatly facilitated by the fact that the same data types exist in both languages.

   In designing and specifying the QM-C data objects (Fig. 6), advantage was taken of the fact that this architecture would be emulated on the QM-1. Thus, the data object declarations in S*A are almost identical to the (predefined) declarations of variables and constants in S*(QM-1). The mapping, in this case, was trivial.

3. The body of an individual procedure in an S*A description is a specification of control of information flow and transformation in the proposed machine. The procedure in the corresponding S*(QM-1) description is a specification of a *program*, i.e., a symbolic representation of the contents of nanostore whose systematic execution will cause the appropriate gates to be controlled in the QM-1. Thus, the greatest difference between the S*A *description* and the S* *implementation* lies in the operations defined on the data objects as opposed to the data objects themselves. For instance, an individual assignment statement in S*A may have to be mapped into one or more machine-specific statements in S*(QM-1).

Example 3: The statement

reg.index.pc:= reg.index.eb + reg.scr1 + 1

in Fig. 9, is represented in S*(QM-1) by the statement sequence (Fig. 10):

alu__carry__in:= 1;
pc:= eb + scr1;

(In S*(QM-1) fields may be referenced without explicit "pathname" (as, e.g., 'pc' or 'scr1') as long as their names are unique. S*A does not allow this.)

Example 4: The statement

reg.scr1:= reg.inst__reg;

in Fig. 9 is transformed into the statement

scr1:= **passl** inst__reg;

in S*(QM-1). **passl** is a predefined machine-specific operator in S*(QM-1) (but not in S*).

The microprocedure (of class *instruction*) for the QM-C CALL instruction is defined in S*(QM-1) as shown by Fig. 10. The declaratives are almost identical to those defined earlier in Fig. 6 and have, therefore, been omitted.

The principal conceptual differences between Figures 9 and 10 are that: (a) the QM-C's main memory is represented by the QM-1's control store; (b) a **cocycle ... coend** statement [4,9] appears in the microprogram for the purpose of specifying the execution of a machine-specific parallel statement. This particular **cocycle** statement indicates that its three constituent assignment statements will begin and complete execution in parallel in the same *microcycle* (which, in the QM-1, corresponds to a single T step [12]); (c) the **repeat** statement is constructed so as to conform to the semantics of a legal test predicates in S*(QM-1); and finally (d), the mechanism calls in the S*A description are replaced by macro calls in the S*(QM-1) version.

To illustrate further the transformation process from an S*A description to a final S*(QM-1) implementation, and to give some idea on how this process might be partially automated, we discuss in the remainder of this section how the **repeat** statement in Fig. 9 was transformed to its equivalent final from in Fig. 10. These examples were hand-compiled from the S*(QM-1) code to the intermediate language acceptable to the compaction phase [17], as that portion of the compiler is still under development [10].

In Figure 11a the **repeat** statement has been transformed to the S*(QM-1) representation. The call to the PUSH__G procedure has been replaced by a **macro** call and the syntax of the statement adjusted to the S*(QM-1) syntax.

The procedure is then compiled and the semantic analyser would indicate the inability of the compiler to generate code for the **until** condition of the **repeat** statement. The programmers knowledge of the QM-1's nano-architecture enables him to detect the reason; the allocation of a scratch register is needed because the semantics of the **until** condition require a test for zero. The code is thus changed to what is shown in Figure 11b.

At this point the compactor indicates its inability to "pack" the **repeat** statement into one nano-word on the QM-1. (The body of the S*(QM-1) **repeat** statement must translate into one nano-word). The programmer decides to expand the macro in-line, in an attempt to locate unnecessary statements (Figure 11c). The statement

ks:= mm__addr__select

sets up the input/output buses of the secondary QM-1 alu (the *index* alu [12]) to the register pointed to by **mm__addr__select**. As this is an invariant expression in the loop (the stack pointer is decremented) it may be replaced by

ks:= c__sp

a constant assignment, not executed in the loop body (set up before execution).

The compactor now generates a one nano-word implementation of the **repeat** statement capable of executing in seven T-periods [12] or 0.6 micro-seconds.

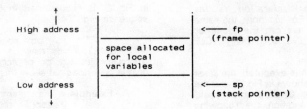

```
High address              |   |  <——— fp
                          |   |      (frame pointer)
                          |———|
                          |space allocated|
                          |for local      |
                          |variables      |
                          |———|
Low address               |   |  <——— sp
                          |   |      (stack pointer)
```

Fig. 7

```
17        12 11                0
 ┌──────────┬──────────────────┐
 │ Reg no.  │  Size            │
 └──────────┴──────────────────┘

 No. of the    Size of the stack
 lowest reg.   space for local
 this subr.    variables of the
 uses          called procedure
```

Fig. 8

```
proc CALL;

      do    reg.index.pc := reg.index.pc+1      /* Point pc to next instruction */
      □     reg.scr1 := reg.inst_reg            /* Save offset from in inst.    */
      □     mm_index_select := n_eb
      od;

      call MAIN_MEM.READ_I_L;                   /* Read mask word onto bus      */
      reg.inst_reg := main_output;              /* Prepare to decode            */

      do    mm_addr_select := n_sp              /* Prepare to save reg's        */
      □     mm_data_select := n_pc+1
      od;

      repeat                                    /* Save registers on stack,     */
            mm_data_select := mm_data_select -1; /* iteratively until the register*/
            call MAIN_MEM.PUSH_G;               /* specified in inst_reg.c has  */
      until mm_data_select = reg.inst_reg.c;    /* been saved                   */

      reg.index.fp := reg.sp;                   /* Set new frame pointer        */
      reg.sp := reg.sp - reg.inst_reg.ab;       /* Allocate for automatics      */
      reg.index.pc := reg.index.eb + reg.scr1 + 1; /* First instruction of proc */

      mm_index_select := n_pc;
      call MAIN_MEM.READ_I;                     /* Read onto bus for decode     */

      act INSTRUCTION_FETCH.NEXT;               /* Activate instr. pipeline     */
endproc;
```

Fig. 9 The CALL instruction as described in S∗A.

```
proc p_call (instruction, mnemonic=call)
    /*
     * Macros  :  INC_PROG_COUNT          - Add one to program counter
     *            MAIN_MEM_READ_I_L       - Read memory (base plus long offset)
     *            MAIN_MEM_READ_I         - Read memry address in index register
     *            MAIN_MEM_PUSH_G         - Push onto stack
     *            INSRUCTION_FETCH_NEXT   - Prefetch (program counter not updated)
     *
     */

    INC_PROG_COUNT;                            /* Point pc to next instruction */
    scr1 := pass1 inst_reg;                    /* Save offset                  */

    cocycle
        mm_index_select := c_eb                /* Read from external base      */
      □ mm_addr_select := c_sp                 /* Save on stack                */
      □ mm_data_select := c_pc_p1              /* PC first saved (c_pc+1)       */
    coend;

    MAIN_MEM_READ_I_L;                         /* Read mask word               */
    inst_reg := main_output;                   /* Prepare to decode            */

    repeat                                     /* Save registers               */
      mm_data_select := mm_data_select -1;
      main_memory[mm_addr_so.reg[mm_addr_select]] := mm_data_so[mm_data_select];
      ks := c_sp;
      reg[ gspec.ks ] := xdecl reg[ gspec.ks];
      f_scr1 := mm_data_select - reg.inst_reg.c
    until (f_scr1 == 0);

    inst_reg.c := 0;                           /* Prep. to allocate automatics */
    fp := pass1 sp;                            /* Set new frame pointer        */
    sp := sp - inst_reg;                       /* Allocate for automatics      */

    alu_carry_in := 1;                         /* Add one to following expr.   */
    pc := eb + scr1;                           /* First instruction of proc    */

    mm_index_select := c_pc;
    MAIN_MEM_READ_I;                           /* Read onto bus for decode     */

    INSTRUCTION_FETCH_NEXT;                    /* Activate instr. pipeline     */

endproc
```

Fig.10 The CALL instruction as implemented in S*(QM-1).

```
repeat                                                              11a
    mm_data_select := mm_data_select -1;
    MAIN_MEM_PUSH_G;
until( mm_data_select == reg.inst_reg.c );
```
```
repeat                                                              11b
    mm_data_select := mm_data_select -1;
    MAIN_MEM_PUSH_G;
    f_scr1 := mm_data_select - reg.inst_reg.c
until( f_scr1 == 0 );
```
```
repeat                                                              11c
  mm_data_select := mm_data_select -1;

  | main_memory[mm_addr_so.reg[mm_addr_select]] := mm_data_so[mm_data_select];
  | ks := mm_addr_select;
  | reg[ gspec.ks ] := xdecl reg[ gspec.ks ];

  f_scr1 := mm_data_select - reg.inst_reg.c
until (f_scr1 == 0);
```
```
repeat                                                              11d
    mm_data_select := mm_data_select -1;
    main_memory[mm_addr_so.reg[mm_addr_select]] := mm_data_so[mm_data_select];

    ks := c_sp;
    reg[ gspec.ks ] := xdecl reg[ gspec.ks ];

    f_scr1 := mm_data_select - reg.inst_reg.c
until (f_scr1 == 0);
```

Fig. 11

127

Even if programming in S*(QM−1) requires a detailed knowledge of the QM−1's architecture, expressing an algorithm using this language is orders of magnitude easier than using a low level *nano-assembler* [12]. The predefined declarations of the QM−1 resources are a fixed part of the S*(QM−1) program and provide an excellent abstract representation of the machine; in fact most of the relevant architectural features of the QM−1 can be deduced from the semantics of the language together with these abstract declarations.

It should be noted, that programming in S*(QM−1) will probably always be an iterative process (similar to what was outlined above). The programmer first represents his algorithm at the highest possible level (very close to the S*A description) within the S*(QM−1) framework. Compiling (especially compacting) the code will reveal that certain portions of the code must be represented at a lower level, closer to the actual machine representation, in order to either achieve correct code, or to improve the quality of the generated machine representation.

6. Conclusions

We have presented here, the outline of a language-based methodology for the description, design, and implementation of computer architectures. The basic idea is the use of a family of closely related, but individually compact, languages to specify an architecture at each major stage of design and implementation. At the present time, the family described here consists of S*A, a language for describing exo-architectures and endo-architectures; and S*, a microprogramming language schema which, for a given microprogrammable host M (say) is instantiated into a specific language S*(M).

S*A and S* may be used collaboratively for the systematic "top-down" design of an architecture until an emulator (interpreter) for the architecture is obtained. The resulting descriptions of architecture and emulator provide, in addition, a complete unified document of the multilevel design process. We have used this technique to describe and design (in S*A), the architecture of the QM-C, a C oriented "abstract" machine, and to write a complete QM−1 emulator for this machine in S*(QM−1) [14].

As noted previously, the present composition of [S*] limits its application to the implementation of architectures on microprogrammable machines. We are presently studying the impact of other implementation techniques, notably bit slice logic, on the structure and composition of [S*]. We are also investigating the incorporation of formal program verification techniques into the [S*] based design methodology, so as to facilitate *architecture design verification*.

Acknowledgements: We thank Richard Heuft, Alynn Klassen, Douglas Rideout and Steven Sutphen for their comments on an earlier version of this paper.

References

[1] Barbacci, M. R., *"A Comparison of Register Transfer Languages for Describing Computers and Digital Systems"*, **IEEE Trans. Comput.**, C-24, 2, Feb 1975 137−150.

[2] Brinch-Hansen, P., **"The Architecture of Concurrent Programs"**, Prentice Hall, N.J., 1977.

[3] Dasgupta, S., *"Towards a Microprogramming Language Schema"*, **Proc. 11th Annual Workshop on Microprogramming** (MICRO 11), IEEE, N.Y., Nov. 1978, 144−153.

[4] Dasgupta, S. *"Some Aspects of High Level Microprogramming"*, **ACM Computing Surveys**, 12(3), Sept. 1980, 295−324.

[5] Dasgupta, S. *"S*A: A Language for Describing Computer Architectures"*, **Proc. 5th Intl. Conf. on Computer Hardware Description Languages, and their Applications**, North Holland, Amsterdam, Sept. 1981.

[6] Dasgupta, S. *"Computer Design and Description Languages"*, in, M.C. Yovits (ed), **Advances in Computers**, Vol. 21, Academic Press, N.Y., 1982.

[7] Kernigan, B.W., D. Ritchie, **The C Programming Language**, Prentice-Hall, N.J., 1978.

[8] Klassen, A., S. Dasgupta *"The Syntax and Semantics of the High Level Microprogramming Language S*(QM-1)"*, Tech. Rept. TR81-3, Dept. of Computing Science, Univ. of Alberta, Edmonton, Canada, June 1981.

[9] Klassen, A., S. Dasgupta *"S*(QM-1): An Instantiation of the High-Level Microprogramming Language Schema S* for the Nanodata QM-1"*, **Proc. 14th Annual Workshop on Microprogramming**, (MICRO 14), IEEE, N.Y., Nov 1981, 124−130.

[10] Klassen, A. *"S*(QM-1): An Experimental Evaluation of the High Level Microprogramming Language Schema S* using the Nanodata QM-1"*, **M.Sc. Thesis**, Univ. of Alberta, 1981.

[11] Mead, C.A., L. Conway, **An Introduction to VLSI Systems**, Addison-Wesley, M.A., 1980.

[12] Nanodata Corporation, **The QM-1 Hardware Users Manual**, (Revised Edition), N.Y., 1979.

[13] Olafsson, M., S. Dasgupta, *"Syntax and Semantics of the Architectural Description Language S*A"*, Tech. Rept. TR81-6, Dept. of Computing Science, Univ. of Alberta, Edmonton, Canada, June 1981.

[14] Olafsson, M., *"The QM-C: A Microprogrammed C-oriented Instruction-Set Architecture for the Nanodata QM-1"* **M.Sc. Thesis**, Univ. of Alberta, 1981.

[15] Parker, A.C., J.J. Wallace, *"SLIDE: An I/O Hardware Descriptive Language"*, **Proc. 1979 Intl. Symp. on Computer Hardware Description Languages and their Applications**, Palo Alto, Ca, Oct. 1979.

[16] Parnas, D.L., *"A Technique for Software Module Specification with Examples"*, **Comm. ACM**, 15(5), May 1972, 330−336.

[17] Rideout, D.J., *"An Application of a Microcode Compaction Technique to the Nanodata QM-1 Nano-Architecture"*, **M.Sc. Thesis**, Univ. of Alberta, 1981.

[18] Salisbury, A.B., **Microprogrammable Computer Architectures**, Elsevier, N.Y., 1975.

[19] Simon, H.A., **Sciences of the Artificial**, MIT Press, Cambridge, MA., 1968.

Chapter 5: Multiprocessor Interconnection Schemes

In a multiple processor system, it is important to appropriately interconnect various functional modules. The performance of such systems largely depends on the suitability and effectiveness of the networks; in fact, they are considered to be the heart of such systems.

The need for these networks was first observed in the communication area[1], and attempts are still being made[2-4] to resolve some of the problems associated with the Benes network.

Advances in semiconductor technology encouraged the use of multiple processor systems, resulting in the introduction of various schemes for providing a connection between functional modules. One of the perfect shuffle type of networks[5-7] was the Omega network[8], still considered to be a standard model and a network for all future comparisons. Description of a general network in the form of graphs is introduced[10], and a data-manipulating network is described by Feng[11].

A topology that describes rules for a class of networks and which shows the topological equivalence of various networks has been developed. Siegel and McMillan[13] offer a versatile cube network that possesses several important characteristics. Barnes and Lundstrom[14] provide design and validation of a network, Wu[15] reviews the major research areas of interconnection networks while Feng[16] offers an excellent survey of existing dynamic and static schemes. An actual design of a switching network for telephony and communication is given by Cotton et al.[17]

Most of the networks mentioned earlier use a 2×2 switch or some modular switches. Others include link-based network design[18-20]. There are several parameters that can indicate the effectiveness of a network. One frequently referred to is the number of simultaneous connections that can be provided by the blocking-type network. Performance and interference analysis are shown[21-27], while the resource sharing issues have been covered in[28-30]. Various models and graph theoretic techniques[31-36] are used to compare the performance of the network while VLSI considerations are covered. Performance of a network is also indicated by the ability of the network to provide a permutation (or state whether a desirable routing is possible) in a conflict-free manner. Many of these issues are addressed[41-51]. These networks can support packet switching if buffers are provided at all or for a few of the intermediate stages. Performance of these networks in such an environment is addressed in[52-60].

Advances in VLSI technology encouraged the implementation of complex logic circuits, and testing of these circuits is becoming more and more complex. But networks are generally modular in nature, and testing of multistage networks has been shown to be relatively simple[61-64]. The demand for improved fault tolerance and the decrease in logic circuit cost encourage researchers to look into fault tolerant and redundant networks[65-77]. Redundancy is usually provided either by adding one or more extra stages or by making the switch more complex than was necessary for a given network configuration. In most cases, for simplicity of analysis, simple stuck-at type permanent faults are considered. These faults could be at the control lines or at the input or output terminals of one or more switches. The question of accessibility in the presence of single and multiple faults is addressed in[78-81]. It is also important to compare single-stage and multistage networks, and it is shown that satisfactory performance for a network with fewer stages could be achieved if it is designed following some specific guidelines[79-81].

Besides multistage networks, the use of multiple buses in multiprocessor systems is advocated because they provide adequate bandwidth at a reasonable cost. Bus contention and memory access problems for such systems have been covered in[82-88].

Three papers are included in Chapter 5 to cover various issues of multi-stage networks and multiple-bus schemes.

References

1   V.E. Benes, *Mathematical Theory of Connecting Networks and Telephone Traffic*, Academic Press, Orlando, Fl., 1965.

2   D. Nassimi and S. Sahni, "A self-Routing Benes Network and Parallel Permutation Algorithms," *IEEE Trans. Computers,* Vol. C-30, No. 5, May 1981, pp. 332-340.

3   S.C. Kothari and S. Lakshmivarahan, "A Condition Known to Be Sufficient for Rearrangeability of the Benes Class of Interconnection Networks with 2×2 Switches Is Also Necessary," *Proc. 1983 Int'l. Conf. Parallel Processing*, IEEE Computer Society, Washington, D.C., 1983, pp. 76-78.

4   K.Y. Lee, "A New Benes Network Control Algorithm," *Proc. 1984 Int'l. Conf. Parallel Processing*, IEEE Computer Society, Washington, D.C., 1984, pp. 51-58.

5   H.S. Stone, "Parallel Processing with the Perfect Shuffle," *IEEE Trans. Computers,* Vol. C-20, No. 2, Feb. 1971, pp. 153-161.

6   T. Lang and H.S. Stone, "A Shuffle-Exchange Network with Simplified Control," *IEEE Trans. Computers,* Vol. C-25, No. 1, Jan. 1976, pp. 55-56.

7   D. Steinberg, "Invariant Properties of the Shuffle-Exchange Network with Simplified Cost-Effective Version of the Omega Network," *IEEE Trans. Computers,* Vol. C-32, No. 5, May 1983, pp. 444-451.

8 D.H. Lawrie, "Access and Alignment of Data in an Array Processor," *IEEE Trans. Computers*, Vol. C-24, No. 12, Dec. 1975, pp. 1145-1155.

9 P.Y. Chen, D.H. Lawrie, D.A. Padua, and P.C. Yew, "Interconnection Networks Using Shuffles," *IEEE Trans. Computers*, Vol. C-30, No.12, Dec. 1981, pp. 55-64.

10 R. Goke and G.J. Lipovski, "Banyan Networks for Partitioning on Multiprocessor Systems," *Proc. 1st Ann. Symp. Computer Architecture*, IEEE Computer Society, Washington, D.C., 1973, pp. 21-30.

11 T.Y. Feng, "Data Manipulation Functions in Parallel Processors and Their Implementations," *IEEE Trans. Computers*, Vol. C-23, No. 3, March 1974, pp. 309-318.

12 C.L. Wu and T.Y. Feng, "On a Class of Multistage Interconnection Networks," *IEEE Trans. Computers*, Vol. C-29, No. 8, Aug. 1980, pp. 694-702.

13 H.J. Siegel and R.J. McMillan, "The Multistage Cube: A Versatile Interconnection Network," *Computer*, Vol. 14, No. 12, Dec. 1981, pp. 458-473.

14 G.H. Barnes and S.F. Lundstrom, "Design and Validation of a Connection Network for Many-Processor Systems," *Computer*, Vol. 14, No. 12, Dec. 1981, pp. 31-41.

15 C.-L. Wu, "Interconnection Networks," *Computer*, Vol. 14, No. 12, Dec. 1981, pp. 8-9.

16 T.Y. Feng, "A Survey of Interconnection Networks," *Computer*, Vol. 14, No. 12, Dec. 1981, pp. 12-27.

17 J.M. Cotton, K. Giesken, A. Lawrence, and D.C. Upp, "ITT 1240 Digital Exchange: Digital Switching Networks," *Electrical Communication, ITT Tech. Journal Quarterly*, Vol. 56, No. 2/3, 1981, pp. 148-160.

18 H.J. Siegel and R.J. McMillen, "Using the Augmented Data Manipulator Network in PASM," *Computer*, Vol. 14, No. 2, Feb. 1981, pp. 25-33.

19 S. Nakamura and G.M. Masson, "Lower Bounds on Crosspoints in Concentrator," *IEEE Trans. Computers*, Vol. C-31, No. 12, Dec. 1982, pp. 1173-1179.

20 C.D. Thompson, "Generalized Connection Networks for Parallel Processor Intercommunication," *IEEE Trans. Computers*, Vol. C-27, No. 12, Dec. 1978, pp. 1119-1126.

21 J.H. Patel, "Performance of Processor-Memory Interconnection for Multiprocessors," *IEEE Trans. Computers*, Vol. C-30, No. 10, Oct. 1981, pp. 771-780.

22 S. Thanawastein and V.P. Nelson, "Interference Analysis of Shuffle/Exchange Network," *IEEE Trans. Computers*, Vol. C-30, No. 4, April 1981, pp. 545-556.

23 L.N. Bhuyan and D.P. Agrawal, "Design and Performance of a General Class of Interconnection Networks," *Proc. 1982 Int'l. Conf. Parallel Processing*, IEEE Computer Society, Washington, D.C., Aug. 1982, pp. 2-9; see also *IEEE Trans. Computers*, Vol. C-32, No. 12, Dec. 1983, pp. 1081-1090.

24 A. Ranade, "Interconnection Networks for Parallel Memory Organizations for Array Processing," *Proc. 1985 Int'l. Conf. Parallel Processing*, IEEE Computer Society, Washington, D.C., 1985, pp. 41-47.

25 D. DeGroot, "Expanding and Contracting SW—Banyan Networks," *Proc. 1983 Int'l. Conf. Parallel Processing*, IEEE Computer Society, Washington, D.C., 1983, pp. 19-24.

26 L.N. Bhuyan and C.W. Lee, "On Interference Analysis of Interconnection Networks," *Proc. 1983 Int'l. Conf. Parallel Processing*, IEEE Computer Society, Washington, D.C., 1983, pp. 2-9.

27 C.P. Kruskal and M. Snir, "The Importance of Being Square," *Proc. 11th Ann. Int'l. Symp. Computer Architecture*, IEEE Computer Society, Washington, D.C., 1984, pp. 91-98.

28 B.W. Wah, "A Comparative Study of Distributive Resource Sharing on Multiprocessors," *IEEE Trans. Computers*, Vol. C-33, No. 8, Aug. 1984, pp. 700-711.

29 M. Lee and C.L. Wu, "Performance of Circuit Switching Baseline Interconnection Networks," *Proc. 11th Ann. Int'l. Symp. Computer Architecture*, IEEE Computer Society, Washington, D.C., 1984, pp. 82-90.

30 J.H. Mirza, "Performance of Self-Routing Shuffle-Exchange Interconnection Network in SIMD Processors," *Proc. 1982 Int'l. Conf. Parallel Processing*, IEEE Computer Society, Washington, D.C., 1982, pp. 13-15.

31 H.J. Siegel, "A Model of SIMD Machines and a Comparison of Various Interconnection Networks," *IEEE Trans. Computers*, Vol. C-28, No. 12, Dec. 1979, pp. 907-917.

32 D.K. Pradhan and K.L. Kodandapani, "A Uniform Representation of Single and Multistage Interconnection Networks Used in SIMD Machines," *IEEE Trans. Computers*, Vol. C-29, No. 9, Sept. 1980, pp. 777-790.

33 C.L. Wu and T.Y. Feng, "Universality of the Shuffle Exchange Network," *IEEE Trans. Computers*, Vol. C-30, No. 5, May 1981, pp. 324-331.

34 D.P. Agrawal, "Graph Theoretic Analysis and Design of Multistage Networks," *IEEE Trans. Computers*, Vol. C-32, No. 7, July 1983, pp. 637-648.

35 H.J. Siegel, "The Theory Underlying the Partitioning of Permutation Networks," *IEEE Trans. Computer*, Vol. C-29, No. 9, Sept. 1980, pp. 791-800.

36 R.J. McMillan, G.B. Adams III, and H.J. Siegel, "Performance and Implementation of 4×4 Switching Modes in an Interconnection Network for PASM," *Proc. 1981 Int'l. Conf. Parallel Processing*, IEEE Computer Society, Washington, D.C., 1981, pp. 229-233.

37 D. Sanjay, M.A. Franklin, and D.F. Wann, "Timing Control of VLSI Based N log n and Crossbar Net-

works," *Proc. 1983 Int'l. Conf. Parallel Processing,* IEEE Computer Society, Washington, D.C., 1983, pp. 59-64.

38 M. Franklin, "VLSI Performance Comparison of Banyan and Crossbar Communications Networks," *IEEE Trans. Computers,* Vol. C-30, No. 4, April 1981, pp. 283-291.

39 D. Steinberg and M. Rodeh, "A Lay Out for the Shuffle-Exchange Network with 0 ($N^2 Log^{3/2}$ N) Area (Corresp.), *IEEE Trans. Computers,* Vol. C-30, No. 12, Dec. 1981, pp. 977-982.

40 L. Bhuyan and D.P. Agrawal, "VLSI Performance of Multistage Interconnection Networks Using 4 × 4 Switches," *Proc. 3rd Int'l. Conf. Distributed Computing Systems,* IEEE Computer Society, Washington, D.C., 1982, pp. 606-613.

41 R.R. Seban and H.J. Siegel, "Performing the Shuffle with the PM 2I and ILLIAC SIMD Interconnection Network," *Proc. 1983 Int'l. Conf. Parallel Processing,* IEEE Computer Society, Washington, D.C., 1983, pp. 117-125.

42 W.R. Quan, Z. Xiang, and G.Q. Shi, "SP2I Interconnection Network and Extension of the Iteration Method of Automatic Vector-Routing," *Proc. 1982 Int'l. Conf. Parallel Processing,* IEEE Computer Society, Washington, D.C., pp 16-25.

43 D.P. Agrawal, T.Y. Feng, and C.L. Wu, "A Survey of Communication Process Systems," *Proc. COMPSAC,* IEEE Computer Society, Washington, D.C., 1978, pp. 668-673.

44 A. Gottlieb and J.T. Schwartz, "Networks and Algorithms for Very Large-Scale Parallel Computation," *Computer,* Vol. 15, No. 1, Jan. 1982, pp. 27-36.

45 L.M. Goldschlager, "A Universal Interconnection Pattern for Parallel Computers," *Journal of the ACM,* Vol. 29, No. 3, July 1982, pp. 1073-1086.

46 P.M. Flanders, "A Unified Approach to a Class of Data Movements on an Array Processor," *IEEE Trans. Computers,* Vol. C-31, No. 9, Sept. 1982, pp. 809-819,

47 U. Banerjee, D. Gajski, and D. Kuck, "Accessing Sparse Arrays in Parallel Memories," *Journal of VLSI and Computer Systems,* Vol. 1, No. 1, Spring 1983, pp. 69-99.

48 M. Lee et al., "Network Facility for a Reconfigurable Computer Architecture," *Proc. 1985 Int'l. Conf. Distributed Computing Systems,* IEEE Computer Society, Washington, D.C., 1985, pp. 264-271.

49 H. Li, C.C. Wang, and M. Lavin, "Structured Process: A New Language Attribute for Better Interconnection of Parallel Architecture and Algorithm," *Proc. 1985 Int'l. Conf. Parallel Processing,* IEEE Computer Society, Washington, D.C., 1985, pp. 247-254.

50 L.N. Bhuyan and D.P. Agrawal, "Performance Analysis of FFT Algorithms on Multiprocessor System," *IEEE Trans. Software Engineering,* Vol. SE-9, No. 4, July 1983, pp. 512-521.

51 C.L. Wu, W. Lin, and M.C. Lin, "Distributed Circuit Switching Starnet," *Proc. 1982 Int'l. Conf. Parallel Processing,* IEEE Computer Society, Washington, D.C., 1982, pp. 26-33.

52 A.R. Tripathi and G.J. Lipovski, "Packet Switching in Banyan Networks," *Proc. 6th Ann. Symp. Computer Architecture,* IEEE Computer Society, Washington, D.C., 1979, pp. 160-167.

53 D.M. Dias and J.R. Jump, "Analysis and Simulation of Buffered Delta Network," *IEEE Trans. Computers,* Vol. C-30, No. 8, Aug. 1981, pp. 273-282.

54 D.M. Dias and J.R. Jump, "Packet Switching Interconnection Networks for Modular Systems," *Computer,* Vol. 14, No. 12, Dec. 1981, pp. 43-53.

55 M. Kumar and J.R. Jump, "Generalized Delta Networks," *Proc. 1983 Int'l. Conf. Parallel Processing,* IEEE Computer Society, Washington, D.C., 1983, pp. 10-18.

56 M. Kumar, D.M. Dias and J.R. Jump, "Switching Strategies in a Class of Packet Switching Networks," *Proc. 10th Ann. Int'l. Symp. Computer Architecture,* IEEE Computer Society, Washington, D.C., 1983, pp. 284-300.

57 C.Y. Chin and K. Hwang, "Packet Switching Networks for Multiprocessors and Data Flow Computers," *IEEE Trans. Computers,* Vol. C-33, No. 11, Nov. 1984, pp. 991-1003.

58 M. Yasrebi, S. Deshpande, and J.C. Browne, "A Comparison of Circuit Switching and Packet Switching for Data Transfer in Two Simple Image Processing Algorithms," *Proc. 1983 Int'l. Conf. Parallel Processing,* IEEE Computer Society, Washington, D.C., 1983, pp. 25-28.

59 C.P. Kruskal, M. Snir, and A. Weiss, "On the Distribution of Design in Buffered Multistage Interconnection Networks for Uniform and Nonuniform Traffic," *Proc. 1984 Int'l. Conf. Parallel Processing,* IEEE Computer Society, Washington, D.C., 1984, pp. 215-219.

60 B.D. Rathi et al., "Specification and Implementation of an Integrated Packet Communication Facility for an Array Computer," *Proc. 1983 Int'l. Conf. Parallel Processing,* IEEE Computer Society, Washington, D.C., 1983, pp. 51-58.

61 D.C.H. Lee and J. Paulshen, "Easily-Testable (N,K) Shuffle/Exchange Networks," *Proc. 1983 Int'l. Conf. Parallel Processing,* IEEE Computer Society, Washington, D.C., 1983, pp. 65-70.

62 D.P. Agrawal, "Testing and Fault Tolerance of Multistage Interconnection Networks," *Computer,* Vol. 15, No. 4, April 1982, pp. 41-53.

63 T.Y. Feng and C.L. Wu, "Fault-Diagnosis for a Class of Multistage Interconnection Networks," *IEEE Trans. Computers,* Vol. C-30, No. 10, Oct. 1981, pp. 743-758.

64 C.S. Raghavendra and D.S. Parker, "Reliability Analysis of an Interconnection Network," *Proc. 4th Int'l.*

Conf. Distributed Computing Systems, IEEE Computer Society, Washington, D.C., 1984, pp. 461-471.

65 G.B. Adams and H.J. Siegel, "The Extra Stage Cube: A Fault-Tolerant Interconnection Network for Supersystems," *IEEE Trans. Computers*, Vol. C-32, No. 5, May 1982, pp. 443-454.

66 R.Q Wang, X. Zhang, and Q.S. Gao, "SP2I Interconnection Network and Extension of the Iteration Method of Automatic Vector-Routing," *Proc. 1982 Int'l. Conf. Parallel Processing*, IEEE Computer Society, Washington, D.C., 1982, pp. 1625.

67 M. Kumar and J.R. Jump, "Generalized Delta Networks," *Proc. 1983 Int'l. Conf. Parallel Processing*, IEEE Computer Society, Washington, D.C., 1983, pp. 10-18.

68 D.S. Parker and C.S. Raghavendra, "The Gamma Network," *IEEE Trans. Computers*, Vol. C-33, No. 4, April 1984, pp. 367-373.

69 S.M. Reddy and V.P. Kumar, "On Fault-Tolerant Multistage Interconnection Networks," *Proc. 1984 Int'l. Conf. Parallel Processing*, IEEE Computer Society, Washington, D.C., 1984, pp. 155-164.

70 G.B. Adams and H.J. Siegel, "Modifications to Improve the Fault-Tolerance of the Extra Stage Cube Interconnection Network," *Proc. 1984 Int'l. Conf. Parallel Processing*, IEEE Computer Society, Washington, D.C., 984, pp. 169-173.

71 D.M. Dias and J.R. Jump, "Augmented and Pruned N Log N Multistage Networks: Topology and Performance," *Proc. 1982 Int'l. Conf. Parallel Processing*, IEEE Computer Society, Washington, D.C., 1982, pp. 10-12.

72 K. Padmanabhan and D.H. Lawrie, "Fault Tolerance Schemes in Shuffle-Exchange Type Interconnection Networks," *Proc. 1983 Int'l. Conf. Parallel Processing*, IEEE Computer Society, Washington, D.C., 1983, pp. 71-75.

73 A. Varma and C.S. Raghavendra, "Realization of Permutations on Generalized INDRA networks," *Proc. 1985 Int'l. Conf. Parallel Processing*, IEEE Computer Society, Washington, D.C., 1985, pp. 328-333.

74 C.Y. Chin and K. Hwang, "Connection Principles for Multipath Packet Switching Networks," *Proc. 11th Ann. Int'l. Symp. Computer Architecture*, IEEE Computer Society, Washington, D.C., 1984, pp. 99-108.

75 S.M. Reddy and V.P. Kumar, "On Multipath Multistage Interconnection Networks," *Proc. 5th Int'l. Conf. Distributed Computing Systems*, IEEE Computer Society, Washington D.C., 1985, pp. 210-217.

76 C.Y. Chin and K. Hwang, "Multipath Packet Switching Networks for Multiprocessors and Dataflow Computers," *IEEE Trans. Computers*, Vol. C-33, No. 11, Nov. 1984, pp. 991-1003.

77 L. Ciminiera and A. Serra, "A Fault-Tolerant Connecting Network for Multiprocessor Systems," *Proc. 1982 Int'l. Conf. Parallel Processing*, IEEE Computer Society, Washington, D.C., 1982, pp. 113-122.

78 J.P. Shen and J.P. Hayes, "Fault-Tolerance of Dynamic Full-Access Interconnection Networks," *IEEE Trans. Computers*, Vol. C-33, No. 3, March 1984, pp. 241-248.

79 J.E. Wirsching and T. Kishi, "Minimization of Path Length in Single Stage Connection Networks," *Proc. of 2nd Int'l. Conf. Distributed Computing Systems*, IEEE Computer Society, Washington, D.C., 1982, pp. 563-571.

80 P.Y. Chen, P.C. Yew, and D. Lawrie, "Performance of Packet Switching in Buffered Single-Stage Shuffle-Exchange Networks," *Proc. 2nd Int'l. Conf. Distributed Computing Systems*, IEEE Computer Society, Washington, D.C., 1982, pp. 622-627.

81 D.P. Agrawal and J.S. Leu, "Dynamic Accessibility Testing and Path Length Optimization of Multistage Interconnection Networks," *Proc. 4th Int'l. Conf. Distributed Computing Systems*, IEEE Computer Society, Washington, D.C., 1984, pp. 266-277.

82 M.A. Marsan and M. Gerla, "Markov Models for Multiple Bus Multiprocessor Systems," *IEEE Trans. Computers*, Vol. C-31, No. 3, March 1982, pp. 239-248.

83 M.A. Jmonemarson et al., "Modeling Bus Contention and Memory Interference in Multiprocessor System," *IEEE Trans. Computers*, Vol. C-32, No. 1, Jan. 1983, pp. 60-72.

84 T.N. Mudge, J.P. Hayes, G.D. Buzzard, and D.C. Winsor, "Analysis of Multiple Bus Interconnection Networks," *Proc. 1984 Int'l. Conf. Parallel Processing*, IEEE Computer Society, Washington, D.C., 1984, pp. 228-232.

85 L.L. Kinney and R.G. Arnold, "Analysis of a Multiprocessor System with a Shared Bus," *Proc. 5th Ann. Symp. Computer Architecture*, IEEE Computer Society, Washington, D.C., 1978, pp. 89-95.

86 M.A. Marsan, G. Balboomed, and G. Conte, "Comparative Performance Analysis of Single Bus Multiprocessor Architecture," *IEEE Trans. Computers*, Vol. C-31, No. 12, Dec. 1982, pp. 1179-1191.

87 T. Lang, M. Valero, and I. Alegre, "Bandwidth of Crossbar and Multiple Bus Connections for Multiprocessors," *IEEE Trans. Computers*, Vol. C-31, No. 12, Dec. 1982, pp. 1227-1234.

88 S. Renben and P.C. Patton," *BCA: A Bus Connected Architecture*," *Proc. 1985 Int'l. Conf. Parallel Processing*, IEEE Computer Society, Washington, D.C., 1985, pp. 79-88.

Design and Performance of Generalized Interconnection Networks

LAXMI N. BHUYAN, MEMBER, IEEE, AND DHARMA P. AGRAWAL, SENIOR MEMBER, IEEE

Abstract—This paper introduces a general class of self-routing interconnection networks for tightly coupled multiprocessor systems. The proposed network, named a "generalized shuffle network (GSN)," is based on a new interconnection pattern called a generalized shuffle and is capable of connecting any number of processors M to any number of memory modules N. The technique results in a variety of interconnection networks depending on how M and N are factored. The network covers a broad spectrum of interconnections, starting from shared bus to crossbar switches and also includes various multistage interconnection networks (MIN's).

The permutation capabilities of these networks are outlined. The performance of the networks with respect to their bandwidth and cost is analyzed and is compared to that of a crossbar. Design procedures for obtaining an optimal network with highest cost efficiency are also presented.

Index Terms—Bandwidth, cost factor, generalized shuffle, *m*-shuffle, mixed radix number system, multistage interconnection networks, network optimization, permutation and combination, probability of acceptance.

I. INTRODUCTION

THE performance of a tightly coupled multiprocessor system rests primarily on an efficient design of the network interconnecting the processors to the memory modules. A crossbar switch [1] allows all possible one-to-one connections between the processors and memories, but the cost grows rapidly with an increase in the network size. As an alternative to crossbars, multistage interconnection networks (MIN's), both nonblocking and blocking have assumed paramount importance in recent times [2]–[9]. Much research has been done in analyzing and studying the equivalences between these networks [9]–[13]. Self-routing networks like Omega [5] and Delta [8] are popular because of the ease in setting the switches by a destination tag generated by the processor itself.

An MIN is basically a blocking network which does not allow all possible permutations but, for a large network, is far less expensive compared to a crossbar switch. A conflict arises when two or more processors need the same link between two successive stages in reaching their destinations. Due to this interference, a subset of processors might be blocked, thus giving a degradation in the performance. Bandwidth (BW) of a network is defined as the expected number of memory modules remaining busy in a cycle or the number of memory requests accepted per cycle. Clearly, this is a parameter which specifies to what extent a network is efficient. In a crossbar, all the memory requests are accepted as long as no two or more processors address the same memory module. In a random mode of request, the memory BW of even a crossbar is much less than the actual capacity [14]. In an MIN, this value should be still less because of the additional conflicts in the network. The interference analysis of such networks has been reported in a few papers recently [8], [15], [16].

The usual design of an MIN employs 2×2 switching elements. However, with advances in LSI technology, it may be better to employ a larger module if the network performance could be improved. It is also known that for a crossbar the BW increases with an increase in the memory modules [14]. So a study on the design of $M \times N$ MIN's with $N > M$ seems appropriate. Patel's Delta network [8] is a logical approach in this direction. The Delta network is a self-routing (digit controlled) network connecting a^n inputs to b^n outputs through $a \times b$ crossbar switches at each stage. Networks like the Omega [5], the indirect binary n-cube [7], the baseline [9], etc., form a subset of Delta networks with $a = b = 2$.

The paper presents a still broader class of networks called a generalized shuffle network (GSN). The M inputs connect to N outputs, for any arbitrary values of M and N. A construction procedure described here is based on the factorization of M and N into the product of r numbers (not necessarily prime). As a result, some existing networks, like the Delta, become a special case of the proposed GSN. An $M \times 1$ GSN represents a shared bus multiprocessor system and an $M \times N$ GSN with $r = 1$ represents a crossbar switch. Although several networks can be obtained by constructing demultiplexer trees [8] from inputs to the outputs, a new interconnection pattern called the "generalized shuffle" will be considered throughout this paper. In Section II, we describe a useful mixed radix number system and define the term "generalized shuffle." Section III builds the details of a GSN. Its permutation capabilities are briefly outlined in Section IV. The main emphasis lies on the probabilistic performance of the network and the aim is to obtain an optimal size for the switches, with a given network size. These are discussed in detail in Sections V and VI. An approximate cost model of the GSN is also developed in Section VI. The optimization is based on a cost factor ξ which is defined as the ratio of bandwidth to cost. Finally, Section VII concludes the paper.

Manuscript received April 2, 1982; revised November 29, 1982, and June 3, 1983. A preliminary version of this paper was presented at the International Conference on Parallel Processing, Bellaire, MI, August 1982. This work was performed when the authors were with the Department of Electrical and Computer Engineering, Wayne State University, Detroit, MI 48202.

L. N. Bhuyan is with the Department of Electrical and Computer Engineering, University of Southwestern Louisiana, Lafayette, LA 70504.

D. P. Agrawal is with the Department of Electrical and Computer Engineering, North Carolina State University, Raleigh, NC 27650.

Reprinted from *IEEE Transactions on Computers*, Volume C-32, Number 12, December 1983, pages 1081-1089. Copyright © 1983 by The Institute of Electrical and Electronics Engineers, Inc.

II. A Mixed Radix Number System

Let M be a decimal number represented as a product of r factors

$$M = m_1 \times m_2 \times \cdots \times m_r.$$

Then, each number X between 0 and $M - 1$ can be expressed as an r-tuple $(x_1 x_2 \cdots x_i \cdots x_r)$ for $0 \leq x_i \leq (m_i - 1)$. x_r is the least significant digit and x_1 is the most significant digit. Associated with each x_i is a weight w_i such that $\sum_{i=1}^{r} x_i w_i = X$ and $w_i = M/m_1 m_2 \cdots m_i$ for all $1 \leq i \leq r$. Note that $w_r = M/m_1 m_2 \cdots m_r = 1$ always. The lowest number $0_{10} = (0\,0 \cdots 0)$ and the highest number $(M - 1) = (m_1 - 1, m_2 - 1, \cdots, m_r - 1)$.

Whenever needed, a number X will be represented as $(X)_{m_1, m_2, \cdots, m_r}$ to specify the radices involved.

Example 1: Let

$$M = 6 = 3 \times 2.$$

Then

$$m_1 = 3, m_2 = 2$$

and

$$w_1 = 2, w_2 = 1$$

$$0_{10} = (00), 1_{10} = (01), 2_{10} = (10)$$

$$3_{10} = (11), 4_{10} = (20), 5_{10} = (21).$$

This mixed radix number system forms the basis of our interconnection. Although the same radix system was used for the Omega networks of Lawrie [6], there are two basic differences between the proposed GSN and Omega. First, GSN is an $M \times N$ network for any arbitrary values of M and N as opposed to an $N \times N$ Omega network. Secondly, the interconnection pattern between two stages of our GSN is completely different and is based on a new term "generalized shuffle" as defined below.

Definition 1: In the above mixed radix system, the generalized shuffle of a number $X = (x_1 x_2 \cdots x_r)_{m_1, m_2, \cdots, m_r}$ will be defined as $S_g(X) = (x_2 x_3 \cdots x_r x_1)_{m_2, m_3, \cdots, m_r, m_1}$.

Example 2: For $M = 3 \times 4$, the numbers are represented from 00 to 23. Any $(x_1 x_2)_{3,4}$ will be connected to $S_g(X) = (x_2 x_1)_{4,3}$ as shown in Fig. 1. The connection procedure is as follows.

Number the inputs in radix (3, 4) and outputs in (4, 3). Make a perfect shuffle of the input and connect to the particular output.

Definition 2: $S_m(X)$, an m-shuffle of an integer X, is given by

$$S_m(X) = mX \bmod (M - 1) \qquad \text{for } 0 \leq X < M - 1$$
$$= X \qquad \text{for } X = M - 1.$$

This is the same as the generalized Faro shuffle with M a multiple of m [17].

As an example, Fig. 1 again, shows a 3-shuffle of 12 inputs. This can be interpreted as follows. Given M cards, divide the cards to m equal piles of M/m cards each. Pick up the first

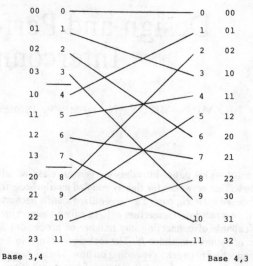

Fig. 1.   A generalized shuffle of $N = 3 \times 4$.

card from the first pile, the first card from the second pile, and so on to form a "new" pile of m cards. Repeat this process for the second cards to constitute a "new" second pile and so on until M/m new piles of m cards each are complete. Obtain a "new" deck by placing the new piles one below the other with the first pile on the top and the last pile at the bottom. There is a definite relationship between "generalized shuffle" and m-shuffle as stated in the following theorem.

Theorem 1: A generalized shuffle of $(X)_{m_1, m_2, \cdots, m_r}$ is identical to an m_1-shuffle of X.

Proof:

a): Let $0 \leq X < M - 1$ be represented in radix $(m_1, m_2, \cdots, m_r)$ as $(x_1, x_2, \cdots, x_r)$.

$$S_{m_1}(X) = m_1 \left(x_1 \cdot \frac{M}{m_1} + x_2 \cdot \frac{M}{m_1 m_2} + x_3 \cdot \frac{M}{m_1 m_2 m_3} + \cdots \right.$$
$$\left. + x_r \cdot \frac{M}{m_1 m_2 \cdots m_r} \right) \bmod (M - 1)$$
$$= \left(x_1 \cdot M + x_2 \cdot \frac{M}{m_2} + x_3 \cdot \frac{M}{m_2 m_3} + \cdots \right.$$
$$\left. + x_r \cdot \frac{M}{m_2 m_3 \cdots m_r} \right) \bmod (M - 1) \cdot$$

Moreover,

$$x_2 \cdot \frac{M}{m_2} + x_3 \cdot \frac{M}{m_2 m_3} + \cdots + x_r \cdot \frac{M}{m_2 m_3 \cdots m_r} \leq (m_2 - 1)$$
$$\cdot \frac{M}{m_2} + (m_3 - 1) \cdot \frac{M}{m_2 m_3} + \cdots + (m_r - 1)$$
$$\cdot \frac{M}{m_2 m_3 \cdots m_r} = M - m_1;$$

and $x_1 M \bmod (M - 1) = x_1$ for any $x_1 < M$. Hence,

$$S_{m_1}(X) = x_2 \cdot \frac{M}{m_2} + x_3 \cdot \frac{M}{m_2 m_3}$$
$$+ \cdots + x_r \cdot \frac{M}{m_2 m_3 \cdots m_r} + x_1$$

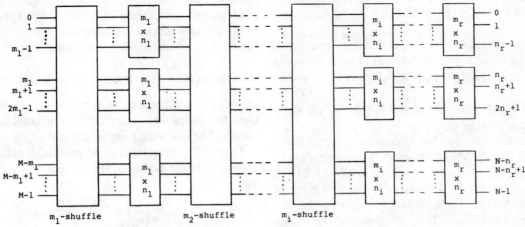

Fig. 2. An $M \times N$ generalized shuffle network, $M = m_1 \times m_2 \times \cdots \times m_r$ and $N = n_1 \times n_2 \times \cdots \times n_r$.

$$= (x_2 x_3 \cdots x_r x_1)_{m_2, m_3, \cdots, m_r, m_1} \text{ with}$$
$$M = m_2 \times m_3 \times \cdots \times m_r \times m_1.$$

b): $X = M - 1$.

Then,

$$X = (m_1 - 1, m_2 - 1, \cdots, m_{r-1}^{-1})_{m_1, m_2, \cdots, m_r}.$$
$$= (m_1 - 1) \cdot m_2 m_3 \cdots m_r + (m_2 - 1) \cdot m_3 m_4 \cdots m_r$$
$$+ \cdots + (m_r - 1)$$
$$= m_1 m_2 m_3 \cdots m_r - 1 = M - 1.$$

Again,

$$(m_2 - 1, m_3 - 1, \cdots, m_r - 1, m_1 - 1)_{m_2, m_3, \cdots, m_r m_1}$$
$$= (m_2 - 1) m_3 m_4 \cdots m_r m_1 + (m_3 - 1) m_4 m_5 \cdots m_r m_1$$
$$+ \cdots + (m_r - 1) m_1 + (m_1 - 1)$$
$$= m_2 m_3 m_4 \cdots m_r m_1 - 1 = M - 1.$$

Hence, $S_r(X) = S_{m_1}(X)$.   Q.E.D.

III. A GENERALIZED SHUFFLE NETWORK (GSN)

The basic element of a GSN is an $m \times n$ crossbar switch. Such a switch has the capability of connecting any one of its m inputs to any one of its n outputs. A self-routing $m \times n$ crossbar switch has a control unit which will select an output depending on the destination tag of the particular input. All the inputs will be connected to the respective outputs provided they are distinct. If two or more inputs request the same output terminal, only one of them would be connected and the others will be blocked or rejected. The permutation capabilities of such a switching element and the probability of blocking, etc., will be treated later.

Let M and N be represented as products of r-terms as $M = m_1 \times m_2 \times \cdots \times m_r$ and $N = n_1 \times n_2 \times \cdots \times n_r$. An $M \times N$ GSN with M inputs and N outputs is an r-stage interconnection network, consisting of a few crossbar switches of size $(m_i \times n_i)$ at the ith stage for all $1 \leq i \leq r$. The inputs and outputs are numbered with base $(m_1, m_2, \cdots, m_r)$ and base $(n_1, n_2, \cdots, n_r)$, respectively, in the mixed radix number system. The switches at stage "i" will be set as per the ith digit of the destination tag. When either M or N is a prime number, the GSN reduces to an $M \times N$ crossbar switch with $r = 1$.

Let M_i and N_i indicate the number of inputs and outputs at the ith stage of switches of the GSN. The first stage will consist of (M/m_1) switches of size $(m_1 \times n_1)$ producing $N_1 = M/n_1 m_1$ outputs with $M_1 = M$. The second stage will have $N_1/m_2 = M \cdot n_1/m_1 m_2$ switches of size $(m_2 \times n_2)$ producing $N_2 = M n_1 n_2/m_1 m_2$ outputs. In general, the ith stage will consist of $M n_1 n_2 \cdots n_{i-1}/m_1 m_2 \cdots m_i$ switches of size $(m_i \times n_i)$ each and will produce $N_i = M n_1 n_2 \cdots n_i/m_1 m_2 \cdots m_i$ outputs. The rth or the final stage will have $M n_1 n_2 \cdots n_{r-1}/m_1 m_2 \cdots m_r = N/n_r$ number of $(m_r \times n_r)$ crossbar switches producing $N_r = N$ outputs.

Demultiplexer trees [8] can now be drawn from a particular input to all outputs for full connectivity and the overlap of such M trees will give rise to a self routing interconnection network. However, the generalized shuffle interconnection pattern is of interest throughout this paper. The ith stage of the GSN will be preceded by an m_i-shuffle for all $1 \leq i \leq r$, as shown in Fig. 2.

Let us consider the interconnection pattern in some more detail. The M inputs are numbered in base $(m_1, m_2, \cdots, m_r)$. The first stage of switches will be preceded by an m_1-shuffle. The inputs to the first stage are numbered in base $(m_2, m_3, \cdots, m_r, m_1)$ following the generalized shuffle. The outputs of the first stage of switches of size $(m_1 \times n_1)$ will be numbered in base $(m_2, m_3, \cdots, m_r, n_1)$. The inputs to the second stage of switches will be numbered in base $(m_3, m_4, \cdots, m_r, n_1, m_2)$ following an m_2-shuffle of interconnection. The outputs of the second stage of switches will be numbered in base $(m_3, m_4, \cdots, m_r, n_1, n_2)$ and so on. We have the following theorem.

Theorem 2: The M-input N-output generalized shuffle network constructed as above is fully connected and is self routing.

Proof: Assume that we wish to connect the source $S = (s_1 s_2 \cdots s_r)_{m_1, m_2, \cdots, m_r}$ to the destination $D = (d_2 d_2 \cdots d_r)_{n_1, n_2, \cdots, n_r}$. The first stage of generalized shuffle modifies the source to $(s_2 s_3 \cdots s_r s_1)_{m_2, m_3, \cdots, m_r, m_1}$ and then it is connected as an input to a switch of the first stage. The particular $(m_1 \times n_1)$ switch at the first stage will connect the source to the output $(s_2 s_3 \cdots s_r d_1)_{m_2, m_3, \cdots, m_r, n_1}$, depending on the destination digit d_1. After the second generalized shuffle, it is moved to $(s_3 s_4 \cdots s_r d_1 s_2)_{m_3, m_4, \cdots, m_r, n_1 m_2}$ at the input of the second stage of switches and $(s_3 s_4 \cdots s_r d_1 d_2)_{m_3, m_4, \cdots, m_r, n_1, n_2}$ at the output. At the output of the ith stage of switches the source reaches $(s_{i+1} s_{i+2} \cdots s_r d_1 d_2 \cdots d_i)_{m_{i+1}, m_{i+2}, \cdots, m_r, n_1, n_2, \cdots, n_i}$.

After the rth stage of switches the source S is connected to $D = (d_1 d_2 \cdots d_r)_{n_1, n_2, \cdots, n_r}$. Since the mixed radix system is unique, there exists a unique path between any input and an output.   Q.E.D.

Example 3: Let $M = 6 = 3 \times 2$ and $N = 8 = 4 \times 2$. $m_1 = 3$, $m_2 = 2$ and $n_1 = 4$, $n_2 = 2$.

The GSN consists of two (3×4) crossbar switches in the first stage and four (2×2) switches at the second stage as shown in Fig. 3. The inputs are numbered in base $(3, 2)$ and the outputs in base $(4, 2)$. The inputs to the first stage of switches are numbered in base $(2, 3)$. The outputs of the first stage are numbered in base $(2, 4)$. The inputs to the second stage of switches are numbered in base $(4, 2)$ following the 2-shuffle interconnection. Finally, the outputs are in base $(4, 2)$. The connection between input $3 = (11)_{3,2}$ and output $1 = (01)_{4,2}$ is shown with a dark line in Fig. 3.

With $r = 1$, any $M \times N$ GSN is equivalent to a crossbar switch. When $N = 1$, M processors share a common memory through an $M \times 1$ switch. This is equivalent to a shared bus system. When $m_1 = m_2 = \cdots m_r = m$ and $n_1 = n_2 = \cdots n_r = n$, the GSN reduces to a delta network with $m = m^2$ and $N = n^2$. Although different interconnection networks can be obtained by constructing demultiplexer trees from input to output, they are all equivalent in terms of total number of permutations, bandwidth, probability of acceptance, etc. The generalized shuffle is just a convenient and useful way of interconnection that has been stressed in the paper. The multistage interconnection networks (MIN's) such as the Omega [5], the indirect binary n-cube [7], the baseline [9], etc., employing 2×2 switches are essentially either a part of or are topologically equivalent to our GSN with $M = N = 2^n$.

IV. PERMUTATION CAPABILITIES OF THE GSN

Let the capacity C be defined as the maximum number of simultaneous input–output connections that can be achieved through a network. For an $M \times N$ crossbar $C = \min\{M, N\}$ [18]. In an $N \times N$ multistage interconnection network, although some permutations are not possible, still the capacity remains equal to N. In a GSN, the capacity is bounded above by the minimum number of inputs/outputs at any stage. For example, in a 6×8 GSN with $M = 6 = 3 \times 2$ and $N = 8 = 2 \times 4$, the number of outputs from the first stage is $N_1 = 4$ which is even less than the number of processors. As a result, no more than four processors can be simultaneously connected to the output. Note that $N = 2 \times 4$ here gives rise to a network different from $N = 4 \times 2$ of Example 3.

Lemma 1: In a GSN, the capacity C is bounded above by $\min \{M, N_i \mid 1 \leq i \leq r\}$, where $N_i = $ the number of outputs at the ith stage of switches.

Proof: The number of inputs to the first stage $= M$. Number of outputs from ith stage $= N_i$ with $N_r = N$. Input to stage $i + 1$ is the output of stage i.

So $M_{i+1} = N_i$, $1 \leq i \leq r - 1$.

Hence, $\{\min M, N_i \mid 1 \leq i \leq r\}$ gives the minimum number of inputs/outputs at any stage in the GSN.   Q.E.D.

In a single $m \times n$ crossbar, the capacity being $\min \{m, n\}$,

it is worthwhile looking into how many possibilities of connections exist. For example, if $m \leq n$, all inputs can be simultaneously connected to m out of n outputs provided no two or more inputs address the same memory module. In an $m \times m$ crossbar, $m!$ such different mappings or permutations are possible. In an $m \times m$ crossbar for $m \leq n$, there can be $\binom{n}{m}$ combinations of choosing m numbers out of n memory modules. Associated with each combination, there are $m!$ permutations. The following lemma results.

Lemma 2: The number of permutations achievable by an $m_i \times n_i$ crossbar module at the ith stage of the GSN is given by

$$s_i = \binom{n_i}{m_i} m_i! \quad \text{for } m_i \leq n_i$$

$$= \binom{m_i}{n_i} n_i! \quad \text{for } m_i \geq n_i.$$

Theorem 3: If a GSN is obtained such that for all $1 \leq i \leq r$, $M_i \geq M_{i+1} = N_i$ (or $m_i \geq m_{i+1} = n_i$) for $M \geq N$ and $M_i \leq M_{i+1} = N_i$ (or $m_i \leq m_{i+1} = n_i$) for $M = N$, the total number of permutations achievable is

$$P = \prod_{i=1}^{r} s_i^{k_i}$$

where k_i is the number of switches at the ith stage and s_i is as given by Lemma 2.

Proof: In a GSN, there exists a unique connection between an input and an output. Each $(m_i \times n_i)$ crossbar module achieves s_i permutations. The total number of permutations is equal to the product of all the permutations. The condition M_i greater than or less than N_i ensures that the capacity $C = \min \{M, N\}$ is satisfied at all the stages. P must be less than or equal to the number of permutations achievable by a single $M \times N$ crossbar module.   Q.E.D.

A conflict is said to occur in a network when two or more sources require the same link between two stages for reaching their destinations. For example, in Fig. 3, the connections $0 \rightarrow 4$ and $2 \rightarrow 5$ require the same link and cannot be simultaneously achieved. In case of conflicts, the connections are usually achieved in two or more cycles. The following theorem characterizes the conflict situation in a GSN.

Theorem 4: In a GSN, there occurs a conflict if at least two sources s_x, s_y try to reach destinations d_x, d_y such that for $1 \leq i \leq r$

$$(d_1 d_2 \cdots d_i)_x = (d_1 d_2 \cdots d_i)_y$$
$$\Updownarrow$$
$$(s_{i+1} s_{i+2} \cdots s_r)_x = (s_{i+1} s_{i+2} \cdots s_r)_y.$$

Proof: s_x and s_y are in base $(m_1, m_2, \cdots, m_r)$. d_x and d_y are in base $(n_1, n_2, \cdots, n_r)$.

From Theorem 2, at the output of the ith stage the source connects to $(s_{i+1} s_{i+2} \cdots s_r d_1 d_2 \cdots d_i)$ in base $(m_{i+1}, m_{i+2}, \cdots, m_r, n_1, n_2, \cdots, n_i)$.

A conflict will occur at the output of the ith stage if

$$(s_{i+1} s_{i+2} \cdots s_r d_1 d_2 \cdots d_i)_x = (s_{i+1} s_{i+2} \cdots s_r d_1 d_2 \cdots d_i)_y.$$

Since both are in base $(m_{i+1}, m_{i+2}, \cdots, m_r, n_1, n_2, \cdots, n_i)$ which is a mixed radix system with a unique representation of

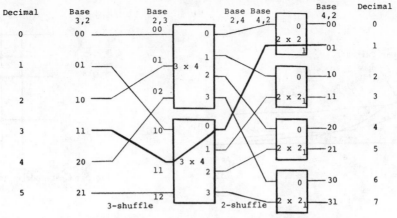

Fig. 3. A 6 × 8 generalized shuffle network with 6 = 3 × 2 and 8 = 4 × 2.

a number, the equality holds only if

$$(s_{i+1}s_{i+2}\cdots s_r)_x = (s_{i+1}s_{i+2}\cdots s_r)_y$$

and

$$(d_1d_2\cdots d_i)_x = (d_1d_2\cdots d_i)_y. \qquad \text{Q.E.D.}$$

V. ANALYSIS OF THE GSN

In this section, we will analyze the GSN with respect to its bandwidth and probability of acceptance of a request, and compare them to those of a crossbar. Bandwidth (BW) is defined as the expected number of memory requests accepted per cycle. Probability of acceptance (PA) is the ratio of the expected BW to the expected number of requests generated per cycle. The GSN and crossbar will be analyzed under the following identical assumptions.

1) The operation is synchronous, i.e., the messages begin and end simultaneously.

2) Each processor generates a random and independent request. The requests are uniformly distributed over all the memory modules.

3) At the beginning of a cycle, each processor generates a new request with a probability p. Thus, p is the average number of requests generated per cycle by each processor.

4) The requests which are not accepted are ignored. The requests issued at a cycle are independent of the requests issued in the previous cycle.

When the requests are random, it is possible for two or more processors to address the same memory module. Assumptions 1 and 4 are there to simplify the analysis. For a network with asynchronous operation, buffers should be provided at each switch to enhance the performance [15]. Assumption 4 is unrealistic because a blocked message will indeed be resubmitted. Various simulation results, however, indicate that the above set of assumptions does not result in a significant difference in the performance. Moreover, it stands well for comparison purposes.

The BW and PA of an $m \times n$ crossbar module are given by [8], [14], [15]

$$\text{BW} = n - n\left(1 - \frac{p}{n}\right)^m$$

$$\text{PA} = \frac{n}{p \cdot m} - \frac{n}{p \cdot m}\left(1 - \frac{p}{n}\right)^m$$

where p is the average number of messages generated per processor per cycle.

The equations are quite simple and they compare well to the exact results [14].

Dividing the bandwidth by n gives us the rate of requests on any one of the n output lines of an $m \times n$ crossbar module, as a function of its input rate

$$p_{\text{out}} = 1 - \left(1 - \frac{p_{\text{in}}}{n}\right)^m.$$

In a GSN, the output rate of the ith stage is also the input rate to the $(i + 1)$th stage. Hence, one can recursively evaluate the output rate of any stage starting with the input rate of the first stage. The output rate of stage r determines the BW of a GSN. This recursive analysis was originally suggested by Patel [8] for computing the BW of the Delta network. We compared the results of a 2×2 Delta network [8] using the above equations with those reported by Thanawastien and Nelson [16]. Patel's analysis is closer to the simulation results. We will simply use these equations for analysis of the GSN instead of pursuing the matter further.

Let p_i be the rate of request at the output of the ith stage. Then $p_i = 1 - (1 - (p_{i-1}/n_i))^{m_i}$, p_0 is the rate of request generated by a processor. A column bandwidth (CBW) is the BW at the output of a particular column.

$$\text{CBW}_i = p_i \times N_i = \frac{Mn_1n_2\cdots n_{i-1}n_ip_i}{m_1m_2\cdots m_i}.$$

The output BW is the CBW at stage n.

$$\text{BW} = N \cdot p_r.$$

The probability that a request will be accepted in a GSN is $P_A = Np_r/Mp_0$.

Conjecture 1: For an $N \times N$ GSN with $N = n_1 \times n_2 \times \cdots \times n_r$, the bandwidth is highest if arranged as $n_1 \geqslant n_2 \geqslant n_3 \geqslant \cdots \geqslant n_r$.

This conjecture is based on the results of computations.

BW is highest if the rate of request at the final stage p_r is highest. Let us consider a two-stage $N \times N$ network with $N = n_1 \times n_2$. The first stage will consist of N/n_1 number of ($n_1 \times n_1$) crossbar modules and the second stage will consist of N/n_2 number of ($n_2 \times n_2$) modules. Fig. 4 shows the variation of the rate of request p with the crossbar size $n \times n$. With $p_0 = 1$,

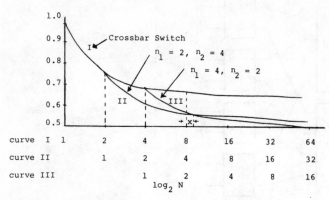

Fig. 4. Probability of acceptance of $N = 4 \times 2$ and $N = 2 \times 4$.

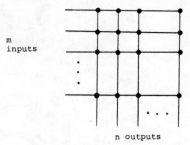

Fig. 5. Cost model of an $m \times n$ switch.

$$p = 1 - \left(1 - \frac{1}{n}\right)^n.$$

The values of p for $n_1 > n_2$ and $n_1 < n_2$ are determined by going down the curve to the required extent. For $n_1 < n_2$, the second curve will start earlier than for $n_1 > n_2$. In Fig. 4, cases with $N = 4 \times 2$ and 2×4 are examined for an 8×8 GSN. For $r = 2$, we have observed that x (Fig. 4) is always positive, however small it may be. A computer simulation was carried out for different values of r, for an $N \times N$ network with N a power of 2. It shows the highest BW when $n_1 \geqq n_2 \geqq n_3 \geqq \cdots \geqq n_r$.

VI. NETWORK OPTIMIZATION

In this section, we present some interesting results on how to design a cost effective interconnection network. The BW reflects the performance of the network. We will define a cost factor ξ as the ratio of the BW to cost. An approximate cost model of the GSN is developed here to carry out the process of optimization. The intent is to underline the design procedures involved in an interconnection network rather than to draw a conclusion from the observations made in this section. In the absence of an established cost criterion, the cost of an $m \times n$ crossbar switch is assumed to be mn units which is equal to the number of cross points shown in Fig. 5. Hence, the results presented in this section are approximate and will change if a different cost model is assumed. Again, we do not have a closed form solution for the BW; most of the results presented here are experimental, obtained through computation. We will study the characteristics of both $M \times N$ and $N \times N$ networks.

Cost Model of the GSN

The cost of an $(m_i \times n_i)$ switch is equal to $m_i \cdot n_i$ units. A GSN employs $Mn_1n_2 \cdots n_{i-1}/m_1m_2 \cdots m_i$ number of $(m_i \times n_i)$ switching modules at the ith stage. The cost of the GSN is

$$\sum_{i=1}^{r} \frac{Mn_1n_2 \cdots n_i}{m_1m_2 \cdots m_{i-1}}.$$

A special case of interest is an $N \times N$ GSN where $m_i = n_i$, $\forall \, 1 \leqq i \leqq r$. The total cost is

$$N \sum_{i=1}^{r} n_i.$$

We get the following results.

Lemma 3: The cost of an $N \times N$ GSN for some fixed r stages of switching elements is minimum when realized as $N = n^r$.

Theorem 5: The overall cost of an $N \times N$ GSN is absolute minimum when realized with all the factors of N as prime numbers.

The proofs of the above lemma and theorem are obvious and, hence, have been omitted.

For a 2×2 switching element, the cost is 4 units. For an MIN employing $\log_2 N$ stages, the total cost = $4 \times (N/2) \times \log_2 N = 2N \log_2 N$. For an $N \times N$ crossbar, cost = N^2. The cost model developed in this section is in agreement with the model developed by Lawrie [6] in terms of logic gates.

Local Optimization of the GSN's

Given a value of N for an $N \times N$ GSN, there may be several ways to factor N into r components. As an example, for $N = 16$ and $r = 2$, N can be expressed as 8×2 or 4×4. The obvious question arises: for given values of N and r, what is the optimum realization of a network? This will be referred to as *local optimization*. The following observation is made.

Conjecture 2: The most cost effective realization of an $N \times N$ GSN in some r-stages is obtained when $m_i = n_i = \sqrt[r]{N}$ for all $i \leqq r$.

The conjecture is obtained from computational results. Let $r = 2$. The cost factor $\xi = \text{BW}/\text{cost}$ is plotted in Fig. 6 for various values of N, a power of 2. The peaks are obtained at a theoretical value of $\sqrt[r]{N}$, even if this is not an integer. A computer search was carried out for a few values of r which resulted in $\sqrt[r]{N}$ as the optimal realization. Since $\sqrt[r]{N}$ may not be an integer for a fixed r, the m_i's should be as close to $\sqrt[r]{N}$ as possible.

Conjecture 3: Given N and r, N should be realized as $N = n_1 \times n_2 \times \cdots \times n_r$ with n_i's $\simeq \sqrt[r]{N}$ and $n_1 \geqq n_2 \geqq \cdots \geqq n_r$.

For given n_i's, the cost is $N \cdot \sum_{i=1}^{r} n_i$. Conjecture 3 is a combination of Conjecture 1 and Lemma 3 and will lead to the most cost effective realization for a given value of N.

Global Optimization of the GSN's

There is another tradeoff in building a GSN. For example, 16 can be factorized as $2 \times 2 \times 2 \times 2$, $4 \times 2 \times 2$, 4×4, etc.

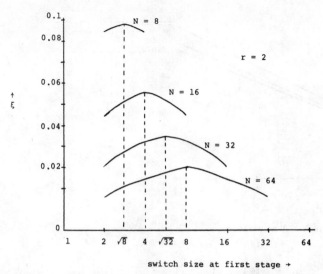

Fig. 6. Cost efficiency versus switch size at the first stage.

TABLE I
DIFFERENT REALIZATION OF A 16 × 16 GSN

N = 16	BW	Cost	ξ
2 x 2 x 2 x 2	7.2	128	0.05626
4 x 2 x 2	7.7833	128	0.0608
4 x 4	8.44	128	0.066
8 x 2	8.78	160	0.0549
16 (crossbar)	10.303	256	0.0402

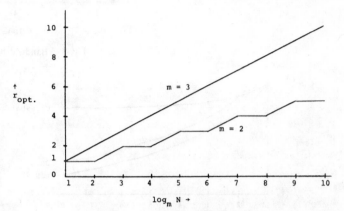

Fig. 7. Value of r_{opt} for $N = m^r$.

The design which gives the highest cost factor is optimal. This will be referred to as *global optimization* of the GSN. Table I shows the relevant information for a 16 × 16 GSN obtained through different factorizations.

It has been impossible to derive a closed form solution for the optimal value of r (r_{opt}). For $N = n^r$ and for values $n = 2$ and 3, the optimal values of r are plotted in Fig. 7 as obtained from computation. For N, a power of 2, the following conjecture states the most important observation.

Conjecture 4: For an $N \times N$ GSN, with N a power of 2, as many 4 × 4 switches as possible should be employed to yield the most cost effective realization.

From Fig. 7 for a 4 × 4 network, $r_{opt} = 1$. This means one 4 × 4 switch should be employed instead of four conventional (2 × 2) switches. For $N = 8$, $r_{opt} = 2$; thus, the realization should be as $N = 4 \times 2$, employing one stage of 4 × 4 switches and another stage of 2 × 2 switches. For $N = 16$, two stages of 4 × 4 switches are desired. So, for N a power of 4, 4 × 4 switches should be employed at all stages, and for N a power of 2 but not a power of 4, the last stage will consist of 2 × 2 switches and all the previous stages should consist of 4 × 4 switches. As illustrated in Fig. 7, for N a power of 3, optimal structure is obtained when 3 × 3 switches are utilized. A study on loosely coupled systems (distributed) with a sort of hypercube topology has also resulted in a similar observation [19]. In general, for any N, a discrete optimization may be carried out to determine the most cost effective realization. The networks realized in this manner will be referred to as optimal GSN's (OGSN) in this paper. The BW, PA, and cost efficiency obtained in an $N \times N$ OGSN for N a power of 2 are compared in Figs. 8, 9, and 10, respectively, with those of a GSN(2) and crossbar. A GSN(2) is the MIN obtained with 2 × 2 switches at each stage, which is equivalent to an Omega network.

Optimal $M \times N$ Networks

We will now examine the performance of an $M \times N$ GSN. It is known from Bhandarkar's analysis [14] that if memory modules are increased compared to the number of processors,

the BW increases. This is evident because, with the availability of more memory modules, less conflicts will occur and more processors can be kept busy in a probabilistic view. The variations of the BW and cost efficiency, resulting by addition of more memory modules, are plotted in Figs. 11 and 12, respectively. The number of processors is kept constant at $M = 16$. Whenever a few memory modules are added, a fresh design of the GSN is carried out and the cost efficiency (ξ) is calculated to yield a new OGSN. The performance of an OGSN is plotted together with that of an $M \times N$ crossbar switch.

As shown in Fig. 11, the BW of a crossbar with $M = 16$ increases with the memory modules and reaches 16 as $N \rightarrow \infty$. For an OGSN, the saturation starts earlier and remains constant at about 10. This is because of the conflicts inherent in a GSN. It may be pointed out here that the OGSN is designed such that the cost efficiency is at the highest level of all the designs. It was observed that the BW improves if other switch sizes are allowed, but this will happen at the expense of cost effectiveness. The crossbar itself is also a part of the GSN anyway.

A similar experiment was carried out to see the effect of adding a processor to a fixed number of memory modules. Figs. 13 and 14 are obtained with various values of M with N kept fixed at 16. The variation of curves obtained for the crossbar can be easily predicted theoretically from the equations

$$\text{BW} = N - N \left(1 - \frac{1}{N}\right)^M, \text{ with } p_0 = 1$$

and cost efficiency $\xi = \dfrac{\text{BW}}{M \cdot N} = \dfrac{1 - \left(1 - \dfrac{1}{N}\right)^M}{M}.$

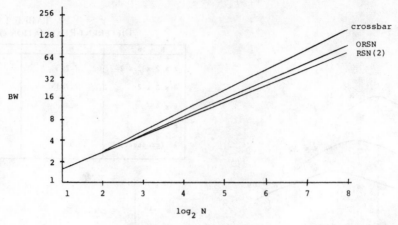

Fig. 8. Bandwidth of $N \times N$ networks.

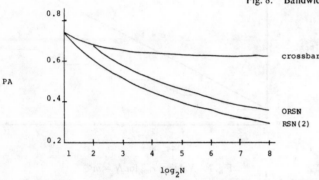

Fig. 9. Probability of acceptance of $N \times N$ networks.

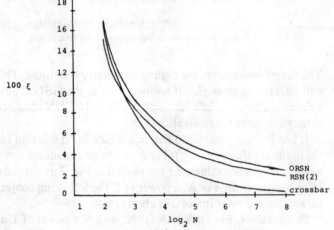

Fig. 10. Cost effectiveness of $N \times N$ networks.

As $M \to \infty$, the BW of a crossbar approaches N. However, with a recursive equation for the BW in the case of a GSN and for the discrete optimization required, it was not possible to theoretically predict the characteristics of the OGSN. The results, however, seem to be quite realistic.

VII. CONCLUSIONS

A broad class of networks called generalized shuffle networks (GSN's) was introduced. The network is self-routing in the sense that the output of the switches at the ith stage is selected by the ith digit of the destination address. The network is so general that it includes systems ranging from a shared bus connection to a crossbar. The cost modeling was approximate, but truly represents the complexity involved. The bandwidth was chosen as a performance measure with the assumption that the cycle time is almost the same for all the realizations of the GSN, including the crossbar. Thus, depending on the actual parameters, the cost efficiency curve may shift a little.

The observations indicate that by adding more memory modules, the bandwidth increases and the GSN provides an efficient design for such an interconnection. Many useful results were presented based on our cost model. An important observation is that an $N \times N$ MIN seems to better employ (4 × 4) switches instead of conventional (2 × 2) switches. A similar conclusion was also drawn in recent papers [20], [21]. When N is a power of 2 but not a power of 4, all the stages can employ (4 × 4) switching elements except the last one which will employ (2 × 2) switches. The generalized shuffle makes that connection possible as illustrated in Fig. 15 for a 32 × 32 network.

REFERENCES

[1] W. A. Wulf and C. G. Bell, "Cmmp—A multiminiprocessor," in *Proc. AFIPS Fall Joint Comput. Conf.*, Dec. 1975, pp. 765–777.
[2] V. E. Benes, *Mathematical Theory of Connecting Networks and Telephone Traffic.* New York: Academic, 1965.
[3] L. R. Goke and G. J. Lipovski, "Banyan networks for partitioning multiprocessor systems," in *Proc. 1st Int. Symp. Comput. Arch.*, FL, Dec. 1973, pp. 21–28.
[4] H. S. Stone, "Parallel processing with the perfect shuffle," *IEEE Trans. Comput.*, vol. C-20, pp. 153–161, Feb. 1971.
[5] D. H. Lawrie, "Access and alignment of data in an array processor," *IEEE Trans. Comput.*, vol. C-24, pp. 1145–1155, Dec. 1975.
[6] ——, "Memory-Processor Connection Networks," Ph.D. dissertation, Univ. Illinois, Urbana, 1973.
[7] M. C. Pease, "The indirect binary N-cube microprocessor array," *IEEE Trans. Comput.*, vol. C-26, pp. 458–473, May 1977.
[8] J. H. Patel, "Performance of processor-memory interconnections for multiprocessors," *IEEE Trans. Comput.*, vol. C-30, pp. 771–780, Oct. 1981.
[9] C. L. Wu and T. Y. Feng, "On a class of multistage interconnection networks," *IEEE Trans. Comput.*, vol. C-29, pp. 694–702, Aug. 1980.
[10] H. J. Siegel, "Analysis techniques for SIMD machine interconnection networks and the effect of processor address masks," *IEEE Trans. Comput.*, vol. C-26, pp. 153–161, Feb. 1977.
[11] D. K. Pradhan and K. L. Kodandapani, "A uniform representation of single and multistage interconnection networks used in SIMD machines," *IEEE Trans. Comput.*, vol. C-29, pp. 777–790, Sept. 1980.
[12] D. P. Agrawal, "Graph theoretic analysis and design of multistage interconnection networks," *IEEE Trans. Comput.*, vol. C-32, July 1983.
[13] D. P. Agrawal and S. C. Kim, "On non-equivalent multistage interconnection networks," in *Proc. Int. Conf. Parallel Processing*, Aug. 1981, pp. 234–237.

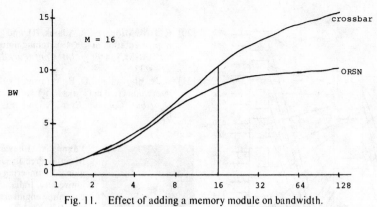

Fig. 11.   Effect of adding a memory module on bandwidth.

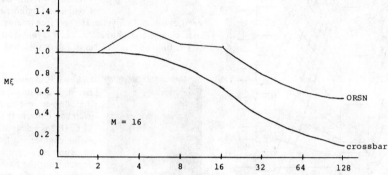

Fig. 12.   Effect of adding a memory module on cost efficiency.

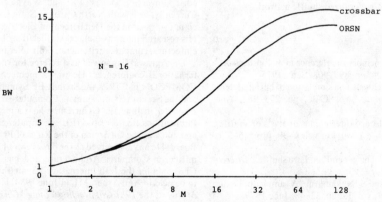

Fig. 13.   Effect of adding a processor on bandwidth.

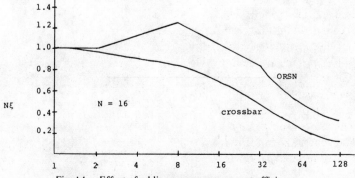

Fig. 14.   Effect of adding a processor on cost efficiency.

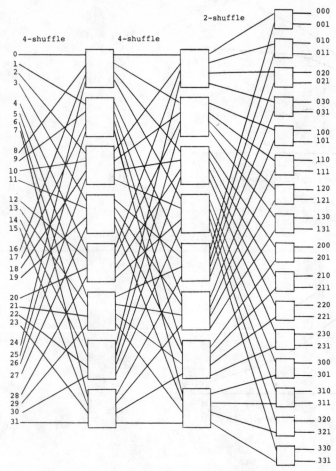

Fig. 15. A 32 × 32 optimal generalized shuffle network.

[14] D. P. Bhandarkar, "Analysis of memory interference in multiprocessor," *IEEE Trans. Comput.*, vol. C-24, pp. 897–908, Sept. 1975.

[15] D. M. Dias and J. R. Jump, "Analysis and simulation of buffered delta networks," *IEEE Trans. Comput.*, vol. C-30, pp. 273–282, Apr. 1981.

[16] S. Thanawastien and V. P. Nelson, "Interference analysis of shuffle/exchange network," *IEEE Trans. Comput.*, vol. C-30, pp. 545–556, Aug. 1981.

[17] S. B. Morris and R. E. Hartwig, "The generalized Faro shuffle," *Discrete Math.*, vol. 15, pp. 333–346, Aug. 1976.

[18] G. M. Masson, G. C. Gingher, and S. Nakamura, "A sampler of circuit switching networks," *Computer*, vol. 12, pp. 32–48, June 1979.

[19] L. N. Bhuyan and D. P. Agrawal, "A general class of processor interconnection strategies," in *Proc. 9th Int. Symp. Comput. Arch.*, Austin, TX, Apr. 1982, pp. 90-98.

[20] R. J. McMillen, G. B. Adams, III, and H. J. Siegel, "Performance and implementation of 4 × 4 switching notes in a interconnection network for PASM," in *Proc. Int. Conf. Parallel Processing*, Aug. 1981, pp. 229–233.

[21] L. N. Bhuyan and D. P. Agrawal, "VLSI performance of multistage interconnection networks using 4 * 4 switches," in *Proc. 3rd Int. Conf. Distribut. Comput. Syst.*, Miami, FL, Oct. 18-22, 1982, pp. 606–613.

Laxmi N. Bhuyan (S'81–M'83) received the M.Sc. degree in electrical engineering from Regional Engineering College, Rourkela, Sambalpur University, India, in 1979 and the Ph.D. degree in computer engineering from Wayne State University, Detroit, MI, in 1982.

During 1982–1983 he was with the Department of Electrical Engineering, University of Manitoba, Winnipeg, Canada. At present he is an Assistant Professor in the Department of Electrical and Computer Engineering, University of Southwestern Louisiana, Lafayette. His research interests include parallel and distributed computer architecture, VLSI layout, and multiprocessor applications.

Dr. Bhuyan is a member of the Association for Computing Machinery.

Dharma P. Agrawal (M'74–SM'79) was born in Balod, India, on April 12, 1945. He received the B.E. degree in electrical engineering from Ravishankar University, Raipur, India, in 1966, the M.E. (Hons.) degree in electronics and communication engineering from the University of Roorkee, Roorkee, India, in 1968, and the D.Sc.Tech. degree from the Swiss Federal Institute of Technology, Lausanne, Switzerland, in 1975.

He has been a member of the faculty at the Motilal Nehru Regional Engineering College, Allahabad, India; the University of Roorkee; the Swiss Federal Institute of Technology; the University of Technology, Baghdad, Iraq; Southern Methodist University, Dallas, TX; and Wayne State University, Detroit, MI. Currently, he is with North Carolina State University, Raleigh, as an Associate Professor in the Department of Electrical and Computer Engineering. His research interests include parallel/distributed processing, computer architecture, computer arithmetic, fault-tolerance, and information retrieval.

Dr. Agrawal has served as a referee for various reputed journals and international conferences. He was a member of Program Committees for COMPCON Fall 1979, the Sixth IEEE Symposium on Computer Arithmetic, and the Seventh Symposium on Computer Arithmetic to be held in Aarhus, Denmark in June 1983. Currently, he is a member and the Secretary of the Publications Board of the IEEE Computer Society, and has recently been appointed as the Chairman of the Rules of Practice Committee of the PUBS Board. He has also served as the Treasurer of the IEEE-CS Technical Committee on Computer Architecture and has been named as the Program Chairman for the 13th International Symposium on Computer Architecture to be held in Ann Arbor, MI, in June 1984. He is listed in *Who's Who in the Midwest*, the *1981 Outstanding Young Men of America*, and the *Directory of World Researchers'* 1980's subjects. He is a member of the Association for Computing Machinery, the Society for Industrial and Applied Mathematics, and Sigma Xi.

DYNAMIC ACCESSIBILITY TESTING AND PATH LENGTH
OPTIMIZATION OF MULTISTAGE INTERCONNECTION NETWORKS

Dharma P. Agrawal and Ja-Song Leu
Department of Electrical and Computer Engineering
North Carolina State University
P.O. Box 7911
Raleigh, NC 27695-7911

ABSTRACT

The emergence of multiple processor systems has seen the increased use of multistage interconnection networks (MINs) built with several stages of 2-input 2-output switching elements (SEs). The connectivity and fault tolerance of these networks are important problems as these MINs are expected to be the heart of these systems. This paper employs a versatile graph model of an SE that could represent all possible stuck type faults at the terminals, and faults at control lines and/or data lines. This technique leads to a graph model of a given MIN amenable to testing of its dynamic full access (DFA) capability. The basic strategy of employing adjacency and reachability matrices enables testing under various multiple faults. Simulation of various networks is carried out to evaluate the average path lengths which illustrates the effect of connection pattern on the network performance. A design methodology for implementing a class of networks is also outlined so that DFA capability and the maximum availability could be ensured. Optimality of such a network is verified by the simulation results that shows a negligible increase in the average path length when a fault is present in the resulting network.

Index terms: Adjacency matrix, average distance, connectivity, distance matrix, dynamic full access capability, graph model, multiple passes, multistage interconnection networks, reachability matrix, simulation, single-stage interconnection networks, stuck-at-faults, switching element.

I. INTRODUCTION

Recent advances in VLSI technology have encouraged the use of multi-processor and multi-computer systems with a large number of processing elements (PE) and memory modules (MM). In such systems, various techniques are utilized to support restructurable data paths between the PEs and MMs. Thus, the intercommunication is becoming an increasingly complex but inevitable issue. Several design techniques for the interprocessor communication have been reviewed [1] and some of them have been constructed. The current trend is to employ multistage interconnection networks (MINs) wherein the network is segmented into several stages and partial input-output connection requirements are satisfied in each stage.

Various design issues of the MINs have been covered in the literature. The main emphasis has been in finding their equivalence and non-equivalence and comparing their permutation capabilities [2-8], designing for conflict-free permutations [9,10], algorithmic adaptability characteristics [11], and understanding relative advantages and disadvantages of the MINs [12]. But, not much attention has been paid to the aspect of fault-tolerance which is crucial to the successful operation of a multiple processor system. The fault-tolerance of MINs are extremely important as they are considered as the heart of parallel systems. This paper is concerned with the fault-tolerant capability of the MINs when employed to provide interprocessor communication in a multi-processor environment. The network should be implemented in such a way that a non-catastrophic fault may not force a complete shut-off and the system should rather continue working with reduced capacity. This graceful degradation characteristics is not only dependent on the processors failure, but also on the MINs. Similarily, the path-length required to provide a logical link between indicates the time-delay involved in transmitting the information from a source to any desired destination. Thus, the average path lengths in both MINs and the single-stage interconnection networks (SSINs) and without and with faults seem to be a good representative of their performance.

The type of multiple processor systems we are concerned with is shown in Fig. 1. In this system model, the PEs with their private memory modules provide desired parallelism while one PE to another PE transfer is achieved through the MIN. Thus, all PEs are connected to both sides of the network so that each PE could transmit data through the input side while the network output is useful in receiving the data from another PE.

A brief introduction of the MINs and an overview of existing testing techniques is covered in section II. Our fault model including multiple stuck-at-faults at input/output and control lines is described in section III. A generalized test procedure and the use of adjacency and reachability matrices are illustrated in section IV. Section V outlines a procedure to compute the static average path length and performance under dynamic loading and various faulty conditions are also observed. Section VI provides an insight to the design methodology of MIN with optimum connectivity. Finally, concluding remarks are included in section VII.

Reprinted from *Proceedings of the 1984 International Conference on Distributed Computing Systems*, 1984, pages 266-277. Copyright © 1984 by The Institute of Electrical and Electronics Engineers, Inc.

II. MULTISTAGE INTERCONNECTION NETWORKS AND EXISTING TESTING TECHNIQUES

Several of the proposed MINs have been designed using 2X2 SE as a basic building block. A simple representation of such an SE is shown in Fig. 2.a and its two possible states are illustrated in Fig. 2.b and 2.c. The parallel and cross-connection of an SE is determined by the logical level applied at its control line. An N-input N-output MIN (for simplicity, N is usually selected as some power of 2 say $N=2^n$) is constructed in several stages with each stage consisting of N/2 SEs. The links between successive stages of the network are assigned in such a way that each input could be connected to as many outputs as possible. An n-stage network can provide a path between each of the N-inputs and the N-outputs and one such network has been reproduced from [2] in Fig.2.d. The control lines are not shown for clarity of the diagram. Thus, the absence of faults allow any input to be connected to any of the outputs in an n-stage MIN.

The problem of communication and data transfer rate tends to be increasingly critical when either network load is heavy, or some of the network lines are faulty. A direct physical link between any input and an arbitrary output may not be possible if a conflict occurs or a line happens to be faulty. In other words, whenever the data is to be transferred between any two PEs in the system of Fig.1, the data may have to be passed to one or more intermediate PEs before reaching the final destination. These considerations encouraged us to look into the MINs with m stages (m<=n).

The fault-diagnosis for a class of switching network has been described by Operfman and Tsao-Wu [14]. They utilize a sequence of tests to ensure the correct operation of two possible states of each SE and they consider faulty state of a SE to be unalterable parallel or cross-connection of the switches. This basically means that they consider stuck-at-faults at the control input lines. Shen and Hayes [15] have used a graph model for illustrating the effect of faults at the control control lines. In their fault model, they consider output side to be fed back to the corresponding input lines as rerouting of data through the PE is possible. They have modeled an SE by a node and each interconnection link is represented by a directed edge connecting the node(s). A faulty SE is indicated by a node partitioned into two sections. Their main concern is to test for a property that determines whether, under a given fault condition, each input of the network could be logically connected to any one of the network outputs in a finite number of passes. They define this property as the dynamic full access (DFA) capability. The control line faults are said to be critical if they destroy the DFA characteristics, i.e., the faulty conditions under which the input-to-output communication is not possible at all.

The same model has been used [16] in analyzing the fault tolerance of various redundant MINs. The major shortcoming in this model is to assume the presence of stuck-at-faults only at the control input(s). In section III, we propose a

graph model which takes care of this limitation.

Narraway and So [17,18] have considered diagnosis model for a general switching network constructed with k-input k-output switches (k > 2). Their basic strategy is to use known good connecting data path in identifying good switches and use this progressively in defining a faulty connecting path. They do not consider faults at the control lines. In another recent paper, Wu and Feng [19] have described a simple testing technique for MINs. In their paper, they have illustrated 16 different possible states of a SE and they consider only two states (parallel or cross-connected) as fault-free situations and all others are interpreted as faults in the SEs. In their novel scheme, they require only four sequences for testing any MIN. In fact only two sequences are needed and are repeated for two different control settings of the network, once when all switches are parallel-connected and another time when all SEs are in cross-connected mode. The two input sequences are also complementary to each other and each sequence is selected in such a way that one out of two code is used in space. This means that only one input (and hence the output) to each SE is made one while the other input remains zero.

It is well known that the probability of logical faults inside an I.C. chip is quite small and most of the faults occur at the pins [20]. Thus, it is more important to consider stuck-at-faults at inputs, outputs and control lines of the SEs. Wu and Feng's algorithm can still test faults at the input and output line(s) of SE(s). Further generalization of their scheme has been covered in [21] wherein the faults at the control lines can also be tested. Another model for the control line faults in Omega [22] and other networks has recently been considered in [23]. Their optimum test sequence allows location of single-stage multiple faults and is helpful in removing the faulty SEs, if a stage is implemented within a single I.C. chip. In another recent work [24], design procedures for (2n-1) stage Benes type network [14] that could tolerate single and multiple faults at the control lines have been outlined. A comprehensive review of testing techniques has appeared in a recent publication [25]. In this paper, we evaluate the DFA capabilities of MINs under stuck-at-faults at the control lines as well as at the inputs and outputs of the SEs.

III. FAULT MODEL

The model for a 2-input 2-output SE of Fig. 2.a, is shown in Fig. 3.a [5,6]. This graph model is based on the connectivity property between the input lines X1 and X2 and output lines Y1 and Y2 of the SE. Each one of them is assigned a node. As X1 (X2) of these (Fig. 2.a) can be connected to either Y1 or Y2 (Y2 or Y1), these are shown by the directed edges in the graph model of Fig. 3.a. It is worth mentioning that the graph model of Fig. 3.a resembles [6] the regular SW Banyan network [26] in appearance. But, instead of using the SE of Fig. 2.a, the Banyan is designed with individually controlled paths and its graph shows the actual link pattern and a link fault eliminates the corresponding edge from the graph. Similarly, the graph model of cross-bar switches [26] utilize one edge for each cross-point and a single switch fault removes an edge in the graph. In this way, our model of 2-input 2-output SE is altogether different from the Banyan network.

Considering the SE of Fig. 2.a again, it could be in either of the two operating modes if no fault is present. But when the control line is stuck-at-zero (s-a-0), the graph of Fig.3.a is reduced to as shown in Fig. 3.b. A similar modification is shown in Fig. 3.c whenever the control line is s-a-1. The stuck-at-faults at the input and output lines of an SE have to be treated in a different way. If a line is faulty (s-a-α,$\alpha\epsilon$0,1) then the line cannot be used to transmit any data. This is reflected in the graph model by removing the corresponding node and hence eliminating all the edges adjacent to the node. This is shown in Fig.4.a for s-a-fault at one of the input lines while Fig. 4.b illustrates the model when a fault is present at one of the output lines. Multiple faults are represented by α, β and γ (α, β, γ ϵ 0,1). Models for the two possible double faults are shown in Figs. 4.c and 4.d. Faults at the two inputs and outputs lead to the model shown in Fig. 4.e while faults at all the inputs and output lines of an SE eliminate all the nodes from the model. If the control line is stuck to 0 or 1, and one of the input or output lines, is also s-a-α, then the graph models are reduced to as shown in Figs. 4.f and 4.g. Two possible combinations of faults with the control line s-a-α and two of the inputs/output lines s-a-α are given in Fig. 4.h and 4.i. In this way, Figs. 3.b, 3.c and 4.a-4.i represent a reduced graph model under all possible single and multiple faults in an SE.

The model of Fig. 3.a could also be used [5,6] to represent the upper and lower broadcast used in Lawries Omega network [22]. In the case of upper broadcast, the upper input X1 is sent to both the outputs Y1 and Y2 while the lower broadcast provides Y1 = Y2 = X2. The graph models of Figs. 3.b, 3.c and 4 remain valid for various faults in the SE for Lawries Omega network. The additional faulty situations and the corresponding reduced graphs for SE which lower and upper broadcast, are shown in Fig. 5.

In this way, once the SEs have been appropriately modeled, the analysis is similar for the MINs using two types of SEs, one with and the other without the upper and lower broadcast capability. For conciseness of the text, we will be considering the networks implemented with SEs having only two valid states and without any broadcast facility.

IV. GRAPH MODEL OF A MIN AND ITS DFA CAPABILITY

Before we go any further, let us define two matrices, the adjacency and the reachability matrix, obtained from the graph model we illustrated earlier. The adjacency matrix A of a graph is the NxN matrix [a_{ij}] with a_{ij}=1 if there is an edge from node i to node j in the graph, otherwise a_{ij}=0. Fig. 6.a show the adjacency matrix of the bipartite directed graph [27] of a 2*2 SE of Fig. 2.a. When the control line is s-a-0 or s-a-1, the matrices are shown in Fig. 6.b and 6.c, respect-

ively.

The reachability matrix R of a graph is defined as and N*N matrix [r_{ij}] with r_{ij}=1 if node j is reachable from node i, and r_{ij}=0 otherwise. Here, the information we need from the reachability matrix is whether an input port of the MIN can reach an output port or not and thereafter, it is not necessary to retain any connectivity information from the input nodes to the intermediate nodes (e.g. node numbers 1 to 16 in Fig. 7.a). The graph model of a 2*2 SE given in Fig. 3.a can be used to obtain the graph model for the baseline network of Fig. 2.d and is shown in Fig. 7.a. The adjacency matrices of each of the three stages are shown in Fig. 7.b, 7.c, and 7.d, respectively.

Corollary 1: In a m-stage MIN let A_i be the adjacency matrix of the bipartite directed graph of the ith stage representing its connectivity, then R, the reachability matrix from input nodes to output nodes of the MIN could be given by

$$R = \pi_{i=1}^{m} A_i$$

Proof: The proof is obvious.

Now we can compute the reachability matrix, R, by multiplying the adjacency matrices A_1, A_2 and A_3 and the resulting R matrix is shown in Fig. 7.e. In a similar way, the model could be obtained for a MIN with any number of stages and with any number of arbitrarily located faults and the R-matrix could be used to test for the DFA capability.

For example, consider the multiple single faults as shown in Fig. 8.a, the corresponding graph model is given in Fig. 8.b, it may be noted that the node No. 11 and a total of 8 edges have been eliminated because of the faults. The adjacency matrices for stage 1, 2, 3 are shown in Fig. 8.c, 8.d, and 8.e respectively. The reachability matrix, R = $A_1 \cdot A_2 \cdot A_3$ given in Fig. 8.f, shows that not all input nodes can reach all the output nodes. If multiple passes are allowed, (i.e. output can be fed back to the input side), then additional nodes can be accessed in successive passes.

Corollary 2: Let R be the reachability matrix of an MIN, then the reachability in K passes (and hence the DFA which indicates the possibility of each input node to reach each one of the output nodes in K passes) could be given by:

$$R_k = R^k$$

Proof: Proof is self-explanatory.

As DFA is defined as a property that provides each input of the network to be connected to any one of its outputs in a finite number of passes (and hence, any PE to any other PE). The R-matrix of Fig. 8.f shows that the network of Fig. 8.a does not allow all input nodes to be connected to each one of the output nodes. But, by multiplying A three times, it could be observed (Fig. 8.h) that three passes through the network of Fig. 8.a is good enough to provide communication paths from any input to any one of the output nodes. Hence the the DFA property is satisfied. It may be noted that its DFA may not be retained for other combinations of faults. For example, an additional s-a-0 at the control input of SE number II in the network of Fig. 8.a, leads to a graph model of Fig. 9.a which is clearly divided into two unconnected sub-graphs, one consisting of the input nodes b and c and the output nodes A, B, and C and the other contains the rest of the input and output nodes. This could also be seen from the reachability matrix of Fig. 9.b which could be partitioned as two smaller nonzero submatrices as shown in the Figure. This is true for any case if R could be postitioned as [27].

$$R = \begin{array}{c|c} R' & 0 \\ \hline 0 & R'' \end{array}$$

Where R' and R" are the two nonzero submatrices. This observation could be easily verified by obtaining the reachability matrices for two, three and four passes as shown in Fig. 9.c, 9.d and 9.e, respectively.

As $R_6 = R_5 = R_4$, it is clear that no matter how hard we try, we will never be able to get any better result. This means the network no longer possesses the DFA capability.

Theorem 1:

In an N-input N-output MIN, the DFA characteristics is ascertained for single or multiple faults at the control line and/or input and output lines of one or more SEs if there exists a reachability matrix R_k ($1 < K < N$) of k passes, such that $r^k_{ij} = 1$ for all i, j; $1 < i, j < N$.

Proof: If a MIN has the DFA property, then any input node of the network could reach at least one output node (different than itself as feedback is assumed) after one pass, and hence, it will be able to reach at least one additional output node in successive passes. Thus, each input node should be able to reach all N output nodes in at most N passes if the network has the DFA capability. This means that an R_k ($1 < K < N$) must exist such that $r^k_{ij} = 1$ for all i,j, $1 < i, j < N$. When this is satisfied, we will be able to connect any input node to any one of the output node in at most K passes. Q.E.D.

It may be noted that the Theorem 1 is applicable to the MINs with M-inputs and N-outputs [7] as long as the configuration satisfies the scheme of Fig. 1.

Corollary 3: If there is any stuck type faults at the input side or the output side of an MIN, (hereinafter called primary inputs and outputs respectively), then the DFA property can not be provided.

Proof: If there is a fault at any one of its output line, then it is obvious that nothing can be transmitted on that line and hence corresponding PE can not receive any data. In terms of the graph model, the output line can not be accessed by any one of the inputs. Similarly, if there is a fault at any one of the input lines, then it can not communicate to the output lines and hence the corresponding PE cannot send any data. Q.E.D.

Theorem 2:

The faults in the MIN may destroy its DFA capability if and only if there exists at least two reachability matrices, R^ℓ and $R^{\ell+1}$, for $1 < \ell < N$, such that $r^\ell = r^{\ell+1}$ for all i, j; $1 < i, j < N$ and at least one $r^\ell_{ij} = 0$ for any i,j; $1 < i,j < N$.

Proof: If some faults in the MIN causes it to lose the DFA property, then there remains at least one pair of input and output nodes i and j, that could not be connect in a finite number of steps and is indicated by an entry of $r^k_{ij} = 0$. Moreover, if $R^{\ell+1} = R^\ell$ then all successive powers of R (i.e. $R^{\ell+2}$ and so on) will remain equal to R^ℓ. This means that the connection from i to j can never be provided for any number of passes. Q.E.D.

Corollary 4: In an N-input N-output MIN, R^{P+1}, the reachability matrix within p+1 passes is equal to R^P for all $P > N$.

Proof: As per Theorem 1, if there exist a path from an input to an output node, then the maximum number of passes required is equal to N. Hence, after N passes, we ought to have the corresponding a^N_{ij} element of R^n as 1 and any further pass should not modify the reachability elements and hence a_{ij} elements. Hence, R^{n+1} ought to remain the same as R^n. Q.E.D.

V. DISTANCE MATRIX AND AVERAGE PATHS LENGTH OF THE MINS

The distance matrix D [27] of an MIN is defined as an NxN matrix $[d_{ij}]$ with the entries,

$d_{ij} = 0$ when $i=j$
     the least ℓ (if any) such that $r = \ell$ in the R ,$1 < \ell < N$
     ∞ otherwise

The entries indicate the number of the passes needed for a request to reach the destination. Figs. 10.a, 10.b and 10.c show the distance matrices of the networks of Figs. 7.a, 8.a and 9.a, respectively.

Corollary 5: If no conflict in data path is assumed for the random requests, then the average of the minimum paths length (called the static average and represented by SAV), can be computed from the distance matrix D as follows:

$$SAV = \frac{d}{N^2} \sum_{i=1}^{N} \sum_{j=1}^{N} d_{ij}$$

Where d represents the delay time needed in each pass.

After we have the entries for the reachability matrices of a MIN, it is easy to have the distance matrix and calculate the average path lengths. Once we have all these results, we may examine the question of whether the network is the best from the SAV viewpoint or not. In other words, could we have better SAV by changing the link connection patterns or doing something else. This aspect could be easily examined at least for some kind of network like single stage interconnection network (SSIN) [4,13]. The minimization of path lengths in a SSIN has been covered in [13] and few rules have been suggested for defining the connection pattern in a SSIN. But the effect of faults on SAV, has never been considered.

A simulation program is implemented to observe the performance of a 16 input, 16 output SSCN network (one stage of the Omega network [22] configuration) and the modified version as shown in Figs. 11.a and 11.b. Fig. 12 indicates the effect of changing the connection pattern when no faults are present. The impact of a single fault on SAV is shown in Fig.13 and the modified version provides a better performance. The next question to be addressed is whether such conclusions are valid for a general MIN with several stages. The answers are obtained from the computer program and under no faults, Fig. 14 shows the effect of changing connection pattern from 2-stage Omega-type network to a modified version. Fig. 15, 16 and 17 shows the performances of these 2-stage network when a single fault occurs in control line at the first stage, second atage or at a link connecting the two stages, respectively.

VI. OPTIMUM DESIGN OF A MIN FOR DFA CAPABILITY

The m-stage MIN design with m = n has been widely covered in the literature [2-4, 7-12]. These networks are designed in such a way that there is one to one correspondence between input and output nodes, i.e., from each input line, there is a unique path to each one of the output lines. This is basically due to the fact that the MINs with m = n utilizes minimum number of stages required to satisfy the full connectivity requirements. Systematic ways of designing these networks, have also been described [6] and hence we will not consider their design procedure here. For m > n, the design will include redundancy in the network by providing alternate paths between each input-output pair and a recent work [28] provides a detailed account of their fault-tolerant capabilities. Our main concern is to describe the design methodology for a class of MINs with m < n so that the availability and graceful degradation of the parallel computing system could be optimized. In other words, the network could be designed such that the DFA property could be retained for as many faults as possible. In the following, we describe a design scheme for any general value of m < n. It may be possible to devise other schemes too. But the proposed methodology does provide a certain degree of optimality from DFA view point.

The design procedure is based on the set theory. The two steps are as follows:

A. Partition the N inputs and outputs into $N/(2^m)$ sets with each set consisting of 2^m inputs and 2^m outputs.

B. Design the m-stages of the network such that 2^m-inputs of one set could be connected to 2^m-outputs of another set.

Thus, each set will consist of m stages, with each stage formed with 2^{m-1} SEs. In this way, each of the subnetworks becomes fully connected network of size 2^m input and 2^m output. One such example for m=2 and n=4 is shown in Fig. 18 wherein the 16 inputs and 16 outputs are divided into four subsets with each groups consisting of four elements. The input subsets are (a,b,c,d), (e,f,g,h), (i,j,k,ℓ) and (m,n,o,p) while the output subsets are (A,B,C,D), (E,F,G,H), (I,J,K,L) and (M,N,O,P). This satisfies part A of the design procedure. Part B is assured by assigning output nodes in such a way so that there are no common alphabet between the inputs and outputs of each sub set. In other words, the outputs from the input node subset (a,b,c,d) are not connected to the output node subset (A,B,C,D). It must be remembered that, for the multiple processor system of Fig. 1, both nodes a and A are logically the same as the corresponding PE works as a communication link between the input-output pair a and A. Hence, no advantage is gained by connecting nodes a and A through the MIN such a design procedure for an arbitrary value of n > m is shown in Fig. 19. Before we consider the optimality of the design procedure, three lemmas are in order.

Lemma 1. In the fault-free partition of $m \cdot 2^{m-1}$ SEs connecting 2^m inputs and corresponding outputs, any input can access any one of its outputs in just one pass.

Proof: The design methodology described earlier makes each of the partitioned network a MIN with 2^m inputs-2^m outputs. Moreover, the R-matrix of each partition could be seen to contain all one elements and hence DFA is satisfied in only one pass. Hence, any of its inputs can access all its outputs lines in one pass. Q.E.D.

Lemma 2. In each partitioned group consisting of $m \cdot 2^{m-1}$ SEs connecting 2m inputs and the corresponding output lines, if some or all SEs have single faults (at the control line or input or the output lines of the SEs except at the primary input lines and output lines), then each primary input line can be connected to at least one of the primary output lines.

Proof: From Figs. 3.b and 3.c, it is obvious that fault at the control line of an SE allows each input to be connected to one output. A single fault at one of the inputs of the SE allows the other input to be connected to both the outputs (Fig. 4.a) and a single fault at an output side of the SE permits both inputs to be connected to the non-faulty output (Fig. 4.b). It may be noted from Figs. 3 and 4 that a fault at an input (output) line is reflected as a fault at the corresponding output (input) line. Hence simultaneous faults at an input and an output line of the same SE are considered as a multiple fault. As the primary input and output lines of the MIN are fault-free, one input can be connected to at least one output lines. This could also be proved using the adjacency matrices for each stage and by using the resultant one-pass reachability matrix. Q.E.D.

Lemma 3: A special case of the Lemma 2 arises when the control lines of all the switches are stuck at zero or one, then the graph model for a partitioned network will contain 2^m unconnected subgraphs, with each one directed from one primary input to only one of the primary outputs.

Proof: From Figs. 3.b and 3.c, whenever the control line of an SE is faulty, there is one to one connection. This means only one input is connected to one and only one of the outputs and hence the adjacency matrix for each stage will have only one nonzero element for each row and each column. Hence, the over all R-matrix will also have only one "1" entry in each row and each column. Hence, we will end up with overall one-to-one connection, with $2^m = 4$ unconnected subgraphs for each group. Q.E.D.

The optimality of the design in terms of DFA capabilty is demonstrated by the following theorem.

Theorem 3: If a 2^n input-2^n output MIN is implemented by m-stages (m < n) according to the design procedures A and B, then DFA capability is ensured for multiple single-faults at the SEs provided $m \cdot 2^{m-1}$ SEs constituting connection for one partition of 2^m inputs and the corresponding outputs are assumed fault-free, and the upper bound for the number of passes required to provide the DFA is (2K-1), where K is given by $K=2^{n-m}$.

Proof: The graph models or possible single faults have been given in Fig. 3.b, 3.c, 4.a and 4.b. The connectivity consideration (and the adjacency matrix), is important for the DFA capability. A typical m-stage MIN is shown in Fig. 19. Then the worst case fault could be said to be present when SEs of all the (K-1) partitions are faulty. For simplicity (and without losing the generality) let us assume that the kth partition is healthy. The reachability matrix R for each partition could be obtained and the R-matrix or first (K-1) partitions would satisfy the Lemma 2 while the Lemma 1 is applicable to the last partition. As interpreted earlier, in the first (K-1) partition, one pass would allow any input to be connected to at least one of the outputs while Kth partition would allow any input to be connected to any one of its outputs in one pass.

Let us assume that we started access from one of the inputs of the 1st partition. Under the assumed faults, the first pass will allow access to at least one of its output nodes and the feedback path through the corresponding PE takes us to a node of the 2nd partition. The second pass takes us to one of the outputs of the 3rd partition and so on. In the worst case, it will take (K-1) passes before we reach the Kth partition. As this group contains all healthy SEs and the corresponding R matrix contains all "1" elements, the next pass can take us to all the output nodes of the Kth partition. Now, the feedback path through PEs takes us back to the first partition and access to all 2^m inputs of the 1st partition is possible. The next pass provides access to all 2^m outputs of the 2nd partition. If this process is continued, a total of (K-1 + K) = (2K -1) passes are required to access any one of the output nodes. Q.E.D.

The graph node of the MIN shown in Fig. 18 which contains several single faults is provided in Fig. 20. The reachabilty marices in various passes are given in Figs. 21.a-21.g. Under the random request loading and close-to-finish arbi-

tration [29], the computer simulation mentioned earlier provides the peformances of the MIN of Fig. 18 and is shown in Fig.22. The average path lengths are computed for the cases when it has a single fault on the control line in either stages or at any one of the links between the two stages, and when no faults are present. The resulting curves indicate that a single fault has a very marginal effect on the average time delay and only slight increase in average delay could be said to be a very valuable simulation result to support our claim that our design is good from a fault-tolerance view point. It has not been possible to compare our design methodology with others, as, to the best of our knowledge, there does not exist any such technique in the literature.

Corollary 6. The restriction imposed by Theorem 3 is not a necessary condition for the DFA property.

Proof: Theorem 3 is sufficient for ensuring DFA, but not necessary, as the faults at the control line might be such that the R-matrix elements may contain arbitrary 1's and the multiple pass (hence, multiplication of the R matrix to itself) may lead to an R^{ℓ} matrix with all "1" entries. Q.E.D.

One such exception, is illustrated in Fig. 23, which can be said to possess a high degree of fault tolerance. Thus, our design procedure is very useful in implementing a MIN with the DFA capability in the presence of faults. Theorem 3 identifies the set of single faults at the SEs so that it is possible to ascertain the DFA characteristic even without obtaining a graph model and without performing a lot of connectivity and reachability computation.

VII. CONCLUDING REMARKS

The fault-model of an SE is used to model the MINs and adjacency matrix and reachability matrices are employed to provides a systematic procedure of testing the networks DFA capability. The versatility of the fault model makes it possible to test the network under multiple stuck-type faults both at the control lines and the input/output lines of the SEs. In addition, the R-matrix in successive passes are also useful in computing the average path length. The network design procedure enables the MIN to possess maximum fault-tolerance and hence, in turn, optimizes the availability of the system. The selection of connection pattern is seen to be a key issue in minimizing the path length in both the SSINs and MINs which could also be used as an index for the performance. If we consider the fault-tolerance as well as the minimization of the path length simultaneously, then the optimization problem of the MIN becomes extremely complex and we hope to present additional results in the near future.

References

1. D.P. Agrawal and T.Y. Feng, "A Study of Communication Processor Systems," Technical Report, Rome Air Development Center, RADC-TR-79-310, Dec. 1979, 179 pages.

2. C.L. Wu and T.Y. Feng, "On a Class of Multistage Interconnection Networks," IEEE Transactions on Computers, Vol. C-29, No. 8, Aug. 1980, pp. 694-702.

3. H.J. Siegel, "The Theory Underlying the Partitioning of Permutation Networks," IEEE Transactions on Computers, Vol. C-29, NO. 9, Sept. 1980, PP. 791-801.

4. D.K. Pradhan and K.L. Kodandapani, "A Uniform Representation of Single-and Multi-stage Interconnection Networks Used in SIMD Machines," IEEE Transactions on Computers, Vol. C-29, No. 9, Sep. 1980, PP. 777-791.

5. D.P. Agrawal, "On Graph Theoretic Approach to n-and (2n-1)-stage Interconnection Networks," Proc. 19th Annual Allerton Conf. on Comm, Control and Computing, Sept 30-Oct. 2, 1981, PP.559-568.

6. D.P. Agrawal, "Graph Theoretic Analysis and Design of Multistage Interconnection Networks," IEEE Transactions on Computers, Vol. C-32, No. 9, Sept. 1983, PP. 637-648.

7. L.N. Bhuyan and D.P. Agrawal, "Design and Performance of a General Class of Interconnection Networks, Proc, 1982 Int. Conf. on Parallel Proc., Aug 24-27, 1982, PP.2-9. (also to appear in IEEE Transactions on Computers, Vol. C-32, No. 11, Dec. 1983, pp. 1081-1090.

8. D.P. Agrawal and S.C. Kim, "On Non-equivalent Multistage Interconnection Networks," Proc. 10th Int. Conf. on Parallel Proc., Aug. 25-28, 1981, PP. 234-237.

9. M.A. Abidi and D.P. Agrawal, "On Conflict-Free Permutations in Multistage Interconnection Network," Journal of Digital Systems, Vol. V, No. 2, Summer 1980, PP.115-134.

10. M. A. Abidi and D.P. Agrawal, "Two Single Pass Permutations in Multistage Interconnection Networks," 1980 Conference on Information Sciences and Systems, March 26-28, 1980, PP. 516-522.

11. D. A. Pauda, D.J. Kuck and D.H. Lawrie, "High-Speed Multiprocessors and Compilation Techniques, " IEEE Transactions on Computers, Vol. C-29, No. 9, Sept. 1980, PP. 763-776.

12. C. L. Wu and T.Y. Feng, "The Reverse-Exchange Interconnection Network," IEEE Transactions on Computers, Vol. C-29, No. 9, Sept. 1980, PP. 801-811.

13. J. E. Wirsching and T. Kishi, "Minimization of Path Lengths in Single Stage Connnection Networks," Proc. 3rd Int. Conf. on Distributed Computing Systems, Oct. 18-22, 1982, PP. 563-571.

14. D. C. Operferman and N.T. Tsao-Wu, "On a Class of Rearrangeable Switching Networks, Part II: Enumeration Studies and Fault Diagnosis," Bell System Technical Journal, May/June 1971, PP.1601-1618.

15. J. P. Shen and J.P. Hayes, "Fault Tolerance of a Class of Connecting Networks," 7th Symposium on Computer Architecture, La Baule, France, May 6-8, 1980, PP. 61-71.

16. J. P. Shen, "Fault Tolerance Analysis of Several Interconnection Networks," Proc., 1982 Int. Conf. on Parallel Processing, Aug. 24-27, 1982, PP. 102-112.

17. K. M. So and J.J. Narraway, "On-line Fault Diagnosis of Switching Networks," IEEE Transactions on Circuits and Systems, Vol. CAS-26, No. 7, July 1979, PP. 575-583.

18. J. J. Narraway and K.M. So, "Fault Diagnosis in inter-Processor Switching Networks," Proc. of the International Conference on Circuits and Computers, Oct. 1-3, 1980, PP. 750-753.

19. C. L. Wu and T.Y. Feng, "Fault-Diagnosis for a Class of Multistage Interconnection Networks," 1979 International Conference on Parallel Processing, Aug. 21-24, 1979, PP. 269-278.

20. D. P. Siewioriek et al., "A Case Study of C*mmp, Cm*, and C*vmp: Part I -Experiences with Fault Tolerance in Multiprocessor Systems," Proceedings of the IEEE, Vol. 66, No. 10, Oct. 1978, PP. 1178-1200.

21. D. P. Agrawal, "Automated Testing of Computer Networks," 1980 International Conference on Circuits and Computers, Oct. 1-3, 1980, PP.717-720.

22. D. K. Lawrie, "Access and Alignment of Data in an Array Processor," IEEE Transactions on Computers, Vol. C-24, No. 12, Dec. 1975, PP. 1145-1155.

23. K. M. Falavarianai and D.K. Pradhan, "Fault-Diagnosis of Parallel Processor Interconnection Networks," Proc. of the 1981 Fault Tolerant Computing Symposium, June 1981.

24. S. Sowrirajan and S.M. Reddy, "A Design for Fault-Tolerant Full Connection Networks," 1980 Conference on Information Sciences and Systems, PP. 536-540.

25. D.P. Agrawal, "Testing and Fault-Tolerance of Multistage Interconnection Networks," IEEE Computer, Vol. 15, No. 4, April 1982, pp. 41-53.

26. L. R. Goke and G.J. Lipovski, "Banyan networks for partitioning of the multiprocessor systems," Proceedings of the First Annual Symp. on Computer Architecture, Dec. 1973, pp. 21-28.

27. F. Harary, "Graph Theory" book, Addison-Wesley Co. 1972.

28. D. P. Agrawal and D. Kaur, "Fault Tolerant Capabilities of Redundant Multistage Interconnection Networks," Proc. Real-time Systems Symp., Dec. 6-8, 1983, pp. 119-127.

29. P. Y. Chen, P.C. Yew and D. Lawrie, "Performance of Packet Switching in Buffered Single-stage Shuffle-exchange Networks," Proc. 3rd Int. Conf. on Distributed Computing Systems, Oct. 18-22, 1982, PP. 622-627.

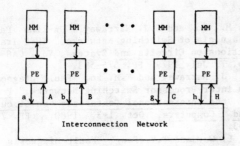

Fig. 1. Multiple Processor System Organization

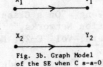

Fig. 3a Graph model of the SE of Fig. 1a.

Fig. 3b. Graph Model of the SE when C s-a-0

Fig. 3c. Graph Model of the SE when C s-a-1

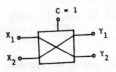

Fig. 2.a. Switching Element

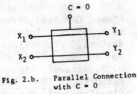

Fig. 2.b. Parallel Connection with C = 0

Fig. 4a. Graph Model of the SE when X_1 s-a-α

Fig. 4b. Graph Model of the SE when Y_2 s-a-α

Fig. 4c. Graph Model of the SE when X_2 s-a-α and Y_2 s-a-β

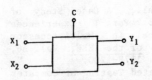

Fig. 2.c. Cross-connection with C = 1

Fig. 4d. Graph Model when X_1 s-a-α and X_2 s-a-β

Fig. 4e. Graph Model when X_2 s-a-α, Y_1 s-a-β and Y_2 s-a-γ

Fig. 4f. Graph Model when control s-a-1 and X_2 s-a-α

Fig. 4g Graph Model when control s-a-0 and Y_1 s-a-α

Fig. 4h. Graph Model when control s-a-1, X_1 s-a-α and Y_2 s-a-β

Fig. 4i. Graph Model when control s-a-α, Y_1 s-a-β and Y_2 s-a-γ

Fig. 4. Graph Models of the SE under various fault conditions.

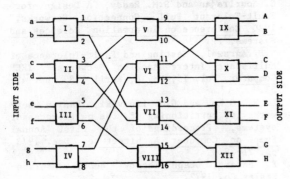

Fig.2.d Base-line Network for N = 8 (n = 3).

Fig. 5.a. Graph Model of a SE for Omega Network when upper broadcast s-a-α

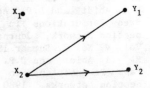

Fig. 5.b. Graph Model with lower broadcast s-a-α

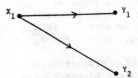

Fig. 5.c. Graph Model when upper broadcast s-a-α and X_2 s-a-γ

Fig. 5.d. Graph Model when lower broadcast s-a-α and Y_2 s-a-γ

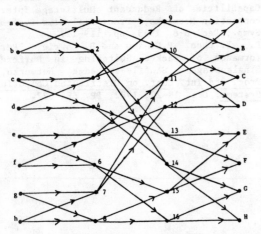

Fig.7.a Graph Model for the Baseline Network of Fig. 2d.

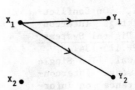

Fig. 6.a Adjacency matrix of the SE of Fig. 2.a.

Fig. 6.b Adjacency matrix of the SE of Fig. 2.b.

Fig. 6.c Adjacency matrix of the SE of Fig. 2.c.

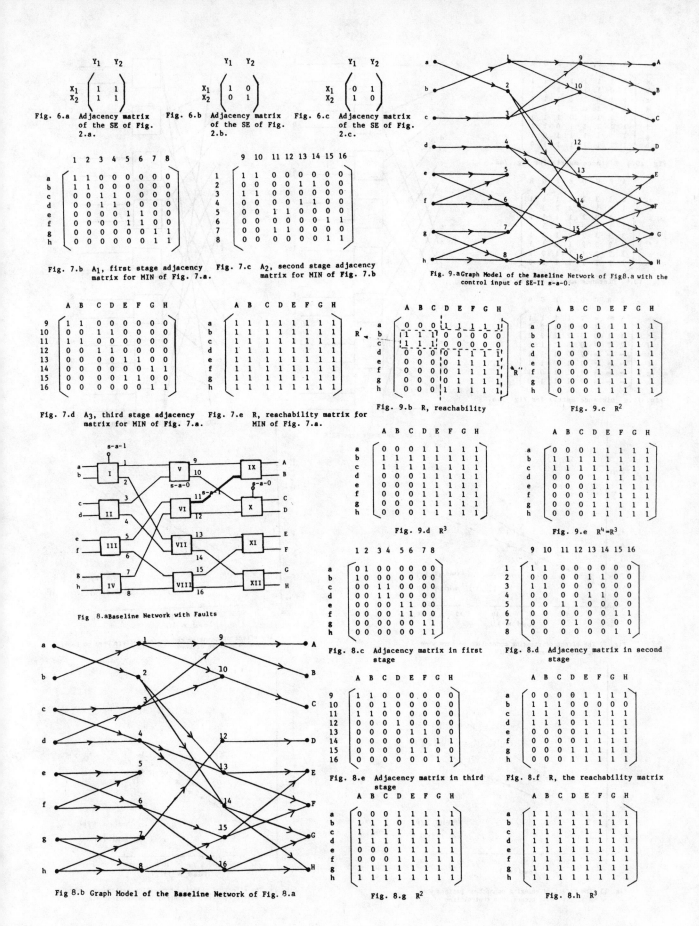

Fig. 6.a Adjacency matrix of the SE of Fig. 2.a.

Fig. 6.b Adjacency matrix of the SE of Fig. 2.b.

Fig. 6.c Adjacency matrix of the SE of Fig. 2.c.

Fig. 7.b A₁, first stage adjacency matrix for MIN of Fig. 7.a.

Fig. 7.c A₂, second stage adjacency matrix for MIN of Fig. 7.b

Fig. 9.a Graph Model of the Baseline Network of Fig8.a with the control input of SE-II s-a-0.

Fig. 7.d A₃, third stage adjacency matrix for MIN of Fig. 7.a.

Fig. 7.e R, reachability matrix for MIN of Fig. 7.a.

Fig. 9.b R, reachability

Fig. 9.c R²

Fig. 9.d R³

Fig. 9.e R⁴=R³

Fig 8.a Baseline Network with Faults

Fig. 8.c Adjacency matrix in first stage

Fig. 8.d Adjacency matrix in second stage

Fig. 8.e Adjacency matrix in third stage

Fig. 8.f R, the reachability matrix

Fig 8.b Graph Model of the Baseline Network of Fig. 8.a

Fig. 8.g R²

Fig. 8.h R³

151

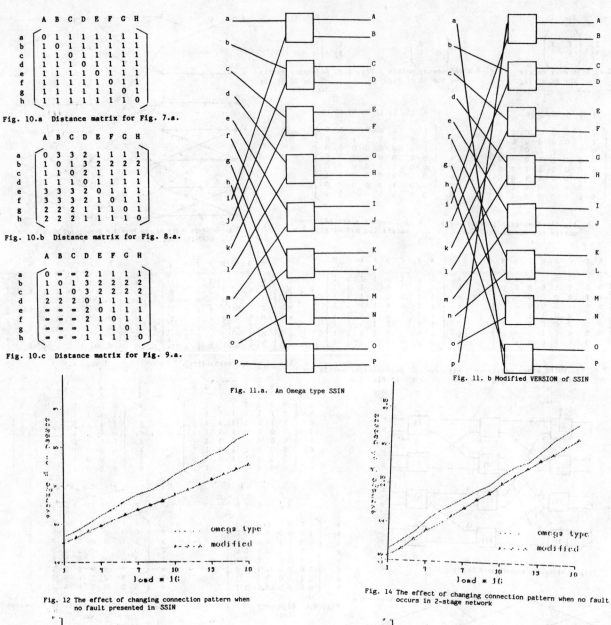

```
    A B C D E F G H
a │ 0 1 1 1 1 1 1 1 │
b │ 1 0 1 1 1 1 1 1 │
c │ 1 1 0 1 1 1 1 1 │
d │ 1 1 1 0 1 1 1 1 │
e │ 1 1 1 1 0 1 1 1 │
f │ 1 1 1 1 1 0 1 1 │
g │ 1 1 1 1 1 1 0 1 │
h │ 1 1 1 1 1 1 1 0 │
```

Fig. 10.a Distance matrix for Fig. 7.a.

```
    A B C D E F G H
a │ 0 3 3 2 1 1 1 1 │
b │ 1 0 1 3 2 2 2 2 │
c │ 1 1 0 2 1 1 1 1 │
d │ 1 1 1 0 1 1 1 1 │
e │ 3 3 3 2 0 1 1 1 │
f │ 3 3 3 2 1 0 1 1 │
g │ 2 2 2 1 1 1 0 1 │
h │ 2 2 2 1 1 1 1 0 │
```

Fig. 10.b Distance matrix for Fig. 8.a.

```
    A B C D E F G H
a │ 0 ∞ ∞ 2 1 1 1 1 │
b │ 1 0 1 3 2 2 2 2 │
c │ 1 1 0 3 2 2 2 2 │
d │ 2 2 2 0 1 1 1 1 │
e │ ∞ ∞ ∞ 2 0 1 1 1 │
f │ ∞ ∞ ∞ 2 1 0 1 1 │
g │ ∞ ∞ ∞ 1 1 1 0 1 │
h │ ∞ ∞ ∞ 1 1 1 1 0 │
```

Fig. 10.c Distance matrix for Fig. 9.a.

Fig. 11.a. An Omega type SSIN

Fig. 11. b Modified VERSION of SSIN

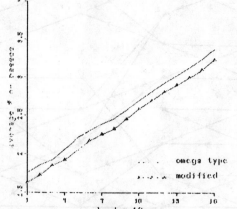

Fig. 12 The effect of changing connection pattern when
no fault presented in SSIN

Fig. 14 The effect of changing connection pattern when no fault
occurs in 2-stage network

Fig. 13 The effect of changing connection pattern when
a single fault occurs in a control line of SSIN

Fig. 15 The effect of changing connection pattern when single
fault occurs in the control line at first stage.

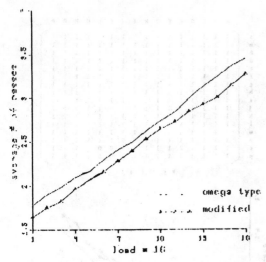

Fig. 16 The effect of changing connection pattern when single fault occurs in the control line at second stage.

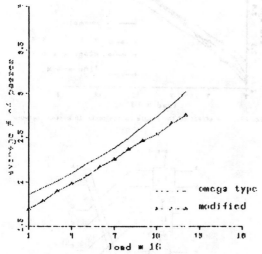

Fig. 17 The effect of changing connection pattern when single fault occurs in the link between 2 stages.

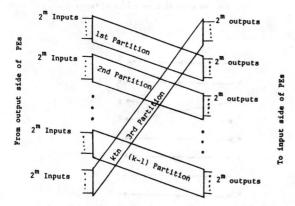

Fig. 19 Optimum design of an m-stage MIN

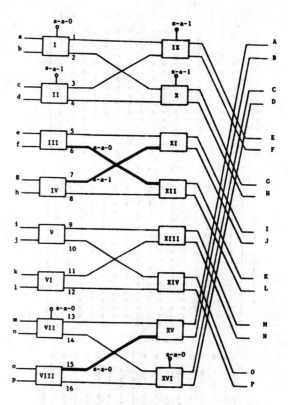

Fig. 18 Two-stage MI network with single stuck type faults at various SEs. (only one group of 4-SEs V, VI, XIII and XIV not faulty)

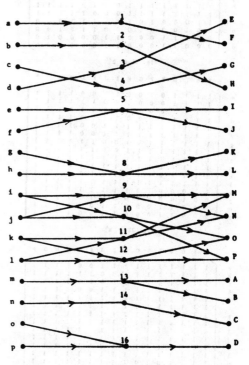

Fig. 20 A Graph Model of Fig. 18.

153

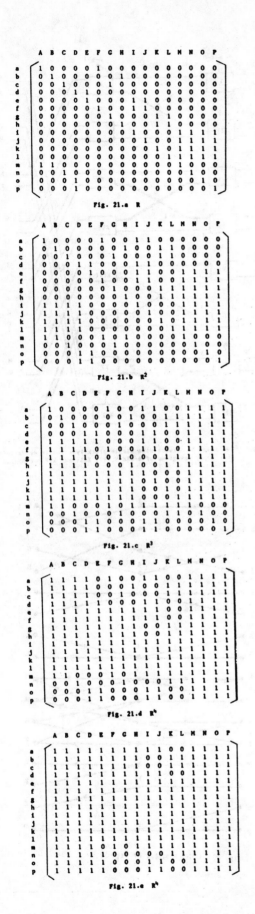

Fig. 21.a R

Fig. 21.b R^2

Fig. 21.c R^3

Fig. 21.d R^4

Fig. 21.e R^4

Fig. 21.f R^5

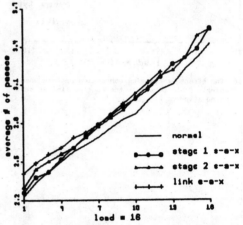

normal
stage 1 s-a-x
stage 2 s-a-x
link s-a-x

average # of passes

load = 16

Fig. 22. The effect of the single faults occur in 2-stage network

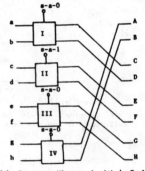

(a). One stage MI network with 4 Faults

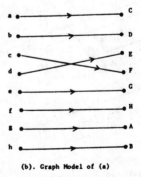

(b). Graph Model of (a)

Fig. 23 One Stage MI network and its graph model

154

ANALYSIS OF MULTIPLE BUS INTERCONNECTION NETWORKS[1]

T.N. Mudge, J.P. Hayes, G.D. Buzzard and D.C. Winsor

University of Michigan
Computing Research Laboratory
Room 1079 East Engineering Bldg.
Ann Arbor, MI 48109 USA

Abstract

A new analytic performance model is presented for multiprocessor systems employing multiple bus interconnection networks. The system bandwidth is analyzed as a two stage process taking into account conflicts arising from memory and bus interference. The analysis covers multiple bus systems in which each memory is connected to every bus, and systems in which each memory is connected to a subset of the buses. The model is compared to previously published simulation data and is shown to be in close agreement.

I. Introduction

A great deal of attention has been paid to the design and analysis of interconnection networks for multiprocessor systems. Most of the previous research has dealt with crossbar networks or multistage networks [1]. While these networks are attractive for applications where high bandwidth is required, their high cost and special implementation requirements have prevented them from being used for the full range of multiprocessor applications. Most commercial systems containing more than one processor employ a single bus; consider, for example, the design philosophy advocated for the iAPX86 family in which the Multibus (IEEE 796 standard bus) provides all the intrasystem communication [2]. Single bus systems are inexpensive and easy to implement but have limited bandwidth and lack fault tolerance. A natural extension is to employ several shared buses to increase bandwidth and fault tolerance at moderate cost. Figure 1 shows typical systems in which B buses are used to interconnect N processors to M memory modules ($B \leq N$). Unlike a crossbar or multistage network, a multiple bus interconnection scheme allows easy incremental expansion of the number of processors and memories in the system. Furthermore, the buses can be configured in a variety of ways to provide a range of trade-offs between bandwidth, connection cost, and reliability.

Recently, Lang, et al. [3,4] have investigated multiple bus systems of the kind depicted in Figure 1. Using simulation they determined the bandwidth characteristics of two representative bus configurations, complete and partial. In the complete case, which is illustrated in Figure 1(a), every processor and memory module is connected to every bus; in the partial case, which is illustrated in Figure 1(b), each memory need only be connected to a subset of the buses. In particular, Lang et al. [3] showed that a complete multiple bus configuration with $B \approx N/2$ has almost the same bandwidth as an $N \times M$ crossbar, as well as higher fault tolerance. Similar advantages can be obtained at lower cost using a partial bus

configuration.

This paper presents an analytic model of the bandwidth of multiple bus systems. Our results are shown to agree closely with the experimental data presented in [3]. Section II defines the underlying assumptions and develops the bandwidth model. Section III then compares the analytic model to the previous simulation results. Finally, some possible extensions of this model are mentioned in Section IV.

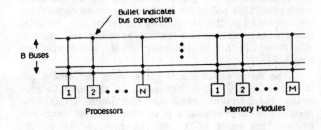

(a)

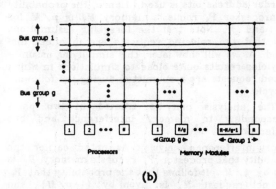

(b)

Figure 1. Two multiprocessor systems with multiple bus interconnection networks: (a) complete; (b) partial.

---

[1]This work was supported by the National Science Foundation, under the Grants No. ECS-8214709 and MCS-8009315.

Reprinted from *Proceedings of the 1984 International Conference on Parallel Processing*, 1984, pages 228-232. Copyright © 1984 by The Institute of Electrical and Electronics Engineers, Inc.

II. The Model

The systems shown in Figure 1 are assumed to be synchronous, and processor-memory transactions are assumed to occur during discrete time intervals termed bus cycles (continuous time analogues of such systems are discussed in [5,6]). For the purposes of this paper, bandwidth will be defined as the expected number of buses in use during a bus cycle. Apart from the configuration of the system, i.e., the values of B, M, N, and the buses grouping used, the most important factors affecting bandwidth are the rate at which memory requests are made by processors, and the degree of conflict that those requests experience.

There are two sources of conflict due to memory requests in a multiple bus system. First, more than one request can be made to the same memory module, resulting in memory interference. Second, there may be an insufficient number of buses available to accommodate all the memory requests, resulting in bus interference. In [3] a two-stage arbitration scheme is used to resolve these conflicts. In the first stage, memory interference is resolved by M 1-out-of-N arbiters each of which selects at most one outstanding request per memory module. In the second stage, bus interference is resolved by a B-out-of-M arbiter which assigns the buses to the memory requests selected in the first stage. The assignment is done on a round robin basis by each arbiter. In a realistic system requests that are blocked by either memory or bus interference are resubmitted during the following bus cycle. This policy for handling rejected requests is implemented in the simulation model of [3]. Analytic models that capture this feature appear to be intractable except in those cases where B, M, and N are very small [7].

The basic assumptions underlying our model follow those of [3]. Each processor is assumed to generate independent requests (Bernoulli trials) for memory with probability p at the start of each bus cycle. This value of p will be referred to as the request rate. Modeling the memory access process as a Bernoulli process has been validated empirically in [8-10], and is widely used as a basis for memory interference models. The memory requests are assumed to be uniformly distributed across all the memories with probability $1/M$; this is a reasonable assumption when address interleaving based on the low-order address bits is used. Hence, the probability that processor P_i requests memory M_j is p/M for all i and j. Note that the foregoing assumptions imply that the rejected requests are in effect discarded. As we will show later, this simplifying assumption yields results quite close to simulations in which blocked requests are resubmitted during the following bus cycle.

The analysis can be treated in two parts corresponding to memory interference and bus interference.

Memory interference analysis: As noted earlier the probability that processor P_i requests memory M_j is given by p/M. It follows that the probability that P_i does not request M_j is given by $(1-p/M)$, and further, that the probability that none of P_i $(i=1,\ldots,N)$ requests M_j is given by $(1-p/M)^N$. This last expression can also be interpreted as the probability that the 1-out-of-N arbiter

associated with M_j has no input requests from which to choose. Conversely, the probability that there is at least one request for M_j is given by

$$q = 1 - (1-p/M)^N \qquad (1)$$

From the behavior of the arbiters, we can conclude that the probability that one request gains access to M_j is q for all j.

Bus interference analysis: Only the requests from at most B of the M 1-out-of-N memory request arbiters can be handled during any bus cycle, since there are only B buses. The probability that exactly i of the M memory-request arbiters output a memory request is given by

$$f(i) = \begin{bmatrix} M \\ i \end{bmatrix} q^i (1-q)^{M-i} \qquad (2)$$

The probability that B or more of the M memory-request arbiters output a memory-request can be written

$$F(B) = \sum_{i=B}^{M} f(i) \qquad (3)$$

This is the probability that all B buses are in use, i.e., the interconnection network is saturated. From equations (2) and (3), the following expression can be derived for the expected number of buses in use during a bus cycle:

$$BW = B \, F(B) + \sum_{i=1}^{B-1} i \, f(i) \qquad (4)$$

By our earlier definition, BW also represents the bandwidth of a complete multiple bus system.

As will be shown, the above expression for BW is in close agreement with the simulation results presented in [3]. The major source of error arises from the assumption that blocked requests are discarded. In reality, and also in the simulations, blocked requests are repeatedly resubmitted or queued until the memory they request allows them access. Equation (4) can be refined by taking this into account in the manner described below.

The probability that a memory request is accepted in the bus cycle in which it is made, is given by

$$P_a = \frac{BW}{Np} \qquad (5)$$

The numerator of (5), i.e., the bandwidth, measures the number of requests that obtain memory access during a bus cycle. The denominator of (5) measures the total number of requests made by all the processors during a bus cycle. It is convenient to define an "adjusted" request rate α, that accounts for resubmission of rejected requests, where $0 \le p \le \alpha \le 1$. By assumption, the memory request process is a Bernoulli trail with success probability p or, in the case of the adjusted rate, α. It follows that the mean number of bus cycles before a request (trial) is $1/p-1$, or in the case of the adjusted rate, $1/\alpha - 1$ [11]. Thus, the ratio of the number of successful requests to the total number of requests, i.e., P_a, is given by

$$P_a = \frac{\frac{1}{\alpha}-1}{\frac{1}{p}-1} \qquad (6)$$

Equations (5) and (6) can be used in an iteration scheme to get an improved estimate for BW due to the adjusted rate α, as follows:

$$\alpha_{k+1} = \left[1 + \frac{BW(\alpha_k)}{Np}\left(\frac{1}{p}-1\right)\right]^{-1} \qquad (7)$$

Here we are using equation (1) for q with α replacing p. Solution of (7) for α_{k+1} yields an improved value, $BW(\alpha_{k+1})$, for the bandwidth. Any remaining deviations from the simulated bandwidth occur because α does not take into account the fact that resubmissions are all directed to the same memory. This iterative technique is an adaptation of a method first proposed by Hoogendoorn [10] (for details see [12]). For large systems, i.e., large M or N, a higher order iterative scheme may be used in place of equation (7) to reduce the number of steps to solution.

It is also possible to derive a analytic expression for the change in bandwidth, ΔBW, due to the removal (or loss) of one bus. Let

$$\Delta BW = BW(B) - BW(B-1) \qquad (8)$$

Then from equation (4) it can be shown that

$$\Delta BW = F(B) \qquad (9)$$

Equation (3) shows that $F(B)$ is the sum of the last $M-B+1$ terms of a binomial series. This can be approximated to the tail of a normal distribution with high accuracy if M is large [11]. In fact, the approximation works well even if M is as small as 10. By approximating ΔBW in this way, it is possible to show that $\Delta BW \approx 2$ percent if the following holds:

$$B > Mq + 2\sqrt{Mq(1-q)} \qquad (10)$$

For example, for $M = N = 16$ and $p = 0.5$, a value of $B > 10$ yields a bandwidth that changes by no more than 2 percent if a bus is removed.

We now generalize equation (4) for the case of partial buses (Figure 1(b)). The memory interference analysis is the same as before, since it is independent of the bus configuration, i.e., equation (1) continues to apply. However, the bus-interference analysis needs modification. If the B buses are grouped into g equal groups (assuming g is a factor of B), equations (2) and (3) become the following:

$$f_g(i) = \binom{M/g}{i} q^i (1-q)^{\frac{M}{g}-i} \qquad (11)$$

$$F_g(B) = \sum_{i=B/g}^{M/g} f_g(i) \qquad (12)$$

Consequently, the bandwidth can be written as

$$BW_g = g\left[\frac{B}{g}\,F_g(B) + \sum_{i=1}^{\frac{B}{g}-1} i\, f_g(i)\right] \qquad (13)$$

which is simply g times the bandwidth of any one of the g subsystems formed from N processors, B/g buses, and M/g memories. Equation (13) can also be incorporated into the iterative scheme of equation (7), as follows:

$$\alpha_{k+1} = 1 - \frac{BW_g(\alpha_k)}{Np}(1-p) \qquad (14)$$

As before, equation (14) yields an improved value, $BW_g(\alpha_{k+1})$, for the bandwidth.

III. Evaluation of Results

In this section we briefly compare the results obtained from our analytic model with the simulation data of Lang et al. [3]. The same $N \times N$ multiprocessor configurations are employed, including systems with complete buses, and systems with two group of partial buses.

Table 1 shows the simulation results presented in [3] for complete bus systems. The bandwidth BW is calculated for various values of B and N, with p, the independent processor request rate, assigned the values 1.0 and 0.5. The data here clearly indicates that BW changes very little after N reaches $B/2$. Table 2 shows BW as predicted by equation (4). The difference between the simulated and analytic values of BW is presented in Table 3. It can be seen that, except for small values of N and p, this difference is less then about 10 percent, indicating reasonable good agreement between our results and those of [3]. Table 4 presents the bandwidth values obtained by using the iterative method. The corresponding percentage deviations from the simulated values (Table 1) appear in Table 5. The maximum difference has now been reduced to less than 7 percent in all cases.

Lang et al. also simulated the partial bus organization of Figure 1(b) with $g = 2$; their results are tabulated in Table 6. The corresponding analytic data, obtained using the iterative method of Section II, is given in Table 7. Comparison of these two sets of results shows good agreement (less than 7 percent) between the analytic and empirical data; see Table 8.

Number of Buses, B	Number of processors N ($=M$)							
	4		8		12		16	
	p=1	p=.5	p=1	p=.5	p=1	p=.5	p=1	p=.5
1	1.00	1.00	1.00	1.00	1.00	1.00	1.00	1.00
2	1.97	1.65	2.00	2.00	2.00	2.00	2.00	2.00
3	2.55	1.77	3.00	2.87	3.00	3.00	3.00	3.00
4	2.62	1.77	3.93	3.33	4.00	3.95	4.00	4.00
5			4.62	3.45	4.99	4.67	5.00	4.98
6			4.90	3.47	5.93	5.03	6.00	5.85
7			4.94	3.47	6.68	5.13	6.98	6.43
8			4.95	3.47	7.12	5.16	7.92	6.70
9					7.27	5.16	8.72	6.82
10					7.28	5.16	9.27	6.83
11					7.30	5.16	9.53	6.83
12					7.30	5.16	9.61	6.83
13							9.63	6.84
14							9.63	6.84
15							9.63	6.84
16							9.63	6.84

Table 1. Bandwidth BW obtained by simulation for the complete bus.

Number of Buses, B	Number of processors N $(=M)$							
	4		8		12		16	
	p=1	p=.5	p=1	p=.5	p=1	p=.5	p=1	p=.5
1	0.99	0.88	1.00	0.98	1.00	1.00	1.00	1.00
2	1.89	1.43	2.00	1.88	2.00	1.98	2.00	2.00
3	2.52	1.63	2.97	2.57	3.00	2.89	3.00	2.98
4	2.73	1.66	3.87	2.99	3.99	3.67	4.00	3.91
5			4.59	3.16	4.97	4.23	5.00	4.74
6			5.04	3.22	5.88	4.57	5.99	5.41
7			5.22	3.23	6.66	4.72	6.97	5.87
8			5.25	3.23	7.24	4.78	7.89	6.15
9					7.58	4.80	8.72	6.29
10					7.73	4.80	9.39	6.35
11					7.77	4.80	9.86	6.37
12					7.78	4.80	10.13	6.37
13							10.25	6.37
14							10.29	6.37
15							10.30	6.37
16							10.30	6.37

Table 2. Bandwidth BW calculated from equation (4).

Number of Buses, B	Number of processors N $(=M)$							
	4		8		12		16	
	p=1	p=.5	p=1	p=.5	p=1	p=.5	p=1	p=.5
1	-1.00	-12.00	0.00	-2.00	0.00	0.00	0.00	0.00
2	-4.06	-13.33	0.00	-6.00	0.00	-1.00	0.00	0.00
3	-1.18	-7.91	-1.00	-10.45	0.00	-3.67	0.00	-0.67
4	4.20	-6.21	-1.53	-10.21	-0.25	-7.09	0.00	-2.25
5			-0.65	-8.41	-0.40	-9.42	0.00	-4.82
6			2.86	-7.20	-0.84	-9.15	-0.17	-7.52
7			5.67	-6.92	-0.30	-7.99	-0.14	-8.71
8			6.06	-6.92	1.69	-7.36	-0.38	-8.21
9					4.26	-6.98	0.00	-7.77
10					6.18	-6.98	1.29	-7.03
11					6.44	-6.98	3.46	-6.73
12					6.58	-6.98	5.41	-6.73
13							6.44	-6.87
14							6.85	-6.87
15							6.96	-6.87
16							6.96	-6.87

Table 3. Percentage difference between calculated (Table 2) and simulated values (Table 1) of BW.

Number of Buses, B	Number of processors N $(=M)$							
	4		8		12		16	
	p=1	p=.5	p=1	p=.5	p=1	p=.5	p=1	p=.5
1	0.99	0.97	1.00	1.00	1.00	1.00	1.00	1.00
2	1.89	1.58	2.00	1.98	2.00	2.00	2.00	2.00
3	2.52	1.77	2.97	2.80	3.00	2.99	3.00	3.00
4	2.73	1.79	3.87	3.27	3.99	3.91	4.00	3.99
5			4.59	3.46	4.97	4.60	5.00	4.95
6			5.04	3.51	5.88	4.99	5.99	5.79
7			5.22	3.52	6.66	5.16	6.97	6.37
8			5.25	3.52	7.24	5.23	7.89	6.71
9					7.58	5.25	8.72	6.88
10					7.73	5.25	9.39	6.95
11					7.77	5.25	9.86	6.98
12					7.78	5.25	10.13	6.98
13							10.25	6.98
14							10.29	6.98
15							10.30	6.98
16							10.30	6.98

Table 4. Bandwidth BW with adjusted rate α calculated from equation (7).

Number of Buses, B	Number of processors N $(=M)$							
	4		8		12		16	
	p=1	p=.5	p=1	p=.5	p=1	p=.5	p=1	p=.5
1	-1.00	-3.00	0.00		0.00	0.00	0.00	0.00
2	-4.06	-4.24	0.00	-1.00	0.00	0.00	0.00	0.00
3	-1.18	0.00	-1.00	-2.44	0.00	-0.33	0.00	0.00
4	4.20	1.13	-1.53	-1.80	-0.25	-1.01	0.00	-0.25
5			-0.65	0.29	-0.40	-1.50	0.00	-0.60
6			2.86	1.15	-0.84	-0.80	-0.17	-1.03
7			5.67	1.44	-0.30	0.58	-0.14	-0.93
8			6.06	1.44	1.69	1.36	-0.38	0.15
9					4.26	1.74	0.00	0.88
10					6.18	1.74	1.29	1.76
11					6.44	1.74	3.46	2.20
12					6.58	1.74	5.41	2.20
13							6.44	2.05
14							6.85	2.05
15							6.96	2.05
16							6.96	2.05

Table 5. Percentage difference between calculated (Table 4) and simulated values (Table 1) of BW

Number of Buses, B	Number of processors N $(=M)$							
	4		8		12		16	
	p=1	p=.5	p=1	p=.5	p=1	p=.5	p=1	p=.5
1+1	1.74	1.50	1.87	1.83	1.92	1.90	1.93	1.93
2+2	2.62	1.77	3.61	3.11	3.81	3.64	3.86	3.79
3+3			4.72	3.44	5.52	4.78	5.73	5.43
4+4			4.93	3.47	6.77	5.10	7.48	6.42
5+5					7.24	5.16	8.79	6.77
6+6					7.28	5.16	9.43	6.83
7+7							9.59	6.84
8+8							9.63	6.85

Table 6. Bandwidth BW_2 obtained by simulation for the partial bus case (2 groups).

Number of Buses, B	Number of processors N $(=M)$							
	4		8		12		16	
	p=1	p=.5	p=1	p=.5	p=1	p=.5	p=1	p=.5
1+1	1.80	1.49	1.97	1.92	2.00	1.99	2.00	2.00
2+2	2.73	1.79	3.73	3.12	3.95	3.76	3.99	3.95
3+3			4.88	3.47	5.71	4.80	5.94	5.58
4+4			5.25	3.52	7.00	5.16	7.71	6.50
5+5					7.63	5.24	9.10	6.86
6+6					7.78	5.25	9.92	6.96
7+7							10.24	6.98
8+8							10.30	6.98

Table 7. Bandwidth BW_2 calculated from equation (14).

Number of Buses, B	Number of processors N $(=M)$							
	4		8		12		16	
	p=1	p=.5	p=1	p=.5	p=1	p=.5	p=1	p=.5
1+1	3.45	-0.67	5.35	4.92	4.17	4.74	3.63	3.63
2+2	4.20	1.13	3.32	0.32	3.67	3.30	3.37	4.22
3+3			3.39	0.87	3.44	0.84	3.66	2.76
4+4			6.49	1.44	3.40	1.18	3.07	1.25
5+5					5.39	1.55	3.53	1.33
6+6					6.87	1.74	5.20	1.90
7+7							6.78	2.05
8+8							6.96	1.90

Table 8. Percentage difference between calculated (Table 7) and simulated values (Table 6).

IV. Conclusion

We have presented new analytic formulas for BW and BW_g. Although they are fairly simple, they are in close agreement with previous simulation results. Possible extension to this work include examining the effects of different arbitration schemes on BW and fault tolerance. Also of interest is obtaining a simple approximation for $BW - BW_g$ to evaluate the bandwidth degradation of different partial bus groupings. After this paper was submitted a result similar to that in equation (4) (BW for a complete system) was derived independently in [13].

V. References

(1) *Computer*, vol.14, no.12, Dec. 1981.

(2) Intel Corp., *iAPX 86,88 User's Manual*, Santa Clara, Calif., 1981.

(3) T. Lang, M. Valero and I. Alegre, "Bandwidth of Crossbar and Multiple-Bus Connections for Multiprocessors," *IEEE Trans. on Computers*, vol.C-31, no.12, pp.1227-1233.

(4) T. Lang, M. Valero and M.A. Fiol, "Reduction of Connections for Multibus Organization," *IEEE Trans. on Computers*, vol.C-32, no.8, pp.707-716.

(5) M.A. Marsan and M. Gerla, "Markov Models for Multiple Bus Multiprocessor Systems," *IEEE Trans. on Computers*, vol.C-31, no.3, pp.239-248, March 1982.

(6) I.H. Onyüksel and K.B. Irani, "A Markovian Queueing Network Model for Performance Evaluation of Bus-Deficient Multiprocessor Systems," *Proc. 1983 Int'l Conf. on Parallel Processing*, pp. 437-439, Aug. 1983.

(7) C.E. Skinner and J.R. Asher, "Effects of Storage Contention on System Performance," *IBM Systems Journal*, vol.8, no.4, pp.319-333, 1969.

(8) D.P. Bhandarkar, "Analysis of Memory Interference in Multiprocessors," *IEEE Trans. on Computer*, vol.C-24, no.9, pp.897-908, Sep. 1975.

(9) F. Baskett and A.J. Smith, "Interference in Multiprocessor Computer Systems with Interleaved Memory," *Comm. of ACM*, vol.19, no.6, pp.327-334, June 1976.

(10) C. H. Hoogendoorn, "A General Model for Memory Interference in Multiprocessors," *IEEE Trans. on Computers*, vol.C-26, no.10, pp.998-1005, Oct. 1977.

(11) W. Feller, *An Introduction to Probability Theory and its Applications*, vol.1, 3rd ed., Wiley, New York, 1968.

(12) D.W.L. Yen, J.H. Patel, and E.S. Davidson, "Memory Interference in Synchronous Multiprocessor Systems," *IEEE Trans. on Computers*, vol.C-31, no.11, pp.1116-1121, Nov. 1982.

(13) A. Goyal and T. Agerwala, "Performance Analysis of Future Shared Storage Systems," *IBM J. Res. Develop.*, vol.28, no.1, pp.95-108, Jan. 1984.

Chapter 6: Multiprocessors and Performance Evaluation

A multiprocessor requires execution of instructions on a set of data. Its performance is greatly influenced by the availability of data in parallel for execution, which necessitates concurrent transfer of data from memory modules to all processors. In general, it may not be possible to satisfy such data transfer requirements, because data pertaining to multiple processors may be located in a single memory module. Techniques have been devised to reduce conflicts and interference in memory units[1-6] for such systems. Several innovative schemes including interleaving[5-6] have been introduced. The concept of cache memories adds another dimension to the usefulness of memory hierarchy[7]. Cache memory provides substantial improvement in speed and leads to a good match between the arithmetic unit processing speed and the memory access time. In a multiprocessor environment, a need for multiple cache memories leads to several important issues, and the placement and effectiveness of cache organization are observed[8-26] to be influenced by such factors as cache-size, shared or distributed cache organization, on-chip cache scheme, cache coherency, replacement policy, etc. Research is still being carried out to address many of the unresolved questions.

An efficient processing of the data also requires an appropriate organization of the processing units. Various vector and array units are being proposed[27-36] to provide the needed speed-up and the processing power. Further enhancements have been attained by introducing instruction pipelining and by defining appropriate languages. The instructions and I/O overlap[37-40] help in improving the performance of the system. In addition, transfer of data from one processor to another (i.e., interprocessor communication) also consumes some time and is considered to be an overhead of parallel architecture. A need to minimize this determines the way the algorithms are defined or modified; the importance of minimal communication overhead is emphasized in[41-45]. Various techniques for indicating the performance of multiprocessor systems are widely covered[46-70]. Several numerical algorithms and optimization techniques for vector processing have been considered. Modeling of algorithms is addressed[71-72] and compiler design issues and scheduling techniques are described in[73-81]. The interdependency of various issues is also illustrated.

Four papers are included in this chapter to cover many aspects of multiprocessor architecture.

References

1 D.P. Bhandarkar, "Analysis of Memory Interference in Multiprocessors," *IEEE Trans. Computers,* Vol. C-24, No. 9, Sept. 1975, pp. 897-908.

2 A.J. Smith, "Multiprocessor Memory Organization and Memory Interference," *Comm. of the ACM,* Vol. 20, No. 10, Oct. 1977, pp. 754-761.

3 D. Chang, D.J. Kuck, and D.H. Lawrie, "On the Bandwidth of Parallel Memories," *IEEE Trans. Computers,* Vol. C-26, No. 5, May 1977, pp. 480-490.

4 K.E. Batcher, "The Multi-Dimensional Access Memory in STARAN," *IEEE Trans. Computers,* Vol. C-26, No. 2, Feb. 1977, pp. 174-177.

5 W. Oed and O. Lange, "On the Effective Bandwidth of Interleaved Memories in Vector Processor Systems," *Proc. 1985 Int'l. Conf. Parallel Processing,* IEEE Computer Society, Washington, D.C., 1985, pp. 33-40.

6 B.R. Rau, "Program Behavior and the Performance of Interleaved Memories," *IEEE Trans. Computers,* Vol. C-28, No. 3, March 1979, pp. 191-199.

7 A. Lehman, "Performance Evaluation and Prediction of Storage Hierarchies," *Proc. ACM SIGMETRICS Performance,* Vol. 9, ACM, New York, N.Y., 1980, pp. 43-54.

8 L.M. Censier and P. Feautrier, "A New Solution to Coherence Problems in Multicache Systems," *IEEE Trans. Computers,* Vol. C-27, No. 12, Dec. 1978, pp. 1112-1118.

9 D. Kroft, "Lockup-Free Instruction Fetch/Prefetch Cache Organization," *Proc. 8th Ann. Symp. Computer Architecture,* IEEE Computer Society, Washington, D.C., 1981, pp. 81-88.

10 F.A. Briggs and M. Dubois, "Cache Effectiveness Multiprocessor Systems with Pipelined Parallel Memories," *Proc. 1981 Int'l. Conf. Parallel Processing,* IEEE Computer Society, Washington, D.C., 1981, pp. 306-313.

11 F.A. Briggs and M. Dubois, "Performance of Cache Based Multiprocessors," *ACM Conf. Measurement Modeling Computer System,* ACM, New York, N.Y., 1981, pp. 181-190.

12 J.H. Patel, "Analysis of Multiprocessors with Private Cache Memories," *IEEE Trans. Computers,* Vol. C-31, No. 4, April 1982, pp. 296-304.

13 A.J. Smith, "Cache Memories," *ACM Computing Survey,* Vol. 14, No. 3, Sept. 1982, pp. 473-530.

14 M. Dubois and F.A. Briggs, "Effects of Cache Coherency in Multiprocessors," *IEEE Trans. Computers,* Vol. C-31, No. 11, Nov. 1982, pp. 1083-1099.

15 R.H. Katz et al., "Implementing a Cache Consistency Protocol," *Proc. 12th Int'l. Symp. Computer Architecture,* IEEE Computer Society, Washington, D.C., 1985, pp. 276-283.

16 F.A. Briggs and M. Dubois, "Effectiveness of Private Caches in Multiprocessor Systems with Parallel-Pipelined Memories," *IEEE Trans. Computers,* Vol. C-32, No. 1, Jan. 1983, pp. 48-59.

17 J.E. Smith and J.R. Goodman, "A Study of Instruction Cache Organizations and Replacement Policies," *Proc. 10th Ann. Int'l. Symp. Computer Architecture*, 1983, pp. 132-137.

18 A.J. Smith, "Cache Evaluation and the Impact of Workload Choice," *Proc. Int'l. Symp. Computer Architecture*, IEEE Computer Society, Washington, D.C., 1985, pp. 64-73.

19 P.C.C. Yeh, J.H. Patel, and E.S. Davidson, "Performance of Shared Cache for Parallel-Pipelined Computer Systems," *Proc. 10th Ann. Int'l. Symp. Computer Architecture*, IEEE Computer Society, Washington, D.C., 1983, pp. 117-123.

20 J.R. Goodman, "Using Cache Memory to Reduce Processor-Memory Traffic," *Proc. 10th Ann. Int'l. Symp. Computer Architecture*, IEEE Computer Society, Washington, D.C., 1983, pp. 124-131.

21 A.R. Pleszkun and E.S. Davidson, "Structured Memory Access Architecture," *Proc. 1983 Int'l. Conf. Parallel Processing*, IEEE Computer Society, Washington, D.C., 1983, pp. 461-471.

22 M.S.P. Marcos and J.H. Patel, "A Low-Overhead Coherence Solution for Multi-Processors with Private Cache Memories," *Proc. 11th Ann. Int'l. Symp. Computer Architecture*, IEEE Computer Society, Washington, D.C., 1984, pp. 348-354.

23 J. Archibald and J.L. Baer, "An Economical Solution to the Cache Coherence Problem," *Proc. 11th Ann. Int'l. Symp. Computer Architecture*, IEEE Computer Society, Washington, D.C., 1984, pp. 355-362.

24 M.D. Hill and A.J. Smith, "Experimental Evaluation of On-Chip Microprocessor Cache Memories," *Proc. 11th Ann. Int'l. Symp. Computer Architecture*, IEEE Computer Society, Washington, D.C., 1984, pp. 158-166.

25 D.A. Patterson, P. Garrison, M. Hill, D. Lioupis, T. Sippel, and K.V. Dyke, "Architecture of a VLSI Instruction Cache for a RISC," *Proc. 10th Ann. Int'l. Symp. Computer Architecture*, IEEE Computer Society, Washington, D.C., 1983, pp. 108-116.

26 L. Rudolph and Z. Segall, "Dynamic Decentralized Cache Schemes for MIMD Parallel Processors," *Proc. 11th Ann. Int'l. Symp. Computer Architecture*, IEEE Computer Society, Washington, D.C., 1984, pp. 340-347.

27 F.J. Burkowski, "A Vector and Array Multiprocessor Extension of the Sylvan Architecture," *Proc. 11th Ann. Int'l. Symp. Computer Architecture*, IEEE Computer Society, Washington, D.C., 1984, pp. 4-11.

28 D.H. Lawrie and C.R. Vora, "The Prime Memory System for Array Access," *IEEE Trans. Computers*, Vol. C-31, No. 5, May 1982, pp. 435-442.

29 V.P. Srini and J.F. Asenjo, "Analysis of CRAY-1 Architecture," *Proc. 10th Ann. Int'l. Symp. Computer Architecture*, IEEE Computer Society, Washington, D.C., 1983, pp. 194-206.

30 E.J. Galloupoulos and S.D. McEwan, "Numerical Experiments with the Massively Parallel Processor," *Proc. 1983 Int'l. Conf. Parallel Processing*, Aug. 1983, pp. 29-35.

31 N. Maron and T.S. Brengle, "Integrating an Array Processor into a Scientific Computing System," *Computer*, Vol. 14, No. 9, Sept. 1981, pp. 41-44,

32 R.H. Sintz, "Optimal Use of a Vector Processor," *Proc. COMPCON*, IEEE Computer Society, Washington, D.C., 1980, pp. 277-281.

33 R.T. Farouki et al., "Computational Astrophysics on the Array Processor," *Computer*, Vol. 16, No. 6, 1983, pp. 73-84,

34 R.H. Perrott et al., "Implementation of an Array and Vector Processing Language," *Proc. 1983 Int'l. Conf. Parallel Processing*, IEEE Computer Society, Washington, D.C., 1983, pp. 232-239.

35 R.N. Ibbett, "MUGV: A Parallel Vector Processing System," *Proc. 12th Int'l. Symp. Computer Architecture*, IEEE Computer Society, Washington, D.C., 1985, pp. 136-144.

36 S.Y. Kung et al., "Wavefront Array Processor: Language, Architecture and Applications," *IEEE Trans. Computers*, Vo. C-31, No. 11, Nov. 1982, pp. 1054-1066.

37 R.W. Holgate and R.N. Ibbett, "An Analysis of Instruction-Fetching Strategies in Pipelined Supercomputers," *IEEE Trans. Computers*, Vol. C-29, No. 4, April 1980, pp. 325-329.

38 G.R. Grohoski and J.H. Patel, "A Performance Model for Instruction Prefetch in Pipelined Instruction Units," *Proc. 1982 Int'l. Conf. Parallel Processing*, IEEE Computer Society, Washington, D.C., 1982, pp. 248-252.

39 S. Weiss and J.E. Smith, "Instruction Issue Logic for Pipelined Supercomputers," *Proc. 11th Ann. Int'l. Symp. Computer Architecture*, IEEE Computer Society, Washington, D.C., 1984, pp. 110-118.

40 H. Hellerman and H.J. Smith, Jr., "Throughput Analysis of Some Idealized Input, Output and Computer Overlap Configurations," *ACM Computing Surveys*, Vol. 2, No. 2, June 1970, pp. 111-118.

41 M. Dubois and F.A. Briggs, "Efficient Interprocessor Communication for MIMD Multiprocessor Systems," *Proc. 8th Ann. Int'l. Symp. Computer Architecture*, IEEE Computer Society, Washington, D.C., 1981, pp. 187-196.

42 K.H. Huang and J.A. Abraham, "Efficient Parallel Algorithms for Processor Arrays," *Proc. Int'l. Conf. Parallel Processing*. IEEE Computer Society, Washington, D.C., 1982, pp. 271-279.

43 L.H. Bhuyan, "On the Performance of Loosely Coupled Multiprocessors," *Proc. 11th Ann. Int'l. Symp. Computer Architecture,* IEEE Computer Society, Washington, D.C., 1984, pp. 256-262.

44 G. Gopal and J.W. Wong, "Delay Analysis of Broadcast Routing in Packet Switching Networks," *IEEE Trans. Computers,* Vol. C-30, No. 12, December 1981, pp. 915-922.

45 H. Fromm et al., "Experiences with Performance Measurement and Modeling of a Processor Array," *IEEE Trans. Computers,* Vol. C-32, No. 1, Jan. 1983, pp. 15-31.

46 K. Irani and K.W. Chen, "Minimization of Interprocessor Communication for Parallel Computation," *IEEE Trans. Computers,* Vol. C-31, No. 11, Nov. 1982, pp. 1067-1075,

47 N. Dimopoulos, "The Homogeneous Multiprocessor Architecture—Structure and Performance Analysis," *Proc. 1983 Int'l. Conf. Parallel Processing,* IEEE Computer Society, Washington, D.C., 1983, pp. 520-523.

48 G.F. Pfister et al., "The IBM Research parallel Processor Prototype (RP3): Introduction and Architecture," *Proc. 1985 Int'l. Conf. Parallel Processing,* IEEE Computer Society, Washington, D.C., 1985, pp. 764-771.

49 B. Lint and T. Agerwala, "Communication Issues in the Design and Analysis of Parallel Algorithms," *Proc. 1981 Int'l. Conf. Parallel Processing,* IEEE Computer Society, Washington, D.C., 1985, pp. 247-254.

50 J.A.B. Fortes and D.I. Moldovan, "Data Broadcasting in Linearly Scheduled Array Processors," *Proc. 11th Ann. Int'l. Symp. Computer Architecture,* IEEE Computer Society, Washington, D.C., 1984, pp. 224-231.

51 L.M. Ni and K. Hwang, "Performance Modeling of Shared Resource Array Processors," *IEEE Trans. Software Engineering,* Vol. SE-7, No. 4, July 1981, pp. 386-394.

52 E.D. Brooks, "Performance of the Butterfly Processor-Memory Interconnection in a Vector Environment," *Proc. 1985 Int'l. Conf. on Parallel Processing,* IEEE Computer Society, Washington, D.C., 1985, pp. 21-24.

53 W.L. Bain, Jr. and S.R. Ahuja, "Performance Analysis of High Speed Digital Buses for Multiprocessing Systems," *Proc. 8th Ann. Symp. Computer Architecture,* IEEE Computer Society, Washington, D.C., 1981, pp. 107-131.

54 E. Nestle and A. Inselberg, "The Synapse Ntl System: Architectural Characteristics and Performance Data of a Tightly-Coupled Multiprocessor System," *Proc. 12th Int'l. Symp. Computer Architecture,* IEEE Computer Society, Washington, D.C., 1985, pp. 233-239.

55 J.W.S. Liu and C.L. Liu, "Performance Analysis of Multiprocessor Systems Containing Functionally Dedicated Processors," *Acta Informatica,* Vol. 10, No. 1, 1978, pp. 95-104,

56 W. Ab-Sufah and A.Y. Kwok, "Performance Prediction Tools for CEDAR: Multiprocessor Supercomputer," *Proc. 12th Int'l. Symp. Computer Architecture,* IEEE Computer Society, Washington, D.C., 1985, pp. 406-413.

57 A.S. Sethi and N. Deo, "Interference in Multiprocessor Systems with Localized Memory Access Probabilities," *IEEE Trans. Computers,* Vol. C-28, No. 2, Feb. 1979, pp. 157-163.

58 D. Parkinson and H.M. Liddell, "The Measurement of Performance on a Highly Parallel System," *IEEE Trans. Computers,* Vol. C-32, No. 1, Jan. 1983, pp. 32-37.

59 I.V. Ramakrishnan and P.J. Varman, "Modular Matrix Multiplication as a Linear Array," *IEEE Trans. Computers,* Vol. C-33, No. 11, Nov. 1984, pp. 952-958.

60 R.L. Sites, "An Analysis of the Cray-1 Computer," *Proc. 5th Ann. Symp. Computer Architecture,* IEEE Computer Society, Washington, D.C., 1978, pp. 101-106.

61 L.M. Ni and K. Hwang, "Vector Reduction Techniques for Arithmetic Pipelines," *IEEE Trans. Computers,* Vol. C-34, No. 5, May 1985, pp. 404-411.

62 C.N. Arnold, "Performance Evaluation of Three Automatic Vectorizer Packages," *Proc. 1982 Int'l. Conf. Parallel Processing,* IEEE Computer Society, Washington, D.C., 1982, pp. 235-242.

63 K. Hwang and L.M. Ni, "Resource Optimization of a Parallel Computer for Multiple Vector Processing," *IEEE Trans. Computers,* Vol. C-29, No. 9, Sept. 1980, pp. 831-836.

64 V.P. Srini and J.F. Asenjo, "Analysis of Cray-1 Architecture," *Proc. 10th Ann. Symp. Computer Architecture,* IEEE Computer Society, Washington, D.C., 1983, pp. 194-206.

65 W.P. Peterson, "Vector Fortran for Numerical Problems on Cray-1," *Comm. of ACM,* Vol. 26, No. 11, Nov. 1983, pp. 1008-1021.

66 D.K. Stevenson, "Numerical Algorithms for Parallel Computers," *Proc. Nat. Computer Conf.,* AFIPS Press, Reston, Va., Vol. 49, 1980, pp. 357-361,

67 A.H. Sameh, "On Two Numerical Algorithms for Multiprocessors," *Proc. NATO Advanced Research Workshop on High Speed Computing,* edited by J.S. Kawalik, Springer-Verlag, W. Germany, 1983.

68 A.J. Krygiel, "Synchronous Nets for Single Instruction Stream-Multiple Data Stream Computers," *Proc. 1981 Int'l. Conf. Parallel Processing,* IEEE Computer Society, Washington, D.C., 1981, pp. 266-273.

69 D. Vrsalovic et al., "The Influence of Parallel Decomposition Strategies on the Performance of Multiprocessor Systems," *Proc. 12th Int'l. Symp. Computer Architecture,* IEEE Computer Society, Washington, D.C., 1985, pp. 396-405.

70 P. Banerji and J.A. Abraham, "Fault-Secure Algorithms for Multiple-Processor Systems," *Proc. 11th Int'l. Symp. Computer Architecture,* IEEE Computer Society, Washington, D.C., 1984, pp. 279-287.

71 K. Hwang and T.P Chang, "Combinatorial Reliability Analysis of Multiprocessor Computers," *IEEE Trans. Reliability,* Vol. R-31, No. 5, Dec. 1982, pp. 469-473.

72 C. Maples, D. Weaver, W. Rathbun, and D. Logan, "The Operation and Utilization of the MIDAS Multiprocessor Architecture," *Proc. 1984 Int'l. Conf. Parallel Processing,* IEEE Computer Society, Washington, D.C., 1984, pp. 190-206.

73 J.L. Baer and C. Ellis, "Model Design and Evaluation of a Compiler for a Parallel Processing Environment," *IEEE Trans. Software Engineering,* Vol. SE-3, No. 6, Nov. 1977, pp. 394-405.

74 C.V. Ramamoorthy and B.W. Wah, "An Optimal Algorithm for Scheduling Requests on Interleaved Memories for a Pipelined Processor," *IEEE Trans. Computers,* Vol. C-30, No. 10, Oct. 1981, pp. 787-800.

75 J.T. Robinson, "Analysis of Asynchronous Multiprocessor Algorithms with Applications to Sorting," *Proc. 1977 Int'l. Conf. Parallel Processing,* IEEE Computer Society, Washington, D.C., 1977, pp. 128-135.

76 J.C. Knight and D.D. Dunlop, "Measurements of an Optimizing Compiler for a Vector Computer," *Proc. 1981 Int'l. Conf. Parallel Processing,* IEEE Computer Society, Washington, D.C., 1981, pp. 58-60.

77 I.A. Newan and M.C. Woodward, "Alternative Approaches to Multiprocessor Garbage Collection," *Proc. Int'l. Conf. Parallel Processing,* IEEE Computer Society, Washington, D.C., 1982, pp. 205-210.

78 J.L. Gula, "Operating System Considerations for Multiprocessor Architecture," *Proc. 7th Texas Conf. Computing Systems,* 1978.

79 M. Dubois and F.A. Briggs, "Performance of Synchronized Iterative Processes in Multiprocessor Systems," *IEEE Trans. Software Engineering,* Vol. SE-8, No. 4, July 1982, pp. 419-431.

80 R.M. Jenevein and J.C. Browne, "A Control Processor for a Reconfigurable Array Computer," *Proc. 9th Ann. Symp. Computer Architecture,* IEEE Computer Society, Washington, D.C., 1982, pp. 81-89.

81 J.T. Robinson, "Some Analysis Techniques for Asynchronous Multiprocessor Algorithms," *IEEE Trans. Software Engineering,* Vol. SE-5, No. 1, Jan. 1979, pp. 24-30.

82 K. Culik, "Towards a Theory of Control-Flow and Data-Flow Algorithms," *Proc. 1985. Int'l. Conf. Parallel Processing,* IEEE Computer Society, Washington, D.C., 1985, pp. 341-348.

83 J. Bannister and K. Trivedi, "Task Allocation in Fault-Tolerant Distributed Systems," *Acta Informatica,* Vol. 20, No. 3, Dec. 1983, pp. 261-281.

84 H.S. Stone, "Multiprocessor Scheduling with the Aid of Network Flow Algorithms," *IEEE Trans. Software Engineering,* Vol. SE-3, No. 1, Jan. 1977, pp. 85-93.

85 S.P. Su and K. Hwang, "Multiple Pipeline Scheduling in Vector Supercomputer," *Proc. of Int'l. Conf. Parallel Processing,* IEEE Computer Society, Washington, D.C., 1982, pp. 226-234.

86 D.A. Padua, D.J. Kuck, and D.H. Lawrie, "High Speed Multiprocessors and Compiling Techniques," *IEEE Trans. Computers,* Vol. C-29, No. 9, Sept. 1980, pp. 763-776.

87 M. Yasumura, Y. Tanaka, and Y. Kanada, "Compiling Algorithms and Techniques for the S-810 Vector Processor," *Proc. 1984 Int'l. Conf. Parallel Processing,* IEEE Computer Society, Washington, D.C., 1984, pp. 285-290.

Effectiveness of Private Caches in Multiprocessor Systems with Parallel-Pipelined Memories

FAYÉ A. BRIGGS, MEMBER, IEEE, AND MICHEL DUBOIS, MEMBER, IEEE

Abstract—A possible design alternative for improving the performance of a multiprocessor system is to insert a private cache between each processor and the shared memory. The caches act as high-speed buffers by reducing the effective memory access time, and affect the delays caused by memory conflicts. In this paper, we study the effectiveness of caches in a multiprocessor system. The shared memory is pipelined and interleaved to improve the block transfer rate, and it assumes a two-dimensional organization, previously studied under random and word access. An approximate model is developed to estimate the processor utilization and the speed-up improvement provided by the caches.

Index Terms—Cache memories, memory organization, multicache consistency, multiprocessors, performance evaluation.

I. INTRODUCTION

IN this paper, we present simulation results and an approximate analytical model to evaluate the performance of multiprocessor systems with private caches. An example of such a system with P processors is depicted in Fig. 1. At the first level, each processor has a private cache (PC). The second memory level comprises a two-dimensional memory called the L-M memory organization, which consists of l lines or banks and m memory modules per line [1]. A line is used to denote the address bus within the shared memory (SM). Associated with each line is a direct memory access (DMA) controller which receives a cache request for a block of size B and issues B internal requests (IR) to consecutive modules on the line. In the following discussion, it is assumed that the interconnection network between the private caches and shared memory modules is a full crossbar. The crossbar is symmetric: the delays along all paths from any processor to any memory module are identical. It can be built with multiplexor chips, as described in [26]. The overhead incurred in traversing the switch has two components. First, there is the delay through the arbitration logic, which, for each memory module, selects one request among all the processor requests submitted to the module. This delay is called the switch setup time (t_a), and does not include the waiting time due to conflicts. Second, there are delays through the mutliplexor chips, which connect the selected processor to the memory module. Such a delay is called the switch transversal time (t_d). In general, t_a and t_d are functions of l, P, and the technology used.

In the architecture of Fig. 1, there is a data coherence problem because several copies of the same block may exist in different caches at any given time. The solution to the coherence problem are *dynamic* or *static*. The dynamic solution consists basically in checking, at run-time, for the presence of the block referenced by the processor in other caches. This can be done by maintaining, dynamically, local and global flags [4], [24]. The dynamic solution is costly and requires conflicting accesses to a central directory shared among all processors. The effects of the enforcement of cache consistency using the dynamic solution have been analyzed in [10].

For the C.mmp [26], the static solution was envisioned but never implemented. In the static solution, each page in shared memory is tagged as *cacheable* or *noncacheable* at compile time. Theoretically, only shared writeable data should be tagged as noncacheable. Examples of noncacheable items are semaphores, process queue and operating system tables. References to noncacheable pages are made directly to the shared memory. Only the blocks contained in cacheable pages are buffered in the private caches. Each page table entry contains a cacheable bit. If the bit is set, the address translation hardware directs the request to the cache. A reset cacheable bit indicates that the data items is to be found in the noncacheable physical space of the shared memory. A similar mechanism was used in the Honeywell 66 Series machines. A modified version of this scheme is proposed for the S-1 multiprocessor system being developed at Lawrence Livermore Laboratory [25]. This scheme works only if a process is not allowed to migrate without the invalidation of its blocks. A similar scheme was introduced [9], in which the noncacheable references are made to a shared cache.

Another method of maintaining multicache consistency may be termed *quasi-dynamic*. In this case, all blocks are initially tagged as cacheable and are stored in the cacheable section of memory. A block which is cached by one processor and is referenced by another processor for a write operation becomes tagged as a shared writeable block. Such a block is "uncached" by transferring the updated block to the noncacheable section of memory where it can be accessed directly by the processors that share the block.

Cacheable and noncacheable data items can be in the same shared memory. Accesses to noncacheable data are made on a word-by-word basis. However, in order to speed-up accesses to noncacheable data the shared memory can be partitioned into cacheable and noncacheable data spaces, where the

Manuscript received February 5, 1982; revised July 22, 1982. This work was supported by the National Science Foundation under Grant ECS 80-16580. Revision of this paper was made while F. A. Briggs was at the IBM Thomas J. Watson Research Center, Yorktown Heights, NY 10598.

F. A. Briggs is with the Department of Electrical Engineering, Rice University, Houston, TX 77001.

M. Dubois is with Thomson-CSF/LCR, Domaine de Corbeville, B.P. 10, 91401, Orsay, France.

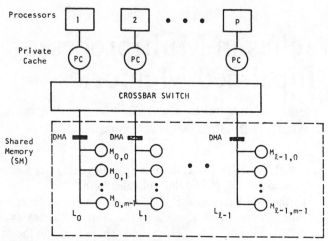

Fig. 1. Cache-based multiprocessor system with L-M shared memory.

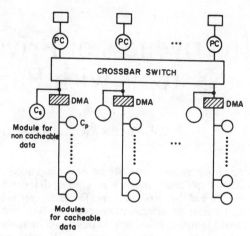

Fig. 2. Cache-based multiprocessor with static or quasi-dynamic coherence check.

noncacheable data are stored in faster memory modules. A typical cache-based multiprocessor system with partitioned shared memory is shown in Fig. 2. The organization of the shared memory will be discussed in Section III.

Most studies to date evaluate the shared memory conflict problem for random-word access [5]. In [2], [3], approximate models were developed to analyze the effect of private caches on the processor utilization. Patel developed a model for a cache-based multiprocessor without pipelined memories [18]. All the above studies ignored the cache coherence problem and thus obtained results that are optimistic. We propose a model which is used to evaluate the degree of memory conflicts in a multiprocessor system with private caches and parallel-pipelined memories. The model developed here incorporates the static and quasi-dynamic coherence checks and hence, is realistic for evaluating the performance of cache-based multiprocessors with software coherence checks. This model permits us to determine the processor utilization and investigate the effects of static and quasi-dynamic cache coherence checks on the performance. Furthermore, we estimate the effect of the caches on the speedup of the multiprocessing system. The performance of the system is a function of the cache hit ratio, h cache organization, processor characteristics and the shared memory characteristics and configuration.

In Section II, we present two cache models, namely, set-associative and fully-associative caches. These models are considered in the analysis to be presented. The organization of the shared memory and its capabilities for handling block transfers are discussed in Section III. Simulation and analytical methodologies are developed in Section IV for the two cache models together with a discussion of the accuracy of the models. Finally, we present an example to illustrate the applicability of the analytical results in the design-decision making phase of the multiprocessor system configuration.

II. THE CACHE MODELS

The processor system consists of P identical processors. In each of these processors, we assume that a machine cycle consists of an integer number, d, of cache cycles. An instruction cycle usually consists of an integer number of machine cycles. Typical machine cycles are instruction-fetch, operand-fetch

and execution cycles, which may involve register-register or memory-register references. It is obvious that in some machine cycles of a processor, no cache memory references will occur. Therefore, let θ be the probability that a memory request is issued by a processor to the cache controller in a machine cycle. Thus, the fraction of references made by the processor to the cache controller in each cache cycle is $x = \theta/d$.

When the cacheable data requested by a processor is not in its private cache, a miss occurs that causes the cache controller to issue a shared memory request for a block transfer. The program behavior in a processor will be characterized by its cache hit ratio, h, or its miss ratio, $1 - h$. The hit ratio of a program as a function of cache size, set size, block size and cache replacement policy has been studied by several authors [14], [19], [23]. We assume that no read-through strategy is implemented. However, the model presented here can easily be adapted for read-through strategy. If the cache is full, the cache replacement algorithm is invoked to decide which block-frame to free in order to create space for the new block containing the referenced data.

Cache management algorithms differ basically in the method of resolving write misses [14]. In a *write-through* strategy, a processor always writes directly in the shared memory, and possibly in the cache if the block is present. Consequently, a block is never copied to shared memory when a block-frame is freed. However, such a policy requires buffering of the write requests or results in the blocking of the processor during write operations. The *write-back-write-allocate* strategy is adopted in this paper. In this strategy, if a cache block-frame which has not been modified is to be replaced, it is overwritten with the new block of data. However, a modified block-frame that is to be replaced must be written to the shared memory (SM) before a block-read from the SM is initiated. In this case, two consecutive transfers are made between the cache and SM. We assume that each time a cache miss occurs, a block-write to SM is required, with a probability w_b, followed by a block-read from SM. w_b, which is the probability that the block-frame to be replaced was modified, depends on the program behavior and the cache organization. It is usually larger than w_t, the probability that a reference is a write [22].

Two methods of organizing the cache for block reads and writes are investigated. In one case, it is assumed that the two consecutive block transfers (one block-write followed by one block-read) are made between a processor and the same line. This assumption will be satisfied if a *set-associative* cache is used in which all the blocks that map to the same set are stored on the same line. Hence, in this method a cache miss requires the transfer of a $2B$-word block with a probability w_b and the transfer of a B-word with a probability $1 - w_b$.

A second method of organizing the cache assumes that the two consecutive block-write and block-read requests are considered independent and hence have equal probability of referencing any SM line. This assumption may be valid in a *fully-associative* cache. The effect of making two consecutive and independent block requests from a processor is to increase the effective rate of requests to the SM.

In our models, the hit ratio, h, and the probability w_b that a miss requires a write back are given. Generally the hit ratio depends on the locality property [8] of the program mix, the cache replacement policy, and the block, set and cache sizes. Various studies have addressed this relationship. In [16], a program is characterized by a simplified mathematical model based on its instruction mix and the model is used to estimate the hit ratio. Smith compares different cache replacement policies [21]. Under the assumption of a linear paging model [20], he shows that the ratio of the miss ratios between the set-associative and the fully associative cache is

$$R(i, N) = \frac{i - \dfrac{1}{N}}{i - 1} \quad \text{for } i \geq 3,$$

where i is the set size (number of blocks in a set) and N is the number of sets. This ratio is always ≥ 1. It tends to 1 when Ni, the cache capacity, increases without limit. This relationship should be considered when comparing the set-associative and fully-associative caches from our models. Strecker presents empirical results for the PDP-11 family computers showing the hit ratio as a function of the cache and block sizes [23]. In [19], an analytical model is proposed. For a *given cache size*, the hit ratio improves as the block size increases from 1, because of the locality of the references to the cache. However, beyond a certain block size, the hit ratio decreases. This is due to the decrease in the usefulness of the extra words in a block as the block size increases. For a given *block size*, the hit ratio increases monotonically with the cache size, for caches with a stack replacement algorithm [6]. If h and w_b can be determined empirically on a uniprocessor machine [23], or theoretically [16], [19], the models given in this paper can then be applied to evaluate the various performance indexes.

For practical purposes, the absolute size of the private cache would be expected to be large enough to accommodate at least the "working set" of the process [8], so that the miss ratio, $1 - h$, is small (in the order of 0.1). Furthermore, we assume that the block transfer time is also small (less than 64 cache cycles). Under these conditions, it is not necessary to perform a task switch on a cache miss to another runnable process. Therefore, in this paper, we shall assume that on a cache miss, the processor enters a *wait state* while waiting for service of the desired block request, and then into a sequence of *transfer states* while the block is being transferred. If a processor is neither in a wait nor a transfer state, it is said to be in an *active state*. Hence, the processor utilization can be computed as the fraction of time the processor is busy processing instructions in an active state. Finally, associated with each DMA controller of a memory line is a buffer which queues the requests for block transfers. The DMA controller schedules these requests to the line, using a first-come-first-served (FCFS) policy.

III. THE SHARED MEMORY ORGANIZATION

The shared memory configuration is derived from the two-dimensional memory organization, which exploits the timing characteristics exhibited by semiconductor memories with address latches [1]. The *address cycle*, or hold time, a_0, which is the minimum duration that the address is maintained on the address bus of the shared memory module for a successful memory operation, is usually less than the shared *memory cycle*, c_0. Throughout this paper, we assume that the basic unit of time is the cache cycle, which is equal to τ s. If the address and shared memory cycles are quantized so that they are expressed as an integer number of cache cycles, then

$$a = \left\lceil \frac{a_0}{\tau} \right\rceil \quad \text{and} \quad c = \left\lceil \frac{c_0}{\tau} \right\rceil$$

so that a set of modules can be multiplexed on a line. In general, $1 \leq a \leq c$. When a memory operation is initiated in a module, it causes the associated line to be active for a units of time, and the module to be active for c units of time.

Recall that the shared memory address space is partitioned into cacheable and noncacheable data spaces. The noncacheable data space (NDS) of shared memory is organized into a set of l interleaved modules, where each module, denoted by ND, is attached to a unique memory line or bank. The memory module characteristic for ND is (a, c_S). The cacheable data space (CDS) of shared memory, which consists of $N = 2^n$ interleaved identical memory modules, is organized in a matrix form in order to exploit the memory module characteristic (a, c_P). Note that each module that stores the cacheable data is denoted by CD and a memory cycle, c_P. As shown in Figs. 1 and 2, a particular memory configuration (l, m) for CDS consists of $l = 2^\beta$ lines and $m = 2^{n-\beta}$ modules of type CD per line, such that $lm = N$, for integer $\beta \geq 0$. The blocks in the memory are interleaved on the lines so that block i is assigned to modules on line $i \bmod l$. It should be noted that this does not contradict the assumption made earlier that blocks of the same set are on the same line for the set-associative cache model. That assumption implies however, that the number of sets is a multiple of the number of lines in SM.

Since the cacheable data space of shared memory is used in the block transfer mode in this paper, we will assume an address cycle of $a = 1$ (i.e., the line holding time is equal to a cache cycle) for the shared memory, in order to obtain a maximum data rate. However, if $a > 1$ for a particular type of memory, the address cycle could be made equal to 1 by incorporating an appropriate address latch in each SM module.

Since $a = 1$, the memory module for cacheable and noncacheable data spaces will be characterized by c_P and c_S respectively. The model developed in [1] is not applicable here, because it was for single-word transfers that are requested by multiple instruction stream pipelined processors.

In order to utilize the SM modules of type CD for the block transfers effectively, the modules on a line are interleaved in a particular fashion, so that the servicing of two SM requests could be overlapped on the same line. The SM modules on a line are interleaved so that a block of data of size $B = 2^b$ is interleaved on consecutive modules on that line. Let line i and module j on that line be referred to as L_i and $M_{i,j}$ respectively for $0 \leq i \leq l - 1$ and $0 \leq j \leq m - 1$. Then the kth word of the block of data that exists on line i is in module $k \bmod m$ on that line for $0 \leq k \leq B - 1$. It is important to note that the first word of a block that exists on line i is in the first module, $M_{i,0}$, on that line. We assume that $B \geq m$. If $B < m$, memory modules $M_{i,B}, M_{i,B+1}, \cdots, M_{i,m-1}$ will not be utilized, because a block starts in module $M_{i,0}$.

When an SM block request is accepted by a line, the DMA controller at the line issues B successive internal requests (IR) to consecutive modules on line i, starting from module $M_{i,0}$. It is assumed that these internal requests are issued at the beginning of every time unit. Therefore, the internal request for the kth word of the block will be issued to module $M_{i,j}$, where $j = k \bmod m$ for $0 \leq k \leq B - 1$. It is obvious that this set of B internal requests is not preemptible. Note that if $B > m$ or if the cache is set-associative, the $(m + 1)$st internal request is for module $M_{i,0}$. Consequently, the first IR must be completed by the time the $(m + 1)$st internal request is issued. This constraint is satisfied if $c_P \leq m$.

IV. PERFORMANCE ANALYSIS

In this section we present assumptions and develop the models that permit us to evaluate the various performance indicators of the cache-based multiprocessor systems. First, we give a model for the system with static coherence check and from this model obtain results for the degenerate case when no sharing occurs.

A. Simulation Preceded by Analysis

For analytical purposes, it is assumed that cache requests to SM are random and uniformly distributed over all l lines of the SM. Similarly, we assume that memory requests to the non-cacheable segment of memory are random and uniformly distributed over all l lines of the SM. These assumptions are justified by the interleaving of the blocks of CDS and words of NDS across the lines. One inference that can be made directly from the above assumptions is that the probability of a request addressing any line is $1/l$. It is also assumed, for simplicity, that while a noncacheabe data item is being accessed, no other processor can initiate a transfer on the same line. This assumption will result in a pessimistic evaluation. In practice, an address latch could be provided at a module for noncacheable data, allowing a block transfer to take place as soon as the address for the noncacheable data items has been latched.

Recall that there is probability x that each processor submits

a request to its cache during a cache cycle. Let us denote by s the probability that such a request is for a noncacheable data item. In this case, the cache controller directs the request to the uncacheable section of shared memory. With probability $1 - s$, the reference is to a cacheable data item, which is first searched for in the cache. It is found in the cache with probability h. Otherwise, a new block is brought into the cache with probability $1 - h$. The handling of this transfer is dependent on the cache organization as described in Section II.

In order to understand the timing characteristics of the servicing of requests for block transfer, we define the time instants t^- and $t+$ as $\lim_{\Delta t \to 0} (t - \Delta t)$ and $\lim_{\Delta t \to 0} (t + \Delta t)$, respectively, for $\Delta t > 0$. A time unit, $\langle t, t + 1 \rangle$, may be thought of as beginning at time t^+ and ending at time $(t + 1)^-$. Hence, as $a = 1$, the successive internal requests which are generated to a line in the servicing of an SM request do not encounter any conflicts.

Recall that when an SM request for a block transfer is accepted, the DMA controller issues B successive IR's. If the request is accepted on line i at time t, then the IR for the kth word of a block of size B is initiated at time $t + k$ to module $M_{i,j}$, for $j = k \bmod m$ and $0 \leq k \leq B - 1$. As the SM module cycle time is c_P, module $M_{i,j}$ will be busy in the intervals $\langle t + k, t + c_P + k \rangle$ for the values of j.

Since $B = 2^b \geq m = 2^{n-\beta}$, then B/m is an integer ≥ 1. Therefore, each module on a line i which accepts an SM request for block transfer at time t receives B/m internal memory requests. In particular, the last IR to module M_{i0} is made at time $t + (B/m - 1)m = t + B - m$. Thus, the last interval in which module $M_{i,0}$ is busy (during the current block transfer) is $\langle t + B - m, t + B - m + c_P \rangle$. After this period, a new block transfer which addresses line i can be accepted. Because the current block transfer was initiated at time t, all block transfer requests arriving at $t + 1, t + 2, \cdots, t + B - m + c_P - 1$ will find line i busy. Note that to an SM request for block transfer, the line is busy for $B - m + c_P$ time units. We refer to this as the *line service time*. However, the *actual service time* of the SM request is $B + c_P - 1$. This is the time taken to access and transfer a block of size B when the request is accepted. Since we do not implement a read-through policy in the cache model, the processor goes through a sequence of transfer states having total duration $B + c_P - 1$ before returning to the active state. That is, the block transfer must be completed before the processor can become active again. Note that the definition of an active processor includes the interval in which the missed data is requested in the cache after the block transfer has been completed. The pipelining of the successive internal requests increases the block transfer speed at low cost. The alternate solution is to fetch the words in parallel. However, in this case the bus width of each line and of the path through the crossbar must be equal to B words, compared with a data path of one word in our organization.

The cache-based multiprocessor system of Fig. 1 may be modeled by the closed queueing network shown in Fig. 3. This network is not a typical "central server model" because it does not have the basic properties which imply solvability [15]. The servers are the shared memory lines, and the requests are issued by a set of P processing nodes, each of each lumps a processor

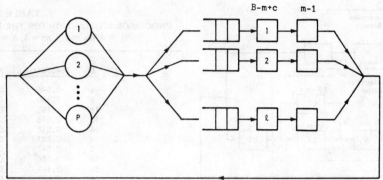

Fig. 3. Central server-like model for the multiprocessor system with private caches.

with its local cache. The two segments of a server model each SM line and reflect the pipeline effect of the L-M memory described above. A similar closed queueing network can be obtained for the system in Fig. 2.

The behavior of each processor in Fig. 2 is illustrated in Figs. 4 and 5 for the set-associative and fully associative cache strategies respectively. Node "A" denotes an active state of the processor and node "W," a waiting state. Node "LT" represents the state for the first part of a transfer during which the line is kept busy (line service time), and "ET," the state in which a transfer is completed without holding a line. These states have to be distinguished because of their different properties. Note that the state graphs, as shown in Figs. 4 and 5, do not constitute Markov graphs, since each state has a different average duration. These average durations are indicated on the graphs. The state of each processor changes asynchronously in an SM request cycle. The SM request cycle C, is the total average time spent in the active state, and the set of transfer states (LT and ET).

When an access to shared memory is made, it can be for one of two reasons: either the reference was for a noncacheable data item (with probability s) or for a cacheable data item absent in the cache [with probability $(1 - s)(1 - h)$]. Hence the fraction of references to SM made to noncacheable data space is $\alpha = s/[s + (1 - h)(1 - s)]$. According to the model assumptions, the visit time (expressed in units of cache cycles) in state A consists of two components. The first component is the processing time during which the processor does not have to reference shared memory. The total probability that a given cache cycle requires an access to the shared memory is $x[s + (1 - h)(1 - s)]$. This can be derived by noting that such an access occurs when a reference is made and the reference is for noncacheable data or is for cacheable data and results in a miss. The mean of the first component of the visit time in state A is thus $1/\{x[s + (1 - h)(1 - s)]\}$, counting the cache cycle in which the access to memory is initiated. The second component of the visit time is the sum of the switch set-up and traversal times in units of cache cycles and is given by $(t_a + t_d)$. So, the total duration of a visit to state A in Figs. 4 and 5 is $1/\{x[s + (1 - h)(1 - s)]\} + t_a + t_d$. The visit time in state ET is a constant with value $m - 1$.

For the set-associative cache (Fig. 4), if a block-write is not required (with probability $1 - w_b$) on a cache miss, then the line which accepts the SM block request is busy for $B - m + c_P$ time units. However, if a block-write is required (with

probability w_b) in addition to the block-read, then two consecutive block transfers (each of size B) are made uninterruptedly on the same SM line. In this case, the line that accepts the block request is busy for $2B - m + c_P$ time units.

The case of the fully-associative cache is simpler (Fig. 5): if a cache miss requires a block-write (with a probability w_b) followed by a block-read, the processor submits these requests as two successive and independent requests to transfer a block of size B in each case because these two blocks may not reside on the same line. Each of the two corresponding LT states thus have a constant duration of $B - m + c_P$.

In both cases, each processor goes through "independent" states (states A and ET), followed by "interactive" states (states W and LT). In an independent state, a processor can proceed freely and does not interfere with the progress of other processors. Interactive states are characterized by a potential for conflicts with other processors. The interactive states are framed in Figs. 4 and 5. During any LT state, the SM line is busy and no other processor can access the line. In order to estimate the average visit time in such states, simulations are required. Note that the foregoing analysis that leads to the state graphs of Figs. 4 and 5 simplifies the simulation significantly. Table I is a compilation of some of the simulation results for an example system configuration with fully-associative caches $s = 0$, $w_b = 0.3$, $c_P = 4$, $x = 0.4$, $h = 0.95$, $m = 4$, $P = 16$). The number of lines, l, and the block size, B, are variable. We have assumed that $t_a + t_d = 0$. The performance index is the average processor utilization, U, defined as the average fraction of time spent by each processor processing instructions in an active state. In our study we found that both cache implementations have practically the same performance for the same value of the hit ratio when slow memories ($c_p > 4$) are used. However, the set-associative organization results in a poorer performance for small number of lines ($l \sim 1$) when faster memories are used. Note that a fully-associative cache usually results in a higher hit ratio than set-associative if a given cache size is applied to both cases. The results obtained from such considerations are discussed in Section IV-B(3).

Because these simulations are still expensive, despite the simplification, we have developed an approximate analytical model to estimate the processor utilization.

B. Approximate Analytical Model

The processor's behavior shown in Figs. 4 and 5 is quite complex to model exactly. We propose an approximate ana-

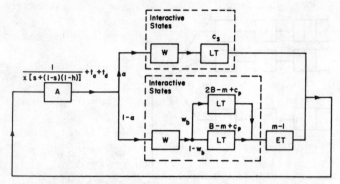

Fig. 4. State graph for set-associative caches system with static or quasi-dynamic coherence check, where $\alpha = s/[s + (1 - s)(1 - h)]$.

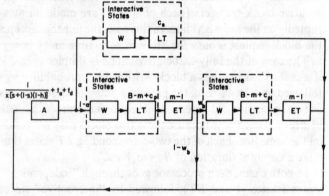

Fig. 5. State graph for fully-associative cache system with static or quasi-dynamic coherence check, where $\alpha = s/[s + (1 - s)(1 - h)]$.

lytical model based on a method applied in [13] for the modeling of random-word accesses in multiprocessor memories. We number the processors from 1 to P and the memory lines from 1 to l. Let

$$I_k(t) = [i_{k,1}(t), i_{k,2}(t), \cdots, i_{k,P}(t)]$$

for $k = 1, \cdots, l$, with $i_{k,j}(t) = 1$ iff processor j is not waiting for or using line k, and $i_{kj}(t) = 0$ iff processor j is waiting for or using line k at time t.

$I_k(t)$ is called the *indicator vector* for line k at time t. Each component, $i_{k,j}(t)$, indicates whether or not processor j is waiting for, or holding line k. Note that a processor waits for or holds a line whenever it is in state W or LT (interactive states), respectively. Let X_s be the probability that a given line is busy and S, the average line service time of a request. Then

X_s = Prob(at least one processor is waiting for, or holding a given line k)

= $1 -$ Prob[no processor is waiting for, or holding line k]

= $1 -$ Prob($i_{k,1} \cdot i_{k,2} \cdots i_{k,P} = 1$)

= $1 - E[i_{k,1} \cdot i_{k,2} \cdots i_{k,P}]$. (1)

This last equality results from the fact that the expectation of a random variable which takes only the values 0 and 1 is equal to the probability of the variable being 1. The rate of *completed* requests by a line is

$$\frac{X_s}{S} \qquad (2)$$

TABLE I
PROCESSOR UTILIZATION FOR THE FULLY-ASSOCIATIVE CACHE
($c = 4$, $w_b = 0.3$, $m = 4$, $h = 0.95$, $P = 16$, $s = 0$)

l	B	Simulation	Model	Error (%)
1	4	0.596	0.601	+0.8
	8	0.300	0.301	+0.3
	16	0.150	0.150	0.0
	32	0.076	0.075	-1.3
	64	0.038	0.038	0.0
2	4	0.789	0.791	+0.2
	8	0.541	0.579	+7.0
	16	0.286	0.301	+5.2
	32	0.145	0.150	+3.4
	64	0.072	0.075	+4.3
4	4	0.929	0.831	+0.2
	8	0.708	0.721	+1.8
	15	0.475	0.511	+7.6
	32	0.261	0.286	+9.9
	64	0.133	0.145	+10.4
8	4	0.839	0.839	+0.0
	8	0.753	0.754	+0.1
	16	0.598	0.603	+0.8
	32	0.390	0.411	+5.4
	64	0.219	0.238	+8.5
16	4	0.842	0.843	+0.1
	8	0.767	0.768	+0.1
	16	0.640	0.642	+0.3
	32	0.467	0.472	+1.1
	64	0.290	0.300	+3.5

In equilibrium, this rate can be equated to the rate of *submitted* requests to a line. To compute this second member of the equation, we note that a processor submits a request whenever it departs from state A. This occurs, for each processor, whenever a cycle in the networks of Figs. 4 and 5 is completed. Recall that C is the average time taken by such a cycle. The rate of submitted requests to the SM by any one processor is $1/C$. Since there are P requesting processors and each request is submitted randomly to any one of the lines, the average rate of submitted request to a given line k is

$$\frac{1}{C} \cdot \frac{P}{l}$$

Let T be the average time between an exit from an interactive state and a visit to the next interactive state. Let Y be the average fraction of time a given processor is in an independent state. By the ergodic property [15], Y is also the probability of being in such a state. The symmetry of the system implies the same value of Y for all the processors. From the above definitions,

$$Y = \frac{T}{C} \cdot$$

Substituting for $1/C$ in the equation for the average rate of submitted request to a given line, and equating this rate to the rate of completed request in (2), we obtain

$$X_s = Y \cdot \frac{S}{T} \cdot \frac{P}{l}$$

Substituting for X_s in (1), we have

$$E[i_{k,1} \cdot i_{k,2} \cdots i_{k,P}] + \rho Y = 1, \qquad (3)$$

where

$$\rho = \frac{S}{T} \cdot \frac{P}{l} \cdot$$

This equation is exact. However, the first term of the left hand side of the equation is very complex to estimate in general. The approximation consists in neglecting the interactions between processors. As a result of the approximation, the components of $I_k(t)$ are not correlated. This approximation performs best for a short and deterministic line service time. Indeed, large instances of the line service time are more likely to result in instantaneous longer queues and more interactions between the processors. Under the noncorrelation conditions,

$$E[i_{k,1} \cdot i_{k,2} \cdots i_{k,P}] = E[i_{k,1}] \cdot E[i_{k,2}] \cdots E[i_{k,P}].$$

If we denote by Z the fraction of time spent by each processor waiting for or holding a given line k, (3) becomes

$$(1 - Z)^P + \rho Y = 1, \tag{4}$$

because of the symmetry of the system.

On the other hand, since a processor is either in an independent state (A or ET), or in an interactive state (waiting for or holding one of the lines), then by the law of total probability in a system with l lines we have

$$Y + l \cdot Z = 1. \tag{5}$$

Using (4) with the condition that $1 - \rho Y > 0$,

$$Z = 1 - (1 - \rho Y)^{1/P}.$$

Consequently, by the substitution for Z in (5) and rearranging, we obtain

$$Y = \frac{1}{\rho}\left[1 - \left(\frac{Y + l - 1}{l}\right)^P\right] \tag{6}$$

with

$$\rho = \frac{P}{l} \cdot \frac{S}{T}.$$

S is the mean line service time and T is the mean time between an exit from an interactive state and a visit to the next interactive state. To compute ρ, we have to distinguish between the two cache implementations. Note that S can be found as the

mean time that a processor spends holding a memory line. Similarly, T is found as the mean time spent *outside* of an interactive state.

Since Y is the average fraction of time spent in state A or ET, the processor utilization, U, which is the fraction of time the processor is busy processing instructions, is given by

$$U = \frac{\dfrac{1}{x[s + (1 - s)(1 - h)]}}{C} = \dfrac{\dfrac{1}{x[s + (1 - s)(1 - h)]}}{T} Y \tag{7}$$

Besides being a good approximation for short line service times with low coefficient of variation, the approximation (6) was proven in [11] to have the following desirable properties.

Property 1: when P tends to ∞ (and all other parameters are kept constant), Y tends to $1/\rho$.

Property 2: Equation (6) has a unique real solution between 0 and min $(1, 1/\rho)$.

As a consequence of the first property, the approximation is correct asymptotically, when the traffic at the memory (and thus the interactions between processors) tends to ∞. This can be seen as follows. When the number of processors increases, the system of Fig. 2 tends to saturate [15]. Under saturated conditions, each line is constantly busy, which implies that X_s tends to 1 for all the lines and thus Y tends to $1/\rho$.

1) *Set-Associative Cache (Fig. 4):* From Fig. 4, the mean time spent holding a line is S and can be obtained from the figure as

$$S = c_S \alpha + [B(1 + w_b) - m + c_P](1 - \alpha), \tag{8}$$

where

$$\alpha = \frac{s}{s + (1 - s)(1 - h)}.$$

The mean time spent in independent states is equal to T and is

$$T = (m - 1)(1 - \alpha) + \frac{1}{x[s + (1 - s)(1 - h)]} + t_a + t_d. \tag{9}$$

Equation (6) is first solved for Y, with the values of S and T above. This equation can be solved by the Newton's iterative methods [7] with initial value $Y_0 = 0.5$. Alternately, (6) can be solved by finding the zero of the function $f(Y) - Y = 0$ via a zero searching algorithm using Property 2, where $f(Y)$ is given by the right hand side of (6).

The processor utilization is

$$U = \frac{\dfrac{1}{x[s + (1 - s)(1 - h)]}}{T} Y.$$

Or

$$U = \frac{Y}{(m - 1)(1 - h)(1 - s)x + (t_a + t_d)x[s + (1 - s)(1 - h)] + 1}. \tag{10}$$

2) *Fully-Associative Cache (Fig. 5):* From Fig. 5 the mean time spent holding a memory line is

$$S = \alpha c_S + (1 - \alpha)(1 + w_b)(B - m + c_P), \tag{11}$$

and

$$T = \frac{1}{x[s + (1 - s)(1 - h)]} + t_a + t_d + (1 - \alpha)(1 + w_b)(m - 1). \tag{12}$$

Again, (6) is first solved for Y, with these values of S and T. Then, the processor utilization is

$$U = \frac{\dfrac{1}{x[s + (1 - s)(1 - h)]}}{T} Y.$$

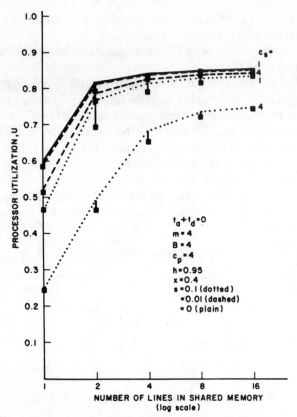

Fig. 6. Processor utilization for the multiprocessor with set-associative caches and static coherence check.

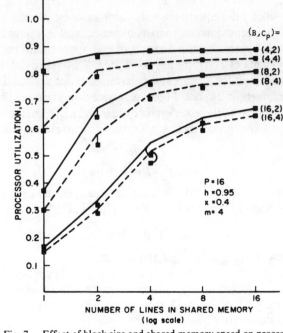

Fig. 7. Effect of block size and shared memory speed on processor utilization for set-associative caches.

configurations. Assuming that the cache size is adjusted to give the same hit ratio when the block size is increased, an increase in the block size deteriorates the utilization. Again, the simulation points are also linked to their analytical estimates in Fig. 7. In all cases (Figs. 6 and 7), the analytical model tends to overestimate the utilization slightly.

Or

$$U = \frac{Y}{(m-1)(1-h)(1-s)(1+w_b)x + (t_a+t_d)x[s+(1-s)(1-h)]+1}. \tag{13}$$

Again, the Newton's iterative or zero searching method can be used to solve for Y.

3) *Accuracy of the Approximate Model:* In order to check the accuracy of approximate model, we have compared it with the simulation. Some typical results that are shown in Table I for the fully-associative case with $s = 0$. The model has been found to be adequate for parameter values corresponding to an effective design, and it is able to detect a poor design.

In order to show the effect of the static coherence check on performance, we display, in Fig. 6, processor utilization curves obtained for the set-associative cache with $B = 4$, $P = 16$, $w_b = 0.3$, and $c_P = 4$, assuming an infinitely fast processor-memory switch. c_S is set to 4 or 1, and s is set to 0.0, 0.01 or 0.1. Note that while $c_S = 1$ and $c_P = 4$ it indicates that noncacheable data space modules are faster than cacheable data space modules. The simulation points (denoted by solid squares) are linked to their analytical estimates. It can be seen that the analytical model approximates the utilization adequately. When the degree of sharing, s, is large ($s = 0.1$), the performance degradations are noticeable. They can be compensated for by using fast modules for the noncacheable data.

The effect of the block size, B, and the shared memory cycle time, c_P, on the processor utilization is illustrated in Fig. 7 for the set-associative cache system with various memory con-

Fig. 8 shows the tradeoffs between the hit ratio, h, and the shared memory cycle time, c_P, for the fully-associative cache system with $s = 0.01$ and $m = B = 8$. Since a change in hit ratio can be due to a change in the cache size, Fig. 8 can be used to study the tradeoffs between cache sizes and memory speeds. In general, as the memory speed decreases, the utilization is reduced. This effect is more pronounced for small l (1 or 2). The diagram shows that a reduction in the memory speed may be compensated for by an appropriate increase in the cache size.

A comparison of set-associative and fully-associative cache systems is shown in Fig. 9. Given the hit ratio, h_{FA}, for a fully-associative cache, we obtained the hit ratio, h_{SA}, for a set associative cache of the same size using the relationship given in Section II for set size $i = 4$ and number of sets, $N = 128$. It can be seen that the hit ratio has a dramatic effect on the processor utilization in both cases.

In order to obtain good estimates with this analytical model, the coefficient of variation of the line service time must be small (say less than 0.5).

For the set-associative cache, the coefficient of variation of the line service time is given by $C_S = \sigma_S/S$, where

$$\sigma_S^2 = \alpha c_S^2 + (1-\alpha)(2B - m + c_P)^2 w_b$$
$$+ (1-\alpha)(1-w_b)(B - m + c_P)^2 - S^2.$$

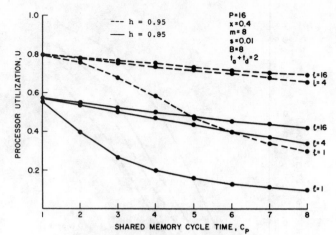

Fig. 8. Effect of block size and shared memory speed on processor utilization for set-associative caches.

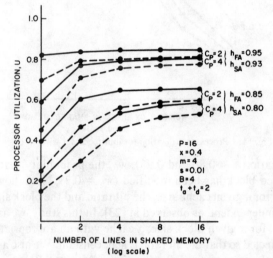

Fig. 9. Comparison of fully-associative and set-associative caches for various memory configurations.

and

$$S = c_S \alpha + [B(1 + w_b) - m + c_P](1 - \alpha),$$

It is interesting to note that the coefficient of variation of the line service time is less than 0.5 in all cases shown except for the case $s = 0.1$ and $c_S = 1$, where it is 0.95.

The coefficient of variation for the worst case of Fig. 7 ($B = 4$, $c_P = 2$) is 0.57. Note that in this case $s = 0$ and hence $\alpha = 0$. The percentage of error is quite small; thus the model is adequate.

For the fully-associative cache model, the coefficient of variation of the line service time is $C_S = \alpha_S/S$, where

$$\sigma_S^2 = \alpha c_S^2 + (1 - \alpha)(1 + w_b)(B - m + c_P)^2 - S^2,$$

and

$$S = \alpha c_S + (1 - \alpha)(1 + w_b)(B - m + c_P).$$

For the fully-associative cache in which $s = 0$, $C_s = 0$ and thus the approximation is very good.

C. Speed-Up of the Cache-Based Multiprocessor

We can derive the speed-up of the cache-based multiprocessor system (called system 1) over another system without caches (called system 2). The system without caches is similar to C.mmp. It consists of a P processor system that has a shared memory with l interleaved modules. The processor and the modules are connected through a crossbar switch. There is no block transfer in system 2, because it is not a cache-based system. The memory modules are interleaved for single-word accesses; i.e., the word with address X is in module X mod l. Each memory reference requires a single-word transfer. Throughout this section, we assume that the degree of sharing is very small and that it can be neglected in order to simplify the computation. Hence $s = 0$ and $\alpha = 0$. Since we assume the same memory parameters, the memory cycle is c_P.

The instruction-mix parameter, θ is the same for both systems. Recall that θ is the probability of a memory request being issued by a processor in a machine cycle. It is important to note that, in system 2, a visit to the SM is part of a useful cycle. The degradation in the processor utilization come uniquely from the waiting time caused by conflicts to the memory.

Because we assume that systems 1 and 2 have identical processors, the absence of the cache in system 2 and the service of each memory reference in the SM elongate the machine cycle time of each processor from T_1 (in system 1) to T_2 (in system 2). It can be easily seen that $T_2 = T_1 - 1 + c_P + t_a + t_d$ time units since every memory reference encounters the delays in the crossbar switch. Note that a cache cycle in system 1 is the time unit. T_1 consists of an integer number, d, of cache cycles. In system 2, a memory reference to SM may encounter a delay in service because of memory conflicts. We denote by A the state in which the processor is active, and by W the state in which the processor is waiting. Furthermore, state M denotes the state of the service of the SM request. From our hypotheses about processor behavior, the number of machine cycles between two successive references to memory are geometrically distributed with parameter θ. The mean number of completed machine cycles between two successive references to memory in system 2 is thus $(1/\theta - 1)$. Fig. 10 depicts the state graph. During a successful memory access, a time c_P is spent in the memory to fetch the requested word. The time spent outside the memory in a successful memory access cycle is thus $T_2 - c_P$. The mean visit time to state A is the mean time spent per cycle through the state graph in the absence of memory conflict, i.e.,

$$\left(\frac{1}{\theta} - 1\right)T_2 + T_2 - c_P = \frac{T_2}{\theta} - c_P.$$

It should be pointed out that the scheduling of requests for single-word transfers in this system is FCFS, as in the system with caches. The model leading to (6) is also applicable to the graph of Fig. 10. Hence

$$Y = \frac{1}{\rho}\left[1 - \left(\frac{Y + l - 1}{l}\right)^P\right],$$

with Y being the fraction of time a given processor is in state A, and

$$\rho = \frac{P}{l} \cdot \frac{S}{T} \cdot = \frac{P}{l} \frac{c_P}{\frac{T_2}{\theta} - c_P}.$$

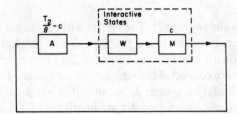

Fig. 10. State graph for the system without caches.

Note that from Fig. 10, $S = c_P$ and T is equal to the mean visit time to state A.

The resulting model is a central server-like model with deterministic servers. In this case, the approximation leading to (6) is accurate, since the coefficient of variation of the memory service time is zero.

The processor utilization, denoted by U_2 is

$$U_2 = \frac{\dfrac{T_2}{\theta}}{C_2} = \frac{T_2 Y}{T_2 - c_P \theta} ,$$

since $Y = (T_2/\theta - c_P)/C_2$ and C_2 is the request cycle in the system without caches. Fig. 11 shows the processor utilization for different values of c_P, t_a and t_d. The accuracy of the analytical model is guaranteed by the fact that the service time at the memory has a coefficient of variation equal to 0 (this is basically a special case of Hoogendoorn's model [13]). Note that the processor utilization for the system with $t_a + t_d = 0$ is worse than for the system with $t_a + t_d = 2$. Indeed, when the switch is faster, the machine cycle of each processor may be reduced and the traffic to memory is more intense, resulting in increased conflicts and thereby reducing the processor utilization.

Let us represent the utilization of system 1 by U_1. U_1 can be obtained from (10) and (13) for the set-associative and fully-associative cache models respectively. The effective machine cycles for a processor of systems 1 and 2 are T_1/U_1 and T_2/U_2, respectively. Since $T_2 = T_1 + c_P - 1 + t_a + t_d$, and $T_1 = d$, the speed-up for the P processor system is

$$S_P = \frac{T_2/U_2}{T_1/U_1} = \frac{T_2}{T_1} \frac{U_1}{U_2} = \left(1 + \frac{c_P - 1 + t_a + t_d}{d}\right)\frac{U_1}{U_2} .$$

The evaluation of the speed-up permits us to compare the effectiveness of the caches in the multiprocessor system. Certainly, this speed-up is a function of many parameters. The discussion of the results given in the next section exposes the effects of the variability of these parameters on the system performance.

V. DISCUSSION AND CONCLUSION

In the following discussion, we assume that the multiprocessor system consists of $P = 16$ processors with private caches. The machine cycle time of the cache-based system is $d = 2$ (all times are expressed in units of cache cycles), and the instruction-mix parameter, θ is 0.8. For system 1, the shared memory has an L-M configuration with $m = 4$, and l (a power of 2) is between 1 and 16. Thus the total number of modules is varaible. Other parameters of the study are B, the block size ($4 \leq B \leq 16$), c_P, the memory cycle time ($2 \leq c_P \leq 4$), h the cache

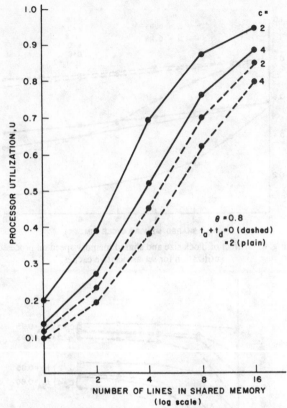

Fig. 11. Processor utilization for multipocessor without caches.

hit ratio ($h = 0.85$ and 0.95), w_b, the probability that a replaced block has been modified ($w_b = 0.3$). Note, however, that for a given cache size, the hit ratio and the block size are not independent, as observed in [23]. In this study, we assume that, for a given block size, a cache with an appropriate size is selected so that the hit ratio is kept constant. We also assume that the degree of sharing is very small ($s \ll 0.01$), so that it can be neglected, as shown in Fig. 6. System 2 does not have any cache, and the shared memory is organized as a set of l interleaved banks.

The processor utilization (U) is a performance index reflecting the degree of matching between the processors and the memory organization. The throughput improvement provided by the introduction of caches is measured by the speed-up (S_p), as defined in Section IV-C. Note that U and S_p are not necessarily related: a system with high speed-up may have an unacceptably low processor utilization. In general, one desires a design with high processor utilization and speed-up to justify the investment in faster processors and expensive cache memories, respectively. For the parameters chosen, there is little difference in the results of the set-associative and fully-associative cache models. Hence, only the results for the set-associative model are given in the figures. To limit the computation cost, the analytical models are used to derive the following curves.

A comparison of Figs. 6 and 11 shows that the caches can have a dramatic effect on processor utilization even when the crossbar delay is neglected ($t_a + t_d = 0$). In general, an increase in the block size or a decrease in the hit ratio causes a significant deterioration of the processor utilization. However, for a reasonable block size (e.g., 4) and high hit ratio (e.g.,

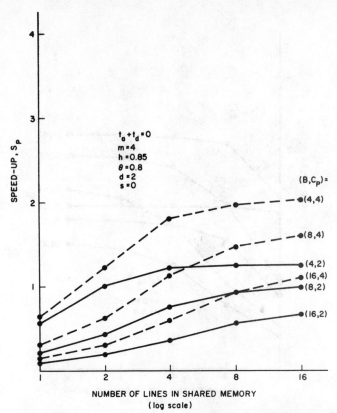

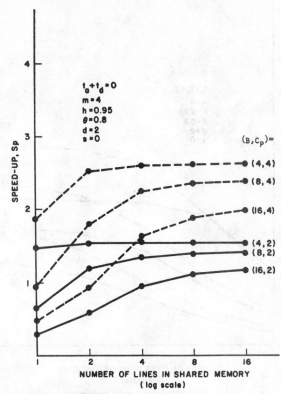

Fig. 12. Effective speed-up for multiprocessor with set-associative caches assuming infinitely fast crossbar switch. (a) Cache with hit ratio, $h = 0.85$. (b) Cache with hit ratio, $h = 0.95$.

0.95), the processor utilization for the system with cache is much better than for the system without caches. This observation is particularly true for small values of l, and was shown experimentally by Nesset [17]. The improvement is more dramatic when the memory cycle time, c_P, is large, as shown in Fig. 8.

The following throughput comparisons between two systems emphasize the design alternatives offered by the use of private caches. Both systems consist of 16 processors. In system 1, a private cache is added to each processor and the memory configuration is characterized by $m = 4$ and $1 \leq l \leq 16$. Hence, the cache controllers access the SM via a $16 \times l$ crossbar switch. In system 2, the processors are connected to an interleaved memory with 16 memory banks through a 16×16 crossbar switch. All the other parameters are as described earlier in this section.

The most significant effect of l in a system is the reduction in complexity of the processor-memory interconnection network and hence in the cost. Figs. 12 and 13 show the effective speed-up achieved by the inclusion of cache memories and the simultaneous reduction in the number of lines l. It can be seen that a significant improvement in the system throughput is still achievable by the simultaneous reduction in l and the inclusion of cache memories even for relatively low hit ratios [Figs. 12(a) and 13(a)]. This performance improvement is even more pronounced for large values of c_P and high hit ratios. A possible significant reduction in l gives the designer a choice. If for a small number of lines, $l < 16$, the incorporation of a per-processor cache with small B and high h results in a speed-up, $S_p \geq 1$, the designer can consider trading off low-cost multiport memories for the expensive 16×16 crossbar switch used in the system without caches. In fact, as is shown in Fig. 12, the incorporation of a per-processor cache results in significant speed-up in most cases, even for small l and when the delay through the crossbar is neglected. This conclusion is much more evident for the case illustrated Fig. 13, in which $t_a + t_d$ has been set to 2.

ACKNOWLEDGMENT

The authors express their gratitude to Dr. O. Ibe of IBM Thomas J. Watson Research Center for his tremendous help in the production of this paper.

REFERENCES

[1] F. A. Briggs and E. S. Davidson, "Organization of semiconductor memories for parallel pipelined processors," *IEEE Trans. Comput.*, vol. C-26, pp. 162–169. Feb. 1977.
[2] F. A. Briggs and M. Dubois, "Performance of cache-based multiprocessors," *Ass. Comput. Mach. Conf. Measurement Modeling Comput. Syst.*, Sept. 1981.
[3] F. A. Briggs and M. Dubois, "Cache effectiveness in multiprocessor systems with pipelined parallel memories," in *Proc. 1981 Int. Conf. Parallel Processing*, Aug. 1981.
[4] L. M. Censier and P. Feautrier, "A new solution to coherence problems in multicache systems," *IEEE Trans. Comput.*, vol. C-27, Dec. 1978.
[5] D. Y. Chang and D. J. Kuck, "On the effective bandwidth of parallel memories," *IEEE Trans. Comput.*, pp. 480–489, May 1977.
[6] E. G. Coffman, Jr. and P. J. Denning, *Operating Systems Theory*. Englewood Cliffs, NJ: Prentice-Hall, 1973.
[7] G. Dahlquist and A. Bjorck, *Numerical Methods*. Englewood Cliffs, NJ: Prentice-Hall, 1974.
[8] P. Denning, "Working sets past and present," *IEEE Trans. Software Eng.*, vol. SE-6, Jan. 1980.
[9] M. Dubois and F. A. Briggs, "Efficient interprocessor communication for MIMD multiprocessor systems," in *Proc. 8th Int. Symp. Comput. Arch.*, May 1981.

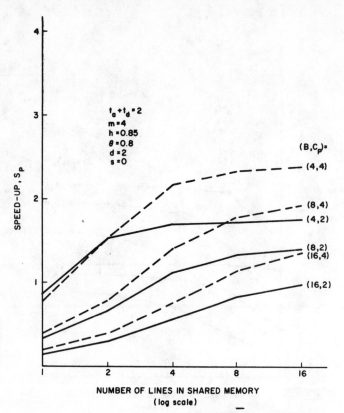
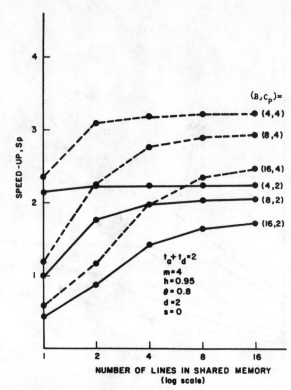

Fig. 13. Effective speed-up for multiprocessor with set-associative caches assuming a finite-speed crossbar switch with $t_a + t_d = 2$. (a) Cache with hit ratio, $h = 0.85$ (b) Cache with hit ratio, $h = 0.95$

[10] M. Dubois and F. A. Briggs, "Effects of cache coherency in multiprocessors," *IEEE Trans. Comput.*, vol. C-31, Nov. 1982.

[11] M. Dubois and F. A. Briggs, "Analytical methodologies for the evaluation of multiprocessing structures," Purdue Univ. Tech. Rep. TR-EE 82-4, Feb. 1982.

[12] M. J. Flynn, "Some computer organizations and their effectiveness," *IEEE Trans. Comput.*, vol. C-21, pp. 998–1005, Sept. 1972.

[13] C. H. Hoogendoorn, "A general model for memory interference in multiprocessors," *IEEE Trans. Comput.*, vol. C-26, pp. 998–1005 Oct. 1977.

[14] K. R. Kaplan and R. O. Winder, "Cache-based computer systems," *Computer*, vol. 6, Mar. 1973.

[15] L. Kleinrock, *Queuing Systems, vols. I and II.* New York: Wiley 1976.

[16] A. Lehman, "Performance evlauation and prediction of storage hierarchies," *ACM SIGMETRICS Perform. '80*, vol. 9, pp. 43–54, May 1980.

[17] D. M. Nessett, "The effectiveness of cache memories in a multiprocessor environment," *Australian Comput. J.*, vol. 7, Mar. 1975.

[18] J. H. Patel, "Analysis of multiprocessors with private cache memories," *IEEE Trans. Comput.*, vol. C-31, Apr. 1982.

[19] G. S. Rao, "Performance analysis of cache memories," *J. Ass. Comput. Mach.*, vol. 25, pp. 378–395, July 1978.

[20] J. H. Saltzer, "A simple linear model of demand paging performance," *Commun. Ass. Comput. Mach.*, vol. 17, Apr. 1974.

[21] A. J. Smith, "A comparative study of set associative memory mapping algorithms and their use for cache and main memory," *IEEE Trans Software Eng.*, vol. SE-4, pp. 121–130, Mar. 1978.

[22] A. J. Smith, "Characterizing the storage process and its effect on the update of main memory by write through," *J. Ass. Comput. Mach.*, vol. 26, Jan. 1979.

[23] W. D. Streker, "Cache memories for PDP-11 family computers," in *Proc. 3rd Ann. Symp. Comput. Arch.*, Jan. 1976.

[24] C. K. Tang, "Cache system design in the tightly coupled multiprocessor system," *Proc. AFIPS*, 1976.

[25] L. C. Widdoes, "The S-1 project: development of high performance digital computers," *Dig. COMPCON '80*, IEEE Comput. Soc., San Francisco, CA, Feb. 1980.

[26] W. A. Wulf, R. Levin and S. P. Harbison, *Hydra/C.mmp: An Experimental Computer System.* New York: McGraw-Hill, 1981.

Fayé A. Briggs (M'77) received the B.Eng. degree from Ahmadu Bello University, Nigeria, in 1971, the M.S. degree from Stanford University, Stanford, CA, in 1974, and the Ph.D. degree from the University of Illinois, Urbana-Champaign in 1977, all in electrical engineering.

He is currently an Associate Professor of Computer Science with the Department of Electrical Engineering at Rice University, Houston, TX. From 1976 to 1982 he was an Associate Professor with the School of Electrical Engineering at Purdue University, West Lafayette, IN. During the Summer of 1982 he was with the IBM Thomas J. Watson Research Center, Yorktown Heights, NY. His current interests include multiprocessor and pipelined computer systems, memory organizations, performance evaluation, operating system, and VLSI computing structures.

Dr. Briggs is a member of the Association for Computing Machinery and the IEEE Computer Society.

Michel Dubois (S'79–M'81) was born in Charleroi, Belgium, in 1953. He received the Ingénieur Civil Electricien degree from the Faculté Polytechnique de Mons, Belgium, the M.S. degree from the University of Minnesota, Minneapolis, in 1978, and the Ph.D. degree from Purdue University West Lafayette, IN, in 1982, all in electrical engineering.

During his studies in the U.S., he was funded by grants from the Faculté Polytechnique de Mons, and by research and teaching positions. He is now with the Central Research Laboratory, Thomson-CSF, Domaine de Corbeville, France, where he designs architectures for very large scale integration. He main interests are in computer architecture and digital image processing.

INSTRUCTION ISSUE LOGIC FOR PIPELINED SUPERCOMPUTERS

Shlomo Weiss
Computer Sciences Department
University of Wisconsin-Madison
Madison, WI 53706

James E. Smith
Department of Electrical and Computer Engineering
University of Wisconsin-Madison
Madison, WI 53706

Abstract

Basic principles and design tradeoffs for control of pipelined processors are first discussed. We concentrate on register-register architectures like the CRAY-1 where pipeline control logic is localized to one or two pipeline stages and is referred to as "instruction issue logic". Design tradeoffs are explored by giving designs for a variety of instruction issue methods that represent a range of complexity and sophistication. These vary from the original CRAY-1 issue logic to a version of Tomasulo's algorithm, first used in the IBM 360/91 floating point unit. Also studied are Thornton's "scoreboard" algorithm used on the CDC 6600 and an algorithm we have devised. To provide a standard for comparison, all the issue methods are used to implement the CRAY-1 scalar architecture. Then, using a simulation model and the Lawrence Livermore Loops compiled with the CRAY FORTRAN compiler, performance results for the various issue methods are given and discussed.

1. Introduction

Although modern supercomputers are closely associated with high speed vector operation, it is widely recognized that scalar operation is at least of equal importance, and pipelining [KOGG81] is the predominant technique for achieving high scalar performance. In a pipelined computer, instruction processing is broken into segments and processing proceeds in an assembly line fashion with the execution of several instructions being overlapped. Because of data and control dependencies in a scalar instruction stream, interlock logic is placed between critical pipeline segments to control instruction flow through the pipe. In an register-register architecture like the CDC 6600 [THOR70], the CDC 7600 [BONS69], and the CRAY-1 [CRAY77, CRAY79, RUSS78], most of the interlock logic is localized to one segment early in the pipeline and is referred to as "instruction issue" logic.

It is the purpose of this paper to highlight some of the tradeoffs that affect pipeline control, with particular emphasis on instruction issue logic. The primary vehicle for this discussion is a simulation study of different instruction issue methods with varying degrees of complexity. These range from the simple and straightforward as in the CRAY-1 to the complex and sophisticated as in the CDC 6600 and the IBM 360/91 floating point unit [TOMA67]. Each is used to implement the CRAY-1 scalar architecture, and each implementation is simulated using the 14 Lawrence Livermore Loops [MCMA72] as compiled by the Cray Research FORTRAN compiler (CFT).

1.1. Tradeoffs

We begin with a discussion of design tradeoffs that centers on four principle issues:

(1) clock period,
(2) instruction scheduling,
(3) issue logic complexity, and
(4) hardware cost, debugging, and maintenance.

Each of these issues will be discussed in turn.

Clock Period. In a pipelined computer, there are a number of segments containing combinational logic with latches separating successive segments. All the latches are synchronized by the same clock, and the pipeline is capable of initiating a new instruction every clock period. Hence, under ideal conditions, i.e. no dependencies or resource conflicts, pipeline performance is directly related to the period of the clock used to synchronize the pipe. Even with data dependencies and resource conflicts, there is a high correlation between performance and clock period.

Historically, pipelined supercomputers have had shorter clock periods than other computers. This is in part due to the use of the fastest available logic technologies, but it is also due to designs that minimize logic levels between successive latches.

Scheduling of Instructions. Performance of a pipelined processor depends greatly on the order of the instructions in the instruction stream. If consecutive instructions have data and control dependencies and contend for resources, then "holes" in the pipeline will develop and performance will suffer. To improve performance, it is often possible to arrange the code, or schedule it, so that dependencies and resource conflicts are minimized. Registers can also be allocated so that register conflicts are reduced (register conflicts caused by data dependencies can not be eliminated in this way, however). Because of their close relationship, in the remainder of the paper we will group code scheduling and register allocation together and refer to them collectively as "code scheduling".

There are two different ways that code scheduling can be done. First, it can be done at compile time by the software. We refer to this as "static" scheduling because it does not change as the program runs. Second, it can be done by the hardware at run time. We refer to this as "dynamic" scheduling. These two methods are not mutually exclusive.

Most compilers for pipelined processors do some form of static scheduling to avoid dependencies. This adds a new dimension to the optimization problems faced by a compiler, and occasionally a programmer will hand code inner loops in assembly language to arrive at a better schedule than a compiler can provide.

Reprinted from *Proceedings of the 11th Annual International Symposium on Computer Architecture*, 1984, pages 110-118. Copyright © 1984 by The Institute of Electrical and Electronics Engineers, Inc.

Issue Logic Complexity. By using complex issue logic, dynamic scheduling of instructions can be achieved. This allows instructions to begin execution "out-of-order" with respect to the compiled code sequence. This has two advantages. First, it relieves some the burden on the compiler to generate a good schedule. That is, performance is not as dependent on the quality of the compiled code. Second, dynamic scheduling at issue time can take advantage of dependency information that is not available to the compiler when it does static scheduling. Complex issue logic does require longer control paths, however, which can lead to a longer clock period.

Hardware Cost, Debugging, and Maintenance. Complex issue methods lead to additional hardware cost. More logic is needed, and design time is increased. Complex control logic is also more expensive to debug and maintain. These problems are aggravated by issue methods that dynamically schedule code because it may be difficult to reproduce exact issue sequences.

1.2. Historical Perspective

It is interesting to review the way the above tradeoffs have been dealt with historically. In the late 1950's and early 1960's there was rapid movement toward increasingly complex issue methods. Important milestones were achieved by STRETCH [BUCH62] in 1961 and the CDC 6600 in 1964. Probably the most sophisticated issue logic used to date is in the IBM 360/91 [ANDE67], shipped in 1967. After this first rush toward more and more complex methods, there was a retreat toward simpler instruction issue methods that are still in use today. At CDC, the 7600 was designed to issue instructions in strict program sequence with no dynamic scheduling. The clock period, however, was very fast, even by today's standards. The more recent CRAY-1 and CRAY-XMP [CRAY82] differ very little from the CDC7600 in the way they handle scalar instructions. The CDC CYBER205 [CDC81] scalar unit is also very similar. At IBM, and later at Amdahl Corp., pipelined implementations of the 360/370 architecture following the 360/91 have issued instructions strictly in order.

As for the future, both the debug/maintenance problem and the hardware cost problem may be significantly alleviated by using VLSI where logic is much less expensive and where replaceable parts are such that fault isolation does not need to be as precise as with SSI. In addition, there is a trend toward moving software problems into hardware, and code scheduling seems to be a candidate. Consequently, tradeoffs are shifting and instruction issue logic that dynamically schedules code deserves renewed study.

1.3. Paper Overview

The tradeoffs just discussed lead to a spectrum of instruction issue algorithms. Through simulation we can look at the performance gains that are made possible by dynamic code scheduling. Other issues like clock period and hardware cost and maintenance are more difficult and require detailed design and construction to make quantitative assessments. In this paper, we do discuss the control functions that need to be implemented to facilitate qualitative judgements. Section 2 examines one endpoint of the spectrum: the CRAY-1. The CRAY-1 uses simple issue logic with a fast clock and static code scheduling only. Section 3 examines the other endpoint of the spectrum: Tomasulo's algorithm. Tomasulo's algorithm is capable of considerable dynamic code scheduling via a complex issue mechanism. Sections 4 and 5 then discuss two intermediate points. The first is a variation of Thornton's "scoreboard" algorithm used in the CDC 6600. Thornton's algorithm is also used to implement the CRAY-1 scalar architecture. The second is an

algorithm we have devised to allow dynamic scheduling while doing away with some of the associative compares required by the other methods that perform dynamic scheduling. Each of the four CRAY-1 implementations is simulated over the same set of benchmarks to allow performance comparisons. Section 6 contains a further discussion on the relationship between software and hardware code scheduling in pipelined processors, and Section 7 contains conclusions.

2. The CRAY-1 Architecture and Instruction Issue Algorithm

2.1. Overview of the CRAY-1

The CRAY-1 architecture and organization are used throughout this paper as a basis for comparison. The CRAY-1 scalar architecture is shown in Figure 1. It consists of two sets of registers and functional units for (1) address processing and (2) scalar processing. The address registers are partitioned into two levels: eight A registers and sixty four B registers. The integer add and multiply functional units are dedicated to address processing. Similarly, the scalar registers are partitioned into two levels: eight S registers and sixty four T registers. The B and T register files may be used as a programmer-manipulated data cache, although this feature is largely unused by the CFT compiler. Four functional units are used exclusively for scalar processing. In addition, three floating point functional units are shared with the vector processing section (vector registers are not shown in Fig. 1).

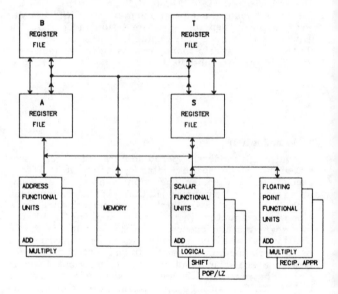

Figure 1 -- The CRAY-1 Scalar Architecture

The instruction set is designed for efficient pipeline processing. Being a register-register architecture, only load and store instructions can access memory. The rest of instructions use operands from registers. Instructions for the B and T registers are restricted to memory access and copies to and from register files A and S, respectively.

The information flow is from memory to registers A (S), or to the intermediate registers B (T). From file A (S) data is send to the functional units, from which it returns to file A (S). Then data can be further processed by functional units, stored into memory or saved in file B (T). Block transfers of operands between memory and registers B and T are also available, thus reducing the number of memory access instructions.

2.2. CRAY-1 Issue Logic

Instructions are fetched from instruction buffers at the rate of one parcel (16 bits) per clock period. Individual instructions are either one or two parcels long. After a clock period is spent for instruction decoding, the issue logic checks interlocks. If there is any conflict, issue is blocked until the conflict condition goes away.

For scalar instructions, the following are the primary interlock checks made at the time of instruction issue:

(1) registers; both the source and destination registers must not be reserved;

(2) result bus; the A and S register files have one bus each over which data can be written into the files. Based on the completion time of the particular instruction, a check is made to determine if the bus will be available at the clock period when the instruction completes.

(3) functional unit; due to vector instructions, a functional unit may be busy when a scalar instruction wishes to use it. Since we are considering scalar performance only, this type of conflict will not occur. The memory system can also be viewed as a functional unit; it can occasionally become busy due to a memory bank conflict, but for scalar code this is a very infrequent occurrence and does not affect performance in any appreciable way.

If all its interlocks pass, an instruction issues and causes the following to take place.

(1) The destination register is reserved; this reservation is removed only when the instruction completes.

(2) The result bus is reserved for the clock period when the instruction completes.

Memory accesses have one further interlock to be checked: memory bank busy. This must be delayed until the indexing register is read and the effective address is computed. Hence, the bank busy check is performed two clock periods after a load or store instruction issues. If the bank happens to be busy, the memory "functional unit" is busied, and no further loads or stores can be issued. Because all loads and stores are two parcels long, they can issue at a maximum rate of one every two clock periods. This means that a bank busy blockage catches a subsequent load or store before it is issued. After a load instruction passes the bank busy check, it places its reservation for the appropriate result bus. A load can only conflict for the bus with a previously issued reciprocal approximation instruction, so the additional interlocking done at that point is minimal.

2.3. CRAY-1 Performance

In this paper performance is measured by simulating the first 14 Lawrence Livermore Loops. These are excerpts from large FORTRAN programs that have been judged to provide a good measure of large scale computer performance. The loops were compiled using the CFT compiler, and instruction trace tapes were generated. These were then simulated with a performance simulator written in C, running on a VAX11/780. With bank busies and instruction buffer misses modeled, the simulator agrees exactly with actual CRAY-1 timings, except when there is a difference in the way a loop fits into the instruction buffers. This particular difference is a function of where the loader chooses to place a program in memory, and for practical use has to be viewed as a nondeterminism.

Since we are interested in scalar performance, the CFT compiler was run with the "vectorizer" turned off so that no vector instructions were produced. When the vectorizer is on, half of the 14 loops contain a substantial

Loop	# instructions executed	# clock cycles
1	7217	18046
2	8448	18918
3	14015	38039
4	9783	22198
5	8347	21707
6	9350	23045
7	4573	10361
8	4031	7841
9	4918	10146
10	4412	10230
11	12002	30011
12	11999	29999
13	8846	18858
14	9915	22391

Table 1 -- CRAY-1 Execution times for the 14 Lawrence Livermore Loops - 1 parcel instructions are issued in 1 cycle, 2 parcel instructions in 2 cycles.

amount of vector code, and half remain scalar.

For the simulations reported here, we have made the following simplifications:

(1) There are no memory bank conflicts.

(2) All loops fit in the instruction buffers.

One reason for this simplification was to simplify the simulator design for the alternative CRAY-1 issue methods to be given later; as mentioned earlier our original CRAY-1 simulator is capable of modeling bank conflicts and instruction buffers. Also, this allows us to concentrate on the performance differences caused by issue logic and to filter the "noise" introduced by other factors (e.g. instruction buffer crossings). Table 1 shows the scalar performance of the CRAY-1 for the first 14 Lawrence Livermore Loops.

3. Tomasulo's Algorithm

The CRAY-1 forces instructions to issue strictly in program order. If an instruction is blocked from issuing due to a conflict, all instructions following it in the instruction stream are also blocked, even if they have no conflicts. In contrast, the scheme in this section allows instructions to begin execution out of program order. It is a variation of the instruction issue algorithm first presented in [TOMA67]. Although the original algorithm was devised for the floating point unit of the IBM 360/91, we show how it can be adapted and extended to control the entire pipeline structure of a CRAY-1 implementation.

Figure 2 illustrates the essential elements of a tag-based mechanism for issue of instructions out-of-order. Fig. 3 illustrates the full CRAY-1 implementation.

Each register in the A and S register files is augmented by a *ready* bit (R) and a *tag* field. Associated with each functional unit is a small number of *reservation stations*. Each reservation station can store a pair of operands; each operand has its own tag field and ready bit. A reservation station also holds a *destination tag* (DTG). When an instruction is issued, a new tag is stored into DTG (see Fig. 2).

New destination tags are assigned from a "tag pool" that consists of some finite set of tags. These are associated with an instruction from the time the instruction is issued to a reservation station until the time it produces a result and completes. The tag is returned to the pool when an instruction finishes. In the original Tomasulo's algorithm, the tags were in 1-to-1 correspondence with the reservation stations. This particular way of assigning tags is not essential, however. Any method will work as long as tags are assigned and released to the pool as described above.

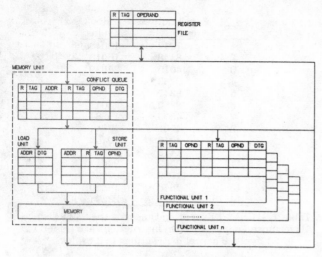

Figure 2 -- Tag based mechanism to issue out-of-order.

We treat the register files B and T as a unit, with one *busy* bit per file, since it is not practical to assign tags to so many registers. When one of these registers awaits an operand, the whole file is set to busy.

To facilitate transfer of operands between the register files, special copy units (AS, SA, AB, and ST) are introduced. These are treated as functional units, with reservation stations and execution time of one clock cycle. These reservation stations (and some others, e.g. reciprocal approximation) have only one operand.

The memory unit appears to the issue logic as a (somewhat more complex) functional unit. Instead of one set of reservation stations, the memory unit has three: *Load* reservation stations, *Store* reservation stations, and a *Conflict Queue*. When a new memory instruction I_i is issued, its effective address (if available) is checked against addresses in the Load and Store reservation stations. If there is a conflict with instruction I_j, I_i is issued and queued in the Conflict Queue. When I_j is eventually processed and the conflict disappears, I_i is transferred from the Conflict Queue to a Load or Store reservation station. If I_i uses an index register that is not ready, the effective address is unknown and there is no way to check for conflicts. In this case, I_i is stored in the Conflict Queue, where it waits for its index register to become ready.

Therefore, instructions from the Load and Store units can be processed asynchronously, since they never conflict with each other (no two instructions in these units have the same effective address). On the other hand, instructions from the Conflict Queue are processed in the order of arrival. This guarantees that two instructions with the same effective address are processed in the right order. The above mechanism takes care of any read after write, write after read or write after write hazards. The Conflict Queue is the only unit in the system in which instructions are strictly processed in the order of their arrival. This is a simpler mechanism that the one employed by the IBM 360/91 Storage System [BOLA67]. The latter has a similar queue for resolving memory conflicts, but instructions stored in this queue can be processed out of order; only two or more requests for a particular address are kept in sequence.

The tag mechanism described above allows decoded instructions to issue to functional units with little regard for dependencies. There are three conditions that must be checked before an instruction can be sent to a functional unit, however.

(1) The requested functional unit must have an available reservation station

(2) There must be an available tag from the tag pool. In Tomasulo's implementation, conditions 1 and 2 are equivalent.

(3) A source register being used by the instruction must not be loaded with a just-completed result during the same clock period as the instruction issues to a reservation station. This hazard condition is often neglected when discussing Tomasulo's algorithm. If it is not handled properly, the source register contents and the instruction that uses the source register will both be transferred during the same clock period. Because the instruction is not in the reservation station at the time of the register transfer, the register's contents will not be correctly sent to the reservation station. When this hazard condition is detected, instruction issue is held for one clock period.

In our simulations, each functional unit had 8 reservation stations. The reason we had a relatively large number of reservation stations was to monitor their usage; in fact most of them were not required. Few functional units need more than one or two reservation stations. Those that need more, usually because they wait for instructions with long latency, such as load or floating point multiply and add, would do very well with 4 reservation stations. Although in our scheme reservation stations are statically allocated to each functional unit, it is possible to reduce their number and optimize their usage by clustering them in a common pool and then allocating as needed.

When an instruction is issued, the following actions take place.

(1) The instruction's source register(s) contents are copied into the requested functional unit's reservation station.

(2) The instruction's source register(s) ready bits are copied into the reservation station.

(3) The instruction's source register(s) tag fields are copied into the reservation station.

(4) A tag allocated from the tag pool is placed in the result register's tag field (if there is a result), the register's ready bit is cleared, and the tag is written into the DTG field of the reservation station.

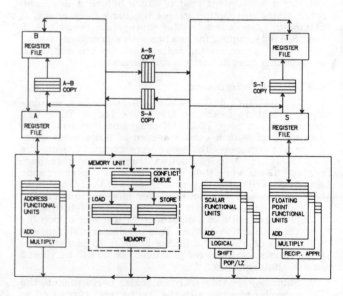

Figure 3 -- A modified CRAY-1 scalar
architecture to issue instructions out-of-order.

Thus, if a source register's ready bit is set, the reservation station will hold a valid operand. Otherwise, it will hold a tag that identifies the expected operand.

In order for an instruction waiting in a reservation station to begin execution, the following must be satisfied.

(1) All its operands must be ready.

(2) It must gain access to the required functional unit; this may involve contention with other reservation stations belonging to the same functional unit that also have all operands ready.

(3) It must gain access to the result bus for the clock period when its result will be ready; again, this may involve contention with other instructions issuing to the same or any other functional unit that will complete at the same time.

When an instruction begins execution, it does the following.

(1) It releases its reservation station.

(2) It reserves the result bus for the clock period when it will complete. Reserving the bus in advance avoids the implementation problems of stopping the pipeline if the bus is busy. An alternative is to request the bus a short time before the end of execution and to provide buffering at the output of the functional unit [TOMA67].

(3) It copies its destination tag into the functional unit control pipeline because the destination tag must be attached to the result when the instruction completes.

When an either a load or functional unit instruction completes, its result and corresponding destination tag appear on the result bus. (In a practical implementation, the tag will probably precede the data by one clock period.) The data is stored in all the reservation stations and registers that have the ready bit clear and a tag that matches the tag of the result. Then the ready bit is set to signal a valid operand.

Because instruction issue takes place in two phases (the first moves an instruction to a reservation station and the second moves it on to the functional unit for execution) we assume that each phase takes a full clock period. In the CRAY-1 there is only a one clock period delay in moving an instruction to a functional unit. We recognize the one clock period difference in our simulation model, so that the minimum time for an instruction to complete is one clock period greater than in the CRAY-1. This takes into account some of the lost time

due to the more complex control decisions that are required. The primary factor that may lead to longer control paths is the contention that takes place among the reservation stations for functional units and busses when more than one are simultaneously ready to initiate an instruction.

When branches are taken, issue is held for at least 5 clock cycles. Since branches test the contents of register A0 for the condition specified in the branch instruction, A0 should not be busy in the previous 2 cycles. These assumptions are in accord with the CRAY-1 implementation and the assumptions made to produce Table 1.

3.1. Performance Results

Table 2 shows the results of simulating the CRAY-1 implemented with Tomasulo's algorithm. The total speedup achieved was 1.43. We recognize that these are in a sense, "theoretical maximum speedups"; any lengthening of the clock period due to longer control paths will diminish this speedup.

Loop	# clock cycles 1 parcel/cp	# clock cycles 1 instr/cp	speedup
1	18046	17244	1.05
2	18918	17717	1.07
3	38039	37037	1.03
4	22198	21163	1.05
5	21707	20709	1.05
6	23045	22045	1.05
7	10361	10241	1.01
8	7841	6874	1.14
9	10146	9744	1.04
10	10230	9430	1.08
11	30011	28013	1.07
12	29999	28001	1.07
13	18858	17957	1.05
14	22391	22087	1.01
total	281790	268262	1.05

Table 3 -- Comparison of the 14 Lawrence Livermore Loops on CRAY-1: one instruction per clock period vs one parcel per clock period.

We noticed while doing the simulations that limiting instruction fetches to the maximum rate of one parcel per clock period appeared to be restricting performance. Hence, we modified the implementation so that a full instruction could be fetched and issued to a reservation station each clock period. This would be slightly more expensive to implement, but for Tomasulo's algorithm it gives a significant performance improvement over one parcel per clock period.

To keep comparisons fair, we went back and modified the original CRAY-1 simulation model so that it, too, could issue instructions at the higher rate. Table 3 gives the results of these simulations, and compares them with the one parcel per clock period results given earlier. Here, the performance improvement is small. This is an interesting result in itself, and shows the wisdom of opting for simpler instruction fetch logic in the original CRAY-1.

Because the higher instruction fetch rate does appear to alleviate a bottleneck that reduces the efficiency of Tomasulo's algorithm, we incorporated it into the model for the studies to follow, and use the CRAY-1 results of Table 3 (1 instruction per clock period) as a basis for further comparisons.

Loop	# clock cycles on CRAY-1	# clock cycles for Tomasulo's algorithm	speedup
1	18046	10838	1.67
2	18918	14102	1.34
3	38039	30017	1.27
4	22198	16534	1.34
5	21707	16925	1.28
6	23045	15042	1.53
7	10361	6513	1.59
8	7841	6780	1.16
9	10146	8238	1.23
10	10230	7421	1.38
11	30011	20006	1.50
12	29999	20000	1.50
13	18858	12314	1.53
14	22391	12780	1.75
total	281790	197510	1.43

Table 2 -- Performance with Tomasulo's Algorithm; One Parcel Issued per Clock Period

Table 4 shows simulation results for Tomasulo's algorithm with one instruction issued per clock period. The speedup achieved is in the range 1.23 - 2.02 (total 1.58). In three out of the four loops whose speedup was

Loop	# clock cycles on CRAY-1	# clock cycles for Tomasulo's algorithm	speedup
1	17244	8832	1.95
2	17717	11062	1.60
3	37037	28012	1.32
4	21163	15418	1.37
5	20709	16898	1.23
6	22045	12956	1.70
7	10241	5069	2.02
8	6874	5195	1.32
9	9744	6332	1.54
10	9430	5318	1.77
11	28013	17871	1.57
12	28001	16001	1.75
13	17957	9364	1.92
14	22087	11713	1.89
total	268262	170041	1.58

Table 4 -- Performance of Tomasulo's Algorithm;
One Instruction Issued per Clock Period

less than 1.5 (i.e. loops 3, 4 and 8) issue was halted due to a busy T file. With an architecture that doesn't have the large number of registers the CRAY-1 has, it would be possible to use tags for all the registers, thus increasing the speedup of the above loops.

3.2. Example

Figure 4 shows a timing diagram of Tomasulo's algorithm compared with that of CRAY-1, both executing loop 12. On the left appear the instructions as generated by the CFT compiler . The timing for two consecutive loop iterations are shown next to each other. Each "|-|" represents one clock period. From the standpoint of issue logic, when store instructions are initiated they go to memory and are no longer considered. Therefore, stores are shown to execute only for the clock period they are initiated. Solid lines indicate that the respective instruction is in execution. For Tomasulo's algorithm, a dotted line shows that an instruction has been issued to a reservation station, and is waiting for operand(s).

With the original CRAY-1 issue algorithm, all instructions in a loop must begin execution and a loop-terminating conditional branch instruction must complete before the next loop iteration can begin. With Tomasulo's algorithm, loop iterations can be "telescoped"; a second loop iteration can begin after all instructions have been sent to reservation stations and the conditional branch is completed. The instructions belonging to the first loop iteration do not necessarily need to begin execution. One could also view this as dynamic rescheduling of the branch instruction. Obviously, the branch instruction is one instruction that can not be moved earlier in the loop as would have to be the case with static rescheduling. The significant speedup of Tomasulo's algorithm for this loop (1.75, see Table 4) is due mainly to the overlap of the loading of registers S6 and S1 with the floating point difference (-F) which uses S6 and S1 as operands. Although -F cannot be executed until the operands return from memory, it can be issued to a reservation station; this allows following instructions to proceed. On the other hand, the CRAY-1 executes the load of S1 and the floating point difference strictly in order.

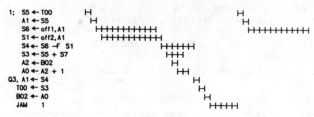

1: S5 ← T00	.COPY T00 TO S5
A1 ← S5	.COPY S5 TO A1
S6 ← off1,A1	.LOAD S6 (ADDRESS INDEXED BY A1)
S1 ← off2,A1	.LOAD S1 (ADDRESS INDEXED BY A1)
S4 ← S6 −F S1	.FLOATING DIFFERENCE OF S6 AND S1 TO S4
S3 ← S5 + S7	.INTEGER SUM OF S5 AND S7 TO S3
A2 ← B02	.COPY B02 TO A2
A0 ← A2 + 1	.INTEGER SUM OF A2 AND 1 TO A0
Q3, A1 ← S4	.STORE S4 (ADDRESS INDEXED BY A1)
T00 ← S3	.COPY S3 TO T00
B02 ← A0	.COPY A0 TO B02
JAM 1	.BRANCH TO LOOP ENTRY

(a) LLL 12 in CRAY Assembly Language;
arrows inserted for readability.

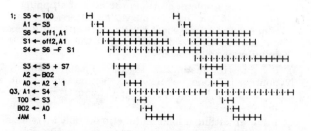

(b) The CRAY-1

(c) Tomasulo's algorithm

Figure 4 -- Timing Diagrams for Lawrence Livermore Loop 12.

One can see from the timing diagrams that with Tomasulo's algorithm only 2 reservation stations are used for more than 1 clock period. The store instruction needs a reservation station that is released a short period of time before the next store is issued. Another reservation station is used extensively by the floating point difference instruction.

4. Thornton's Algorithm

Tomasulo's algorithm leads to complex issue logic and may be quite expensive to implement. Therefore, in this section and in the next section, we consider ways to reduce the cost. One major cost is the associative hardware needed to match tags. When an operand and its attached tag appear on a bus, register files A and S and all the reservation stations have to be searched simultaneously. The operand is stored in any register or reservation station with a matching tag.

In this section, we implement the CRAY-1 scalar architecture with an issue method that is a derivative of Thornton's "scoreboard" algorithm used in the CDC6600. Here, control is more distributed (there is no global scoreboard), and reservation stations have been added to functional units. The primary difference between Thornton's algorithm and Tomasulo's is that instruction issue is halted when the destination of an instruction is a register that is busy. This simplifies the issue logic hardware in the following ways.

(1) The associative compare with the register file tags is eliminated.

(2) Tag allocation and de-allocation hardware is eliminated because the result register designator acts as the tag.

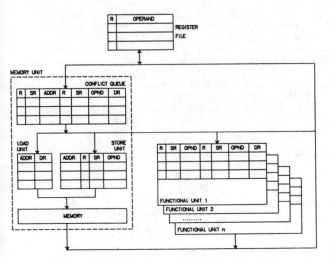

Figure 5 -- Thornton's issue logic.

Figure 5 illustrates the algorithm. Most reservation stations hold two operands (although some need only one, depending on the functional unit) and the address of the destination register (DR). Attached to each operand is the source register designator (SR) and a ready flag (R). Also, attached to each register in the register file is a ready bit (R). (These are the same as the reserved bits used in the original CRAY-1 control.)

The following operations are performed when an instruction is issued:

(1) A reservation station of the requested functional unit, if available, is reserved. Otherwise, issue is blocked.

(2) If a source register is ready, it is copied into the reservation station and the ready bit is set. Otherwise, the ready bit is cleared and the source register's designator is stored into the SR field.

The conditions for moving an instruction from a reservation station to begin execution are the same as given for Tomasulo's algorithm in the previous section. When a functional unit is finished with an instruction the result register designator is matched against all the SR fields in the reservation stations, and the result is written into the reservation stations where there is a match. The corresponding operand ready bits are then set. The result is also stored into the destination register, and it is set ready.

Although the above is derived from Thornton's original algorithm, there are some differences. The functional units of the CDC 6600 do not have reservation stations (one could say that they have reservation stations of depth 1 that are not able to hold operands, only control information). This imposes some additional restrictions. An instruction to be executed on a particular functional unit can be issued even if its source registers are not ready, but a second instruction requiring the same functional unit will block issue until the first one is done. On the other hand, with reservation stations, several instructions can wait for operands at the input of the functional unit. For example,

    S1 <- S2 *F S3
    S4 <- S5 *F S6

with the CDC 6600 scoreboard the second instruction will block, while with the algorithm here it will be issued.

Another restriction of the scoreboard is the following. In this example,

    S1 <- S2 *F S3
    S2 <- S4 + 1

we assume that S2 and S4 are ready, while S3 is not (e.g. it awaits an operand from memory). The second instruction will be completed before the first one, but on the CDC 6600 the result cannot be stored into S2 since it serves as a source register for the first instruction. Therefore, the add functional unit will remain busy until the first instruction completes as well. On the other hand, with the algorithm we have given, S2 has been copied into the floating point multiply reservation station when the first instruction was issued, and therefore the second instruction can complete before the first one.

4.1. Performance Results

We originally planned to simulate the scoreboard as designed by Thornton, but decided that it would lead to a more interesting comparison if multiple reservation

Loop	# clock cycles on CRAY-1	# clock cycles for Thornton's algorithm	speedup
1	17244	12434	1.39
2	17717	13500	1.31
3	37037	28020	1.32
4	21163	19578	1.08
5	20709	17030	1.22
6	22045	18370	1.20
7	10241	8671	1.18
8	6874	6381	1.08
9	9744	8634	1.13
10	9430	7820	1.21
11	28013	18001	1.56
12	28001	16003	1.75
13	17957	14870	1.21
14	22087	20273	1.09
total	268262	209585	1.28

Table 5 -- Performance of Thornton's Algorithm; One Instruction Issued per Clock Period

stations were allowed. The results of the simulation are shown in Table 5. The total speedup is 1.28. We discuss ways this can be improved by static code scheduling in Section 6.

5. An Issue Method Using a Direct Tag Search

In this section we propose an alternative issue algorithm that is related to Tomasulo's algorithm, but which eliminates the need for associative tag comparison hardware in the reservation stations. This algorithm instead uses a direct tag search (DTS), and will be referred to as the "DTS" algorithm. The DTS algorithm imposes the restriction that a particular tag can be stored only in one reservation station. This is easily implemented by associating with each tag in the tag pool a *used* bit. Whenever a register that is not ready is accessed for the first time, its tag is copied to the respective reservation station and the used bit is set. A second attempt to use the same tag will block issue.

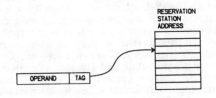

Figure 6 -- Tag Search Table for the DTS Algorithm.

The DTS algorithm allows implementation of the tag search mechanism by a table indexed by tags (Fig. 6), rather than associative hardware. For each tag there is one entry in the table that stores the address of a reservation station. The table is small since there are few tags (we used 5 bits for each tag; there are 32 tags).

5.1. Performance Results

A comparison of the results for the DTS algorithm with Tomasulo's algorithm reveals that for 9 out of the 14 loops the DTS algorithm achieves speedup similar to Tomasulo's algorithm. This shows that the restriction imposed by the DTS algorithm, namely that a tag can be in no more than one reservation station at a given time, has only a limited effect on performance. The reason is that the following pattern is quite common:

```
S1  <-  off1,A1
S2  <-  off2,A1
S3  <-  S1 *F S2
S5  <-  S3 +F S4
```

That is, two registers are loaded and are sent to a functional unit whose result is input to another functional unit, and so on. The DTS algorithm is able to process such code at full speed.

On the other hand, if a register is used as an input to a functional unit and at the same time has to be stored (in the memory, or temporarily in the T or B file), then the register, and its tag, have to be used twice, so the DTS algorithm blocks issue. Such cases account for the lower speedup of 5 out of 14 loops.

Loop	# clock cycles on CRAY-1	# clock cycles for the DTS algorithm	speedup
1	17244	8832	1.95
2	17717	11083	1.60
3	37037	28020	1.32
4	21163	20534	1.03
5	20709	17690	1.17
6	22045	17027	1.29
7	10241	5069	2.02
8	6874	5361	1.28
9	9744	6732	1.45
10	9430	8518	1.11
11	28013	17871	1.57
12	28001	16001	1.75
13	17957	14356	1.25
14	22087	17421	1.27
total	268262	194515	1.38

Table 6 -- Performance of DTS Issue Logic.

6. Further Comments on Code Scheduling

For all the various issue logic simulations, we used as input the object code generated by the CRAY-1 optimizing FORTRAN compiler, without any changes. Therefore, the level of code optimization and scheduling is realistic for the CRAY-1. Tomasulo's algorithm is less sensitive to the order of the instructions, since it does a great deal of dynamic scheduling. It is also capable of dynamic register re-allocation so it is not as susceptible to the compiler's register allocation method. On the other hand, static scheduling and register allocation has a significant impact on the performance of the DTS issue logic and Thornton's algorithm. Since we have not reorganized the code for the latter two schemes, many dependencies and resource conflicts that appear in the compiled code contribute to lower performance as compared with Tomasulo's algorithm.

Figure 7 illustrates an example, extracted from Lawrence Livermore Loop 4. The instruction "T02 <- S5" saves register S5 for use during the next pass through the loop. For the DTS issue logic, this instruction has to be blocked, since it attempts to use register S5 as a source for the second time (register S5 is not ready and was used for the first time by the previous instruction). However, neither S5 nor T02 are used before the branch instruction, so this interlock could be postponed by moving instruction "T02 <- S5" down, just before the

```
      do 175 l=7,107,50
      lw = l
      do 4 j=30,870,5
      x(l-1) = x(l-1) - x(lw)*y(j)
    4 lw = lw + 1
      x(l-1) = y(5)*x(l-1)
  175 continue
```

(a) Fortran code for Lawrence Livermore Loop 4 (banded linear equations).

```
LOOP4:  S6  <-  T00
        S1  <-  T01
        A3  <-  S1
        A2  <-  S6
        S3  <-  off2,A3      ; x(lw)
        S5  <-  off3,A2      ; y(j)
        S4  <-  S5 *R S3
        S3  <-  T02
        S5  <-  S3 -F S4
        S4  <-  S1 + S2
        A1  <-  B02
        S3  <-  S6 + S7
   off4,A7  <-  S5      ; x(l-1)
        T02  <-  S5
        T01  <-  S4
        A0  <-  A1 + 1
        T00  <-  S3
        B02  <-  A0
        JAM      LOOP4
```

(b) Compiled object code (the inner loop) extracted from Lawrence Livermore Loop 4.

Figure 7 -- Example of interlock for the DTS Issue Logic.

branch. The 4 clock cycles thus saved, multiplied by the number of iterations through the loop, result in a 4% performance improvement.

Figure 8 shows another example, extracted from loop 1. Registers S2, S6, S1, S3 and S4 are designated as destination registers for the first time in the upper half of the loop, and then for the second time, almost in the same order, in the lower half of the loop. The second usage of S2 (S2 <- S4 *R S6) as a destination register causes an immediate blockage for Thornton's algorithm, since S2 is still busy from the previous load instruction (S2 <- off1,A1). Any independent instruction inserted just before instruction "S2 <- S4 *R S6" will execute for free. There are 3 such instructions before the branch:

```
A2  <-  B02
A0  <-  A2 + 1
B02  <-  A0
```

This simple rescheduling gives a performance improvement of 10.7%.

```
       q = 0.0
       do 1 k = 1,400
    1     x(k) = q + y(k)*(r*z(k+10) + t*z(k+11))
```

(a) Fortran code for Lawrence Livermore Loop 1
(hydro excerpt).

```
  LOOP1: S5  <- T00
         A1  <- S5
         S2  <- off1,A1      ; z(k+10)
         S6  <- off2,A1      ; z(k+11)
         S1  <- T02
         S3  <- S1 *R S2
         S4  <- T01
         S2  <- S4 *R S6
         S6  <- off3,A1
         S1  <- S2 +F S3
         S4  <- S6 *R S1
         S3  <- S5 + S7
         A2  <- B02
         A0  <- A2 + 1
off4,A1      <- S4
         T00 <- S3
         B02 <- A0
         JAM     LOOP1
```

(b) Assembly code extracted from
Lawrence Livermore Loop 1.

Figure 8 -- Example of interlock for Thornton's Algorithm.

Since there is a large gap between Tomasulo's and Thornton's algorithms for loop 1 (1.95 vs 1.39), we tried to see if this gap could be closed by reallocating registers for Thornton's algorithm. The following code does the processing of loop 1, except for index and address calculations:

```
     S1 <- off1,A1
     S2 <- off2,A1
     S4 <- S1 *F S3
     S6 <- S2 *F S5
     S7 <- S4 +F S6
     S8 <- off3,A1
     S9 <- S7 *F S8
off4,A1 <- S9
```

Since registers are not re-used during the same pass through the loop, Thornton's algorithm would run as fast as Tomasulo's. But we need 9 scalar registers, more than available on the CRAY-1. The high speedup achieved by Tomasulo's algorithm demonstrates the importance of its ability to reallocate registers dynamically.

7. Summary and Conclusions

We have discussed design tradeoffs for control of pipelined processors. Performance of a pipelined processor depends greatly on its clock period and the order in which instructions are executed. Simple control schemes allow a short clock period and place the burden of code scheduling on the compiler. Complex control schemes generally require a longer clock period, but are less susceptible to the order of the instructions generated by the compiler. The latter are also able to take advantage of information only available at run time and "dynamically" reschedule the instructions. Additional factors to be considered are hardware cost, debugging and maintenance.

We have presented a quantitative measure of the speedup achievable by sophisticated issue logic schemes. The CRAY-1 scalar architecture is used as a basis for comparison. Simulation results of the 14 Lawrence Livermore Loops executed on 4 different issue logic mechanisms show the performance gain achievable by various degrees of

issue logic complexity. Tomasulo's algorithm gives a total speedup of 1.58. The direct tag search (DTS) algorithm, introduced in this paper, allows dynamic scheduling while eliminating the need for associative tag comparison hardware. The DTS issue logic achieves a total speedup of 1.38, and thus retains much of the performance gain of Tomasulo's algorithm. A derivative of Thornton's algorithm gives a total gain of 1.28.

In our model, the large intermediate register files of the CRAY-1 (B and T) are treated as a unit, since it is not practical to assign tags to so many registers. With Tomasulo's algorithm, this was the cause of a relatively low performance improvement for three loops. With an architecture that does not have the large number of registers the CRAY-1 has, it would be possible to use tags for all the registers, thus increasing the speedup of the above loops.

Finally, we have discussed the impact of code scheduling on the simulation results. Tomasulo's algorithm is less sensitive to the order of the instructions, since it does a great deal of dynamic scheduling and register reallocation. On the other hand, static scheduling has a significant impact on the performance of the DTS and Thornton's algorithms. We gave specific examples how the performance of the latter two algorithms can be improved even by simple code scheduling.

8. Acknowledgements

This is material based upon work supported by the National Science Foundation under Grant ECS-8207277.

The authors would like to thank Nick Pang for the CRAY-1 simulators used for generating the results in Tables 1 and 3.

9. References

[ANDE67] D.W. Anderson, F.J. Sparacio, F.M. Tomasulo, "The IBM System/360 Model 91: Machine Philosophy and Instruction-Handling", IBM Journal, V 11, Jan 1967

[BOLA67] L.J. Boland, G.D. Granito, A.U. Marcotte, B.U. Messina, J.W. Smith, "The IBM System/360 Model 91: Storage System", IBM Journal, V 11, Jan 1967.

[BONS69] P. Bonseigneur, "Description of the 7600 Computer System," Computer Group News, May 1969.

[BUCH62] W. Bucholz,ed., *Planning a Computer System*, McGraw-Hill, New York, 1962.

[CDC81] "CDC CYBER 200 Model 205 Computer System Hardware Reference Manual," Control Data Corp., Arden Hills, MN, 1981.

[CRAY77] "The CRAY-1 Computing System", Cray Research, Inc., Publication number 2240008 B, 1977.

[CRAY79] "CRAY-1 Computer Systems, Hardware Reference Manual", Cray Research, Inc., Chippewa Falls, WI, 1979.

[CRAY82] "CRAY X-MP Computer Systems Mainframe Reference Manual", Cray Research, Inc., Chippewa Falls, WI,1982.

[KOGG81] P. M. Kogge, *The Architecture of Pipelined Computers*, McGraw-Hill, 1981.

[MCMA72] F. H. McMahon, "FORTRAN CPU Performance Analysis," Lawrence Livermore Laboratories, 1972.

[RUSS78] R.M. Russell, "The CRAY-1 Computer System", Comm. ACM, V 21, N 1, January 1978, pp. 63-72.

[THOR70] J.E. Thornton, *Design of a Computer - The Control Data 6600*, Scott, Foresman and Co., Glenview, IL, 1970

[TOMA67] R.M. Tomasulo, "An Efficient Algorithm for Exploiting Multiple Arithmetic Units", IBM Journal, V 11, Jan 1967

SYNCHRONOUS NETS FOR SINGLE INSTRUCTION STREAM - MULTIPLE DATA STREAM COMPUTERS

Annette J. Krygiel
Defense Mapping Agency
Washington, D.C. 20305

Abstract -- Synchronous Nets, or S Nets, are developed as a modeling tool particularized for describing processes on Single Instruction Stream - Multiple Data Stream (SIMD) computers. S Nets are a modification of Petri Nets, using transitions and places to model events and conditions. However, S Nets introduce vector-mask places to model the conditions of the array resources of SIMD machines. These places are distinguished from scalar places which model the scalar resources. S Nets also introduce a new kind of transition. One type correlates with the Petri Net transition, but the mask firing transition is particularized to the SIMD environment, modeling the inherent capability of a computation executing on a SIMD machine to alter the participation of the vector aggregates in successor events.

Introduction

This paper is concerned with the problem of mapping algorithms onto certain classes of parallel processors to exploit parallelism in the algorithm to the maximum extent supportable by the machine on which it is to be implemented. The approach taken is one of providing a tool -- a graph-based modeling system called Synchronous Nets or S Nets -- to describe such an implementation.

SIMD Architectures

The processors of interest are of the single instruction stream-multiple data stream (SIMD) architectures as described by Flynn [1] who distinguishes four classes:

> Single instruction stream - single data stream (SISD)
>
> Single instruction stream - multiple data stream (SIMD)
>
> Multiple instruction stream - single data stream (MISD)
>
> Multiple instruction stream - multiple data stream (MIMD)

Figure 1 illustrates an SIMD architecture, which typically consists of a control unit with its own memory, and (possibly) some limited processing capability; an array or vector unit consisting of N Processing Elements (PEs) and at least N memories (PEMs); and an interconnection network for interprocessor communication. Associated with each PE is some indicator (mask) for signaling participation or non-participation in

instructions. In implementation, usually a conventional sequential machine is attached to the control unit, i.e. a mini-host.

A Multiple-SIMD (MSIMD) architecture is configured as two or more independent SIMD machines, each with its own control unit, array unit, etc., and with one interconnection network. These SIMD components have the ability to perform synchronously, and using the same instruction stream or different instruction streams. Such an architecture is illustrated by Figure 2.

SIMD machines are considered "special purpose." They perform spectacularly on problems to which they are well suited [2, 3, 4, 5]. To derive high performance, the application should have a high degree of parallelism, with the algorithm consistent with the topology of the machine. Unfortunately there are no simple means to gauge this desired isomorphism. Modeling is one approach that can be employed. S Nets were specifically developed to accomplish and facilitate this, and are a modification of Petri Nets [6, 7, 8, 9] supplying constructs particularized to SIMD (and MSIMD) architectures.

Definition of Synchronous Nets

System Overview

A Synchronous Net, or S Net, is a directed graph with a marking and a set of descriptors [10]. The vertices of the graph are vector-mask places, scalar places, and transitions. Scalar places and vector-mask places are connected with arcs to transitions and vice versa. A marking associates a non-negative integer with each scalar place, and associates a tuple of non-negative integers with each vector-mask place. The non-negative number is called the number of tokens. Descriptors are associated with each transition and characterize the behavior of the transition.

As with Petri Nets S Nets use transitions to model events and places to model conditions with arcs representing the paths allowed for passage of control. Analogous to Petri Nets S Nets exhibit dynamic behavior resulting from the firing of transitions. The firing of a transition models the occurrence of an event; tokens in a place can model the holding of a condition.

The key differences between Petri Nets and S Nets are the S Net innovations of vector-mask places and mask firing transitions. Vector-mask places model aggregates of logically associated and homogeneous conditions whose initial and

Reprinted from *Proceedings of the 1981 International Conference on Parallel Processing*, 1981, pages 266-273. Copyright © 1981 by The Institute of Electrical and Electronics Engineers, Inc.

ceasing events are synchronized, i.e., the conditions of a set of array processors. These aggregates are further characterized by the fact that the marking of some members of the aggregate may be relevant to the firing of a successor transition while others may not. This characteristic can model the participation or non-participation of some elements of the array processor in subsequent events.

Unique to S Nets is the concept of two kinds of transition firings -- one of which -- the mask firing -- provides for alternatives in the markings of the aggregates. This enables modeling of changes in the participation or non-participation of the elements of an array processor as it proceeds from event to event. These alternatives are formalized by descriptors associated with each transition.

S Net Graphs

S Nets will be defined in terms of sets. The element of a set will be designated within { }. The CARDINALITY of any set shall be designated | | and refers to the number of elements in the set, i.e., $|S|$ represents the number of elements in S. For example,

$$\text{if } S = \{s_1, s_2, \ldots s_j\}, \text{ then } |S| = j.$$

Also important in the S Net definition is the notion of tuples denoted by < > and consisting of ordered components. The cardinality of a tuple is also designated | |, but it is more appropriately called its DIMENSIONALITY.

An S Net Graph will be a quadruple (T,S,U, A), with an initial marking K_0 and a set of transition descriptors D, where:

T = A finite set of transitions $\{t_1, t_2, \ldots t_{|T|}\}$.

S = A finite set of scalar places $\{s_1, s_2, \ldots s_{|S|}\}$.

U = A finite set of vector-mask places $\{<V_1, M_1>, <V_2, M_2>, \ldots <V_{|U|}, M_{|U|}>\}$.

A = A finite set of directed arcs $\{a_1, a_2, \ldots a_{|A|}\}$, such that

$A \subseteq (P \times T) \cup (T \times P)$, where $P = U \cup S$ and P is called the set of places.

Thus the elements of A are of the form $<p_j, t_k>$ or $<t_j, p_k>$, so that an arc either connects a place to a transition or a transition to a place.

The set U is defined as a subset of $V \times M$, where:

V = A finite set of elements called vector places $\{V_1, V_2, \ldots V_{|V|}\}$; each element of V, designated V_i, is a tuple containing some number

of ordered components, i.e.,
$V_i = <v_{i1}, v_{i2}, \ldots v_{ip}>$, $p > 1$, and $|V_i|$ does

necessarily equal $|V_j|$ when $i \neq j$, but

$|V| = |U|$.

M = A finite set of elements called masks $\{M_1, M_2, \ldots M_{|M|}\}$; each element of M,

designated M_i, is a tuple containing some number of ordered components, i.e.,

$M_i = <m_{i1}, m_{i2}, \ldots m_{iq}>$, $q > 1$, and $|M_i|$ does

not necessarily equal $|M_j|$ when $i \neq j$,

but $|M| = |U|$.

If P is $U \cup S$, and A is as defined, the triple (P,T,A) is a bipartite directed graph since all nodes can be partitioned into two sets, transitions and places, such that each arc directed FROM an element of one set is directed TO an element of the other set, and vice versa. Therefore arcs from(to) a vector-mask place or a scalar place are always directed to(from) a transition.

In the S Net Graph, transitions are represented by ╎ , the scalar places are represented by ◯ , and the vector-mask places by

. Within that last symbol, the vector

symbol V_i is and the mask symbol M_i is

or . The dimensionality of V_i

or $|V_i|$ in is portrayed as .

The dimensionality of M_i is not noted on the graph, but is specified in the formal designation of M_i components, i.e.,

$$<m_{i1}, m_{i2}, \ldots m_{i|M_i|}>. \text{ Arcs are}$$

denoted as ⟶ .

Given the S Net shown in Figure 3, we shall delineate the graph of the S Net as follows:

$T = \{t_1, t_2, t_3, t_4, t_5, t_6\}$

$S = \{s_1, s_2, s_3\}$

$V = \{V_1, V_2, V_3, V_4\}$

$$V_1 = \langle v_{11}, v_{12}, v_{13} \rangle$$

$$V_2 = \langle v_{21}, v_{22}, v_{23} \rangle$$

$$V_3 = \langle v_{31}, v_{32}, v_{33} \rangle$$

$$V_4 = \langle v_{41}, v_{42}, v_{43} \rangle$$

$$M = \{M_1, M_2, M_3, M_4\}$$

$$M_1 = \langle m_{11}, m_{12}, m_{13} \rangle$$

$$M_2 = \langle m_{21}, m_{22}, m_{23} \rangle$$

$$M_3 = \langle m_{31}, m_{32}, m_{33} \rangle$$

$$M_4 = \langle m_{41}, m_{42}, m_{43} \rangle$$

$$U = \{\langle V_1, M_1 \rangle, \langle V_2, M_2 \rangle, \langle V_3, M_3 \rangle, \langle V_4, M_4 \rangle\}$$

$$A = \{\langle s_1, t_1 \rangle, \langle t_1, \langle V_1, M_1 \rangle\rangle, \langle\langle V_1, M_1 \rangle, t_2 \rangle,$$
$$\langle t_2, \langle V_2, M_2 \rangle\rangle, \langle\langle V_2, M_2 \rangle, t_3 \rangle, \langle t_3, s_2 \rangle,$$
$$\langle t_1, \langle V_3, M_3 \rangle\rangle, \langle\langle V_3, M_3 \rangle, t_4 \rangle, \langle t_4, \langle V_4,$$
$$M_4 \rangle\rangle, \langle\langle V_4, M_4 \rangle, t_3 \rangle, \langle s_2, t_5 \rangle, \langle t_5, s_1 \rangle,$$
$$\langle s_2, t_6 \rangle, \langle t_6, s_3 \rangle\}$$

S Net Structure

Analogously to a Petri Net, the structure of an S Net is defined so as to make clear the relationship of places and transitions. The INPUT PLACES of a transition $I(t)$ are all scalar places and vector-mask places directed immediately TO the transition. The OUTPUT PLACES of a transition $O(t)$ are all scalar places and vector-mask places directed immediately FROM the transition.

Markings

The infinite set of non-negative integers $\{0, 1, \ldots\}$ is designated N; the set of Boolean numbers $\{0, 1\}$ is designated B; the set $\{0\}$ is designated Z. Also the r-fold Cartesian products are defined:

$N^r = N \times N \ldots N$; each member is of the form $\langle N_1, N_2, \ldots N_r \rangle$

$B^r = B \times B \ldots B$; each member is of the form $\langle B_1, B_2, \ldots B_r \rangle$

$Z^r = Z \times Z \ldots Z$; each member is of the form $\langle 0, 0, \ldots 0 \rangle$

where N_i and B_i, are elements of N and B, respectively.

A MARKING is a function K where

$$K: \quad S \to N; \quad V_1 \to N^{|V_1|} \quad \text{for all } V_1 \in V;$$
$$M_1 \to B^{|M_1|} \quad \text{for all } M_1 \in M.$$

The marking associates a non-negative integer with each scalar place — $K(s)$ for each $s \in S$ — and two vectors of non-negative integers with each vector-mask place, one of those associated vectors being a Boolean vector — $K(V_1)$ for each $V_1 \in V$ and $K(M_1)$ for each $M_1 \in M$.

A marking for an S Net must specify all three components.

An INITIAL MARKING K_0 is defined as the first marking of the S Net.

A MASK MARKING for a mask M_1 is a function K such that $M_1 \to B^{|M_1|}$.

The set of possible mask markings for any M_1 is $W(M_1)$ and denotes the co-domain of a mask marking, consisting of designated tuples of $B^{|M_1|}$, or if appropriate, the entire product set $B^{|M_1|}$.

Notation for Markings. The convention adopted to show markings will be that of ( ) and $\langle \;\; \rangle$. The former is used to distinguish the marking of a single element or component, and the latter is used when more than one element or component is involved, thereby denoting an ordering with respect to markings of elements or components.

As an example, markings for places s_1, s_2, s_3 are designated $K(s_1) = (0)$; $K(s_2) = (0)$; $K(s_3) = (0)$.

If $V = \{V_1, V_2\}$, and if $V_1 = \langle v_{11}, v_{12}, v_{13} \rangle$, then K: $V_1 \to Z^3$ is equivalent to: $K(V_1) = \langle 0, 0, 0 \rangle$; alternately $K(v_{11}) = (0)$; $K(v_{12}) = (0)$; $K(v_{13}) = (0)$. Similarly, for $M_1 = \langle m_{11}, m_{12}, m_{13} \rangle$, a marking $K(M_1) = \langle 1, 0, 0 \rangle$ designates that $K(m_{11}) = (1)$, $K(m_{12}) = (0)$, $K(m_{13}) = (0)$.

Graphic Portrayal of Markings. Markings are illustrated with the presence of tokens. Dots in any place represent tokens. Tokens in masks may, alternatively, be represented by Boolean symbols for legibility.

The symbol ⌷ for M_1 shows a token in m_{11} and m_{12}. This is synonomous to the symbol

Using the S Net example of Figure 3, Figure 4 illustrates a marking where masks are marked with tokens but vector places are not marked with tokens. This example assumes the initial marking is:

$$K_0(s_1) = (1); \; K_0(s_2) = (0); \; K_0(s_3) = (0)$$

$$K_0(V_1) = K_0(V_2) = K_0(V_3) = K_0(V_4) = <0, 0, 0>$$

$$K_0(M_1) = K_0(M_2) = <1, 0, 0>$$

$$K_0(M_3) = <1, 1, 1>$$

$$K_0(M_4) = <0, 0, 1>$$

An assignment of tokens to a vector place V_i may leave some of the component places marked with tokens and others empty, i.e., all elements v_{ij} of V_i may not have tokens. Since the $|V_i|$ may be large, graphic designation of which components are marked must necessarily be limited. For example, a ⊘③ portrays a V_i with three components; then ⊘⑫ indicates that two $v_{ij} \varepsilon V_i$ are marked. Synonomous are the symbols

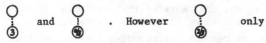

⊘③ and ⊘⑫ . However ⊘⑫ only

conveys that two v_{ij} are marked but does not distinguish the individual elements, nor does it indicate how many tokens are in each marked v_{ij}. However S Nets use vector-mask places to model conditions resulting from and leading to events, and V_i is always expressed graphically in conjunction with M_i. It is M_i which will be used graphically to enhance comprehension of which v_{ij} are marked — at least in markings resulting from an execution of the S Net.

Rules for Execution

The graph and structure of S Nets have been addressed in previous Sections. Now discussed is the dynamic behavior of S Nets.

Enabled Transitions. A scalar place is HOLDING if it has at least one token in it. A vector-mask place $<V_i, M_i>$ is HOLDING if:

at least one $K(m_{ij}) = (1)$, $j = 1, 2, \ldots |V_i|$, and $v_{ij} \varepsilon V_i$ has a non-zero marking for all those j for which $m_{ij} \varepsilon M_i$ has a non-zero marking.

A holding for a vector-mask place is in contrast to a marking of that place. Whereas a marking associates some set of integers with vector-mask places, a holding for a vector-mask place REQUIRES that the components of V_i be marked with tokens everywhere that their associated M_i components are marked with tokens.

A transition t is ENABLED also called FIRABLE under the following conditions: t is ENABLED if all scalar places in I(t) are holding and all vector-mask places in I(t) are holding.

Firing Transitions. A FIRING is a function of a transition which has for its domain and range the marking of the input places and output places of the transition. There is a firing associated with every enabled transition t. When a transition t is enabled, its firing function is defined at a given marking K_n of the S Net, and the firing yields K_{n+1}, a new marking.

Transition Types. A TRANSITION TYPE specifies the firing capabilities of the transition — either simple or mask firing — designated SFT and MFT respectively.

Transition Descriptors. A TRANSITION DESCRIPTOR D[t] specifies the transition type, either SFT or MFT, and for every vector-mask output place $<V_i, M_i>$ of the transition, specifies $W(M_i)$, the set of markings for M_i. Descriptors for a transition t with vector-mask output places $<V_i, M_i>$, $<V_j, M_j>, \ldots <V_r, M_r>$ are specified:

$$D[t] = [type; \; K(M_i) \; \varepsilon \; W(M_i),$$

$$K(M_j) \; \varepsilon \; W(M_j), \ldots K(M_r) \; \varepsilon \; W(M_r)].$$

Rules for a Simple Firing. A SIMPLE FIRING associated with an enabled transition t is such that:

For every scalar input place s, then

$$K_{n+1}(s) = K_n(s) - 1$$

For every scalar output place s, then

$$K_{n+1}(s) = K_n(s) + 1$$

For every vector-mask input place $<V_i, M_i>$,

then: for $v_{ij} \varepsilon V_i$, $j = 1, 2, \ldots |V_i|$,

$$K_{n+1}(v_{ij}) = K_n(v_{ij}) - 1 \text{ for those j for}$$

which $m_{ij} \varepsilon M_i$ has a non-zero marking; and for $m_{ij} \varepsilon M_i$,

$$K_{n+1}(m_{ij}) = K_n(m_{ij}) \text{ for all j.}$$

For every vector-mask output place $<V_i, M_i>$,

then: for $v_{ij} \varepsilon V_i$, $j = 1, 2, \ldots |V_i|$,

$$K_{n+1}(v_{ij}) = K_n(v_{ij}) + 1 \text{ for those j for}$$

which $m_{ij} \varepsilon M_i$ has a non-zero marking; and for $m_{ij} \varepsilon M_i$,

$$K_{n+1}(m_{ij}) = K_n(m_{ij}) \text{ for all j.}$$

As seen from the firing rules, SFTs do not alter their input or output masks.

Rules for a Mask Firing. A MASK FIRING is associated with an enabled transition t that has at least one $<V_i, M_i>$ output place, and is such that:

For every scalar input place s, then

$$K_{n+1}(s) = K_n(s) - 1$$

For every scalar output place s, then

$$K_{n+1}(s) = K_n(s) + 1$$

For every vector-mask input place $<V_i, M_i>$,

then: for $v_{ij} \in V_i$, $j = 1, 2, \ldots |V_i|$,

$K_{n+1}(v_{ij}) = K_n(v_{ij}) - 1$ for those j for which $m_{ij} \in M_i$ has a non-zero marking; and for $m_{ij} \in M_i$,

$$K_{n+1}(m_{ij}) = K_n(m_{ij}) \text{ for all j.}$$

For every vector-mask output place $<V_i, M_i>$, then for M_i,

$K_{n+1}(M_i) \in W(M_i)$, where $W(M_i)$ is specified by the transition descriptor D[t], and $K_{n+1}(M_i)$ is non-deterministically chosen.

For every vector-mask output place $<V_i, M_i>$, then for $v_{ij} \in V_i$, $j = 1, 2, \ldots |V_i|$,

$K_{n+1}(v_{ij}) = K_n(v_{ij}) + 1$ for those j for which $m_{ij} \in M_i$ has a non-zero marking, i.e., where $K_{n+1}(m_{ij}) = (1)$.

The assignment of a Boolean vector to M_i by MFT is a mapping of M_i INTO $W(M_i)$, where the domain is M_i and the co-domain consists of the elements of $W(M_i)$, i.e., $M_i \xrightarrow{\text{INTO}} W(M_i)$.

By the firing rules, firings remove tokens from places and add tokens to other places, and in the case of the mask firing mark the masks of the vector-mask output places. It should be noted that the number of tokens subtracted by a transition firing does not necessarily equal the number that it adds.

Transitions and Their Descriptors. As seen from the firing definitions, SFTs on firing do not change the $K(M_i)$ of their $<V_i, M_i>$ input and output places. The transition descriptor is noted simply as D[t] = [SFT;_].

For MFTs, the $|W(M_i)| \geq 1$ for all output masks, and since these markings are determined by the transition firing and not the initial marking, the set of markings must be listed

in the transition descriptor, i.e.,

$$D[t] = [MFT; K(M_i) \in \{<\quad>, <\quad> \ldots\}]$$

Example of Mask Firing Transitions. Figure 5 through Figure 8 show MFTs in an S Net and illustrate their graphic portrayal and behavior. Given an initial marking and descriptors:

$$K_0(s_1) = (1): K_0(s_2) = (0); K_0(s_3) = (0)$$

$$K_0(V_1) = K_0(V_2) = <0, 0, 0>$$

$$D[t_1] = [MFT; K(M_1) \in \{<1, 0, 0>, <0, 0, 1>\}]$$

$$D[t_2] = [MFT; K(M_2) \in \{<1, 0, 0>, <0, 0, 1>\}]$$

$$D[t_3] = D[t_4] = D[t_5] = [SFT;\_]$$

Figure 5 reflects the initial marking and shows that t_1 is enabled. Transition t_1 has one output mask and $|W(M_1)| = 2$, both elements of which are shown on the graph. When transition t_1 fires, the results are shown in Figure 6. The marking assigned to M_1 by t_1 was $<1, 0, 0>$ which is designated in $D[t_1]$ and is shown on the graph as one member of the set $W(M_1)$. (At the time of firing the mask marking that is chosen by the transition is arbitrary.) After t_1 fires, v_{11} receives one token since m_{11} is marked with a token, and a token is removed from s_1.

The v_{11} token enables t_2 since m_{11} also holds a token, so that the firing of t_2 can commence. If t_2 fires changing the marking $K(M_2)$ to $<1, 0, 0>$, and if the firing sequence t_1, t_2, t_3, t_4 is assumed, then Figure 7 illustrates the marking after t_4 has fired. In Figure 7 a token is again in s_1; $K(M_1)$ is $<1, 0, 0>$ from the previous firing of t_1; $K(M_2)$ is $<1, 0, 0>$ as marked from the previous firing of t_2; $K(V_1)$ is $<0, 0, 0>$ since the token in v_{11} placed there as a result of the first t_1 firing was removed at the firing of t_2. $K(V_2)$ is $<0, 0, 0>$ since the token in v_{21} placed there after the firing of t_2 was removed at the firing of t_3.

Where Figure 7 shows t_1 enabled, Figure 8 shows the results after the second firing of t_1. Here $K(M_1) = <0, 0, 1>$, a marking alternative also described in $D[t_1]$. (The selection of the marking is arbitrary, and could have been $<1, 0, 0>$ again.) Given $K(M_1) = <0, 0, 1>$, by firing definition v_{13} now receives a token. Since m_{13} also holds a token, t_2 is enabled, and so on.

To analyze an algorithm, a sequence of S Net transition firings can be examined. The sequence resolves conflict, or indeterminacies in computational flow, in that a particular order of firings is assumed. (Conflict is typified in Figures 5 through 8 by t_4 and t_5 which share an input place;

when one token resides in the place, only one transition can fire and which transition fires is indeterminate [6, 7, 8, 9, 10]). Analogously, in modeling a specific computation, the indeterminacy of mask selection by MFTs is not troublesome by assuming an order of mask selections.

S NET APPLICATION

To apply S Nets it is necessary to relate the model to the actual algorithm. An INTERPRETATION of an S Net is an assignment of labels to the transitions and/or places of the Net to indicate for the transition the event that it models and for the place the condition that it models.

Consider the example of summing the rows of a 4x4 matrix A, multiplying the sum by a 4x1 vector B, and storing results in the first column of A. The FORTRAN description is:

```
        DO 200 I = 1, 4
        DO 100 J = 1, 3
100     A(I, 1) = A(I, 1) + A(I, J+1)
200     A(I, 1) = A(I, 1) * B(I)
```

Assume an 8 PE SIMD machine is available. A data storage scheme for the vectors is depicted in Figure 9, which indicates that PE_0 has the first row of A in its PEM, PE_1 has the second row, etc. With parallel hardware available, the four row sums can be formed simultaneously. This is shown in the S Net model of Figure 10 which is marked to reflect a holding of condition after a t_2 firing. The S Net uses vector-mask places to model conditions in array resources and scalar places to model conditions in scalar resources. The masks of the vector-mask places model control over the participation of the array resources.

Transition t_2 models the event which adds the Jth column of matrix A to the first column of matrix A. Places s_4 and s_5 model the conditions resulting from the test of J. Assuming a sequence of firings such that t_4 and t_5 have conflict resolved by the status of loop index J, when t_4 fires, all rows have been summed; then t_7 models a parallel multiplication of all four sums by the appropriate element of vector B. The utilization of the array resources is a byproduct of this S Net execution, i.e., the marking on the vector-mask output place resulting from the t_2 firing is depicted on Figure 10 as 4/8. Both the parallelism achieved by the array resource (4) and the utilization with respect to the maximum parallelism supportable by the array hardware (8) becomes apparent. Also, the marking of the mask suggests some additional management activity required of the vector resource and is specific as to which PEs will participate -- PE_0 through PE_3.

With every execution of the array events modeled by SFTs t_2 and t_7, PE_0 through PE_3 always participate. However if the problem context is changed to require the alternative of using PE_4

through PE_7 in a different iteration of the computation, these array events are more aptly modeled by MFTs, i.e.,

$$D(t_2) = [MFT; K(M_1) \; \varepsilon \; \{<1^4, \; 0^4>, \; <0^4, \; 1^4>\}]$$

$$D(t_7) = [MFT; K(M_2) \; \varepsilon \; \{<1^4, \; 0^4> \; <0^4, \; 1^4>\}]$$

For analysis, an assumption would then be made about the order of selection of the masks, i.e., $<1^4, \; 0^4>$, then $<0^4, \; 1^4>$. This capability for alternation is readily distinguishable on the graph, contributing more detail for analysis.

More exposition of the modeling capability of S Nets, particularly the properties of concurrency and conflict, is supplied in [10] as are additional (and less simple) examples. SIMD algorithms can be modeled with Petri Nets, but with increased modeling complexity. S Nets are distinct from Petri Nets in the notions of vector-mask places and mask firing transitions. Many Petri Net places are created in lieu of a single vector-mask place. It requires many Petri Net transitions in forward conflict to model the more concise mask firing transition [10].

The richer detail of S Nets is illustrated by modeling Flynn's classes of architectures shown in Figure 11. Because of the availability of vector-mask places in addition to scalar places, the multiplicity of the data stream can now be depicted; also scalar and vector activity can be distinguished. The SIMD architecture is readily distinguished from SISD by the added detail of vector-mask places. The MIMD-2 architecture which allows both scalar and vector concurrency, is distinguishable from the MIMD-3 architecture which allows concurrent SIMD resources (MSIMD). Both are clearly different from the MIMD-1 architecture of conventional distributed processors.

SUMMARY

In this paper, Synchronous Nets, or S Nets, have been formally defined. S Nets are a modification of Petri Nets, specifically developed to provide richer detail for modeling the SIMD environment. It is possible to model SIMD computations with Petri Nets but at the expense of increased modeling complexity. However, the relationship of S Nets and Petri Nets is explored elsewhere [10].

REFERENCES

[1] Flynn, Michael J., "Very High-Speed Computing Systems", Proceedings of the IEEE, Volume 54, No. 12, December 1966, pp. 1901-1909.

[2] Thurber, Dennis J., and Wald, L. D., "Associative and Parallel Processors", Computing Surveys, Volume 7, No. 4, December 1975, pp. 215-255.

[3] Ruben, Sherwin, et al., "Application of a Parallel Processing Computer in LACIE", Proceedings of the 1976 International Conference on Parallel Processing, pp. 24-32.

[4] Krygiel, Annette J., "An Implementation of the HADAMARD Transform on the STARAN Associative Array Processor", Proc. 1976 International Conference on Parallel Processing, p. 34.

[5] Daley, J. S., and Underwood., B. D., "Short-Term Weather Prediction on ILLIAC IV", Proc. 1975 Sagamore Computer Conference on Parallel Processing, p. 240.

[6] Petri, Carl A., "Kommunikation mit Automaten", Translation by C. F. Greene, Supplement 1 to RADC-TR-65-337, Vol 1, RADC, Griffiss AFB, New York, 1962.

[7] Holt, A. W., et al, "Information System Theory Project", Applied Data Research, Inc., RADC-TR-68-305, Rome Air Development Center, Griffiss AFB, New York, September 1968.

[8] Holt, A. W., and Commoner, Frederic, "Events and Conditions", Applied Data Research, Inc., New York, 1979.

[9] Peterson, James L., "Petri Nets", Computing Surveys, Volume 9, pp. 223-252.

[10] Krygiel, Annette J., "Synchronous Nets for Single Instruction Stream - Multiple Data Stream Computers", D. Sc Dissertation, Sever Institute of Technology, Washington University, St. Louis, MO, May 1980.

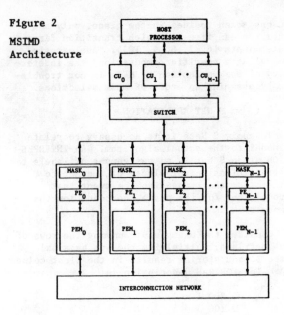

Figure 2   MSIMD Architecture

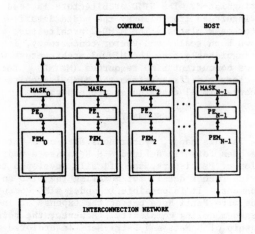

Figure 1   SIMD Architecture

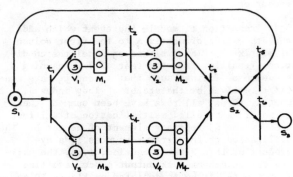

Figure 3   An S Net

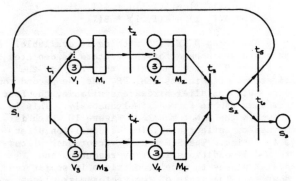

Figure 4   An S Net With M_1 Marked

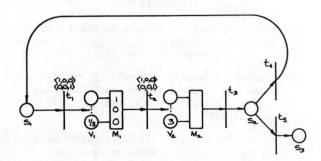

Figure 6   MFTS t_1 and t_2 at K_1

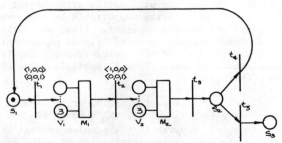

Figure 5   MFTs t_1 and t_2 at K_0

192

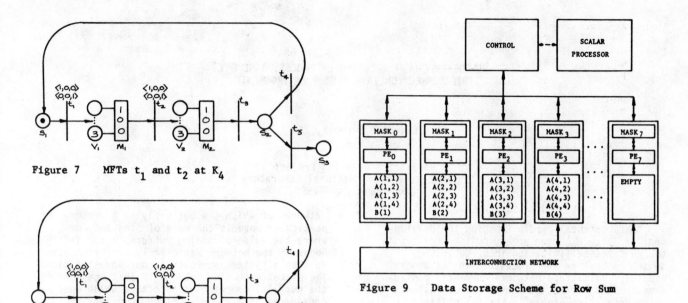

Figure 7   MFTs t_1 and t_2 at K_4

Figure 8   MFTs t_1 and t_2 at K_5

Figure 9   Data Storage Scheme for Row Sum

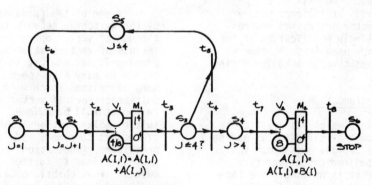

Figure 10   S Net Model for Row Sum

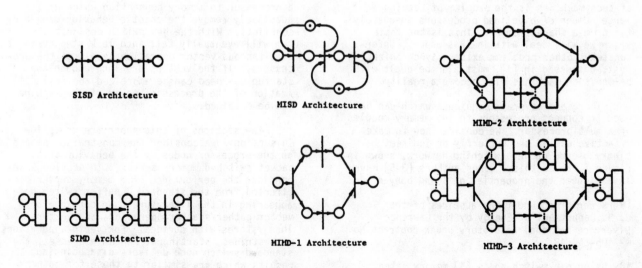

SISD Architecture

MISD Architecture

MIMD-2 Architecture

SIMD Architecture

MIMD-1 Architecture

MIMD-3 Architecture

Figure 11   S Nets Depicting Machine Architectures

PERFORMANCE OF THE BUTTERFLY PROCESSOR-MEMORY INTERCONNECTION IN A VECTOR ENVIRONMENT[†]

Eugene D. Brooks, III

Parallel Processing Project
Lawrence Livermore National Laboratory
Livermore, CA 94550

Abstract

A fundamental hurdle impeding the development of large N common memory multiprocessors is
the performance limitation incurred in the
switch connecting the processors to the memory
modules. Multistage networks currently considered for this connection have a memory latency
which grows like $\alpha\log_2 N$[*]. For scientific
computing, it is natural to look for a multiprocessor architecture that will enable the use
of vector operations to mask memory latency.
The problem to be overcome here is the chaotic
behavior introduced by conflicts occurring in
the switch. In this paper we examine the performance of the butterfly or indirect binary
n-cube network in a vector processing environment. We describe a simple modification of the
standard 2x2 switch node used in such networks
which adaptively removes chaotic behavior during
a vector operation.

1. Introduction

The VLSI revolution, which has drastically
reduced the cost of computer circuits, is making
large N multiprocessor designs possible. VLSI
implementations of pipelined processors have
become so cheap that cost is no longer the factor which inhibits the development of high performance shared memory multiprocessors. One of
the stumbling blocks preventing the development
of such machines is the problem of keeping a
large number of pipelined processors adequately
fed from a shared memory. This is the topic
which we will deal with in this paper. Unfortunately, other problems exist. Synchronization
cost, discussed in [1], must also be dealt with
before such machines will become a reality.

There are several techniques which can be
used to connect processors to the memory modules
of a multiprocessor. We consider how to make
effective use of the butterfly or indirect
binary n-cube packet switching network, shown in
figure 1, to do this. Other authors [3-5] have
investigated the properties of δ and banyan

networks of which the butterfly is a member. Of
particular note is the work of Dias and Jump,
where the value of adding buffers to the switch
nodes of the network was clearly demonstrated.
We take a systems approach in our investigation.
The packet switching network is just one part of
the parallel computer architecture which must be
considered as a whole. Only by considering the
system of interacting components, in this case
the user application, the cpu nodes, the switching network and the memory modules, can one put
the performance analysis of the switching network into context.

As one of the fundamental problems imposed
by the switching network is latency, we consider
the use of vector operations in multiprocessors.
The use of vectorization to deal with a latency
problem is not new, it is the technique of
choice in many high speed computers. There are
many algorithms which will run efficiently on
multiprocessors if vector operatins can be made
to run at full bandwidth. In the standard
switch implementations considered to connect
processors to memory modules in large N multiprocessors, fluctuations in timing caused by
conflicts lead to further conflicts in the
switch. This chaotic behavior causes a bandwidth reduction for vector operations. By introducing a modification to the standard 2x2
switch node used in such networks, we construct
a processor to memory connection which will
adaptively remove the chaotic behavior caused by
conflicts. With the new switch design the system will eventually fall into lock step during a
simultaneous vector operation by all of the processors. If the vectors are long enough the
startup overhead can be amortized and full utilization of the processing power of the machine
can be obtained.

The sections of this paper are as follows.
In section 2 we consider the constraints placed
on the processor nodes by the behavior of a
packet switched memory server. In section 3 we
consider the performance of a memory server constructed from the standard 2 buffer switch node
appearing in the literature. We consider both
vector gather/scatter operations and vector
loads/stores with strides. For vector operations
with strides, starting at random addresses, the
standard switch node delivers disappointing
results which are similar to those for gather/
scatter addressing. In section 4 we introduce

[†]Work performed under the auspices of the
U. S. Department of Energy by the Lawrence
Livermore National Laboratory under contract No.
W-7405-ENG-48.

[*]By using n∗n switch nodes [5] memory latency
can be reduced to $\alpha\log_n N$.

our modified 2x2 switch node with 4 internal buffers. For random addressing, a switch made of these nodes delivers a normalized bandwidth approaching unity as the lengths of the buffers are increased. When we consider vector loads and stores, with random starting addresses, we get surprising results. The new switch adaptively removes the chaotic behavior caused by conflicts and after a settling time achieves a normalized bandwidth of unity. Every processor, or memory module for vector stores, receives a vector element on each clock cycle. Finally, in section 5, we discuss these results and their implications for the future of large N common memory multiprocessors.

2. The Architecture of the CPU Node

In order to put our simulations of the butterfly switch into context, we briefly describe a cpu architecture that would be useful on such a system. We envision a RISC architecture [2], with vector instructions, that cleanly separates memory operations from the other functions of the cpu. The vector instructions can be envisioned as a sequence of scalar instructions that are executed in microcode.

The key feature of the packet switched memory server network is its indeterminate memory latency. The minimum latency is $2\log_2 N$ but the actual latency will vary due to conflicts in the network. The cpu makes memory requests by submitting request packets to the network. A request packet contains information giving the memory operation to perform, the location to affect, the cpu issuing the request and the register to fill with the result if the operation was a read. When the cpu submits a read request packet it marks the destination register empty. Should the cpu require the register in a later instruction it will wait until the memory server has filled the register. Having empty/full flags is important even for the individual elements of a vector register. Although the vector request packets are submitted to the memory server in order the response packets can arrive back from the server out of order due to conflicts in the switch. By having empty/full flags on each register in a vector set the cpu can be properly synchronized for an operation which is chained behind the load.

In order to be viable for use in a multiprocessor our cpu node must also have synchronization instructions. Due to the possibility of a synchronization operation beating a memory operation through the switch, return receipt packets are included for write requests. A counter in the cpu node keeps track of the pending read or write requests and a synchronization instruction waits until all memory requests have been satisfied. By using a return receipt mechanism for all memory operations the integrity of shared data can be guaranteed.

3. The Performance of the Standard Switch

Consider a memory server constructed from

the 2x2 switch node shown in figure 2. Packets enter the two input ports on the left and feed the internal buffers. A single bit of the packet is used to determine the output port that will be used to exit the switch. If this bit is 0 then the packet will exit output port 0. Otherwise the packet will exit output port 1. The heads of the two buffers compete for access to the output ports. If both packets are destined for the same output port one must wait while the other moves through the port.

Using this switch model we simulated a memory server for a saturated random addressing load, which would occur for a gather/scatter vector operation with random addresses, and for a stride 1 vector load with random starting addresses. The system was started with an empty network and all processors began making requests simultaneously. In table 1 we show the normalized bandwidth, the bandwidth divided by N, as a function of network size and buffer length. The poor performance of the switch for a buffer size of 1 is clearly demonstrated. As the buffer size is lengthened the normalized bandwidth approaches 75%. This would not be a bad performance level for random gather/scatter addressing but we would prefer that the normalized bandwidth approach 100% as the buffer length is increased. When stride 1 vector addressing with random starting addresses was simulated we obtained results similar to those shown in table 1. The conflicts caused by the random starting addresses led to chaotic behavior. Although 75% of ideal performance might be acceptable even for vector operations with strides, we would prefer a multiprocessor system that could adaptively remove the conflicts and eventually achieve ideal bandwidth.

4. The Modified 4 Buffer Switch Node

Why is the bandwidth of the 2 buffer switch node limited to 75%? Examining figure 2 we can see the root of the problem. If the two packets at the heads of the buffers need to be routed to the same output port one of them must wait for the next clock cycle. The waiting packet blocks any packet sitting further back in the buffer which is destined for the unused port. If we could implement a 2x2 switch that could manage to slip a packet past this block, full bandwidth would be maintained. In figure 3 we show a 2x2 switch capable of performing this feat. This switch has 4 internal buffers. Packets entering the input ports are sorted into the buffers according to the output port they are destined for. With this presorting of packets into separate buffers the only way we can have a blocked port is to have zero packets in the switch destined for the port. If the buffers are long enough this is unlikely to happen.

It is not surprising that a butterfly network constructed from this new switch node gives a limiting normalized bandwidth of 1 for gather/scatter operations with random addressing. In table 2 we show the bandwidth of the system for such operations as a function of N and the buffer length. When we tried stride 1 vector operations, with random starting addresses, we would have been happy with similar results. Instead the new network delivered a surprise. After an initial settling in period the system fell into lock step with every cpu getting a vector element each clock cycle. The new switch adaptively absorbed the conflicts caused by the random starting addresses and eventually reached a bandwidth of 1.

The vector elements, however, do not arrive in the exact order of request. They arrive in a bunny hop[†] which is dependent on initial conditions. The approximate ordering allows chaining of arithmetic operations if the cpu is properly designed. The result is not restricted to a stride of 1. If suitable constraints on the initial starting addresses are met, for instance if the stride is 2 then exactly half of the starting addresses must be even, the network locks in to a normalized bandwidth of 1 for any stride. This restriction on the starting addresses is just the one required for full bandwidth on a crossbar.

The first question that one asks, given the results discussed above for vector operations, is how long must the vectors be. In table 3 we provide the answer for stride 1 vectors with random starting addresses. The column labeled by $n_{1/2}$, $n_{3/2}$, and $n_{9/10}$ give the vector lengths required for an average normalized bandwidth of 1/2, 3/4, and .9 respectively. The column labeled L_b gives the buffer length required to achieve lock step. As can be seen in the table, the vector lengths required for efficient operation do not grow too rapidly with the number of cpu nodes N. The buffer lengths required grow very modestly with N.

It is interesting to consider the functional dependence of the vector lengths $n_{1/2}$, $n_{3/2}$, and $n_{9/10}$ on N for large N. By plotting n vs $\log_2 N$ on a log-log plot we find that the points fit a power curve very well for large N. Performing a standard power curve fit to the last 8 points we find the following relationships.

$$n_{1/2} = 0.850(\log_2 N)^{2.04} \qquad (1)$$

$$n_{3/2} = 1.91(\log_2 N)^{2.30} \qquad (2)$$

$$n_{9/10} = 4.09(\log_2 N)^{2.52} \qquad (3)$$

We are well into the large N regime with our simulations.

5. Conclusions

We have presented a modified butterfly memory server network that is capable of delivering

[†] A very dated dance craze.

full bandwidth to a large number of processors performing simultaneous vector operations. The memory server adaptively absorbs conflicts and timing fluctuations making it suitable for general purpose large N pipelined multiprocessors. Scalar fetches through the memory server still incur a latency of $\alpha\log_2 N$ which limits scalar performance of the machine. The switch saturation caused by vector operations will reduce scalar fetch performance even further. In a real machine one would of course include local memory in order to increase speed for scalar data which does not need to be shared. It may also be profitable to include a separate memory server switch for scalar fetches from shared memory. Examining these issues is beyond the scope of this paper.

We have not investigated banyan networks[5] to see if the same basic switch node modification yields adaptive behavior for vector operations. This is an interesting proposition as these networks offer a much lower latency of $\alpha\log_j N$ where j is the number of ports on the basic switch node. The lower memory latency would improve the speed of scalar operations and would reduce the vector lengths required for efficient vector performance. We will report on banyan and other networks with interesting features in a future paper.

References

[1] T. S. Axelrod, "Effects of Synchronization Barriers on Multiprocessor Performance," submitted to IEEE Trans. Comput., LLNL, Livermore, UCRL 92175 (1985).

[2] D. A. Patterson, "Reduced Instruction Set Computers,", Commun. ACM, Vol. 28, Num. 1, pp. 8-21 (Jan. 1985).

[3] J. H. Patel, "Performance of Processor-Memory Interconnections for Multiprocessors," IEEE Trans. Comput., Vol. C30, pp. 771-780 (Oct. 1981).

[4] D. M. Dias and J. R. Jump, "Analysis and Simulation of Buffered Delta Networks," IEEE Trans. Comput., Vol. C30, pp.273-282 (Apr. 1981).

[5] S. Cheemalavagu and M. Malek, "Analysis and Simulation of Banyan Interconnection Networks with 2x2, 4x4, and 8x8 Switch Elements," Proc. Real-Time Systems Symposium, pp. 83-89, Los Angeles, California (Dec. 1982).

[6] E. D. Brooks, "A Butterfly Processor-Memory Interconnection for a Vector Processing Environment," submitted to IEEE Trans. Comput., LLNL, Livermore, UCRL 92325 (1985).

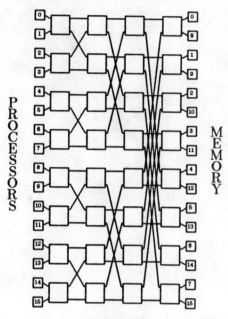

Figure 1
The butterfly multiprocessor architecture.

N	buffer length					
	1	2	4	8	16	32
2	.40	.75	.75	.75	.75	.75
4	.31	.59	.67	.71	.73	.74
8	.25	.51	.63	.69	.72	.74
16	.22	.46	.60	.67	.71	.72
32	.20	.43	.58	.67	.70	.72

Table 1

Normalized random fetch bandwidth for the standard 2 buffer switch node.

N	buffer length					
	1	2	4	8	16	32
2	.40	.83	.92	.96	.98	.99
4	.31	.66	.86	.93	.96	.98
8	.25	.60	.82	.91	.94	.96
16	.22	.55	.79	.89	.93	.96
32	.20	.53	.77	.88	.93	.96

Table 2

Normalized random fetch bandwidth for the 4 buffer switch node.

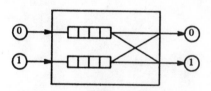

Figure 2
The standard 2 buffer switch node.

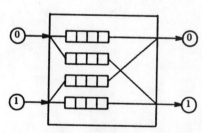

Figure 3
The modified 4 buffer switch.

Performance for stride 1 vector loads					
$\log_2 N$	N	$n_{1/4}$	$n_{1/2}$	n_9	L_b
1	2	2	6	19	1
2	4	7	21	64	2
3	8	11	33	100	2
4	16	14	48	145	2
5	32	21	72	226	4
6	64	34	114	370	6
7	128	50	177	550	12
8	256	84	225	712	12
9	512	71	297	1099	21
10	1024	88	393	1396	20
11	2048	110	453	1783	NA

Table 3

Vector lengths required for stride 1 vector operations.

Chapter 7: Multicomputer Interconnection Schemes

As the number of interconnected computers increases, the interconnection among them plays an increasingly important role in influencing the performance of the multicomputer system. A network configuration is considered ideal if it possesses a direct communicating link between any two interacting computers or between any two processes that need to transfer data to each other. To provide a reasonable capability, various mesh-connected types and other schemes[1-4] are described. A taxonomy, covering interconnection structures, has been given[5]. For multiple instruction/multiple data computation, a simple loop structure[6] is described, and several modifications[7-12] for increasing the bandwidth and reducing the communication delay by adding appropriate additional links, are described. It is also clearly shown that increasing one network parameter may adversely affect another network parameter. For example, addition of links increases the number of I/O ports and, hence, the cost of the system. Some compromises have to be made to satisfy various requirements.

A tree scheme has become quite popular for searching and sorting. The same notion is used in designing a multicomputer structure in the form of a tree. However, this necessitates going through the root node, if a leaf node belonging to the left subtree has to communicate to the right subtree. Additional links have been proposed[13-15] to reduce the communication delays between leaf nodes belonging to separate subtrees. The suitability of tree schemes in implementing a hierarchical multicomputer structure is shown by Shin[16]. Various other alternative strategies are also introduced[17-21].

Another important class of structure includes a binary cube connection[22-24], which is suitable for many applications and provides a good compromise between the communication delay and the total number of links needed to connect the computers together in the cube configuration. Preparata and Vullemin[25] describe a further variation that requires replacing each node of a binary cube by a loop network, thereby limiting the number of I/O ports to three while substantially increasing the number of processors. Its suitability for VLSI implementation and for searching-sorting applications has also been demonstrated. Other large scale homogenous interconnection schemes are described[26-33].

The diameter (i.e., maxima of the minimum distance between any two computers or nodes) is considered to be a good representative indicating the maximum communication delay of the network if the queueing effect is ignored. The cost of the network is related to the number of communication links (or connectivity) per node. Thus, one would like to maximize the number of nodes while minimizing the diameter and connectivity. In general, it is not possible to design such networks with any arbitrary parameter values. This is known as the (d,k) graph problem; several related issues including fault tolerance are addressed[34-46]. Communication mechanisms, ways to reduce intercomputer communication, and cost-performance bounds are also addressed[47-52].

Four papers dealing with various aspects of multicomputer interconnection schemes are included in this chapter.

References

1 R. Miller and Q.F. Stout, "Computational Geometry on a Mesh-Connected Computer," *Proc. 1984 Int'l. Conf. Parallel Processing,* IEEE Computer Society, Washington, D.C., 1984, pp. 66-73.

2 C.S. Raghavendra and V.K.P. Kumar, "Permutations on ILLIAC IV-Type Networks," *Proc. 1984 Int'l. Conf. Parallel Processing,* IEEE Computer Society, Washington, D.C., 1984, pp. 59-62.

3 A.P. Reeves, "A Systematically Designed Binary Array Processor," *IEEE Trans. Computers,* Vol. C-29, No. 4, April 1980, pp. 278-287.

4 T. Hoshino, T. Shirakawa, T. Kamimura, T. Kageyama, K. Takenouchi, H. Abe, S. Sekiguchi, Y. Oyanagi, and T. Kawai, "Highly Parallel Processor Array 'PAX' for Wide Scientific Applications, *Proc. 1983 Int'l. Conf. Parallel Processing,* IEEE Computer Society, Washington, D.C., 1983, pp. 95-105.

5 G.A. Anderson and E.D. Jensen, "Computer Interconnection Structures: Taxonomy, Characteristics, and Examples." *ACM Computing* Surveys, Vol. 7, No. 4, Dec. 1975, pp. 197-213.

6 M.T. Liu, "Distributed Loop Computer Networks," *Advances in Computers,* Vol. 17, Academic Press, Orlando, Fl., 1978, pp. 164-216.

7 R.M. Keller, S.S. Patil, and G. Lindstorm, "A Loosely Coupled Applicative Multiprocessing System," *Proc. Nat. Computer Conf.,* AFIPS Press, Reston, Va., 1979, pp. 613-622.

8 C.H. Sequin, "Doubly Twisted Torus Networks for VLSI Processing Arrays," *Proc. 8th Ann. Symp. Computer Architecture,* IEEE Computer Society, Washington, D.C., 1981, pp. 471-480.

9 S.B. Wu, and M.T. Liu, "A Cluster Structure as an Interconnection Network for Large Multimicrocomputer Systems," *IEEE Trans. Computers,* Vol. C-30, No. 4, April 1981, pp. 254-265.

10 B.W. Arden and H. Lee, "Analysis of Chordal Ring Network," *IEEE Trans. Computers,* Vol. C-30, No. 4, April 1981, pp. 254-265.

11 B.W. Arden and H. Lee, "A Regular Network for Multicomputer Systems," *IEEE Trans. Computers,* Vol. C-31, No. 1, Jan. 1982, pp. 60-69.

12 K.W. Doty, "Large Regular Interconnection Networks," *Proc. 2nd Int'l. Conf. Distributed Computing Systems,* IEEE Computer Society, Washington, D.C., 1982, pp. 312-317.

13 A.M. Despain and D.A. Patterson, "X-Tree: A Tree Structured Multiprocessor Computer," *Proc. 5th Ann. Symp. Computer Architecture*, IEEE Computer Society, Washington, D.C., April 1978, pp. 144-151.

14 J.R. Goodman and C.H. Sequin, "Hypertree: A Multiprocessor Interconnection Topology," *IEEE Trans. Computers,* Vol. C-30, No. 12, Dec. 1981, pp. 923-933,

15 E. Horowitz and A. Zorat, "The Binary Tree as an Interconnection Network: Applications to Multiprocessor Systems and VLSI," *IEEE Trans. Computers,* Vol. C-30, No. 4, April 1981, pp. 247-253.

16 K.G. Shin et al., "Design of HM2P—A Hierarchical Multiprocessor for General Purpose Applications," *IEEE Trans. Computers,* Vol. C-31, No. 11, Nov. 1982, pp. 1045-1053.

17 R.A. Finkel and M.H. Solomon, "Processor Interconnection Strategies," *IEEE Trans. Computers,* Vol. C-29, No. 5, May 1980, pp. 360-371.

18 J.E. Wirshing and T. Kishi, "CONET: A Connection Network Model," *IEEE Trans. Computers,* Vol. C-31, No. 4, April 1981, pp. 298-301.

19 R.A. Finkel and M.H. Solomon, "The Lens Interconnection Strategy," *IEEE Trans. Computers,* Vol. C-30, No. 12, Dec. 1981, pp. 960-965.

20 B.W. Arden and R. Ginosar, "MP/C: A Multi-Microprocessor Architecture," *IEEE Trans. Computers,* Vol. C-31, No. 5, May 1982, pp. 455-473.

21 Y.K. Dalal, "Use of Multiple Networks in the Xerox Network System," *Computer,* Vol. 15, No. 10, Oct. 1982, pp. 82-92.

22 M.C. Pease, "The Indirect Binary n-cube Microprocessor Array," *IEEE Trans. Computers,* Vol. C-25, No. 5, May 1977, pp. 458-473.

23 H.J. Siegel and R.J. McMillen, "The Cube Network as a Distributed Processing Test-Bed Switch," *Proc. 2nd Int'l. Conf. Distributed Computing Systems*, IEEE Computer Society, Washington, D.C., 1981, pp. 377-387.

24 A.Y. Oruc, "A Classification of Cube Connected Networks with a Simple Control Scheme," *Proc. 1983 Int'l. Conf. Parallel Processing,* IEEE Computer Society, Washington, D.C., 1983, pp. 126-131.

25 F.P. Preparata and J. Vullemin, "The Cube Connected Cycles: A Versatile Network for Parallel Computation," *Commun. of the ACM,* Vol. 24, No. 5, May 1981, pp. 300-309.

26 H. Sullivan and T.R. Bashkow, "A Large Scale, Homogenous, Fully Distributed Parallel Machine I," *Proc. 4th Ann. Symp. Computer Architecture,* IEEE Computer Society, Washington, D.C., 1977, pp. 105-117.

27 M.J. O'Donnel and C.H. Smith, "A Combinational Problem Concerning Processor Interconnection Networks," *IEEE Trans. Computers,* Vol. C-31, No. 2, Feb. 1982, pp. 163-164.

28 W.L. Leland and M.H. Solomon, "Dense Trivalent Graphs for Processor Interconnection," *IEEE Trans. Computers,* Vol. C-31, No. 3, March 1982, pp. 219-222.

29 J.P. Fishburn and R.A. Finkel, "Quotient Networks," *IEEE Trans. Computers,* Vol. C-31, No. 4, April 1982, pp. 288-295.

30 V. Conta, "Torus and Other Networks as Communication Networks with up to Some Hundred Points," *IEEE Trans. Computers,* Vol. C-32, No. 7, July 1983, pp. 657-667.

31 K.W. Doty, "Dense Bus Connection Networks," *Proc. Int'l. 1983 Conf. Parallel Processing,* IEEE Computer Society, Washington, D.C., 1983, pp. 158-160.

32 K.W. Doty, "New Designs for Dense Processor Interconnection Networks," *IEEE Trans. Computers,* Vol. C-33, No. 5, May 1984, pp. 58-160.

33 K.W. Doty, "New Designs for Dense Processor Interconnection Networks," *IEEE Trans. Computers,* Vol. C-33, No. 5, May 1984, pp. 447-450.

34 P. Erdos, S. Fajtlowicz, and A.J. Hoffman, "Maximum Degree in Graphs of Diameter 2," *Networks,* Vol. 10, No. 1, May 1984, pp. 87-90.

35 M. Imase and M. Itoh, "Design to Minimize Diameter on Building-Block Network," *IEEE Trans. Computers,* Vol. C-30, No. 6, June 1981, pp. 439-442.

36 M. Maekawa, "Optimal Processor Interconnection Tonologies," *Proc. 8th Ann. Symp. Computer Architecture*, IEEE Computer Society, Washington, D.C., 1981, pp. 171-186.

37 L.N. Bhuyan and D.P. Agrawal, "A General Class of Processor Interconnection Strategies," *Proc. 9th Ann. Int'l. Symp. Computer Architecture*, IEEE Computer Society, Washington, D.C., April 1982.

38 G. Memmi and Y. Raillard, "Some New Results about the (d,k) Graph Problem," *IEEE Trans. Computers,* Vol. C-31, No. 8, Aug. 1982, pp. 784-790.

39 D.K. Pradhan and S.M. Reddy, "A Fault-Tolerant Communication Architecture for Distributed Systems," *IEEE Trans. Computers,* Vol. C-31, No. 9, Sept. 1982, pp. 863-870.

40 M.A. Fiol, I. Alegre, and J.L.A. Yebra, "Line Diagraph Iterations and the (d,k) Problem for Directed Graphs," *Proc. 10th Ann. Int'l. Symp. Computer Architecture*, IEEE Computer Society, Washington, D.C., 1983, pp. 174-177.

41 S.M. Reddy, P. Raghavan, and J.G. Kuhl, "A Class of Graphs for Processor Interconnection," *Proc. 1983 Int'l. Conf. Parallel Processing*, IEEE Computer Society, Washington, D.C., 1983, pp. 154-157.

42 M.R. Samatham and D.K. Pradhan, "The De Bruijn Multiprocessor Network: A Versatile Sorting Network," *Proc. 12th Int'l. Symp. Computer Architecture*, IEEE Computer Society, Washington, D.C., 1985, pp. 360-367.

43 M.R. Jerrum and S. Skyum, "Families of Fixed Degree Graphs for Processor Interconnection," *IEEE Trans. Computers*, Vol. C-33, No. 2, Feb. 1984, pp. 190-194.

44 L.N. Bhuyan and D.P. Agrawal, "Generalized Hypercube and Hyperbus Structures for a Computer Network," *IEEE Trans. Computers*, Vol. C-33, No. 4, April 1984, pp. 323-333.

45 M.A. Fiol, J.L.A. Yebra, and I.A. De Miquel, "Line Diagraph Iterations and the (d,k) Diagraph Problem," *IEEE Trans. Computers*, Vol. C-33, No. 5, May 1984, pp. 400-403.

46 C. Delorme and G. Farjo, "Large Graphs with Given Degree and Diameter—Part I," *IEEE Trans. Computers*, Vol. C-33, No. 9, Sept. 1984, pp. 857-860.

47 J.A. Stankovic, "Software Communication Mechanisms: Procedure Calls Versus Messages," *Computer*, Vol. 15, No. 4, April 1982, pp. 19-25.

48 K.B. Irani and N.G. Khabbaz, "A Methodology for the Design of Communication Networks and the Distribution of Data in Distributed Super Computer Systems," *IEEE Trans. Computers*, Vol. C-31, No. 5, May, 1982, pp. 419-434.

49 D.A. Reed and H.D. Schwetman, "Cost-Performance Bounds for Multicomputer Networks," *IEEE Trans. Computers*, Vol. C-32, No. 1, Jan. 1983, pp. 83-95.

50 B.D. Rathi, "Specification and Implementation of an Integrated Packet Communication Facility for an Array Computer," *Proc. 1983 Int'l. Conf. Parallel Processing*, IEEE Computer Society, Washington, D.C., 1983, pp. 51-58.

51 K.B. Irani and W.S. Wu, "Minimization of Inter-Processor Communication for Parallel Computations on a SIMD Multicomputer Interconnected with an Omega Network," *Proc. 1984 Int'l. Conf. Parallel Processing*, IEEE Computer Society, Washington, D.C., 984, pp. 63-65.

52 W.W. Chu, M.T. Lan, and J. Hellerstein, "Estimation of Intermodule Communication (IMC) and Its Application in Distributed Processing Systems," *IEEE Trans. Computers*, Vol. C-33, No. 8, Aug. 1984, pp. 691-699.

Reprinted from *IEEE Transactions on Computers*, Volume C-30, Number 4,
April 1981, pages 291-295. Copyright © 1981 by The Institute of Electrical
and Electronics Engineers, Inc.

Analysis of Chordal Ring Network

BRUCE W. ARDEN AND HIKYU LEE

Abstract—A family of regular graphs of degree 3, called *Chordal Rings*, is presented as a possible candidate for the implementation of a local network of message-connected (micro) computers. For a properly constructed graph in this family having n nodes the diameter, or maximum length message path, is shown to be of $0(n^{1/2})$. The symmetry of the graphs makes it possible to determine message routing by using a simple distributed algorithm. The given algorithm is also potentially useful for the determination of alternate paths in the event of node or link failure.

Index Terms—Chordal Ring, distributed routing, message-passing, multi-(micro) computer systems, regular networks.

I. INTRODUCTION

A common theme in current studies of computer system architecture is in the exploitation of parallel, or concurrent, computation. There are many approaches. Concurrence can be achieved by the simultaneous, synchronous execution of many relatively simple operation sequences. The local averaging operation often used in the numerical solution of partial differential equations is an example. Such specialized algorithms have a regularity that is attractive for integrated circuit implementation. On the other hand, the remarkable capabilities of modern microprocessors suggest that a processor, with its associated memory (i.e., a computer), be used as the basic computer element. In this case the "size" of the algorithm will generally be much larger; the unit of execution can be regarded as a "process"

in the operating system sense. Here, asynchronous system operation is an option.

Tightly coupled, multiprocessor systems, where the processors share a common high performance random access memory suffer from connection complexity that is costly and thus tends to offset the favorable economics of microprocessors [9], [11], [12]. In multicomputer systems processor-memory units are interconnected in a network and computation-enabling data are passed using a message passing protocol. Although the interconnection is much simpler, messages may pass through a number of network nodes before reaching their destinations. The message processing load and message delay can offset the advantage of simple connectivity.

When considering such multicomputer systems, regular networks of low degree having small maximum message path lengths (or graph diameters) are of interest. The regularity permits a local network to be implemented, or extended, using a "standard" building block. Given the pin limitation on microcomputers, a relatively small number of bidirectional buses at a node is a natural limitation. Clearly a node with two buses, or degree 2 limit the regular network to cycles. With $2n + 1$ nodes in a cycle the maximum message path length is n [2], [10], [13]. This diameter is acceptable if n is relatively small, but even for several tens of computers path lengths become too large. There are many families of regular graphs of degree 3 [1], [3]–[8] and it is, of course, possible to greatly reduce the graph diameter for a given number of nodes in comparison to the degree 2 case, or cycle. This paper is concerned with a particular family of degree 3 graphs called *Chordal Rings* which can be formed by adding chords to a simple cycle, or ring.

For regular graphs it is possible to compute, at each node, the path(s) between any source and destination node—as opposed to using a tabular representation of the network stored at each node. This path determination is particularly simple with the Chordal Ring geometry and an algorithm is given.

Manuscript received June 2, 1980; revised October 29, 1980. This work was supported by the National Science Foundation under Grant MCS 74-21939.

B. W. Arden is with the Department of Electrical Engineering and Computer Science, Princeton University, Princeton, NJ 08544.

H. Lee is with the Department of Electrical Engineering and Computer Science, Northwestern University, Evanston, IL 60201.

II. Description of a Chordal Ring

The Chordal Ring is a ring structured network in which each node has an additional link, called a *chord,* to some other node across the network. The number of nodes in a Chordal Ring is assumed to be even and nodes are indexed $0, 1, 2, \cdots, n-1$ around the ring. In the present correspondence we restrict our attention to the case in which each odd-numbered node i ($i = 1, 3, \cdots, n-1$) is connected to a node $(i+w)$ *mod* n. Accordingly, each even-numbered node j ($j = 0, 2, \cdots, n-2$) is connected to a node $(j-w)$ *mod* n. The w is called *chord length* and is assumed to be positive odd. Without loss of generality, we assume that $w \leq n/2$. For a given number of nodes n, a number of Chordal Rings can be obtained for different values of chord length w. An example of a Chordal Ring for $n = 18$ and $w = 5$ is shown in Fig. 1. Note that the Chordal Ring structure is incrementally extensible by adding multiples of two nodes to the original configuration. However, as the number of nodes increases, the optimal chord length giving the minimum diameter changes.

III. Diameter of a Chordal Ring

For a given number of nodes n and chord length w, we are interested in computing the maximum of minimum path length between all pairs of nodes in a Chordal Ring, where the length of a path is determined by the number of links in the path.

Suppose we are given two nodes, *source* and *destination*. Without loss of generality, we assume that the source is node 0 and destination is node x for $0 \leq x < n$. One obvious way of finding a path is simply to traverse ring-edges, either in clockwise or in counterclockwise direction, along the periphery of the ring. However, it is obvious that proper chordal traversals should be included in the path since this simple strategy does not guarantee the shortest path between the two nodes. Since the chord length w is less than or equal to $n/2$, we call a chordal traversal from node i to node $(i+w)$ *mod* n a *clockwise chordal traversal* for each odd-numbered node i. Similarly, a chordal traversal from node j to node $(j-w)$ *mod* n is called a *counterclockwise chordal traversal* for each even-numbered node j.

In a ring network there are two *noncyclic* paths from node 0 to node x, i.e., one traversing the ring in clockwise direction and the other in counterclockwise direction. The optimal path is then determined by the shorter of the two. Similarly, in a Chordal Ring we have two types of paths from node 0 to node x. They are paths consisting of clockwise chordal traversals plus appropriate ring-edge traversals, and paths consisting of counterclockwise chordal traversals plus appropriate ring-edge traversals. For convenience, we call the former *clockwise paths* and the latter *counterclockwise paths.* Then the length of the shortest path from node 0 to node x, which we denote as $\text{DIST}(x)$, is given by

$$\text{DIST}(x) = \min\{\text{dist}_R(x), \text{dist}_L(x)\}$$

where $\text{dist}_R(x)$ and $\text{dist}_L(x)$ denote the length of a shortest clockwise path and that of a shortest counterclockwise path, respectively. Note that in Fig. 1 $\text{dist}_R(5) = 3$. The corresponding clockwise paths are $0 \to 1 \to 6 \to 5$ and $0 \to 17 \to 4 \to 5$. Similarly, $\text{dist}_L(5) = 5$ and the corresponding counterclockwise paths are $0 \to 13 \to 12 \to 7 \to 6 \to 5$, $0 \to 17 \to 16 \to 11 \to 10 \to 5$, $0 \to 13 \to 12 \to 11 \to 10 \to 5$, and $0 \to 13 \to 14 \to 9 \to 10 \to 5$. Hence, we have $\text{DIST}(5) = 3$.

We compute $\text{dist}_R(x)$ as follows: We define a composite move of one clockwise ring-edge traversal at an even-numbered node followed by a clockwise chordal traversal as an α-move. A β-move is similarly defined as a composite move of one counterclockwise ring-edge traversal at an even-numbered node followed by a clockwise chordal traversal. Then we observe:

1) By using α-move i times, we reach node $i(w+1)$.
2) By using β-move i times, we reach node $i(w-1)$.
3) Even-numbered nodes between node $i(w-1)$ and node $i(w+1)$ can be reached by using combination of α- and β-moves i times.

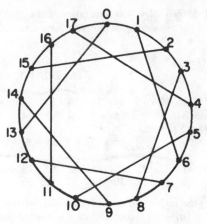

Fig. 1.   Chordal Ring with $n = 18$ and $w = 5$.

More specifically, node $i(w+1) - 2s$ ($0 \leq s \leq i$) will need $(i-s)$ α-moves and s β-moves. Likewise, odd-numbered nodes between node $i(w-1)$ and node $i(w+1)$ can be reached by using combination of α- and β-moves i times plus one ring-edge traversal at the end. More specifically, node $i(w+1) - (2s+1)$ will need $(i-s)$ α-moves and s β-moves followed by one counterclockwise ring-edge traversal, or equivalently $(i-s-1)$ α-moves and $(s+1)$ β-moves followed by one clockwise ring-edge traversal.

Since each α-move is equivalent to $(w+1)$ ring-edge traversals, we divide the nodes into *clockwise intervals,* each of size $w+1$, such that the ith ($1 \leq i \leq \lfloor n/(w+1) \rfloor$) interval contains nodes $(i-1)(w+1) + 1, \cdots, i(w+1)$ *mod* n and examine how many traversals will be needed to reach the nodes in each interval. Obviously, the first node in the ith interval can be reached by $(2i-1)$ traversals, i.e., $(i-1)$ α-moves plus one clockwise ring-edge traversal will do. From the observations 1)–3) above, the last $\min(2i+1, w)$ nodes in the ith interval, i.e., nodes $i(w+1) - \min(2i+1, w) + 1, \cdots, i(w+1)$ will require either $2i$ or $2i+1$ traversals depending on whether the node is even- or odd-numbered.

Hence, if $2i + 1 \geq w$, then all the even-numbered nodes in the ith interval can be reached with $2i$ traversals and all the odd-numbered nodes, except the first one which only takes $2i-1$ traversals, can be reached with $2i + 1$ traversals.

If $2i + 3 \leq w$, then the first and the second node will need $2i - 1$ and $2i$ traversals, respectively; the 3rd, 4th, $\cdots$, $(3 + (w - 2i - 3)/2)$th nodes as well as $(w - 2i)$th, $(w - 2i - 1)$th, $\cdots$, $(w - 2i - (w - 2i - 3)/2)$th nodes will need $2i + 1, 2i + 2, \cdots, 2i + (w - 2i - 1)/2$ traversals, respectively; for the last $(2i + 1)$ nodes, $2i$ traversals are needed for even-numbered nodes and $2i + 1$ traversals for odd-numbered ones. The fact that node x is in the $\lceil x/(w+1) \rceil$th interval leads to the following expression for $\text{dist}_R(x)$, where Δ_x denotes x *mod* $(w+1)$:

1) When $\left\lceil \dfrac{x}{w+1} \right\rceil \geq \dfrac{w-1}{2}$, $\text{dist}_R(x) = 2\left\lceil \dfrac{x}{w+1} \right\rceil - 1$ if $\Delta_x = 1$;

$$2\left\lceil \frac{x}{w+1} \right\rceil + \left[(-1)^{x+1}\frac{1}{2}\right] \text{ if } \Delta_x = 0 \text{ or } 2 \leq \Delta_x \leq w.$$

2) When $\left\lceil \dfrac{x}{w+1} \right\rceil \leq \dfrac{w-3}{2}$, $\text{dist}_R(x) = 2\left\lceil \dfrac{x}{w+1} \right\rceil + \Delta_x$

$$\text{if } 1 \leq \Delta_x \leq \frac{w+1}{2} - \left\lceil \frac{x}{w+1} \right\rceil;$$

$$(w+1) - \Delta_x \text{ if } \frac{w+3}{2} - \left\lceil \frac{x}{w+1} \right\rceil \leq \Delta_x \leq w - 2\left\lceil \frac{x}{w+1} \right\rceil;$$

$$2\left\lceil \frac{x}{w+1} \right\rceil + \left[(-1)^{x+1}\frac{1}{2}\right] \text{ if } \Delta_x = 0 \text{ or } w - 2\left\lceil \frac{x}{w+1} \right\rceil + 1 \leq \Delta_x \leq w.$$

Example 1: Shown below is an illustration of $\text{dist}_R(x)$ of the nodes in the 2nd and the 5th clockwise intervals for a Chordal Ring with $n = 100$ and $w = 9$.

2nd interval $(i = 2)$

$$\min(2i + 1, w) = 5$$

node (x):	11	12	13	14	15	16	17	18	19	20
$\text{dist}_R(x)$:	3	4	5	6	5	4	5	4	5	4

5th interval $(i = 5)$

$$\min(2i + 1, w) = 9$$

node X:	41	42	43	44	45	46	47	48	49	50
$\text{dist}_R(x)$:	9	10	11	10	11	10	11	10	11	10	□

By dividing the nodes into *counterclockwise intervals* such that the ith $(1 \le i \le \lfloor n/w + 1 \rfloor)$ counterclockwise interval contains nodes $n - (i-1)(w+1) - 1, n - (i-1)(w+1) - 2, \cdots, n - i(w+1)$, and following a similar analysis to the one for $\text{dist}_R(x)$, expression for $\text{dist}_L(x)$ is accordingly obtained [5]. Having computed $\text{dist}_R(x)$ and $\text{dist}_L(x)$, we are ready to compute the diameter k. That is, the diameter k is given by

$$k = \max\{\text{DIST}(x)\}$$

$$= \max[\min\{\text{dist}_R(x), \text{dist}_L(x)\}] \quad \text{for all } x(0 \le x < n).$$

Theorem 1: For a Chordal Ring with n nodes and chord length w, let $i = \left\lfloor \dfrac{n}{2(w+1)} \right\rfloor$ and $\Delta = \dfrac{n}{2} \bmod (w+1)$. Then the diameter k of a Chordal Ring is given by

1) When $i \ge \dfrac{w-1}{2}$, $k = 2i - 1$ if $\Delta = 1$; $2i$ if $2 \le \Delta \le \dfrac{w+3}{2}$;

$$2i + 1 \text{ if } \Delta = 0 \text{ or } \dfrac{w+5}{2} \le \Delta \le w.$$

2) When $i = \dfrac{w-3}{2}$, $k = w - 3$ if $1 \le \Delta \le 2$;

$$w - 2 \text{ if } \Delta = 0 \text{ or } 3 \le \Delta \le w.$$

3) When $i < \dfrac{w-3}{2}$, $k = i + \dfrac{w-3}{2}$ if $1 \le \Delta \le \dfrac{w+1}{2} - 1$

or $\dfrac{w+5}{2} - i \le \Delta \le w - i$; $i + \dfrac{w-1}{2}$ if $\Delta = 0$, $\dfrac{w+3}{2} - i$

$$\text{or } w - i + 1 \le \Delta \le w.$$

Proof: Refer to related result in [5]. Q.E.D.

In Fig. 1, we have $n = 18$ and $w = 5$. Hence, $\left\lfloor \dfrac{n}{2(w+1)} \right\rfloor \ge \dfrac{w-1}{2}$.

Since $\Delta \left(= \dfrac{n}{2} \bmod (w+1) \right) = 3$, $k = 2\left\lfloor \dfrac{n}{2(w+1)} \right\rfloor = 4$. For the special

case in which n is a square, we have the following.

Theorem 2: For a Chordal Ring with n nodes $(n \ge 8^2)$, where n is a square, the diameter is greater than or equal to $\sqrt{n} - 1$. Furthermore, the equality holds when $\sqrt{n} + 3 \le w \le \sqrt{n} + 2h + 1$, where h is the largest integer satisfying $\sqrt{n} \ge 2(2h^2 + h + 1)$.

Proof: Refer to related result in [5]. Q.E.D.

IV. ROUTING IN THE CHORDAL RING

In the Chordal Ring there is more than one shortest path for most pairs of nodes. To utilize this property to its full extent, we present a *distributed, computational* routing algorithm in this section.

The *routing record*, from which all the shortest paths between *source* and *destination* can be retrieved, is initially computed at the source. It is updated at each intermediate node on the way to the

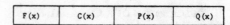

F(x)	C(x)	P(x)	Q(x)

Fig. 2. Routing record for destination node x. ROUTE(x).

destination in such a way that the current routing record contains information on the rest of the path, that is, on the shortest paths from that intermediate node to the destination. The actual implementation of the routing algorithm will determine the next node to visit according to the routing record and the current states of the neighboring nodes. The described routing strategy is *adaptive* and *fail-soft* in the sense that, when there is more than one alternative for the next node to visit, we may choose one according to certain rules. Obviously, the choice would exclude a broken link or a malfunctioning processor, if these conditions are detectable. Also, any idle or lightly loaded successor node could be preferentially chosen.

In the following we illustrate a computation of routing record for a Chordal Ring. Without loss of generality, we assume that node 0 is source and an arbitrary node $x(0 \le x < n)$ is destination.

We denote the routing record for a destination node x as ROUTE(x). ROUTE(x) consists of four fields: $F(x)$, $C(x)$, $P(x)$, and $Q(x)$. Each field contains the following information on the shortest paths from node 0 to node x.

$F(x)$: flag specifying traversal direction, i.e., "+" denotes clockwise and "−" denotes counterclockwise direction.

$C(x)$: the number of chordal traversals in the direction specified by $F(x)$ in the shortest paths from node 0 to node x.

$P(x)$: the number of ring-edge traversals in the direction specified by $F(x)$ in the shortest paths from node 0 to node x.

$Q(x)$: the number of ring-edge traversals in the opposite direction specified by $F(x)$ in the shortest paths from node 0 to node x.

Note that the length of shortest paths from node 0 to node x, i.e., $\text{DIST}(x)$, is then equal to $|\text{ROUTE}(x)|$, where

$$|\text{ROUTE}(x)| = C(x) + P(x) + Q(x).$$

To obtain the expression for ROUTE(x), we first consider the case in which $\text{dist}_R(x) \le \text{dist}_L(x)$. In this case, $F(x)$ is set to "+." In the previous section we observed that nodes were divided into intervals in the clockwise direction and a node in each interval was reached by using a combination of α- and β-moves plus additional ring-edge traversals, if necessary. The derivation for $C(x)$, $P(x)$, and $Q(x)$ for a given destination node x is, therefore, a straightforward computation in which

$C(x) = $ (number of α-moves) + (number of β-moves);
$P(x) = $ (number of α-moves) + (number of additional ring-edge traversals in clockwise direction);
$Q(x) = $ (number of β-moves) + (number of additional ring-edge traversals in counterclockwise direction).

Therefore, when $\text{dist}_R(x) \le \text{dist}_L(x)$, $F(x) = $ "+" and the values of $C(x)$, $P(x)$, and $Q(x)$ are obtained from the following equations, where Δ_x denotes $x \bmod (w+1)$.

Case 1a): If $\left\lfloor \dfrac{x}{w+1} \right\rfloor \ge \dfrac{w-1}{2}$ and $0 \le \Delta_x \le 1$, then $C(x)$

$= \left\lfloor \dfrac{x}{w+1} \right\rfloor$, $P(x) = \left\lfloor \dfrac{x}{w+1} \right\rfloor + \Delta_x$ $Q(x) = 0$.

Case 1b): If $\left\lfloor \dfrac{x}{w+1} \right\rfloor \ge \dfrac{w-1}{2}$ and $2 \le \Delta_x \le w$, then $C(x)$

$= \left\lfloor \dfrac{x}{w+1} \right\rfloor$, $P(x) = \left\lfloor \dfrac{x}{w+1} \right\rfloor$ and $Q(x) = \left\lfloor \dfrac{w - \Delta x}{2} \right\rfloor + \left[(-1)^{x+1} \dfrac{1}{2} \right]$.

Case 2a): If $\left\lfloor \dfrac{x}{w+1} \right\rfloor \le \dfrac{w-3}{2}$ and $0 \le \Delta_x \le \dfrac{w+1}{2} - \left\lfloor \dfrac{x}{w+1} \right\rfloor$,

same as Case 1a).

Case 2b): If $\left\lfloor\dfrac{x}{w+1}\right\rfloor \le \dfrac{w-3}{2}$ and $\dfrac{w+3}{2} - \left\lfloor\dfrac{x}{w+1}\right\rfloor \le \Delta_x$

$\le w - 2\left\lfloor\dfrac{x}{w+1}\right\rfloor$, then $C(x) = \left\lfloor\dfrac{x}{w+1}\right\rfloor$, $P(x) = 0$ and $Q(x)$

$= w + 1 - \left\lfloor\dfrac{x}{w+1}\right\rfloor - \Delta_x$.

Case 2c): If $\left\lfloor\dfrac{x}{w+1}\right\rfloor \le \dfrac{w-3}{2}$ and $w - 2\left\lfloor\dfrac{x}{w+1}\right\rfloor + 1$

$\le \Delta_x \le w$, same as Case 1b).

Similar expression for ROUTE(x) can be obtained [5] for the case in which $\mathrm{dist}_L(x) \le \mathrm{dist}_R(x)$.

Example 2: Shown below is an illustration of ROUTE(x) for the nodes in the 2nd and the 5th clockwise intervals for a Chordal Ring with $n = 100$ and $w = 9$. Each row denotes number of α-moves, number of β-moves, number of additional ring-edge traversals, and $C(x)$, $P(x)$, and $Q(x)$ values. For these nodes $\mathrm{dist}_R(x) \le \mathrm{dist}_L(x)$, hence $F(x) =$ "+." The "+" sign on the number of additional ring-edge traversals denotes clockwise direction and "−" sign denotes counterclockwise direction. DIST(x)($= \mathrm{dist}_R(x)$) is shown for reference.

2nd interval ($i = 2$) — min ($2i + 1, w = 5$)

x:	11	12	13	14	15	16	17	18	19	20
α:	1	1	1	0	0	0	1	1	2	2
β:	0	0	0	2	2	2	1	1	0	0
ring-edge:	+1	+2	+3	−2	−1	0	−1	0	−1	0
$C(x)$:	1	1	1	2	2	2	2	2	2	2
$P(x)$:	2	3	4	0	0	0	1	1	2	2
$Q(x)$:	0	0	0	4	3	2	2	1	1	0
DIST(x):	3	4	5	6	5	4	5	4	5	4

5th interval ($i = 5$) — min ($2i + 1, w = 9$)

x:	41	42	43	44	45	46	47	48	49	50
α:	4	1	2	2	3	3	4	4	5	5
β:	0	4	3	3	2	2	1	1	0	0
ring-edge:	+1	0	−1	0	−1	0	−1	0	−1	0
$C(x)$:	4	5	5	5	5	5	5	5	5	5
$P(x)$:	5	1	2	2	3	3	4	4	5	5
$Q(x)$:	0	4	4	3	3	2	2	1	1	0
DIST(x):	9	10	11	10	11	10	11	10	11	10

Having computed the routing record ROUTE(x), we apply the routing algorithm depicted in Fig. 3 to ROUTE(x), starting from the source node. At each intermediate node, denoted as CUR, including the source node, appropriate traversals (marked (1), (2), and (3) in Fig. 3) to the next node is determined according to the values of CUR and ROUTE(x). CUR and ROUTE(x) are modified after each traversal (marked (4) in Fig. 3) in such a way that the modified ROUTE(x) contains information on the rest of the path, that is, on the shortest paths from CUR to the destination. Note that there can be more than one candidate for the next node to visit. For example, in Fig. 3, if both $P(x)$ and $Q(x)$ are nonzero before (1), then we may either visit node CUR + 1 or CUR − 1.

At each intermediate node CUR on the routing path, the following assertion on ROUTE(x), which contains information on the shortest paths from CUR to the destination, should hold.

$$P(x) + Q(x) \ge C(x) \text{ if } F(x) = \text{"+" and CUR = even,}$$
$$\text{or } F(x) = \text{"−" and CUR = odd.}$$
$$\text{and } P(x) + Q(x) + 1 \ge C(x) \text{ if } F(x) = \text{"+" and CUR = odd,}$$
$$\text{or } F(x) = \text{"−" and CUR = even.}$$

For instance, suppose $F(x) =$ "+" and CUR is even. Since chordal traversals in the routing path are made at odd-numbered nodes and the node visited after each chordal traversal is even-numbered, each

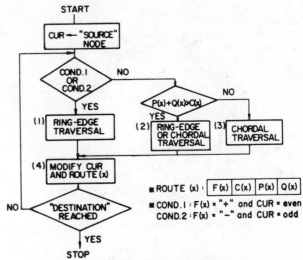

Fig. 3. Routing algorithm for a Chordal Ring.

chordal traversal in the routing path from CUR to node x is preceded by at least one ring-edge traversal (either in clockwise or in counterclockwise direction). Therefore, $P(x) + Q(x) \ge C(x)$. Similar argument leads to the rest of the above assertion, which we call *routing invariant*. It can be easily shown [5] that the routing algorithm depicted in Fig. 3 correctly finds the shortest routing path from source to destination by observing that the above routing invariant holds for ROUTE(x) at each intermediate node in the path.

At each intermediate node, we may apply the following modification rules to ROUTE(x), if necessary, in certain circumstances.

Rule 1: Decrease (resp. increase) P by $\dfrac{w+1}{2}$ and correspondingly increase (resp. decrease) C by 1 and Q by $\dfrac{w-1}{2}$.

Rule 2: Increase both P and Q by 1.

Note that *Rule 1* permits us to have additional alternate paths without increasing the path length. However, in applying *Rule 1*, the routing invariant should not be violated. By applying *Rule 2*, we still reach the same destination, but, at the expense of increasing the path length by two. These strategies can be exploited in case we need alternate paths due to link or node failures in the system.

In Fig. 4, a Chordal Ring with $n = 36$ and $w = 5$ is shown with two eligible routing records, ROUTE$_1(x)$ and ROUTE$_2(x)$ for $x = 14$. ROUTE$_1(14)$ is computed from the presented equations and ROUTE$_2(14)$ is obtained by interchanging 3 P with 1 C plus 2 Q. Note that there are six alternate shortest paths of length 6 from node 0 to node 14.

We finish this section by presenting the following example of sending a message from node 0 to node 14 in Fig. 4. In the beginning, CUR is node 0 and routing record is ROUTE$_1(14)$ shown in Fig. 4. Suppose node 1 is not functioning properly. With ROUTE$_1(14) = [+, 2, 4, 0]$, node 1 is the only candidate for the next node from the routing algorithm of Fig. 3. Hence, we apply *Rule 1* to get alternate routing record ROUTE$_2(14) = [+, 3, 1, 2]$. Now we can avoid the inoperative node 1 by visiting node 35 instead. After the traversal, ROUTE(14) becomes $[+, 3, 1, 1]$ and CUR = 35. Since CUR is odd and $P(14) + Q(14) < C(14)$ at node 35, a chordal traversal, i.e., traversal to node 4, should be made. Therefore, if node 4 is operational, the destination can be reached via nodes 3, 8, and 9 or via nodes 5, 10, and 9. On the contrary, let us assume that node 4 is also out of operation (or we may assume that link connecting node 35 and node 4 is broken). Note that *Rule 1* cannot be applied to ROUTE$_2(x) = [+, 3, 1, 1]$ at node 35 since the resulting routing record will violate the routing invariant. Hence, we try *Rule 2* instead to get modified

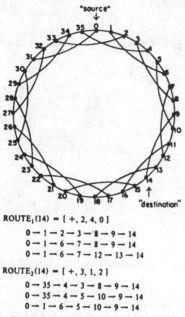

ROUTE$_1$(14) = [+, 2, 4, 0]

0 → 1 → 2 → 3 → 8 → 9 → 14
0 → 1 → 6 → 7 → 8 → 9 → 14
0 → 1 → 6 → 7 → 12 → 13 → 14

ROUTE$_2$(14) = [+, 3, 1, 2]

0 → 35 → 4 → 3 → 8 → 9 → 14
0 → 35 → 4 → 5 → 10 → 9 → 14
0 → 1 → 6 → 5 → 10 → 9 → 14

Fig. 4. Routing records, ROUTE$_1$(14) and ROUTE$_2$(14), and corresponding routing paths for a Chordal Ring with $n = 36$ and $w = 5$.

ROUTE$_2$(x) = [+, 3, 2, 2]. Now we can avoid both node 1 and node 4 and can reach the destination by taking, for example, a path 35 → 34 → 33 → 2 → 3 → 8 → 9 → 14. Corresponding ROUTE$_2$(14)'s at these intermediate nodes are [+, 3, 2, 2], [+, 3, 2, 1], [+, 3, 2, 0], [+, 2, 2, 0], [+, 2, 1, 0], [+, 1, 1, 0], [+, 1, 0, 0], and [+, 0, 0, 0].

V. MAXIMAL CHORDAL RING

For given diameter k, we call a Chordal Ring with maximal number of nodes $n_{max}(k)$ a *maximal Chordal Ring*. The chord length, which achieves $n_{max}(k)$, is called *optimal chord length* and denoted as $w_{opt}(k)$.

Theorem 3: For a given diameter k, the maximal number of nodes $n_{max}(k)$ and the optimal chord length $w_{opt}(k)$ for a Chordal Ring are given by

1) $k = 2$; $n_{max}(2) = 6$ and $w_{opt}(2) = 3$;
2) $k = 3$; $n_{max}(3) = 14$ and $w_{opt}(3) = 5$;
3) $k = 4$ or 6; $n_{max}(k) = k^2 + 2k - 4$ and $w_{opt}(k) = k + 3$ (also $k + 1$ when $k = 4$);
4) k is odd and ≥ 5; $n_{max}(k) = k^2 + 3k - 6$ and $w_{opt}(k) = k + 4$ (also $k + 2$ when $k = 5$);
5) k is even and ≥ 8; $n_{max}(k) = k^2 + 3k - 12$ and $w_{opt}(k) = k + 5$ (also $k + 3$ when $k = 8$).

Proof: Refer to related result in [5]. Q.E.D.

Fig. 5 shows maximal Chordal Ring for $k = 5$, where $n_{max}(5) = 34$ and $w_{opt}(5) = 7$.

VI. CONCLUSION

A multi-(micro) computer interconnection network called a Chordal Ring has been presented. The diameter of a Chordal Ring with n nodes and properly chosen chord length is shown to be $0(n^{1/2})$. Compared with two-dimensional array interconnections [3], [15], which also has a diameter of $0(n^{1/2})$, Chordal Ring networks are of lower degree and consequently have fewer links. A distributed computational routing algorithm for a Chordal Ring has been presented. The Chordal Ring network provides increased reliability and failsoftness compared to the ring network due to its multiple routing paths and appropriate use of the described modification rules in case of node or link failures.

Message switching is assumed for the communication between processors since circuit or line switching causes potential congestion

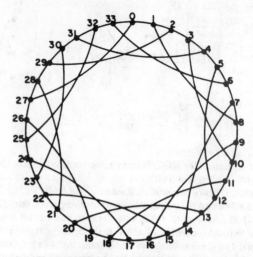

Fig. 5. Maximal Chordal Ring for $k = 5$.

by tying up a long path through the network. However, future implementation of networks comprising hundreds of computer nodes might use both message passing and buses [14]. The fact that proposed Chordal Ring structure is based on a ring network which connects all the nodes in a cycle provides a systematic organization for the study of this combined strategy.

ACKNOWLEDGMENT

The authors would like to thank M. Condry for stimulating discussions and comments.

REFERENCES

[1] B. Arden and H. Lee, "A multi tree structured network," in *Proc. COMPCON 1978 Fall*, Sept. 1978, pp. 201–210.

[2] D. J. Farber *et al.*, "The distributed computing system," in *Proc. COMPCON 1973 Spring*, Feb. 1973, pp. 31–34.

[3] G. A. Anderson and E. D. Jensen, "Computer interconnection networks: Taxonomy, characteristics and examples," *ACM Comput. Surveys*, vol. 7, pp. 197–213, Dec. 1975.

[4] R. A. Finkel and M. H. Solomon, "Processor interconnection strategies," *IEEE Trans. Comput.*, vol. C-29, pp. 360–370, May 1980.

[5] H. Lee, "Modeling of multi-microcomputer networks," Ph.D. dissertation, Princeton Univ., Princeton, NJ, Nov. 1979.

[6] H. J. Seigel, R. J. McMillen, and P. T. Muller, Jr., "A survey of interconnection methods for reconfigurable parallel processing systems," in *AFIPS Conf. Proc. 1979 NCC*, June 1979, pp. 529–542.

[7] R. S. Wilkov, "Analysis and design of reliable computer networks," *IEEE Trans. Commun.*, vol. COM-20, pp. 660–678, June 1972.

[8] H. Sullivan and T. R. Bashkow, "A large scale, homogeneous fully distributed, parallel machine: I," in *Proc. 4th Symp. on Comput. Arch.*, Apr. 1977, pp. 105–117.

[9] K. J. Thurber and H. A. Freeman, "Local computer network architectures," in *Proc. COMPCON 1979 Spring*, Feb. 1979, pp. 258–261.

[10] M. T. Liu, "Distributed loop computer networks," in *Advances in Computers*, vol. 17. New York: Academic, 1978, pp. 163–221.

[11] A. Frank *et al.*, "Some architectural and system implications of local computer networks," in *Proc. COMPCON 1979 Spring*, Feb. 1979, pp. 272–276.

[12] P. H. Enslow, Jr., *Multiprocessor and Parallel Processing*. New York: Wiley, 1974.

[13] H. J. Jafari, J. Spragins, and T. Lewis, "A new modular loop architecture for distributed computer systems," in *Trends and Applications 78: Distributed Processing*, 1978, pp. 72–77.

[14] H. F. Jordan, "A special purpose architecture for finite element analysis," ICASE Rep. 78-9, 1978.

[15] G. H. Barnes *et al.*, "The Illiac IV computer," *IEEE Trans. Comput.*, vol. C-17, pp. 746–757, Aug. 1968.

Reprinted from *IEEE Transactions on Computers*, Volume C-33, Number 1,
April 1984, pages 323-333. Copyright © 1984 by The Institute of Electrical
and Electronics Engineers, Inc.

Generalized Hypercube and Hyperbus Structures for a Computer Network

LAXMI N. BHUYAN, MEMBER, IEEE, AND DHARMA P. AGRAWAL, SENIOR MEMBER, IEEE

Abstract — A general class of hypercube structures is presented
in this paper for interconnecting a network of microcomputers in
parallel and distributed environments. The interconnection is
based on a mixed radix number system and the technique results
in a variety of hypercube structures for a given number of processors N, depending on the desired diameter of the network. A
cost optimal realization is obtained through a process of discrete
optimization. The performance of such a structure is compared to
that of other existing hypercube structures such as Boolean n-cube
and nearest neighbor mesh computers.

The same mathematical framework is used in defining a corresponding bus oriented structure which requires only two I/O ports
per processor. These two types of structures are extremely suitable for local area computer networks.

Index Terms — Distributed computers, hyperbus structures,
hypercube structures, local area networks, multistage interconnection networks, parallel computers, topological optimization.

I. INTRODUCTION

SEVERAL structures have been proposed in the literature
for interconnecting a large network of computers in
parallel and distributed environments [2]–[12]. In this paper,
we present a generalized hypercube structure and reveal
some interesting properties of hypercubes. An interconnection structure in general should have a low number of
links per node (degree of a node), a small internode distance
(diameter), and a large number of alternate paths between a
pair of nodes for fault tolerance. The distance between any
two nodes is defined as the number of links traversed by a
message, initiated from one node and sent to another via
intermediate nodes. In a network of N nodes, the diameter is
defined as $D = \max\{d_{ij} \mid 1 \leq i, j \leq N\}$, where $d_{ij} =$
distance between nodes i and j along the shortest path. Designing a network with a low message traffic density and
good modularity is also desirable.

The Boolean n-cube computer [7] is an interconnection of
$N = 2^n$ processors which may be thought of as placed at the
corners of an n-dimensional cube with each edge of the cube
having two processors. The degree of a node and the diameter
of this type of structure are equal to $n = \log_2 N$. A loop
structure with additional links is imbedded in this structure,

Manuscript received March 24, 1983; revised October 12, 1983. A preliminary version of this paper was presented at the 9th Annual International
Symposium on Computer Architecture, April 1982.

L. N. Bhuyan is with the Department of Electrical and Computer Engineering, University of Southwestern Louisiana, Lafayette, LA 70504.

D. P. Agrawal is with the Computer Systems Laboratory, Department of
Electrical and Computer Engineering, North Carolina State University,
P. O. Box 7911, Raleigh, NC 27650.

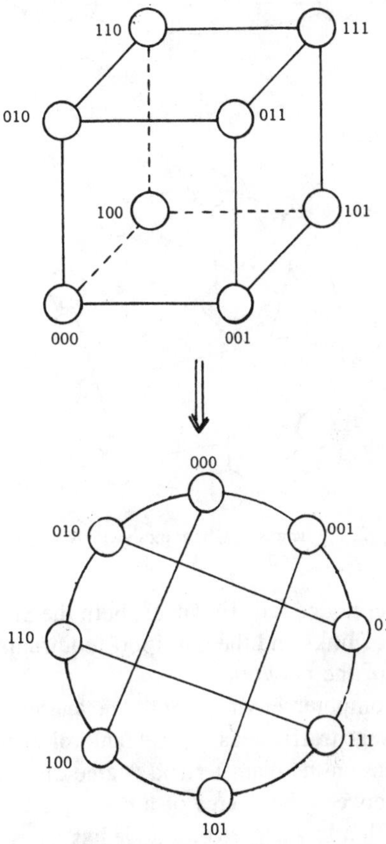

Fig. 1. A Boolean n-cube computer with $N = 8$.

and for $N = 8$, this is illustrated in Fig. 1. When the total
number of nodes N equals W^D, W and D both being integers,
the nodes can be arranged as a D-dimensional hypercube with
W nodes in each dimension. If a node is connected to its two
nearest neighbors in each dimension, a nearest neighbor
mesh hypercube is obtained. The degree of a node in such a
structure is $2D$ and the diameter is $WD/2$ for $W > 2$ [8].
There is also a loop structure associated with a nearest neighbor mesh as shown in Fig. 2 for a two-dimensional mesh with
9 nodes. We can also deduce that a bidirectional single loop
structure [3] is equivalent to a nearest neighbor connection
with dimension $D = 1$. This structure has a minimum number of links and a diameter of $N/2$. Any two nonadjacent
faulty nodes will disconnect the loop. With the addition of an
extra link to the loop structure the diameter is reduced to
$0(\sqrt{N})$ [4]. On the other hand, a completely connected structure has $(N - 1)$ links per node with a distance of one
between any two nodes. Any two nodes remain connected

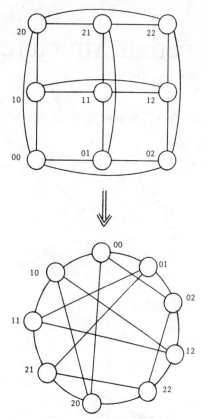

Fig. 2. A nearest neighbor mesh with $N = 3^2$.

generalized hypercube (GHC) and generalized hyperbus (GHB) structures. They possess the following characteristics:

1) The interconnection supports any number of nodes N. This is in contrast with the existing hypercube structures, where $N = W^D$ for some integer values of W and D.

2) The design is based on the allowable diameter of the network. If the diameter can be increased, a structure with a lower degree of a node can be obtained.

3) These structures are highly fault tolerant, they possess a small average message distance and a low traffic density.

4) The structures presented here are very general in nature. Single loop, Boolean n-cube, nearest neighbor mesh hypercube and fully connected systems can be considered as a part of this generalized structure.

5) The GHB structures have only two links per node, and hence require only two I/O ports per processor.

The paper is organized as follows. Section II describes a useful mixed radix number system used in [14], [15], the topology, the properties, and the routing and broadcasting algorithms of the GHC structures. Section III analyzes the GHC structures with respect to a cost parameter defined by (degree of a node) * (diameter). The section also outlines the procedure for obtaining an optimal GHC (OGHC) structure. Section IV considers the parameters like average distance, cost, traffic density, and fault tolerance, etc. to compare the performance of an OGHC to other hypercube structures. Section V obtains the equivalent m-cube multistage interconnection networks (MIN's) of the GHC structures. Section VI presents the GHB structures and derives the expressions for internode distances.

II. THE GENERALIZED HYPERCUBE (GHC) STRUCTURE

A. A Mixed Radix Number System

Let N be the total number of processors and be represented as a product of m_i's, $m_i > 1$ for $1 \leq i \leq r$.

$$N = m_r * m_{r-1} * \cdots * m_1.$$

Then, each processor X between 0 to $N - 1$ can be expressed as an r-tuple $(x_r x_{r-1} \cdots x_1)$ for $0 \leq x_i \leq (m_i - 1)$. Associated with each x_i is a weight w_i, such that $\sum_{i=1}^{r} x_i w_i = X$ and $w_i = \prod_{j=1}^{i-1} m_j = m_{i-1} * m_{i-2} * \cdots * m_1$ for all $1 \leq i \leq r$. Hence, $w_1 = 1$ always.

Example 1:

$$\text{Let} \quad N = 24 = 4 * 3 * 2.$$

$$m_1 = 2, \quad m_2 = 3, \quad m_3 = 4.$$

$$w_1 = 1, \quad w_2 = 2, \quad w_3 = 6.$$

Then, $X = (x_3 x_2 x_1)$, $0 \leq x_1 \leq 1$, $0 \leq x_2 \leq 2$, $0 \leq x_3 \leq 3$ for any X in the range 0–23. $0_{10} = (000)$, $23_{10} = (321)$ in this mixed radix system.

B. Description of the GHC Structure

Each processor $X = (x_r x_{r-1} \cdots x_{i+1} x_i x_{i-1} \cdots x_1)$ will be connected to processors $(x_r x_{r-1} \cdots x_{i+1} x_i' x_{i-1} \cdots x_1)$ for all $1 \leq i \leq r$, where x_i' takes all integer values between 0 to $(m_i - 1)$ except x_i itself. This type of interconnection will be

even if all other nodes fail. However, both the high cost of a large number of links and the multiport requirement of $0(N)$ limit the size of the network.

In a multicomputer environment, the average internode distance, message traffic density, and fault tolerance are very much dependent on the diameter and degree of a node. There is a tradeoff between the degree of a node and the diameter. A structure with a low degree of a node has a large diameter and a structure that has a low diameter usually possesses a large degree of a node. A single loop structure and a completely connected structure as described above represent the two extremes. The (diameter * degree of a node) is therefore a good criterion to measure the performance of a structure. The hypercube structures seem to offer a reasonable characteristic. One commonly noted disadvantage of the Boolean n-cube computer is that the number of I/O ports is $\log_2 N$. However, keeping in mind the simple routing, the low diameter, and the large ($\log_2 N$) number of disjoint paths, this topology seems extremely suitable for a local computer network. Moreover, with current advances in technology, the number of I/O ports per processor up to 1000 has become quite feasible [13]. Recently, a few structures have been proposed with better graph theoretic properties [9]–[12]. Their fault tolerance is basically limited by the fixed number of I/O ports per node. What we present here is a complete generalization of the hypercube and some interesting analyses of hypercube structures, where good fault tolerance is guaranteed. The present study should therefore be viewed in that context.

This paper presents two new hypercube structures, called

called the generalized hypercube (GHC) throughout this paper. In general, the total number of links (L) is greater than the total number of processors (N) in this GHC topology.

Example 2: For $N = 24$, any processor can be expressed in the mixed radix system between (000) and (321). Processor (000) is connected to processors (001), (010), (020), (100), (200), and (300). Processor (001) is connected to processors (000), (011), (021), (101), (201), and (301) and so on as shown in Fig. 3. For the sake of clarity, connection is not completed in the figure for the nodes shown by dotted lines. Imbedded in this structure is a loop structure arranged as (000) → (001) → (011) → (021) → (121) → (221) → (321) → (311) → (301) → (300) → (310) → (320) → (220) → (120) → (020) → (010) → (110) → (210) → (200) → (201) → (211) → (111) → (101) → (100) → (000) with 4 extra links per node.

The GHC structure consists of r-dimensions with m_i number of nodes in the ith dimension. A node in a particular axis is connected to all other nodes in the same axis. Accordingly, we make the following observations.

1) From any particular node $X = (x_r x_{r-1} \cdots x_{i+1} x_i x_{i-1} \cdots x_1)$, there are $(m_i - 1)$ number of links in the ith direction. Hence, for all i, $1 \leq i \leq r$, the total number of links per node or the degree of a node $\ell = \sum_{i=1}^{r} (m_i - 1)$.

2) Each link is connected to two processors. Hence, the total number of links in GHC structure $L = N/2 \cdot \sum_{i=1}^{r}(m_i - 1)$.

3) d_{xy} = distance between any two nodes x and y in terms of number of hops = Hamming distance between the nodes. Hamming distance between two nodes differing in their addresses in the ith coordinate only is unity and the total Hamming distance is the sum of the number of coordinates in which the addresses differ.

4) The addresses can differ at maximum in all the r-coordinates. Thus, the diameter of the structure = r.

C. Routing Procedure

A message is formatted at the source node with source address, destination address and a few tag bits. The source and destination addresses are specified in the binary equivalent of the mixed radix numbers. The ith digit of the address can take a maximum value of $(m_i - 1)$, and hence can be expressed in $\lceil \log_2 m_i \rceil$ binary bits, where $\lceil x \rceil$ is the smallest integer greater than or equal to x. As a result, any processor $0 \leq X \leq N - 1$ can be specified completely in $\sum_{i=1}^{r} \lceil \log_2 m_i \rceil$ binary bits. At each node, the destination address is compared to its own address, contained in a register. If the addresses match, the node accepts the message. If they do not, a digit by digit comparison takes place and the node transmits the message along the direction of the first differing digit. The process continues until the destination is reached. However, at each node the message goes through a certain delay, waiting for the particular link to be free.

Based on the above routing procedure, we can deduce the following.

1) If two nodes differ in their address by d coordinates (dimensions), then d is the shortest distance between these two nodes. A message can start from the source node along

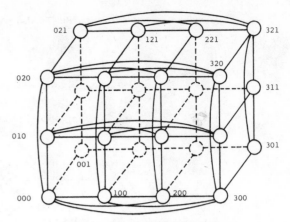

Fig. 3. A 4 * 3 * 2 GHC-structure.

any one of these d coordinates and then follow the above routing procedure to reach the destination node. These paths, illustrated in Fig. 4(a), are disjoint and cover a distance d each. This observation is similar to the characteristics of a Boolean n-cube computer [16].

2) From any node $(x_r x_{r-1} \cdots x_i \cdots x_2 x_1)$, the message can go to an intermediate neighboring node and travel to the corresponding neighboring node of the destination $(y_r y_{r-1} \cdots y_i \cdots y_2 y_1)$. In the previous case, a message could start along a particular node in the ith coordinate only if the source and destination addresses differed in their ith coordinate. Note in Fig. 4(b), that a message can start along any of the nodes in the ith coordinate for $1 \leq i \leq r$ without depending on whether or not the source and destination addresses mismatch in their ith coordinate. Then the intermediate nodes encountered on a single path have their ith coordinate fixed at a particular digit. The paths are therefore disjoint. A suitable reference to the path generation process is [10]. Hence, there are ℓ alternate paths between any two nodes of the GHC structure where "ℓ" is the degree of a node.

3) For any number of faults less than "ℓ" in the system, the worst case distance between two connected nodes is $r + 1$. This is also clear from Fig. 4(b).

Alternate Routing Procedures: As mentioned above, there are d disjoint paths of equal length d between any two nodes separated by Hamming distance d. If the channels in one path are busy or faulty, a message can be routed in a different path with the same distance d. This is possible if the status of every link is updated at each node. In that case, the source node can route the message along an alternate path thus saving the delay in transmission. This process requires additional hardware and software and the path computation may be time consuming. If the link is busy another simple method is to route the message along the next digit of the first differing digit. For example, with $N = 24$, while routing from (001) to (221), instead of routing through (021) first, the message can be routed to (201) and then to (221), if the previous channel is busy.

D. Broadcasting

Any processor can send a message to all other processors in just r steps by using the following algorithms.

The structure is an r-dimensional hypercube with $(m_i - 1)$

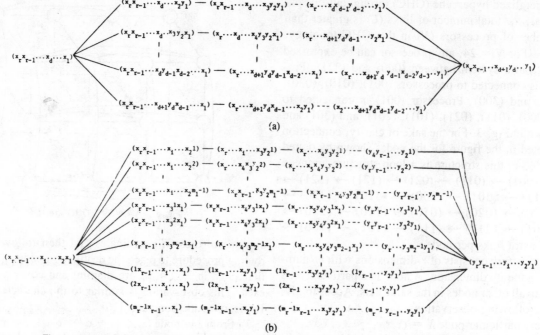

Fig. 4. (a) "d" disjoint paths of length "d" each between nodes at Hamming distance "d." (b) "ℓ" alternate paths between any source and destination.

numbers of links in the ith dimension. Each link in the machine is numbered, with the links in the ith dimension being numbered "i" for all $1 \leq i \leq r$. Let us assume node A $(00 \cdots 0)$ wishes to broadcast a message. To do so, it sends messages with a weight "i" in the links along the ith dimension. In the second step, all the receiving nodes reduce the weight by one and transmit the messages along all those dimensions whose numbers do not exceed the reduced weight. The process continues for r steps until all the nodes have received the message. It may be noted that r is the lower bound for the minimum number of steps required for broadcasting in a graph with a diameter of r.

Example 3: The structure for $N = 24$ is shown in Fig. 3. In the first step, nodes (001) will receive the message with a weight "1," nodes (010) and (020) will receive the message with weight "2," and nodes (100), (200), (300) will receive the message with weight "3." In the next step, all these nodes will reduce their weights by one and transmit the messages as shown below.

(001) → no transmission
(010) and (020) → (011) and (021) respectively with weight "1"
(100), (200) and (300) → (101), (201) and (301) respectively with weight "1," and
(110), (120), (210), (220), (310) and (320) with weight "2."

In the third and final step,

(110) → (111), (120) → (121), (210) → (211), (220) → (221), (310) → (311), (320) → (321) with weight "1."

The complete broadcasting is achieved in three steps, as shown in Fig. 5.

III. ANALYSIS OF GHC STRUCTURES

A. Structure Optimization

When an interconnection of N processors is desired with the constraint that the maximum distance between any two nodes along the shortest path or the diameter does not exceed r, N has to be expressed as a product of r quantities as $N = m_r * m_{r-1} * \cdots * m_1$. The number of links per node $= \sum_{i=1}^{r} (m_i - 1)$. In fact, there are several ways to factor N into r components. For example, 16 can be factored as $8 * 2$ or $4 * 4$. An optimized structure with diameter r is obtained when the total number of links in the structure is at the minimum.

Lemma 1: When $\sqrt[r]{N}$ is an integer, a cost optimal GHC with diameter "r" is obtained if $m_i = \sqrt[r]{N}$ for all $1 \leq i \leq r$.

Proof: Since the number of links per node "ℓ" is the same for all the nodes, a minimization of "ℓ" with respect to m_i's gives the desired result

$$m_1 = \frac{N}{m_r m_{r-1} \cdots m_2}$$

$$\ell = \sum_{i=2}^{r} (m_i - 1) + \left(\frac{N}{m_r m_{r-1} \cdots m_2} - 1 \right)$$

$$\frac{\partial \ell}{\partial m_r} = \frac{\partial \ell}{\partial m_{r-1}} = \frac{\partial \ell}{\partial m_2} = 0.$$

This results in $m_r = m_{r-1} = \cdots = m_2 = m_1 = \sqrt[r]{N}$. Q.E.D.

Since $\sqrt[r]{N}$ may not be an integer, all m_i's should lie as close to $\sqrt[r]{N}$ as possible. When $N = m^r$, the mathematics involved is simply a higher radix system, each x_i lying between 0 and $(m - 1)$ for all $1 \leq i \leq r$.

There is another aspect of the GHC structures. The number of links per node is different for different values of diameter

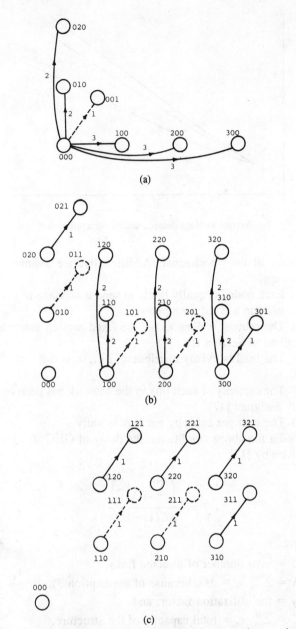

Fig. 5. (a) Broadcasting at the first step, (b) broadcasting at the second step, (c) broadcasting at the third step.

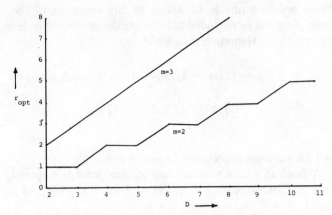

Fig. 6. r_{opt} for number of processors $= m^D$.

r. Again, for example, 16 can be expressed as $4 * 4$, $4 * 2 * 2$, $2 * 2 * 2 * 2$ with diameters 2, 3, and 4, respectively. As mentioned earlier, a structure with a lower degree of a node usually has a higher diameter. If a cost factor ξ is defined as the product of the diameter and the links per node, a discrete optimization of $r \sum_{i=1}^{r} (m_i - 1)$ with respect to r and subject to the constraint that $\prod_{i=1}^{r} m_i = N$ and integer values of m_i's, yields an optimized structure. As an example, the optimal values of r for processors equal to 2^D and 3^D, are plotted in Fig. 6. Because of the discrete optimization involved, it was not possible to derive a closed form solution for r_{opt}.

Conjecture 1: For N, a power of two, an absolute cost optimal GHC (OGHC) is obtained when $r = \lfloor \log_4 N \rfloor$, where $\lfloor x \rfloor$ is the largest integer smaller than or equal to x.

This deduction follows from Fig. 6. Up to $N = 2^3$, $r_{opt} = 1$ indicates a fully connected system. For $N = 2^4$, $r_{opt} = 2$

results in a two-dimensional GHC with 4 nodes in each dimension. For $N = 2^5$, there are 4 nodes in one dimension and 8 nodes in the other. For $N = 2^6$, $r_{opt} = 3$ and so on. Also, for N and m powers of two a GHC with m nodes in each dimension has a cost of $(m - 1) \log_m^2 N$ which has a local minimum at $m = 4$.

For N, a power of four, the degree of a node of an OGHC is $3 \log_4 N = 1.5 \log_2 N$. The diameter is $\log_4 N = 0.5 \log_2 N$. Hence, the cost $= 0.75 (\log_2^2 N)$. The cost of other structures [9]–[12] are proportional to $(\log_2 N)$ instead of $(\log_2^2 N)$. However, they do not possess as good a fault tolerance as the GHC structures do. For N, a power of 5, the cost is $0.742 \log_2^2 N$ when $m = 5$. However, only values of N which are powers of two are considered in conjecture 1 for later use in Section IV.

B. Internode Distance and Queueing Delay

Distance between any processor $X = (x_r x_{r-1} \cdots x_{i+1} x_i x_{i-1} \cdots x_2 x_1)$ and $X' = (x_r x_{r-1} \cdots x_{i+1} x_i', x_{i-1} \cdots x_2 x_1)$, $x_i' \in \{0, 1, 2, \cdots, m_i - 1\}$ and $x_i' \neq x_i$, is unity. In general, the distance between any two processors is equal to the Hamming distance between them; that is, in how many coordinates their addresses differ. The average internode distance plays a key role in determining the queueing delay in a computer network. For calculating the number of nodes at different distances, the node $(00 \cdots 0)$ can be assumed to be the source node without any loss in generality. There are $(m_i - 1)$ number of nodes which differ from the source node only in the ith dimension. Hence, $N_1 = $ total number of nodes differing by distance 1

$$= \sum_{i=1}^{r} (m_i - 1).$$

The nodes which have distance 2 from the source node must differ in their addresses by two coordinates i and j. In these two dimensions, $(m_i - 1)(m_j - 1)$ different combinations can occur. Again, these two dimensions are selected out of r such dimensions existing in the address space. Hence, the total number of nodes differing by the shortest distance 2,

$$N_2 = \sum (m_i - 1)(m_j - 1)$$

$$i, j \in \{1, 2, \cdots, r\} \quad \text{and} \quad i \neq j.$$

There are $\binom{r}{2}$ terms to be added in this summation. The same ideas can be extended to calculate the number of nodes differing by a Hamming distance d,

$$N_d = \sum (m_i - 1)(m_j - 1)(m_k - 1)\cdots d \quad \text{such terms}$$

$$i, j, k \cdots \ \varepsilon \ \{1, 2, \cdots, r\}$$

$$i \neq j \neq k \neq \cdots$$

and the summation includes $\binom{r}{d}$ such items.

A Boolean n-cube structure can be considered as a special case of GHC structures, where $m_i = 2$ for $1 \leqslant i \leqslant r$. As a result, $N = 2^r$ and $r = \log_2 N = n$.

$$\prod (m_i - 1) = 1 \quad \text{and} \quad N_d = \binom{n}{d} = \frac{n!}{d!(n-d)!}.$$

Once the number of nodes at a distance d is known, the average message distance is $\bar{d} = (\sum_{d=1}^{r} dN_d)/(N - 1)$.

To get an idea how the average message distance varies, let us consider the case when $N = m^r$. Also, as mentioned earlier, m_i's should be as close as possible to $\sqrt[r]{N}$ for an optimized structure with diameter r, and hence this should give approximate results for any N that can be factored into r-components.

When all m_i's are equal to m, the number of nodes at a distance d, $N_d = \binom{r}{d}(m-1)^d$, and

$$\bar{d} = \left[\sum_{d=1}^{r} d\binom{r}{d}(m-1)^d\right]/(N - 1)$$

$$= (m - 1)\left[\sum_{d=0}^{r} \binom{r}{d}\frac{\partial(m-1)^d}{\partial(m-1)}\right]/(N - 1)$$

$$= (m - 1)\frac{\partial}{\partial(m-1)}\left[\sum_{d=0}^{r} \binom{r}{d}(m-1)^d\right]/(N - 1)$$

$$= \left[(m - 1)\frac{\partial}{\partial(m-1)}(m - 1 + 1)^r\right]/(N - 1)$$

$$= r \cdot (m - 1) \cdot m^{r-1}/(N - 1), \quad m = \sqrt[r]{N}.$$

Fig. 7 shows the variation of average message distance $(\bar{d})$ with respect to r for a few values of m. When $m = 2$, it is simply a Boolean n-cube structure. For an OGHC, $\bar{d} \cong 0.375 \log_2 N$.

The average message traffic density in a link of GHC structures is defined as

$$\rho = \frac{\text{Average message distance} * \text{number of nodes}}{\text{total number of links}}$$

$$= \frac{\bar{d}N}{\frac{N}{2}\sum_{i=1}^{r}(m_i - 1)} = \frac{2\bar{d}}{\sum_{i=1}^{r}(m_i - 1)}.$$

For $N = m^r$, $\rho = \dfrac{2\bar{d}}{r(m - 1)} = 0.5$ for an OGHC structure.

The GHC structures can be modeled as a communication net with the ith channel represented as an $M/M/1$ system with Poisson arrivals at a rate λ_i and exponential service time of mean $1/\mu c_i$ [17]. μ = average service rate and c_i =

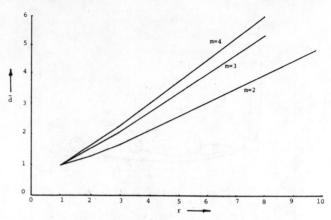

Fig. 7. Average message distance in GHC-structure with $N = m^r$.

capacity of the ith channel. Additionally, we assume the following.

1) Each node is equally likely to send a message to every other node in a fixed time period.

2) The routing is done as per the fixed routing algorithm described in Section II.

3) The load is evenly distributed, i.e., λ_i is the same for all i.

4) The capacity of each link in the network has been optimally assigned [17].

5) The cost per capacity per link is unity.

Under the above conditions, the delay of GHC structures is given by [17]

$$T = \frac{\bar{d}\left(\sum_{i=1}^{M} \sqrt{\frac{\lambda_i}{\lambda}}\right)^2}{\mu C(1 - \bar{d}\gamma)}$$

where

M = total number of directed links,

$\lambda = \sum_{i=1}^{M} \lambda_i = M\lambda_i$ because of assumption 3),

γ = the utilization factor, and

$C = \sum_{i=1}^{M} c_i$ = total capacity of the structure.

With N nodes and ℓ bidirectional links per node,

$$M = \left(\frac{N}{2}\right) \cdot 2\ell.$$

Hence,

$$T = \frac{\bar{d}\left(\frac{N}{2}\right) \cdot 2\ell}{\mu C(1 - \bar{d}\gamma)}.$$

With constants μ, C, and N, the above delay can be normalized as

$$T' = \frac{\bar{d}2\ell}{(1 - \bar{d}\gamma)}.$$

The delay increases exponentially with increased utilization and saturates at a particular load, given by $\gamma_{sat} = 1/\bar{d}$. In a fully connected system, $\gamma_{sat} = 1$ since $\bar{d} = 1$, and hence the computer network performs very well under heavy load con-

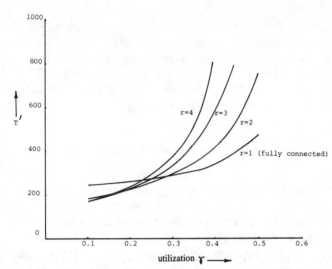

Fig. 8. Normalized queueing delay in GHC-structures with $N = 16$.

TABLE I
CHARACTERISTICS OF GHC STRUCTURES

N	Factors	Diameter r	Links per node ℓ	Cost Factor ξ	Average Message Distance $\bar{d}$	γ_{sat}
	$2*2*2*2$	4	4	16	2.13	0.47
	$4*2*2$	3	5	15	1.87	0.535
16	$4*4$	2	6	12	1.6	0.625
	16 (fully connected)	1	15	15	1	1
	$3*2*2*2$	4	5	20	2.26	0.442
	$4*3*2$	3	6	18	2.0	0.5
24	$6*4$	2	8	16	1.65	0.606
	24 (fully connected)	1	23	23	1	1

ditions. In general, the performance of the GHC structures will lie between a loop structure and a fully connected net. The average delay in different GHC structures for $N = 16$ is plotted in Fig. 8. As expected, the optimized structure with $N = 4*4$, performs well both in light load and heavy load conditions. Table I presents a summary of some relevant information for different GHC structures with $N = 16$ and 24.

IV. PERFORMANCE OF GHC STRUCTURES

In this section, the performance of the GHC structures will be compared to that of other hypercube structures. The number of nodes N will be assumed to be a power of two and the GHC considered here is the OGHC as obtained in Section III. The loop structure is a nearest neighbor mesh in one dimension, whereas a completely connected structure is a one-dimensional GHC. The Boolean n-cube computer, although it is a part of the GH and the nearest neighbor mesh, is a well known topology and will therefore be considered separately. The nearest neighbor mesh considered here is an optimal structure as described below.

Nearest Neighbor Mesh Hypercube Structures: If N can be expressed as a product of r-terms, a generalized nearest neighbor mesh hypercube is obtained when a node $(x_r x_{r-1} \cdots x_{i+1} x_i x_{i-1} \cdots x_2 x_1)$ is connected to $[x_r x_{r-1} \cdots x_{i+1}(x_i + 1) \bmod m_i x_{i-1} \cdots x_2 x_1]$ and $[x_r x_{r-1} \cdots x_{i+1}(x_i - 1) \bmod m_i x_{i-1} \cdots x_2 x_1]$ for all $1 \le i \le r$. Such a structure for $N = 4*3*2$ is shown in Fig. 9. The degree of a node is $2r$ when all the factors are greater than two. The diameter of such a structure is $\sum_{i=1}^{r} \lfloor m_i/2 \rfloor$. For a fixed value of N, there can be several ways to factor N into r components. The degree of a node being fixed at $2r$, an optimal structure is obtained when $\sum_{i=1}^{r} \lfloor m_i/2 \rfloor$ is minimum. For high values of m_i, the floor function can be neglected. The following lemma results.

Lemma 2: An optimal nearest neighbor mesh with some fixed r dimensions is obtained when $m_i \cong \sqrt[r]{N}$.

Again, for a fixed value of N, there can be several ways to design a nearest neighbor mesh. A discrete optimization of the product of the degree of a node and the diameter, for various values of r, will give rise to an optimal design. The

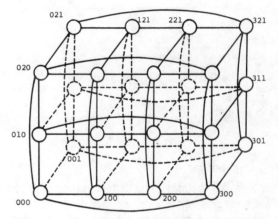

Fig. 9. A generalized nearest neighbor mesh hypercube with $N = 4*3*2$.

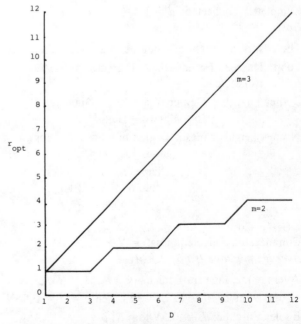

Fig. 10. r_{opt} for nearest neighbor mesh hypercube with $N = m^D$.

values of r_{opt} for N, powers of 2 and 3 are plotted in Fig. 10. For N, a power of two, an optimal structure is obtained when there are 8 nodes in each dimension, as can be seen from the computation.

Conjecture 2: For N, a power of two, an optimal nearest neighbor mesh hypercube is obtained when $r = \lceil \log_8 N \rceil$. Throughout this section, such an optimal structure (8-cube) will be considered for performance comparison.

Average Message Distance ($\bar{d}$):

Loop:
$$\bar{d} = \frac{2\left(1 + 2 + 3 + \cdots + \frac{N-1}{2}\right)}{N-1}$$

$$= \frac{1}{4}(N + 1) \quad \text{for} \quad N \quad \text{odd}$$

$$= \frac{2\left(1 + 2 + 3 + \cdots + \frac{N-2}{2}\right) + \frac{N}{2}}{N-1}$$

$$= \frac{1}{4} \frac{N(N-2)}{N-1} \quad \text{for} \quad N \quad \text{even}$$

$$\cong 0.25\, N \qquad \text{for any} \quad N.$$

Boolean n-cube:
$$\bar{d} = \sum \binom{n}{d} d = \frac{n}{2} \cdot \frac{N}{N-1}$$

$$\cong 0.5 \log_2 N.$$

Nearest neighbor mesh:

With $N = W^r$, the maximum distance along each direction is $W/2$. The average distance along each dimension is $0.25\,W$ as in the case of a loop. For r dimensions, $\bar{d} \cong 0.25\,rW$. With an optimal design, $W = 8$ and $\bar{d} = 0.25 \times \log_8 N \times 8 = 0.667 \log_2 N$.

OGHC: $\bar{d} = 0.375 \log_2 N$.
Completely connected: $\bar{d} = 1$.
Cost:

The cost of a structure = degree of a node * diameter

Loop: Degree of a node = 2, Diameter = $0.5N$.
      Hence, cost = N.

Boolean n-cube: Degree of a node = Diameter = $\log_2 N$, cost = $\log_2^2 N$.

Nearest neighbor mesh: Degree of a node = $2 \log_8 N = 0.667 \log_2 N$
      Diameter = $r \cdot (W/2)$ = $4 \log_8 N = 1.333 \log_2 N$
      Cost = $0.889 \log_2^2 N$.

OGHC: Cost = $0.75 \log_2^2 N$.
Completely connected: Cost = $N - 1$.
Average message traffic density:

Average message traffic density $\rho = (\bar{d} \times N)/L$
Loop: Number of links $L = N$; hence $\rho = \bar{d} = 0.25N$
Boolean n-cube: $L = 0.5N \log_2 N$; $\rho = \bar{d}/0.5 \log_2 N = 1$
Nearest neighbor mesh: $L = r \cdot N = 0.334N \log_2 N$
      $\rho = \bar{d}/0.334 \log_2 N = 2$.

OGHC: $\rho = 0.5$.

Fault Tolerance: The fault tolerance of a structure is the connectivity or the number of node disjoint paths between any two nodes. The connectivity for a loop is 2; for a Boolean n-cube, it is $\log_2 N$; for a nearest neighbor mesh it is $2r$ [18], i.e., $0.667 \log_2 N$ here; for an OGHC it is $1.5 \log_2 N$ and for a completely connected structure it is $(N - 1)$.

V. m-CUBE INTERCONNECTION NETWORKS

An $N \times N$ multistage interconnection network (MIN) [19]–[21] is capable of connecting N number of processing elements (PE's) to N number of memory modules (MM's). Various MIN's described in the literature [19] employ 2-input 2-output switching elements (SE's). Here, we illustrate the use of GHC structures in designing $N \times N$ MIN's implemented with $m \times m$ SE's. We limit our discussions to only values of N and m which are powers of two.

An m-cube multicomputer is a GHC structure with m number of nodes in each dimension. When N is a power of m, there are m nodes in each of $r = \log_m N$ dimensions of the hypercube. When N is not a power of m, there will be $r - 1 = \lfloor \log_m N \rfloor$ dimensions with m nodes each and one dimension with $N/_m r - 1$ number of nodes. All the nodes in a dimension are connected to each other by dedicated links. A completely connected multicomputer corresponds to a crossbar [22] in a circuit switched multiprocessor. When an m-cube GHC is unfolded, an m-cube MIN results. By unfolding we mean that the ith stage of the MIN is connected as per the ith dimension of the GHC structure for $1 \leq i \leq r$. An m-cube MIN will consist of $\log_m N$ stages of N/m number of $m \times m$ crossbar modules at each stage when N is a power of m. When N is not a power of m, there will be $\lfloor \log_m N \rfloor$ stages of $m \times m$ crossbar modules followed by $N/_m r - 1 \times N/_m r - 1$ crossbar modules at the last stage. This also results by unfolding an m-cube GHC. The construction of a 32×32 4-cube MIN is illustrated in Fig. 11. When a Boolean n-cube structure with $m = 2$ is unfolded, a generalized cube interconnection network [20] results. Some recent studies [15], [23], [24] have shown that a 4-cube MIN gives optimal performance in terms of bandwidth and cost.

VI. GENERALIZED HYPERBUS (GHB) STRUCTURES

In the preceding section, N specifies the number of processors in the structure. If, however, it specifies the number of buses, a different configuration results. Then, each processor is connected to two adjoining buses, running in different dimensions of the generalized hypercube. Such a structure for $N = 3 * 2$ is shown in Fig. 12. These types of structures will be referred to as generalized hyperbus (GHB) structures. The number of processors P in a GHB structure will be greater than the number of buses N. The distance between two processors is specified by the number of buses a message has to travel from one processor to the other. Since GHB structures have fewer links than nodes, these structures will give rise to a high message traffic density in a bus, and hence will saturate rapidly. However, having only two I/O

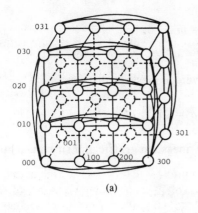

(a)

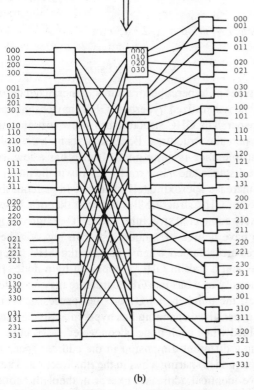

(b)

Fig. 11. (a) A 4 * 3 * 2 GHC structure, (b) a 32 × 32 4-cube network.

ports per processor, the cost is very small as compared to the GHC structures.

The GHB structure consists of N buses with $N = m_r * m_{r-1} * \cdots * m_i * \cdots * m_2 * m_1$. A bus in the GHB structure is denoted by an r-tuple $(x_r x_{r-1} \cdots x_i \cdots x_2 x_1)$ for $0 \leq x_i \leq m_i - 1$ for $1 \leq i \leq r$. A processor will be denoted $(x_r x_{r-1} \cdots x_{i+1} [y_i z_i] x_{i-1} \cdots x_1)$, i.e., with x_i replaced by a 2-tuple $[y_i z_i]$ for $y_i, z_i \varepsilon \{0, 1, \cdots (m_i - 1)\}$. This means that the processor is connected to buses $(x_r x_{r-1} \cdots x_{i+1} y_i x_{i-1} \cdots x_1)$ and $(x_r x_r - 1 \cdots x_{i+1} z_i x_{i-1} \cdots x_1)$. $y_i, z_i \varepsilon \{0, 1, \cdots, (m_i - 1)\}$ and the ith position can vary between 1 and r. The Hamming distance between a pair $[y_i z_i]$ and some v_i is 0 if v_i is equal to y_i or z_i or $[y_i w_i]$ or $[w_i z_i]$ and equals 1, otherwise. Similarly, Hamming distance between x_i and v_i is 0 if $x_i = v_i$ and equals 1 if $x_i \neq v_i$. The actual distance between any two different processors = Hamming distance between them +1.

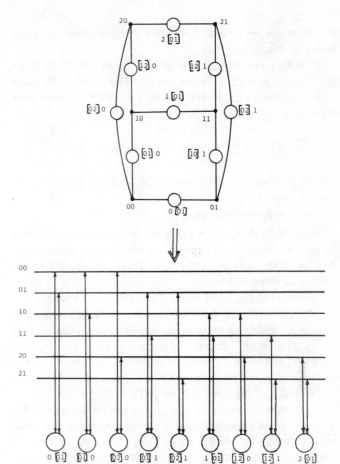

Fig. 12. A GHB structure with $N = 3 * 2$.

The GHB structures have the following features:
1) Each processor has only two I/O ports.
2) The number of processors connected to a bus is

$$p = \sum_{i=1}^{r} (m_i - 1).$$

3) Total number of processors in the system.

$$P = \frac{N}{2} \sum_{i=1}^{r} (m_i - \overset{\bullet}{1}).$$

4) Two processors can differ in their addresses in all the r-coordinates. Thus, the diameter of the structure = $r + 1$.
5) There are p bus disjoint paths between any two buses. A bus disjoint path also corresponds to a node disjoint path.
6) There are d disjoint paths of equal distance d between any two buses with a Hamming distance d.
7) A processor is disconnected if both the adjoining buses fail.

Internode Distance: Since the structure is symmetrical, let us consider $0^{r-1} [01]$ as the source node. 0^{r-1} means $000 \cdots$ up to $(r - 1)$ terms.

Nodes differing by unit distance:
1) When nodes have addresses $\{w0\}$ and $\{w1\}$, where w is a set of $(r - 1)$ terms $000 \cdots [0x_i] \cdots 0$ for all

$1 \leq x_i \leq (m_i - 1)$ and $2 \leq i \leq r$. The number of such nodes $= 2 \sum_{i=2}^{r} (m_i - 1)$

2) When the nodes are of the form $\{0^{r-1}[0x_1]\}$ or $\{0^{r-1}[1x_1]\}$, $x_1 \, \varepsilon \, \{2, 3, \cdots (m_1 - 1)\}$. The number of such nodes $= 2(m_1 - 2)$. Hence, the total number of nodes with distance 1

$$N_1 = 2 \sum_{i=2}^{r} (m_i - 1) + 2(m_1 - 2).$$

When $N = m^r$, $N_1 = 2(r - 1)(m - 1) + 2(m - 2) = 2rm - 2r - 2$.

Nodes differing by distance d:

When $N = m_r * m_{r-1} * \cdots * m_1$, it is extremely difficult to derive closed form expressions for N_d. Let us consider $N = m^r$ with $m_i = m$, $1 \leq i \leq r$. There are several possibilities as discussed below.

1) Nodes of the form $\{w[0x_1]\}$ and $\{w[1x_1]\}$, where w is a $r - 1$ tuple differing from 0^{r-1} in $(d - 1)$ dimensions. For each $[0x_1]$ and $[1x_1]$ in the least significant digit (lsd), there are $\binom{r-1}{d-1}(m - 1)^{d-1}$ number of nodes and there are $(m - 1)$ such $[0x]$ and $(m - 2)$ such $[1x]$ in the lsd. Hence, number of nodes $= (2m - 3)\binom{r-1}{d-1}(m - 1)^{d-1}$.

2) Nodes of the form $\{w0\}$ or $\{w1\}$.

(a) When w contains one $[0x_i]$ in the ith dimension for $2 \leq i \leq r$. As a result of $[0x_i]$ in the ith dimension, the node must differ in its address by $(d - 1)$ places out of $(r - 2)$ dimensions. There are $(r - 1)$ values i can take and there are $(m - 1)$ different values for x_i. Hence, the number of nodes $= 2(r - 1)\binom{r-2}{d-1}(m - 1)^{d-1}(m - 1)$.

(b) When w contains $[yz]$, $y, z \neq 0$ in the ith dimension. There are $\binom{m-1}{2}$ such elements possible in one dimension and for each $[yz]$ there are $\binom{r-2}{d-2}(m - 1)^{d-2}$. Again, $[yz]$ can occupy $(r - 1)$ dimensions except lsd and the total number of nodes $= 2 (r - 1)\binom{m-1}{2}\binom{r-2}{d-2}(m - 1)^{d-2}$.

3) Nodes of the form $\{wx\}$, $x \, \varepsilon \, \{2, 3, \cdots (m - 1)\}$.

(a) When w contains $[0y]$ in the ith dimension, for each x in the lsd, there can be $(m - 1)$ such $[0y]$ in a particular dimension. The number of nodes for each such $[0y] = \binom{r-2}{d-2}(m - 1)^{d-2}$. There are $(r - 1)$ dimensions and $(m - 1)$ number of $[0y]$ in each dimension; number of nodes for each $x = (r - 1)(m - 1)\binom{r-2}{d-2}(m - 1)^{d-2}$. Again, there can be $(m - 2)$ such x in the lsd. Hence, the total number of nodes $= (m - 2)(r - 1)(m - 1)\binom{r-2}{d-2}(m - 1)^{d-2}$.

(b) When w contains $[yz]$, $y, z \neq 0$ in the ith dimension, there can be $\binom{m-1}{2}$ such pairs in each dimension with each having $\binom{r-2}{d-3}(m - 1)^{d-3}$ nodes. For $(r - 1)$ such dimensions and $(m - 2)$ such x in the lsd, the total number of nodes $= (m - 2)(r - 1)\binom{m-1}{2}\binom{r-2}{d-3}(m - 1)^{d-3}$.

4) Nodes of the form $\{w[yz]\}$, $y, z \, \varepsilon \, \{2, 3, \cdots (m - 1)\}$. There are $\binom{m-2}{2}$ such pairs in the lsd. For each pair there will be $\binom{r-1}{d-1}(m - 1)^{d-2}$ nodes differing by distance d. Hence, the total number of nodes $= \binom{m-2}{2}\binom{r-1}{d-2}(m - 1)^{d-2}$.

The total number of nodes N_d differing by a distance d in the GHB structure will be the sum of all the nodes in the above four possibilities. The maximum possible distance $= r + 1$. The total number of nodes in GHB struc-

ture with $N = m^r$

$$P = 1/2 \cdot N \cdot r(m - 1).$$

Hence, the average message distance is

$$\bar{d} = 2\left(\sum_{d=1}^{r+1} dN_d\right) / N \cdot r \cdot (m - 1).$$

The average message traffic density in a bus in GHB structure is

$$\rho = \frac{\bar{d} \cdot \dfrac{N}{2} \cdot \sum_{i=1}^{r} (m_i - 1)}{N} = 1/2 \cdot \bar{d} \sum_{i=1}^{r} (m_i - 1)$$

and when $N = m^r$, $\rho = 1/2 \cdot \bar{d} \cdot r(m - 1)$.

VII. Conclusion

Two types of hypercube structures, generalized hypercube (GHC) and generalized hyperbus (GHB) have been presented in this paper. The GHC structure has a low cost compared to other hypercube structures. Because of its high connectivity, the fault tolerance is quite good. It also has a low average message distance and a low traffic density in the links. These factors increase approximately as log N. In general, the performance of GHC structure lies between that of a loop and a completely connected structure. In a GHC design it is impossible to have degree of a node less than $\log_2 N$. The GHB structures are obtained when a node in the GHC is replaced by a bus and a link in GHC is replaced by a node. Hence, traffic density on a bus in a GHB structure may be quite high. However, the number of I/O ports per processor is fixed at two. A generalized spanning bus hypercube [8] can similarly be obtained when each node is connected to 'r' buses, each spanning a different dimension in the address space and m_i number of nodes sharing a bus in the ith direction. The nodes will have identical addresses except in their ith coordinate.

The study provides clean design methodologies for a computer network based on the desired diameter. It also reveals many interesting properties of the hypercubes.

Acknowledgment

The authors are thankful to R. Finkel and W. Leland of the University of Wisconsin, Madison for their constructive criticisms and helpful comments.

References

[1] L. N. Bhuyan and D. P. Agrawal, "A general class of processor interconnection strategies," in *Proc. 9th Annu. Int. Symp. on Comput. Arch.*, Austin, TX, Apr. 1982, pp. 90–98.
[2] G. A. Anderson and E. D. Jenson, "Computer interconnection structures: Taxonomy, characteristics and examples," *ACM Comput. Surveys*, vol. 7, pp. 197–213, Dec. 1975.
[3] M. T. Liu, "Distributed loop computer networks," in *Advances in Computers, Vol. 17.* New York: Academic, 1978.
[4] B. W. Arden and H. Lee, "Analysis of chordal ring network," *IEEE Trans. Comput.*, vol. C-30, pp. 291–295, Apr. 1981.

[5] D. P. Agrawal, T. Y. Feng, and C. L. Wu, "A survey of communication processor systems," in *Proc. COMPSAC*, Chicago, IL, pp. 668–673, Nov. 1978.

[6] A. M. Despain and D. A. Patterson, "X-tree: A tree structured multiprocessor computer architecture," in *Proc. 5th Symp. on Comput. Arch.*, Apr. 1978, pp. 144–151.

[7] H. Sullivan and T. R. Bashkow, "A large scale, homogeneous, fully distributed parallel machine I," in *Proc. 4th Symp. Comput. Arch.*, Mar. 1977, pp. 105–117.

[8] L. D. Wittie, "Communication structures for large networks of microcomputers," *IEEE Trans. Comput.*, vol. C-30, pp. 264–273, Apr. 1981.

[9] F. P. Preparata and J. Vullemin, "The cube connected cycles: A versatile network for parallel computation," *Commun. Ass. Comput. Mach.*, vol. 24, pp. 300–309, May 1981.

[10] D. K. Pradhan and S. M. Reddy, "A fault-tolerant communication architecture for distributed systems," *IEEE Trans. Comput.*, vol. C-31, pp. 863–870, Sept. 1982.

[11] H. S. Stone, "Parallel processing with the perfect shuffle," *IEEE Trans. Comput.*, vol. C-20, 1971, pp. 153–161, Feb. 1971.

[12] R. Finkel and M. H. Solomon, "The lens interconnection strategy," *IEEE Trans. Comput.*, vol. C-30, pp. 960–965, Dec. 1981.

[13] L. S. Haynes *et al.*, "A survey of highly parallel computing," *Computer*, vol. 15, pp. 9–24, Jan. 1982.

[14] D. H. Lawrie, "Memory-processor connection networks," Ph.D. dissertation, Univ. of Illinois, 1973.

[15] L. N. Bhuyan and D. P. Agrawal, "Design and performance of a general class of interconnection networks," in *Proc. 1982 Int. Conf. on Parallel Processing*, Bellaire, MI, Aug. 1982, pp. 2–9; see also, *IEEE Trans. Comput.*, vol. C-32, Dec. 1983.

[16] J. G. Kuhl, "Fault-diagnosis in computing networks," Univ. of Iowa, ECE Tech. Rep. R-80-1, Aug. 1980, 183 pages.

[17] L. Kleinrock, *Queueing Systems: Vol. II, Computer Applications*. New York: Wiley, 1976.

[18] K. Bhat, "On the properties of arbitrary hypercubes," *Computer and Mathematics with Applications*, to be published.

[19] T. Y. Feng, "A survey of interconnection networks," *Computer*, vol. 14, pp. 12–27, Dec. 1981.

[20] H. J. Siegel and R. J. McMillan, "The multistage cube: A versatile interconnection network," *Computer*, pp. 458–473, Dec. 1981.

[21] D. P. Agrawal, "Graph theoretic analysis and design of multistage interconnection networks," *IEEE Trans. Comput.*, vol. C-32, pp. 637–648, July 1983.

[22] W. A. Wulf and C. G. Bell, "C.mmp—A multiminiprocessor," in *Proc. AFIPS, Fall Joint Comput. Conf.*, Dec. 1972, pp. 765–777.

[23] R. J. McMillan, G. B. Adams, III, and H. J. Siegel, "Performance and implementation of 4 × 4 switching modes in an interconnection network for PASM," in *Proc. 1981 Int. Conf. on Parallel Processing*, Aug. 1981, pp. 229–233.

[24] L. N. Bhuyan and D. P. Agrawal, "VLSI performance of multistage interconnection networks using 4 * 4 switches," in *Proc. 3rd Int. Conf. on Distributed Computing Systems*, Oct. 1982, pp. 606–613.

Laxmi N. Bhuyan (S'81–M'83) received the M.Sc. degree in electrical engineering from Regional Engineering College, Rourkela, Sambalpur University, India, in 1979, and the Ph.D. degree in computer engineering from Wayne State University, Detroit, MI, in 1982.

During 1982–83, he taught at the University of Manitoba, Winnipeg, Canada. Since September 1983, he has been with the Department of Electrical and Computer Engineering, University of Southwestern Louisiana, Lafayette, as an Assistant Professor. His research interests include parallel and distributed computer architecture, VLSI layout, and multiprocessor performance evaluations.

Dr. Bhuyan is a member of the Association for Computing Machinery.

Dharma P. Agrawal (M'74–SM'79) was born in Balod, M.P., India, on April 12, 1945. He received the B.E. degree in electrical engineering from the Ravishankar University, Raipur, M.P., India, in 1966, the M.E. (Hons.) degree in electronics and communication engineering from the University of Roorkee, Roorkee, U.P., India in 1968, and the D.Sc. Tech. degree from Federal Institute of Technology, Lausanne, Switzerland in 1975.

He has been a member of the faculty in the M.N. Regional Engineering College, Alahabad, India, the University of Roorkee, Roorkee, India, the Federal Institute of Technology, Lausanne, Switzerland, the University of Technology, Baghdad, Iraq; Southern Methodist University, Dallas, TX, and Wayne State University, Detroit, MI. Currently, he is with the North Carolina State University, Raleigh, NC, as an Associate Professor in the Department of Electrical and Computer Engineering. His research interests include parallel/distributed processing, computer architecture, computer arithmetic, fault tolerance, and information retrieval. He has served as a referee for various reputed journals and international conferences. He was a member of Program Committees for the COMPCON Fall of 1979, the Sixth IEEE Symposium on Computer Arithmetic, and Seventh Symposium on Computer Arithmetic held in Aarhus, Denmark in June 1983. Currently, he is a member and the Secretary of the Publications Board, IEEE Computer Society, and recently, he has been appointed as the Chairman of the Rules of Practice Committee of the PUBS Board. He served as the Treasurer of the IEEE-CS Technical Committee on Computer Architecture and has been named as the Program Chairman for the 13th International Symposium on Computer Architecture to be held in Ann Arbor in June, 1984. He is also a distinguished visitor of the IEEE Computer Society.

Dr. Agrawal is a member of the ACM, SIAM, and Sigma Xi. He is listed in *Who's Who in the Midwest*, the *1981 Outstanding Young Men of America*, and in the *Directory of World Researchers'* 1980's subjects published by the International Technical Information Institute, Tokyo, Japan.

Reprinted from *IEEE Transactions on Computers*, Volume C-31, Number 8, August 1982, pages 784-791. Copyright © 1982 by The Institute of Electrical and Electronics Engineers, Inc.

Some New Results About the (d, k) Graph Problem

GERARD MEMMI AND YVES RAILLARD

Abstract—The (d, k) **graph problem which is a still open extremal problem in graph theory, has received very much attention from many authors due to its theoretic interest, and also due to its possible applications in communication network design. The problem consists in maximizing the number of nodes** n **of an undirected regular graph** (d, k) **of degree** d **and diameter** k. **In this paper, after a survey of the known results, we present two new families of graphs, and two methods of generating graphs given some existing ones, leading to further substantial improvements of some of the results gathered by Storwick [21] and recently improved by Arden and Lee [3] and also by Imase and Itoh [11].**

Index Terms—**Communication network, diameter minimization,** (d, k) **graph, graph generating operations, graph theory, Moore graph.**

Manuscript received February 26, 1980; revised July 20, 1981 and February 1, 1982.

G. Memmi is with the Central Research Laboratory, Thomson-CSF, Orsay Cedex, France.

Y. Raillard is with Thomson-CSF Telephone, Boulogne-Billaucourt, France.

I. INTRODUCTION

RAPID advances in very large scale integrated circuit technology have stimulated a great interest in microprocessor networks. In such networks, minimizing the distance between every couple of microprocessors obviously leads to more efficient communication networks (reducing delays and load on the lines). Furthermore, the cost of the interconnection among the microprocessors increases with the number of physical lines between two microprocessors in the network.

In graph theoretic terms microprocessors are called nodes; lines edges and the network are then modeled by an undirected graph. In this context, the main practical problem to be solved can be stated as follows: given a number of nodes, interconnect them minimizing both the number of edges and the distance between nodes. Conversely, given a maximum degree d (i.e., the number of edges incident at a node), and a maximal distance k find a graph of maximal order. This last formulation is known as the (d, k) graph problem [6].

This paper proposes several approaches to this problem. First, various results appearing in the open literature are reviewed and compared. A synoptic table summarizes these results. Then, two novel families of graphs are presented. Finally, after recalling local procedures for increasing the number of nodes in a graph, some methods of generating graphs, given some existing graphs and parameters are introduced.

Other constraints such as reliability [23] or extensibility are not dealt with in this paper.

II. KNOWN RESULTS

After recalling some basic graph notions and posing the (d, k) graph problem, we recall some known upper bounds for (d, k) graphs. Then we briefly exhibit several families of (d, k) graphs which can be found in the literature [1], [3], [7], [10], [11], [12], [13], [15], [22].

A. The (d, k) Graph Problem

Let $G = (X, E)$ be an undirected finite graph where X is a nonempty set of n nodes and E is the set of undirected edges.

The distance $d(x, y)$ is the length of a shortest path between two nodes x, y; accordingly, the diameter k of a graph G is the longest distance between any pair of nodes, i.e.

$$k = \max_{(x,y) \in X^2} (d(x, y))$$

A graph of maximum degree d and diameter k is called a (d, k) graph. A graph is said regular when all its nodes have the same degree. The problem of (d, k) graphs was first set by Elspas [6]. It consists in maximizing the order $n(d, k)$ of a graph given its maximum degree d and its diameter k.

B. Upper Bounds for the (d, k) Graph Problem

The (d, k) graph problem is an extremal problem (i.e., optimizing some characteristics of a graph given other ones) and a difficult theoretic problem. So, it would be very helpful to have an upper bound as a guideline in view to construct optimal solutions.

An upper bound can be obtained by considering Moore graphs. A Moore graph is a regular (d, k) graph which can be viewed as a tree-based: taking one node as the root with $d(d - 1)^{k-1}$ nodes at distance k. We call such a set of nodes the level k of the tree. For $d > 2$,

$$n_M(d, k) = \frac{d(d - 1)^k - 2}{d - 2}$$

is an upper bound for any (d, k) graph.

Recently, Erdös, Fajtlōwicz, and Hoffman [8] have slightly improved this bound for the $(d, 2)$ graphs:

$$n(d, 2) \leq d^2 - 1 \qquad \text{for } d \neq 2, 3, 7, 57.$$

C. Moore–Singleton Graphs

From the Moore graphs construction we see that the stumbling block is to join nodes of the level k.

When existing, Moore graphs are indeed optimal for the extremal problem. Hoffman and Singleton [11] have proved

that Moore graphs of diameter 2 exist only for $d = 2, 3, 7$ and possibly for $d = 57$.

For Singleton graphs we have

$$n_S(d, k) = \frac{2(d - 1)^k - 2}{d - 2}.$$

Sachs [19] proved that for $k = 3$, these graphs exist only if $d - 1$ is a power of a prime number. Longyear [15] gives a construction when $d - 1$ is a prime number. Another construction for $d \in \{2, 3, 4, 5, 6\}$ can be found in [24].

D. Other Results

Other known interesting constructions which give a lower bound to some values of the (d, k) graph problem are worth mentioning.

Akers [1] constructs $(d, d - 1)$ graphs based upon coding theory. They have

$$n_A(d, d - 1) = \binom{2d - 1}{d} \text{ nodes.}$$

Friedman's construction [10] is based upon tree developing of $\left\lfloor \dfrac{k}{2} \right\rfloor$ levels (where $\lfloor x \rfloor$ is the greatest integer less or equal than x). We have

$$n_F(d, k) = \frac{2d}{d - 2} ((d - 1)^{\lfloor k/2 \rfloor} - 1) \text{ nodes}$$

and

$$n_F(d, d - 1) > n_A(d, d - 1)$$

$$\text{for } d \in [13] \cup [15, 16 \cdots].$$

Korn [13] points out that $n_F(d, 2r) = n_F(d, 2r + 1)$ and improves Friedman's construction for $k = 2r + 1$ with

$$n_K(d, k) = \frac{2}{d - 2} (2(d - 1)^{r+1} - d).$$

This last remark is a starting point for one of the constructions and for one of the generating procedures we proposed below.

Storwick [22] introduces two constructions based upon Friedman's construction and the substitution for the nodes at the zero levels by complete graphs with n_1 or n_2 nodes, under the conditions

$$n_2(d - n_2 + 1) \leq n_1(d - n_1 + 1)$$
$$\leq n_2(d - n_2 + 1)(d - 1).$$

Then,

$$\bullet \; n_{S1}(d, k) = \frac{1}{(d - 2)} (n_1(n_1 - 3)(d - 1) + n_2(n_2 - 3)$$
$$+ (d - 1)^{r-2}(n_1(2d - 3)(d - n_1 + 1)$$
$$+ n_2(d - 1)(d - n_2 + 1)))$$

where

$$k = 2r \qquad \text{for } n_1 > 1, n_2 > 1$$
$$k = 2r - 1 \qquad \text{otherwise}$$

$$\bullet \ n_{S2}(d, k) = \frac{n_1^2(d - n_1 + 1)(d - 1)^{r-2}}{d - 2}$$

$$\times (d(n_1 - 3) + 2(d - n_1 + 1)(d - 1)^{r-1})$$

$$+ \frac{n_2(d - 1)}{d - 2} (n_2 - 3 + (d - n_2 + 1)(d - 1)^{r-1})$$

$$- \frac{n_1(d - 1)}{d - 2} (n_1 - 3 + (d - n_1 + 1)(d - 1)^{r-2}).$$

where

$$k = 4r - 3 \qquad \text{if } n_1 = 1$$
$$k = 4r - 2 \qquad \text{if } n_1 > 1 \text{ and } n_2 = 1$$
$$k = 4r - 1 \qquad \text{if } n_1 > 1 \text{ and } n_2 > 1.$$

These graphs are not necessarily regular.

The multitree-structured (MTS) construction of Arden and Lee [3] is defined as follows.

1) There are m trees of $t - 1$ levels.
2) The m roots are connected to form a cycle.
3) Each leaf is connected to $d - 1$ other leaves.
4) All the leaves are interconnected in at least one complete cycle.

The construction is no longer explicited for $d > 3$. For $d = 3$ a procedure is given to connect the leaves. But it does not seem that there exists a formula to obtain the diameter. Nevertheless, the authors give for $d = 3$ and $k \in [5, 8]$ the best solutions to our knowledge (see Table I).

Imase and Itoh [12] give a nice construction which works in the case where we consider directed graphs.

This construction leads to $n_I(d, k) = (d/2)^k$ for d even. The nodes are numbered from 0 to $(d/2)^k - 1$. Nodes i and j are connected iff

$$j = id + \alpha \bmod (n)$$

or

$$i = jd + \alpha \bmod (n) \qquad \text{where } \alpha = 0, \cdots, d - 1.$$

This construction had already been found with the notion of d-circulants which verify the matrix equation $A^m = \lambda J$ in [14] and [25].

III. NOVEL CONSTRUCTIONS

Here, we describe two novel constructions which improve some (d, k) graphs. Table I summarizes for (d, k) graphs first values, the range of which is of practical use in communication or local networks.

A. Construction C1

Each graph of this family is defined by two integers: the degree d of the graph, and m the number of rows in a graph as defined below.

A $C1$ graph is a regular graph with $m(d/2)^{m-1}$ nodes distributed around a cylinder in m rows of $(d/2)^{m-1}$ nodes each (see Fig. 1). The construction is defined for d even and $m \geq 3$.

Each node x is identified by the pair (i, j) with $0 \leq i < m$ and $0 < j \leq (d/2)^{m-1}$; x is the node j of the row i. Each node (i, j) is connected to $d/2$ nodes of the row $i - 1 \pmod m$, and

$d/2$ nodes of the row $i + 1 \pmod m$ with the following rule. (i, j) is connected to node (k, l) if

$$\begin{cases} k = i + 1 \bmod (m) \\ l = \left(\alpha + \frac{d}{2} (j - 1) \right) \bmod \left(\left(\frac{d}{2} \right)^{m-1} \right) \end{cases}$$

$$\text{with } \alpha = 1, 2, \cdots, \frac{d}{2}.$$

The diameter of such graphs is given by use of the following property.

Theorem: The diameter k of a $C1$ graph defined by d and m is given by

$$\begin{cases} k = m \qquad \text{for } m = 3 \\ k = m + \left\lceil \frac{m - 1}{2} \right\rceil - 2 \qquad \text{if } m > 3. \end{cases}$$

Therefore, we have, as for the preceding results

$$n_{C1}(d, 3) = \frac{3}{4} d^2$$

$$n_{C1}(d, k) = \frac{2}{3} (k + 2) \left(\frac{d}{2} \right)^{(2k + 1)/3} \qquad \text{if } k = 1 \pmod 3$$

$$n_{C1}(d, k) = \frac{2k + 5}{3} \left(\frac{d}{2} \right)^{2(k + 1)/3} \qquad \text{if } k = 2 \pmod 2$$

There does not exist $C1$ graph with $k = 0 \pmod 3$.

Proof: First, it is easy to show that each node is not topologically distinguished from any other one (i.e., the graph is node-transitive) so, we can restrict ourselves in finding the maximal distance between the node $(0, 1)$ and any other one. Then one notices that:

all nodes of rows 1 and $m - 1$ are at distance at most $m - 1$ from $(0, 1)$

all nodes of rows 0, 2 and $m - 2$ are at distance at most m from $(0, 1)$ and so on.

All nodes of rows i and $m - i$ are at distance at most $m + i - 2$ from $(0, 1)$:

$$\text{if } m - 1 = 2n \qquad \text{then } k = m + n - 2$$
$$\text{if } m - 1 = 2n + 1 \qquad \text{then } k = m + n - 1.$$

In any case, all nodes of all rows are reached at distance at most

$$m + \left\lceil \frac{m - 1}{2} \right\rceil - 2 \text{ from } (0, 1).$$

In fact, this upper bound is attained.

Finally, one remarks that for $d = 2$ there exist isomophic topologies [17], [19]. Another generalization of the network described in [17] is given in [21] for d even; but the results are suboptimal.

B. Construction C2

This family is based upon Friedman's construction and, as Korn's construction [13], is restricted to odd values of k. d identical trees of $\lfloor k/2 \rfloor$ are constructed; but instead of sharing their lowest level nodes (i.e., leaves) as in Friedman's or Korn's

TABLE I

k / d	1	2	3	4	5	6	7	8	9	10
2	3 *	5 *	7 *	9 *	11 *	13 *	15 *	17 *	19 *	21
3	4 *	10 *	20 *	30 S (46)	56 AL (94)	72 AL (190)	120 AL (382)	124 AL (766)	138 C2,S1 (1534)	216 S2 (3070)
4	5 *	15 *	35 A (53)	48 T (161)	80 C1 (485)	114 S2 (1457)	212 C2 (4373)	448 C1 (131 121)	644 C2 (39 365)	1024 C1,I (118 097)
5	6 *	24 *	42 S (106)	126 A (426)	130 C2 (1706)	232 S2 (6826)	530 C2 (27306)	850 F (109 226)	2 130 S2 (436 906)	3 512 S2 (1 747 626)
6	7 *	31 S (35)	62 S (187)	108 C1 (937)	462 A (4687)	729 I (23437)	2187 I (117187)	6561 I (585 937)	19 683 I (2 929 687)	59 049 I (14 648 137)
7	8 *	50 *	80 (302)	150 (1814)	378 A (10 886)	1716 A (65318)	2114 C2 (391910)	3626 F (3 351 462)	12 698 C2 (14 108 774)	22 836 S2 (84 652 646)
8	9 *	57 S (63)	114 S (457)	256 C1,I (3201)	1280 C1 (22 409)	4096 I (156 865)	16 384 I (1 098 057)	65 536 I (7 686 401)	262 144 I (53 804 809)	1 048 576 I 376 633 665)
9	10 *	74 (80)	150 (658)	240 (5266)	738 C2 (42 130)	1904 S2 (337 042)	5 922 C2 (2 696 338)	24 310 A (21 570 706)	47 394 C2 (172 565 648)	94 416 S2 (1 380 525 202)
10	11 *	91 (99)	200 (911)	625 I (8201)	3125 C1,I (73 811)	15625 I (664 301)	78 125 I (5 978 711)	390 625 I (53 808 401)	1 953 125 I (484 275 611)	9 765 625 I (4 358 480 501)

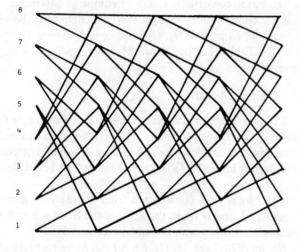

Row :   0   1   2   3   0

Fig. 1.   The construction $C1$ where $d = 4$, $m = 4$. We have $k = 4$ and $n_{C1}(4, 4) = 32$.

construction, each leaf is connected to exactly one leaf of each other tree (see Fig. 2).

An easy method for connecting the leaves is to label the leaves of each tree, then to connect together all the leaves having the same label. We have then

$$n_{C2}(d, k) = \frac{d}{d-2}(d(d-1)^{\lfloor k/2 \rfloor} - 2).$$

IV. COMPARISONS

A. Table I

Table I gives the first values of (d, k) graphs for $d \in [1, 10]$ and $k \in [1, 10]$. Starred values are maximal (d, k) graphs. Those marked with an A are due to Akers [1]; AL to Arden and Lee [3]; S to Singleton [15] or [24]; F to Friedman [10];

I to Imase and Itoh [12]; $S1$, $S2$ to Storwick [22]; T to Toueg and Steiglitz [23]; $C1$ and $C2$ refer to our constructions. All other values are from Elspas [7]. Values in brackets are the upper bounds obtained from Moore formula or derived from [8].

B. Analytical Comparisons

Comparing the different formulas of the constructions, one can derive the following results, provided the constructions are possible:

$$n_{C2}(d, k) > n_F(d, k) \qquad \text{for all } d, \text{ for all } k$$
$$n_{C2}(d, k) > n_K(d, k) \qquad \text{for } d \geq 2, \text{ for all } k$$
$$n_{C2}(d, k) > n_{S1}(d, k) \qquad \text{for } d \geq 3, \text{ for all } k \geq 4.$$

Let $C2_{\cup}F$ denote Friedman's construction for d even, the $C2$ construction for d odd we have

$$n_{C2_{\cup}F}(d, d - 1) > n_A(d, d - 1) \qquad \text{for } d > 12.$$

Between $C1$ and $C2$ we have

$$n_{C1}(d, k) > n_{C2}(d, k) \qquad \text{for } d \geq 4 \text{ for } k \geq 7.$$

Between the Itoh and Imase's construction and the $C1$ construction

$$n_I(d, k) > n_{C1}(d, k) \qquad \text{when } k = 4 \, d > 8$$
$$k = 5 \, d > 10$$
$$k = 7 \, d \geq 5$$
$$k = 8 \, d \geq 6$$
$$k = 10 \, d > 4$$
$$k = 11 \, d \geq 5$$
$$k \geq 13, d > 4.$$

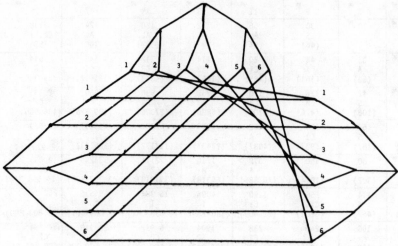

Fig. 2. Here $d = 3$, $k = 5$, $N = 30$.

Asymptotically, we have the following behavior. When $d \to \infty$

$$n_{C1}(d, k) \sim \frac{2k + 5}{3} \left(\frac{d}{2}\right)^{2(k+1)/3}$$

$$n_{C2}(d, k) \sim d^{(k+1)/2}$$

$$n_I(d, k) \sim \left(\frac{d}{2}\right)^k.$$

When $k \to \infty$

$$n_{C1}(d, k) \sim \frac{d^2}{d - 2} (d - 1)^{k/2}$$

$$n_{C2}(d, k) \sim \frac{2k}{3} \left(\frac{d}{2}\right)^{2k/3}$$

$$n_I(d, k) \sim \left(\frac{d}{2}\right)^k.$$

One notices that Itoh and Imase's construction reaches the order of the Moore bound.

V. Two Other Ways for Increasing the Lower Bound of the (d, k) Graph Problem

Beside the construction of families of graphs, one can find in the literature two other ideas to improve some results in the (d, k) graph problem. The first one is to find an algorithm which locally modifies a given graph and slightly, step-by-step improves the characteristics of the graph. Such procedures can be found in [23] or [24]. This kind of algorithm has two serious limitations. One is the lack of knowledge of the structure of the graph; the other one is its complexity that makes impractical the treatment of graphs with order greater than 150 [23]. The second idea consists in making operations of graphs. For instance, the product graph [4] was used in [6] for designing communication network. Given p graphs: $G_1, \cdots, G_p$, q parameters $\alpha_1, \cdots \alpha_q$, the operation Op, one can more generally generate the family of graphs: $Op\ (G_1, \cdots, G_p; \alpha_1, \cdots, \alpha_q)$ where the parameters $\alpha_1 \cdots \alpha_q$ can vary.

In this paper, we introduce two generating operations. The generating scheme for the first operation, namely $T(G, h)$, is a tree-based construction as in Friedman's construction or in our $C2$ construction. The generating scheme for the second operation, namely $B(G_1, G_2)$, is a complete bipartite graph. Finally Table II shows how these two operations improve several values for (d, k) graphs.

A. $T(G, h)$ Operation

Let G be a graph of order N, degree d and diameter k. The nodes of G are from 1 to N. N trees numbered from 1 to N are then constructed. They have h levels and are of degree $d + 1$ and so they have $L = (d + 1)d^{h-1}$ leaves numbered from 1 to L.

$T(G, h)$ is then constructed from L graphs G numbered from 1 to L and N trees: the leaf j of the tree i is identified to the node i of the graph G numbered j (see Fig. 3).

So, let $NT(G, h), DT(G, h), KT(G, h)$ be respectively the order, the degree and the diameter of $T(G, h)$; we clearly have

$$NT(G, h) = \frac{N}{d - 1} ((d + 1)d^h - 2)$$

$$DT(G, h) = d + 1$$

$$KT(G, h) = 2h + k.$$

Let $C(d - 1)$ denote the complete graph of degree $d - 1$. Applying T operation on $C(d - 1)$, one generates graphs obtained with construction $C2$. Then we have

$$n_{C2}(d, k) = NT(C(d - 1), \lfloor k/2 \rfloor).$$

When G is a circuit of 4 nodes ($d = 2$), for $h = 1$ we get the graph $T(G, 1)$ as seen in Fig. 3.

B. $B(G_1, G_2)$ Operation

Let G_1 and G_2 be two graphs of order N_1, N_2; degree d_1, d_2 and diameter k_1, k_2 respectively. Let us assume that $d_1 \geq d_2$.

TABLE II

d \ k	1	2	3	4	5	6	7	8	9	10
2	3	5	7	9	11	13	15	17	19	21
3	4	10	20	30 S (46)	56 AL (94)	72 AL (190)	120 AL (382)	124 AL (766)	154 T(2,3;3) (1534)	230 T(2,2;4) (3070)
4	5	15	35 A (53)	50 T(3,2;1) (161)	100 T(3,3;1) (485)	200 B(3,2;3,2) (1457)	448 T(3,3;2) (4373)	800 B(3,3;3,3) (131 121)	1060 T(3,3;3) (39 365)	1800 B(3,4;3,4) (118 097)
5	6	24	42 S (106)	126 A (426)	210 T(4,3;1) (1706)	450 B(4,2;3,2) (6826)	1050 B(4,3;3,2) (27 306)	2450 B(4,3;4,3) (109 226)	3710 T(4,3;3) (436 906)	6390 T(4,2;4) (1 747 626)
6	7	31 (35)	62 S (187)	168 T(5,2;1) (937)	462 A (4687)	1152 B(5,2;5,2) (23 437)	2520 B(5,2;4,3) (117 187)	5670 B(5,4;4,2) (585 937)	19 683 I (2 929 687)	59 049 I (14 648 137)
7	8	50	80 (302)	248 T(6,2;1) (1 814)	520 B(4,1;6,2) (10 885)	1922 B(6,2;6,2) (65 318)	4340 B(4,3;6,2) (391 910)	11718 B(6,2;5,4) (3 351 462)	33 264 B(5,2;6,5) (14 108 774)	64 880 B(4,3;6,5) (84 652 646)
8	9	57 (63)	114 S (457)	450 T(7,2;1) (3 201)	1280 C1 (22 409)	5000 B(7,2;7,2) (155 865)	16 384 I (1 098 057)	65536 I (7 686 401)	262 144 I (53 804 809)	1 048 576 I (376 633 665)
9	10	74 (80)	150 (658)	570 T(8,2;1) (5 266)	1710 B(5,1;8,2) (42 130)	8550 B(7,2;8,2) (337 042)	17100 B(7,2;8,3) (2696338)	67500 B(7,2;8,4) (21570706)	192 000 B(7,2;8,5) (172565648)	750 000 B(7,2;8,6) (1380525202)
10	11	91 (99)	200 (911)	814 T(9,2;1) (8201)	3125 C1,I (73811)	15625 I (664 301)	78125 I (5978711)	390625 I (53808401)	1953125 I (484275611)	9 765 625 I (4358480501)

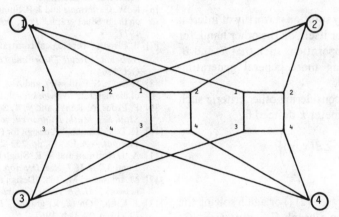

Fig. 3.   Circled values number the four trees of one level.

$B(G_1, G_2)$ is then constructed from N_2 graphs G_1 numbered from 1 to N_2 and $(d_1 - d_2 + 1) N_1$ graphs G_2 numbered from 1 to $(d_1 - d_2 + 1) N_1$.

The node i of the jth graph G_1 is connected to the node j of the graphs G_2 numbered $kN_1 + i$ with $k = 0, 1, \cdots, d_1 - d_2$. The node i of the jth graph G_2 is connected to the node j of the i-th graph G_1 (see Fig. 4).

Let $NB(G_1, G_2), DB(G_1, G_2), KB(G_1, G_2)$ be respectively the order, the degree, and the diameter of $B(G_1, G_2)$, we clearly have

$$\begin{cases} NB(G_1, G_2) = N_1 N_2 (d_1 - d_2 + 2) \\ DB(G_1, G_2) = d_1 + 1 \\ KB(G_1, G_2) = k_1 + k_2 + 2. \end{cases}$$

C. Improvement of Table I

Applying the operations T and B on graphs described in Table I we get new lower bounds for the (d, k) graph problem. In Table II, $T(d, k, h)$ is a short notation for the graph obtained from the best (d, k) graph by the T operation with parameter k; $B(d_1, k_1; d_2, k_2)$ is a short notation for the graph obtained from the best (d_1, k_1) graph and (d_2, k_2) graph by the B operation. Circled values have permitted the best improvement of the Table I with the help of operations T and B.

VI. CONCLUSION

We have presented two novel families of graphs and two operations to deal with the (d, k) graph problem. One can

223

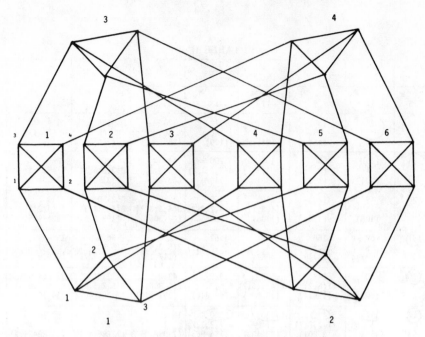

Fig. 4. G_1 is such that $N_1 = 4$, $d_1 = 3$, $k_1 = 1$. G_2 is such that $N_2 = 3$, d_2 = 2, $k_2 = 1$. $NB(G_1, G_2) = 36$; $DB(G_1, G_2) = 4$; $KB(G_1, G_2) = 4$.

point out that only three Akers graphs remain in Table II. Thus, the conjecture of their optimality is invalidated. But the (d, k) graph problem remains open. This paper covers only the results known to us in the years 1979/1980. We are sure they can again be improved upon.

Proving the optimality of any solution is worthy of interest on two grounds; on one hand for itself, on the other hand, for generating other graphs with operations such that T and B. We are currently investigating more general generating methods derived from T and B.

Designing networks implies considering other criteria such as minimizing the average diameter $\bar{k}$ defined by

$$\bar{k} = \frac{1}{N} \Sigma \left(\frac{1}{N} \Sigma d(x, y) \right)$$

$$x \in X \qquad y \in Y$$

or maximizing the connectivity (see [21]) or again solving the extensibility problem, i.e., given a graph G finding $G_1 \subset G_2 \subset \cdots \subset G_n = G$ such that G_i keeps properties (optimal connectivity, diameter) close to the final graph G.

For our constructions the average diameter can be improved, but the structure of the graph then becomes difficult to describe. The operations B and T lead to good heuristics for the extensibility problem. In an earlier version of this paper, we conjectured that the graphs of our two families had the maximum possible connectivity. This has been recently proved by Amar [2]. Some of our constructions have been generalized by Bermond, Delorme, Farhi and Quisquatter [5].

REFERENCES

[1] S. B. Akers, Jr. "On the construction of (d, k) graphs," *IEEE Trans. Electron. Comput.*, vol. EC-14, p. 488, June 1965.
[2] D. Amar, "On the connectivity of some telecommunication networks," L. R. I. Univ. Paris-Sud, Orsay, France, Res. Rep. 95; submitted to *IEEE Trans. Comput.*
[3] B. W. Arden and H. Lee, "A multi-tree-structured network," in *Proc. COMPCON 78*, Sept. 1978, pp. 201-210.
[4] C. Berge, *Graphes et Hypergraphes*. Paris: Dunod, 1970.
[5] J. C. Bermond, C. Delorme, G. Farhi, and Quisquatter, "Large graphs with given degree and diameter," L. R. I. Univ. Paris-Sud, Orsay, France, to be published.
[6] K. W. Cattermole and J. P. Summer, "Communication networks based on the product graph," *Proc. Inst. Elec. Eng.*, vol. 124, pp. 38-48, Jan. 1977.
[7] B. Elspas, "Topological constraints on interconnection limited logic," *Switching Circuit Theory and Logical Design*, vol. S.164, pp. 133-147, Oct. 1964.
[8] P. Erdös, S. Fajtlowicz, and A. J. Hoffman, "Maximum degree in graphs of diameter 2," *Networks*, vol. 10, pp. 87-90, 1980.
[9] P. Erdös, A. Rényi, and V. T. Sos, "On a problem of graphic theory," *Stud. Sci. Math. Hungarica*, vol. 1, pp. 215-235, 1966.
[10] H. D. Friedman, "A design for (d, k) graphs," *IEEE Trans. Electron. Comput.*, vol. EC-15, pp. 253-254, 1966.
[11] A. J. Hoffman and R. R. Singleton, "On Moore graphs with diameter 2 and 3," *IBM J. Res. Develop.*, vol. 4, pp. 497-504, 1960.
[12] M. Imase and M. Itoh, "Design to minimize diameter on building-block network," *IEEE Trans. Comput.* vol. C-30, pp. 439-442, June 1981.
[13] J. Korn, "On (d, k) graphs," *IEEE Trans. Electron. Comput.*, vol. EC-16, p. 90, Feb. 1967.
[14] C. W. H. Lam, "On some solution of $A^k = dI + \lambda J$," *J. Combinatorial Theory*, A-23, pp. 140-147, 1977.
[15] J. Q. Longyear, "Regular d-valent graphs of girth 6 and 2 $(d^2 - d + 1)$ vertices," *J. Combinatorial Theory*, vol. 9, pp. 420-422, 1970.
[16] G. Memmi, "Etude de graphes pour le projet Sycomore," ERIA, ECA Automation, Saint-Cloud Cedex, France, Rep. 7T40719, Aug. 1979.
[17] M. C. Pease, "The undirected binary n-cube microprocessor array," *IEEE Trans. Comput.*, vol. C-26, May 1977.
[18] F. Preparata and J. Vuillemin, "The cube-connected cycles: A versatile network for parallel computation," *Commun. Ass. Comput. Mach.*, vol. 4, pp. 300-309, May 1981.
[19] H. Sachs, "On regular graphs with given girth," in *Theory of Graphs and its Applications.* New York: Academic, 1964 pp. 91-97.
[20] H. J. Siegel and R. J. McMillen, "The cube network as a distributed processing test bed switch," in *Proc. 2nd Int. Conf. Distrib. Comput. Syst.*, Paris, France, Apr. 1981, pp. 377-387.
[21] M. R. Sleep and F. W. Burton, "Towards a zero assignment parallel processor," in *Proc. 2nd Int. Conf. Distrib. Comput. Syst.*, Paris, France, Apr. 1981, pp. 80-85.
[22] R. M. Storwick, "Improved construction techniques for (d, k) graphs," *IEEE Trans. Comput.*, vol. C-19, pp. 1214-1216, Dec. 1970.
[23] S. Toueg and K. Steiglitz, "The design of small-diameter networks by

local search," *IEEE Trans. Comput.*, vol. C-28, pp. 537–542, July 1979.

[24] R. S. Wilkov, "Construction of maximally reliable communication networks with minimum transmission delay," in *Proc. 1970 IEEE Int. Conf. Commun.*, vol. 6, June 1970, pp. 4210–4215.

[25] K. Wang, "On the matrix equation $A^m = \lambda J$," *J. Combinatorial Theory*, A-29, pp. 134–141, 1980.

Gerard Memmi received the engineering degree from the Ecole Nationale Supérieure des Télécommunications and the degree of Docteur-Ingénieur from the University of Paris VI, France, in 1976 and 1978, respectively.

From 1978 to 1980 he was with ECA-Automation, St. Cloud, where he was involved in software reliability studies and began research on switching systems design. Presently, he is with the Central Research Laboratory, Thomson-CSF, Orsay, France, where he participates in a project in the area of formal specification and verification of real-time systems (in particular using Petri nets theory).

Yves Raillard was born in Montbard, France, on September 11, 1948. He graduated from the Ecole Centrale de Paris in 1972.

From 1972 to 1974, he was employed by the Compagnie Generale de Construction Telephoniques in Paris, where he was involved in theoretic teletraffic studies. Since 1974, he has been with Thomson-CSF Telephone, Boulogne Billancourt, France. His main interests are design of voice and data switching networks, and performance evaluation of telecommunication systems. Now, he applies these mathematical tools to the design of broad-band networks.

A SIMULATION STUDY OF MULTIMICROCOMPUTER NETWORKS

Daniel A. Reed[†]

Department of Computer Sciences
Purdue University
West Lafayette, Indiana 47907

Abstract: Recent developments in VLSI have made it feasible to interconnect large numbers of single chip computers to form a multimicrocomputer network. Using task precedence graphs to represent the time varying behavior of parallel computations, we investigate the performance of interconnection topologies for multimicrocomputer networks.

Introduction

Current evolutionary trends in integrated circuit fabrication suggest that it will soon be cost effective to consider a new parallel processing paradigm based on large networks of interconnected single chip computers. The single VLSI chip comprising each network node would contain a processor with a modicum of locally addressable memory, a communication controller capable of routing internode messages without delaying the processor, and a small number of connections to other nodes.

Among the suggested application areas for these multimicrocomputer networks are partial differential equations solvers and divide and conquer algorithms. The cooperating tasks of a parallel algorithm for solving one of these problems would execute asynchronously on different nodes and communicate via internode message passing. The limited node fanout implied by the VLSI implementation, as well as the absence of shared memory, make it crucial to select an interconnection network capable of efficiently supporting message passing. In this paper we discuss computation paradigms for multimicrocomputer networks and techniques for assessing the performance of network interconnections.

Models of Computation

In one view of parallel computation, all parallel tasks are known *a priori* and are statically mapped onto the network nodes before the computation begins. In this case, queueing theoretic models can be used to estimate the performance of a given multimicrocomputer network executing a particular algorithm [4].

In the alternate view, a parallel computation is defined by a dynamically created task precedence graph. Tasks are created and destroyed as the computation proceeds, and the mapping of tasks onto network nodes is done dynamically.

Because most queueing theoretic models assume steady state behavior, they are not generally applicable to study of time dependent parallel computations. In particular, models of time dependent computation must account for time varying workloads, distribution of data to multiple tasks, and dynamic mapping of tasks onto network nodes using only partial knowledge of the global network state. Because we know of no analytic technique capable of accurately representing this behavior, we have adopted simulation as a means of study.

Subsequent sections of this paper present five multimicrocomputer interconnection networks, outline a task precedence model of time dependent computation, and discuss the results of a parametric simulation study of these interconnection networks when supporting time dependent computations.

Interconnection Networks

Because of the computational expense of simulation, we limited our study to five interconnection networks that earlier analysis suggested were worthy of further investigation: the 2-D spanning bus hypercube [6], 2-D toroid [4], cube-connected cycles [3], 2-ary N-cube [1], and the complete connection. We have included the complete connection to determine the performance degradation attributable to incompletely connected networks.

Task Precedence Graphs

As stated earlier, our model of time varying computation is the task precedence graph. A precedence graph represents a computation as a series of dependencies. The results of all computations providing input to a task, its antecedents, must become available before the task is eligible for execution.

In each precedence graph, three types of tasks can be distinguished: fork tasks, join tasks, and regular tasks. A *fork* task has a single antecedent task and one or more consequent tasks; it represents the computation prior to initiation of parallel subtasks to solve a problem. A *join* task has one or more antecedent tasks and a single consequent task; it represents the combination of subproblem solutions to yield a solution to an entire problem. Finally, a *regular* task is any task that is not a fork or join task; it represents a simple computation. If we interpret the juxtaposition AB of tasks to mean "A is an antecedent of B", a task precedence graph can be formally defined by the following grammar.

$$\langle precedence\ graph \rangle ::= \langle regular\ task \rangle \ |$$
$$\langle fork\ task \rangle \langle precedence\ graph \rangle^+ \langle join\ task \rangle$$

As summarized in Table I, the characteristics of a precedence graph are determined by several parameters. Because the number of possible graph parameterizations is so large, we have somewhat arbitrarily selected a set of values, also given in Table I, to be used as a reference point in our study. By systematically varying subsets of these parameters, we obtain different performance results. By comparing these results to those obtained using the reference parameters, we can estimate the effect of the variations.

Simulation Methodology

For comparative purposes, we generated twenty five task precedence graphs using the reference parameters shown in Table I. All service times were drawn from negative exponential distributions, the number of consequents of each fork task was uniformly distributed between B_{min} and B_{max}, and all graphs were

---

[†]Present address: Department of Computer Science, University of North Carolina, Chapel Hill, North Carolina 27514

Reprinted from *Proceedings of the 1983 International Conference on Parallel Processing*, 1983, pages 161-163. Copyright © 1983 by The Institute of Electrical and Electronics Engineers, Inc.

constrained to have between *Maxtasks* / 2 and *Maxtasks* tasks. Each node was assumed to possess complete knowledge of the network state, and each task eligible for execution was scheduled on the idle node nearest its location. We will return to this assumption when discussing distributed scheduling algorithms. Finally, to model the fact that each network node is a single chip with fixed bandwidth, we scaled the mean data communication times by the number of link connections to each node.

The average parallelism P attained when evaluating a precedence graph on a network has been taken as the measure of performance. This is

$$P = \frac{\sum_{i=1}^{Numtasks} S_i}{parallel\ execution\ time} \qquad where \quad S_i \in \{ S_F, S_R, S_J \} .$$

Simulation Experiments

Using the assumptions discussed above, we explored five different variations of precedence graph parameters and network characteristics and their effect on network performance: precedence graph structure, the event horizon of a distributed task scheduler, the maximum task branching factor, the mean computation time/communication time ratio, and the number of network nodes. The first two of these are discussed below; an analysis of the other variations can be found in [5].

Precedence Graph Structure

Figure I shows the graph parallelism when each of the twenty five graphs derived from the reference graph parameters was simulated on the five networks with 64 nodes. The precedence graphs were sorted in increasing order of parallelism on the complete connection. Table II shows the average parallelism over the set of graphs using each network.

Two features of Figure I are of particular interest. The first is the way networks other than the complete connection exhibit the same performance trends from precedence graph to graph. This suggests that something inherent to the graphs is affecting the time required for their evaluation. To determine what this might be, we examined two precedence graphs, numbers nine and eleven in the figure, that represented two extremes of behavior. Figure II shows the time varying parallelism when the two graphs were evaluated on a 2-*D* toroid with 64 nodes. The simulation of precedence graph nine exhibits a striking decrease in the number of parallel tasks near time 90. Because a similar simulation on the complete connection exhibits no such decrease, we can only conclude that this variation is caused by the collapse of a parallel subgraph requiring the transmission of results across several communication links. During the delay caused by this transmission, tasks otherwise eligible for execution were forced to wait for these results.

Figure I also points out the performance differential between the spanning bus hypercube and the networks using dedicated links. Although, this behavior may appear somewhat anomalous in light of the apparently greater communication bearing capacity of the dedicated link networks, this is not the case. A detailed examination of the simulation results shows that tasks generally execute on nodes near their point of origin. In other words, the precedence graph evaluation exhibits considerable communication locality. For this communication pattern and the given ratio of computation time to communication time for tasks, the utilization of the communication links is low. Because of this, the buses of the spanning bus hypercube permit more rapid distribution of tasks to other nodes than the dedicated links of the other networks. For the same reason, distinct differences among the dedicated link networks are also not apparent.

Event Horizon of a Distributed Scheduler

Heretofore we have assumed that the task scheduler at each node always possesses complete knowledge of the global network state. In practice, only limited information is available, and it is often no longer completely accurate when it is received.

To determine a scheduler's operation in the face of partial knowledge, we postulated the existence of an *event horizon* for each network node. We assume the scheduler at each node has no knowledge of network activity at any nodes beyond its event horizon and that it must schedule all eligible tasks on nodes within its event horizon. Using the reference precedence graph parameters, Figure III shows the average graph parallelism as a function of the distance to the event horizon from a node. Similar results are obtained when the ratio of computation times to communication times varies from 1:1 to 100:1. Based on this limited evidence, it appears that state knowledge of nodes within a small distance from each source node is sufficient to achieve reasonable results. This is encouraging because it suggests that efficient distributed schedulers can be constructed for multimicrocomputer networks.

Two final observations about distributed schedulers should be made. First, this dynamic scheduling strategy does not use the precedence graph structure to aid its decisions. It should be possible to design heuristics that take advantage of some graph specific information.

Second, the acquisition of state information from nodes within an event horizon is decidedly more difficult for networks connected by buses than for those using dedicated communication links. This is primarily because so many more nodes are within a small number of bus crossings from a source node. Communicating state information to other nodes on the same bus could conceivably consume a significant portion of the available communication bandwidth. Additional work is needed to determine the cost of acquiring state information.

Summary

We have presented a model of time dependent parallel computation and studied the behavior of five multimicrocomputer interconnection networks supporting computations similar to those of the model. Among the issues considered were the relative performance of interconnection networks and the efficacy of distributed scheduling using incomplete information.

For small, dynamically created tasks, the spanning bus hypercube appears to have better performance than the dedicated link networks because it can diffuse work more rapidly. This is not always true; if message routing does not exhibit enough locality (i.e., messages must cross many links to reach their destination), the smaller communication bearing capacity of the spanning bus hypercube will be saturated, and the dedicated link networks will be preferred. Clearly, the selection of a network must be made with knowledge of communication patterns and task sizes required by an algorithm.

Finally, dynamic task scheduling using only local information seems successful for the class of algorithms represented by precedence graphs, suggesting that efficient distributed schedulers can be designed.

References

[1] F. W. Burton and M. R. Sleep, "Executing Functional Programs on a Virtual Tree of Processors," *Proc of the 1981 Conf on Functional Prog Lang and Computer Arch*, Oct. 1981, pp. 187-194.

[2] M. C. Pease, "The Indirect Binary n-cube Microprocessor Array," *IEEE Trans on Comput*, Vol. C-26, No. 5, May 1977, pp. 458-473.

[3] F. P. Preparata and J. Vuillemin, "The Cube-Connected Cycles: A Versatile Network for Parallel Computation," *Comm of the ACM*, Vol. 24, No. 5, May 1981, pp. 300-309.

[4] D. A. Reed and H. D. Schwetman, "Cost-Performance Bounds for Multimicrocomputer Networks," *IEEE Trans on Comput*, Vol. C-32, No. 1, Jan. 1983, pp. 83-95.

[5] D. A. Reed, "A Simulation Study of Multimicrocomputer Networks," *Tech Rep CSD-TR-435*, Department of Computer Sciences, Purdue University.

[6] L. D. Wittie, "Communication Structures for Large Multimicrocomputer Systems," *IEEE Trans on Comput*, Vol. C-30, No. 4, Apr. 1981, pp. 264-273.

Table I Precedence graph parameters

Quantity	Definition	Reference Value
B_{min}	minimum number of consequents of a fork task	1
B_{max}	maximum number of consequents of a fork task	4
C_F	mean data communication time to initiate a fork or regular task	1
C_J	mean data communication time to initiate a join task	1
Maxpath	maximum length path through the graph	60
Numtasks	number of tasks in the graph	1024
S_F	mean fork task service time	10
S_R	mean regular task service time	10
S_J	mean join task service time	10

Table II
Average graph parallelism for 64 node networks using the reference precedence graph parameters

Network	Average parallelism	Fraction of complete connection
Complete Connection	22.17	1.00
Cube-connected Cycles	15.33	0.69
2-ary 4-cube	15.42	0.70
2-D Spanning Bus Hypercube	18.04	0.81
2-D Toroid	14.75	0.67

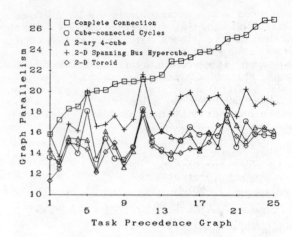

Figure I
Graph parallelism for 64 node networks using the reference precedence graph parameters

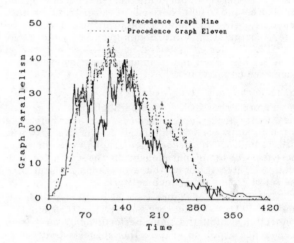

Figure II
Time varying parallelism for two precedence graphs on a 64 node toroid

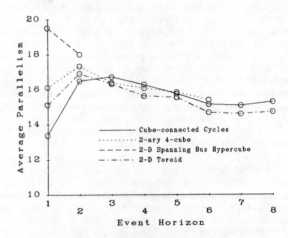

Figure III
Average parallelism for 64 node networks with varying amounts of scheduler information

Chapter 8: Problems Associated with Multicomputer Architecture

Various issues influence the design and implementation of multicomputers. In earlier systems, hardware cost played an important role in defining the architecture, but the decreasing cost of hardware and increasing manpower requirements for the software development now force researchers to think differently. Programming a multicomputer system is altogether different and substantially more complex than programming single-computer system. It is much more difficult to provide useful software support to the users so that the multicomputer systems can be easily usable. In this respect, various architectural issues[1-7] ought to be considered carefully.

One of the most important architectural issues is intercomputer communication strategy with the necessary hardware support. It is generally believed that in a multicomputer environment, it is better to minimize the communication overhead as much as possible. Ideally, it is desirable to interconnect all the individual computers together. While too expensive to provide interconnection, it is still necessary to have a reasonable level of connectivity. Several papers report evaluation studies of various topologies[8-14], and techniques that help in reducing interprocessor communication and for broadcasting data are given in[15-25].

Another important consideration in solving a given problem on a multicomputer system is to partition it into several subtasks that can be run concurrently. Various models have been used to represent a given application algorithm. Some of the techniques for obtaining models are demonstrated[26-46]. Some of them use instruction-level data dependency graphs (commonly known as data-flow graphs) and some employ a higher level of abstract representation with certain attributes associated with the model. The first scheme achieves a larger degree of parallelism while necessitating increased interprocessor communication. A higher level abstraction may not exploit all possible concurrency in a given application, even though the communication overhead is minimal. The level of parallelism is also known as the "grain" size. Because there are pros and cons of larger versus smaller granularity, there is no consensus as to what the optimal grain size should be. Several researchers are working in this area to determine and establish general guidelines.

Some of the algorithms may be synchronous, while others may be asynchronous and the best modeling strategy in general is problem dependent[47-56]. These models are used to obtain a match between algorithms and architectures[57-65]. This problem is also called mapping of algorithms onto architectures. Allocation of channels or tasks and scheduling of non-iterative and data-dependent processes are fairly complex issues, and optimal solutions are either NP-complete or intractable, which has led to several heuristic schemes[66-69] shown to perform well for a given environment. Some of these techniques[70-91] are to be used before/at the actual compilation process and may not provide good results for all possible applications. Various performance measures and optimization criteria include speed up, turn-around time, processor utilization, channel utilization, queueing delay, etc., and have been widely covered[92-96]. Appropriateness of file placement depends on the allocation of processes[97-99]. Allocation of processes at run time is known as dynamic allocation, and models for such allocation and other hardware and software issues have been proposed[100-106] Specific algorithms like sorting extremum search, merging, branch and bound, etc., have been discussed[108-113] projections and an overview of the next generation of computers have been described[114-116].

Case studies are very useful in understanding the shortcomings of existing architectures and in defining future strategies. Case studies for various MIMD-based machines have been reported in the literature, and some of them are[117-123]. Evaluation of some other schemes including those for AI applications have also been given[124-127].

Four papers have been included in this chapter to cover various problems associated with multicomputers.

References

1   H.F. Jordan, M. Scalabrin, and W. Calvert, "A Comparison of Three Types of Multiprocessor Algorithms," *Proc. 1979 Int'l. Conf. Parallel Processing*, IEEE Computer Society, Washington, D.C., 1979, pp. 231-238.

2   A.K. Jones and E.F. Gehringer, (eds.), *The Cm* Multiprocessor Project: A Research Review*, Computer Science Dept., Carnegie-Mellon University, Pittsburgh, Penn., Tech. Report CMU-CS-80-131, July 1980.

3   K. Hwang and Z. Ku, "Remps: A Reconfigurable Multiprocessor for Scientific Supercomputing," *Proc. 1985 Int'l. Conf. Parallel Processing*, IEEE Computer Society, Washington, D.C., 1985, pp. 102-111

4   J. Edler et al., "Issues related to MIMD Shared-Memory Computers: The NYU Ultra Computer Approach," *Proc. 12th Int'l. Symp. Computer Architecture*, IEEE Computer Society, Washington, D.C., 1985, pp. 126-135.

5   J. Beetem et al., "The GF11 Supercomputer," *Proc. 12th Int'l. Symp. Computer Architecture*, IEEE Computer Society, Washington, D.C., 1985, pp. 108-115.

6   D. Naedel, "Closely Coupled Asynchronous Hierarchical and Parallel Processing in an Open Architecture," *Proc. 12th Int'l. Symp. Computer Architecture*, IEEE Computer Society, Washington, D.C., 1985, pp. 215-220.

7   M.J. Gonzalez and B.W. Jordan, "A Framework for the Quantitative Evaluation of Distributed Computer Systems," *IEEE Trans. Computers*, Vol. C-29, No. 12, Dec. 1980, pp. 1087-1094.

8   D.A. Reed, "A Simulation Study of Multimicrocomputer Networks," *Proc. 1983 Int'l. Conf. Parallel Processing*, IEEE Computer Society, Washington, D.C., 1983, pp. I61-163.

9 Y.-H. Yang and T. W. Sze, "An Evaluation Study of Topologies of Parallel Computer Architectures for Scene Matching," *Proc. 1983 Int'l. Conf. Parallel Processing,* IEEE Computer Society, Washington, D.C., 1983, pp. 258-250.

10 Arvind and R.A. Iannucci, "A Critique of Multiprocessing von Neumann Style," *Proc. 10th Ann. Int'l. Symp. Computer Architecture,* IEEE Computer Society, Washington, D.C., 1983, pp. 426-436.

11 V.K. Janakiram and D.P. Agrawal, "Multicomputer Architecture Evaluation," *Tech. Report, CCSP,* North Carolina State University, Raleigh, N.C., 1983.

12 H.F. Jordan, "Experience with Pipelined Multiple Instruction Streams," *Proc. IEEE,* Vol. 72, No. 1, Jan. 1984, pp. 113-123.

13 J.E. Smith and A.R. Pleszkun, "Implementation of Precise Interrupts in Pipelined Processors," *Proc. 12th Int'l. Symp. Computer Architecture,* IEEE Computer Society, Washington, D.C., 1985, pp. 36-44.

14 L.N. Bhuyan, "On the Performance of Loosely Coupled Multiprocessors," *Proc. 11th Int'l. Symp. Computer Architecture,* IEEE Computer Society, Washington, D.C., 1984, pp. 256-262.

15 D. Nasimni and S. Sahni, "Data Broadcasting in SIMD Computers," *IEEE Trans. Computers,* Vol. C-30, No. 2, Feb. 1981, pp. 101-107.

16 D. Nassimi and S. Sahni, "Optimal BPC Permutations on a Cube Connected SIMD Computer," *IEEE Trans. Computers,* Vol. C-31, No. 4, April 1982, pp. 338-341.

17 K.B. Irani and K.W. Chen, "Minimization of Interprocessor Communication for Parallel Computations," *IEEE Trans. Computers,* Vol. C-31, No. 11, Nov. 1982, pp. 1067-1075.

18 A. Wilson, D. Siewiorek, and Z. Segall, "Evaluation of Multiprocessor Interconnect Structures with the CM* Testbed," *Proc. 1983 Int'l. Conf. Parallel Processing,* IEEE Computer Society, Washington, D.C., 1983, pp. 164-171.

19 F. Sovis, "Uniform Theory of the Shuffle-Exchange Type Permutation Networks," *Proc. 10th. Ann. Symp. Computer Architecture,* IEEE Computer Society, Washington, D.C., 983, pp. 334-340.

20 L. Philipson, B. Nilsson, and B. Breidgard, "A Communication Structure for a Multiprocessor Computer with Distributed Global Memory" *Proc. 10th Ann. Int'l. Symp. Computer Architecture,* IEEE Computer Society, Washington, D.C., 1983, pp. 334-340.

21 S.P. Kartashev and S.I. Kartashev, "Optimal Routing Algorithms in Multicomputer Networks Organized as Reconfigurable Binary Trees," *Proc. 1983 Int'l. Conf. Parallel Processing,* IEEE Computer Society, Washington, D.C., 1983, pp. 206-213.

22 K.B. Irani and K.W. Chen, "Minimization of Interprocessor Communication for Parallel Computation," *IEEE Trans. Computers,* Vol. C-31, No. 11, Nov. 1982, pp. 1067-1075.

23 K.B. Irani and N.G. Khabbaz, "A Methodology for the Design of Communication Networks and the Distribution of Data in Distributed Super Computer Systems," *IEEE Trans. Computers,* Vol. C-31, No. 5, May 1982, pp. 419-434.

24 M.A. Marsan, G. F. Balbo, G. Conte, and F. Gregoretti, "Modeling Bus Contention and Memory Interference in a Multiprocessor System," *IEEE Trans. Computers,* Vol. C-32, No. 1, Jan. 1983, pp. 60-71.

25 R. Cezzar and D. Kloppholz, "Process Management Overhead in a Speed-Up Oriented MIMD System," *Proc. 1983 Int'l. Conf. Parallel Processing,* IEEE Computer Society, Washington, D.C., 1983, pp. 395-403.

26 O. Wing and J.W. Huang, "A Computational Model of Parallel Solution of Linear Equations," *IEEE Trans. Computers,* Vol. C-29, No. 7, July 1980, pp. 632-638.

27 D.A. Reed and M.I. Patrick, "Interactive Solution of Large, Sparse, Linear Systems on a Static Data Flow Architecture: Performance Studies," *Proc. 1985 Int'l. Conf. Parallel Processing,* IEEE Computer Society, Washington, D.C., 1985, pp. 25-32.

28 J.R. McGraw, "Data Flow Computing-Software Systems Development," *IEEE Trans. Computers,* Vol. C-29, No. 12, December 1980, pp. 1095-1103.

29 J. Deminet, "Experience with Multiprocessor Algorithms," *IEEE Trans. Computers,* Vol. C-31, No. 4, April 1982, pp. 278-288.

30 J.R. McGraw and S.K. Skedzielewski, "Streams and Iteration in Val: Additions to a Data Flow Language," *Proc. 3rd Int'l. Conf. on Distributed Computing Systems,* IEEE Computer Society, Washington, D.C., 1982, pp. 733-739.

31 B.W. Weide, "Modeling Unusual Behavior of Parallel Algorithms," *IEEE Trans. Computers,* Vol. C-31, No. 11, Nov. 1982, pp. 1126-1130.

32 M.D. Ercegovac and W.J. Karplus, "On a Dataflow Approach in High-Speed Simulation of Continuous Systems," *Proc. Int'l. Workshop on High-Level Computer Architecture,* edited by Y. Chu, University of Maryland, College Park, Md., 1979, pp. 2.1-2.8.

33 D. Gelernter, "Dynamic Global Name Spaces on Network Computers," *Proc. 1984 Int'l. Conf. Parallel Processing,* IEEE Computer Society, Washington, D.C., 1984, pp. 25-31.

34 J.L. Peterson, "Petri Nets," *ACM Computing Surveys,* Vol. 9, No. 3, Sept. 1977, pp. 223-252.

35 J.D. Brock and L.B. Montz, "Translation and Optimization of Data Flow Programs," *Proc. 1979 Int'l. Conf. Parallel Processing,* IEEE Computer Society, Washington, D.C., 1979,. pp. 46-54.

36 M.J. Flynn and J.L. Hennessy, "Parallelism and Representation Problems in Distributed Systems," *IEEE Trans. Computers,* Vol. C-29, No. 12, Dec. 1980, pp. 1080-1086.

37 D. Klappholz, "The Symbolic High-Level Language Programming of an MIMD Machine," *Proc. 1981 Int'l. Conf. Parallel Processing,* IEEE Computer Society, Washington, D.C., 1981, pp. 61-53.

38 D.J. Kuck, R.H. Kuhn, D.A. Padua, B. Leasure, and M. Wolfe, "Dependence Graphs and Compiler Optimizations," *Proc. 8th ACM Symp. Principles Programming Languages,* ACM, New York, N.Y., Jan. 1981, pp. 207-218.

39 A.L. Davis and R.M. Keller, "Data Flow Program Graphs," *Computer,* Vol. 15, No. 2, Feb. 1982, pp. 26-40.

40 D. Klappholz et al., "Toward a Hybrid Data-Flow/ Control-Flow MIMD Architecture," *Proc. 5th Int'l. Conf. Distributed Computing Systems,* IEEE Computer Society, Washington, D.C., 1985, pp. 10-15.

41 B. Jayaraman, "Constructing a Parallel Implementation from High-Level Specification: A Case Study Using Resource Ex-

pressions," *Proc. 1983 Int'l. Conf. Parallel Processing,* IEEE Computer Society, Washington, D.C., 1983, pp. 416-420.

42 D. Logan, C. Maples, D. Weaver, and W. Rathbun, "Adapting Scientific Programs to the MIDAS Multiprocessor System," *Proc. 1984 Int'l. Conf. Parallel Processing,* IEEE Computer Society, Washington, D.C., 1984, pp. I5-24.

43 K. Oflazer, "Partitioning in Parallel Processing of Production Systems," *Proc. 1984 Int'l. Conf. Parallel Processing,* IEEE Computer Society, Washington, D.C., 1984, pp. 92-100.

44 A.J. Bernstein, "Analysis of Programs for Parallel Processing," *IEEE Trans. Electronic Computers,* Vol. EC-15, No. 5, Oct. 1966, pp. 757-763.

45 T.P. Barnwell, III, and C.J.M. Hodges, "Optimal Implementation of Signal Flow Graphs on Synchronous Multiprocessors," *Proc. 1982 Int'l. Conf. Parallel Processing,* IEEE Computer Society, Washington, D.C., 1982, pp. 90-95.

46 P. Heidelberger and K.S. Trivedi, "Analytical Queueing Models for Programs with Internal Concurrency," *IEEE Trans. Computers,* Vol. C-22, No. 1, Jan. 1983, pp. 73-82.

47 P.C. Treleaven, "Exploiting Program Concurrency in Computing Systems," *Computer,* Vol. 12, No. 1, Jan. 1979, pp. 42-50.

48 G.J. Li and B.W. Wah, "Computational Efficiency of Parallel Approximate Branch-and-Bound Algorithms," *Proc. 1984 Int'l. Conf. Parallel Processing,* IEEE Computer Society, Washington, D.C., 1984, pp. 473-480.

49 R.H. Barlow, D.J. Evans, and J. Shanchi, "Comparative Study of the Exploitation of Different Levels of Parallelism on Different Architectures," *Proc. 1982 Int'l. Conf. Parallel Processing,* IEEE Computer Society, Washington, D.C., 1982, pp. 34-40.

50 G.M. Baudet, "Asynchronous Iterative Methods for Multiprocessors," *Journal of the ACM,* Vol. 25, No. 2, April 1978, pp. 226-244,

51 M. Dubois and F.A. Briggs, "An Approximate Analytical Model for Asynchronous Processes in Multiprocesses in Multiprocessors," *Proc. 1982 Int'l. Conf. Parallel Processing,* IEEE Computer Society, Washington, D.C., 1982, pp. 290-297.

52 M. Dubois and F.A. Briggs, "Performance of Synchronized Iterative Process in Multiprocessor Systems," *IEEE Trans. Software Engineering,* Vol. SE-8, No. 4, July 1982, pp. 419-431.

53 R.C. Pearce and J.C. Majithia, "Analysis of a Shared Resource MIMD Computer Organization," *IEEE Trans. Computers,* Vol. C-27, No. 1, Jan. 1978, pp. 64-67.

54 F.A. Briggs, M. Dubois, and K. Hwang, "Throughput Analysis and Configuration Design of a Shared-Resource Multiprocessors Systems: PUMPS," *Proc. 8th Ann. Symp. Computer Architecture,* IEEE Computer Society, Washington, D.C., May 1981, pp. 67-80.

55 R. Cezzer and D. Klappholz, "Process Management Over head in a Speedup-Oriented MIMD System," *Proc. of 1983 Int'l. Conf. Parallel Processing,* IEEE Computer Society, Washington, D.C., 1983, pp. 395-403.

56 B.W. Wah, "A Comparative Study of Distributed Resource Sharing on Multiprocessors," *Proc. 10th Ann. Int'l. Symp. on Computer Architecture,* IEEE Computer Society, Washing-

ton, D.C., 1983, pp. 301-308.

57 Y. Chiang and K.S. Fu, "Matching Parallel Algorithm and Architecture," *Proc. 1983 Int'l. Conf. Parallel Processing,* IEEE Computer Society, Washington, D.C., 1983, pp. 374-380.

58 D. Gannon, "On Mapping Non-uniform PDE Structures and Algorithms onto Uniform Array," *Proc. 1981 Int'l. Conf. Parallel Processing,* IEEE Computer Society, Washington, D.C., 1981, pp. 100-105.

59 M. Tadjan, R.E. Buehrer, and W. Haelg, "Parallel Simulation by Means of a Prescheduled MIMD-System Featuring Synchronous Pipelined Processors," *Proc. 1982 Int'l. Conf. Parallel Processing,* IEEE Computer Society, Washington, D.C., 1982, pp. 280-283.

60 I.V. Ramakrishnan, D.S. Fussell, and A. Silberschatz, "On Mapping Homogeneous Graphs on a Line Array-Processor Model," *Proc. 1983 Int'l. Conf. Parallel Processing,* IEEE Computer Society, Washington, D.C., 1983, pp. 440-447.

61 G.R. Gao, "Pipelined Mapping of Homogeneous Dataflow Programs," *Proc. 1984 Int'l. Conf. Parallel Processing,* IEEE Computer Society, Washington, D.C., 1984, pp. 532-538.

62 F. Berman and L. Snyder, "On Mapping Parallel Algorithms into Parallel Architectures," *Proc. 1984 Int'l. Conf. Parallel Processing,* IEEE Computer Society, Washington, D.C., 1984, pp. 307-309.

63 M.F.M. Tenorio and D.I. Moldovan, "Mapping Production Systems into Multiprocessors," *Proc. 1985 Int'l. Conf. Parallel Processing,* IEEE Computer Society, Washington, D.C., 1985, pp. 56-62.

64 C.P. Kriskal and A. Weiss, "Allocating Independent Subtasks on Parallel Processors," *Proc. 1984 Int'l. Conf. Parallel Processing,* IEEE Computer Society, Washington, D.C., 1984, pp. 236-240.

65 F. Berman and L. Snyder, "On Mapping Parallel Algorithms into Parallel Architecture," *Proc. 1984 Int'l. Conf. Parallel Processing,* IEEE Computer Society, Washington, D.C., 1984, pp. 307-309.

66 C. Maples, D. Weaver, D. Logan, and W. Rathbun, "Performance of a Modular Interactive Data Analysis System (MIDAS)," *Proc. 1983 Int'l. Conf. Parallel Processing,* IEEE Computer Society, Washington, D.C., 1983, pp. 514-519.

67 H.J. Sips, "Task Distribution on Clustered Parallel or Multiprocessor Systems," *Proc. 4th Int'l. Conf. Distributed Computing Systems,* IEEE Computer Society, Washington, D.C., 1984, pp. 126-130.

68 J.A. Stankovic and I.S. Sidhu, "An Adaptive Bidding Algorithm for Processes, Clusters and Distributed Groups," *Proc. 4th Int'l. Conf. Distributed Computing Systems,* IEEE Computer Society, Washington, D.C., 1984, pp. 49-59.

69 U.I. Gupta, D.T. Lee, and J.Y.-T. Leung "An Optimal Solution for the Channel-Assignment Problem," *IEEE Trans. Computers,* Vol. C-28, No. 11, Nov. 1979, pp. 807-810.

70 K. Hovesty and C.J. Jenny, "Partitioning and Allocating Computational Objects in Distributed Computing Systems," *Proc. IFIP 80,* North-Holland, Amsterdam, The Netherlands, 1980.

71 W.W. Chu, L.J. Holloway, M.T. Lan, and K. Efe, "Task Allocation in Distributed Data Processing," *Computer*, Vol. 13, No. 11, Nov. 1980, pp. 57-69.

72 U. Lauther, "Comments on 'An Optimal Solution for the Channel-Assignment Problem' by U.I. Gupta, et al.," *IEEE Trans. Computers*, Vol. C-30, No. 6, June 1981, pp. 455.

73 P. Ma, E.Y.S. Lee, and M. Tsuchiya, "On the Design of a Task Allocation Scheme for Time-Critical Applications," *Proc. Real-Time Systems Symp.*, IEEE Computer Society, Washington, D.C., pp. 121-126.

74 L.M. Ni and C.F.E. Wu, "Design Trade-Offs for Process Scheduling in Tightly Coupled Multiprocessor Systems," *Proc. 1985 Int'l. Conf. Parallel Processing*, IEEE Computer Society, Washington, D.C., 1985, pp. 63-70.

75 Y. Takuhaski, "Partitioning and Allocation in Parallel Computation of Partial Differential Equations," *Proc. 19th IMACS World Congress*, Vol. 1, 1982, pp. 311-313.

76 G. Persky, B.N. Tien, and B.S. Ting, "Comments on 'An Optimal Solution for the Channel-Assignment Problem' by U.I. Gupta, et al.," *IEEE Trans. Computers*, Vol. C-30, No. 6, June 1981, p. 454.

77 P. Ma, P.Y. Richard, E.Y.S. Lee, and M. Tsuchiya, "A Task Allocation Model for Distributed Computing Systems," *IEEE Trans. Computers*, Vol. C-31, No. 1, Jan. 1982, pp. 41-47.

78 C.A. Niznik, "A Quantization Approximation for Modeling Computer Network Nodal Queueing Delay," *IEEE Trans. Computers*, Vol. C-32, No. 3, March 1983, pp. 245-253.

79 E. Williams, "Assigning Processes to Processors in Distributed Systems," *Proc. 1983 Int'l. Conf. Parallel Processing*, IEEE Computer Society, Washington, D.C., 1983, pp. 404-406.

80 V.M. Lo, "Heuristic Algorithms for Task Assignment in Distributed Systems," *Proc. 4th Int'l. Conf. Distributed Computing Systems*, IEEE Computer Society, Washington, D.C., 1984, pp. 30-39.

81 C.E. Houstis, E.N. Houstis, and J R. Rice, "Partitioning and Allocation of PDE Computations in Distributed Systems," *PDE Software: Modules, Interfaces and Systems*, edited by B. Engquist, North-Holland, New York.

82 M.J. Gonzalez, "Deterministic Processor Scheduling," *ACM Computing Surveys*, Vol. 9, No. 3, Sept. 1977, pp. 173-204.

83 T. Gonzalez and S. Sahni, "Preemptive Scheduling of Uniform Processor Systems," *Journal of the ACM*, Vol. 25, No. 1, Jan. 1978, pp. 92-101.

84 F. Rubin, "Comments on 'An Optimal Solution for the Channel-assignment Problem' by U.I. Gupta, et al.," *IEEE Trans. Computers*, Vol C-30, No. 6, June 1981, pp. 455.

85 K. Efe, "Heuristic Models of Task Assignment Scheduling in Distributed Systems," *Computer*, Vol. 15, No. 6, June 1982, pp. 50-56.

86 E. Delel and S. Sahni, "Binary Trees and Parallel Scheduling Algorithms," *IEEE Trans. Computers*, Vol. C-32, No. 3, March 1983, pp. 307-315.

87 S.P. Su and K. Hwang, "Multiple Pipeline Scheduling in Vector Super Computers" *Proc. 1982 Int'l. Conf. Parallel Processing*, 1982, pp. 226-234.

88 M.A. Srinivas, "Optimal Parallel Scheduling of Gaussian-Elimination Directed Acyclic Graphs," *IEEE Trans. Computers*, Vol. C-32, No. 12, Dec. 1983, pp. 1109-1117.

89 D. Klappholz and H.C. Park, "Parallelized Process Scheduling for a Tightly-coupled MIMD Machine," *Proc. 1984 Int'l. Conf. Parallel Processing*, IEEE Computer Society, Washington, D.C., 1984, pp. 315-321.

90 G.C. Pathak and D.P. Agrawal, "Automated Design of Multicomputer Architecture for Real-Time Applications," *IEEE-CS Distributed Processing Newsletter*, Vol. 6, No. SI-1, IEEE Computer Society, Washington, D.C., 1984, pp. 35-38.

91 S. Uchida, "Inference Machine: From Sequential to Parallel," *Proc. 10th Ann. Int'l. Symp. Computer Architecture*, IEEE Computer Society, Washington, D.C., 1983, pp. 410-416.

92 S. Sahni, "Scheduling Multipipeline and Multiprocessor Computers," *Proc. 1984 Int'l. Conf. Parallel Processing*, IEEE Computer Society, Washington, D.C., 1984, pp. 333-337.

93 J.A.B. Fortes and F.P. Presicce, "Optimal Linear Time Schedules for the Parallel Execution of Algorithms," *Proc. 1984 Int'l. Conf. Parallel Processing*, IEEE Computer Society, Washington, D.C., 1984, pp. 322-329.

94 D. Klappholz and H.C. Park, "Parallelized Process Scheduling for a Tightly-Coupled MIMD Machine," *Proc. 1984 Int'l. Conf. Parallel Processing*, IEEE Computer Society, Washington, D.C., 1984, pp. 315-321.

95 R. Mehrotra and S.N. Talukdar, "Scheduling of Tasks for Distributed Processors," *Proc. 11th Ann. Int'l. Symp. Computer Architecture*, IEEE Computer Society, Washington, D.C., 1984, pp. 263-270.

96 R. Manner, "Hardware Task/Processor Scheduling in a Polyprocessor Environment," *IEEE Trans. Computers*, Vol. C-33, No. 7, July 1984, pp. 626-636.

97 H. Garcia-Molina, "Elections in a Distributed Computing System," *IEEE Trans. Computers*, Vol. C-31, No. 1, Jan. 1982, pp. 48-59.

98 D.L. Tuomenoksa and H.J. Siegel, "Preloading Schemes for the PASM Parallel Memory System," *Proc. 1983 Int'l. Conf. Parallel Processing*, IEEE Computer Society, Washington, D.C., 1983, pp. 407-415.

99 B.W. Wah, "File Placement on Distributed Computer Systems," *Computer*, Vol. 17, No. 1, Jan. 1984, pp. 23-32.

100 Y.C. Chow and W.H. Kohler, "Models for Dynamic Load Balancing in a Heterogeneous Multiple Processor System," *IEEE Trans. Computers*, Vol. C-28, No. 5, May 1979, pp. 354-361.

101 P. Li and C. Johnsson, "The Tree Machine: An Evaluation of Strategies for Reducing Program Loading Time," *Proc. 1983 Int'l. Conf. Parallel Processing*, IEEE Computer Society, Washington, D.C., 1983, pp. 202-205.

102 D.P. Siewiorek et al., "A Case Study of C.mmp, Cm and C.vmp, Part I: Experience with Fault-Tolerance in Multiprocessor Systems," *Proc. IEEE*, Vol. 66, No. 10, Oct. 1978, pp. 1178-1199.

103 G.J. Nutt, "A Parallel Processor Operating System," *IEEE Trans. Software Engineering*, Vol. SE-3, No. 6, Nov. 1977, pp. 467-475.

104 W.J. Karplus and D. Cohen, "Architectural and Software Issues in the Design and Application of Peripheral Array

Processors," *Computer,* Vol. 14, No. 9, Sept. 1981, pp. 11-17

105 Arvind and K.P. Gostelow, "The U Interpreter," *Computer,* Vol. 15, No. 2, Feb. 1982, pp. 42-50.

106 R.G. Avizienis, "Reliability Optimization in the Design of Distributed System," *Proc. 2nd Int'l. Conf. Distributed Computing Systems,* IEEE Computer Society, Washington, D.C., 1982, pp. 388-393.

107 B. W. Wah, G.-J. Li, and C.-F. Yu, "The Status of MANIP-A Multicomputer Architecture for Solving Combinatorial Extremum-Search Problems," *Proc. 11th Ann. Int'l. Symp. Computer Architecture,* IEEE Computer Society, Washington, D.C., 1984, pp. 56-63.

108 F.G. Gray, W.M. McCormack, and R.M. Haralick, "Significance of Problem Solving Parameters on the Performance of Cominatroial Algorithms on Multi-Computer Parallel Architectures," *Proc. 1982 Int'l. Conf. on Parallel Processing,* IEEE Computer Society, Washington, D.C., 1982, pp. 185-192.

109 C. Kruskal, "Searching, Merging and Sorting in Parallel Computation," *IEEE Trans. Computers,* Vol. C-32, No. 10, Oct. 1983, pp. 942-947.

110 Q.F. Stout, "Sorting, Merging, Selecting and Filtering on Tree and Pyramid Machines," *Proc. 1983 Intl. Conf. Parallel Processing,* IEEE Computer Society, Washington, D.C., 1983, pp. 214-221.

111 C.D. Thompaon and H.T. Kunf, "Sorting on a Mesh-Connected Parallel Computer," *Comm. of the ACM,* Vol. 20, No. 4, April 1977, pp. 263-271.

112 B.W. Wah and Y.W. Ma, "Manip-A Parallel Computer System for Implementing Branch and Bound Algorithms," *Proc. 8th Ann. Symp. Computer Architecture,* IEEE Computer Society, Washington, D.C., 1981, pp. 239-262.

113 Y. Ishikawa and M. Tokoro, "The Design of an Object Oriented Architecture," *Proc. 11th Ann. Int'l. Symp. Computer Architecture,* IEEE Computer Society, Washington, D.C., 984, pp. 178-187.

114 R.G. Arnold, R.O. Berg, and J.W. Thomas, "A Modular Approach to Real-time Supersystems," *IEEE Trans. Computers,* Vol. C-31, No. 5, May 1982, pp. 385-398.

115 J. Lewell, "Turning Dreams into Reality with Super Computers and Super Visions," *Computer Pictures,* Jan./Feb. 1983, p. 40.

116 T. Moto-Oka, "Overview of the Fifth Generation Computer System Project," *Proc. 10th Ann. Int'l. Symp. Computer Architecture,* IEEE Computer Society, Washington, D.C., 1983, pp. 417-422.

117 J.S. Emer and D. W. Clark, "A Characterization of Processor Performance in the VAX-11/780," *Proc. 11th Ann. Int'l. Symp. Computer Architecture,* IEEE Computer Society, Washington, D.C., 1984, pp. 301-309.

118 T. Cheung and J. E. Smith, "An Analysis of the CRAY X-MP Memory System," *Proc. 1984 Int'l. Conf. Parallel Processing,* IEEE Computer Society, Washington, D.C., 1984, pp. 499-505.

119 A. Wilson, D. Siewiorek, and Z. Segall, "Evaluation of Multiprocessor Interconnect Structures with the Cm* Testbed," *Proc. 1983 Int'l. Conf. Parallel Processing,* IEEE Computer Society, Washington, D.C., 1983, pp. 164-171.

120 H.F. Jordan, "Performance Measurements on HEP-A Pipelined MIMD Computer," *Proc. 10th Ann. Int'l. Symposium on Computer Architecture,* IEEE Computer Society, Washington, D.C., 1983, p. 207-212.

121 E.F. Gehringer et al., "The Cm* Testbed," *Computer,* Vol. 15, No. 10, Oct. 1982, pp. 38-50.

122 P. Civera, et al., "The μ* Project: An Experience with a Multimicroprocessor System," *IEEE Micro,* Vol. 2, No. 2, May 1982, pp. 38-50.

123 H. Fromm et. al., "Experiences with Performance Measurement and Modeling of a Processor Array,": *IEEE Trans. Computers,* Vol. C-32, No. 1, Jan. 1983, pp. 15-31.

124 K.P. Gostelow and R. E. Thomas, "Performance of a Simulated Dataflow Computer," *IEEE Trans. Computers,* Vol. C-32, No. 1, Jan. 1983, pp. 15-21.

125 Gelenbe et al., "Experience with the Parallel Solution of Partial Differential Equations on a Distributed Computing System," *IEEE Trans. Computer,* Vol. C-31, No. 12, Dec. 1982, 1157-1164.

126 K.D. Fennell and V.R. Lesser, "Parallelism in Artificial Intelligence Problem Solving: A Case Study of Hearsay II," *IEEE Trans. Computer,* Vol. C-26, No. 3, March, 1977, pp. 98-11.

127 A. Gupta, "Implementing OPS5 Production Systems on DADO," *Proc. 1984 Int'l. Conf. Parallel Processing,* IEEE Computer Society, Washington, D.C., 1984, pp. 83-91.

Predicting execution times in the complex, parallel environment can be risky. Techniques developed for NASA's Finite Element Machine provide accurate performance estimates and minimize the risk.

Modeling Algorithm Execution Time on Processor Arrays

Loyce M. Adams, Institute for Computer Applications in Science and Engineering

Thomas W. Crockett, Kentron International, Inc.

The performance of a numerical algorithm on a sequential computer is usually measured by the number of arithmetic operations required to complete the algorithm. Generally, this number is expressed as a function of the size of the application problem. For instance, it is well known that the solution of a system of n linear equations using Gaussian elimination takes $0(n^3)$ arithmetic operations.[1] On sequential machines, the execution time of the algorithm is assumed to be directly proportional to the arithmetic operation count. This approach has worked well as a means of comparing sequential algorithms.

However, it has been pointed out repeatedly that this standard arithmetic complexity analysis is not sufficient to analyze parallel algorithms.[2-5] Additional operations—such as data transmissions between processors, synchronization of processors, and global decision making—may add to the execution time of the algorithms. The number of these operations and the time required for each operation may vary with the algorithm, with the number of processors used to solve the problem, and with the problem size. The time required for these operations is dependent not only upon the particular architecture in use, but also upon the software required to implement them. These considerations suggest that an adequate performance analysis of a parallel algorithm must include a model for its execution time.

This article describes an approach for modeling the execution time of algorithms on parallel arrays; this time is expressed as a function of the number of processors and system (hardware and software) parameters.

Performance model

The execution time of an algorithm running on multiple, cooperating processors is defined as the time elapsed from when the first processor begins execution to when the last processor finishes. Furthermore, if we let the execution time of an algorithm on a given processor be the sum of the busy and idle times of that processor, the execution time will be the same for all processors (see Figure 1). Consequently, to determine the execution time of any given processor, it may be necessary to model all processors to account for the effect of interactions between them.

The execution time, E, of a parallel algorithm can be broken down into four broad categories: A, arithmetic time; C, communication time; S, synchronization time; and W, idle or wait time:

$$E = A + C + S + W \tag{1}$$

This model assumes one process per processor and no overlap of arithmetic, communication, and synchronization times.

The value for A includes the time for floating-point operations, integer arithmetic, loop overhead, and array indexing. These integer operations are rarely included in sequential algorithmic analysis; however, since they may be a function of the number of processors as well as the problem size in the parallel environment, they should be included.

The value for C includes the time to communicate values from one processor to another. If the processors are connected to a shared memory, communication time will be realized as the time to read and write into the shared memory. If, instead, the processors communicate directly with each other by passing messages over communication links, it will be the time required to both send information to and receive information from cooperating processors.

The value for S includes the times required for synchronization between processors and global decision making. For example, in parallel iterative algorithms, the processors must synchronize after each iteration and then determine if a global stopping criterion is met. For processors connected to a shared memory, S will be the time required for all processors to write and then read a shared variable. If the processors are connected to special hard-

Reprinted from *Computer*, July 1984, pages 38-43. Copyright © 1984 by The Institute of Electrical and Electronics Engineers, Inc.

ware for this purpose, it is the time required for the hardware and its software interface to perform the operations. For some hardware array designs, synchronization and global decision making may be more appropriately modeled as communication time.

The value for W includes the time that the processor spends (1) waiting on values from other processors to arrive if communication links are used, or (2) contending for shared memory if the processors communicate in that fashion. Also included in W is the time that a processor is idle either prior to or following the execution of a task (see Figure 1).

An iterative algorithm example

The conjugate gradient algorithm[6] for solving a system of linear equations that arise from discretizing a partial differential equation problem domain can be used to illustrate how the number of operations in equation (1) is determined.

For this problem, suppose that each computational node from an x by y block of nodes (see Figure 2) contributes two equations to the system of linear equations to be solved. Each processor is therefore responsible for the solution of $2xy$ equations. If there are N equations total and p processors are used, the value of $2xy$ will be N/p. We now describe the components of the execution time for a processor in the interior of the processor array.

The parallel conjugate gradient algorithm for this problem can be shown[7] to require the following number of floating-point arithmetic operations (the number of iterations of the algorithm is represented by I):

$$
\begin{array}{ll}
\text{multiply/add pairs} & \dfrac{19NI}{p} \\
\text{adds} & 2I(p-1) \\
\text{or} & \\
\text{divides} & 2I \qquad\qquad (2)
\end{array}
$$

On each iteration, two values for each computational node on the border of the x by y block must be sent to adjacent processors. Values going to the same processor may be sent as one or more packages, depending on the structure of the particular architecture. Likewise, on each iteration, a processor must receive the two values for each border node of adjacent processors. Again, the values coming from a given processor may be received in one or more packages. In addition, the algorithm requires one value to be broadcast to the $p-1$ other processors and $p-1$ values to be received from the other processors twice each iteration. These communication components are summarized in the following list (we assume that c numbers are sent per package and d numbers received per package):

$$
\begin{array}{ll}
\text{packages sent:} & 4I(x+y+1)\div c \\
\text{numbers sent:} & 4I(x+y+1) \\
\text{packages broadcast:} & 2I \\
\text{numbers broadcast:} & 2I \\
\text{packages received:} & 4I(x+y+1)\div d + 2I(p-1) \\
\text{numbers received:} & 4I(x+y+1)+2I(p-1) \qquad (3)
\end{array}
$$

For each iteration, the processors must be synchronized and the global convergence test made. Therefore, the number of these components are

number of synchronizations: I
number of convergence checks: I $\qquad$ (4)

On sequential computers, the time for convergence checking is rarely counted in the complexity of the algorithm. However, this operation requires cooperation between the processors for the parallel algorithm and may be costly depending on the hardware and software available to perform these operations.

The wait time for this algorithm is assumed to be zero since each processor in the interior of the processor array has the same amount of work to perform and the same code to execute. Unlike the situation shown in Figure 1, the processors will calculate, communicate, and synchronize more or less at the same time for this algorithm.

The times for each of the operations for the conjugate gradient algorithm depend upon the parallel array and its software, as we will illustrate for the Finite Element Machine.

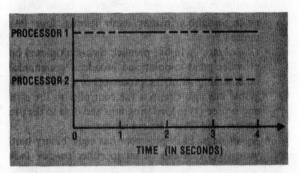

Figure 1. Two processors working together to solve a problem. The solid line indicates busy time and the dotted line represents idle time. The total execution time of the algorithm is four seconds, even though processor 1 is busy for two seconds and processor 2 is busy for three seconds.

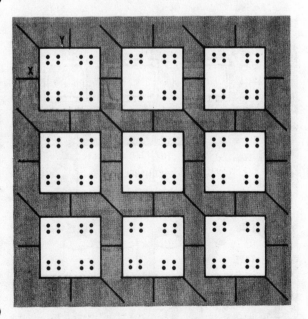

Figure 2. The assignment of a problem to processors. A rectangular domain is discretized into computational nodes with an x by y block of nodes assigned to each processor in the processor array.

The Finite Element Machine

The FEM[8-11] is a research computer being built at NASA's Langley Research Center to investigate the application of parallel processing to structural engineering analysis. FEM consists of a minicomputer front end, called the controller, attached to an MIMD array of asynchronous microcomputers, referred to as the array (see Figure 3). Each processor in the array is based on a TMS9900 microprocessor[12] with an associated Am9512 floating-point unit,[13] 32K bytes of RAM, and 16K bytes of EPROM. Each processor has its own clock and runs its own program on its own data (there is no shared memory in the system). Additional circuitry provides a rich interconnection environment for communication and cooperative computation, which includes

- *Local communication links.* Each processor has 12 bidirectional serial ports that provide dedicated I/O paths to neighboring processors. For this study, we chose the interconnection topology to be an eight nearest-neighbor planar mesh leaving four links unused.
- *Global bus.* A 16-bit, parallel, time-multiplexed bus provides point-to-point and broadcast communications among all of the processors in the array. The global bus also connects the controller to the array and is used (1) to load programs and data to the processors, and (2) to retrieve results.
- *Signal flags.* Each processor has eight binary hardware flags that can be set to either *true* or *false*. Distributed circuitry allows each processor to inspect the global status of each flag. Status signals include ANY (one or more processors have set the flag to *true*), ALL (every processor has set the flag to *true*), and a special SYNC signal that is used for synchronization.

- *Sum/maximum network.* The sum/max network aids in global calculations by determining the sum and maximum of the inputs from all processors.[14] This network is logically a tree with special-purpose computation nodes residing on each processor. The results of the computation are made available to all processors in the array.

The current machine has eight processors operational (minus the sum/max network) and plans call for expansion first to 16, and eventually to 36, processors.

System software for FEM consists of three major components: (1) FEM array control software, or FACS, (2) Nodal Exec operating system, and (3) Paslib (Pascal library) subroutine library. FACS[15] is a set of about 40 programs that provide the user interface to the array. Nodal Exec is a small special-purpose operating system which resides in EPROM on each processor in the array. It is divided into two major sections, one of which provides the usual operating system support services such as memory management, I/O primitives, interrupt handling, and timing. The other section is a set of routines that carry out operations requested by the FACS software.

Application programs for the array are written in Pascal. Programs are compiled and linked on the controller, and downloaded to the appropriate processor(s) using FACS. Access to the special architectural features of the machine is provided by a library of subroutines called Paslib.[16] Some Paslib operations are implemented directly, while others are carried out through Nodal Exec. Services provided by Paslib include communication with the controller and other processors, flag and sum/max operations, mathematical subroutines, and timing.

Interprocessor communication is provided by three subroutines: SEND, SENDALL, and RECV. SEND transmits the requested number of data words at a given address to a particular neighboring processor. SENDALL is

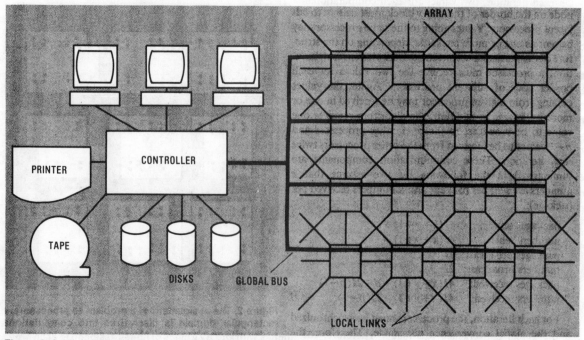

Figure 3. A 16-processor finite element machine.

similar, but transmits the data to all neighboring processors. RECV accepts the requested number of data words from a neighboring processor and stores them at the given address. Nodal Exec provides buffering services so that communicating processors need not be tightly synchronized.

Model parameters for FEM

The software component of the various operations performed by FEM (see Table 1) dominates the hardware time required. Although proposed parallel architectures are frequently analyzed based on hardware arguments, our experience indicates that performance estimates can only be justified when the times for realistic software implementations are included. In many cases, accurate estimates of software overhead can only be obtained by writing the code and determining the execution time, either by summing instruction times, simulating execution at the instruction level, or running on the actual hardware.

The figures in Table 1 were obtained by either of two techniques: (1) adding up the instruction times required for the operation, or (2) performing timing experiments on the actual hardware.

The time for single-precision floating-point operations on FEM is dominated by the time required to load operands and retrieve results from the Am9512, which has an eight-bit-wide data path. Since actual computation time is operand-dependent, a range of times for floating-point arithmetic operations is given, along with a typical time.

Communication times include software overhead for parameter validation, table look-ups, buffering, and interrupt overheads. The times used here are based on Knott's study of the Paslib SEND and RECV routines.[17] Broadcast times for FEM have not been measured, but are similar to those for nonbroadcast SENDs. These times are subject to some variation caused by dynamic interactions among asynchronous processors.

The synchronization operation uses the SYNC flag signal to achieve synchronization among all processors. The synchronization value in Table 1 excludes any time that is spent waiting for slower processors to catch up. Actual wait times are dependent on the algorithm and the variation in workload between processors; minor effects are caused by operand dependencies in floating-point operations and slight differences in clock speeds between processors. This is one of the most efficient operations implemented by Paslib; most of the software time is attributable to subroutine call overhead.

Global flag status checks, like synchronization operations, are relatively efficient with subroutine entry and exit code constituting the major overhead. In parallel iterative algorithms, for example, they are used to determine global convergence.

Performance measurement tools

System software for FEM provides several tools that aid in the analysis of program behavior on the array. These include timers, operation counters, and a statistical trace facility. Two interval timers are available on each processor. Nodal Exec uses one of them to measure elapsed program execution time, with a resolution of 16 ms. This timer can be interrogated from user programs to yield the elapsed execution time at any point. The second timer, which can be started and stopped under control of the user program, has programmable resolution from one to 349 ms.

In addition, Nodal Exec and Paslib maintain counters during program execution to record the number of floating-point and flag operations, SEND and RECV calls, buffer allocations, I/O interrupts, and data words transmitted and received. This information can be retrieved by the controller and postprocessed to give an execution statistics report that includes not only the operation counts, but derived performance measures such as average I/O data rates, average number of data words processed per I/O interrupt, and the overall floating-point rate. The operand counts provide accurate data to validate the numbers in the performance model and the derived statistics give a rough idea of communication and floating-point efficiencies.

While the execution statistics can be used to validate the number of operations in the model, an additional tool is needed to validate the percentage of time spent in these operations and to pinpoint discrepancies between predicted and observed behavior. This capability is provided by Nodal Exec in the form of a statistical tracer. The tracer works by sampling the processor's program counter at regular intervals and sending the observed value to the controller, which, in turn, stores the value in a file. If enough samples are taken, the resulting distribution of program counter addresses will reflect the time spent in various portions of the program, including system code. The trace file saved by the controller is sorted by processor number and program counter address, and the result can be correlated with the program's link map to give the approximate percentage of time spent in each routine. Since the trace resolution is at the instruction level, time spent in specific loops can be pinpointed.

Because the trace data is only a statistical sample, it is subject to some error, and trace results may vary somewhat from run to run. The recommended procedure is to make several runs of the same program and average the trace results. There is sufficient asynchrony between the trace mechanism (driven by a timer interrupt) and program execution that identical trace results from one run to the next have not been observed. The variance of trace

Table 1. FEM model parameters.

COST PARAMETER	TIME (ms)
Multiply/Add Pair	0.997-1.195 (1.032 typical)
Addition	0.475-0.662 (0.516 typical)
Division	0.520-0.538 (0.526 typical)
Package Receive Overhead	1.308
Receive a Number	0.510
Package Send Overhead	1.672
Send a Number	0.221
Package Broadcast Overhead	1.672
Broadcast a Number	0.221
Synchronize	0.129
Global Flag Check	0.278

results among several runs can be used to obtain a measure of confidence for the mean result.

Results

The conjugate gradient algorithm was run on an eight-processor FEM arranged as two rows and four columns of processors for two problems. For the first problem, each processor was assigned a 1×3 block of computational nodes; for the second problem, each processor had a 3×3 block of nodes. Each problem was run and the execution statistics matched exactly the number of operations predicted by the model. The problems were then run three times each with the tracer enabled using a 50-ms trace interval. The tracer increased execution time by about 0.9 percent and no effect on execution behavior was noticed in the execution statistics. The results of the three runs were averaged and compared against those predicted by the model. Tables 2 and 3 summarize the findings. The model predictions agreed closely with the trace results for the time required for the floating-point arithmetic and communication and synchronization operations. The tracer also indicated that integer arithmetic, array indexing, and loop overhead should be modeled since this accounted for about 20 percent of the execution time in both problems.

This model can be used to predict the performance of the example iterative algorithm on larger processor arrays. As an illustration, assume that one number per package is sent and received and that the time to broadcast a package is equal to the time required to send or receive it. Furthermore, define the ratio of the communication time to arithmetic time, α, as

$$\alpha = \frac{\text{time to send a package}}{\text{time to do a multiply-add pair}}$$

Table 2. Execution time components for processors with a 1 × 3 block of nodes.

TYPE OF OPERATION	TRACER RESULTS TIME (SEC)	% TIME	MODEL PREDICTIONS TIME (SEC)
Floating Point Arithmetic	8.96	56.7	8.57
Integer Arithmetic and Indexing	2.81	17.8	——
Communication and Synchronization	4.03	25.5	4.33

Table 3. Execution time components for processors with a 3 × 3 block of nodes.

TYPE OF OPERATION	TRACER RESULTS TIME (SEC)	% TIME	MODEL PREDICTIONS TIME (SEC)
Floating Point Arithmetic	34.93	67.3	34.44
Integer Arithmetic and Indexing	10.27	19.8	——
Communication and Synchronization	6.70	12.9	6.28

With this definition, the execution time for our example algorithm can be expressed in terms of α and p, the number of processors. As an example, we consider the problem size to be fixed at a 16×48 block of nodes and let the number of processors vary from 1, 4, 16, 64, to 256 (the block of nodes per processor will vary from 16×48, 8×24, 4×12, 2×6, and 1×3, respectively). Figure 4 shows the execution times of this problem as a function of the number of processors for machines with an α parameter of 10 and 1, respectively. In both cases, there will be a point where adding more processors to solve the problem is not beneficial, since the execution time will increase: As the number of processors increases, the adds in equation (2) and the receives in equation (3)—both $O(p)$—begin to dominate the execution time. To avoid this situation, these operations could be done with special hardware like the sum/maximum circuit on the FEM that requires only $O(log_2 p)$ operations.

This model for the execution time of parallel algorithms on processor arrays captures many of the additional complexity measures unique to a parallel environment. The model was applied to a parallel implementation of the conjugate-gradient algorithm on NASA's FEM.

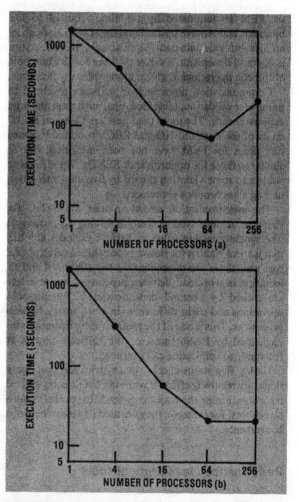

Figure 4. Graphs of execution times for machines with communications to arithmetic time ratios [α] of 10 (a) and one (b), respectively.

Experiments were performed to compare the model predictions against actual behavior; results showed that the floating-point arithmetic, communication, and synchronization components of the parallel algorithm execution time were being modeled correctly. In particular, these results pointed out that the overhead caused by the interaction of the system software and the actual parallel hardware must be reflected in the model parameters.

The model was used to predict the performance of the conjugate gradient algorithm on a given problem as the number of processors and machine characteristics varied. In fact, the model can be used to address other issues such as algorithm speedup as a function of the number of processors; machine reliability as a function of the number of processors and machine parameters; algorithm comparisons as a function of problem size, number of processors, and machine parameters; and comparison of parallel and serial algorithms. ✱

Acknowledgments

This research was supported by NASA under (1) contract NAS1-16000 while Thomas W. Crockett was employed at the Aerospace Technologies Division of Kentron International, Inc., Hampton, Virginia; and (2) contracts NAS1-17070 and NAS1-17130 while Loyce M. Adams was in residence at ICASE, NASA Langley Research Center, Hampton, Virginia.

References

1. A. George and J. Liu, *Computer Solution of Large Sparse Positive Definite Systems,* Prentice-Hall, Englewood Cliffs, N.J., 1981, p. 21.

2. J. Ortega and R. Voigt, "Solutions of Partial Differential Equations on Vector Computers," *Proc. Army Numerical Analysis Conf.,* 1977, pp. 475-526.

3. B. Buzbee, "Implementing Techniques for Elliptic Problems on Vector Computers," tech. report *LA-UR 80-2343,* Los Alamos Scientific Laboratory, Los Alamos, N.M.

4. A. Jones and R. Schwarz, "Experience Using Multiprocessor Systems—A Status Report," *Computing Surveys,* Vol. 12, No. 2, June 1980, pp. 121-165.

5. R. Hockney, "Characterizing Computers and Optimizing the FACR(1) Poisson-Solver on Parallel Unicomputers," *IEEE Trans. Computers,* Vol. C-32, No. 10, Oct. 1983, pp. 933-941.

6. A Hageman and D. Young, *Applied Iterative Methods,* Academic Press, New York, 1981, pp. 139-145.

7. L. M. Adams, "Iterative Algorithms for Large Sparse Linear Systems on Parallel Computers," tech. report CR-166027, NASA Langley Research Center, Nov. 1982, pp. 155-157.

8. H. F. Jordan and P. L. Sawyer, "A Multi-Microprocessor System for Finite Element Structural Analysis," *Trends in Computerized Structural Analysis and Synthesis,* A. K. Noor and H. G. McComb, Jr., eds., Pergamon Press, Oxford, England, 1978, pp. 21-29.

9. H. F. Jordan, ed., *The Finite Element Machine Programmer's Reference Manual,* CSDG-79-2, Computer Systems Design Group, University of Colorado, Boulder, 1979.

10. O. O. Storaasli et al., "The Finite Element Machine: An Experiment in Parallel Processing," *Research in Struct. & Solid Mechanics,* NASA Conf. Pub. 2245, Washington, D.C, Oct. 1982, pp. 201-217.

11. D. D. Loendorf, "Advanced Computer Architecture for Engineering Analysis and Design," PhD dissertation, Department of Aerospace Engineering, University of Michigan, Ann Arbor, 1983.

12. *TMS 9900 Microprocessor Data Manual,* Semiconductor Group, Texas Instruments Inc., Dallas, Tex., Nov. 1975.

13. *Am9512 Floating-Point Processor,* Advanced Micro Devices, Sunnyvale, Calif., Apr. 1980.

14. H. F. Jordan, M. Scalabrin, and W. Calvert, "A Comparison of Three Types of Multiprocessor Algorithms," *Proc. Int'l Conf. Parallel Processing,* Aug. 1979, pp. 231-238.

15. J. D. Knott, "FEM Array Control Software User's Guide," NASA CR-172189, NASA Langley Research Center, Hampton, Va., Aug. 1983.

16. T. W. Crockett, "Paslib Programmer's Guide for the Finite Element Machine," NASA CR-172281, NASA Langley Research Center, Hampton, Va., Apr. 1984.

17. J. D. Knott, "A Performance Analysis of the Paslib Version 2.1X SEND and RECV Routines On The Finite Elememt Machine," NASA CR-172205, NASA Langley Research Center, Hampton, Va., Aug. 1983.

Loyce M. Adams, a research scientist with the Institute for Computer Applications in Science and Engineering, or ICASE, at NASA Langley Research Center, has been developing, implementing, and analyzing parallel numerical algorithms for the finite element machine. She is a member of SIAM and AMS.

Adams received a PhD from the Department of Applied Mathematics and Computer Science, University of Virginia, in 1983.

Thomas W. Crockett, a system software engineer with Kentron International, Inc., has been developing software for the Finite Element Machine since 1980, under contract to NASA. Before joining Kentron, he was a systems programmer for the Computer Center at the College of William and Mary, where he worked on performance measurement and computer graphics. Crockett worked briefly for ICASE at NASA Langley in the areas of distributed computing and computer graphics.

Crockett received his BS degree in mathematics/computer science from the College of William and Mary in 1977.

Questions about this article can be addressed to Thomas W. Crockett, Aerospace Technologies Division, Kentron International, Inc., 3221 N. Armistead Ave., Hampton, VA 23665.

OPTIMAL LOAD BALANCING STRATEGIES FOR
A MULTIPLE PROCESSOR SYSTEM

Lionel M. Ni
Department of Computer Science
Michigan State University
East Lansing, MI. 48824

Kai Hwang
School of Electrical Engineering
Purdue University
West Lafayette, IN. 47907

Abstract -- To balance the workload among multiple processors is of fundamental importance in enhancing the performance of a multiple processor system (MPS). Optimal probabilistic load balancing policies are studied in this paper. Multiple processor systems are classified into four categories according to homogeneous versus heterogeneous processors and single-job class versus multiple-job classes. Closed-form solutions are derived for scheduling an MPS with single job class. An optimal load balancing algorithm is developed for an MPS with multiple job classes. The probabilistic scheduling policy is easy to be implemented in an MPS and can be extended to optimize message routing in a computer communications network.

I. Introduction

A loosely coupled Multiple Processor System (MPS) consists of multiple number of independent processors receiving jobs from a common job scheduler [2,3]. Such MPSs are considered a kind of distributed computer systems. The motivation to develop MPS is to allow resources sharing and to achieve higher system throughput and reliability. The objective of this study is to develop optimal load balancing techniques for achieving the above goals. The system performance of such an MPS is generally indicated by the average job turnaround time.

In an MPS, the job scheduler is responsible to dispatch jobs among several processors. An arriving job is routed to one of the processors according to the scheduling policy and the job characteristics. Load balancing can be done either deterministically or probabilistically. The deterministic routing assigns the next processor depending on the current state of the system. The probabilistic routing dispatches jobs in a proportionate approach, which is independent of the system state.

Only probabilistic routing strategies are considered in this paper. The job scheduling probabilities are solved for each job class to each of the processors with given workload and job assignment pattern. As a result, the minimal average job turnaround time can be achieved. An optimal deterministic routing policy (if exist) should provide a better system performance than that provided by an optimal probabilistic routing policy [6]. To prove the optimality of a specific deterministic routing policy is a nontrivial task. Usually, a deterministic routing policy must be compared with other routing policies to display its superiority. Most performance evaluation under a deterministic routing policy is conducted on MPS with only two or three processors [2,3,5]. A probabilistic job routing policy is easier to implement in MPSs with arbitrary number of processors. The scheduling overhead is low, because current processor information is not needed. The probabilistic approach can be also used to evaluate existing deterministic routing policies.

Recently, Chow and Kohler [3] presented a queueing model to analyze a single-job-class and heterogeneous MPS. They proposed a proportional branching policy, which assigns the job scheduling probability in proportional to the processing speed of the processor. The proportional branching policy can prevent the queue from saturation, but cannot minimize the average job turnaround time. For the deterministic case, they presented an approximated numerical method to analyze a two-processor heterogeneous MPS. Towley studied the deterministic routing in a closed queueing network [9]. A single-server processor-sharing system with many job classes has been studied by [4]. Baskett, et al. studied the behavior of queueing networks with different classes of customers [1].

Some related researches were conducted by [6,7] in packet switched computer communications networks. Computer network generally assumes fixed routing (probabilistic routing), since it is easy to describe by means of a routing table. Adaptive routing (deterministic routing), on the other hand, is complex to describe, and requires simulation to evaluate channel flows and delays. Furthermore, it was shown by [7] that at steady state, flow patterns and delays induced by good adaptive routing policies are very close to those obtained with optimal fixed routing policies. Foschini [6] studied deterministic routing policies in a packet switched network with multiple packet classes, where the outgoing trunks have different capabilities. He employed a diffusion analysis to study the effect of routing strategies under a nearly overloaded situation.

Optimal solutions to the load balancing problem are developed in this paper for a multiple processor system with single job class. The proportional branching policy suggested by Chow and Kohler [3] is formally proved to be nonoptimal. This study extends the MPS environment from single job class to multiple job classes. An optimal algorithm is developed to calculate the optimal job scheduling probabilities for each processor with multiple job classes. A comparison of various load balancing policies for MPSs is also given.

II. System Classification and Scheduling Models

A homogeneous MPS contains identical processors. Whereas, a heterogeneous MPS contains different processors. Depending on the processor

Reprinted from *Proceedings of the 1981 International Conference on Parallel Processing*, 1981, pages 352-357. Copyright © 1981 by The Institute of Electrical and Electronics Engineers, Inc.

capability and assignability, jobs are classified into multiple classes. Different classes of jobs are to be assigned to different subsets of processors. In terms of processor capabilities and job classes, an MPS can be classified into one of the following four categories.

SCHO: Single job Class HOmogeneous system.
SCHE: Single job Class HEterogeneous system.
MCHO: Multiple job Classes HOmogeneous system.
MCHE: Multiple job Classes HEterogeneous system.

Queues of jobs are formed at each processor based on the stochastic nature of job arrival and given job classification. The single most important performance measure of an MPS is the average job turnaround time. This includes the time from the submission of a job through the dispatcher to its completion by one of the processors. SCHE systems have been studied by Chow and Kohler [2]. A queueing model for an SCHE system is shown in Fig.1a. Jobs from the same class are dispatched to the j-th processor with probability S_j. The model can be generalized to consider multiple classes of job arrivals to the dispatcher as depicted in Fig.1b. This queueing network is used to model the scheduling environment of an MCHE system. With minor modification, it can be applied to other three classes of multiple processor systems as well.

Each processor in the MPS is modeled by an M/M/1 queue. Let n be the total number of processors and m be the total number of distinct job classes. For n processors, we have n independent M/M/1 queues. The i-th job class has a Poisson arrival rate with mean λ_i. The j-th processor has an exponentially distributed service rate with mean μ_j. Upon the arrival of a new job, the job dispatcher is responsible for assigning the job to one of the processors. The probabilistic scheduling policy is independent of the state of the system. The state of the system is represented by the number of jobs in each of the queues at any instance. The first-come first-served (FCFS) queueing discipline is assumed, and jockeying is not allowed in this study.

Let $M=\{1,2,\ldots,m\}$ and $N=\{1,2,\ldots,n\}$ be two sets representing indices of job classes and processors respectively. Jobs in different classes arrive independently. The total job arrival rate , λ, is the sum of all different classes of job arrival rates, λ_i. The job assignment matrix A $=(a_{ij})$ is an m by n matrix, where a_{ij} indicates that the i-th class job can be executed on the j-th processor; $a_{ij}=0$ otherwise. The job scheduling matrix $S=(s_{ij})$ is an m by n matrix, where s_{ij} is the probability of the i-th class job being assigned to the j-th processor. Obviously, $s_{ij}=0$ if $a_{ij}=0$. After the job scheduling matrix is determined, the actual job arrival rate, λ_j' , to the j-th processor can be expressed by

$$\lambda_j' = \sum_{i \in M} s_{ij} \lambda_i$$

Since each arrival source is a Poisson process, the linear combination of them is also a Poisson process with mean arrival rate λ_j' . Hence, we have

$$\lambda = \sum_{i \in M} \lambda_i = \sum_{j \in N} \lambda_j' \qquad (1)$$

Once the scheduling matrix $\underline{S}$ is determined, the model in Fig.1b can be decomposed into n independent M/M/1 queues, where the j-th queue has mean arrival rate λ_j' and service rate μ_j respectively. All queues behave independently but constrained by the linear relation in Eq.(1).

An M/M/1 queue is solvable under the unsaturated condition, $\lambda_j' < \mu_j$. At equilibrium state, the average job turnaround time among jobs serviced by the j-th processor is calculated by $T_j = 1/(\mu_j - \lambda_j')$ for all j. We want to find a particular assignment of λ_j' satisfying Eq.(1) to minimize the average of all T_j's. Specifically, we define the average job turnaround time

$$T = \sum_{j \in N} T_j (\lambda_j' / \lambda) \qquad (2)$$

The problem of finding an optimal job scheduling matrix resulting in a minimal average job turnaround time can be formulated as a nonlinear programming problem as follows:

Minimize $T = \sum_{j \in N} T_j (\lambda_j' / \lambda)$

provided that

$$\lambda_i < \sum_{j \in N} a_{ij} \mu_j \qquad \text{for } i \in M \qquad (3)$$

$$\lambda < \sum_{j \in N} \mu_j \qquad (4)$$

subject to

$$s_{ij} \geq 0 \qquad \text{for } i \in M, j \in N \qquad (5)$$

$$\sum_{j \in N} s_{ij} = 1 \qquad \text{for } i \in M \qquad (6)$$

$$\lambda_j' = \sum_{i \in M} \lambda_i s_{ij} < \mu_j \qquad \text{for } j \in N \qquad (7)$$

Condition in Eq.(3) prevents any one class of jobs from saturating the system. Condition in Eq.(4) ensures that the total job arrival rate is less than the total service rate. Constraint in Eq.(7) prevents any processor from saturation during the scheduling process.

III. Optimal Load Balancing with Single Job Class

In a single job class environment, the job assignment matrix $\underline{A}$ is a 1 by n row matrix with all components equal to 1. Also m=1, $\lambda = \lambda_1$. We shall use S_j to represent the probability s_{1j}. The optimization problem stated in Sec.II can be simplified to

$$\text{Minimize } T = \sum_{j \in N} S_j / (\mu_j - \lambda S_j) \qquad (8)$$

provided that

$$\lambda < \sum_{j \in N} \mu_j \qquad (9)$$

subject to

$$S_j \geq 0 \qquad \text{for } j \in N \qquad (10)$$

$$\sum_{j \in N} S_j = 1 \qquad (11)$$

$$\lambda S_j < \mu_j \qquad \text{for } j \in N \qquad (12)$$

To minimize the objective function T in Eq. (8), we employed the Method of Lagrange multiplier. Due to page limitations, proofs of all the following theorems are skipped. Interested readers may refer to [8] for details of all the proofs.

The objective function in Eq.(8) can be proved convex with respect to S_j for all j. In an SCHE system, processors may have different processing speeds. Obviously, a processor with higher service rate should have higher probability to be assigned with jobs. Without loss of generality, the service rates $\{\mu_j\}$ of the n processors are denoted in descending order

$$\mu_1 \geq \mu_2 \geq \cdots \geq \mu_n > 0 \qquad (13)$$

Theorem 1:
In an SCHE system, the job scheduling matrix S, which minimizes T and satisfies the constraints in Eqs.(10)-(12), has the following probabilities.

$$S_j = [\mu_j - \sqrt{\mu_j}(\theta_k - \lambda)/\beta_k]/\lambda \qquad \text{for } 1 \leq j \leq k$$
$$= 0 \qquad \text{for } k < j \leq n \qquad (14)$$

where

$$\theta_k = \sum_{i=1}^{k} \mu_i \quad \text{and} \quad \beta_k = \sum_{i=1}^{k} \sqrt{\mu_i}$$

and k is determined by the job arrival rate λ as follows:

$$\theta_k - \sqrt{\mu_k}\beta_k < \lambda \leq \theta_{k+1} - \sqrt{\mu_{k+1}}\beta_{k+1} \qquad \text{for } 1 \leq k < n \qquad (15)$$
or

$$\theta_n - \sqrt{\mu_n}\beta_n < \lambda < \theta_n \qquad \text{for } k = n \qquad (16)$$

with this optimum assignment, we obtain

$$T_j = \beta_k / (\sqrt{\mu_j}(\theta_k - \lambda)) \qquad \text{for } 1 < j < k$$

and the minimized average job turnaround time

$$T = \frac{\beta_k^2 - k(\theta_k - \lambda)}{\lambda(\theta_k - \lambda)} \qquad (17)$$

Note that $\lambda_j' = \lambda S_j$. This means that the actual job arrival rate to the j-th processor is equal to the service rate of the j-th processor subtracting a term which is proportional to the square root of the service rate of the j-th processor. In an SCHO system ($\mu_{j=\mu}$, for all j), the job scheduling matrix S has equal probability $S_j = 1/n$ for all j. This means that jobs are assigned randomly among processors with equal probability as expected.

In a light traffic environment, only the first k processors are assigned with jobs as stated in Theorem 1. The average job turnaround time under this circumstance is faster than the service time of any of the remaining n-k slower processors. This fact is proved in [8] by showing that $T < 1/\mu_j$ for all j>k.

Chow and Kohler proposed a proportional branching policy for an SCHE system [3]. The scheduling probabilities are proportional to the service rate of processors, but independent of the job arrival rate, i.e., $S_j = \mu_j / \theta_n$ for all j. We have discovered in [8] that this proportional branching policy is not necessarily optimal.

Most scheduling studies on loosely coupled MPSs were conducted in a single-class job environment. In what follows, we compare our scheduling policy with two known policies in a single-class job environment.

(1) the proportional branching policy proposed by Chow and Kohler.
By Eq.(8), the average job turnaround time for the proportional branching policy, T_1, can be expressed as $T_1 = n/(\theta_n - \lambda)$.

(2) the optimal probabilistic scheduling policy proposed by Ni and Hwang.
The average job turnaround time for the optimal probabilistic scheduling policy, T_2, was stated in Eq.(17).

(3) the deterministic scheduling policy proposed by Foschini.
A deterministic policy routes an arriving job to the processor that offers the least expected turnaround time. An arriving job is sent to the queue which has the minimum ratio of the queue length to service rate. If minimum ratio is not unique, the job dispatcher selects from the ties the one with maximum service rate. A generalized version of this policy was studied by Foschini [6]. This policy is considered the best scheduling policy for an SCHE system [3].

(4) The ideal scheduling with a single fast processor.
This corresponds to the case when a system has single processor whose service rate is the sum of service rates of all n individual processors in an MPS. This is an ideal case because the single processor has the same capability of the whole MPS but the ill effect due to load unbalancing disappeared. This ideal case is included for comparison purpose only. The single processor is a standard M/M/1 queue with service rate θ_n. The average job turnaround time of such a system equals $T_4 = 1/(\theta_n - \lambda)$.

There is no doubt that the deterministic scheduling policy will result in the least turnaround time. However, closed-form solution of the average job turnaround time can not be obtained for deterministic scheduling. One approach to obtain a meaningful solution requires to perform extensive simulation experiments which are rather time-consuming. Chow and Kohler developed an efficient technique for analyzing deterministic scheduling in a two-processor SCHE system. Their solutions are accurate only for a light traffic environment. When the job arrival rate approaches the total service rate, the accuracy begins to deteriorate.

Consider a two-processor SCHE system. When $\mu_1 = 4$ and $\mu_2 = 1$, we observed from Fig.2 that

$$T_1 \geq T_2 \geq T_3 \geq T_4 \qquad (18)$$

for any choice of λ. Note that when λ is close to the total service rate, T_3 can not be obtained due to the light traffic assumption made by Chow and Kohler. Under light load conditions, T_2 and T_3 approach the performance of the single fast processor, because most of the jobs are assigned to the fast processor. When the arrival rate increases, the deterministic scheduling policy displays its superiority over the probabilistic scheduling policy. The rapidly declined performance of the proportional branching policy is due to its failure considering the effect of the arrival rate.

IV. Environment of Multiple Job Classes

The number of unknown scheduling probabilities for a multiple-job-classes environment equals the number of nonzero elements in the assignment matrix $\underline{A}$. In terms of the unknown scheduling probabilities, s_{ij}, the objective function can be expressed as

$$T = \frac{1}{\lambda} [\sum_{j=1}^{n} (\sum_{i=1}^{m} \lambda_i s_{ij})/(\mu_j - \sum_{i=1}^{m} \lambda_i s_{ij})] \qquad (19)$$

There are two obstacles which prevent a direct solution of Eq.(19). First, the objective function T can not be proved to be convex. Secondly, even if T is convex, the method of Lagrange multiplier cannot be used to simplify the problem, because at least m Lagrange multipliers are required.

In our model, the average service rate of each processor is assumed time-invariant. In other words, different classes of jobs assigned to the same processor have the same average service time. From the viewpoint of a processor, job classes do not make any difference in achieving the average service rate once a job has been assigned to it. Let us temporarily ignore the job preference restriction, that is, each job can be assigned to any of the processors. The total job arrival rate can be calculated by Eq.(1). The optimal job arrival rate assigned to each processor can be derived directly from Theorem 1. Specifically, if δ_j denotes the optimal job assignment rate to the j-th processor, then $\delta_j = \lambda S_j$ for

all j. This does suggest how an optimal assignment in an MPS with multiple job classes can be achieved. If we distribute different job classes to multiple processors such that the actual job arrival rate, λ_j', equals the optimal job assignment rate, δ_j, for each of the processors, the optimal job scheduling matrix can then be calculated. More specifically,

$$\delta_j = \sum_{i \in M} \lambda_i s_{ij} = \lambda_j' \qquad \text{for } j \in N \qquad (20)$$

Equation (20) is basically a set of n linear equations over more than n variables. This implies that there may exit none, or one, or infinitely many solutions to Eq.(20) subject to the constraints given in Eqs.(5) to (7). The case of no solution must be avoided; whereas, the other two cases are acceptable in the search of an optimal scheduling matrix. The following example shows a singular case in which solution does not exist.

Consider an MCHO system with two processors and two different job classes as illustrated in Fig.3 with $\lambda_1 = 4, \lambda_2 = 2$, and $\mu = 10$. Also only $a_{12}=0$ for the job assignment matrix $\underline{A}$.

From Theorem 1, we obtain $S_1 = 0.5$ and $S_2 = 0.5$. Therefore, both δ_1 and δ_2 are equal to 3. Substituting these values into Eq.(20), we obtain

$$\begin{cases} 4s_{11} + 2s_{21} = 3 \\ 2s_{22} = 3 \end{cases}$$

Obviously, $s_{22} = 1.5 > 1$ violates the constraint. Therefore, the solution does not exist. In this example, the first job class must be assigned to the first processor. The optimization problem becomes how to find the optimal scheduling probabilities, s_{21} and s_{22}, provided that λ_1 was assigned to the first processor ($s_{11}=1$). In general, the problem of finding the optimal job assignment rate, δ_j, with some preassignment of jobs can be formulated as follows.

Let c_j be the preassigned job arrival rate to the j-th processor. The preassigned rate may come from any of the job classes, but equally treated by the processor. Let η_i be the arrival rate of the i-th job class, in which the assignment has not been determined. We shall refer η_i as the unassigned job arrival rate of the i-th job class. The preassigned and the unassigned job arrival rates are related by

$$\eta = \sum_{i \in M} \eta_i = \lambda - \sum_{j \in N} c_j = \lambda - \gamma_n \quad \text{where } \gamma_k = \sum_{j=1}^{k} c_j \quad (21)$$

Let S_j be the probability of jobs assigned to the j-th processor over the total unassigned jobs with arrival rate η. The problem of finding the optimal assignment rate to each processor, with some preassigned arrival rates, $\{c_j\}$, and a given total unassigned arrival rate, η, is formulated as follows:

$$\text{Minimize } T = \sum_{j=1}^{n} \frac{\eta S_j + c_j}{\lambda (\mu_j - \eta S_j - c_j)} \qquad (22)$$

provided that

$$\lambda_i < \sum_{j \in N} a_{ij}\mu_j \qquad \text{for } i\varepsilon M \qquad (23)$$

$$\lambda = \eta + \gamma_n < \sum_{j \in N} \mu_j = \theta_n \qquad (24)$$

$$c_j < \mu_j \qquad \text{for } j\varepsilon N \qquad (25)$$

subject to

$$S_j \geq 0 \qquad \text{for } j\varepsilon N \qquad (26)$$

$$\sum_{j \in N} S_j = 1 \qquad (27)$$

$$\eta S_j + c_j < \mu_j \qquad \text{for } j\varepsilon N \qquad (28)$$

It can be easily proved that the objective function in Eq.(22) is convex. Closed-form solution for the above constrained minimization problem is stated in Theorems 2 for heterogeneous multiple processor systems. Without loss of generality, we order the subscript j such that

$$(\mu_1-c_1)/\sqrt{\mu_1} \geq (\mu_2-c_2)/\sqrt{\mu_2} \geq \ldots \geq (\mu_n-c_n)/\sqrt{\mu_n} \qquad (29)$$

Theorem 2:

The optimal job assignment $\{\delta_j\}$ to a heterogeneous MPS with unassigned total arrival rate η and some preassigned rates c_j for all j, which minimizes T in Eq.(22) subject to the constraints in Eqs.(26)-(28), can be evaluated by

$$\delta_j = \begin{cases} (\mu_j-c_j)-\sqrt{\mu_j}(\theta_k-\gamma_k-\eta)/\beta_k & \text{for } 1\leq j\leq k \\ 0 & \text{for } k<j\leq n \end{cases} \qquad (30)$$

where k is determined by the unassigned job arrival rate η as follows:

$$(\theta_k-\gamma_k)-\beta_k(\mu_k-c_k)/\sqrt{\mu_k} < \eta \leq (\theta_{k+1}-\gamma_{k+1})-$$

$$\beta_{k+1}(\mu_{k+1}-c_{k+1})/\sqrt{\mu_{k+1}} \qquad \text{for } 1\leq k<n$$

or

$$\qquad (31)$$

$$(\theta_n-\gamma_n)-\beta_n(\mu_n-c_n)/\sqrt{\mu_n} < \eta < \theta_n-\gamma_n \quad \text{for } k=n$$

The physical meaning of the optimal assignment in Eq.(30) can be interpreted as follows. If the traffic is very heavy, i.e. $\lambda=\eta+\gamma_n$ approaches θ_n, the optimum assignment is very close to the available capacity of the processor, i.e., $\mu_j - c_j$ for the j-th processor. When the traffic becomes light, the optimal job assignment is formed by subtracting a value proportional to $\sqrt{\mu_j}$ from the available capacity of that processor. If $c_j=0$ for all j, Theorem 2 becomes equilivalent to Theorem 1. If $\mu_j=\mu$ for all j in Theorem 2, Theorem 2 can be applied to a homogeneous MPS.

V. An Optimal Load Balancing Algorithm

A recursive optimal load balancing algorithm is developed below to generate the scheduling matrix $\underline{S}$ for an MPS in a multiple-job-class environment. Although there may be many solutions to $\underline{S}$, the average job turnaround time is unique and minimized for all possible solutions of $\underline{S}$. Our purpose is to find a systematic procedure to generate at least one of the possible solutions of $\underline{S}$. The notation c_{ij} is used to denote the rate of the i-th class job assigned to the j-th processor. All a_{ij}, c_{ij}, η_i, and μ_j (for $1\leq i\leq m$, $1\leq j\leq n$) are global variables. M is a set of active job classes. $i\varepsilon M$ indicates that the assignment of the i-th job class has not been determined, i.e., $\eta_i \neq 0$. N is a set of active processors. $j\varepsilon N$ indicates that $a_{kj}\neq 0$ for at least one $k\varepsilon M$. Both M and N sets are local variables.

The Load Balancing Algorithm:

Input: Global variables: a_{ij}, c_{ij}, η_i, and μ_j.
    Local variables: M and N sets.
Output: Changes on those global variables.
Procedure:
1. For each $i\varepsilon M$ with $\sum a_{ij}=1$, find a particular k such that $a_{ik}=1$. Then set $c_{ik} \leftarrow c_{ik}+\eta_i$, $\eta_i \leftarrow 0$, and $a_{ik} \leftarrow 0$ for that i. Update M and N.
2. For those $j\varepsilon N$, calculate the corresponding job assignment rates δ_j for $j\varepsilon N$ by applying Theorem 2, where $\eta=\sum\eta_i$ and $c_j=\sum c_{ij}$.
3. Form a set N', where $j\varepsilon N'$ if $j\varepsilon N$ and $\sum\eta_i a_{ij}<\delta_j$. Form a set M', where $i\varepsilon M'$ if $i\varepsilon M$ and there is at least a $j\varepsilon N'$ such that $a_{ij}=1$. If $N'\neq\emptyset$, invoke this algorithm with inputs M' and N'.
4. Form $M''=M-M'$ and $N''=N-N'$. For each $j\varepsilon N''$ with $\sum a_{ij}=1$, find a particular k such that $a_{kj}=1$ and $\delta_j\neq 0$. Set $c_{kj} \leftarrow c_{kj}+\delta_j$ and $\eta_k \leftarrow \eta_k-\delta_j$.
5. If $N'=0$ in (3) or at least one particular k was found in (4), invoke this algorithm again with local inputs M'' and N''.
6. Update M and N. Solve the following set of linear equations.

$$\begin{cases} \sum_{i \in M} \eta_i X_{ij}=\delta_j & \text{for } j \varepsilon N \\ \sum_{j \in N} X_{ij} = 1 & \text{for } i \varepsilon M \end{cases}$$

where X_{ij}'s are unknown variables satisfying

$$X_{ij}=0 \text{ if } a_{ij}=0 ; X_{ij}\geq 0 \text{ if } a_{ij}=1 \text{ for } i\varepsilon M, j\varepsilon N$$

This set of linear equations always has infinitely many solutions. Picking any one solution is sufficient.
7. For $i\varepsilon M$ and $j\varepsilon N$, set $c_{ij} \leftarrow c_{ij}+X_{ij}\eta_i$ and $a_{ij} \leftarrow 0$.

In the main program:
1. Given m job classes with average arrival rates λ_i, n processors with average service rate μ_j, an m by n job assignment matrix $\underline{A}$, and conditions in Eqs.(5)-(7).
2. Initialize local variables $M=\{1,2,\ldots,m\}$ and $N=\{1,2,\ldots,n\}$.
3. Initialize global variables; $c_{ij} \leftarrow 0$ and $\eta_i \leftarrow \lambda_i$ for all $i\varepsilon M$ and $j\varepsilon N$.
4. Invoke the load balancing algorithm.

5. For $1 \leq i \leq m$ and $1 \leq j \leq n$, calculate $s_{ij} = c_{ij}/\lambda_i$.

VI. Conclusions

Optimal probabilistic load balancing policies are developed for a multiple processor system with either single job class or multiple job classes. Those policies provide a test bed to determine the superiority of any deterministic scheduling policy over probabilistic ones. With the high implementation overhead of deterministic policy, we conclude that the proposed probabilistic scheduling policy is more feasible and can be systematically implemented in commercial multiple processor systems.

Acknowledgements

This work was supported in part by the NSF research grant MCS-78-18906A02 and in part by DOT research contract R920044.

References

[1] Baskett, F., et al. "Open, closed, and mixed networks of queues with different classes of customers", J. of ACM, (April, 1975), pp. 248-260.

[2] Chow, Y.C. and Kohler, W.H., "Dynamic load balancing in a homogeneous two-processor distributed system", Computer Performance, (Eds. K.M. Chandy and M. Reiser), pp.39-52.

[3] Chow, Y.C. and Kohler, W.H., "Models for dynamic load balancing in a heterogeneous multiple processor system", IEEE Trans. on Computer, (May, 1979), pp.354-361.

[4] Fayolle, G., et al. "Sharing a processor among many job classes", J. of ACM, (July 1980), pp.519-532.

[5] Flatto, L., Two parallel queues with equal servicing rates, IBM Research Rep. RC 5916, (March 1976).

[6] Foschini, G.J., "On heavy traffic diffusion analysis and dynamic routing in packet switched networks", Computer Performance, (Eds. K.M. Chandy and M. Reiser), pp.499-513.

[7] Gerla, M. and Kleinrock, L., "On the topological design of distributed computer networks", IEEE Trans. on Comm. (January 1977), pp.48-60.

[8] Ni, L.M. and Hwang, K., Probabilistic load balancing in a multiple processor system with many job classes, School of Electrical Engineering, Purdue University, TR-EE 81-1, (January 1981), 41 pp.

[9] Towsley, D., "Queueing network models with state-dependent routing", J. of ACM, (April 1980), pp.323-337.

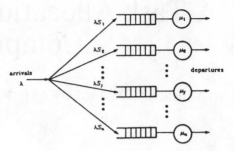

(a) A queueing model for probabilistic load balancing in an SCHE system.

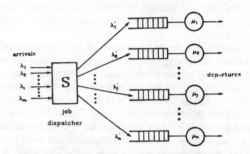

(b) A queueing model for probabilistic load balancing in an MCHE system.

Fig. 1. Probabilistic load balancing models for a multiple processor system.

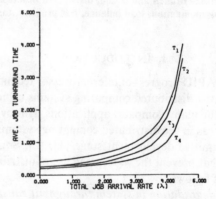

Fig. 2. Comparison of three load balancing policies for a two-processor heterogeneous system with single job class.

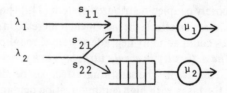

Fig. 3. The queueing model of an MCHO system with two processors and two job classes.

A Task Allocation Model for Distributed Computing Systems

PERNG-YI RICHARD MA, EDWARD Y. S. LEE, MEMBER, IEEE, AND MASAHIRO TSUCHIYA, MEMBER, IEEE

Abstract—This paper presents a task allocation model that allocates application tasks among processors in distributed computing systems satisfying: 1) minimum interprocessor communication cost, 2) balanced utilization of each processor, and 3) all engineering application requirements.

A cost function is formulated to measure the interprocessor communication and processing costs. By employing various constraints, the model efficiently generates minimum-cost allocation using a branch and bound technique. With suitable modification of these constraints, both application requirements and load balance can be achieved.

For evaluation, this allocation model was applied to an Air Defense (AD) case study which involves the allocation of 23 real-time software tasks into a network of processors. Simulation was used to validate the resultant allocations against the three goals. The result indicates that the allocation model is applicable to large practical problems. It satisfies all application requirements and generates an allocation that counterbalances interprocessor communication cost and load balancing.

Index Terms—Branch and bound, distributed processing, interprocessor communication, load balance, NP problem, task allocation.

I. INTRODUCTION

THE RAPID progress of microprocessor technology has made the distributed computing systems economically attractive for many computer applications. However, many problem areas in the distributed computing systems are still in their primitive development stage [1], [2]. Some major problems that prevent the widespread use of distributed systems are as follows.

1) The degradation in system throughput caused by the "saturation effect" [3]: A saturation effect is caused by heavy communication traffic induced by data transfers from one task to another residing in separate processors. The interprocessor traffic is always the most costly and the least reliable factor in the loosely coupled distributed system [1], [4]. As a result of this saturation effect, the incremental increase in computing resources could actually degrade system throughput.

2) The difficulty in evenly utilizing each processor in the distributed system: The saturation effect can be alleviated by loading the tasks with high communication demands into the same processor. However, this often creates load imbalance

and thus lowers system throughput. It is very important to balance these two competing forces to achieve a greater system throughput [3], [5].

3) A large gap between the engineering application requirements and the existing distributed network architecture [6]: Application tasks defined by the process designers to meet the engineering requirements do not often map optimally into the existing distributed architecture [6]. Conversely, a gap exists in the design of the distributed architecture to meet the software and system requirements. Hence, a software tool is badly needed for the practical allocation of engineering application tasks in the distributed systems.

4) The difficulty in verifying allocations resulted from any allocation model: Due to the scarcity of real-life data, most research results are limited to theoretical and mathematical models [1], [4], [7], [8] and their merits are difficult to compare [9].

Several approaches to the allocation model have been identified. They are basically graph theoretical, integer programming, and heuristic methods. The graph theoretical approach uses a graph to represent application tasks [4]. It minimizes the total interprocessor communication cost by performing a min-cut algorithm on the graph. The limitation on its generalization is the high computing time complexity when more than two processors are used in the allocation model. Furthermore, it is difficult to incorporate various constraints into such a model.

The integer programming method [10], [11] is based on the implicit enumeration algorithm subject to the additional constraints. It allows constraints to be easily incorporated into the allocation model to meet various application requirements. This approach is limited by the amounts of time and memory needed to obtain an optimal solution since they grow as exponential functions of the problem order.

The heuristic method is to provide fast and effective algorithms for a suboptimum solution [1]. This technique requires less computation time than integer programming methods. They are useful in applications where an optimum solution is not obtainable within a critical time limit. They are also applicable to larger dimensional problems.

This paper presents a task allocation model for distributed computing systems based on a zero-one programming technique, the branch-and-bound method. For a given distributed system configuration and a set of constraints, it generates an optimal solution for medium-size problems satisfying all application requirements. For a large-size problem, the allocation

Manuscript received April 3, 1981; revised July 17, 1981. This work was supported in part by the Ballistic Missile Defense Advanced Technology Center under Contract DASG60-79-C-0039 and the independent research and development project of the TRW Systems Engineering and Integration Division under Project 8100692.

The authors are with TRW, Redondo Beach, CA 90278.

Reprinted from *IEEE Transactions on Computers*, Volume C-31, Number 1, January 1982, pages 41-47. Copyright © 1982 by The Institute of Electrical and Electronics Engineers, Inc.

model is judged by the practical engineering application requirements. In order to verify its validity, the allocation model was tested on an Air Defense (AD) case study which involves the allocation of 23 real-time software tasks into three processors. The results show that the model is applicable to large practical problems and that it generates very effective allocation.

II. Problem Statement

The problem involves the development of task allocation model for the distributed computing system. The model must allocate tasks among distributed processors to achieve the following goals:

1) allow specification of a large number of constraints to facilitate a variety of engineering application requirements,

2) balance the utilization of individual processors in the distributed computing system, and

3) minimize interprocessor communication cost.

In order for the task allocation model to effectively satisfy these goals, it should have a structure with supporting functions as shown in Fig. 1. The task preprocessor analyzes the application tasks to acquire relevant information such as coupling factors among tasks and task attribute sizes. The coupling factor between tasks is measured by the number of data units transferred from one task to another. The unit of data is dependent on the application task; it may be word, byte, or bit. The attributes are the inherent characteristics of tasks, e.g., the number of executable statements, or the maximum allowable execution time.

The network preprocessor examines the distributed network and provides information on the network architecture which includes the interprocessor distance and processor constraints. The interprocessor distance is conceptually the physical distance between two processors. However, it may represent any type of cost that can be measured in time or in dollars [4]. Every processor has its hardware constraints which are called processor attributes. For example, the attributes may be the MIPS (million instructions per second) rate, storage space, etc.

Based on the assumption that all necessary information on the tasks and processors is provided by the two preprocessors, this paper presents the development and application of a task allocation model and verification of its results using a simulator.

III. Functional Design of the Allocation Model

The design of a mathematical model for task allocation for a distributed computing system involves the following steps: 1) formulate the cost function to measure the interprocessor communication (IPC) cost and processing cost, 2) formulate a set of constraints to meet the diverse requirements, and 3) derive an iterative algorithm to obtain a minimum total cost solution.

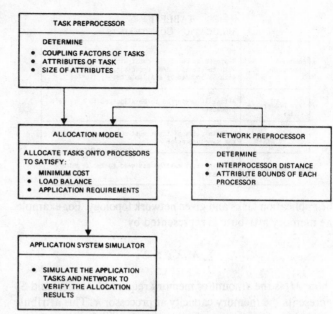

Fig. 1.   General structure of the allocation model and its supporting functions.

A. Cost Function

The cost function is formulated as the sum of the IPC cost and the processing cost. IPC cost is a function of both task coupling factors and interprocessor distances. Coupling factor C_{ij} is the number of data units transferred from task i to task j. Interprocessor distance d_{kl} is certain distance-related communication costs associated with one unit of data transferred from processor k to processor l. If tasks i and j are assigned to processors k and l, respectively, the interprocessor cost is $(C_{ij} * d_{kl})$. If $k = l$ then $d_{kl} = 0$. The unit of IPC cost is application dependent. For example, if the unit of C_{ij} is word and d_{kl} is \$/word, the IPC unit is in dollars.

Processing cost q_{ik} represents the cost to process task i on processor k. It can be used to control the processor assignment. For example, if task i must not be executed on processor k, a very large value can be assigned to q_{ik} to inhibit the assignment.

The assignment variable is defined as follows:

$$X_{ik} = \begin{cases} 1, & \text{if task } i \text{ is assigned to processor } k. \\ 0, & \text{otherwise.} \end{cases}$$

The total cost for processing the tasks is stated as [3]

$$\sum_i \sum_k \left(wq_{ik}X_{ik} + \sum_l \sum_j (c_{ij}*d_{kl})X_{ik}X_{jl} \right).$$

The normalization constant w is used to scale processing cost and IPC cost to account for any difference in measuring units.

B. Constraints

Several constraints are incorporated in the allocation model to achieve the load balance and meet the application requirements (Table I). Attributes are a collection of constraints from

TABLE I
ALLOCATION CONSTRAINTS

Bounded Attributes	Representation of the constraints associated with the tasks and/or processor, e.g., task size is bounded by available memory storage
Task Preference	A task is preferred to be allocated to a certain processor
Task Exclusion	Certain pairs of tasks must not be assigned to the same processor
Task Redundancy	Certain tasks must be assigned to two or more processors

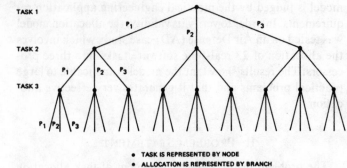

- TASK IS REPRESENTED BY NODE
- ALLOCATION IS REPRESENTED BY BRANCH

Fig. 2.   Decision tree with three tasks and three processors.

the application tasks and given network topology. For example, the memory attribute is represented by

$$\sum_i M_i X_{ik} \leq S_k$$

where M_i is the amount of memory required by task i, and S_k represents the memory capacity at processor k. This attribute states that the amount of memory required for all tasks assigned to a processor must not exceed the processor memory capacity.

The task preference matrix, task exclusive matrix, and task redundancy are implemented to increase the model capability. The *task preference matrix* indicates that certain tasks can only be executed in the specified processor. It is represented by an $m \times n$ matrix P (m is the number of tasks and n is the number of processors), where $P_{ik} = 0$ implies that task i cannot be assigned to processor k; and $P_{ik} = 1$, otherwise.

The *task exclusive* matrix defines mutually exclusive tasks. It is represented by an $m \times m$ matrix E, where $E_{ij} = 1$ implies that tasks i and j cannot be assigned to the same processor; otherwise, $E_{ij} = 0$.

The *task redundancy* may be provided for system reliability. This permits multiple copies of a task. For example, if task i has a redundancy of three, new tasks $i + 1$ and $i + 2$ are added to the original set of tasks. They have identical constraints to task i. In addition, an additional constraint is added such that tasks i, $i + 1$, and $i + 2$ cannot be assigned to the same processor.

C. Algorithm Derivation

The algorithm was derived from a branch and bound (BB) method. To employ the BB technique, the allocation problem is represented by a search tree. The allocation decision represents a branching at the node corresponding to the given task. Consider a problem of allocating m tasks among n processors. Starting with task 1, each task is allocated to one of the n processors subject to the constraints imposed on the relations on tasks and processors. The number of tree levels m corresponds to m tasks. A feasible sequence of successive branches is called a path. A path from the root node to the last node corresponds to a *complete allocation;* otherwise, it is a *partial allocation*. The cost of a path is computed according to the cost equation. An example of a three-level search tree with three processors is shown in Fig. 2.

The BB method defined by Kohler and Steiglitz [12] consists of nine rules: $(B, S, F, D, L, U, E, BR, RB)$. *Branching rule B* defines the scheme for generating sons of each node. *Selection rule S* selects the next branching node from the currently active nodes. *Characteristic function F* eliminates nodes known to have no completion from the set of feasible solutions. *Dominance relation D* defined on the set of partial solutions is used by rule E to eliminate nodes from the search tree before extending them. *Lower bound function L* assigns a cost lower bound to each partial solution. *Cost upper bound U* of a complete solution is known at the beginning of the algorithm. *Elimination rules E* use D, L, and U to eliminate newly generated and currently active nodes. *Termination rule BR* shows the desired derivation of the optimal cost from an acceptable solution. *Resource bound vector RB* has components that are upper bounds of the resources used in the allocation model. This Kohler and Steiglitz BB method has been modified for our task allocation algorithm.

The following rules determine whether the selected branch i for a given node k should be eliminated.

1) Rule F checks the preference matrix P for task k and processor i. If $P_{ik} = 0$, the branch is eliminated.

2) Rule E checks the exclusive matrix for task k. If task l which is mutually exclusive to task k has already been allocated to processor i, branch i for node k is eliminated.

3) Rule RB checks the cumulative memory requirement of tasks against the processor memory capacity. As task k is assigned to processor i, its size is added to all tasks which are already in processor i. If the cumulative size of all tasks exceeds the processor's memory capacity, branch i for node k is eliminated.

4) Rule D compares the partial cost L with the complete cost U. If L is greater than U, the solution cannot be improved. Hence, branch i for node k is eliminated.

If branch i of node k satisfies all these four rules, the allocation is made. The *iteration count* is incremented indicating that one branch has been investigated for a node.

These rules constitute a depth-first search method. In addition to the elimination rules, the following rules are applied to select the next node and to terminate the algorithm.

5) Selection rules S select the next node to be expanded. It may be the current node, say, node k, the precedent node ($k - 1$), or the descendant node ($k + 1$). Branching rule B selects the branch (processor allocation) for a given node.

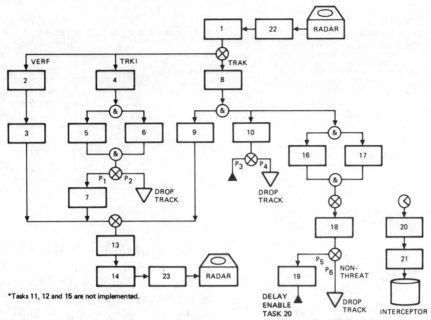

Fig. 3.   Task flow diagram for a model AD application.

*Tasks 11, 12 and 15 are not implemented.

6) Termination rule *BR* terminates the algorithm when all possible paths have been investigated or the prespecified number of iterations has been reached. This number limits the time allowed for the algorithm to enable trading an optimal solution for a fast algorithmic result.

IV. APPLICATION

The Air Defense (AD) application is shown in Fig. 3. This depicts the data processing system interfacing with the radar and the interceptor of a model AD system. Sensor data from the radar are input to the system which tracks and keeps under constant surveillance all possible attacking reentry vehicles (RV) and commands the radar and the interceptor to prevent any RV from penetrating the defended areas. This scenario will have definite influence on the design of the data processing tasks. Twenty three tasks are identified in Fig. 3 (only 20 are shown here; the other three are not implemented yet). These tasks are arranged into seven major processing threads, each consisting of a number of tasks as shown in Fig. 4. These threads can be executed in parallel to a certain extent. Because of the real-time critical nature of this application, they must meet the shown port-to-port (PTP) processing times which confines the total execution time of the specified thread within a certain prescribed limit. Therefore, any allocation of the tasks to the processors must first satisfy these PTP time requirements in order to be qualified as a valid allocation. Since the processing load is scenario dependent, the allocation can be optimized only for a given scenario.

To justify the allocation result, a simulator [13] was designed to simulate the AD data processing system which includes twenty tasks and three processors. The three processors were simulated as homogeneous, fully connected computers with 1.5 million instruction per second (MIPS) rate each. The task attributes and task coupling factors used as inputs to the allocation model were also built into the simulator. The at-

THREADS	PTP DELAY LIMIT (MSEC)
(22, 1, 2, 3, 13)	100
(22, 1, 4, 13)	50
(22, 1, 4, 5, 6, 7, 13)	40
(22, 1, 8, 9, 13)	40
(22, 1, 8, 10)	40
(22, 1, 8, 16, 17, 18)	40
(22, 1, 8, 17, 18, 19)	50

Fig. 4.   Major processing threads and port-to-port time requirements.

tribute includes the task sizes in machine language instructions. Task coupling factors are in words. Some examples are shown in Table II(A) and (B). The interprocessor distance between any two processors is assumed to be unity.

The rest of this section reports two applications of the allocation model. In Section IV-A the allocation model is applied to the AD data processing system and its results are compared with those obtained from engineering experience. Section IV-B discusses improvement in allocation results by making suitable modifications to the model inputs.

A. Allocation

Two allocation policies were studied. Twenty tasks were allocated into three processors in the AD data processing system. Allocation *A*-1 [Fig. 5(a)], based on the engineering experience, was designed to satisfy the PTP time by evenly loading the tasks on the processors with an equal MIPS rate.

Allocation *A*-2 [Fig. 5(b)] was based on the allocation algorithm derived in this paper. In the current allocation model, only IPC cost is used in the cost function. The IPC cost is a function of interprocessor distances and coupling factors among tasks. In this model, the units for coupling factor and distance are word and $/word, respectively, and the distance is assumed to be unity.

TABLE II
(A) Size of Tasks (Machine Language Instructions). (B) Coupling Factor Among Tasks (Words)

Task	TASK SIZE (MLI)
1	200
13	1200
14	350
22	150
23	350

(A)

Task \ Task	13	14	20	21	23
13		1000			
14	1000				100
20				200	
21			200		
23		100			

(B)

TABLE III
Performance of Allocation A-1 and A-2 as Measured by the Simulator

	A-1	A-2
PTP-	PASS	PASS
CPU$_1$	39%	40%
CPU$_2$	55%	52%
CPU$_3$	42%	40%
IPC	222	184

A - 1

	P_1	P_2	P_3
Tasks	1	2	3
	4	5	6
	7	8	9
	10	13	16
	17	14	19
	20	18	23
	22	21	

(a)

A - 2

	P_1	P_2	P_3
Tasks	13	2	1
	14	3	4
	17-19	6	5
		8	7
		9	10
		23	16
			20-22

(b)

Fig. 5. (a) Engineering experience allocation to achieve load balance. (b) Allocation from the allocation model.

A critical engineering requirement in this AD application is the PTP time. If the execution time of any thread exceeds the specified PTP time, the allocation fails. The simulator can explicitly display the thread PTP time. The second goal, load balance, is expressed by the simulator as the CPU utilization of each processor during every 10 ms interval. The third goal, minimizing IPC cost, is measured by the simulator as the number of words that are transmitted among the three processors within every one ms interval. Note that the unit of IPC cost of simulator is different from that of the allocation model.

Two allocations, A-1 and A-2, were tested on the simulator. The result is shown in Table III. A-1 satisfies the PTP time requirement and achieves good load balancing at the expense of high IPC cost. A-2 shows a similar load balancing effects, but at a lower IPC cost. Note that these results are based on the assumption that homogeneous computers are employed in the experiment.

B. Using the Algorithm

If the distributed system is varied, the user can modify the allocation constraints (algorithm input) to meet the network requirements. Two allocations are designed to trade off IPC cost and load balance. If load balancing is more critical for the system application, two tasks which are heavy CPU users should not be allocated to the same processor. This can be controlled through the exclusive matrix. On the other hand, if minimization of IPC cost is important, tasks with large coupling factor should be allocated together. This is controlled by assigning their coupling factor a large dummy value.

With suitable modifications to algorithmic constraints [5], allocations A-3 [Fig. 6(a)] and A-4 [Fig. 6(b)] are obtained. A-3 is designed mainly for load balance, and A-4 is designed mainly for lower IPC cost. The result is shown in Table IV. If the network requires high throughput and is tightly coupled, then A-3 is a good candidate. Conversely, if the network is loosely coupled, and IPC cost is extremely high, then A-4 is better.

V. Evaluation

The task allocation algorithm was implemented in Fortran IV on a CDC 6600. Several sets of input data [5] were applied to test the optimality and time complexity of the algorithm.

A. Algorithmic Time Complexity

Using a BB method to find an optimum solution in the search tree is known to be an NP problem [10]. As m tasks are allocated into n processors, total number of enumerations (complete allocations) in the search tree is n^m. However, imposing a large number of constraints on the BB technique greatly reduces the feasible solution space. All enumerations are not necessary because the elimination rules eliminate infeasible solutions before the subtree expansion. As mentioned earlier, the preference matrix limits the candidate processors for each task. Let n_i be the number of 1's appeared in row i of the preference matrix, i.e., task i has n_i choices of possible allocation. The upper bound for algorithmic time is $\Pi_{i=1}^{m}(n_i)$ due to the elimination rule F. This upper bound can be further reduced by other elimination rules. If a branch from a node on level k is eliminated by any of these rules, $n^{(m-k)}$ complete allocations are pruned. For example, in Fig. 2 if branch P_2 from node 1 is eliminated, then $3^{3-1} = 9$ paths are eliminated.

	A-3		
	P_1	P_2	P_3
Tasks	2	8	1
	3	9	4
	13	20	5
	14	21	6
	17	23	7
	18		10
	19		16
			22

(a)

	A-4		
	P_1	P_2	P_3
Tasks	4	6	1
	5	8	2
	7	10	3
	9	16	22
	13	18	
	14	19	
	17	20	
	23	21	

(b)

Fig. 6. (a) Allocation to achieve load balance. (b) Allocation to achieve lower IPC cost.

TABLE IV
PERFORMANCE OF ALLOCATION A-3 AND A-4 AS MEASURED BY THE SIMULATOR

	A-3	A-4
PTP	PASS	PASS
CPU_1	45%	63%
CPU_2	53%	25%
CPU_3	42%	33%
IPC	236	114

Since pruning is heavily dependent on the input constraints, the lowest upper bound for the algorithm's run time has not been determined.

In the AD case study, the upper bound is $0(10^{10})$ iterations. Each iteration is equivalent to the checking of a branch for a node. Three different allocations A-2, A-3, and A-4 are made. The numbers of iterations required for A-2 and A-3 are each $0(10^3)$, and for A-4 is $0(10^4)$. The CDC 6600 computing power is $0(10^3)$ iterations/s.

B. Algorithm Optimality

Theoretically, the algorithm generates an optimum solution with respect to IPC cost. Several sets of input constraints with small upper bound for algorithm computation time were used to test the algorithm optimality [5]. This upper bound was less than 10^4 iterations for the selected inputs. The final solutions from these tests did provide the minimum IPC cost.

For practical applications with larger upper bound values the optimality is judged by the engineering requirements. Compare allocations A-3 and A-4, for instance. A-3 utilizes processors evenly and would be more suitable for a system which requires a high throughput. Allocation A-4 incurrs a smaller IPC cost, suggesting that it is a better solution for loosely-coupled distributed system whose IPC cost is high.

VI. CONCLUSION

The task allocation model presented was derived by using the BB technique. This model can accommodate a large number of constraints and hence is able to incorporate various engineering requirements. Load balance can be achieved by suitable control of model input parameters such as the preference matrix and exclusive matrix. The minimum cost solution is obtained by the model automatically within the constraints.

This model was applied to a large scale practical problem, the AD distributed processing system, and the resultant allocations were tested on the simulator. Results from the simulation indicate that the allocation generated by the model can achieve the multiple goals. Most allocation algorithms [1], [4], [7], [8] are limited to finding the minimum cost solution and/or seldom consider the complexities of constraints and multiple objectives of the practical system design problem.

Obviously, there is still a considerable gap between the engineering problem and the mathematical model. To fully exploit this allocation model, the following are being explored further.

1) *Unit Value for Cost Function:* Cost unit must be uniform. Cost function must represent both IPC and processing costs that are inherently different in their measurement units. One approach would be to assign weights that reflect the criticality of the costs to particular applications. This would enable the allocation model to incorporate tradeoffs between IPC cost and load balance.

2) *Time Complexity:* In general, to obtain an optimum solution by the BB technique is an NP problem. However, the constraints placed on the problem greatly reduce the time complexity. A better estimate of the lowest upper bound on time complexity needs to be determined from both the model inputs and the elimination rules.

3) *Allocation Model Verification:* The allocation results from the model must be validated by testing them either with actual implementation or with simulation. For obvious reasons the latter approach is preferred [14]. More flexible and powerful simulators are needed for this purpose. Currently, the simulator for the AD data processing system is being modified to increase the number of processors that can be simulated.

4) *Application Dependence:* The allocation model was designed to be a general purpose model. When a specific requirement exists in the application, it takes an engineering experience to tailor the inputs to the model. For example, in order to meet PTP time requirement, a designer must realize that any task should not wait too long in the waiting queue. Hence, the user of the model must translate this requirement into model inputs to achieve the effect of allocating large tasks to separate processors. How to properly identify all application requirements is thus an important research topic.

In order to provide more representative task attributes to the allocation model, some form of requirement engineering methodologies is needed. Currently, there are some research activities in the requirements engineering for distributed systems [15], but further work is necessary. With further progress in this area, the allocation model should prove to be a valuable tool for the design of distributed systems.

Acknowledgment

The authors wish to thank E. Swartzlander for his support as Project Manager of the Distributed Process Design Technology Development Program, and also the following people who worked on various segments of this project: M. L. Green, D. S. Shannon, and R. H. Hoffman developed and implemented the simulator; Y. Fukuda encoded the first version of the allocation algorithm; and H. Wang patiently typed the many versions of this paper.

References

[1] V. B. Gylys and J. A. Edwards, "Optimal partitioning of workload for distributed systems," in *Dig. COMPCON Fall 1976*, 1976, pp. 353–357.

[2] W. W. Chu, "Introduction in the Special Issue on distributed processing systems," *IEEE Trans. Comput.*, vol. C-29, pp. 1037–1038, Dec. 1980.

[3] W. W. Chu, L. J. Holloway, M. Lan, and K. Efe, "Task allocation in distributed data processing," *Computer*, vol. 13, pp. 57–69, Nov. 1980.

[4] H. S. Stone, "Multiprocessor scheduling with the aid of network flow algorithm," *IEEE Trans. Software Eng.*, vol. SE-3, pp. 85–93, Jan. 1977.

[5] E. Y. S. Lee and P. Ma, "Final report of the distributed processing design technology development (DPDTD) program—Vol. II research results," TRW Defense Space Syst. Group, Mar. 1981.

[6] C. R. Vick, "A next generation of supercomputers: From mainframes to micros," presented at Euromicro 1980, London, England, Sept. 1980.

[7] B. W. Wah, "An efficient heuristic for file placement on distributed database," in *Proc. COMPSAC 1980*, Oct. 1980, pp. 462–468.

[8] C. C. Price, "The assignment of computational tasks among processors in a distributed system," in *Proc. Nat. Comput. Conf.*, May 1981, pp. 291–296.

[9] P. Chen and J. Akoka, "Optimal design of distributed information system," *IEEE Trans. Comput.*, vol. C-29, pp. 1068–1079, Dec. 1980.

[10] O. I. El-Dessouki and W. H. Huan, "Distributed enumeration on network computers," *IEEE Trans. Comput.*, vol. C-29, pp. 818–825, Sept. 1980.

[11] W. W. Chu, "Optimal file allocation in a multiple computing system," *IEEE Trans. Comput.*, vol. C-18, pp. 885–889, Oct. 1969.

[12] E. G. Coffman, Jr., Ed., *Computer and Job-Shop Scheduling Theory*. New York: Wiley, 1976.

[13] M. L. Green *et al.*, "The DDP underlay simulation experiment: Tactical applications and d-RTOS models," TRW Defense Space Syst. Group, May 1980.

[14] R. H. Hoffman, R. W. Smith, and J. T. Ellis, "Simulation software development for the BMDATC DDP underlay experiment," in *Proc. COMPSAC 1980*, Chicago, Oct. 1980, pp. 569–577.

[15] M. W. Alford, "A requirements engineering methodology for real-time processing requirements," *IEEE Trans. Software Eng.*, vol. SE-3, pp. 60–68, Jan. 1977.

Perng-yi Richard Ma received the B.S.E.E. degree from Taiwan Maritime College in 1972, and the M.S. and Ph.D. degrees in electrical engineering from Oregon State University, Corvallis, in 1976 and 1978, respectively.

From 1978 to 1979 he was with the Rockwell Space Division. Currently, he is with TRW, Redondo Beach, CA. His present research interests include the static and dynamic allocation in distributed computing, and closed-loop design among application tasks, software mapping system, and network architecture.

Edward Y. S. Lee (M'73) received the B.S. degree in physics from Portland State University, Portland, OR, and the M.S. and Ph.D. degrees in physics from Purdue University, West Lafayette, IN.

He is currently a Senior Staff Engineer at TRW Defense and Space System Group, System Engineering and Integration Division, Redondo Beach, CA. As the Assistant Project Manager for Distributed Processing Design Technology Development (DPDTD) Program, he participates in the research and development of distributed system design methodologies, allocation models, distributed databases, and the development and implementation of an experimental distributed real-time operating system for a simulation experiment in DPDTD. Prior to TRW, he led the development of information retrieval systems for the Image Laboratory at the Jet Propulsion Laboratory in conjunction with several NASA unmanned space missions.

Dr. Lee is active in both National and the Los Angeles Chapters of the Association for Computing Machinery (ACM). He was Program Chairman for the LA Chapter from 1978 to 1979 and received the Outstanding Member award. He was the General Chairman of the Joint ACM–ASM Springs System Seminar and the Vice Chairman for the Chapter in 1980. He became Chairman in July 1981. As a member of the IEEE Computer Society, he participates in both the Technical Committees on Distributed Data Processing as well as Data Base Engineering. He is currently a member of the IEEE 802 Local Area Network Standards Committee. Dr. Lee is a frequent speaker in many national conferences and symposiums and has published many technical papers and reports. He is also a frequent contributor to the ACM *Computing Reviews*. He is currently teaching an introductory course in Data Base Management Systems in the TRW After Hour Class Program.

Masahiro Tsuchiya (S'70–M'73) received the B.S. degree in management information systems from Konan University, Kobe, Japan, and the Ph.D. degree in computer sciences from the University of Texas, Austin.

He is currently with TRW, Redondo Beach, CA. Prior to joining TRW, he was a faculty member at the University of Hawaii, Manoa, the University of California, Irvine, and Northwestern University, Evanston, IL. In 1975 he was a Visiting Computer Scientist at Datalogisk Afdeling, Aarhus Universitet, Aarhus, Denmark, and in 1972 he was a Visiting Lecturer at Konan University, Konan, Japan. His research interests include computer architecture, distributed processing systems, and database systems.

Evaluating the Performance of Multicomputer Configurations

Reprinted from *Computer*, May 1986, pages 23-37. Copyright © 1986 by
The Institute of Electrical and Electronics Engineers, Inc.

Dharma P. Agrawal and Virendra K. Janakiram,
North Carolina State University

Girish C. Pathak, Texas Instruments Inc.

Interconnections for multicomputers can be evaluated using such parameters as distance between nodes, number of communication links, degree of fault tolerance, and machine expansion capability.

As ever more powerful computers were developed, so did the demands made upon them (which is, of course, just an instance of Parkinson's law in action). However, there is a limit to the maximum speed obtainable from a computer based on a single processor. The closer we approach this limit, the more rapidly does the cost of such a computer rise. An alternative and radically different solution is to move from this uniprocessor architecture to a newer architecture employing the time-tested device of parallelism, i.e., using a number of cooperating processors. The concept underlying parallel architectures is not new. Nature is full of instances where seemingly powerless creatures, such as ants and bees, achieve incredible feats by collective endeavor. All modern technology is the result of joint human effort. In fact, this approach has another point in its favor: because of advances made in VLSI technology, it has become possible to fabricate cheaply many processors on a single chip. Undoubtedly, there are many problems to be overcome, some of which seem almost insurmountable. We will discuss here some of the most fundamental of these, and show the various ways in which these are being overcome.

A crucial decision that must be made in the design of such Multi-Computer Systems, or MCS, is the level of parallelism, or, in other words, the size of the subtasks that the original task is split into. Different design philosophies have favored different sizes.[1] Each has its own strengths and weaknesses. At one end of the spectrum is the Data Flow Machine, or DFM, where each subtask is a single operation. The DFM has a problem in the amount of the communication overhead involved as each processor sends or receives data from another. On the other hand, using large subtasks, while reducing this burden, involves another (nontrivial) problem of properly partitioning the given algorithm into reasonably sized chunks, and then mapping these resulting subtasks on the available architecture in the most efficient manner.

There have been many approaches to these new architectures that employ parallelism. In one of the simpler implementations, numerous relatively simple processors work on different sets of the data, performing the same set of instructions on each set. These processors will need to interact often in order to synchronize themselves. Alternatively, we can have processors working independently, interacting only briefly and not very often. These processors can be geographically distant from one another.

The approach we discuss here takes a middle road. This architecture consists of medium-power processors (such as those used in single-board computers), which are physically close together so that they may communicate easily, via dedicated links or communication paths, but which at the same time work relatively independently of one another.

Flynn[2] categorized the various classes of computers based on the way they operate and handle data. These categories are: SISD (Single Instruction Stream, Single Data Stream), SIMD (Single Instruction Stream, Multiple Data Stream), MISD (Multiple Instruction Stream, Single Data Stream), and MIMD (Multiple Instruction Stream, Multiple Data Stream). The classification is fairly logical and self-explanatory. In this article we are concerned with MIMD schemes, where different processors work on different or multiple data schemes, with each possibly executing different instructions. It would be extremely useful to have a reasonable methodology to evaluate the performance of various MIMD schemes, and thereby provide a possible design tool for use in such systems. Thus far, new architecture designs have been done mainly on an ad hoc basis. There is a need to replace such intuitive techniques with some systematic methodology. Although the MCS can conceptually provide a linear speedup over a uniprocessor system, practical systems fall far short of this because of problems with mismatch between the algorithm and architecture, overheads associated with data management and communications, etc.[3]

What can be done to optimize the performance of an MCS? From a commonsense point of view, three factors that could have a bearing on performance come to mind: (1) the interconnection scheme that ties all the processors together, (2) the scheduling and mapping of the algorithm on the architecture, and (3) the mechanism for detecting parallelism and partitioning the algorithm into modules, or subtasks, which, when run on an MCS, will achieve a computational speedup. The last of these issues is quite involved, and space will not permit a summary that would do it justice.

Interconnection scheme issues

When several processors are required to work cooperatively on a single task, one expects frequent exchange of data among the several subtasks that comprise the main task. The amount of data, the frequency with which they are transmitted, the speed of their transmission, and the route that they take are all significant in affecting this intercommunication. The first two factors depend on the algorithm itself and how well it has been partitioned. The speed of transmission is a function of the hardware used and is not the point of the discussion here. In this section, we concern ourselves with the last factor.

Ideally, if one processor wants to communicate with another, then it should do so over a channel that directly connects the two. A channel between every pair of processors would yield a system that is most versatile. Given a sufficient number of processors, there would be little or no problems with scheduling. Such a system is undoubtedly the most desirable. It would also be prohibitively expensive. A channel between every pair of processors would require $O(n^2)$ channels for n processors. For any significant n the total cost of these channels would swamp all other costs. We must, therefore, trade cost for speed and versatility. The compromise that is made involves routing data from one processor to another via intermediate processors, in cases where there is no direct link between the two processors. This has several repercussions. First, there is now an extra delay added in data transmission because of possible intermediate stages. Second, and perhaps more important, is the added capability that must be built into each processor that would allow it to perform this routing intelligently. The processor must know whether a block of data it has received is for itself or is en route to another processor, in which case it must forward this block to the appropriate processor, which could be the destination processor or another intermediate processor. And conversely, when a processor wishes to acquire data from another, it must know how and when to access this data. In other words, the processors must be aware of some routing and synchronization rules, and these should be, preferably,

both simple and efficient. The interconnection scheme must take into account all these factors.

There have been many approaches that try to address this problem, viz., given these n processors, how to connect them in the most cost-effective manner.

Broadly speaking, a viable interconnection strategy (or topology) must have a small number of channels, and relatively easy routing rules. There are also such other considerations as fault tolerance: how to reroute data and recover gracefully in case a processor fails. Each of the schemes has been proposed with a certain class of applications in mind. Therefore, it would not be possible to directly compare these schemes as there is, in general, no "best" scheme. Instead, what we have is a number of schemes, each of which has its particular area of usefulness. With the range of possible applications in mind, the designer must choose the most cost-effective one for his purposes. Any evaluation of the performance of these schemes must be, to a certain extent, qualitative. However, once a few candidate networks have been tentatively selected, detailed (and expensive) evaluation including simulation can be carried out and the "best" one selected for the proposed application.

It is instructive to examine, at least qualitatively, some of the important characteristics of these interconnection schemes. We will first describe and define these characteristics and then evaluate various interconnection schemes vis-a-vis these characteristics. In what follows a distinction is made between two classes of interconnection schemes. *Link*-oriented structures or schemes comprise those interconnection schemes in which there is a dedicated link or channel available for data transfer between two computers that are to be connected. *Bus*-oriented structures consist of multiple buses. Each bus is shared by a group of computers; communication takes place in a series of hops, from computer to computer, via these buses.

Network characteristics. We now look at some of the considerations in the evaluation of interconnection networks. In all these networks, it should be emphasized that improving one parameter might adversely affect some other parameters: what is sought is an optimization of the network.

Average distance. One of the more important evaluative measures of an interconnection network is the *average distance*. This is the distance messages must travel, on an average, in the network. It is advantageous to make this as short as possible. The average distance (in terms of the number of links) is defined as:[4]

$$\text{AvgDist} = \frac{\sum\limits_{d=1}^{r} d\, N_d}{N-1}$$

where N_d is the number of computers at a distance d links away, r is the diameter (maximum of the minimum distance between any two pairs of nodes), and N is the total number of computers.

For regular networks, i.e., those in which each computer is connected to the same number of other computers, the AvgDist is a constant. For irregular networks, the formula will yield different results, depending on the node from which d is measured. A network that has a low average distance may require an unreasonable number of communication ports for each computer. In order to distinguish these cases, a *normalized average distance* is defined[4] for link-based structures:

$$\text{NormAvgDist (link)} = \text{AvgDist} \times \text{Ports/comp} \quad (2)$$

where Ports/comp is the number of communication ports required of each computer.

In the case of bus structures, the distance d is the number of buses a message has to cross on the way to its destination. Also, the number of computers tied to a bus is of importance as several computers on a single bus may create bottlenecks due to bus contentions. To account for this, we define the normalized average distance for bus structures as the average distance weighted by the number of computers that may have access to a single bus.

$$\text{NormAvgDist (bus)} = \text{AvgDist} \times \text{Ports/bus} \quad (3)$$

Communication links. The total number of communication links in a network of given size is another useful measure. Clearly, among two networks, the one that has fewer connecting links is the more desirable, assuming (naively) all else is equal.

Routing algorithm. When a message is to be routed from one computer to another, the route it must take is obtained from the *routing algorithm*. It is desirable that the routing algorithm be simple and not require a complete knowledge of the entire network. In particular, it would be convenient if, by merely having the destination address, it is possible to obtain the exact—and preferably the shortest—sequence of computers the message must traverse.

Fault tolerance. If one of the computers along this route were to be faulty, then a breakdown in communication would result, and this could make any further computation pointless. To preclude such a possibility, networks must be fault tolerant. Fault-tolerant networks have at least one redundant path between any two computers; and these redundant paths are used in the case of a fault in a connecting channel. Another fault that is potentially more dangerous is the failure of a computer. Should such a fault arise, it is desirable that the system bypasses this faulty computer in all future computations and remain functional although possibly impaired. This "graceful degradation" feature is desirable in certain critical areas, such as space and military applications.

Expansion capability. Any large system must be capable of expansion in such a way that it causes a minimum of disruption of the existing setup. Clearly, a network that requires a complete rebuilding, with fresh demands on the number of communication ports of individual computers, every time extra computers are added is less preferable to one that can be extended in a natural way, without major upheaval of the entire system.

Link-oriented structures

In this section we analyze some link-oriented structures. The issues mentioned in the previous section are dealt with in seriatim.

The ring network. The ring structure is one of the simplest networks. The routing is simple and the structure has been well analyzed, mainly because, along with the star and tree networks, it is among the

> The routing algorithm of link-oriented structures is relatively straightforward, because of the simplicity of the network.

most popular of the topologies used in Local Area Networks, or LANs. The topology has also been used in a Dataflow machine architecture.[5,6] It consists of a number of computers connected in the form of a ring, i.e., each connected to its two neighbors. Although most LAN topologies use a unidirectional ring (i.e., one in which data flows in one direction only around the ring), because of its obvious problem of poor fault tolerance, we will assume a bidirectional ring.

Average distance. The average distance is easily found to be $(N+1)/4$, for a ring of N computers, where N is odd. The case for N even is also easy to deal with, but the relations are not so neat. The normalized average distance is, of course, $(N+1)/2$, as there are two ports on each computer. This linear relationship means that the distance may become unacceptably large for large N.

Communication links. The total number of communication links is N.

Routing algorithm. The routing algorithm is relatively straightforward, because of the simplicity of the network. It is simplest for unidirectional rings and only slightly more involved for bidirectional rings.

Fault tolerance. The fault tolerance of the ring structure is questionable. If any node in a unidirectional ring fails, it may render the entire system nonfunctional. In a bidirectional ring the failure of two nodes will cause the same result. In order to alleviate this problem, several variants

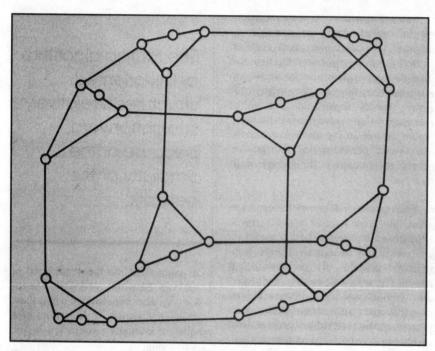

Figure 1. A 32-node cube connected cycles network (k = 5).

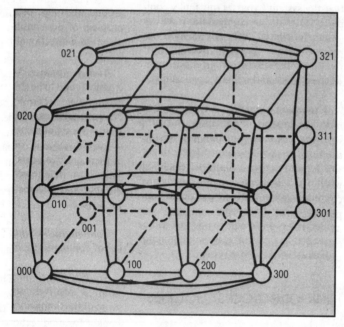

Figure 2. A $4 \times 3 \times 2$ alpha network.

F, B, and L (for Forward, Backward, and Lateral) provided on each computer, and the interconnection rule is:

F(l,p) is connected to B(l, ($p+1$)mod2^r);
B(l,p) is connected to F(l, ($p-1$)mod2^r);
L(l,p) is connected to L($l + \epsilon^p$);

where $\epsilon = 1 - 2 \times (p^{th}$ bit of l). An example of such a structure for $k = 5$ is shown in Figure 1.

Average distance. The average distance for the CCC is obtained as the product of the average distance of the subgroup of 2^r processors (which form a ring) and the main ($k - r$) cube network. The number of ports in each computer is three, so the normalized distance is simply the average distance times three.

Communication links. The total number of communication links is at most $(3/2)N$, where N is the total number of nodes in the network.[7]

Routing algorithm and fault tolerance. Wittie[8] gives a simple algorithm to route messages between computers. Even when a node is faulty, an alternative path may be found with ease.

Expansion capability. Because of the cube structure employed, expansion is not easy. Not only must the expansion be in powers of two, but the system must be completely restructured.

The alpha network. This is a generalized hypercube structure.[4] Unlike the hypercube, which needs the number of nodes to be of the form $N = W^D$, the alpha network is valid for all nonprime values of N. The alpha network is constructed in the following manner: Let $m_1, m_2, ..., m_D$ be chosen such that m_i is integer and

$$\prod_{i=1}^{d} m_i = N$$

Then each node can be expressed in a mixed radix form as a D-tuple ($x_D, x_{D-1}, ..., x_1$), which forms the address of the node. Connections are made from each node to every node whose address differs by 1 in any one coordinate. An example of an alpha network is shown in Figure 2.

Average distance. The average distance in a network is given by

$$\text{AvgDist(alpha)} = \frac{D(W-1)W^{N-1}}{N-1} \quad (4)$$

have been considered by different researchers.

Expansion capability. The ring network is obviously one of the simplest to expand.

The cube connected cycles network. This network, proposed by Preparata,[7] connects 2^k computers (k is an integer) in such a way that groups of 2^r (r is the smallest integer such that $r + 2^r \geq k$) are interconnected so as to form a ($k-r$)-dimension cube. Each computer has a k-bit address that is expressed as a pair (l,p) of integers, l having ($k-r$) bits, and p having r bits. There are three ports, called

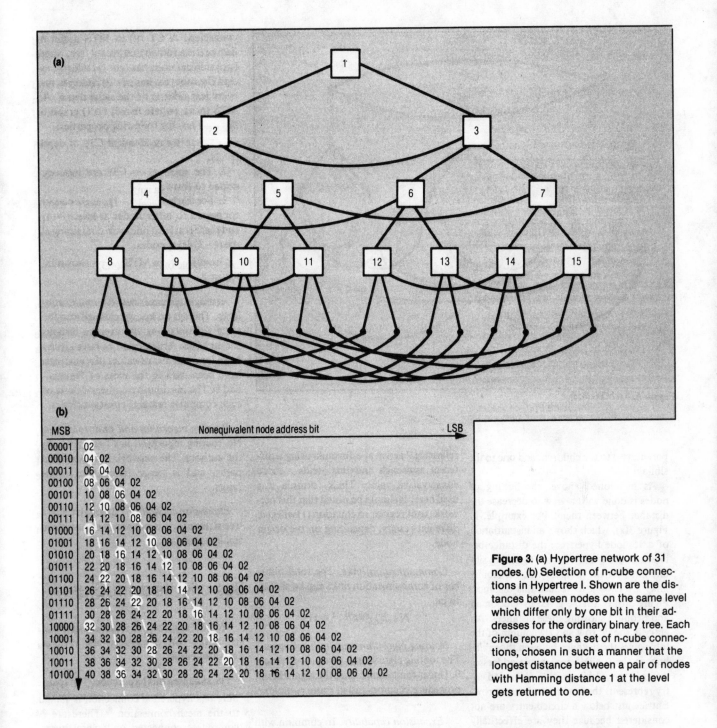

Figure 3. (a) Hypertree network of 31 nodes. (b) Selection of n-cube connections in Hypertree I. Shown are the distances between nodes on the same level which differ only by one bit in their addresses for the ordinary binary tree. Each circle represents a set of n-cube connections, chosen in such a manner that the longest distance between a pair of nodes with Hamming distance 1 at the level gets returned to one.

The number of ports on each processor is given by

$$\text{Ports (alpha)} = D(W - 1) \qquad (5)$$

Communication links. The total number of links is

$$\text{Links (alpha)} = N \times \text{Ports}/2 \qquad (6)$$

Routing algorithm and fault tolerance. A simple routing algorithm is given in reference 4. Because of the several redundant paths that exist, this network is highly fault tolerant.

Expansion capability. Since this network is a generalized cube network, expansion is not easy as the number of ports is dependent on network size. Unlike cube networks, however, any nonprime value of N can be accommodated.

The hypertree network. The hypertree[9] is basically a binary tree network, which by the judicious addition of extra edges connecting sibling nodes, has been made to have a smaller average distance, and a measure of fault tolerance. These new edges are chosen to be n-cube connections; i.e., they link nodes that have (binary) addresses that differ in only one bit. Each processor has four ports—one from the

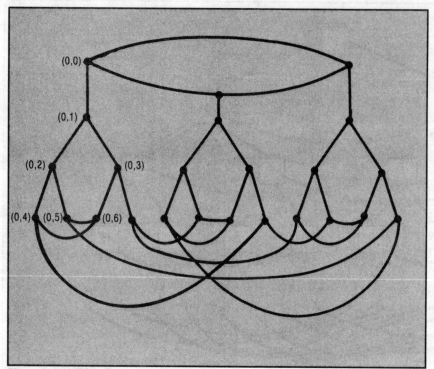

Figure 4. An MTS (4:3).

parent, two to the children, and one to the sibling.

As mentioned above, the linking of nodes is done with a view to decrease the distance between them. For example, in Figure 3(a), which shows an instantiation of a 15-node hypertree, the distance between nodes 8 and 15 is six (ignoring sibling links for the moment). So the sibling links are chosen to reduce this distance. Figure 3(b) is a table given by Goodman and Sequin[9] showing these distances. An entry in the ith row and j^{th} column of the table gives the distance between those siblings in the $(i+1)^{th}$ row whose addresses differ in the jth bit position. A circled entry represents the maximum for that row. Entries just below a circled entry are not considered because they are effactually reduced to three by the sibling links in the previous level. Entries two rows below a circled entry are reduced to five, and so on. With this table, the sibling links may be chosen in a fairly straightforward manner. For every level i, links are given by the value of the circled entry of the table.

Average distance. The average distance of the hypertree is tedious to calculate using equation (1). The authors of reference 9 arrive at a formula using a different approach and this yields a more conservative value. Their formula was used here. It should be noted that this network is not regular so equation (1) will give different results, depending on the origin node.

Communication links. The total number of communication links can be shown to be

$$N + 2(2^{\lceil \log_2 N \rceil - 1} - 1)$$

Routing algorithm and fault tolerance. The routing algorithm is given in reference 9. Under fault conditions, the algorithmic procedure becomes rather more complex.

Expansion capability. In common with tree structures, the network is easily extensible, and expansion requires a minimum disruption of the rest of the system.

The multitree structure. The multitree structure[10] is another tree type structure that uses connections to sibling nodes to reduce the distance between them. An MTS (m:t) consists of m identical Component Trees, or CTs, each of t levels, which have their roots and their leaves circularly connected. A CT of an MTS graph of degree d is a rooted undirected tree, where each nonleaf node has $(d-1)$ children, except the root that has $(d-2)$ children, and every leaf node is of the same depth. An MTS (m:t), (where $m \geq 3$, $t \geq 1$) graph of degree d has the following properties:

1. There are m identical CTs of depth $(t-1)$.
2. The roots of m CTs are interconnected to form a ring.
3. For each level $(t-1)$, each node is connected to other nodes at level $(t-1)$, and there is at least one cycle containing all the $(t-1)$-level nodes.

An example of an MTS(4:3) is shown in Figure 4.

Average distance and communication links. There is no known closed-form formula for obtaining the average distance for an MTS. Arden and Lee have given a table for a number of values of n and these have been used in the plots of Figures 7 and 8. The maximum number of ports on each computer remains constant (four).

Routing algorithm and fault tolerance. No routing algorithm has been given by the authors. The network has redundant paths, and is hence tolerant of single faults.

Expansion capability. Although this is a tree structure, it is not easily extensible in small increments.

Bus-oriented structures

We now analyze two representative bus structures with regard to the criteria described earlier.

The spanning bus hypercube. The spanning bus hypercube connection is similar to the mesh connection.[8] There are N computers connected on several buses. Each computer is connected to D buses that span each of the D dimensions of the hypercube space. Nodes that have all their coordinates—except the ith—the same are connected to the ith bus. Figure 5 shows a 3^3 spanning bus hypercube structure.

Average distance. The average distance for the spanning bus hypercube is given by equation (4), the alpha structure formula, because of the similarity of the addressing

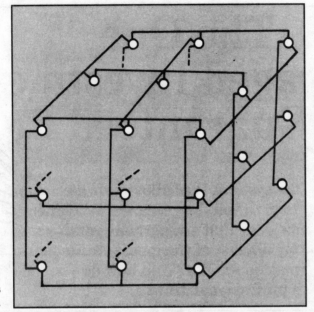

Figure 5. A 3^3 spanning bus hypercube.

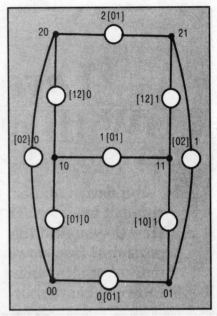

Figure 6. A 2 × 3 beta network.

schemes between these networks.

The number of buses used is[8] DW^{D-1}.

Routing algorithm and fault tolerance. Wittie[8] gives the routing algorithm for this network. A single fault in a bus can be tolerated by such networks.

Expansion capability. Spanning bus hypercube structures may be expanded by increasing D or W. Increasing W has the advantage of not requiring fresh ports in each computer.

Beta networks. The beta structure[4] is of the same topology as the alpha structure. However, a link in the alpha structure is substituted for a node (computer) in the beta. The node of an alpha network is a bus in a beta structure. Figure 6 is an example of a beta network.

Average distance. There exists no known closed-form relation for directly computing the average distance of such a network. The plots of Figures 7 and 8 were obtained by numerical methods.

Communication links. The number of buses is given by W^D. The number of nodes is given by

$$N = \frac{W^D(W-1)}{2} \qquad (7)$$

(*continued on p. 32*)

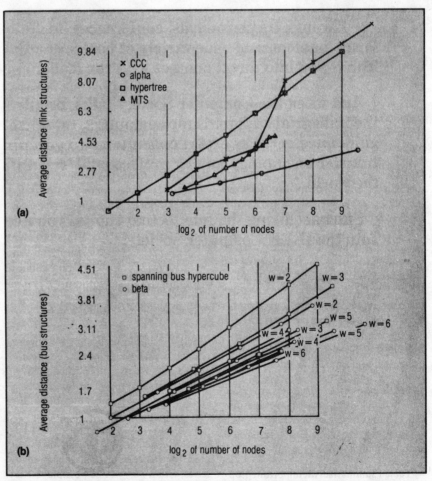

Figure 7. (a) Average distance (link structures) versus number of nodes. (b) Average distance (bus structures) versus number of nodes.

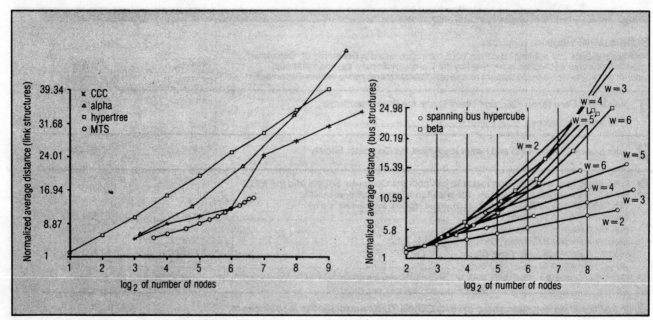

Figure 8. (a) Normalized average distance (link structures) versus number of nodes. (b) Normalized average distance (bus structures) versus number of nodes.

Routing algorithm and fault tolerance. The routing procedure is simple and similar to that of the spanning bus hypercube. Beta networks are also fault tolerant.

Expansion capability. An expansion of the beta network does require rerouting of the network, but the number of ports demanded of each computer remains fixed at two.

Figures 7 and 8 show plots of the average distance and normalized average distance vs. the number of computers for these networks. Among link structures, alpha networks have the smallest average distance. The next best structure is the MTS, followed by the CCC structure. The MTS has the best normalized average distance. However, the routing poses a significant hurdle to its performance. The CCC is the next best and, together with its simple routing algorithm and its fault tolerance, looks attractive indeed.

In the case of bus structures, the beta network possesses smaller average distance, but its normalized average distance is larger and also increases at a faster rate than the spanning bus hypercube.

Table 1 summarizes the important properties of these interconnection schemes. Note that the formulae given therein for the average distances are empirical and approximate, and to be used for comparison only. The term *message density* is defined as

$$\text{Mess. Dens.} = \frac{\text{Avg. Dist.} \times \text{no. of nodes}}{\text{Total no. of links}}$$

As was mentioned earlier, no concrete conclusion can be drawn at this stage as to the relative merit of any scheme based on these figures alone. For example, the CCC seems to be a reasonable choice from a consideration of only the average distance, but from an application viewpoint the alpha structure is the most versatile, as is shown later in a simulation study.

Mapping and scheduling issues

Suppose we have at hand a computational task and, to perform it, we are also given a suitable algorithm to be used. In addition, assume this algorithm has been divided into some number of subtasks in a way that some of these subtasks may be run concurrently. As these subtasks run (on the different processors), they may need to exchange data amongst themselves, and it may not be possible to start the execution of one subtask before the completion of some other subtasks. If we

can estimate the extent of this data exchange, i.e., communication between subtasks (see, for example, reference 5), and their data dependencies, then we can estimate the general behavior of the algorithm on the system. The scheduling problem is: How does one find an optimum allotment of these subtasks among the processors so that the maximum possible speedup (or, equivalently, some other performance parameter) may be achieved? For example, if two subtasks exchange data frequently, they should be allotted to two processors that are adjacent, i.e., directly connected to one another.

So, on one hand we have the several subtasks and their interrelationships with respect to data dependency; and on the other, we have the many (not necessarily identical) processors, with their interrelationships, i.e., interconnection scheme. We now need to "map" one on the other. In a most general purpose computer, no information will be available beforehand on the nature of the tasks to be performed on it, so the mapping described above must be done at runtime, dynamically, as subtasks are created. The time spent on this mapping will contribute to the total time that it takes to complete the task. This mapping time is not negligible, and may significantly detract from the performance of the system, especially in real-time applications, where time is of the greatest im-

Table 1. Properties of interconnection schemes.

	Average distance	Ports/node (link structures) or ports on a bus (bus structures) (P)	Normalized average distance (L)	Message density	Number of links (buses)	Fault tolerance (link failures)
Fully connected network	1	$N-1$	N	N	(N^2-N)	$N-1$
Ring (bidirectional)	$(N+1)/4$	2	$(N+1)/2$	$(N+1)/4$	N	2
Cube connected cycles	$\approx 0.8 \log_2 N - 2.4$	3	$\approx 2.4 \log_2 N - 7.2$	$5D/4$	$\dfrac{3N}{2}$	2
Alpha	$\approx k \log_2 N + 0.2$ $k \approx 0.3$ to 0.5	$D(W-1)$	$D(W-1)L$	$\dfrac{2L}{D(W-1)}$	$\dfrac{ND}{2}$	$D(W-1)-1$
Hypertree	$\approx 1.1 \log_2 N - 0.7$	4	$\approx 4.4 \log_2 N - 2.8$	$\dfrac{L}{2}$	$\approx 2(N-1)$	3
MTS	$\approx \log_2 N - 2$	3	$\approx 3 \log_2 N - 6$	$2 \log_2 N - 4$	–	2
Single global bus	1	N	N	N	1	$N-1$
Spanning bus hypercube	$\approx k \log_2 N + 0.2$ $k \approx 0.3$ to 0.5	W	$\approx W \log_2 N + 0.2W$ $k \approx 0.3$ to 0.5	W	DW^{D-1}	$W-1$
Beta	$\approx k \log_2 N + 0.25$ $k \approx 0.30$ to 0.37	$D(W-1)$	$D(W-1)L$	L	W^D	$D(W-1)-1$

portance. The performance parameter to be optimized could be just the total execution time, or a weighted combination of execution and communication times, or channel and processor utilization. Numerous authors have considered the problem of allocating noninteracting tasks in a distributed environment. They have not considered the effects of data dependency or communication amongst these tasks. But in a multiprocessor environment, interprocessor communication overheads play an important part in determining the performance of the system.

An optimal assignment of subtasks, or modules, to a two-processor system has been considered by Stone,[11] in which the cost of interprocessor communication has been taken into account, in addition to the communication and other collective costs. The basic idea used by Stone is to apply a maximal-flow algorithm to the graph model of a modular program, i.e., one in which each module is represented by a node and the weight on the edge connecting two nodes represents the cost of an intermodule reference when the two nodes (or modules) are assigned to different computers. Each cutset of this graph partitions the graph into two disjoint subsets, and each subset could be assigned to each processor such that the weights of the edges comprising the cutset (which account for all costs) could be minimized. This, in turn, will minimize the total runtime. Stone also provides a way of extending this technique for systems with more than two processors.

A more complete solution to this issue for an arbitrary number of processors was provided by Bokhari.[12] His method assumes that the intermodule communication requirements (which form a precedence relationship) could be represented by a tree-like structure. The method then uses a dynamic programming approach, and minimizes the sum of execution and interprocessor communication costs for an arbitrarily connected distributed system.

Tilborg and Wittie[13] introduced another method called *wave scheduling*, which is applicable to a large homogeneous multicomputer system. The method assumes that there is a hierarchical level of control in the form of a tree (although the computers themselves need not necessarily be connected in a tree-like form). It also assumes that any task can be executed on any one of the processors, and that all cooperating tasks form a *task force*, and that these are known a priori. A task force needing a specific number of nodes is entered in a queue at any node, and the hierarchical control at the root of the subtree schedules the enqueued task forces that are no larger than the number of nodes in the subtree. Tilborg and Wittie have observed that decentralized wave scheduling works well with at low to moderate levels of work load and its efficiency is comparable to that of centralized scheduling.

There are several other scheduling and load balancing strategies advocated by various researchers. But these efforts are limited to scheduling of noninteractive and independent tasks on multiprocessors of distributed systems, where the major concern has been optimization of execution times, and the appropriate placement of distributed databases. As applied to the

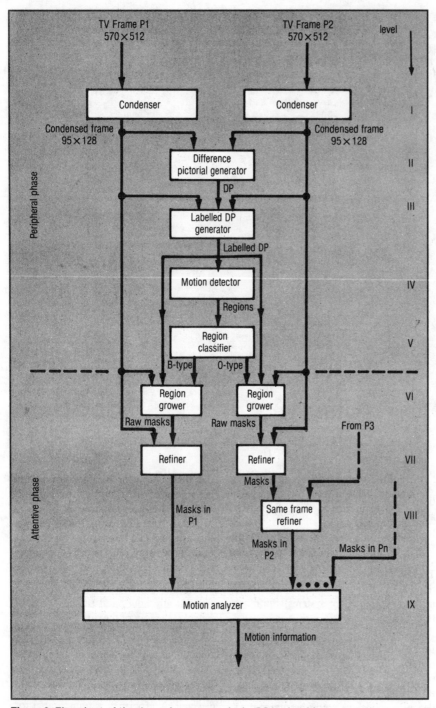

Figure 9. Flowchart of the dynamic-scene-analysis (DSA) algorithm.

physically or directly connected processors. In other words, it gives a number indicating how well the algorithm has mapped on the architecture in a physical sense. It has been shown [12,14] that the mapping problem falls into a class of intractable problems, called *NP-Complete*. In order to solve the allocation problem with the expenditure of reasonable effort, some approximations have to made and some heuristics employed. Furthermore, if some of the typical algorithms that will be used are known previously, then the various attributes of the subtasks can be estimated and this mapping can be done before the actual runtime of the algorithm. This is called *static allocation*. Many real-time applications can be easily served by using static allocation, and, as we will see later, pipelining.

The heuristic employed by Bokhari allows pairwise interchange of mapped nodes. The exchange that leads to the maximum increase in cardinality of the mapping is selected. The rationale behind the optimization of cardinality is to reduce the communication overhead in incompletely connected systems of multicomputers.

Bokhari's work, though important, has some shortcomings. It assumes the processors are identical and that the channel bandwidths are the same for all the channels. No consideration is given to the amount of computation to be done at each node, and the amount of data to be transferred along each connecting edge.

Some of these issues have been addressed by Pathak.[14] The heuristic he employs is the one known as the *greedy* heuristic. For each node, the algorithm looks at the node's immediate surroundings and obtains the optimal mapping, in an attempt to eventually achieve a global optimization. The algorithm makes use of two graph theoretic constructs called the *Computation Flow Graph* and the *Computation Resource Graph*. It is common practice to model the software for parallel machines in the form of directed graphs with directed edges representing the data dependencies, and other parameters being associated with each node and the connecting edges. In the same way the processors and their resources could be modeled by graphs. The CFG is a directed graph that shows the data dependency or the interrelationships with respect to data ex-

architecture we are discussing, the crucial issues of data dependency between subtasks and the interprocessor communication overhead has been neglected.

Bokhari [12] showed that when assigning tasks to the processors, pairs of tasks, or modules, that need to communicate with each other should be placed, if possible, on processors that are directly connected. The property that characterizes such an assignment is known in graph theory as the *cardinality* of the mapping. Cardinality refers to the number of data transfers of the communicating subtasks falling upon

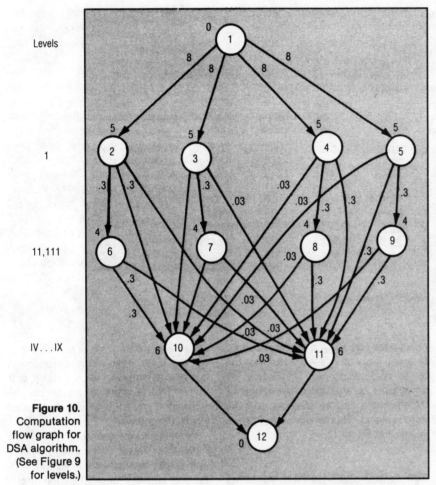

Figure 10.
Computation
flow graph for
DSA algorithm.
(See Figure 9
for levels.)

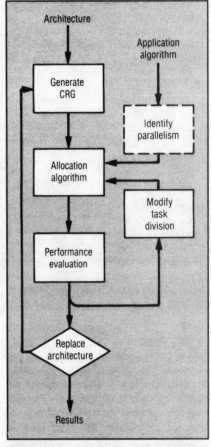

Figure 11. Flowchart for suboptimal mapping.

change between the various subtasks. Each node of this graph represents a subtask and each edge in it has a value equal to the amount of data that will need to be transferred. The CFG is defined to be acyclic.

The CRG is an undirected graph in which the nodes are the processors and the edges denote the channel between the two adjacent processors. The mapping algorithm accepts these two graphs as input, and produces as output the mapping of the CFG on the CRG. Each node of the CFG can be associated with a level. A node has level 1 if it is a source node; i.e., it does not need any input data from any other node. Nodes that need data from level 1 nodes are at level 2, and so on. The algorithm works as follows: Allocation starts from level 1 nodes. For each level l, a node of the CFG of level l is chosen per a criterion that selects nodes with the maximum computation and data communication. A match for this node is searched for in the CRG. A node of the CRG that would minimize the

total communication and computation time is selected. Once all the nodes at level l have been matched, scheduling is continued for level $l+1$, and so on, until all the nodes of the CFG have been mapped. The algorithm assumes that the number of processors are at least equal to the number of nodes of the CFG.

Once the mapping is done, a simulation program is run that will give an estimate of some important parameters that can be used to judge the effectiveness of the architecture/algorithm combination that has been employed. If the results are not encouraging, another combination may be tried.

A simple example would serve to illustrate the procedure.

An application example

The Dynamic Scene Analysis algorithm[15] provides a method for extracting images of moving objects. The algorithm

works in several stages and thus can be pipelined. Recall that the CFG was stipulated to be acyclic. Also, since each subtask of the algorithm maps on a unique processor, when a processor is done with a subtask, it will not be used again in this instance of the algorithm. These two conditions allow for pipelining. Figure 9 shows the various stages of the algorithm. The algorithm yields a CFG that is shown in Figure 10. For a more complete description, see reference 13. It is required to find a suitable architecture on which the algorithm could be mapped so as to achieve a respectable speedup.

The next stage in the evaluation process is to consider possible architectures, and by studying the results of the evaluation, pick the most suitable one. From Figure 7(a), which gives a plot of the average distance, the alpha structure, the CCC, and the MTS seem to be reasonable choices. Now with each of these schemes, the mapping algorithm is run and an allocation is made. Next, using the software described

Table 2. Simulation results for various architectures.

	Number of processors	Degree	Cardinality	Average communicating distance	Average mapping distance	Channel utilization*	Resource utilization*	Speed up*	Turnaround time*
Alpha	24	6	10	2.000	1.833	1.193	1.035	0.955	1.064
B-Cube	16	4	8	2.133	1.792	1.025	0.772	0.603	1.383
B-Tree	13	3	3	3.282	3.000	1.679	0.837	0.371	1.935
CCC	24	3	4	3.217	3.458	1.641	0.810	0.359	1.985
Full	13	12	24	1.000	1.000	1.000	1.000	1.000	1.000
H-Tree	13	4	5	2.269	2.417	1.497	0.807	0.407	1.754
Mesh	16	4	6	2.667	2.583	1.276	0.864	0.639	1.286
EAMesh	16	4	6	2.133	1.958	1.229	0.847	0.639	1.317
Ring	13	2	2	3.500	3.292	1.494	0.833	0.491	1.552
Star	13	12	3	1.846	1.875	1.839	0.780	0.214	2.990

*Normalized with respect to fully connected scheme.
Normalizing factors are 0.0143, 0.7248, 6.034 and 1.514, respectively.

in reference 13, a simulation is done, which yields estimates of important parameters. The results of such a simulation are given in Table 2, which compares the results for various architectures. The second column gives the number of processors (or computers) The third column gives the degree, or the number of processors connected directly to a given processor. Column 4 gives the cardinality of mapping. The fifth column gives the average communicating distance between two processors (in number of hops). The next column gives the average mapping distance, which is the average data communication distance of subtasks on the particular architecture. Column 7 gives the channel utilization, and column 8 the resource utilization. By utilization we mean the proportion of time the item is kept busy. The next column (9) gives the speed-up over a conventional uniprocessor. The last column gives the turnaround time, which is the total time for execution. Note that the last four columns have been normalized so that the fully connected scheme has value 1 for these parameters. The computing power and the data transfer rates are assumed to be 1 MIPS and 0.5M bytes/s, respectively.

An examination of the table shows that the alpha and mesh structures perform close to the fully connected, ideal scheme. The cube connected cycles scheme that, after a study of Figure 7(a), seemed to be a reasonable network to use turns out to be a rather poor performer in this application. If at this stage, it was concluded that the results obtained are not satisfactory for any scheme, an alternative partitioning of the algorithm may be tried out and the steps repeated. This iterative procedure is depicted in Figure 11.

The methodology outlined here serves two purposes. One, it provides a way of choosing the appropriate architecture for a class of applications and, two, gives a method of determining how good this choice was by actually doing the mapping of the algorithm on the architecture and performing a simulation of the execution.

We have tacitly assumed so far that the algorithms that will be used have somehow been already partitioned into their respective subtasks. At present this partitioning must be done by the programmer. On the one hand, this has the advantage that it forces the programmer to think in a "concurrent" way; future algorithms may benefit from this way of thinking. On the other hand, there is a vast body of programs that has already been written, and which may be speeded up by exploiting any inherent parallelism each may possess. It would be tedious to rewrite all these programs. Instead, it would be extremely helpful to have an intelligent compiler that could extract parallelism from a program written for a sequential machine. Already

some work is being done in this direction. But this is not a trivial task. Parallelism may exist in terms of a single do loop, or it may be that an entire subroutine may be executed in parallel with others. In other words, the *granularity*[16] is variable.

By incorporating such a compiler in the flowchart of Figure 11 the whole mapping process may be automated to yield an optimum or near-optimum allocation after a few iterations. The (appropriately named) B-HIVE project is a nascent multicomputer project at North Carolina State University.[17] Here the ideas contained in this article have been incorporated in a 24-computer network, using the alpha interconnection scheme. Each node (or computer) consists of two processors: an Application processor that actually executes the application program, and a Communication processor that takes care of the details of sending and receiving data, routing, etc. This hierarchical construction of each node serves to keep separate the two logically different functions. The philosophy behind the B-HIVE project is to build a functional MCS using a "no-frills" approach. It is hoped that the hands-on experience we gain from such a working system will prove invaluable in future designs. □

Acknowledgments

This work is part of the B-HIVE multi-computer project currently being implemented at North Carolina State University. It has been partially supported by NASA Ames Research Center contract no. NAG 2-337, and a summer grant from the Center for Communication and Signal Processing and the Electrical and Computer Engineering Department, North Carolina State University.

References

1. P. C. Treleaven, D. R. Brownbridge, and R. P. Hopkins, "Data-driven and Demand-driven Computer Architecture," *ACM Computing Surveys,* Vol. 14, No. 1, pp. 93-143, March 1982.

2. M. J. Flynn, "Some Computer Organizations and Their Effectiveness," *IEEE Trans. Computers,* Vol. C-21, No. 9, pp. 948-960, Sept. 1972.

3. B. Lint and T. Agerwala, "Communication Issues in the Design and Analysis of Parallel Algorithms," *IEEE Trans. Software Engineering,* Vol. SE-7, pp. 174-188, March 1981.

4. L. N. Bhuyan and D. P. Agrawal, "A General Class of Processor Interconnection Strategies," *Proc. 9th. Ann. Symp. Computer Architecture,* Austin, Texas, pp. 90-98, April 26-29, 1982.

5. W. W. Chu et al., "Task Allocation in Distributed Data Processing," *Computer,* Vol. 13, No. 11, pp. 57-69, Nov. 1980.

6. K. P. Gostelow and R. E. Thomas, "Performance of a Simulated Data-flow Computer," *IEEE Trans. Computers,* Vol. C-29, No. 10, pp. 905-919, Oct. 1980.

7. F. P. Preparata and J. V. Vullemin, "The Cube Connected Cycles: A Versatile Network for Parallel Computers," *CACM,* Vol. 24, pp. 300-309, May 1981.

8. L. D. Wittie, "Communication Structures for Large Networks of Microcomputers," *IEEE Trans. Computers,* Vol. C-30, No. 4, pp. 284-273, April 1981.

9. J. R. Goodman and C. H. Sequin, "Hypertree: A Multiprocessor Interconnection Topology," *IEEE Trans. Computers,* Vol. C-30, No. 12, pp. 923-933, Dec. 1981.

10. B. W. Arden and H. Lee, "A Regular Network for Multicomputer Systems," *IEEE Trans. Computers,* Vol. C-30, pp. 60-69, Jan. 1982.

11. H. S. Stone, "Multiprocessor Scheduling with the Aid of Network Flow Algorithms," *IEEE Trans. Software Engineering,* Vol. SE-3, pp. 85-94, Jan. 1977.

12. S. H. Bokhari, "On the Mapping Problem," *IEEE Trans. Computers,* Vol. C-30, No. 3, pp. 207-214, March 1981.

13. A. M. van Tilborg and L. D. Wittie, "Wave Scheduling—Decentralized Scheduling of Task Forces in Multicomputers," *IEEE Trans. Computers,* Vol. C-33, No. 9, pp. 835-844, Sept. 1984.

14. G. C. Pathak, "Towards Automated Design of Multicomputer System for Real-time Applications," PhD. dissertation, N.C. State Univ., Raleigh, July 1984.

15. D. P. Agrawal and R. Jain, "A Pipelined Pseudoparallel System Architecture for Real Time Dynamic Scene Analysis," *IEEE Trans. Computers,* Vol. C-31, No. 10, pp. 952-962, Oct. 1982.

16. R. G. Babb II, "Parallel Processing with Large-Grain Data Flow Technique," *Computer,* Vol. 17, No. 7, pp. 55-61, July 1984.

17. D. P. Agrawal and W. E. Alexander, "B-HIVE: A Heterogeneous, Interconnected, Versatile and Expandable Multicomputer System," *ACM Computer Architecture News,* Vol. 12, No. 2, pp. 7-13, June 1984.

Virendra K. Janakiram is currently working toward the PhD degree at North Carolina State University at Raleigh. His research interests include parallel processing and functional and logic programming.

Girish C. Pathak received the BE degree in electronics and communication engineering from the University of Roorkee, India, the MTech degree from IIT, Kanpur, India, and the PhD degree in computer engineering from North Carolina State University, Raleigh, NC, in 1984.

In 1984, he joined Texas Instruments as a Member of Technical Staff. He is currently involved in the design of the architecture for AI machines. His research interests include multiprocessor systems and database management systems.

Dharma P. Agrawal is a professor of electrical and computer engineering at North Carolina State University, Raleigh. His research interests include both software and hardware aspects of parallel and distributed processing, computer architecture, and fault-tolerant computing. Currently, he is the Chairman of the Policy and Practices Committee of the IEEE-CS Publications Board and is an editor of the *Journal on Parallel and Distributed Computing.*

Agrawal holds a BE from the Ravishankar University, Raipur, an MS from the Roorkee University, and a DSc from the Federal Institute of Technology, Lausanne, Switzerland.

Readers may write to Agrawal at N.C. State University, Dept. of Electrical and Computer Engineering, Box 7911, Raleigh, NC 27695-7911.

Although multiprocessors are theoretically cost-effective and reliable, we aren't really using them. Experiments with a 50-processor architecture are uncovering practical ways to realize these benefits.

The Cm* Testbed

Edward F. Gehringer, Anita K. Jones, and Zary Z. Segall
Carnegie-Mellon University

Interest in multiprocessor architecture has grown steadily over the past ten to fifteen years. With VLSI technology we can build multiprocessors that are substantially larger than present computers to solve problems that cannot be solved today. Yet despite the substantial number of multiprocessor designs, only a few multiprocessors have been built with a high degree of parallelism, say thirty or more processors.

Although multiprocessors appear to have cost/performance and reliability benefits, the computing community has relatively little experience in their actual use. Consequently, little is known about how well the potential of multiprocessors can be realized, which is exactly the thrust of the Cm* research project.

We can view a distributed system as being composed of an architectural component and a behavioral component. The first component consists of hardware, firmware, and software elements, and the relationships between them. The behavioral component is characterized by the way the architecture acts in the presence of a workload. The architectural component should be flexible, and the behavioral component should provide a controllable and measurable behavior.

These two characteristics are embodied in the Cm* testbed, which has a programmable interconnection network for hardware-architecture flexibility. The two operating systems StarOS and Medusa provide adaptable mechanisms and policies for running experiments with application programs. The workload, the measurement tools, and the experimentation control are integrated into an experimentation environment, which complements the other support programs such as compilers and loaders with facilities for specifying, monitoring, and analyzing experiments.

The Cm* project has successfully constructed a 50-processor multiprocessor and two operating systems, thus demonstrating the feasibility of several aspects of multiprocessing. In this article we describe not only Cm* hardware and software but also experimental results, how well various algorithm structures exploit the potential parallelism of the Cm*, and the results of extended measurements on the hardware itself.

The Cm* experimentation environment

Cm* hardware. The Cm* hardware consists of 50 processor-memory pairs called Cm's, which are connected by a hierarchical, distributed switching structure. Cm* is partitioned into five *clusters* of up to 14 Cm's each; the Cm's in an individual cluster are connected via a *map bus* to a mapping processor, called a *Kmap*, through which they communicate with each other (Figure 1). The clusters are interconnected via *intercluster buses*. For a Cm to communicate with a Cm in a remote cluster, it first sends a request to the Kmap in its cluster, which forwards it to the Kmap in the *remote* cluster, which in turn passes the request to the target Cm.

Consequently, any Cm can reference memory anywhere in the system, and the memory appears to be a single large one. Nevertheless, the communication paths are of different length and induce a performance hierarchy: references by a Cm to its local memory take about 3 μsec.; references to another Cm in the same cluster require 8.6 μsec.; and intercluster references take about 35.3 μsec.[1]

Each Cm is a DEC LSI-11 with 64K or 128K bytes of memory, modified by the addition of a local switch, or *Slocal,* which examines each memory reference generated by the processor. Using its internal mapping tables, the Slocal decides whether the reference is to the processor's local memory. If it is, the reference takes no longer than a

Reprinted from *Computer*, October 1982, pages 38-50. Copyright © 1982 by The Institute of Electrical and Electronics Engineers, Inc.

memory reference by an unmodified LSI-11. If not, the Slocal passes the reference on to the Kmap. The Kmap is a high-speed microprogrammable communication controller with a cycle time of 157 nsec., a control store of 4K 80-bit words, and a data RAM of 4K 80-bit words. Since the Kmap is programmable, we can experiment with different processor-memory and interprocessor communication strategies. Further, the border between software and firmware is fluid and can be moved to investigate different operating system implementations. For example, important operating system functions can be placed in the Kmap to improve performance or to protect them from user programs.

Each Kmap has two bidirectional ports, and each port can be connected to a separate intercluster bus, permitting clusters to be connected in many different ways. At present, all five Kmaps are attached to two intercluster buses, allowing a direct path between each pair of Kmaps and ensuring that messages need never be forwarded via intermediate Kmaps. All communication between Kmaps and from the Kmap to a Cm is performed by packet switching rather than circuit switching to avoid deadlock over dedicated switching paths. The Kmap is provided with eight process-state contexts so that it can service up to eight requests concurrently by switching from one context to another. Typically, it switches away from a context while awaiting completion of a memory access emanating from that context.

A major advantage of the Cm* structure is its extensibility. Because the switching structure is not centralized, it does not grow more complicated as the number of processors increases. By contrast, C.mmp,[2] an earlier multiprocessor constructed at CMU, used a 16×16 crosspoint switch to route memory references to its sixteen processors. The complexity of such a switch grows by a factor of n^2 as n, the number of processors, increases. Cm* is built from clusters of limited size, which may be interconnected arbitrarily. Thus the number of processors or the amount of shared memory is virtually unlimited. Because intercluster messages are not passing through a central switch or bus, the overall intercommunication bandwidth has no architectural limit. Indeed, it has been estimated that a Cm* structure of up to 10,000 processors can be built.[3]

Flexibility of the switching network. Multiple-processor computer systems vary from shared-memory multiple-ALU machines like the Illiac IV,[4] to multiprocessors in which each processor is directly connected to one portion of memory and can access any portion of memory, to computer networks where each processor can directly address only its own memory. The Cm* Kmaps can be microprogrammed to emulate either of the latter two structures or other interconnection structures such as rings and cubes.

For example, if the Kmap is loaded with microcode that cannot map an address generated by one processor to the memory of another, Cm* becomes, in effect, a network of LSI-11s. Comparing the performance of a multiprocessor with a network is useful, since we tend to think

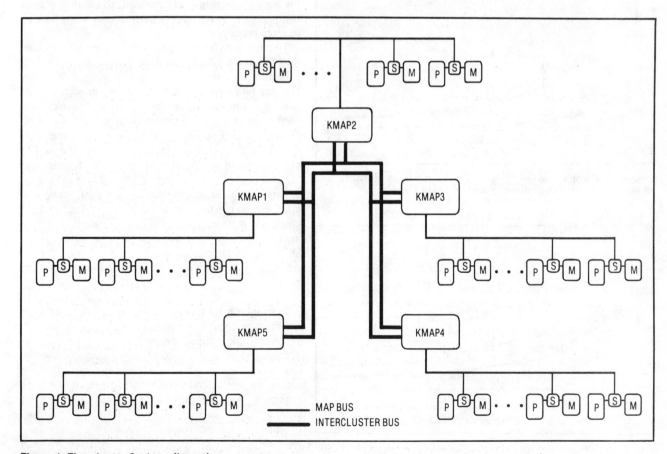

Figure 1. Five-cluster Cm* configuration.

that given the same processor-memory pairs, a network should be cheaper than a multiprocessor because of the relative simplicity of the interconnection hardware.

Levy Raskin[5] performed two experiments comparing Cm* as a multiprocessor with Cm* as a network. His results show that, at least for some practical multiprocessing algorithms, a network can compete with a multiprocessor. The first experiment used the following integer-programming application that exhibited rather low communication traffic:

Set-partitioning integer programming. The set-partitioning algorithm implemented for Cm* uses an enumeration algorithm that performs an *n*ary tree search in a large, relatively sparse binary matrix for a minimum-cost solution. The matrix is two dimensional with a size usually on the order of hundreds by thousands. The problem is to solve

$$\min(\underline{c}\cdot\underline{x}\,|\,A\underline{x} = \underline{e}\,, x_j = 0 \text{ or } 1 \text{ for } 0 \le j \le N)$$

where A is an $M \times N$ binary matrix, $\underline{c}$ is a vector of length N, and $\underline{e}$ is the identity vector of length M.

As an example, consider the airline-crew scheduling problem. The rows of the A matrix correspond to a set of flight legs to be covered during a specified period, and the columns of A correspond to a possible sequence of tours of flight legs made by one crew; $\underline{c}$ is a vector containing the cost of each tour. A feasible solution consists of a set of tours that satisfy all the flight legs (one and only one crew makes a flight leg). The algorithm seeks the solution with the lowest cost.

This algorithm was run on both Cm* configurations. In the network configuration, all interprocessor communication was via messages (transmitted by value) rather than shared memory, and the shortest message could be transmitted in 85 μsec. The algorithm was tested on five sets of data. When the matrix and other read-only global variables were replicated in each processor, the communication overhead was moderate, about 1.3M bps. Nonetheless, the network configuration actually performed better than the multiprocessor configuration (Figures 2 and 3), perhaps because its microcode is simpler.

The second network experiment involved a speech-recognition task with complex and intense communication demands. In the experiment Harpy, a speech-recognition system developed at CMU,[6,7] was used to implement a voice-input "desk calculator" and a 32-word command vocabulary. Despite the fact that the algorithm was carefully tuned to minimize interprocessor communication, the optimal number of processors in the network configuration was only three; as additional processors were added, execution time increased because of the high message rate. By contrast, the multiprocessor configuration could achieve performance gains with up to seven processors.

To implement large programs on Cm* we must expand the LSI-11's 16-bit address space. Here, too, the Cm* architecture provides considerable latitude. Each Slocal has one map bit and one relocation register for each 4K-byte page of its Cm's address space. The Kmap can selectively set the map bits, causing various portions of the Cm's address space to be mapped, via the Kmap, to remote Cm's or remote clusters. References that are not mapped to other Cm's can be relocated within the local memory of the same Cm. The Slocal relocation registers too can be updated by the Kmap microcode. Hence a running program can be given access to different portions of Cm* memory at different times. The Kmap's data RAM can be used to cache recently accessed mapping information. Different Kmap microcodes have used very different strategies for mapping addresses and managing the cache.

External control of experiments on Cm*. Cm* needs to communicate with other computers for several reasons. When multiple groups are using Cm* simultaneously for operating system development, some external machine must keep track of who has what resources so that the groups do not interfere with each other. When large multiprocessor experiments are performed, perturbation is minimized if an external computer archives performance data. Another reason is that we may occasionally want to perform an application cooperatively between Cm* and other computers. Finally, as a research com-

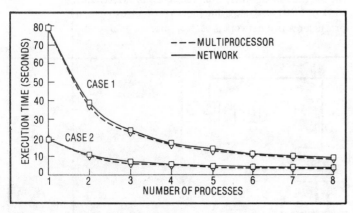

Figure 2. Comparison of integer programming on network and multiprocessor configurations, using data sets 1 and 2.

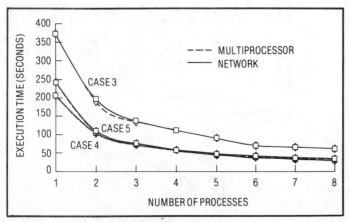

Figure 3. Comparison of integer programming on network and multiprocessor configurations, using data sets 3 through 5.

puter, Cm* does not warrent a fully developed set of utilities, but software development can be streamlined if the compilers and editors on other machines can conveniently operate on Cm* code.

Some of these functions are provided by a PDP 11/10 known as the *Cm* Host*. Users who want to access Cm* first log into the host from a terminal anywhere in the Computer Science Department and then reserve some set of resources, usually individual Cm's or entire clusters. To use a preloaded Cm* operating system, users need to reserve only a single serial line attached to one Cm. To load an operating system, one or more entire clusters are required. During the daytime, two different operating systems are normally running in two different partitions of Cm*.

The host can be used to start, stop, and single-cycle Cm's. It can also be used to "listen to" serial lines selectively so that if several processors are sending output simultaneously, the user can temporarily "gag" all but one of them to look at output without being interrupted. If users choose to listen to all processors, the host will prefix each line of output with the name of the processor that sent it.

Through the host, users gain access to the three *Hooks processors,* which are special microprocessors attached to the Kmaps. The Hooks run a powerful debug-

ging tool known as *KDP,* which can load, start, stop, and single-step a Kmap and examine its registers or RAMs. With KDP, microcode can be debugged on the Cm* itself, rather than on a software simulator. This ability is important, because in a multiprocessor, microcode bugs are often timing dependent and cannot be re-created in a simulator.

The *diagnostic processor* is a PDP 11/10 connected to the host. It runs diagnostic programs on unused Cm's and maintains an error log. These records are important for the management of a large multiprocessor.

Cm* communicates with other general-purpose computers over the Computer Science Department's Ethernet. Files, particularly object-code files, are transferred over this link to Cm*. The data-aggregation facilities of the *Simon* monitor[8] run on a VAX and gather data, which are shipped in packets from the resident monitor running on the Cm*. Commands are sent to the resident monitor from the VAX, making possible the control of Cm* experiments from an external machine. Figure 4 is a diagram showing how Cm* is interfaced to other devices and computers.

Software in the experimentation environment. Cm* provides a flexible, layered experimentation environment. The experimenter may use as many of the layers as

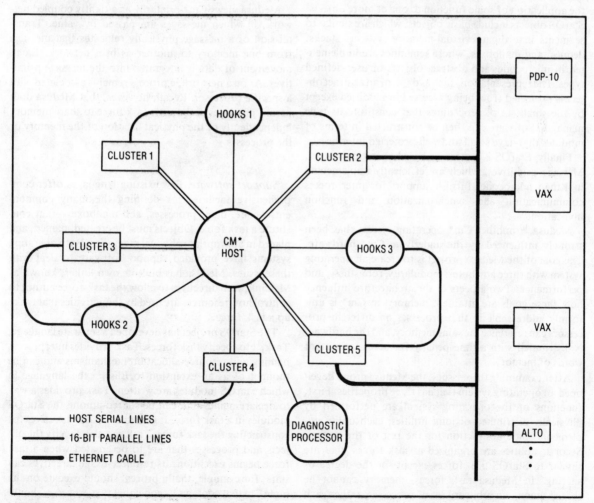

HOST SERIAL LINES
16-BIT PARALLEL LINES
ETHERNET CABLE

Figure 4. The Cm* hardware environment.

appropriate for the application—from the "bare" hardware to sophisticated experiment-management tools.

One component of the environment is the operating system, of which Cm* has two, StarOS and Medusa. They are instrumented with sensors to allow monitoring, and the utilities run as user programs on top of an operating system. On Cm* they are heavily oriented towards providing facilities for creating and controlling sets of concurrent processes. The top level of the experimentation environment consists of three components—a schema manager, a monitor, and a workload generator—which allow speedy construction of synthetic tasks to exercise various portions of the multiprocessor.

Operating systems. StarOS[9] is an operating system for the support of task forces, which are collections of processes that work towards a single goal. They are usually small, with less responsibility than the average process that runs on a uniprocessor, and they proceed in parallel to take advantage of the multiprocessor architecture. StarOS strives to make processes cheap enough to permit many functions that are ordinarily accomplished by procedure calls—requests for operating system services such as memory allocation, for example—to be performed by separate, concurrent processes.

In addition, StarOS is an object-oriented operating system; that is, every action performed by the system is the application of some function to one or more objects. StarOS objects include basic objects, which are similar to segments in ordinary virtual-memory systems; stacks, deques, and mailboxes, whose semantics are implemented in microcode; and abstract objects of user-defined types. The representation, such as data, of an abstract object is protected from being accessed or modified except by the small set of procedures that constitute its type manager. Software can then be constructed in terms of modules that have small and well-protected interfaces.

Finally, StarOS is a message-based operating system. Message primitives, which are efficiently implemented in Kmap microcode, furnish support for interprocess communication and synchronization and function invocation.

Medusa,[10] another Cm* operating system, has been strongly influenced by the underlying Cm* hardware. The goal of the Medusa project is to create an operating system with three attributes: modularity, robustness, and performance. Two aspects of the architecture influence how these goals are attained: memory, in Cm* is uniformly addressable in that processes on different processors can reference the same memory, and the hardware is distributed with a time penalty for accessing distant words of memory.

After examining these issues, the Medusa group developed an operating system that has three properties. First, functions of the operating system are performed by physically distributed disjoint utilities; each utility implements some abstraction for the rest of the system. Second, utilities are organized as task forces that are similar to StarOS task forces except for the degree of sharing. In Medusa task forces, memory cannot be shared among an arbitrary set of processes; rather each segment is either global to the task force or private to a particular *activity*—the Medusa term for a component process of a task force. Third, utilities communicate via messages, as in StarOS.

As in StarOS, the Medusa message operations are microcoded for efficiency. The main difference is that Medusa messages are byte streams sent through pipes, similar to the pipes in Unix. A pipe can be nearly 4K bytes long, so a rather long message can be sent if the pipe is not too full. On the other hand, StarOS messages are generally communicated by reference—a pointer to the data is passed—while Medusa messages are passed by value.

To promote an efficient implementation, Medusa has attempted to adhere more closely to the Cm* hardware structure than has StarOS. For example StarOS supports a full *capability*-based addressing scheme, in which an address names a capability, which indirects through a descriptor to a segment of memory. A Medusa address names a descriptor directly, avoiding one level of indirection, but affording less flexibility in sharing.

Many differences between the designs of the two systems can be explained as follows. StarOS views Cm* basically as a multiprocessor. Task forces consist of processes that share global data. Hence, a convenient and efficient way for processes to communicate is by passing references. All physical movement of data is explicitly requested by some process, and processes can migrate from one processor to another.

Medusa views Cm* primarily as a tightly coupled network, in which messages are passed by value. Transmission of a message physically relocates that message from one memory to another as in a network. Block movement of data is integrated into the message primitives. As on a network, a process remains associated with a specific processor. Recall, however, that Medusa does permit processes in the same task force to share memory independently of the physical location of the memory or the processes.

Support software. Few existing languages offer comprehensive facilities for defining the many components—code, data, processes, and mailboxes—that constitute a task force. Objects must be created, named, and placed in appropriate physical memories. Both operating systems have provided support software to deal with these issues. Medusa has built its own linker, known as Medlink, with directives to allow the task-force author to control how resources are used by the activities that make up a task force.

The StarOS project has developed a separate language, Task,[11] to specify task forces. Task provides interprocess naming and resource-allocation mechanisms and can be thought of as an extension to Bliss,[12] the language in which StarOS modules are written. Task provides a way to declare names that can be shared among the StarOS modules in a task force. It generates loader directives for constructing the task force. Task can also specify the objects and processes that are to be created when a task force begins execution. Its resource-usage directives can state, for example, that a process should execute on the same Cm that contains its code; that two processes should share the same Cm; or that two other processes should execute on different Cm's or in different clusters—to decrease contention, for instance.

Support for experimentation. Several elements make up the Cm* integrated instrumentation environment, or IIE:

- The *schema manager* manages the experiment. That is, it takes a description of the experiment, causes it to be run, and stores its results.

- The Simon monitor[8] gathers resource-utilization data while the experiment is running. It gets its information from sensors embedded in the operating system, each of which records the state of a resource.

- The task force to be measured is called the *stimulus*. It may be either an application program or a synthetically generated workload. The Cm* workload generator is Pegasus.[13]

Figure 5 shows how these components fit together. At experiment run time, the instrumented stimulus, the instrumented operating system, and the resident monitor are active. The resident monitor is a process that enables and disables the sensors and collects data from them.

A *schema* is a complete experiment description, consisting of a task force to be measured, monitoring directives, system configuration information, and experiment directives written in the workload-generator language. The results of an individual experiment are captured in a *schema instance*. Schemata are archived by the schema manager. They may be created either from scratch with a conventional text editor or generated automatically during a series of runs by having the schema manager record the commands that are used. The schema manager scans the schema and sends directives to the runtime system, including global initialization commands for the entire experiment and commands to set up, start, and terminate each run.

Simon is a high-level multiprocessor monitoring program. The user asks a high-level question, which Simon attempts to map into low-level questions. For example, when asked for the utilization of a particular processor, Simon consults its relational database to discover where the resource is located and what kind of sensor exists to record the use of the resource. It then enables the sensor. Some of the entries in the database tables contain information that does not vary much with time—for example, the list of processors in the system. Other entries instead contain descriptors for sensors embedded into the operating system, and when one of these entries is read, the corresponding sensor is activated. Simon itself runs on a VAX and communicates with the resident monitor on Cm* under StarOS. A compatible resident monitor will soon be built for Medusa.

The final component of the IIE is the workload generator, Pegasus. Some measurements are best made with synthetic workloads that exert precise loads on particular components of the system. In addition, composing directives for a workload generator is usually quicker than writing an application program with the same characteristics.

Pegasus represents a task force as a graph, where the nodes of the graph are the subtasks (processes or activities) and the arcs are buffers, such as mailboxes, that can queue data variables flowing from one subtask to another. The firing rules are Boolean expressions that state which arcs must contain tokens (input firing rule) before the node fires, and which arcs receive tokens when the node fires (output firing rule). The output firing rule can be expressed probabilistically. For example the rule can state that an output token will be placed on arc $B3$

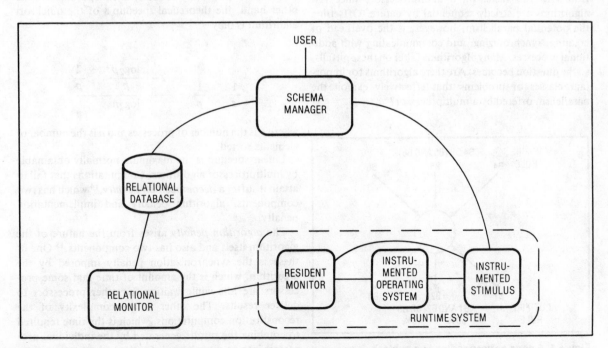

Figure 5. The integrated instrumentation environment. Arcs indicate transfer of data.

with a proability of 40 percent or on both arcs B1 and B2 with a probability of 40 percent (see Figure 6).

The subtasks are programmed in terms of simple statements and control constructs. A simple statement says that a particular action is performed a given number of times. For example, $<a_i, r_j>$ says that action a_i is performed r_j times. An action consists of a memory reference or the firing of a token. Simple statements can be arranged sequentially or encapsulated in loops. The *Select* statement allows one of the branches of a case-like statement to be chosen probabilistically. Another statement varies the values of parameters each time a loop is performed, allowing an experiment to be repeated automatically under slightly different conditions each time. Pegasus has been interfaced to Medusa, and a StarOS implementation is in progress.

Research in distributed systems

A multiprocessor like Cm* is a versatile testbed. We can test algorithms to see how efficiently they decompose for multiprocessing, and compare interprocess communication systems, such as the StarOS and Medusa message systems. We can also experiment with different ways of organizing task forces. We can even evaluate the hardware to decide which components are performance bottlenecks and deserve close attention in future multiprocessor designs.

One important question is whether multiprocessors can be cost-effective computational engines; in other words, can they perform a substantial amount of computing more efficiently than alternative architectures—like fast uniprocessors or networks of smaller computers? Germane to this question is the issue of *speedup*.

Speedup. At first glance, we would expect most algorithms to run faster on a multiprocessor, since few algorithms are strictly sequential by nature. Offsetting the potential parallelism, however, is the overhead of creating, synchronizing, and communicating with additional processes. Many algorithms falter on these pitfalls, so the question becomes: Are there algorithms for important classes of problems that effectively exploit the parallelism offered by a multiprocessor?

Speedup is a useful measure of whether an algorithm succeeds in harnessing the potential parallelism of a computer like Cm*. It is defined as E_u/E_m, the ratio of the elapsed time required by a uniprocessor algorithm to the elapsed time taken by a multiprocessor algorithm for the same computation. If n processors are used, the speedup is generally between 1 and n. Sometimes when a multiprocessor algorithm is run on a uniprocessor configuration, the speedup is less than one; an algorithm designed specifically for uniprocessors would be faster. Occasionally we encounter a speedup of more than n. For most algorithms, the speedup curve is the convex in the number of processors. Up to a certain point, speedup rises as processors are added, then begins to fall; in other words, adding more processors actually slows down the computation. Thus, another interesting issue is the optimal number of processors for executing each algorithm.

During the past few years, we have measured the speedup of several algorithms on Cm*, under widely varying conditions. Early experiments involved only a 10-processor Cm* system, precluding realistic multicluster investigation. In later experiments, the number of Cm's per cluster changed from time to time because of breakage and varying repair times. Some experiments had the full support of an operating system; others were built from scratch, using only rudimentary Kmap microcode. Among these algorithms are a quicksort, a partial differential equation solver, a railway-network simulation, and the integer-programming algorithm mentioned previously.

Theoretical and practical speedup. Some algorithms lend themselves to more speedup than others. We say that the algorithm exhibits a linear speedup if the time taken by an n-processor version is one nth of the time required by the uniprocessor version. Algorithms for solving partial differential equations and integer programming have a theoretical possibility of nearly linear speedup. On the other hand, the theoretical speedup s of the quicksort algorithm is only

$$\frac{1}{s} = \frac{1}{p} + \frac{2 - \dfrac{\log_2 p}{p} - \dfrac{2}{p}}{\log_2 n}$$

where p is the number of processes and n is the number of elements sorted.

Linear speedup is the maximum normally obtainable by multiprocessor algorithms. Computations that fail to attain it suffer a *decomposition penalty*,[14] which has two components, algorithm penalty and implementation penalty.

The *algorithm penalty* arises from the nature of the algorithm itself and also has two components.[15] One of these is the synchronization penalty imposed by the algorithm, which is the amount of time that some processors are idle while waiting for other processors to deliver results. The other is the complexity of the reconstitution computations, which is the time required to combine the results generated by the individual processors into an overall result for the entire computation.

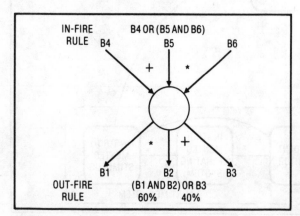

Figure 6. A node corresponding to a subtask.

This component is insignificant in the algorithms presented in this paper, but not for all algorithms—for example, the power systems simulation implemented on Cm* by Carey, Dugan, and Durham.[15-18]

The *implementation penalty*, also comprising two components, is a consequence of executing the algorithm on a particular hardware and system-software configuration. The first component is the degree of coupling between the parallel processors, which reflects the overhead of the interprocess communcation (e.g., via global data or message passing) required by the algorithm. This penalty diminishes, for example, as the message-communication microcode is optimized. The second component is the impact of process and data placement: the Cm* memory-reference hierarchy slows down processes that need to reference nonlocal data.

Algorithms with little decomposition penalty show the most speedup. This characteristic implies little synchronization or communication, few references to large global data structures, and simple reconstitution computations—in short, processes that are relatively small and independent.

The influence of synchronization. How much does synchronization cost? As a case in point, consider the algorithm for solving partial differential equations:

Partial differential equations. The objective is to solve Laplace's partial differential equation, or PDE, with given boundary conditions (Dirichlet's problem) using the finite differences method. The equation

$$\frac{\partial^2 z}{\partial x^2} + \frac{\partial^2 z}{\partial y^2} = 0$$

is solved for points of an $m \times n$ rectangular grid, where only the values at the outer edges of the grid are given. The solution is found iteratively. On each iteration, the new value of every element is set to the arithmetic mean of the values of its four adjacent neighbors. Each process runs on its own dedicated processor and performs the iteration for a fixed, continuous subset of the grid array, which is called a task. Thus, the processes are distinguishable. The algorithm was implemented on the 10-processor Cm* by Levy Raskin[5] and updated by Jarek Deminet[19] for the 50-processor system.

Several different variations[20] of this algorithm have been implemented on Cm*. All the following methods use one process per processor, so these terms can be used interchangeably. The processors iterate on equal-size partitions of the grid.

1. *Jacobi's method.* At the beginning of each iteration, a processor retrieves its partition from a global array. New values are computed for each element of the partition, then stored back into the global array. This storing is performed inside a critical section. The processor then checks its error vector (computed from the difference of the new and old values in its partition). If the error vector is smaller than a specified limit, the processor reports that it has finished. Otherwise it blocks, until the other processors have completed the current iteration. Iterations are performed until all processors have finished.

2. *Asynchronous Jacobi method.* This method is the same as method 1 except that a processor does not wait for the other processors to finish before starting on the next iteration.

3. *Asynchronous Gauss-Seidel method.* This method is similar to method 2 except that the processor uses newly computed values as soon as they are available, instead of using the values known at the beginning of the iteration.

4. *Purely asynchronous method.* To compute new array values, this method uses the most recent values of all components by reading them directly from the global array and writing the updated values back to the global array (without any critical sections or synchronization). It uses a critical section only for a processor to report that it has finished.

Raskin compared these algorithms using a 21×24 array (504 elements) on a one-cluster Cm* system with a maximum of eight processors (Figure 7). With eight processors, method 1 yields a speedup of just over 5.0; method 3 gives a speedup of better than 5.3; method 2 yields 6.4; and method 4, almost 7.3.

An apparent anomaly in these figures is the lower speedup of method 2 compared with that of method 3, though the values used in method 3 are nominally more up to date. However, the uniprocessor Gauss-Seidel algorithm is almost twice as efficient as the uniprocessor Jacobi algorithm. Because it cannot quite maintain this advantage as the number of asynchronous processes in-

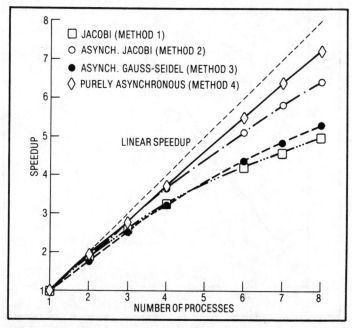

Figure 7. Comparison of speedup for different methods of the partial differential equation algorithm.

creases, the speedup of method 2 is greater. In fact, all asynchronous algorithms take more iterations as the number of processors increases;[20] but the rate of increase with method 3 is greatest, followed by method 2 and then method 4. (The number of iterations taken by the synchronous Jacobi algorithm is independent of the number of processors.) Nonetheless, method 3 is still faster than method 2 for eight processors, by a margin of 38 percent. Beware of confusing speedup with speed; a slower algorithm may display a better speedup.

Note that methods 2 and 3 are the only two that demand precisely the same amount of synchronization (critical sections at the beginning and end of an iteration, no waiting for other processors). Regardless of execution time, each time the synchronization requirements decrease—from method 1 to methods 2 and 3, and then again to method 4—speedup improves. Hence, the degree of synchronization seems to have the greatest influence on the speedup of the algorithm.

The cost of synchronization is also illustrated by comparing the following two methods of simulating the structure of liquids.

Simulation of molecular motion. Given the microscopic interactions between particles, we want to predict the static and dynamic properties of a collection of such particles. We obtain macroscopic quantities by averaging according to one of two methods—ensemble averaging or time averaging. The Metropolis method[21] employs ensemble averaging. To generate each new configuration, a single particle is moved. The bottleneck of the calculation for each move is the computation of the binding energy for each particle, which involves $O(N)$ calculations. The parallel algorithm uses K processors in an attempt to reduce the complexity of this step to $O(N/K)$. The interactions can be evaluated in parallel without interprocessor communication, but the contributions calculated by each processor must be added together. The complexity of this step is $O(N)$. In addition, the computation must be synchronized at each move.

The molecular-dynamics algorithm[22] uses time averaging. First an initial set of velocities for the particles is calculated. Given an initial set of coordinates, the velocities are used to predict a set of coordinates at a later time. A summation is again performed to find the binding energy, but with this algorithm, the summation can be reordered to allow a processor to sum its subset of binding energies locally, with the global summation required only once at the end of the computation.

These simulations are described by Ostlund, Hibbard, and Whiteside.[23] The results of the problem, which is representative of the general problems involved in the theoretical study of molecular motion, are shown in Figure 8 for a system of 50 particles.

The molecular-dynamics algorithm shows better speedup than the Metropolis algorithm. One factor is that in the molecular-dynamics algorithm, we do not have to sum shared variables. In addition, since particles move simultaneously rather than one at a time, the $O(N^2)$ serial computation of the binding energy is converted to an $O(N^2/K)$ parallel computation using K processors. A processor computes $O(N^2/K)$ interactions between synchronizations, instead of $O(N/K)$ interactions as in the Metropolis algorithm.

Both graphs exhibit a zig-zag pattern because the particles are parceled out among the processors as evenly as possible. Each time the number of particles handled by the "busiest" processor decreases, speedup increases markedly. Note, for example, the large jump in going from 24 to 25 processors; in the latter case, no processor has to handle more than two particles.

Both algorithms for molecular motion are synchronous, requiring lock-step iteration, and no asynchronous molecular-dynamics equation is known. An asynchronous algorithm for molecular dynamics would be difficult to develop, since it would have to average the interactions between particles occupying different positions in space and time. In general, even if an asynchronous algorithm exists, it is more difficult to prove its convergence. It must reliably attain the same final state each time it is repeated, yet it passes through a sequence of intermediate states that is unpredictable because of slight variations in processor speeds.

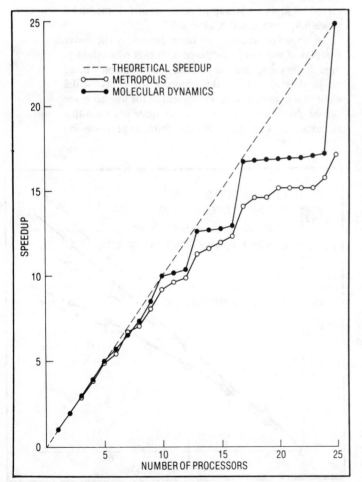

Figure 8. Speedup for the molecular-motion simulation algorithm. Results are based on a system of 50 particles.

The placement of processes. On a multiprocessor like Cm* with a nonuniform reference time to different portions of memory, the placement of processes and data can severely impact algorithm performance. What factors must we consider in deciding how they are to be distributed? The first is *locality of reference.* To expedite memory references, data should be local to the processor that references them. Although this condition is not feasible for shared global data structures, we can still minimize the distance between processors and their data.

For example, Raskin's version of the PDE (partial differential equation) assigned processors to array partitions essentially at random, but not all of the processors had the same amount of work to perform. Those that operate on partitions in the "middle" of the grid require more iterations than the ones that are close to the boundary, so ideally they should be solved by the fastest processes. When Deminet reimplemented the algorithm for the multicluster StarOS, he created a version that satisfied this criterion, which we call the improved processor selection version.

Figure 9 displays the effect of improved processor selection. The effect is significant when the number of processors is greater than 16, meaning that more than two clusters are involved. At 35 processors, the improvement is about 20 percent.

Distribution of data. While thoughtful placement of processes can greatly improve locality of reference, it does little to reduce memory contention. If a global data structure is deposited in the local memory of a single Cm, then many processors compete for access to the same Slocal and memory, so response deteriorates. The impact can be substantial because many multiprocessor algorithms, such as the PDE, make a large part of their memory references to a single, shared data structure.

Deminet[19] performed an experiment to determine the effects of data placement. Method 4 of the PDE was run on a 150 × 150 grid. In one case, data were centralized in the memory of a single Cm. In the other, the pages of the array were distributed between clusters to maximize cluster locality of reference (Figure 10). The centralized-data version achieved a maximum speedup of 16, while the distributed-data version yielded a speedup of 28 with 37 processors (the most processors for which it was run), apparently without reaching its maximum. We can also see these effects by considering the degradation of an individual processor's performance. In the distributed-data version, all processors ran at least 68 percent as fast as the fastest processor, while in the centralized-data version, the slowest processor ran at only 28 percent of the speed of the fastest.

A tradeoff exists between locality of reference and memory contention. When data are too centralized, many processors contend for the same memory. When data are too widely distributed, processors must make too many expensive intercluster references. Consider again the PDE. When processors are added to the experiment, the strategy is to fill up one cluster before beginning the next. The curve in Figure 11 shows a dropoff in speedup at about 20 processors, just as the experiment moves into its third cluster. The explanation is that data are now distributed between

three clusters instead of two. All processors but one need to perform intercluster accesses to access data in the third cluster, and the extra intercluster references slow down the entire experiment. Notice the additional and more pronounced drops in performance as the experiment crosses into its fourth and fifth clusters. Deminet calls this the *crossover phenomenon.*

As we have seen, many factors must be taken into account when deciding how to distribute data. We have no straightforward way to estimate the interplay of these factors and determine how to place the data objects in the

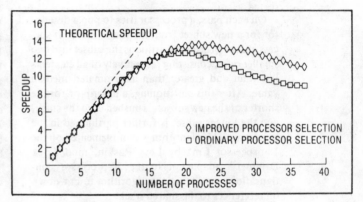

Figure 9. Effects of improved processor selection.

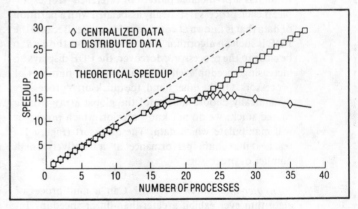

Figure 10. Effects of data distribution.

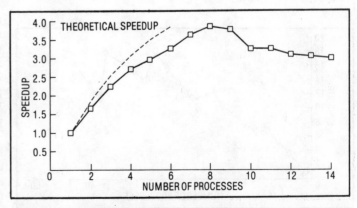

Figure 11. Deminet's crossover phenomenon illustrated in the partial differential equation algorithm.

most desirable location. The Cm* operating systems provide no automatic distribution algorithms, and while Task permits the programmer to specify constraints on object placement and uses heuristics in an attempt to satisfy them, it cannot guarantee optimal placement.

The Cm* quicksort is another algorithm that operates on a large shared data structure:

> *Quicksort.* In the multiprocessor quicksort,[24] a number of indistinguishable processes, one per processor, sort a global array of integers. The processors share a stack, which contains descriptors for continuous subsets of the array that are not yet sorted.
>
> On each pass, a processor tries to pop a descriptor for a new subset from the shared stack. If successful, the processor partitions the subset into two smaller ones, consisting respectively of all elements less than and greater than an estimated median value. After this partitioning, a descriptor for the shorter of the new subsets is pushed onto the stack, and the longer subset is further partitioned in the same way. This algorithm was implemented on the 10-processor Cm* by Levy Raskin,[5] and Jarek Deminet[19] adapted it to the 50-processor configuration, modifying the algorithm to cut down on references to the shared stack.

Placement decisions are simpler to make if an algorithm has a predictable pattern of reference—for example, if each process is statically associated with a partition of data that is known at compile or load time. Because the PDE is such an algorithm, we can arrange for the data to be close to the processor. Moreover, the PDE displays an increasing speedup even for relatively large numbers of processors. On the other hand, the quicksort's processors dynamically choose subsets of the global array from a shared stack; we do not know a priori which processor will manipulate which data. The quicksort (Figure 12) reaches maximum performance at a relatively small number of processors.

Greater-than-linear speedup? Can a multiprocessor algorithm ever exhibit greater-than-linear speedup? Intuitively, the answer is no, because such an implementation would do less total work than its uniprocessor counterpart. By simply turning its independent processes into coroutines, we could produce a faster uniprocessor version of the same algorithm, assuming, of course, that as much memory is available to the uniprocessor version as to the total multiprocessor version. (Otherwise more frequent swapping would retard its execution speed.) Also, if process switching were much slower than synchronization primitives, the multiprocessor version might gain a greater-than-linear advantage over the coroutine version, but this gain could not properly be called speedup.

Nonetheless, we do occasionally encounter a particular algorithm *execution* with greater-than-linear speedup. One such case occurred with the integer-programming algorithm mentioned earlier, which Raskin implemented for the 10-processor Cm*. In this algorithm's initialization phase, a large number of possible solutions are put in a global stack, from which all the processors choose their work. As the search proceeds, a global variable holds the cost of the best solution found so far by any processor. All processors compare their current cost value to it, and begin to backtrack in the search when the global cost is lower.

The multiprocessor version could be "lucky," in that one of its processors might encounter a near-optimal solution at the outset and then none of the processors would have very much work. The uniprocessor version, which does not encounter the near-optimal solution until later, has the disadvantage of having done a more complete search over the earlier possible solutions. But the multiprocessor algorithm could also be "unlucky." Suppose the near-optimal solution turned up first? Then the uniprocessor and multiprocessor versions would enter it at the same time. Before its cost could be determined, however, the other processors in the multiprocessor version would have wasted processing time on their initial solutions.

Hence, the multiprocessor version cannot be lucky all the time. A search program can occasionally exhibit greater-than-linear speedup, but it cannot "on average" show greater-than-linear speedup, over all possible sets of input data. The results in Figure 13 show that only one of the five integer-programming runs managed to surpass linear speedup.

Task-force organization. Implementations of the algorithms introduced in the previous section are quite simple. A single *master* process is responsible for setting up and starting each of the other processes, known as *slaves*. The slaves execute in parallel, perhaps synchronizing from time to time, until they have completed their portion of the computation. They then notify the master. When all the slaves have completed, the master reports the results of the experiment.

Master-slave organization is one of the simplest task-force structures, and one that allows us to take meaningful speedup measurements, since the multiprocessor algorithms have a uniprocessor analog that can be used for speed comparisons. Some algorithms like the following railway-network simulation have no uniprocessor version.

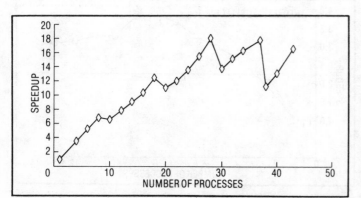

Figure 12. Speedup for the quicksort algorithm.

COMPUTER

Railway-network simulation. The task force consists of a fixed number of processes (63 in this version), each of which represents a station. Two stations may be connected by a unidirectional track. For a given station *A*, a set of previous stations includes each station *B* for which a track exists from *B* to *A*. The stations exchange messages representing trains. The route of each train is an attribute of the train that is determined when the train is created. Each station serves the trains in the order in which they arrive.

Each process maintains its own simulated time. At a given moment, the simulated time is probably different in different processes; thus the simulated time of sending a train from one station to another is unrelated to the real time that the message representing the train was created. Even the real-time order of events may be different from the simulated-time order. Suppose, for example, that station *A* sends a message to station *C* at real time 5. At this moment station *A*'s clock may show the simulated time 50. Station *B* may send a message to *C* at real time 7, but its clock may then show the simulated time 40. The second message should be serviced by *C* before the first one, since only the simulated time is relevant. In general, a station process blocks until it knows the simulated arrival time of the next train from each station.

Unlike the previous experiments, several processes may run on each processor. One additional process, the reporter, records data sent to it by the stations. As programmed, the application cannot be run on a uniprocessor configuration, since the reporter must be running throughout the experiment. In fact, this task force will fit in a minimum of four Cm's. (This algorithm was programmed by Jarek Deminet in 1979.)

Estimating speedup for this algorithm is very difficult because running time depends not only on the number of processors but also on the distribution of processes among them. In the implemented version, processes cannot move from one processor to another. If they did, we would probably have to move their local data to avoid the penalty of remote references, and such a move would impose an overhead. Thus the runtime of the experiment depends heavily on the initial assignment of processes to processors. Figure 14 graphs the runtime as a function of the number of processors. The graph shows an initial decrease, where the average number of runnable processes is greater than the number of processors, and then random fluctuations, which may be due to variations in the suitability of the initial process-to-processor assignments.

Hardware reliability tests. To obtain long-term reliability data for the components of Cm* we used the Auto-Diagnostic program, which continuously exercises the hardware by running diagnostic programs on all otherwise idle computer modules. Four distinct components were tested: the memory, the instruction set, the traps and interrupts, and the Slocal and a small part of the

Kmap. The memory test consists of 13 subtests, including a gallop test, marching ones and zeros, and shifting ones. The instruction-set test and the trap-and-interrupt test check the functioning of the LSI-11 processor. The Slocal diagnostic tests the registers and data path of the Slocal, among other things.

In continuous measurements over an eight-month period, transient errors were noted more than 20 times as often as hard failures (permanent faults that reflect an irreversible change in the hardware). Of the transient errors, 83 percent were local, confined to only one Cm (Table 1).[25] A burst error consists of multiple errors in the same Cm within a short span of time, simultaneous errors affect more than one Cm, and an isolated error is a single

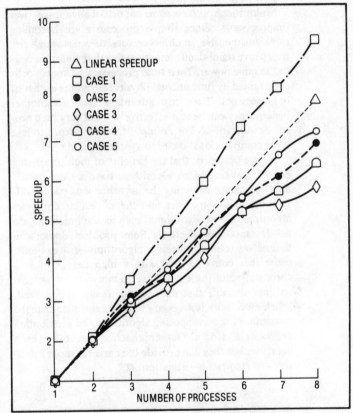

Figure 13. Speedup for the integer-programming algorithm.

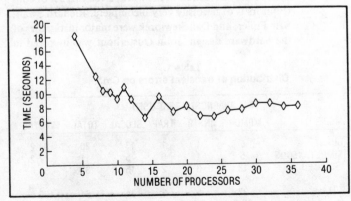

Figure 14. Speedup for the railway-network simulation algorithm.

error in a single Cm. Transient errors followed a decreasing failure-rate Weibull distribution. This pattern is in contrast to the usual assumption of exponentially distributed transient errors. Studies done on several other computers also reported a decreasing failure rate.[26]

These general observations about the cost-effectiveness of multiprocessor computation constitute only a sample of the work that has been done with Cm*. With the experimental support provided by the Cm* testbed, we are continuing to broaden the range of our investigations. The long-range issue is not whether Cm* itself, with its relatively primitive microprocessors, is a useful vehicle for solving large problems, but whether multiprocessor architectures in general have an important role to play in providing computational power.

Multiprocessors have some important advantages over uniprocessors. Since simple processors are becoming quite inexpensive, multiprocessors of substantial size may prove significantly less expensive than uniprocessors of the same power. Their total processing power is not as constrained by fundamental physical constants as that of uniprocessors. Their cost advantage leads to another benefit: they can be cost-effective without very high processor utilizations. For example, they can afford to lose some computational cycles to synchronization.

We are optimistic that the benefits of multiprocessing can be realized. Many algorithms have a theoretically linear speedup, including the asynchronous partial differential equation solver and the molecular dynamics algorithm. Other algorithms, such as the quicksort, do not decompose as effectively. Some problems do not lend themselves to multiprocessor algorithms—for example, those that converge only with a high degree of synchronization or those that have memory-access patterns so unpredictable that data cannot really be localized. Much more work is necessary to refine and automate the techniques for decomposing algorithms and distributing processes and data. Our approaches have often been heuristic, but they can provide the basis for more extensive and rigorous investigation. ∎

Acknowledgments

Cm* is a large project. We wrote the paper but performed only a fraction of the work. Even this list of contributors is of necessity very incomplete. Richard Swan, Sam Fuller, and Dan Siewiorek were major instigators of the hardware design. John Ousterhout was involved in the software effort from the start, and with Pradeep Sindhu, was primarily responsible for the Medusa operating system. Anita Jones, Bob Chansler, and Ivor Durham, together with Karsten Schwans, Steve Vegdahl, Mike Kazar and Joe Mohan, designed most of the StarOS system. Zary Segall, Rick Snodgrass, and Ajay Singh were the driving force behind the IIE. Levy Raskin was the first experimenter, followed by Jarek Deminet, Neil Ostlund, and Bob Whiteside. Sarosh Talukdar oversaw the power-systems simulation work.

Research for this article was supported by the Defense Advanced Research Projects Agency (ARPA Order No. 3597, monitored by the Air Force Avionics Laboratory under Contract F33615-81-K-1539), the Digital Equipment Corporation, and the Ballistic Missle Defense Advanced Technological Center (DASG 60-81-0077). The views and conclusions are those of the authors and should not be interpreted as representing the official policies, either expressed or implied, of DARPA, DEC, BMDATC, or the US government.

References

1. Anita K. Jones and Edward F. Gehringer, eds., "The Cm* Multiprocessor Project: A Research Review," Tech. Report CMU-CS-80-131, Computer Science Department, Carnegie-Mellon University, July 1980.

2. William A. Wulf, Roy Levin, and Samuel P. Harbison, *Hydra/C.mmp: An Experimental Computer System*, McGraw-Hill, 1981.

3. Richard J. Swan, "The Switching Structure and Addressing Architecture of an Extensible Multiprocessor, Cm*," PhD dissertation, Carnegie-Mellon University, Aug. 1978.

4. G. H. Barnes et al., "The Illiac IV Comuter," *IEEE Trans. Computers*, Vol. C-17, Aug. 1968, pp. 746-757.

5. Levy Raskin, "Performance Evaluation of Multiple Processor Systems," PhD dissertation, Carnegie-Mellon University, Aug. 1978, also Tech. Report CMU-CS-78-141.

6. B. T. Lowerre, *The Harpy Speech Recognition System*, Tech. Report, Computer Science Department, Carnegie-Mellon University, Apr. 1976.

7. Peter Feiler, "Harpy," *Cm* Review*, S. H. Fuller, A. K. Jones, and I. Durham, eds., Computer Science Department, Carnegie-Mellon University, June 1977, pp. 57-64.

8. Richard Snodgrass, "Monitoring Distributed Systems," PhD dissertation, Carnegie-Mellon University, 1982, to be completed.

9. A. K. Jones et al., "StarOS, a Multiprocessor Operating System for the Support of Task Forces," *Proc. Seventh Symp. Operating Systems Principles,* ACM/SIGOPS, California, Dec. 1979, pp. 117-127.

10. J. K. Ousterhout, D. A. Scelza, and P. S. Sindhu, "Medusa: An Experiment in Distributed Operating System Sturcture," *Comm. ACM*, Vol. 23, No. 2, Feb. 1980, pp. 92-105.

11. Anita K. Jones and Karsten Schwans, "Task Forces: Distributed Software for Solving Problems of Substantial Size," *Proc. Fourth Int'l. Conf. Software Engineering*, ACM/SIGSOFT, Munich, Sept. 1979.

Table 1.
Distribution of transient errors on Cm*.

MODE	DIAGNOSTIC TEST USED					
	MEMORY	INSTR.	TRAP	SLOCAL	TOTAL	% TOTAL
BURST	5	1	1	13	20	31.2
SIMULTANEOUS	5	1	0	5	11	17.2
ISOLATED	13	3	2	15	33	51.6
TOTAL	23	5	3	34	64	100.0
% TOTAL	35.9	7.8	4.7	51.6		

12. William A. Wulf et al., *Bliss-11 Programmer's Manual*, Digital Equipment Corporation, 1970.

13. Z. Segall et al., "An Integrated Instrumentation Environment for Multiprocessors," *IEEE Trans. Computers* (to be published).

14. Sarosh N. Talukdar, "On Using MIMD-Type Multiprocessors—Some Performance Bounds, Metrics, and Algorithmic Issues," *Proc. 10th Pittsburgh Modeling and Simulation Conf.*, 1979, pp. 1167-1173.

15. Michael J. Carey, "Parallel Processing for Power System Transient Simulation: A Case Study," Master's thesis, Carnegie-Mellon University, Dec. 1980.

16. R. C. Dugan, I. Durham, and S. N. Talukdar, "An Algorithm for Power System Simulation by Parallel Processing," *Text of Abstracts, Summer Power Meeting*, IEEE Power Eng. Soc., 1979.

17. I. Durham et al., "Power System Simulation on a Multiprocessor," *Text of Abstracts, Summer Power Meeting*, IEEE Power Eng. Soc., 1979.

18. S. N. Talukdar, M. J. Carey, and S. S. Pyo, "Multiprocessors for Power System Problems," *Joho-Shori, Info. Proc. Soc. Japan*, Vol. 22, No. 12, Dec. 1981.

19. Jarek Deminet, "Experience With Multiprocessor Algorithms," *IEEE Trans. Computers,* Vol. C-31, No. 4, April 1982, pp. 278-287.

20. G. M. Baudet, "The Design and Analysis of Algorithms for Asynchronous Multiprocessors," PhD dissertation, Carnegie-Mellon University, Apr. 1978.

21. N. Metropolis et al., "Equation of State Calculations by Fast Computing Machines," *J. Chemistry and Physics,* Vol. 21, 1953, pp. 1087-1092.

22. L. Verlet, "Computer Experiments on Classical Fluids: Thermodynamic Properties of Lennard-Jones Molecules," *Physical Review*, Vol. 159, 1967, pp. 98-103.

23. N. S. Ostlund, P. G. Hibbard, and R. A. Whiteside, "A Case Study in the Application of a Tightly-Coupled Multiprocessor to Scientific Computations," *Parallel Computations*, B. Alder, S. Fernbach, and M. Rotenberg, eds., Academic Press, 1982.

24. R. Sedgewick, "Implementing Quicksort Programs," *Comm. ACM,* Vol. 21, No. 10, Oct. 1978, pp. 847-857.

25. M. M. Tsao, "A Study of Transient Errors on Cm*," Master's thesis, Carnegie-Mellon University, Dec. 1978.

26. S. R. McConnel, D. P. Siewiorek, and M. M. Tsao, "The Measurement and Analysis of Transient Errors in Digital Computer Systems," *FTCS9*, IEEE Computer Society, 1979, pp. 67-70.

Edward F. Gehringer is a lecturer in computer science at Carnegie-Mellon University. He has been with CMU since receiving his PhD from Purdue University in 1979. His research interests include operating systems, high-level computer architectures, distributed systems, and protection.

Gehringer is a member of the ACM and six honor societies, including Sigma Xi and Phi Kappa Phi. In 1981, he held a Fulbright Postdoctoral Fellowship to work on the Monads project at Monash University in Melbourne, Australia.

Anita K. Jones is an associate professor of computer science at CMU and is a senior scientist at Tartan Laboratories, Inc., in Pittsburgh, Pennsylvania. She has been on the CMU faculty since she received her PhD there in 1973. Her professional interests include operating systems, distributed systems, protection, parallel algorithms, and the manufacture of software.

Jones is a member of the ACM, Sigma Xi, and the IEEE Computer Society. She has been a member of program committees for several recent conferences as well as the operating systems editor for *Communications of the ACM*. She is also the editor-in-chief of the *ACM Transactions on Computer Systems*, which will commence publication in 1983.

Zary Z. Segall is on the computer science faculty at Carnegie-Mellon University and is the head of the Cm* research project. His research interests are in parallel computation, fault tolerance, performance evaluation, and design automation. Segall received an EE degree from the Polytechnical Institute in Bucharest, Romania, and an MSc and PhD in computer science from Technion in Haifa, Israel.

Chapter 9: VLSI And Computer Architecture

Advances in VLSI technology have profound and unparalleled impact on computer architecture. Logic circuits that seemed impossible just a few years ago can now be implemented on a small silicon area. The impact of technology and design trade offs has been widely covered in the literature[1-15]. The area-time optimality[16-21] is considered crucial in characterizing the effectiveness of VLSI circuits. Similarly, mapping of parallel algorithms into a fixed size VLSI circuits is very important to present-day logic designers[22-23]. In VLSI, techniques for designing special-purpose VLSI chips and for providing synchronization in a large chip are critical issues[24-31].

Various factors are considered while preparing VLSI layout of a circuit. One of the intrinsic features usually emphasized from the fabrication process standpoint is the uniformity and regularity in the structure of the logic circuit. This led to the design of arithmetic cellular arrays with identical cells and a regular interconnection pattern which also helps in having the same time delay in each cell. The same strategy is used in designing systolic arrays[33-52], especially for those applications that require similar operations on a set of data and the same data-transfer pattern. These arrays have been made versatile by making them programmable so that they could be pre-programmed to perform different operations in various cells. This has opened a new area of research, and its use in various application areas is currently being explored.

The capabilities offered by VLSI are explored by designing special-purpose chips that can satisfy the requirements for signal- and image-processing applications[53-62]. Reconfigurable and adaptable chips[63-73] are also proposed to conform to the communication and processing requirements. The restructurable capability is achieved by incorporating switches at various places in the logic circuit.

Other general and special purpose VLSI-based schemes including database and dictionary machines[69-76] have been designed. VLSI layout for the cross-bar and multistage interconnection networks[71-80] which are useful in interconnecting various functional modules, have also been done, and time-delay and silicon area requirements have been computed. Other VLSI chips[81-88] include those for sorting and solving graph problems.

Six papers are included in this chapter to cover those aspects of VLSI that are considered to have maximum impact on the architecture.

References

1   C.A. Mead and L.A. Conway, *Introduction to VLSI Systems* Addison-Wesley, Reading, Mass., March 1980.

2   D.J. Theis, guest editor: Special Issue: "Array Processor Architecture," *Computer,* Vol. 14, No. 9, Sept. 1981, pp. 8-9.

3   C.E. Leiserson and J.B. Saxe, "Optimizing Synchronous Systems," *Proc. 22nd Ann. Symp. Foundations of Computer Science,* IEEE Computer Society, Washington, D.C., Oct. 1981, pp. 23-26.

4   R. Egan, "The Effect of VLSI on Computer Architecture," *ACM Computer Architecture News,* Vol. 10, No. 5, Sept. 1982, pp. 19-22.

5   P.L. Stanat and J.S. Nolen, "Performance Comparisons for Reservoir Simulation Problems on Three Supercomputers," *Paper SPE 10640,*1982.

6   N R. Lincoln, "Technology and Design Trade Offs in the Creation of a Modern Supercomputer," *IEEE Trans. Computers,* Vol. C-31, No. 5, May 1982, pp. 363-376.

7   R.M. Burger et al., "The Impact of ICs on Computer Technology," *Computer,* Vol. 17, No. 10, Oct. 1984, pp. 88-95.

8   F. Faggin, "How VLSI Impacts Computer Architecture," *IEEE Spectrum,* Vol. 15, No. 5, May 1978, pp. 28-31.

9   E.E. Swartzlander, Jr. and B.K. Gilbert, "Arithmetic for Ultra-High-Speed Tomography," *IEEE Trans. Computers,* Vol. C-29, No. 5, May 1980, pp. 341-354.

10   D.A. Paterson and C.H. Sequin, "Design Considerations for Single-Chip Computers of the Future," *IEEE Trans. Computers,* Vol. C-29, No. 2, Feb. 1980, pp. 108-116.

11   W. Fichtner, L.W. Nagal, B.R. Penumali, W.P. Peterson, and J.L. D'Arcy, "The Impact of Supercomputers on IC Technology Development and Design," *Proc. IEEE,* Vol. 72, No. 1, Jan. 1984, pp. 96-112.

12   D.G. Fairbairn, "VLSI: A New Frontier for System Designers," *Computer,* Vol. 15, No. 1, Jan. 1982, pp. 87-96.

13   J.D. Ullman, *Principles of VLSI Computations*, Computer Science Press, Rockville, Md., 1984.

14   L.S. Haynes, "Highly Parallel Computing," Guest Editor Special Issue, *Computer,* Vol. 15, No. 1, Jan. 1982, pp. 7-8.

15   L.B. Lee and A.L. Wiemann, "New Design Methodologies and Circuits Needed for Parallel VLSI Supercomputers," *Proc. Int'l. Conf. on Circuits and Computers,* IEEE Computer Society, Washington, D.C., 1982, pp. 224-231.

16   J.E. Savage, "Area-Time Tradeoffs for Matrix Multiplication and Related Problems in VLSI Models," *Journal of Computers and System Science*, Vol. 27, No. 2, 1980, pp. 230-242,

17   P.Y.T. Hsu et al., "TIOBITS: Speedup via Trim-Delay Bit-Slicing in ALU Design for VLSI technology," *Proc. Int'l. Symp. Computer Architecture,* IEEE Computer Society, Washington, D.C., 1985, pp. 28-35.

EH0246-9/86/0000/0281$01.00 © 1986 IEEE

18 P.S. Liu and T.Y. Young, "VLSI Array Design under Constraint of Limited I/0 Bandwidth, *IEEE Trans. Computers,* Vol. C-32, No. 12, Dec. 1983, pp. 1160-1170.

19 R.P. Brent and L.M. Goldschlager, "Some Area-Time Tradeoffs for VLSI," *SIAM Journal Computers,* Vol. 11, No. 4, Nov. 1982, pp. 737-747.

20 J. Vuillemin, "A Combinational Limit to the Computing Power of VLSI Circuits," *IEEE Trans. Computers,* Vol. C-32, No. 3, March 1983, pp. 294-300.

21 G.M. Bandet, F.P. Preparata, and J.E. Vuillemin, "Area-Time Optimal VLSI Circuit for Convolution," *IEEE Trans. Computers,* Vol. C-32, No. 7, July 1983, pp. 684-688.

22 D.I. Moldovan, C.I. Wu and J.A.B. Fortes, "Mapping on Arbitrarily Large QR Algorithm into a Fixed Size VLSI Array," *Proc. 1984 Int'l. Conf. Parallel Processing,* IEEE Computer Society, Washington, D.C., 1984, pp. 365-373.

23 Y.P. Chiang and K.S. Fu, "Matching Parallel Algorithm and Architecture," *Proc. 1983 Int'l. Conf. Parallel Processing,* IEEE Computer Society, Washington, D.C., 1983, pp. 374-380.

24 M.J. Foster and H.T. Kung, "The Design of Special-Purpose VLSI Chips," *Computer,* Vol. 13, No. 1, Jan. 1980, pp. 26-40.

25 L.L. Kinney et al., "An Architecture for a VHSIC Computer," *Proc. of 8th Ann. Symp. Computer Architecture,* IEEE Computer Society, Washington, D.C., 1981, pp. 459-470.

26 J. Tuazon et al., "CALTECH/JPL Mark II Hypercube Concurrent Processor," *Proc. 1985 Int'l. Conf. Parallel Processing,* IEEE Computer Society, Washington, D.C., 1985, pp. 666-673.

27 D.A. Patterson and C.H. Sequin, "RISC 1: A Reduced Instruction Set VLSI Computer," *Proc. of 8th Ann. Symp. Computer Architecture,* IEEE Computer Society, Washington, D.C, 1981, pp. 443-458.

28 A.L. Fisher and H.T. Kung, "Synchronizing Large VLSI Processor Arrays," *Proc. 10th Ann. Symp. Computer Architecture,* IEEE Computer Society, Washington, D.C, 1983, pp. 54-58.

29 H. Li, "A VLSI Modular Architecture Methodology for Real Time Signal Processing Applications," *Proc. 1983 Int'l. Conf. Parallel Processing,* IEEE Computer Society, Washington, D.C., 1983, pp. 319-324.

30 W.D. Moeller and G. Sandweg, "The Peripheral Processor PP4-A Highly Regular VLSI Processor," *Proc. 11th Ann. Int'l. Symp. Computer Architecture,* IEEE Computer Society, Washington, D.C, 1984, pp. 312-318.

31 S. Abraham and D.D. Gajski, "A Communication Algorithm for a Wafer Scale Integrated Multiprocessor," *Proc. 1984* Int'l. Conf. Parallel Processing, IEEE Computer Society, Washington, D.C., 1984, pp. 147-154.

32 H.T. Kung and C.E. Leiserson, "Systolic Arrays (for VLSI)," *Spare Matrix Proc.,* edited by I.W. Duff et al., Society of Indust. and Appl. Math., Philadelphia, Penn., 1978.

33 H.T. Kung and P.L. Leham, "Systolic (VLSI) Arrays for Relational Database Operations," *Proc. ACM-SIG-MOD 1980 Int'l. Conf. Management of Data,* ACM, New York, N.Y., 1980, pp. 105-116.

34 W.M. Gentleman and H.T. Kung, "Matrix Triangularization by Systolic Arrays," *Proc. SPIE, Real Time Signal Processing IV,* Vol. 298, Society of Photo-Optical Instrumentation Engineer, Bellingham, Wash.

35 D.W.L. Yen and A.V. Kulliarm, "The ESL Systolic Processors for Signal and Image Processing," *Proc. 1981 Workshop Computer Architecture for Pattern Analysis and Image Data-Base Management,* IEEE Computer Society, Washington, D.C., 1981, pp. 265-272.

36 K. Bromley, J.J. Symanski, J.M. Spieser, and H.J. Whitehouse, "Systolic Array Processor Developments," *VLSI Systems and Computations,* edited by H.T. Kung, R.F. Sproull, and A.L. Steele, Jr., Carnegie-Mellon University, Computer Science Press, Pittsburgh, Penn., 1981, pp. 273-284.

37 M.J. Foster and H.T. Kung, "Recognize Regular Languages with Programmable Building Blocks," *VLSI 81,* Academic Press, Orlando. Fl., 1981, pp. 75-84.

38 H.T. Kung and S.W. Song, "A Systolic 2-D Convolution Chip, *Technical Report CMV-CS-81-110,* Carnegie-Mellon University, Computer Science Dept., Pittsburgh, Penn., March 1981.

39 A. Bode et al., "Multi-Grid Oriented Computer Architecture," *Proc. 1985 Int'l. Conf. Parallel Processing,* IEEE Computer Society, Washington, D.C., 1985, pp. 89-95.

40 A. Khurshid and P.D. Fisher, "Algorithm Implementation on Reconfigurable Mixed Systolic Arrays," *Proc. 1985 Int'l. Conf. Parallel Processing,* IEEE Computer Society, Washington, D.C., 1985, pp. 748-755.

41 A.R. Hurson and B. Shirazi, "A Systolic Multiplier Unit and Its VLSI Design," *Proc. 12th Ann. Int'l. Symp. Computer Architecture,* IEEE Computer Society, Washington, D.C., 1985, pp. 302-309.

42 L.J. Guibas and F.M. Liang, "Systolic Stacks, Queues and Counters," *Proc. Conf. Advanced Research in VLSI,* MIT, Cambridge, Mass., 1982, pp. 155-164.

43 H.T. Kung, "Why Systolic Architectures," *Computer,* Vol. 15, No. 1, Jan. 1982, pp. 37-46.

44 A.L. Fisher, H.T. Kung, and L.M. Monier, "Architecture of the PSC: A Programmable Systolic Chip," *Proc. 10th Ann. Int'l. Symp. Computer Architecture,* IEEE Computer Society, Washington, D.C., 1983, pp. 48-53.

45 D.I. Moldovan, "On the Design of Algorithms for VLSI Systolic Array," *Proc. IEEE,* Vol. 71, No. 1, Jan. 1983, pp. 113-120.

46 K. Culik, J. Graska, and A. Salomaa, "Systolic Automata for VLSI on Balanced Trees," *Acta Informatica,* 1983.

47 J. Grinberg, G.R. Nudd, and R.D. Etchells, "A Cellular VLSI Architecture," *Computer,* Vol. 17, No. 1, 1984, pp. 69-81.

48 H.T. Kung and M. Lam, "Wafer-Scale Integration and Two-Level Pipelined Implementations of Systolic Arrays," *Journal of Parallel and Distributed Computing,* Vol. 1, No. 1, August 1984, pp. 32-63.

49 S.I. Tanimoto, "A Hierarchical Cellular Logic for Pyramid Computers," *Journal of Parallel and Distributed Computing,* Vol. I, No. 2, November 1984, pp. 105-132.

50 P.R. Cappello and K. Steiglitz, "Digital Signal Processing Applications of Systolic Algorithms," *VLSI Systems and Computations,* edited by H.T. Kung, R.K. Sproull, and G.L. Steele, Jr., Carnegie-Mellon University, Computer Science Press, Pittsburgh, Penn., 1981, pp. 245-254.

51 P.L. Lehman, "A Systolic (VLSI) Array for Processing Simple Relational Oueris," *VLSI System and Computations,* edited by H.J. Kung, R.F. Sproull, and G.I. Steele, Jr., Carnegie-Mellon University, Computer Science Press, Pittsburgh, Penn., Oct. 1981, pp. 285-295.

52 C. Savage. "A Systolic Date Structure Chip for Connecting Problems," *VLSI Systems and Computations,* edited by H.T. Kung, R.F. Sproull, and G.L. Steele, Jr., Carnegie-Mellon University, Computer Science Press, Pittsburgh, Penn., 1981, pp. 296-300.

53 H.T. Kung, "Special-Purpose Devices for Signal and Image Processing, *Real-Time Signal Processing III,* Vol. 241, Society of Photo-Optical Instrumentation Engineer, Bellingham, Wash., 1980, pp. 76-84.

54 M.J. Foster and H.T. Kung, "The Design of Special-Purpose VLSI Chips," *Computer,* Vol. 13, No. 1, Jan. 1980, pp. 26-40.

55 V. Weiser and A. Davis, "A Wavefront Natational Tool for VLSI Array Design," *VLSI Systems and Computations,* edited by H.T. Kung, R.F. Sproull, and G.L. Steele, Jr., Carnegie-Mellon University, Computer Science Press, Pittsburgh, Penn., 1981, pp. 226-234.

56 H.T. Kung, L.M. Ruane, and D.W.L. Yen, A Two-Level Pipelined Systolic Array for Convolutions," *VLSI Systems and Computations,* edited by H.T. Kung, R.F. Sproull, and G.L. Steele, Jr., Carnegie-Mellon University, Computer Science Press, Pittsburgh, Penn., 1981, pp. 255-264.

57 H.T. Kung and R.L. Picard, "Hardware Pipeliners for Multi-Dimensional Convolution and Resampling," Proc. *1981 Workshop on Computer Architecture for Pattern Analysis and Image Database Management,* IEEE Computer Society, Washington, D.C., 1981, pp. 273-278.

58 S.Y. Kung, K.S. Arun, R.J. Galezer, and D.V.B. Rao, "Wavefront Array Processor: Language, Architecture, and Applications," *IEEE Trans. Computers,* Vol. C-31, No. 11, Nov. 1982, pp. 1054-1066.

59 S-Y. Xung, "On Supercomputing with Systolic/Wavefront Array Processors," *Proc. IEEE,* Vol. 72, No. 7, July 1984, pp. 867-884.

60 T. Murata and M.Y. Chern, "Efficient Matrix Multiplications a Concurrent Data-Loading Array Processor," *Proc. 1983 Int'l. Conf. Parallel Processing,* IEEE Computer Society, Washington, D.C., 1983, pp. 90-94.

61 G. Wolf and J.R. Jump, "Matrix Multiplication in an interleaved array processing architecture," *Proc. 12th Int'l. Symp. Computer Architecture,* IEEE Computer Society, Washington, D.C., 1985, pp. 11-17.

62 M.Y. Chern and T. Murata, "A Fast Algorithm for Concurrent LU Decomposition and Matrix Inversion," *Proc. 1983 Int'l. Conf. on Parallel Processing,* IEEE Computer Society, Washington, D.C., 1983, pp 79-86.

63 C.R. Vick, S.P. Kartashev, and S.I. Kartashev, "Adaptable Architectures for Super-Systems," *Computer,* Vol. 13, No. 11, Nov. 1980, pp. 17-35.

64 I. Koren, "A Reconfigurable and Fault-Tolerant VLSI Multiprocessor Array," *Proc. 8th Ann. Symp. Computer Architecture,* IEEE Computer Society, Washington, D.C., 1981, pp. 425-442.

65 A. Rosenfeld and A.Y. Wu, "Reconfigurable Cellular Computers," *Information and Control,* Vol. 50, No. 1, July 1981, pp. 64-84.

66 L. Snyder, "Introduction to the Configurable Highly Parallel Computer," *Computer,* Vol. 15, No. 1, Jan. 1982, pp. 47-64.

67 A. Kapauan, K.Y. Wang, D. Gannon, J. Cuny, and L. Snyder, "The Pringle Experimental System for Parallel Algorithm and Software Testing," *Proc. 1984 Int'l. Conf. Parallel Processing,* IEEE Computer Society, Washington, D.C., 1984, pp. 1-6.

68 A. Kapauan, J.T. Field, D.B. Gannon, and L. Snyder, "The Pringle Parallel Computer," *Proc. 11th Ann. Int'l. Symp. Computer Architecture,* IEEE Computer Society, Washington, D.C., 1984, pp. 12-20.

69 T. Ottman, A.L. Rosarberg, and L.J. Stockmerger, "A Dictionary M/C (for VLSI)," *Technical Report RC 9060 (#39615),* IBM T.J. Watson Research Center, Yorktown Heights, N.Y., 1981.

70 R.A. Wagner, "The Boolean Vector Machine (BVM)," *Proc. 10th Ann. Symp. Computer Architecture,* IEEE Computer Society, Washington, D.C., 1983, pp. 59-66.

71 M.A. Bonuccelli, E. Lodi, F. Luccio, P. Maestrini, and L. Pagli, "A VLSI Tree Machine for Relational Data Bases," *Proc. 10th Ann. Int'l. Symp. Computer Architecture,* IEEE Computer Society, Washington, D.C., 1983, pp. 67-73.

72 M.A. Bonuccelli et al., "A VLSI Area Machine for Relational Data Bases," *Proc. 10th Ann. Symp. Computer Architecture,* IEEE Computer Society, Washington, D.C., 1983, pp. 67-75.

73 K. Hwang and K.S. Fu, "Integrated Computer Architectures for Image Processing and database Management," *Computer,* Vol. 16, No. 1, Jan. 1983, pp. 51-61.

74 D. Ungar, R. Blau, P. Foley, D. Samples, and D. Patterspm, "Architecture of SOAR: Smalltalk on a RISC," *Proc. 11th Ann. Int'l. Symp. Computer Architecture,* IEEE Computer Society, Washington, D.C., 1984, pp. 151-156.

75 A.L. Fisher, "Dictionary Machines with a Small Number of Processors," *Proc. 11th Ann. Int'l. Symp. on Computer Architecture,* IEEE Computer Society, Washington, D.C., 1984, pp. 151-156.

76 A.K. Somani and V.K. Agarwal, "An Efficient VLSI Dictionary Machine," *Proc. 11th Ann. Int'l. Symp. Computer Architecture,* IEEE Computer Society, Washington, D.C., 1984, pp. 142-150.

77 M.R. Samatham and D.K. Pradhan, "A Multi-processor Network Suitable for Single-Chip VLSI Implementation," *Proc. 11th Ann. Int'l. Symp. Computer Architecture,* IEEE Computer Society, Washington, D.C., 1984, pp. 328-337.

78 M.A. Franklin, "VLSI Performance Comparison of Banyan and Crossbar Communication Networks," *IEEE Trans. Computers,* Vol. C-30, No. 4, April 1981, pp. 283-291.

79 D.F. Wann and M.A. Franklin, "Asynchronous and Clocked Control Structures for VLSI Based Interconnection Networks," *IEEE Trans. Computers,* Vol. C-32, No. 3, March 1983, pp. 284-293.

80 L. Bhuyan and D.P. Agrawal, "VLSI Performance of Multistage Interconnection Networks Using 4 × 4 Switches," *Proc. 3rd Int'l. Conf. Distributed Computing Systems,* IEEE Computer Society, Washington, D.C., 1982, pp. 606-613.

81 H. Yasuura, N. Takagi, and S. Yajima, "The Parallel Enumeration Sorting Scheme for VLSI," *IEEE Trans. Computers,* Vol. C-31, No. 12, Dec. 1982, pp. 1192-1201.

82 C.C. Hsiao and L. Snyder, "Ominisort: A Versatile Data Processing Operation for VLSI," *Proc. 1983 Int'l. Conf. Parallel Processing,* IEEE Computer Society, Washington, D.C., 1983, pp. 222-225.

83 G. Miranker, L. Tang, and C.K. Wong, "A Zero-Time VLSI Sorter," *IBM Journal of Research and Development,* Vol. 27, No. 2, March 1983, pp. 140-148.

84 L. Philipson, "VLSI Based Design Principles for MIMD Multiprocessor Computers with Distributed Memory Management," *Proc. 11th Ann. Int'l. Symp. Computer Architecture,* IEEE Computer Society, Washington, D.C., 1984, pp. 319-327.

85 G. Bilari and F.P. Preparata, "An Architecture for Bitonic Sorting with Optimal VLSI Performance," *IEEE Trans. Computers,* Vol. C-33, No. 7, July 1984, pp. 646-651.

86 S.E. Hambrusch, "VLSI Algorithms for the Connected Component Problems," *SIAM Journal Computers,* Vol 12, No. 2, May 1983, pp. 354-365.

87 J.L. Bentley, "A Parallel Algorithm for Constructing Minimum Sparing Trees," *Journal of Algorithms,* Vol. 1, No. 1, March 1980, pp. 51-59.

88 J.W. Hong and H.T. Kung, "I/0 Complexity: The Red-Blue Pebble Game," *Proc. 13th Ann. ACM Symp. Theory of Computing,* ACM, New York, N.Y., 1981, pp. 326-333.

NEW DESIGN METHODOLOGIES AND CIRCUITS NEEDED FOR PARALLEL VLSI SUPERCOMPUTERS

Ruby B. Lee*
Alan L. Wiemann*

Computer Systems Laboratory
Stanford University
Stanford, California 94305

Abstract

The degree of parallelism dictated by the high performance requirements of special-purpose supercomputers motivates a departure from the design methodology of inherently sequential von Neumann computers. A new design methodology is proposed which integrates the functions of processing, memory, control, and timing into primitive, autonomous operators. These operators act on the principle of the production and consumption of data, both on the conceptual level and on the hardware level. An extra "empty" state is introduced for self-synchronization. Systems are constructed by interconnecting the operators according to the logical data and control dependencies imposed by the particular application. The reflection of the these dependencies in the physical implementation produces both correctness of computation and maximality of parallelism. Although these primitive operators can be fabricated using existing CMOS technology, it is recommended that new semiconductor circuits be designed to implement these operators more directly. Rather than designing computers around the capabilities and limitations of new technologies, this paper indicates the need to develop new circuits and technologies as dictated by computer design requirements.

1. Introduction

A *supercomputer* is a computer organization that achieves a high performance level for a certain class of problems. Although a supercomputer may also perform general-purpose computations, it will only achieve superior performance, usually in terms of the speed of execution, for the special class of problems for which it was designed. This special class of problems may be quite broad, like all floating-point scientific computation, or quite narrow, like matrix multiplication.

A *VLSI supercomputer* may be viewed as a set of chips, some of which may implement the usual functions of a general-purpose computer. Other chips implement the special-purpose, high-performance algorithms which give the entire computer organization its supercomputer flavor. These chips may be viewed as super coprocessors, or *superprocessors*.

With the advent of very large scale integration and the promise of very powerful computer-aided design tools, the design and implementation of such special-purpose superprocessors, and hence, supercomputers, become economically and physically feasible. Unfortunately, many successful design techniques developed for general-purpose serial computers do not appear to be applicable to the design of parallel VLSI supercomputers. Also, a study of the designs of the few existing supercomputers like the ILLIAC IV, the STARAN, the CRAY I, and others,[1-5] do not reveal many common design features that carry over well into the design of parallel architectures for VLSI implementation.

Section 2 gives an empirical analysis of the ideal design requirements for parallel VLSI architectures and how these requirements differ from those for conventional serial von Neumann computers. Section 3 presents the proposed solution to these ideal design requirements. Section 4 shows the feasibility of our proposed solution with an implementation in current CMOS technology. Section 5 describes how the new parallel VLSI systems are constructed.

2. Differences with Conventional Computer Design

The main differences in the new approach to the design of parallel VLSI supercomputers versus the old approach to the design of serial general-purpose computers are itemized below and then discussed in greater detail in sections 2 and 3.

- Parallel execution versus serial execution.
- Hardware implemented algorithms versus software implemented algorithms.
- Decentralized control versus centralized control.
- Asynchronous, self-regulated control versus synchronous, clock-regulated control.
- Self-activated operators versus externally-activated operators.
- Implicit synchronization versus explicit synchronization.

---

*
This work was done while Dr. Lee was assistant professor and Mr. Wiemann was a graduate student at Stanford University. Dr. Lee is now with the Computer Research Center, Hewlett Packard Laboratories, 1501 Page Mill Road, Palo Alto, California, 94304. Mr. Wiemann is now with Bell Telephone Laboratories, Crawfords Corner Road, Holmdel, New Jersey, 07733.

Reprinted from *International Conference on Circuits and Computers*, 1982, pages 224-231. Copyright © 1982 by The Institute of Electrical and Electronics Engineers, Inc.

- Sending of results when they are produced to successive operators who are ready to receive them, versus the independent storing of results and the subsequent fetching of operands when needed by operators.
- Processing, memory, control, and timing functions built into primitive operators rather than implemented as separate subsystems.
- Explicit representation and detection of the "empty" state in addition to the valid states for a data bit, versus the explicit representation of only valid states for a data bit.
- Active consumption of data versus passive use of data.

2.1 Basic Design Goals

Dramatic speed increases in the past have usually been achieved via technological advances. However, we are approaching the theoretical limit of speed increases via technological improvements. The computer organizational technique for achieving higher bandwidths uses multiple resources with overlapped execution. *This indicates parallel versus serial computer organizations for high speed computations.*

Conventional computers depend on the stored program concept to achieve their general-purpose computing capability. This means that algorithms are first expressed in software programs, usually in some high-level language, which is then compiled into machine language before being executed. The execution of each machine language instruction involves much overhead. The basic instruction execution cycle (see figure 1) con-

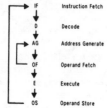

Figure 1. Basic Instruction Execution Cycle

sists of fetching the instruction from a passive memory unit to the control unit, decoding the fields of the instruction, calculating the effective addresses of the operands specified in the instruction, fetching these operands from the memory unit to the appropriate functional unit, and finally executing the required operation in a functional unit. The whole process is then repeated for the next instruction. *For special-purpose machines, the general-purpose nature of the stored program concept is not necessary. For high performance machines, the overhead of the stored program concept is undesirable, leading to the concept of the direct implementation of algorithms in hardware.*

2.2 Control Philosophy

Most conventional serial computers have some form of centralized control for both computation control and communication control. For example, there is a central control unit that fetches

instructions, decodes them, and sends appropriate control signals to activate memory, functional, and input-output units to execute the current instruction. Usually, there is also a global bus system to which all units are attached and which is controlled by a centralized bus controller. All requests for communication over the bus are directed to the centralized bus controller, which arbitrates in case of contention. *For highly parallel computer organizations a centralized controller represents a definite bottleneck in the system. Some form of decentralized control is indicated.*

A central clock usually exists in conventional computers which is used in combination with control signals sent by a central control unit to synchronize explicitly the activation of functional units. The concept of such global, synchronous, clock-regulated control is contraindicated for parallel VLSI computers, because of the magnified problem of clock-skew in VLSI technology and the large number of units that have to be activated simultaneously. Instead of having the speed of execution artificially regulated by an independent clock, it seems desirable to have the speed regulated by the complexity of the operations to be performed and the severity of their dependency constraints. *This indicates the desirability of an asynchronous, self-regulated system for computations with large amounts of potential concurrency. In lieu of a central clock and a central controller, we propose autonomous, self-activating hardware units, where synchronization is implicitly built into the primitive operators from which the system is constructed.*

2.3 Communication and Memory Usage

In conventional computers there is some form of global control, like a central bus controller, that ensures that the production of results and their subsequent use is properly ordered. In a system with no central control each hardware unit has to take responsibility for sending its results to all subsequent units which need it and to save its results in the event that a successor unit is not ready to receive it. Furthermore, in conventional systems the only connection between an instruction that produces a result and one that uses it is via an explicit memory location. *The active sending of results by individual operators and their interim storage eliminates the overhead of, and contention involved in storing and retrieving data from passive shared memory resources. It also eliminates the artificial sequentiality of instructions which use the same memory location as a communication medium.*

3. Characteristics of Proposed Solution

To achieve all the above desirable qualities of a parallel VLSI supercomputer with decentralized, asynchronous control of implicity synchronized, self-activating, self-regulating, result-saving-and-sending operators, *we propose the construction of new primitive operators that integrate the functions of processing, memory, control and timing.*

To implement implicit synchronization of operators, we propose that the self-activation of operators depend on the arrival of valid input data, and the sending of new results depend on the consumption of prior results. This implies that not only the presence of valid or unused data must be detected, but also its absence. Hence, *we propose the explicit representation of the "empty" state in addition to the valid logical states*. For example, in binary logic systems we now have three states: logic "0", logic "1", and the empty state "E". This is not the usual ternary logic system, since boolean operations are still performed only on the two valid, or nonempty, states, "0" and "1". The third explicit state, "E", is used only for self-synchronization purposes.

In addition to being able to represent and detect an explicit "empty" state, we need to be able to *create* such an empty state. *This implies the active consumption of input data after they are used by the operator, so that new input data can then be sent to the operator to activate it again.*

3.1 Definition and Properties of an Operator

An operator is an atomic hardware unit that combines the functions of processing, memory, control, and timing. It is represented symbolically as a node (circle or polygon) with n input arcs and m output arcs (see figure 2). The n

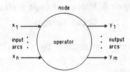

Figure 2. Symbolic Representation of
an Operator

input arcs represent n pieces of input data to the operator. The m output arcs represent m results produced by the operator.

An operator has the following properties:
1. An operator can detect the presence and absence of valid input data.
2. An operator activates itself when a predefined subset of its input data has arrived, and a predefined subset of its previous results has been sent to, and consumed by, the appropriate successor operators.
3. Upon activation an operator performs its specified function on its input data and sends the results to the successor operators, saving these results until they have been consumed by these successor operators.
4. Upon completion of the execution of its function an operator consumes all its input data, leaving the input lines in the "empty" state.

Usually, the predefined subset of inputs and predefined subset of outputs refer to all the inputs or outputs respectively. However, there are certain operators, used for directing the flow of data, whose activation is based on only a subset of the inputs and outputs. These will be

defined in section 5.

3.2 Conceptual Structure of an Operator

Figure 3 gives a conceptual block diagram of

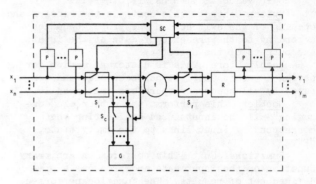

Figure 3. Conceptual Block Diagram of
an Operator

an operator. The six types of basic blocks are shown in figure 4 and are described below.

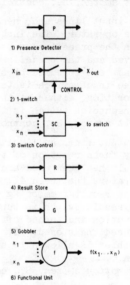

Figure 4. Six Types of Basic Blocks

Presence Detector This is a boolean function that maps the n valid logic states into "True" and the explicit "empty" state into "False". For example, in binary logic where n=2 the two valid logic states are "0" and "1", and the empty state is denoted "E". Denoting the presence detector as "P", we have:
$$P(0) = 1,$$
$$P(1) = 1, \text{ and}$$
$$P(E) = 0.$$
Switch This can be turned on or off depending on a control input value. When the switch is on, it allows data to pass through, acting as a closed circuit. When the switch is off, acting as an open circuit, no data can pass through. There are as many types of switches as there are valid logic states. For example, in binary logic there are

two types of switches:
- 0-switch: turns on when the control input has logic value "0", turns off otherwise.
- 1-switch: turns on when the control input has logic value "1", turns off otherwise.

<u>Switch Control</u> This controls the closing and opening of the switches in the proper sequence according to the presence of data at the inputs and outputs of the operator.

<u>Result Store</u> This is a storage medium for saving a result until it has been used and consumed by all successor operators that need it.

<u>Gobbler</u> This performs the action of "consuming" all the inputs used and setting the corresponding input lines to the empty state, "E".

<u>Functional Unit</u> This performs an arbitrary function on the input data and produces a predefined set of results. The function performed may be a simple "NOT," "AND", "OR", "NAND", or "NOR" function or a more complex function like a "MULTIPLY-and-ADD" function.

There are three switches in the conceptual block diagram of an operator given in figure 3:

The *input switch*, S_i, controls the flow of data from the input lines and, hence, the activation of the operator. The input switch is turned on when the predefined subset of input data has arrived and the predefined subset of output data has been consumed by successor operators. The input switch is turned off at the end of the operation, either at the same time, or after, the consumtpion switch is turned off.

The *result switch*, S_r, controls the flow of data to the output lines and isolates the result store from any further action of the operator until the result has been used and consumed by all successor operators that need it. In particular, it protects the result from being consumed by the gobbler. The result switch is turned on at operator activation and turned off after the result has been produced and stored. It is turned off *before* the gobbler is allowed to start consuming the input data.

The *consumption switch*, S_c, controls the flow of data into the gobbler. This switch is turned off before the operator is activated to allow the input data to be used by the functional unit to produce the results. After the results have been isolated by the result switch, the consumption switch is turned on, so that the input data may be consumed by the gobbler. After consumption has occurred, the consumption is turned off.

Figure 5 summarizes the sequence of events

```
repeat forever
begin
    if  [P(x₁) and P(x₂) and ... and P(xₙ) and P(y)]
      then begin
        ┌ Sᵢ on  ┌ Sᵣ on
        │        │    compute y = f(x₁, x₂, ..., xₙ)
        │        │    save y in result store
        │        └ Sᵣ off
        │        ┌ Sᶜ on
        │        │    consume input data, i.e., x₁ = x₂ = ... = xₙ = E
        └ Sᵢ off └ Sᶜ off
      end if
end repeat
```

Figure 5. Sequence of Events for an Operator

starting with the activation of an operator which produces a single result, y, based on a function of n inputs, $x_1, x_2, \ldots, x_n$.

Based upon our empirical analysis of the requirements of parallel VLSI supercomputers we contend that new circuits are needed that can implement efficiently, in both time and space, the properties of an operator defined in section 3.1. The conceptual structure of an operator described in section 3.2 is based upon our proposed implementation of such operators in CMOS circuits, which is described in section 4.

4. CMOS Implementations

In order to realize the three states defined above with simple circuitry, conventional CMOS circuits, with p-channel and n-channel field-effect transistors used in a complementary fashion, are proposed for implementation. Two power supply voltages are required and are denoted by +V and -V, since they are equal in magnitude and of opposite polarity. The mapping of logic states to circuit voltages is shown in figure 6. The empty

State	Voltage
0	-V volts
E	0 volts
1	+V volts

Figure 6. Mapping of Logic States to Circuit Voltages

state, "E", is represented by 0 volts.

4.1 Basic Blocks

The implementation of the six basic blocks in figure 4 is described below.

<u>Presence Detector</u> The circuit diagram of the presence detector and its truth table are shown in figure 7. Its function is to indicate the

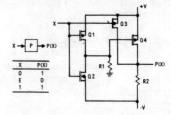

Figure 7. Circuit Diagram of Presence Detector and its Symbol

presence of a valid datum at its input. Note that its output is never equal to "E".

Transistors Q1 and Q2 and resistor R1 form an inverter. When a "0" or "1" (-V or +V volts) is present at the input, the inverter ensures that either Q3 or Q4 conducts. Thus, the output of the detector is "1" (+V volts). When the input is "E" (0 volts) the output of the inverter is "E" and neither Q3 nor Q4 conducts. The resistor R2 pulls the voltage at the output down to -V volts. Thus, the output is "0" when no valid state is present. In order to verify the operation of this circuit, an ADVICE[6] simulation was performed using transistors with a turn-on threshold of 5.5 volts and power supply voltages of +5 and -5 volts. The input-output transfer function shown in figure 8

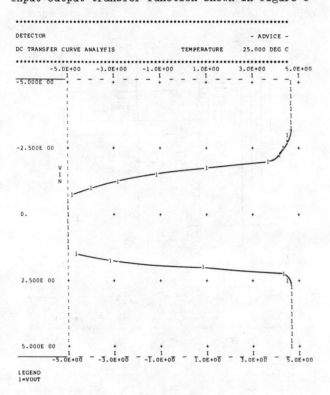

Figure 8. Results of ADVICE Simulation of
Presence Detector

shows that logic states "0" and "1" are mapped to "1" and the state "E" is mapped to "0".

Switch The circuit diagram of the switch is shown in figure 9. The interchange of transistors

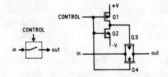

Figure 9. Circuit Diagram of 1-switch and
its Symbol

Q3 and Q4 forms a 0-switch and is represented symbolically by a negation bubble at the CONTROL input.

Switch Control In general, switches are controlled by functions of the outputs and, in some operators, the inputs of presence detectors. Inserting delay elements in signal paths or other methods may be needed to ensure that the various switches open and close in the proper sequence.

Result Store The proposed implementation of the result store is a CMOS capacitor (figure 10). Upon production of a result by the functional unit, the capacitor is charged to either

Figure 10. Circuit Diagram of Result Store and
its Symbol

+V or -V volts (logical "1" or "0"). Upon consumption it is discharged to 0 volts, corresponding to the empty state, "E". The size of the capacitor is determined by the on- and off-resistance of the FETs in the switches, the input resistance of FETs used in logic gates, and its own leakage resistance. This type of result store will retain data for a relatively short period of time, and some sort of refresh mechanism or a more permanent storage medium may be necessary if operators are required to store their results for longer periods of time.

Gobbler The gobbler is simply a connection to ground (figure 11). When the consumption

Figure 11. Circuit Diagram of Gobbler and
its Symbol

switch is closed (see figure 3) the capacitors at the output of the previous operators are discharged.

Functional Unit The functional unit is composed of logic gates which perform binary logic operations and recognize and respond to the empty state. Circuit diagrams for three gates with their respective truth tables are shown in figures 12 (NOT), 13 (NAND), and 14 (NOR). They function

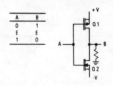

Figure 12. Circuit Diagram of NOT Gate
and its Truth Table

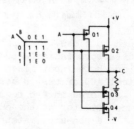

Figure 13. Circuit Diagram of NAND Gate
and its K-map

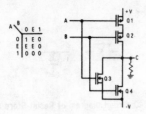

Figure 14. Circuit Diagram of NOR Gate
and its K-map

in a manner similar to conventional CMOS logic
gates. Since all logical operations are defined
only for the two values "0" and "1", the entries
in the rows and columns headed by "E" are not to
be interpreted as logical results; they are included only for completeness and reflect the
operation of the circuits used to realize the
functions. Transitions of input data to or from
"E" do not produce spurious spikes at the output.

4.2 Example of an Operator

An example of a simple operator is shown in
figure 15. The operator performs the logical
AND of its input data. The input switch control

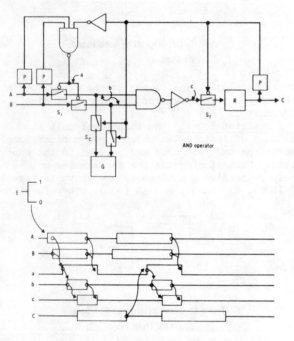

Figure 15. Block Diagram of AND Operator
and its Timing Diagram

logic is designed to close the input switches
when presence detectors indicate that the result
store is empty and both input lines have valid
data. The logical AND of the inputs is computed
and the result is stored in the result store.
When the presence detector at the output of the
operator indicates a non-empty state, the result
switch is opened, isolating the result, and the
consumption switch is closed, consuming the input.
The propagation delay of the switch control logic
guarantees that S_i opens after S_c has closed,
consuming the input data. In general it may be

necessary to insert delay elements in the paths
of switch control signals to ensure correct
operation. The timing diagram in figure 15
details the dynamic behavior of the operator.

An implementation of the AND operator using
conventional technology and design techniques is
shown in figure 16. Two control lines for each

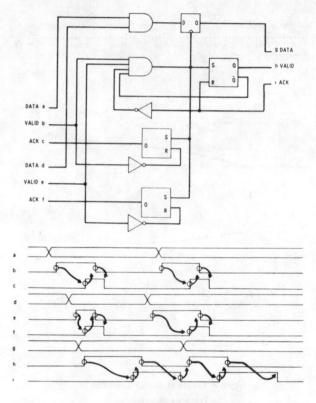

Figure 16. Implementation of AND Operator
With Conventional Logic and its
Timing Diagram

data line are required to indicate the presence of
a new datum. The signals VALID and ACK operate
in a handshake mode to coordinate the passing of
data and to synchronize the operators. Referring
to the timing diagram in figure 16, when data
arrive at each of the inputs to the operator, the
corresponding VALID signals are raised. The
operator stores the AND of the data, acknowledges
receipt of the data by raising the two ACK signals,
and indicates to the successor operator that the
new datum is ready by raising the output VALID
signal. The operator does not respond to the
arrival of new data until the successor operator
has acknowledged receipt of the current result.
In general, two control wires and one latch are
required for each input word and for each output
word. The new proposed operators require no
control wires but do require one presence detector
for each input word and an additional power wire.
In this particular example the conventional
implementation requires more circuit elements than
the proposed implementation.

5. Synthesis of Parallel VLSI Architectures

5.1 Flow Operators

A custom VLSI architecture implements an algorithm in hardware. Hence, analogous to the implementation of algorithms in software, there must exist some means for expressing conditional actions or conditional dataflow patterns in hardware. This is achieved by flow operators which either replicate data or conditionally direct their flow based on some predicate. Three canonical flow operators are described below.

The DUPLICATE operator is required since

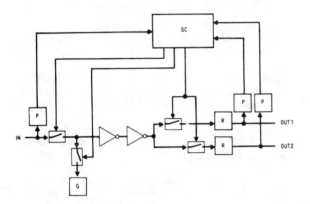

Figure 17. Block Diagram of DUPLICATE Operator

fanout points are not allowed due to the independent consumption of data by different successor operators. It produces a copy of its input datum at each of its outputs. When no data are at either of the outputs and a datum is present at the input, the input switch is closed. The datum at the input is reproduced and stored in each of the result stores, where they may be consumed independently. When both results have been consumed, the operator is ready to respond to the next input datum.

The MULTIPLEXER allows the selection of an

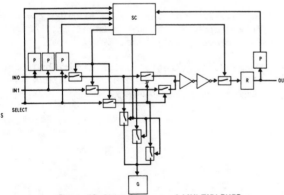

Figure 18. Block Diagram of MULTIPLEXER Operator

input datum to be passed to a successor operator based on the value of the SELECT signal. If SELECT=0 and there is a datum present on IN0, or

if SELECT=1 and there is a datum present on IN1, then the corresponding input switches are closed and the datum is stored in the result store. After the result has been stored, the input data are consumed. When the result has been consumed, the operator is ready to respond to new input data.

The DEMULTIPLEXER allows the routing of a datum to one of two successor operators based on

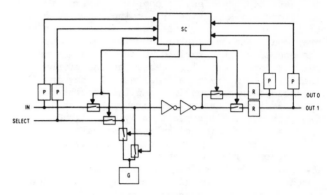

Figure 19. Block Diagram of DEMULTIPLEXER Operator

the value of the SELECT signal. When there are data on the IN line and the SELECT line and there is no datum on the selected output line, the operator responds by closing the input switches. If SELECT=0, the input datum is routed to OUT0 by closing the corresponding result switch. If SELECT=1, the input datum is routed to OUT1 in the same manner. When the datum has been stored in the appropriate result store, the input data are consumed. The DUPLICATE operator, the MULTIPLEXER, and the DEMULTIPLEXER may be extended to operators with more than two inputs or outputs.

5.2 Flownets

A parallel VLSI architecture may be expressed as a *flownet*. A flownet is an interconnection of functional operators and flow operators which expresses the functional requirements and data dependencies of the algorithm to be implemented. It is like a data-dependency graph[7,8] with firing rules similar to those of Petri nets[9].

The concept of a flownet, derived from an empirical analysis of the design requirements of high-performance, special-purpose parallel architectures, is similar to the concept of a dataflow graph.[10] However, the proposed software implementation of dataflow graphs via general-purpose machines[10,11] is distinctly different from the hardware implementation of flownets proposed in this paper.

After the flownet description of an architecture has been specified, it remains to design only the functional operators, some of whose circuit descriptions may already exist in a library. No further design of timing or control subsystems is required, since the operators are asynchronous, self-regulating units.

6. Conclusions

The need for highly parallel, special-purpose computer architectures motivates a departure from conventional hardware design methodology. New hardware is designed by synthesizing a flownet, which is a graphical representation of a system of operators connected according to their control and data dependencies. A complete system of operators which combine processing, memory, control, and timing functions into the same unit is proposed. The particular CMOS implementation of the operators as described in section 4 may not suffice for practical systems, because of the inability to store data indefinitely, the increased power consumption, and the possibly decreased circuit density compared to conventional CMOS circuits. To exploit fully the high degree of parallelism afforded by these operators, either advanced semiconductor technology or an altogether different technology will be necessary. It is hoped that the need for very high speed, parallel computing circuits with shorter design cycles and enhanced correctness of computation will stimulate interest and further research in these operators and their practical realizations.

7. Acknowledgements

The authors wish to express their gratitude to Michael Flynn for his support, to Levy Gerzburg for his valuable comments on the implementation, to Victor Herrero for his assistance with the ADVICE simulations, and to other colleagues at Hewlett Packard Laboratories, Bell Laboratories, and Stanford for their interesting comments.

8. References

1. Barnes, G., Brown, R. M., Kato, M., Kuck, D. J., Slotnick, D. L., and Stocks, R. A., "The ILLIAC IV Computer," *IEEE Transactions on Computers*, Vol. C-17, No. 8, August, 1968.

2. Batcher, K. E., "STARAN Parallel Processor System Hardware," National Computer Conference, 1974.

3. Russell, R. M., "The CRAY-1 Computer System," *Communications of the ACM* Vol. 21, No. 1, January, 1978.

4. Thurber, K. J., "Parallel Processor Architectures – Part 1: General Purpose Systems," *Computer Design*, Vol. 18, No. 1, January, 1979.

5. Thurber, K. J., "Parallel Processor Architectures – Part 2: Special Purpose Systems," *Computer Design*, Vol. 18, No 2, February, 1979.

6. Nagel, L., "ADVICE for Circuit Simulation," *1980 IEEE International Symposium on Circuits and Systems*, 1980.

7. Karp, R., and Miller, R., "Properties of a Model for Parallel Computations: Determinacy, Termination, Queuing," *SIAM Journal Appl. Math.*, Vol. 14, No. 6, November, 1966.

8. Kuck, D. J., "A Survey of Parallel Machine Organization and Programming," *Computing Surveys*, Vol. 9, No. 1, March, 1977, pp. 29-58.

9. Petri, C. A., "Interpretations of Net Theory," *Interner Bericht 75-07*, Gesellschaft fuer Mathematik und Datenverarbeitung, Bonn, W. Germany, July, 1975.

10. Dennis, J. B., "The Varieties of Data Flow Computers," *Proceedings of the First International Conference on Distributed Computing Systems*, October, 1979.

11. Watson, I., and Gure, J., "A Prototype Data Flow Computer with Token Labeling," *AFIPS Conference Proceedings*, 1979.

12. Kung, H. T., "Let's Design Algorithms for VLSI Systems," *Proceedings of Caltech Conference on VLSI*, January, 1979.

THE PERIPHERAL PROCESSOR PP4
A HIGHLY REGULAR VLSI PROCESSOR

W.D. Moeller and G. Sandweg

Corporate Laboratories for Information Technology
Siemens AG, Muenchen, Germany

ABSTRACT

The architecture of an experimental 8/16-bit peripheral processor is described. The chip was fabricated in a 2-μm NMOS technology with two metal layers. There are about 300 000 transistors on a chip area of 105 mm^2. The average time for a read-modify-write instruction is 200 ns. A highly modular and regular design style and some automatically generated layouts resulted in a short design time.

1.   Introduction

1.1 Goals of the Work

After our research group had successfully developed a 32-bit execution unit as a model of a VLSI chip /1/, we were looking for a real VLSI chip with more than 100 000 transistors. We found a suitable object in the peripheral processor PP4. This processor has to control the data flow between mass storage devices (e.g. discs) and a mainframe computer. At this time it was under development employing a printed circuit board with some standard ICs like the Am29116, Am2911, SAB8253, some memory chips and some glue chips. As an alternative our goal was to integrate all these functions on one VLSI chip. During the project it became evident that a stand-alone VLSI chip would not result in economic advantages. This could be reached only by designing a whole system in a VLSI style. But in spite of this problem we decided to go ahead with our PP4 chip claiming it to be an experimental chip with a realistic task. We used this chip as a test vehicle for advanced design methods and a risky technology.

1.2 Definition of the Processor

The processor is intended to control the data flow between high speed peripheral devices and the CPU of a mainframe computer. The requirements for such a processor are very challenging:
- High data rates (up to 5 MByte/s), resulting in a cycle time in the range of 200 ns.
- Real-time operation, i.e. worst-case conditions for timing must be assumed.
- Flexible programming, as the specifications of future peripheral units cannot be foreseen.
- Powerful instructions for 8 and 16 bit data.

General purpose microprocessors, even the most advanced ones, are not fast enough to fulfill these requirements, therefore a special processor with some dedicated hardware is necessary. To meet these stringent requirements, the following decisions were taken with respect to the architecture of the processor:
- Horizontally coded instruction format (similar to microinstructions) to speed the decoding.
- Instructions as simple as possible, e.g. no multiplication or division in hardware (RISC architecture /2/).
- Registers and data path operating in 16 bit mode and 8 bit mode (low byte only).
- Instruction format is 32 bit.
- Control registers in the external devices are included in the register address space (256) to allow fast access.
- Registers are addressed directly in the instructions.
- Memory has an address space of 64 Kwords.
- Part of the memory is placed on the processor chip (1.5K words).
- Memory locations may be addressed directly or indirectly.
- Data (e.g. parameter tables) may be stored in memory.
- Overlap of instruction fetch and execution.
- Instruction cycle with a variable number of steps.

1.3 Technology

The processor chip was fabricated in an advanced NMOS technology with 2-μm structures, 2 metal layers and one polysilicide layer for gates and short interconnections. The total chip size is about 105 mm^2. It contains about 300 000 transistors.

2.   Global Architecture of the PP4 Processor

Main goal in the design of the PP4 processor was to achieve a very regular und modular structure. This should be accomplished by use of ROM, RAM, PLA und highly repetitive structures wherever possible. Apart from some minor units for synchronizing and interrupt, the processor is divided into three sections: data unit, control unit and memory unit (cf. fig. 1).

Reprinted from *Proceedings of the 11th International Symposium on Computer Architecture*, 1984, pages 312-318. Copyright © 1984 by The Institute of Electrical and Electronics Engineers, Inc.

The <u>data unit</u> consists of a data port, an execution unit, a timer block and a sequencer.

The data port serves as an interface to external registers and for data to and from the memory.

The execution unit handles all data manipulation.

The timer block consists of three timers which fit structurally very well into the concept of the data unit.

The sequencer is normally located in the control section. But as the main task of the sequencer is 16-bit address manipulation, its structure is very similar to the structure of the other modules in the data unit. Therefore the sequencer fits better into the data unit than into the control unit where mainly single bit processing is performed.

The <u>control unit</u> has to provide the control signals for all other units of the processor. It is normally considered to be the most irregular part of a processor. But due to the modular instruction format and by putting the sequencer into the data unit a very regular 2-stage decoding scheme with PLA-like structures could be realized. The instruction word is 32 bit wide with 1 parity bit per byte additionally.

Address space for program memory is 64K words. The memory may be used for data storage as well. Data transfer between the data unit and the memory is done via the data port, which transforms 32-bit words into 8- and 16-bit words, and vice versa.

The whole addressable memory would be too large to be placed on the processor chip itself. But to reduce long access times to the memory we tried to provide as much <u>internal memory</u> as possible. Thus a ROM section of 512 words for bootstrap and selftest programs avoids the hardware overhead of an external ROM with control logic. A RAM of 1K words allows for rapid access to parameter tables and to subroutines used often. The external memory is accessed via the 16-bit memory address bus and the 36-bit data bus (32 data bits and 4 parity bits).

Both register and memory address space contain internal and external storage locations. To exploit the full advantages of short access time to internal storage, a variable-length timing scheme was introduced (timing steps).

The maximum number of steps per instruction cycle is 9 for an instruction with 2 accesses to the external memory. The minimum of 3 steps occurs for an internal register-to-register operation with next instruction in the internal memory.

The time for one step is 40 ns, thus one instruction takes between 120 and 360 ns. The average instruction time is 200 ns.

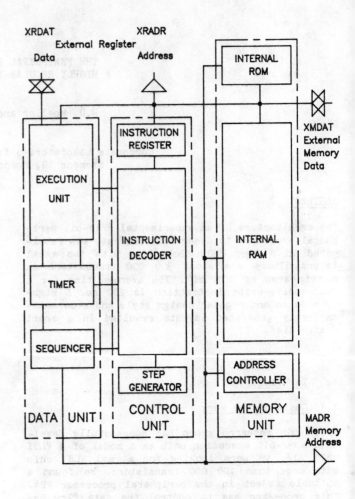

Fig. 1 VLSI-PP4: Block architecture

3. Data Unit

3.1 Structure of the Data Unit

The data unit is composed in a matrix structure by bit slices and function slices. This concept allows for an easy interconnection scheme, high regularity, and a clear hierarchial description of a socalled data path.

The number of hierarchial levels depends on the complexity of the data path and of the single blocks. The first division into blocks is done according to the function, e.g. register file, arithmetic-logic unit (cf. fig. 2). Lower levels of hierarchy depend on the complexity of the single functions and on the reusability of cells, e.g. the basic 1-bit register cell may be used in the data register file and in the program stack.

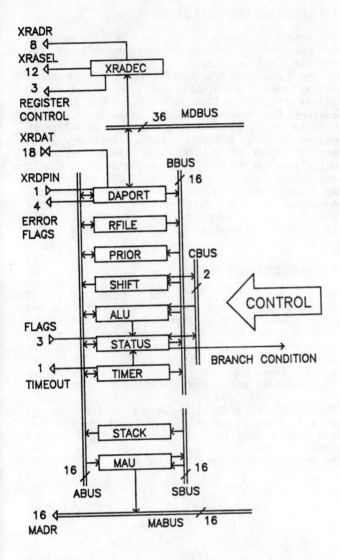

Fig. 2 Structure of the data unit

3.2 Data Path Busses and Timing

The instruction set of the PP4 consists mainly of 1-operand and 2-operand instruction. Thus a 2-bus system (A-Bus and B-Bus) and dual port registers for the internal register file are adequate regarding the speed requirements of a peripheral processor. In an ordinary 2-operand instruction the two operands are fetched simultaneously from the registers via the A-bus and the B-bus. The result is written into the destination register reusing the A-bus.

There were wishes for some 3-operand instructions. But the provision of the 3rd operand via a special register was discarded introducing too much irregularity into the architecture. Thus 3-operand instructions have to be replaced by a sequence of 2-operand instructions.

To keep the clock rate at a moderate level, a timing scheme was selected with phases as long as possible. For an ordinary register-to-register operation two phases are necessary. This allows for switching between read and write mode. The data manipulation can be executed asynchronously during the read and write phase (cf. fig. 3). This scheme precludes any precharge on the busses, as during phase 2 the data stabilizes on the bus in the middle of the phase only. Input data is stored in input latches of the manipulation function slices over phase 2.

3.3 Data Path Function Slices

The data path consists of 6 units (cf. fig. 2).

At the upper end of the data path the data port (DAPORT) acts as gateway to the external registers and the memory to exchange data. Parity for the external register data bus and the memory data bus is generated here. This introduces slight irregularities in the design, as 9 bits have to be accommodated in the same width where 8 bits are located in the data path.

The register file (RFILE) contains 32 general purpose and 5 special registers, one of which is a hardwired zero. Two different registers may be read out to the A-bus and B-bus simultaneously.

The priority encoder (PRIOR) finds the position of a leading "1" and expresses this Position in a 5-bit number.

The barrel shifter (SHIFT) executes various multiple bit shift operations in one cycle. Logic and arithmetic shift with sign handling is possible.

The arithmetic-logic unit (ALU) performs the standard logic and arithmetic functions. For symmetry both subtract functions (A-B, B-A) are provided. Increment, decrement and masking operations are possible with all powers of 2.

Internal states of the processor (e.g. zero, carry, overrun, negative) and external states (e.g. timeout) are stored in the 16-bit status register inside the slice STATUS. A condition decoder for conditional branches is also included. The output of this condition logic is sent to the control part via a 1-bit branch condition signal.

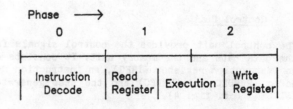

Fig. 3 Timing of register-to-register instruction

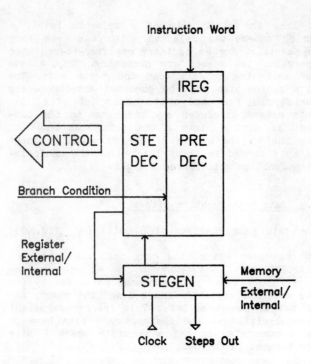

Fig. 4 Structure of the control unit

3.4 Sequencer

The sequencer is not as usual included in the control unit but is placed at the lower end of the data path. There it fits very well to the width of the data path (16-bit data and addresses). Beside this, the sequencer may be regarded as a simple address processing unit which is controlled by the control unit and not as a part of it. The sequencer contains the program stack (8 words) and the program counter.

Destination addresses for all branch instructions (direct and indirect call and jump, return) are transferred to the program counter via the A-bus, with acts as a general purpose connection between the execution unit and the sequencer.

Memory addresses for memory data accesses are passed through the sequencer from the A-bus to the memory address bus.

4. Control Unit

The control unit provides the control signals for the data path and the memory unit. It consists of an instruction register (IREG), an instruction decoder (PREDEC and STEDEC) and the step generator (STEGEN) (cf. fig. 4).

Because 95% of the 200 control signals concern the data path the structure of the control unit is tailored to the structure of the data path.

4.1 Function Slices in the Decoder

The matrix structure of the data path is extended to the control unit by "function slicing" the decoder. In parallel with the function slices in the data path, the control lines are generated in the same topological order as they are needed in the data path. Thus only river routing is necessary for interconnection. Each control line has its decoding and timing logic in an adjoining region of the decoder. Single function slices may be added or omitted with local influences only. Even geometrical fitting between data path and decoder can be achieved easily by adding dummy slices in the data path or in the decoder, depending on which part must be stretched. This helps a lot in order to keep the width of the interconnect channel small.

4.2 Instruction Decoding

At the beginning of each instruction the actual instruction code is transferred to the output of the instruction register. From there the control signals for the data path and the memory are decoded by a 2-stage decoding scheme. The first stage is a predecoder (PREDEC). The output of the predecoder is stable from the end of the first step to the end of the whole instruction.

The PREDEC is a PLA-like structure (cf. fig. 5) with 33 input lines (32 bit instruction word plus one branch condition bit) and about 500 product terms in the AND-plane. The OR-plane is reduced to an OR-line with some 300 outputs.

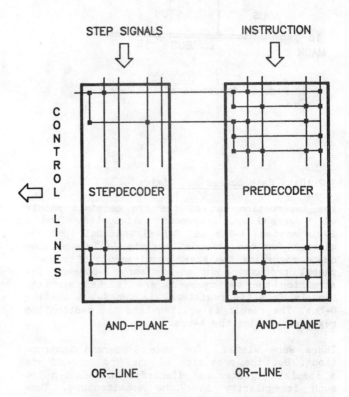

Fig. 5 Instruction Decoding with PLA structures

The final timing of the control lines is accomplished in the second stage, the step decoder (STEDEC). Each output of the PREDEC is gated with the appropriate step. Control lines which are active during two or more steps have multiple outputs from the PREDEC.

The STEDEC is a PLA structure with an additional input on each product term (outputs of PREDEC, cf. fig. 5).

The instruction decoder was generated fully automatically from an alphanumeric input file, which contains the names and the topological order of the control lines together with the decoding and timing information. The PLA parts were generated with modified PLA generators, while placing, spacing and wiring was done by an automatic router. Fig. 6 gives an example of an input listing for the generator program.

```
-WLAIO   =.....11..#.I...............I111000001...0...0
 -       =.....11..#.I........I00000...I.........I.0110..0
 -       =.......11#.I........I............I11100000I00.....
 -       =.......11#.I........I00000...I..........I01.....0
-WLBIO   =.....11..#.I........I...00000I...........0..0
-WLAI1   =.....11..#.I...............I111000011...0...0
 -       =.....11..#.I........I00100...I.........I.0110..0
 -       =.......11#.I........I............I11100000I00.....
 -       =.......11#.I........I00100...I..........I01.....0
-WLBI1   =.....11..#.I........I...00001I...........0..0

-IBPR    =..1......#.I0010....I........I..........I.......0
-PRC2    =....1....#.I0010..10I........I..........I.......0
-PRC3    =....1....#.I00100..0I........I..........I.......0
-PRC1    =....1....#.I001001001........I..........I.......0
-PRBM    =....1....#.I0010....I........I..........I....0..0
-OPRA    =...1.....#.I0010....I........I..........I.......0

-IBSH    =..1......#.I1010....I........I..........I.......0
 -       =..1......#.I00011...I........I..........I.......0
 -       =..1......#.I01......I........I..........I.......0
-NBYTE   =....1..1.#.I01......I........I.100.....I....1.0
 -       =....1..1.#.I00110...I........I.100.....I..1.0
-ROLB    =....1..1.#.I1010....I........I..........I.....0.0
-EXT     =....1..1.#.I101000001000101101.1.......I.......0
 -       =....1..1.#.I01110....I11000110I.1.......I..0.0
-SHO     =.1..1....#.I.1..00001........I..........I.......0
 -       =.1..1....#.I1...00001........I..........I.......0
-SH15    =....1....#.I.1..1111I........I..........I.......0
 -       =....1....#.I1...1111I........I..........I.......0
 -       =....1....#.I001101..I........I..........I.......0
-SH14    =....1....#.I.1..1110I........I..........I.......0
 -       =....1....#.I1...1110I........I..........I.......0
-SH13    =....1....#.I.1..1101I........I..........I.......0
 -       =....1....#.I1...1101I........I..........I.......0
```

Fig. 6 Example input listing for PREDEC/STEDEC generation

4.3 Step Generation

The timing signals are called steps because they represent not only timing information but functional decisions also. All steps for the processor are delivered from the central step generator (STEGEN). With these steps a variable-length instruction cycle can be performed (cf. fig. 8). Depending on the location (wether internal or external) of the operands and the next instruction word steps of the full cycle are omitted (cf. fig. 7).

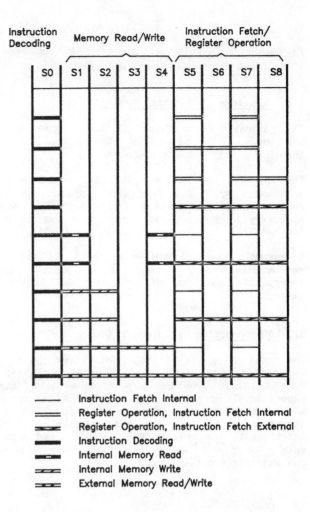

Fig. 7 Variable timing scheme of the PP4

The step generator is basically a finite state machine with a flip-flop row as state memory and 3 PLA's for control and generation of nonoverlapping steps. It is clocked by an external master clock with a period of 40 ns. The processor may be halted at any time by stopping the clock or synchronously at the end of any instruction by a gating signal.

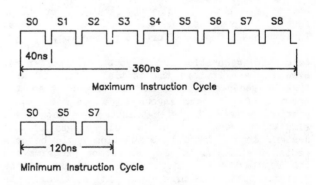

Fig. 8 Longest and shortest instruction cycle of the PP4

5.   Memory Unit

The memory space is 64K words of 36 bit each. This includes one parity bit per byte.

5.1   Structure of Internal Memory

The internal ROM contains 18K bit, organized in 512 words by 36 bit. This storage capacity is enough for selftest and bootstrapping.

The internal RAM contains 36K bit, organized in 1024 words by 36 bit. For reasons of fast access and compability with the technology for logic circuitry a static 6-transistor cell was chosen for the RAM.

A memory address controller monitors the addresses on the memory address bus and enables the appropriate sections of internal and external memory.

5.2   Disconnection of Internal Memory

The total chip size of the PP4 is about 105 mm^2. Two thirds of this area are occupied by RAM and ROM. As yield problems were expected with this experimental chip, the ROM and/or RAM sections may be switched off by test signals to allow the operation of the PP4 with external memory only. Additionally the RAM and ROM may be tested separately by direct access via the memory address bus and the data bus.

6.   Experiences

From the beginning the PP4 was designed with all aspects of VLSI in mind. Regular modules were taken whenever possible. There are only few active parts that have not a RAM, ROM, PLA or slice structure. We are now convinced that it is possible to realize processor chips very efficiently by regular structures if there is some freedom in the instruction set and in the instruction format.

Interconnection of blocks was thought of in a topological floorplan long before the first layout of subblocks was completed. So local wiring could be achieved mostly by abutment or river routing. Global wiring was realized by busses. In both cases design effort is rather low.

Automatic generation of layout was preferred, even in cases, where the initial effort of writing a generation program was higher than the drawing of the same layout on a graphics workstation by hand. Register-transfer and gate-level simulation were employed at all stages of the design. Errors found by simulation could be corrected easily due to the generation programs and the regularity and hierarchial structure of the design. Optimization cycles, in particular in the control unit, were possible only because of the use of generation programs. Optimizing the

layout by hand would have involved too many steps and would have created too many new errors to be acceptable.

We got first silicon in Oct. 83. A chip microphotograph is shown in fig. 9. The tests indicated design errors in some central parts (e.g. step generator, RAM decoder). Most of these errors would have been found by an electrical rule check program. But at the time of finishing the layout the check programs available to us could not handle the huge amount of data. We have got now these programs but there is still the problem of too long computing times. Nowadays most of the CAD tools do not exploit the hierarchy brought along by modern architectures. Taking advantage of this hierarchy to reduce data amount and computing time is a must for the future work.

To estimate the real design effort for the PP4 is rather difficult because in our research group there were other activities not related directly to the PP4 project. Over a period of two years about 5 engineers were involved in specification, architecture, circuit design and layout of the PP4. One engineer has tested the chip and corrected all found errors within half a year. We expect silicon of a redesigned and shrinked version in the mid of 1984.

REFERENCES

/1/   Pomper, M.; Beifuss, W.;   Horninger, K.; Kaschke, W.: A 32-bit Execution Unit in an Advanced NMOS Technology. IEEE Journal of Solid-State Circuits, Vol. SC-17, No. 3, June 1982.

/2/   Patterson, D.; Sequin, C.: A VLSI RISC. IEEE Computer Magazine, vol. 15, no. 9, Sept. 82, pp. 34-38.

/3/   Pomper, M.; Augspurger, U.; Mueller, B.; Stockinger, J.; Schwabe, U.: A 300 K transistor NMOS peripheral processor. ESSCIRC 1983, Lausanne. Digest of Technical Papers.

/4/   Stockinger, J.; Wallstab, S.: A Regular Control Unit for VLSI Microprocessors. ESSCIRC 1983, Lausanne. Digest of Technical Papers.

/5/   Pomper, M.; Stockinger, J.; Augspurger, U.; Mueller, B.; Horninger, K.: A 300K Transistor NMOS Peripheral Processor. Paper to be published in the IEEE Journal of Solid-State Circuits, vol. SC-19, no. 3, June 1984.

This work was supported by the Technological Program of the Federal Department of Research and Technology of the Federal Republic of Germany (Project Number NT 2588/6). The authors alone are responsible for the contents. The authors are with the Corporate Laboratories for Information Technology, Siemens AG, Muenchen, Germany.

Fig. 9 Microphotograph of the peripheral processor PP4

*Systolic architectures, which permit multiple computations
for each memory access, can speed execution of
compute-bound problems without increasing I/O requirements.*

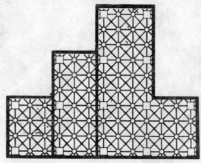

Why Systolic Architectures?

H. T. Kung
Carnegie-Mellon University

High-performance, special-purpose computer systems are typically used to meet specific application requirements or to off-load computations that are especially taxing to general-purpose computers. As hardware cost and size continue to drop and processing requirements become well-understood in areas such as signal and image processing, more special-purpose systems are being constructed. However, since most of these systems are built on an ad hoc basis for specific tasks, methodological work in this area is rare. Because the knowledge gained from individual experiences is neither accumulated nor properly organized, the same errors are repeated. I/O and computation imbalance is a notable example—often, the fact that I/O interfaces cannot keep up with device speed is discovered only after constructing a high-speed, special-purpose device.

We intend to help correct this ad hoc approach by providing a general guideline—specifically, the concept of systolic architecture, a general methodology for mapping high-level computations into hardware structures. In a systolic system, data flows from the computer memory in a rhythmic fashion, passing through many processing elements before it returns to memory, much as blood circulates to and from the heart. The system works like an automobile assembly line where different people work on the same car at different times and many cars are assembled simultaneously. An assembly line is always linear, however, and systolic systems are sometimes two-dimensional. They can be rectangular, triangular, or hexagonal to make use of higher degrees of parallelism. Moreover, to implement a variety of computations, data flow in a systolic system may be at multiple speeds in multiple directions—both inputs and (partial) results flow, whereas only results flow in classical pipelined systems. Generally speaking, a systolic system is easy to implement because of its regularity and easy to reconfigure (to meet various outside constraints) because of its modularity.

The systolic architectural concept was developed at Carnegie-Mellon University,[1-7] and versions of systolic processors are being designed and built by several industrial and governmental organizations.[8-10] This article

reviews the basic principle of systolic architectures and explains why they should result in cost-effective, high-performance special-purpose systems for a wide range of problems.

Key architectural issues in designing special-purpose systems

Roughly, the cycle for developing a special-purpose system can be divided into three phases—task definition, design, and implementation. During task definition, some system performance bottleneck is identified, and a decision on whether or not to resolve it with special-purpose hardware is made. The evaluation required for task definition is most fundamental, but since it is often application-dependent, we will concentrate only on architectural issues related to the design phase and will assume routine implementation.

Simple and regular design. Cost-effectiveness has always been a chief concern in designing special-purpose systems; their cost must be low enough to justify their limited applicability. Costs can be classified as nonrecurring (design) and recurring (parts) costs. Part costs are dropping rapidly due to advances in integrated-circuit technology, but this advantage applies equally to both special-purpose and general-purpose systems. Furthermore, since special-purpose systems are seldom produced in large quantities, part costs are less important than design costs. Hence, the design cost of a special-purpose system must be relatively small for it to be more attractive than a general-purpose approach.

Fortunately, special-purpose design costs can be reduced by the use of appropriate architectures. If a structure can truly be decomposed into a few types of simple substructures or building blocks, which are used repetitively with simple interfaces, great savings can be achieved. This is especially true for VLSI designs where a single chip comprises hundreds of thousands of components. To cope with that complexity, simple and regular designs, similar

Reprinted from *Computer*, January 1982, pages 37-46. Copyright © 1982 by
The Institute of Electrical and Electronics Engineers, Inc.

to some of the techniques used in constructing large software systems, are essential.[11] In addition, special-purpose systems based on simple, regular designs are likely to be modular and therefore adjustable to various performance goals—that is, system cost can be made proportional to the performance required. This suggests that meeting the architectural challenge for simple, regular designs yields cost-effective special-purpose systems.

Concurrency and communication. There are essentially two ways to build a fast computer system. One is to use fast components, and the other is to use concurrency. The last decade has seen an order of magnitude decrease in the cost and size of computer components but only an incremental increase in component speed.[12] With current technology, tens of thousands of gates can be put in a single chip, but no gate is much faster than its TTL counterpart of 10 years ago. Since the technological trend clearly indicates a diminishing growth rate for component speed, any major improvement in computation speed must come from the concurrent use of many processing elements. The degree of concurrency in a special-purpose system is largely determined by the underlying algorithm. Massive parallelism can be achieved if the algorithm is designed to introduce high degrees of pipelining and multiprocessing. When a large number of processing elements work simultaneously, coordination and communication become significant—especially with VLSI technology where routing costs dominate the power, time, and area required to implement a computation.[13] The issue here is to design algorithms that support high degrees of concurrency, and in the meantime to employ only simple, regular communication and control to enable efficient implementation.

Balancing computation with I/O. Since a special-purpose system typically receives data and outputs results through an attached host, I/O considerations influence overall performance. (The host in this context can mean a computer, a memory, a real-time device, etc. In practice, the special-purpose system may actually input from one "physical" host and output to another.) The ultimate performance goal of a special-purpose system is—and should be no more than—a computation rate that balances the available I/O bandwidth with the host. Since an accurate a priori estimate of available I/O bandwidth in a complex system is usually impossible, the design of a special-purpose system should be modular so that its structure can be easily adjusted to match a variety of I/O bandwidths.

Suppose that the I/O bandwidth between the host and a special-purpose system is 10 million bytes per second, a rather high bandwidth for present technology. Assuming that at least two bytes are read from or written to the host for each operation, the maximum rate will be only 5 million operations per second, no matter how fast the special-purpose system can operate (see Figure 1). Orders of magnitude improvements on this throughput are possible only if multiple computations are performed per I/O access. However, the repetitive use of a data item requires it to be stored inside the system for a sufficient length of time. Thus, the I/O problem is related not only to the available I/O bandwidth, but also to the available memory internal to the system. The question then is how to arrange a computation together with an appropriate memory structure so that computation time is balanced with I/O time.

The I/O problem becomes especially severe when a large computation is performed on a small special-purpose system. In this case, the computation must be decomposed. Executing subcomputations one at a time may require a substantial amount of I/O to store or retrieve intermediate results. Consider, for example, performing the n-point fast Fourier transform using an S-point device when n is large and S is small. Figure 2 depicts the n-point FFT computation and a decomposition scheme for $n = 16$ and $S = 4$. Note that each subcomputation block is sufficiently small so that it can be handled by the 4-point device. During execution, results of a block must be temporarily sent to the host and later retrieved to be combined with results of other blocks as they become available. With the decomposition scheme shown in Figure 2b, the total number of I/O operations is $O(n \log n/\log S)$. In fact, it has been shown that, to perform the n-point FFT with a device of $O(S)$ memory, at least this many I/O operations are needed for any decomposition scheme.[14] Thus, for the n-point FFT problem, an S-point device cannot achieve more than an $O(\log S)$ speed-up ratio over the conventional $O(n \log n)$ software implementation time, and since it is a consequence of the I/O consideration, this upper bound holds independently of device speed. Similar upper bounds have been established for speed-up ratios achievable by devices for other computations such as sorting and matrix multiplication.[14,15] Knowing the I/O-imposed performance limit helps prevent overkill in the design of a special-purpose device.

In practice, problems are typically "larger" than special-purpose devices. Therefore, questions such as how a computation can be decomposed to minimize I/O, how the I/O requirement is related to the size of a special-purpose system and its memory, and how the I/O bandwidth limits the speed-up ratio achievable by a special-purpose system present another set of challenges to the system architect.

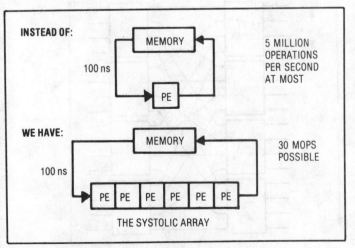

Figure 1. Basic principle of a systolic system.

Systolic architectures: the basic principle

As a solution to the above challenges, we introduce systolic architectures, an architectural concept originally proposed for VLSI implementation of some matrix operations.[5] Examples of systolic architectures follow in the next section, which contains a walk-through of a family of designs for the convolution computation.

A systolic system consists of a set of interconnected cells, each capable of performing some simple operation. Because simple, regular communication and control structures have substantial advantages over complicated ones in design and implementation, cells in a systolic system are typically interconnected to form a systolic array or a systolic tree. Information in a systolic system flows between cells in a pipelined fashion, and communication with the outside world occurs only at the "boundary cells." For example, in a systolic array, only those cells on the array boundaries may be I/O ports for the system.

Computational tasks can be conceptually classified into two families—compute-bound computations and I/O-bound computations. In a computation, if the total number of operations is larger than the total number of input and output elements, then the computation is compute-bound, otherwise it is I/O-bound. For example, the ordinary matrix-matrix multiplication algorithm represents a compute-bound task, since every entry in a matrix is multiplied by all entries in some row or column of the other matrix. Adding two matrices, on the other hand, is I/O-bound, since the total number of adds is not larger than the total number of entries in the two matrices. It should be clear that any attempt to speed up an I/O-bound computation must rely on an increase in memory bandwidth. Memory bandwidth can be increased by the use of either fast components (which could be expensive) or interleaved memories (which could create complicated memory management problems). Speeding up a compute-bound computation, however, may often be accomplished in a relatively simple and inexpensive manner, that is, by the systolic approach.

The basic principle of a systolic architecture, a systolic array in particular, is illustrated in Figure 1. By replacing a single processing element with an array of PEs, or cells in the terminology of this article, a higher computation throughput can be achieved without increasing memory bandwidth. The function of the memory in the diagram is analogous to that of the heart; it "pulses" data (instead of blood) through the array of cells. The crux of this approach is to ensure that once a data item is brought out from the memory it can be used effectively at each cell it passes while being "pumped" from cell to cell along the array. This is possible for a wide class of compute-bound computations where multiple operations are performed on each data item in a repetitive manner.

Being able to use each input data item a number of times (and thus achieving high computation throughput with only modest memory bandwidth) is just one of the many advantages of the systolic approach. Other advantages, such as modular expansibility, simple and regular data and control flows, use of simple and uniform cells, elimination of global broadcasting, and fan-in and (possibly) fast response time, will be illustrated in various systolic designs in the next section.

A family of systolic designs for the convolution computation

To provide concrete examples of various systolic structures, this section presents a family of systolic designs for the convolution problem, which is defined as follows:

Given the sequence of weights $\{w_1, w_2, \ldots, w_k\}$ and the input sequence $\{x_1, x_2, \ldots, x_n\}$,

compute the result sequence $\{y_1, y_2, \ldots, y_{n+1-k}\}$ defined by

$$y_i = w_1 x_i + w_2 x_{i+1} + \ldots + w_k x_{i+k-1}$$

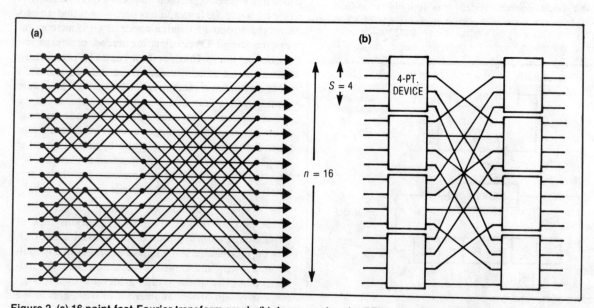

Figure 2. (a) 16-point fast-Fourier-transform graph; (b) decomposing the FFT computation with $n = 16$ and $S = 4$.

January 1982

302

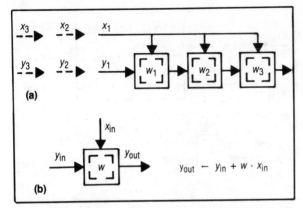

Figure 3. Design B1: systolic convolution array (a) and cell (b) where x_i's are broadcast, w_i's stay, and y_i's move systolically.

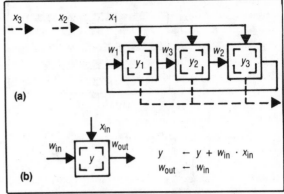

Figure 4. Design B2: systolic convolution array (a) and cell (b) where x_i's are broadcast, y_i's stay, and w_i's move systolically.

We consider the convolution problem because it is a simple problem with a variety of enlightening systolic solutions, because it is an important problem in its own right, and more importantly, because it is representative of a wide class of computations suited to systolic designs. The convolution problem can be viewed as a problem of combining two data streams, w_i's amd x_i's, in a certain manner (for example, as in the above equation) to form a resultant data stream of y_i's. This type of computation is common to a number of computation routines, such as filtering, pattern matching, correlation, interpolation, polynomial evaluation (including discrete Fourier transforms), and polynomial multiplication and division. For example, if multiplication and addition are interpreted as comparison and boolean AND, respectively, then the convolution problem becomes the pattern matching problem.[1] Architectural concepts for the convolution problem can thus be applied to these other problems as well.

The convolution problem is compute-bound, since each input x_i is to be multiplied by each of the k weights. If the x_i is input separately from memory for each multiplication, then when k is large, memory bandwidth becomes a bottleneck, precluding a high-performance solution. As indicated earlier, a systolic architecture resolves this I/O bottleneck by making multiple use of each x_i fetched from the memory. Based on this principle, several systolic designs for solving the convolution problem are described below. For simplicity, all illustrations assume that $k = 3$.

(Semi-) systolic convolution arrays with global data communication. If an x_i, once brought out from the memory, is broadcast to a number of cells, then the same x_i can be used by all the cells. This broadcasting technique is probably one of the most obvious ways to make multiple use of each input element. The opposite of broadcasting is fan-in, through which data items from a number of cells can be collected. The fan-in technique can also be used in a straightforward manner to resolve the I/O bottleneck problem. In the following, we describe systolic designs that utilize broadcasting and fan-in.

Design B1—broadcast inputs, move results, weights stay. The systolic array and its cell definition are depicted

in Figure 3. Weights are preloaded to the cells, one at each cell, and stay at the cells throughout the computation. Partial results y_i move systolically from cell to cell in the left-to-right direction, that is, each of them moves over the cell to its right during each cycle. At the beginning of a cycle, one x_i is broadcast to all the cells and one y_i, initialized as zero, enters the left-most cell. During cycle one, $w_1 x_1$ is accumulated to y_1 at the left-most cell, and during cycle two, $w_1 x_2$ and $w_2 x_2$ are accumulated to y_2 and y_1 at the left-most and middle cells, respectively. Starting from cycle three, the final (and correct) values of $y_1, y_2, \ldots$ are output from the right-most cell at the rate of one y_i per cycle. The basic principle of this design was previously proposed for circuits to implement a pattern matching processor[16] and for circuits to implement polynomial multiplication.[17-20]

Design B2—broadcast inputs, move weights, results stay. In design B2 (see Figure 4), each y_i stays at a cell to accumulate its terms, allowing efficient use of available multiplier-accumulator hardware. (Indeed, this design is described in an application booklet for the TRW multiplier-accumulator chips.[21] The weights circulate around the array of cells, and the first weight w_1 is associated with a tag bit that signals the accumulator to output and resets its contents.* In design B1 (Figure 3), the systolic path for moving y_i's may be considerably wider than that for moving w_i's in design B2 because for numerical accuracy y_i's typically carry more bits than w_i's. The use of multiplier-accumulators in design B2 may also help increase precision of the results, since extra bits can be kept in these accumulators with modest cost. Design B1, however, does have the advantage of not requiring a separate bus (or other global network), denoted by a dashed line in Figure 4, for collecting outputs from individual cells.

Design F—fan-in results, move inputs, weights stay. If we consider the vector of weights $(w_k, w_{k-1}, \ldots, w_1)$ as being fixed in space and input vector $(x_n, x_{n-1}, \ldots, x_1)$ as sliding over the weights in the left-to-right direction, then the convolution problem is one that computes the inner product of the weight vector and the section of input vector it overlaps. This view suggests the systolic array

---

*To avoid complicated pictures, control structures such as the use of tag bits to gate outputs from cells are omitted from the diagrams of this article.

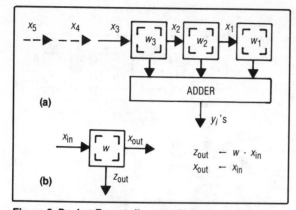

Figure 5. Design F: systolic convolution array (a) and cell (b) where w_i's stay, x_i's move systolically, and y_i's are formed through the fan-in of results from all the cells.

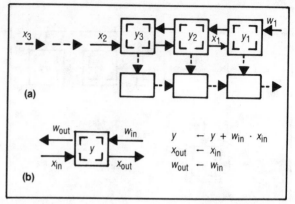

Figure 6. Design R1: systolic convolution array (a) and cell (b) where y_i's stay and x_i's and y_i's move in opposite directions systolically.

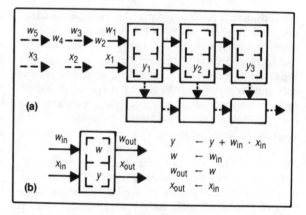

Figure 7. Design R2: systolic convolution array (a) and cell (b) where y_i's stay and x_i's and w_i's both move in the same direction but at different speeds.

shown in Figure 5. Weights are preloaded to the cells and stay there throughout the computation. During a cycle, all x_i's move one cell to the right, multiplications are performed at all cells simultaneously, and their results are fanned-in and summed using an adder to form a new y_i. When the number of cells, k, is large, the adder can be implemented as a pipelined adder tree to avoid large delays in each cycle. Designs of this type using unbounded fan-in have been known for quite a long time, for example, in the context of signal processing[33] and in the context of pattern matching.[43]

(Pure-) systolic convolution arrays without global data communication. Although global broadcasting or fan-in solves the I/O bottleneck problem, implementing it in a modular, expandable way presents another problem. Providing (or collecting) a data item to (or from) all the cells of a systolic array, during each cycle, requires the use of a bus or some sort of tree-like network. As the number of cells increases, wires become long for either a bus or tree structure; expanding these non-local communication paths to meet the increasing load is difficult without slowing down the system clock. This engineering difficulty of extending global networks is significant at chip, board, and higher levels of a computer system. Fortunately, as will be demonstrated below, systolic convolution arrays without global data communication do exist. Potentially, these arrays can be extended to include an arbitrarily large number of cells without encountering engineering difficulties (the problem of synchronizing a large systolic array is discussed later).

Design R1—results stay, inputs and weights move in opposite directions. In design R1 (see Figure 6) each partial result y_i stays at a cell to accumulate its terms. The x_i's and w_i's move systolically in opposite directions such that when an x meets a w at a cell, they are multiplied and the resulting product is accumulated to the y staying at that cell. To ensure that each x_i is able to meet every w_i, consecutive x_i's on the x data stream are separated by two cycle times and so are the w_i's on the w data stream.

Like design B2, design R1 can make efficient use of available multiplier-accumulator hardware; it can also use a tag bit associated with the first weight, w_1, to trigger the output and reset the accumulator contents of a cell.

Design R1 has the advantage that it does not require a bus, or any other global network, for collecting output from cells; a systolic output path (indicated by broken arrows in Figure 6) is sufficient. Because consecutive w_i's are well separated by two cycle times, a potential conflict—that more than one y_i may reach a single latch on the systolic output path simultaneously—cannot occur. It can also be easily checked that the y_i's will output from the systolic output path in the natural ordering $y_1, y_2, \ldots$. The basic idea of this design, including that of the systolic output path, has been used to implement a pattern matching chip.[1]

Notice that in Figure 6 only about one-half the cells are doing useful work at any time. To fully utilize the potential throughput, two independent convolution computations can be interleaved in the same systolic array, but cells in the array would have to be modified slightly to support the interleaved computation. For example, an additional accumulator would be required at each cell to hold a temporary result for the other convolution computation.

Design R2—results stay, inputs and weights move in the same direction but at different speeds. One version of design R2 is illustrated in Figure 7. In this case both the x and w data streams move from left to right systolically, but the x_i's move twice as fast as the w_i's. More precisely,

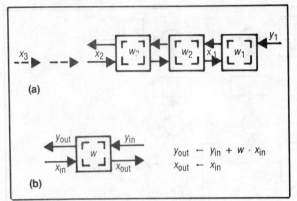

Figure 8. Design W1: systolic convolution array (a) and cell (b) where w_i's stay and x_i's and y_i's move systolically in opposite directions.

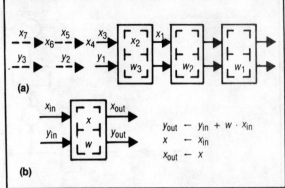

Figure 9. Design W2: systolic convolution array (a) and cell (b) where w_i's stay and x_i's and y_i's both move systolically in the same direction but at different speeds.

each w_i stays inside every cell it passes for one extra cycle, thus taking twice as long to move through the array as any x_i. In this design, multiplier-accumulator hardware can be used effectively and so can the tag bit method to signal the output of the accumulator contents at each cell. Compared to design R1, this design has the advantage that all cells work all the time when performing a single convolution, but it requires an additional register in each cell to hold a w value. This algorithm has been used for implementing a pipeline multiplier.[22]

There is a dual version of design R2; we can have the w_i's move twice as fast as the x_i's. To create delays for the x data stream, this dual design requires a register in each cell for storing an x rather than a w value. For circumstances where the w_i's carry more bits than the x_i's, the dual design becomes attractive.

Design W1—weights stay, inputs and results move in opposite directions. In design W1 (and design W2, below), weights stay, one at each cell, but results and inputs move systolically. These designs are not geared to the most effective use of available multiplier-accumulator hardware, but for some other circumstances they are potentially more efficient than the other designs. Because the same set of weights is used for computing all the y_i's and different sets of the x_i's are used for computing different y_i's, it is natural to have the w_i's preloaded to the cells and stay there, and let the x_i's and the y_i's move along the array. We will see some advantages of this arrangement in the systolic array depicted in Figure 8, which is a special case of a proposed systolic filtering array.[3] This design is fundamental in the sense that it can be naturally extended to perform recursive filtering[2,3] and polynomial division.[23]

In design W1, the w_i's stay and the x_i's and y_i's move systolically in opposite directions. Similar to design R1, consecutive x_i's and y_i's are separated by two cycle times. Note that because the systolic path for moving the y_i's already exists, there is no need for another systolic output path as in designs R1 and R2. Furthermore, for each i, y_i outputs from the left-most cell during the same cycle as its last input, x_{i+k-1} (or x_{i+2} for $k = 3$), enters that cell. Thus, this systolic array is capable of outputting a y_i every two cycle times with constant response time. Design W1, however, suffers from the same drawback as design R1,

namely, only approximately one-half the cells work at any given time unless two independent convolution computations are interleaved in the same array. The next design, like design R2, overcomes this shortcoming by having both the x_i's and y_i's move in the same direction but at different speeds.

Design W2—weights stay, inputs and results move in the same direction but at different speeds. With design W2 (Figure 9) all the cells work all the time, but it loses one advantage of design W1, the constant response time. The output of y_i now takes place k cycles after the last of its inputs starts entering the left-most cell of the systolic array. This design has been extended to implement 2-D convolutions,[6,24] where high throughputs rather than fast responses are of concern. Similar to design R1, design W2 has a dual version for which the x_i's move twice as fast as the y_i's.

Remarks. The designs presented above by no means exhaust all the possible systolic designs for the convolution problem. For example, it is possible to have systolic designs where results, weights, and inputs all move during each cycle. It could also be advantageous to include inside each cell a "cell memory" capable of storing a set of weights. With this feature, using a systolic control (or address) path, weights can be selected on-the-fly to implement interpolation or adaptive filtering.[24] Moreover, the flexibility introduced by the cell memories and systolic control can make the same systolic array implement different functions. Indeed, the ESL systolic processor[8,10] utilizes cell memories to implement multiple functions including convolution and matrix multiplication.

Once one systolic design is obtained for a problem, it is likely that a set of other systolic designs can be derived similarly. The challenge is to understand precisely the strengths and drawbacks of each design so that an appropriate design can be selected for a given environment. For example, if there are more weights than cells, it's useful to know that a scheme where partial results stay generally requires less I/O than one where partial results move, since the latter scheme requires partial results to be input and output many times. A single multiplier-accumulator hardware component often represents a cost-effective implementation of the multiplier and adder

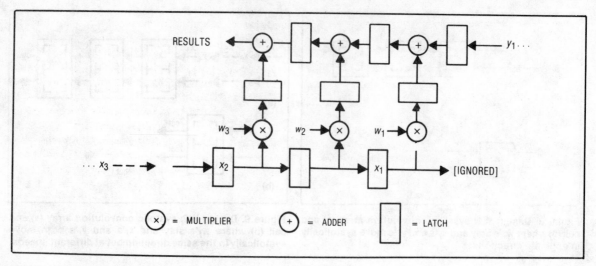

Figure 10. Overlapping the executions of multiply and add in design W1.

needed by each cell of a systolic convolution array. However, for improving throughput, sometimes it may be worthwhile to implement multiplier and adder separately to allow overlapping of their executions. Figure 10 depicts such a modification to design W1. Similar modifications can be made to other systolic convolution arrays. Another interesting scenario is the following one. Suppose that one or several cells are to be implemented directly with a single chip and the chip pin bandwidth is the implementation bottleneck. Then, since the basic cell of some semi-systolic convolution arrays such as designs B1 and F require only three I/O ports, while that of a pure-systolic convolution array always requires four, a semi-systolic array may be preferable for saving pins, despite the fact that it requires global communication.

Criteria and advantages

Having described a family of systolic convolution arrays, we can now be more precise in suggesting and evaluating criteria for the design of systolic structures.

(1) *The design makes multiple use of each input data item.* Because of this property, systolic systems can achieve high throughputs with modest I/O bandwidths for outside communication. To meet this criterion, one can either use global data communications, such as broadcast and unbounded fan-in, or have each input travel through an array of cells so that it is used at each cell. For modular expansibility of the resulting system, the second approach is preferable.

(2) *The design uses extensive concurrency.* The processing power of a systolic architecture comes from concurrent use of many simple cells rather than sequential use of a few powerful processors as in many conventional architectures. Concurrency can be obtained by pipelining the stages involved in the computation of each single result (for example, design B1), by multiprocessing many results in parallel (designs R1 and R2), or by both. For some designs, such as W1, it is possible to completely overlap I/O and computation times to further increase concurrency and provide constant-time responses.

To a given problem there could be both one- and two-dimensional systolic array solutions. For example, two-dimensional convolution can be performed by a one-dimensional systolic array[24,25] or a two-dimensional systolic array.[6] When the memory speed is more than cell speed, two-dimensional systolic arrays such as those depicted in Figure 11 should be used. At each cell cycle, all the I/O ports on the array boundaries can input or output data items to or from the memory; as a result, the available memory bandwidth can be fully utilized. Thus, the choice of a one- or two-dimensional scheme is very dependent on how cells and memories will be implemented.

As in one-dimensional systolic arrays, data in two-dimensional arrays may flow in multiple directions and at multiple speeds. For examples of two-dimensional systolic arrays, see Guibas et al.[26] and Kung and Lehman[4] (type R), Kung and Leiserson[5] and Weiser and Davis[27] (type H), and Bojanczyk et al.[28] and Gentleman and Kung[29] (type T). In practice, systolic arrays can be chained together to form powerful systems such as the one depicted in Figure 12, which is capable of producing on-the-fly the least-squares fit to all the data that have arrived up to any given moment.[29]

For the systolic structures discussed in the preceding section, computations are pipelined over an array of cells. To permit even higher concurrency, it is sometimes possible to introduce another level of pipelining by allowing the operations inside the cells themselves to be pipelined. (Note that pipelined arithmetic units will become increasingly common as VLSI makes the extra circuits needed for

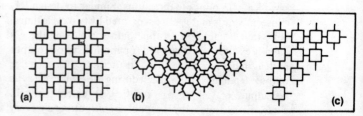

Figure 11. Two-dimensional systolic arrays: (a) type R, (b) type H, and (c) type T.

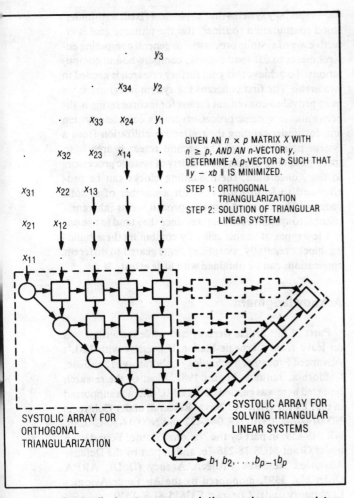

GIVEN AN $n \times p$ MATRIX X WITH $n \geq p$, AND AN n-VECTOR y, DETERMINE A p-VECTOR b SUCH THAT $\| y - xb \|$ IS MINIMIZED.

STEP 1: ORTHOGONAL TRIANGULARIZATION
STEP 2: SOLUTION OF TRIANGULAR LINEAR SYSTEM

SYSTOLIC ARRAY FOR ORTHOGONAL TRIANGULARIZATION

SYSTOLIC ARRAY FOR SOLVING TRIANGULAR LINEAR SYSTEMS

$b_1 b_2, \dots, b_{p-1} b_p$

Figure 12. On-the-fly least-squares solutions using one- and two-dimensional systolic arrays, with $p = 4$.

staging affordable.) Both designs W1 and W2 support two-level pipelining.[25] Since system cycle time is the time of a stage of a cell, rather than the whole cell cycle time, two-level pipelined systolic systems significantly improve throughput.

(3) *There are only a few types of simple cells.* To achieve performance goals, a systolic system is likely to use a large number of cells. The cells must be simple and of only a few types to curtail design and implementation costs, but exactly how simple is a question that can only be answered on a case by case basis. For example, if a systolic system consisting of many cells is to be implemented on a single chip, each cell should probably contain only simple logic circuits plus a few words of memory. On the other hand, for board implementations each cell could reasonably contain a high-performance arithmetic unit plus a few thousand words of memory. There is, of course, always a trade-off between cell simplicity and flexibility.

(4) *Data and control flows are simple and regular.* Pure systolic systems totally avoid long-distance or irregular wires for data communication. The only global communication (besides power and ground) is the system clock. Of course, self-timed schemes can be used instead for synchronizing neighboring cells, but efficient implementations of self-timed protocols may be difficult. Fortunately, for any one-dimensional systolic array, a global clock

parallel to the array presents no problems, even if the array is arbitrarily long. The systolic array (with data flowing in either one or opposite directions) will operate correctly despite the possibility of a large clock skew between its two ends.[30] However, large two-dimensional arrays may require slowdown of the global clock to compensate for clock skews. Except for this possible problem in the two-dimensional case, systolic designs are completely modular and expandable; they present no difficult synchronization or resource conflict problems. Software overhead associated with operations such as address indexing are totally eliminated in systolic systems. This advantage alone can mean a substantial performance improvement over conventional general-purpose computers. Simple, regular control and communication also imply simple, area-efficient layout or wiring—an important advantage in VLSI implementation.

In summary, systolic designs based on these criteria are *simple* (a consequence of properties 3 and 4), *modular* and *expandable* (property 4), and yield *high performance* (properties 1, 2, and 4). They therefore meet the architectural challenges for special-purpose systems. A unique characteristic of the systolic approach is that as the number of cells expands the system cost and performance increase proportionally, provided that the size of the underlying problem is sufficiently large. For example, a systolic convolution array can use an arbitrarily large number of cells cost-effectively, if the kernel size (that is, the number of weights) is large. This is in contrast to other parallel architectures which are seldom cost-effective for more than a small number of processors. From a user's point of view, a systolic system is easy to use—he simply pumps in the input data and then receives the results either on-the-fly or at the end of the computation.

Summary and concluding remarks

Bottlenecks to speeding up a computation are often due to limited system memory bandwidths, so called *von Neumann bottlenecks*, rather than limited processing capabilities per se. This problem can certainly be expected for I/O-bound computations, but with a conventional architectural approach, it may be present even for compute-bound computations. For every operation, at least one or two operands have to be fetched (or stored) from (or to) memory, so the total amount of I/O is proportional to the number of operations rather than the number of inputs and outputs. Thus, a problem that was originally compute-bound can become I/O-bound during its execution. This unfortunate situation is the result of a mismatch between the computation and the architecture. Systolic architectures, which ensure multiple computations per memory access, can speed up compute-bound computations without increasing I/O requirements.

The convolution problem is just one of many compute-bound computations that can benefit from the systolic approach. Systolic designs using (one- or two-dimensional) array or tree structures are available for the following regular, compute-bound computations.

Signal and image processing:
• FIR, IIR filtering, and 1-D convolution[2,3,31];

- 2-D convolution and correlation[6,8,10,24,25];
- discrete Fourier transform[2,3];
- interpolation[24];
- 1-D and 2-D median filtering[32]; and
- geometric warping.[24]

Matrix arithmetic:
- matrix-vector multiplication[5];
- matrix-matrix multiplication[5,27];
- matrix triangularization (solution of linear systems, matrix inversion)[5,29];
- QR decomposition (eigenvalue, least-square computations)[28,29]; and
- solution of triangular linear systems.[5]

Non-numeric applications:
- data structures—stack and queue,[34] searching,[15,35,36] priority queue,[7] and sorting[7,15];
- graph algorithms—transitive closure,[26] minimum spanning trees,[37] and connected components[38];
- language recognition—string matching[1] and regular expression[39];
- dynamic programming[26];
- encoders (polynomial division)[23]; and
- relational data-base operations.[4,40]

In general, systolic designs apply to any compute-bound problem that is regular—that is, one where repetitive computations are performed on a large set of data. Thus, the above list is certainly not complete (and was not intended to be so). Its purpose is to provide a range of typical examples and possible applications. After studying several of these examples, one should be able to start designing systolic systems for one's own tasks. Some systolic solutions can usually be found without too much difficulty. (I know of only one compute-bound problem that arises naturally in practice for which no systolic solution is known, and I cannot prove that a systolic solution is impossible.) This is probably due to the fact that most compute-bound problems are inherently regular in the sense that they are definable in terms of simple recurrences. Indeed, the notion of systolicity is implicit in quite a few previously known special-purpose designs, such as the sorting[41] and multiply designs.[22] This should not come as a surprise; as we have been arguing systolic structures are essential for obtaining any cost-effective, high-performance solution to compute-bound problems. It is useful, however, to make the systolic concept explicit so that designers will be conscious of this important design criterion.

While numerous systolic designs are known today, the question of their automatic design is still open. But recent efforts show significant progress.[27,42] Leiserson and Saxe, for instance, can convert some semi-systolic systems involving broadcasting or unbounded fan-in into pure-systolic systems without global data communication.[42] A related open problem concerns the specification and verification of systolic structures. For implementation and proof purposes, rigorous notation other than informal pictures (as used in this article) for specifying systolic designs is desirable.

With the development of systolic architectures, more and more special-purpose systems will become feasible—especially systems that implement fixed, well-understood computation routines. But the ultimate goal is effective use of systolic processors in general computing environments to off-load regular, compute-bound computations. To achieve this goal further research is needed in two areas. The first concerns the system integration: we must provide a convenient means for incorporating high-performance systolic processors into a complete system and for understanding their effective utilization from a system point of view. The second research area is to specify building-blocks for a variety of systolic processors so that, once built, these building blocks can be programmed to form basic cells for a number of systolic systems. The building-block approach seems inherently suitable to systolic architectures since they tend to use only a few types of simple cells. By combining these building-blocks regularly, systolic systems geared to different applications can be obtained with little effort. ∎

Acknowledgment

Parts of this article were written while the author was on leave from Carnegie-Mellon University with ESL's Advanced Processor Technology Laboratory in San Jose, California, January-August 1981. Most of the research reported here was carried out at CMU and was supported in part by the Office of Naval Research under Contracts N00014-76-C-0370, NR 044-422 and N00014-80-C-0236, NR 048-659, in part by the National Science Foundation under Grant MCS 78-236-76, and in part by the Defense Advanced Research Projects Agency (DoD), ARPA Order No. 3597, monitored by the Air Force Avionics Laboratory under Contract F33615-81-K-1539.

References

1. M. J. Foster and H. T. Kung, "The Design of Special-Purpose VLSI Chips," *Computer*, Vol. 13, No. 1, Jan. 1980, pp. 26-40.
2. H. T. Kung, "Let's Design Algorithms for VLSI Systems," *Proc. Conf. Very Large Scale Integration: Architecture, Design, Fabrication*, California Institute of Technology, Jan. 1979, pp. 65-90.
3. H. T. Kung, "Special-Purpose Devices for Signal and Image Processing: An Opportunity in VLSI," *Proc. SPIE, Vol. 241, Real-Time Signal Processing III*, Society of Photo-Optical Instrumentation Engineers, July 1980, pp. 76-84.
4. H. T. Kung and P. L. Lehman, "Systolic (VLSI) Arrays for Relational Database Operations," *Proc. ACM-Sigmod 1980 Int'l Conf. Management of Data*, May 1980, pp. 105-116.
5. H. T. Kung and C. E. Leiserson, "Systolic Arrays (for VLSI)," *Sparse Matrix Proc. 1978*, Society for Industrial and Applied Mathematics, 1979, pp. 256-282.
6. H. T. Kung and S. W. Song, *A Systolic 2-D Convolution Chip*, Technical Report CMU-CS-81-110, Carnegie-Mellon University Computer Science Dept., Mar. 1981.
7. C. E. Leiserson, "Systolic Priority Queues," *Proc. Conf. Very Large Scale Integration: Architecture, Design, Fabrication*, California Institute of Technology, Jan. 1979, pp. 199-214.
8. J. Blackmer, P. Kuekes, and G. Frank, "A 200 MOPS systolic processor," *Proc. SPIE, Vol. 298, Real-Time Signal Processing IV*, Society of Photo-Optical Instrumentation Engineers, 1981.

9. K. Bromley, J. J. Symanski, J. M. Speiser, and H. J. Whitehouse, "Systolic Array Processor Developments," in *VLSI Systems and Computations,* H. T. Kung, R. F. Sproull, and G. L. Steele, Jr., (eds.), Carnegie-Mellon University, Computer Science Press, Oct. 1981, pp. 273-284.

10. D. W. L. Yen and A. V. Kulkarni, "The ESL Systolic Processor for Signal and Image Processing," *Proc. 1981 IEEE Computer Society Workshop on Computer Architecture for Pattern Analysis and Image Database Management,* Nov. 1981, pp. 265-272.

11. C. A. Mead and L. A. Conway, *Introduction to VLSI Systems,* Addison-Wesley, Reading, Mass., 1980.

12. R. N. Noyce, "Hardware Prospects and Limitations," in *The Computer Age: A Twenty-Year Review,* M. L. Dertouzos and J. Moses (eds.), IEEE Press, 1979, pp. 321-337.

13. I. E. Sutherland and C. A. Mead, "Microelectronics and Computer Science," *Scientific American,* Vol. 237, No. 3, Sept. 1977, pp. 210-228.

14. J-W. Hong and H. T. Kung, "I/O Complexity: The Red-Blue Pebble Game," *Proc. 13th Annual ACM Symp. Theory of Computing,* ACM Sigact, May 1981, pp. 326-333.

15. S. W. Song, *On a High-Performance VLSI Solution to Database Problems,* PhD dissertation, Carnegie-Mellon University, Computer Science Dept., July 1981.

16. A. Mukhopadhyay, "Hardware Algorithms for Nonnumeric Computation," *IEEE Trans. Computers,* Vol. C-28, No. 6, June 1979, pp. 384-394.

17. D. Cohen, *Mathematical Approach to Computational Networks,* Technical Report ISI/RR-78-73, University of Southern California, Information Sciences Institute, 1978.

18. D. A. Huffman, "The Synthesis of Linear Sequential Coding Networks," in *Information Theory,* C. Cherry (ed.), Academic Press, 1957, pp. 77-95.

19. K. Y. Liu, "Architecture for VLSI Design of Reed-Solomon Encoders," *Proc. Second Caltech VLSI Conf.* Jan. 1981.

20. W. W. Peterson and E. J. Weldon, Jr., *Error-Correcting Codes,* MIT Press, Cambridge, Mass., 1972.

21. L. Schirm IV, *Multiplier-Accumulator Application Notes,* TRW LSI Products, Jan. 1980.

22. R. F. Lyon, "Two's Complement Pipeline Multipliers," *IEEE Trans. Comm.,* Vol. COM-24, No. 4, Apr. 1976, pp. 418-425.

23. H. T. Kung, "Use of VLSI in Algebraic Computation: Some Suggestions," *Proc. 1981 ACM Symp. Symbolic and Algebraic Computation,* ACM Sigsam, Aug. 1981, pp. 218-222.

24. H. T. Kung and R.L. Picard, "Hardware Pipelines for Multi-Dimensional Convolution and Resampling," *Proc. 1981 IEEE Computer Society Workshop on Computer Architecture for Pattern Analysis and Image Database Management,* Nov. 1981, pp. 273-278.

25. H. T. Kung, L. M. Ruane, and D. W. L. Yen, "A Two-Level Pipelined Systolic Array for Convolutions," in *VLSI Systems and Computations,* H. T. Kung, R. F. Sproull, and G. L. Steele, Jr. (eds.), Carnegie-Mellon University, Computer Science Press, Oct. 1981, pp. 255-264.

26. L. J. Guibás, H. T. Kung, and C. D. Thompson, "Direct VLSI Implementation of Combinatorial Algorithms," *Proc. Conf. Very Large Scale Integration: Architecture, Design, Fabrication,* California Institute of Technology, Jan. 1979, pp. 509-525.

27. U. Weiser and A. Davis, "A Wavefront Notation Tool for VLSI Array Design," in *VLSI Systems and Computations,* H. T. Kung, R. F. Sproull, and G. L. Steele, Jr. (eds.), Carnegie-Mellon University, Computer Science Press, Oct. 1981, pp. 226-234.

28. A. Bojanczyk, R. P. Brent, and H. T. Kung, *Numerically Stable Solution of Dense Systems of Linear Equations Using Mesh-Connected Processors,* Technical Report, Carnegie-Mellon University, Computer Science Dept. May 1981.

29. W. M. Gentleman and H. T. Kung, "Matrix Triangularization by Systolic Arrays," *Proc. SPIE, Vol. 298, Real-Time Signal Processing IV,* Society of Photo-optical Instrumentation Engineers, 1981.

30. A. Fisher and H. T. Kung, CMU Computer Science Dept. technical report, Jan. 1982.

31. P. R. Cappello and K. Steiglitz, "Digital Signal Processing Applications of Systolic Algorithms," in *VLSI Systems and Computations,* H. T. Kung, R. F. Sproull, and G. L. Steele, Jr. (eds.), Carnegie-Mellon University, Computer Science Press, Oct. 1981, pp. 245-254.

32. A. Fisher, "Systolic Algorithms for Running Order Statistics in Signal and Image Processing," in *VLSI Systems and Computations,* H. T. Kung, R. F. Sproull, G. L. Steele, Jr. (eds.), Carnegie-Mellon University, Computer Science Press, Oct. 1981, pp. 265-272.

33. E. E. Swartzlander, Jr., and B. K. Gilbert, "Arithmetic for Ultra-High-Speed Tomography," *IEEE Trans. Computers,* Vol. C-29, No. 5, May, 1980, pp. 341-354.

34. L. J. Guibas and F. M. Liang, "Systolic Stacks, Queues, and Counters," *Proc. Conf. Advanced Research in VLSI,* MIT, Jan. 1982.

35. J. L. Bentley and H. T. Kung, "A Tree Machine for Searching Problems," *Proc. 1979 Int'l Conf. Parallel Processing,* Aug. 1979, pp. 257-266. Also available as a Carnegie-Mellon University Computer Science Dept. technical report, Aug. 1979.

36. T. Ottmann, A. L. Rosenberg, and L. J. Stockmeyer, "A Dictionary Machine (for VLSI)," Technical Report RC 9060 (#39615), IBM T. J. Watson Research Center, Yorktown Heights, N.Y., 1981.

37. J. L. Bentley, *A Parallel Algorithm for Constructing Minimum Spanning Trees," Journal of Algorithms,* Jan. 1980, pp. 51-59.

38. C. Savage, "A Systolic Data Structure Chip for Connectivity Problems," in *VLSI Systems and Computations,* H. T. Kung, R. F. Sproull, and G. L. Steele, Jr., (eds.), Carnegie-Mellon University, Computer Science Press, Oct. 1981, pp. 296-300.

39. M. J. Foster and H. T. Kung, "Recognize Regular Languages With Programmable Building-Blocks," in *VLSI 81,* Academic Press, Aug. 1981, pp. 75-84.

40. P. L. Lehman, "A Systolic (VLSI) Array for Processing Simple Relational Queries," in *VLSI Systems and Computations,* H. T Kung, R. F. Sproull, and G. I. Steele, Jr. (eds.), Carnegie-Mellon University, Computer Science Press, Oct. 1981, pp. 285-295.

41. S. Todd, "Algorithm and Hardware for a Merge Sort Using Multiple Processors," *IBM J. Research and Development,* Vol. 22, No. 5, 1978, pp. 509-517.

42. C. E. Leiserson and J. B. Saxe, "Optimizing Synchronous Systems," *Proc. 22nd Annual Symp. Foundations of Computer Science,* IEEE Computer Society, Oct. 1981, pp. 23-36.

43. C. A. Mead et al., "128-Bit Multicomparator," *IEEE J. Solid-State Circuits,* Vol. SC-11, No. 5, Oct. 1976, pp. 692-695.

H. T. Kung is an associate professor of computer science at Carnegie-Mellon University, where he leads a research group in the design and implementation of high-performance VLSI systems. From January to September 1981 he was an architecture consultant to ESL, Inc., a subsidiary of TRW. His research interests are in paradigms of mapping algorithms and applications directly on chips and in theoretical foundations of VLSI computations. He serves on the editorial board of the *Journal of Digital Systems* and is the author of over 50 technical papers in computer science.

Kung graduated from National Tsing-Hua University, Taiwan, in 1968, and received his PhD from Carnegie-Mellon University in 1974.

*Architectures for this computer family are built around
a lattice of programmable switches and data paths that allows arbitrary
connection patterns — an approach that preserves locality.*

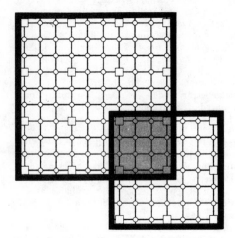

Introduction to the Configurable, Highly Parallel Computer

Lawrence Snyder, Purdue University

polymorphism, *n.*(1): capability of assuming different forms; capability of wide variation.
Webster's Third International Dictionary

When von Neumann computers were still new and exciting, scientists noted in popular accounts that unlike mechanical devices, computers are polymorphic—their function can be radically changed simply by changing programs. Polymorphism *is* fundamental, but this familiar and obvious fact receives little mention any more, even though it underlies important advances such as time-sharing and programmable microcode. Now, however, as we are confronted with the potential for highly parallel computers made possible by very-large-scale integrated circuit technology, we may ask: What is the role of polymorphism in parallel computation? To answer this question, we must review the characteristics of parallel processing and the benefits and limitations of VLSI technology.

Algorithmically specialized processors

Perhaps the most important characteristic of VLSI circuit technology is that the manufacturing processes use photolithography to create copies of a circuit.[1] Fabrication by photolithography (or the newer X-ray lithography) requires a fixed number of steps to produce a circuit, independent of the circuit's complexity. It costs no more to make copies of a chip containing a NAND gate than to make copies of a chip containing a microprocessor, although yields will likely be higher for the former and wire bonding costs higher for the latter. Because preparing and debugging the lithographic masks is expensive,

the technology favors parallel processing techniques that employ many copies of the same circuit, even if it is complex.

Uniformity is the source of leverage in VLSI, and recognition of this caused a flurry of research during the past five years that resulted in a number of proposals for devices we may call *algorithmically specialized processors*. By focusing on computationally intensive problems and carefully dissecting algorithms for them, researchers have developed algorithmically specialized processors with several important characteristics:

- Construction is based on a few easily tessellated processing elements.
- Locality is exploited; that is, data movement is often limited to adjacent processing elements.
- Pipelining is used to achieve high processor utilization.

Examples of algorithmically specialized processors include designs for LU decomposition,[2,3] the main step in solving systems of linear equations; the solution of linear recurrences[2]; tree processors,[4-6] used in searching, sorting, and expression evaluation; dynamic programming,[7] a general problem-solving technique with numerous applications; join processing,[8] for data base querying; and many others.

Algorithmically specialized processing components must be joined together to solve a large, computationally intensive problem. This composition step is crucial, since whole problems tend to be multiphased and these components tend to be specialized to an algorithm used in only one phase. For example, to solve a system of linear equations $(Ax=b)$, one might use a processor component to form the LU decomposition of the matrix A $(A=LU)$ and then use a linear recurrence solver component to perform the substitution phases $(Ly=b$ and $Ux=y)$. As another example, queries in data-base query languages are formed by composing operations such as "search" and "join."

If the component processors are implemented on chips, one way to compose them is to wire them together. This solution is inflexible because the components are dedicated to a particular problem and cannot be used for another problem. Another compositional scheme is to join the processors to a bus as "peripherals." This is more flexible since a processor can be used in different phases, but the bus becomes a bottleneck and time is wasted in interphase data movement.

Still another approach is to replace the dedicated processing elements with more general microprocessors and simply program the algorithmically specialized processing function. This solution is much more flexible because different components can use the same devices by changing programs, provided the interconnection pattern is the same. The bus bottleneck is eliminated. There is a loss in performance with this polymorphism, however, since circuit implementation of the primitive actions is replaced by the slower process of instruction execution.

But the main problem with this approach is that algorithmically specialized processors often use different interconnection structures (Figure 1). There is no guarantee that the consecutive phases of the computation can be done efficiently in place. For example, if we have an $n \times n$ mesh-connected microprocessor structure and want to find the maximum of n^2 elements stored one per processor, $2n - 1$ steps are necessary and sufficient to solve the problem. But a faster algorithmically specialized processor for this problem uses a tree interconnection pattern to find the solution in $2 \log n$ steps. For large n this is a benefit worth pursuing. Again, a bus can be introduced to link several differently connected multiprocessors, including mesh- and tree-connected multiprocessors. Data could be transferred when a change in the processor structure would be beneficial. But the bottleneck is quite serious; in the example, data has to be transferred at a rate proportional to $n^2/\log n$ words per step to make the

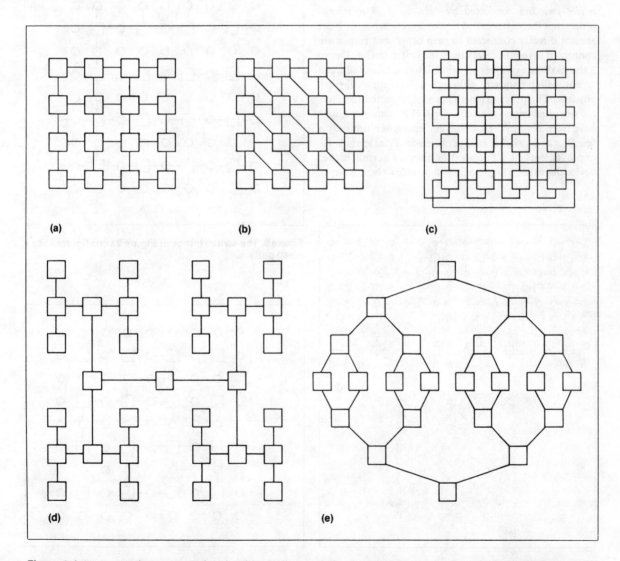

Figure 1. Interconnection patterns for algorithmically specialized processors: (a) mesh, used for dynamic programming[7]; (b) hexagonally connected mesh used for LU decomposition[2]; (c) torus used for transitive closure[7]; (d) binary tree used for sorting[4]; (e) double tree used for searching.[5]

COMPUTER

transfer worthwhile. What we need is a more polymorphic multiprocessor that does not compromise the benefits of VLSI technology.

The configurable, highly parallel, or CHiP computer is a multiprocessor architecture that provides a programmable interconnection structure integrated with the processing elements. Its objective is to provide the flexibility needed to compose general solutions while retaining the benefits of uniformity and locality that the algorithmically specialized processors exploit.

The CHiP architecture overview

The CHiP computer is a family of architectures each constructed from three components: a collection of homogeneous microprocessors, a switch lattice, and a controller. The switch lattice is the most important component and the main source of differences among family members. It is a regular structure formed from programmable switches connected by data paths. The microprocessors (hereafter called processing elements, or PEs) are not directly connected to each other, but rather are connected at regular intervals to the switch lattice. Figure 2 shows three examples of switch lattices. Generally, the layout will be square, although other geometries are possible. The perimeter switches are connected to external storage devices. A production CHiP computer might have from 2^8 to 2^{16} PEs. (With current technology only a few PEs and switches can be placed on a single chip. As improvements in fabrication technology permit higher device densities, a single chip will be able to host a larger region of the switch lattice. Moreover, as discussed below, the CHiP architecture is quite suitable for "wafer-level" fabrication.)

Each switch in the lattice contains local memory capable of storing several configuration settings. A configuration setting enables the switch to establish a direct, static connection between two or more of its incident data paths. (This is circuit switching rather than packet switching.) For example, we achieve a mesh interconnection pattern of the PEs for the lattice in Figure 2a by assigning north-south configuration settings to alternate switches in odd-numbered rows and east-west settings to switches in the odd-numbered columns. Figure 3 illustrates the configuration; Figure 4 gives the configuration settings of a binary tree.

The controller is responsible for loading the switch memory. (This task is performed via a separate intercon-

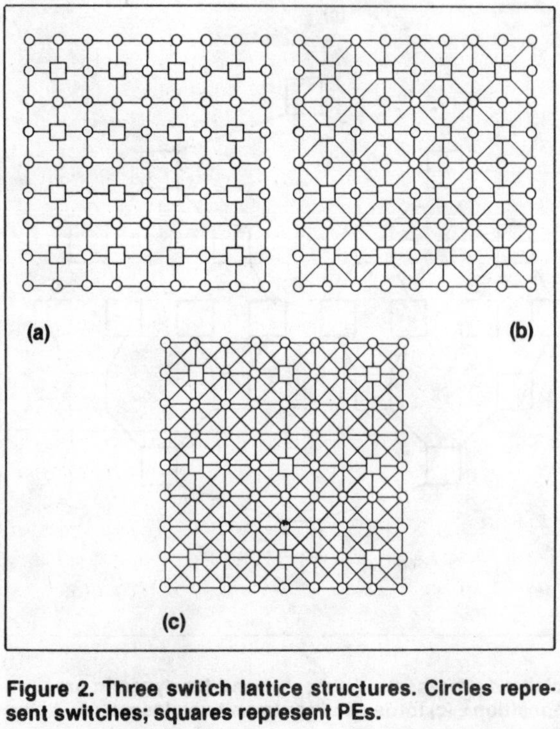

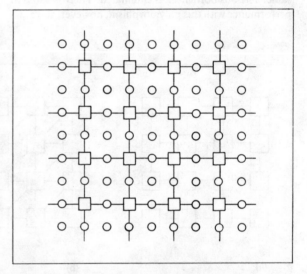

Figure 3. The switch lattice of Figure 2a configured into a mesh pattern.

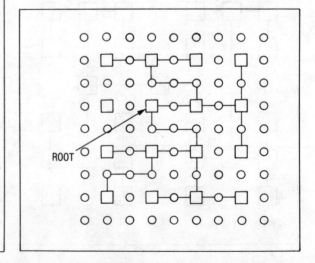

Figure 4. The switch lattice of Figure 2a configured into a binary tree.

![Figure 2 switch lattice structures showing three diagrams labeled (a), (b), and (c)]

Figure 2. Three switch lattice structures. Circles represent switches; squares represent PEs.

nection "skeleton.") The switch memory is loaded preparatory to processing and is performed in parallel with the PE program memory loading. Typically, program and switch settings for several phases can be loaded together. The chief requirement is that the local configuration settings for each phase's interconnection pattern be assigned to the same memory location in all switches. For example, in each switch, location 1 might be used to store the local configuration to implement a mesh pattern; location 2 might store the local configuration for the tree interconnection pattern, etc.

CHiP processing begins with the controller broadcasting a command to all switches to invoke a particular configuration setting. For example, suppose it is the setting stored at location 1 that implements a mesh pattern. With the entire structure interconnected into a mesh, the individual PEs synchronously execute the instructions stored in their local memory. PEs need not know to whom they are connected; they simply execute instructions such as READ EAST, and WRITE NORTHWEST. The configuration remains static. When a new phase of processing is to begin, the controller broadcasts a command to all switches to invoke a new configuration setting, for instance the one stored at location 2 implementing a tree. With the lattice thus restructured, the PEs resume processing, having taken only a single logical step in interphase structure reconfiguration.

A closer look at switches and lattices

The members of the CHiP computer family are distinguished by different characteristics of the switches and lattices.

Switches. It is convenient to think of switches as being defined by several parameters:

m—the number of wires entering a switch on one data path or data path width,

d—the degree or number of incident data paths,

c—the number of configuration settings that can be stored in a switch.

The value of m reflects the balance struck between parallel and serial data transmission. This balance will be influenced by several considerations, one of which is the limited number of pins on the package containing the chips of the CHiP lattice. Specifically, if a chip hosts a square region of the lattice containing n PEs, then the number of pins required is proportional to $m\sqrt{n}$.

The value of d will usually be 4, as in Figure 2a, or 8, as in Figure 2c. Figure 2b shows a mixed strategy that exploits the tendency of switches to be used in two different roles. Switches at the intersection of the vertical and horizontal switch corridors tend to perform most of the routing, while those interposed between two adjacent PEs act more like extended PE ports for selecting data paths from the "corridor buses." Specializing the degree of the switch to these activities reduces the number of bits required to specify a configuration setting and thus saves area.

The value of c is influenced by the number of configurations that may be needed for a multiphase computa-

tion and the number of bits required per setting. The latter number depends on the degree and the crossover capability of the switch.

Crossover capability is a property of switches and refers to the number of distinct data path groups that a switch can simultaneously connect. We speak of data path groups rather than data path pairs because fanout is permitted at a switch, allowing it to connect more than a pair of data paths. Crossover capability is specified by an integer g in the range 1 to $d/2$. Thus 1 indicates no crossover and $d/2$ is the maximum number of distinct paths intersecting at a degree d switch. Like the three parameters mentioned above, the crossover capability g is fixed at fabrication time.

The number of bits of storage needed for a switch is a modest dgc. This provides a bit for each direction of each crossover group of each configuration setting. This value can be reduced by providing for the loading of switch settings while the CHiP processor is executing. This quality, called asynchronous loading, permits a smaller value of c by taking advantage of two facts: algorithms often use configurations that differ in only a few places, and configurations often remain in effect long enough to prepare for future settings.

Lattices. From Figure 2 it is clear that lattices can differ in several ways. The PE degree, like the switch degree, is the number of incident data paths. Most algorithms of interest use PEs of degree eight or less. Larger degrees are probably not necessary since they can be achieved either by multiplexing data paths or by logically coupling processing elements (e.g., two degree-four PEs could be coupled to form a degree-six PE where one serves only as a buffer). The latter method leads to some loss in PE utilization, however.

We can call the number of switches that separate two adjacent PEs the corridor width, w. (See Figure 2c for a $w = 2$ lattice.) This is perhaps the most significant parameter of a lattice, since it influences the efficiency of PE utilization, the convenience of interconnection pattern embeddings, and the overhead required for the polymorphism.

To see the impact of corridor width, let us embrace graph embedding parlance and say that a switch lattice "hosts" a PE interconnection pattern. In theory, even the simplest lattice (like the one in Figure 2a) can host an arbitrary interconnection pattern, but to do so may require the PEs to be underutilized. There are two reasons for this: First, PEs may be coupled to achieve high PE degree, as mentioned at the beginning of this section. Second, and more important, adjacent PEs in the (logical) guest interconnection pattern may have to be assigned to widely spaced PEs in the hosting lattice (i.e., separated by unused PEs) in order to provide enough data paths for the edges. (Figure 5 shows the embedding of the complete bipartite graph, $K_{4,4}$, in the lattice of Figure 2c where the center column of PEs is unused.) Increasing corridor width improves processor utilization when complex interconnection patterns must be embedded because it provides more data paths per unit area.

How wide should corridors be? It depends on which interconnection patterns are likely to be hosted and how economically necessary it is to maximize PE utilization.

For most of the algorithmically specialized processors developed for VLSI implementation, a corridor width of two suffices to achieve optimal or near optimal PE utilization. However, to be sure of hosting all planar interconnection patterns of n nodes with reasonably complete processor utilization, a width proportional to $\log n$ suffices and may in fact be necessary.[9] To host patterns such as the shuffle-exchange graph efficiently will require even wider corridors; on the average w must be at least proportional to $n/\log n$.[10]

Selecting a corridor width is difficult, especially if it is a nonconstant width. The benefit, in some cases, is higher PE utilization; the cost is a loss of some locality (in all cases), more area overhead, and increased problems with pin limitations. Preliminary evidence indicates that $w \leq 4$ provides a reasonable cost/benefit trade-off, but further experimentation and analysis are required.[11]

Embedding an interconnection pattern

In addition to the conventional polymorphism derived from PE programming, we have provided for a second variety in the programmable switches. This requires interconnection pattern programming, i.e., specification of a global interconnection pattern. When viewed in a programming language context, the source program is a global interconnection pattern that a compiler translates into an object code of individual switch settings suitable for loading into the switches by the CHiP controller. Our concern here, however, is limited to one particular interconnection pattern: the complete binary tree. This example will illustrate the differences between embedding into the plane and embedding into the CHiP lattice.

The complete binary tree has $2^p - 1$ PEs, one at each node. One possible layout of this structure in the CHiP lattice is a direct translation of the hyper-H strategy[1] illustrated in Figure 1d. Figure 6 illustrates this embedding into the lattice of Figure 2a, and it is clear that many (asymptotically one half) of the PEs are unused in this naive approach. The problem is that although the hyper-H is an excellent embedding on plain silicon where the placement of PEs and data paths is arbitrary, CHiP lattice embeddings must conform to the prespecified PE and data path sites. As we shall see, this constraint is not onerous.

To illustrate an optimal embedding in terms of maximizing the use of PEs, let's assume that we have an $n \times n$ CHiP lattice where $n = 2^k$ for some integer k. This gives 2^{2k} PEs, so a binary tree of depth $2k$ fits with only one unused PE, since it has $2^{2k} - 1$ nodes. We'll call this unused PE a "spare."

We proceed inductively by pairing two embedded subtrees to form a new tree one level higher. For the basis of the induction it is convenient to use a three-node binary tree embedded with one spare in a 2×2 portion of the lattice. Pairing square subtree embeddings produces rectangles with sides in ratio 2:1. Pairing these rectangles yields squares again. In general, we pair two subtrees, each with $2^{2k} - 1$ nodes and a spare, to produce a new $2^{2k+1} - 1$ node tree in which one of the subtree spares becomes the root of the new tree and the other spare

becomes the spare of the new tree. The challenge is to place the spares at the proper sites for the next step in the induction.

If we adopt the strategy of the hyper-H embedding and locate the root at the center of the tree, it makes sense to place a spare at the middle of one side. Then, when this

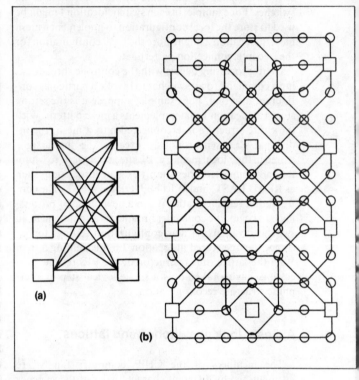

Figure 5. Graph $K_{4,4}$ shown in (a) is embedded into the lattice of Figure 2c using a switch with crossover value $g = 2$.

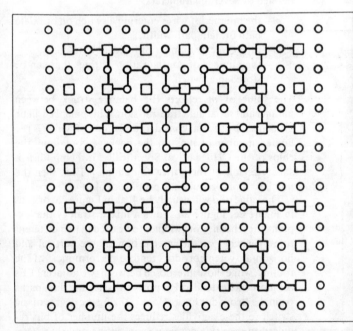

Figure 6. The hyper-H tree (Figure 1d) directly embedded into the switch lattice of Figure 2a; the switches are not shown.

tree is paired to form the next larger tree, there is a spare at the interface ready to become the new root. This will be in the center of the new tree as we intend. (Of course, since the sides always have an even number of PEs, "middle" here means adjacent to the midpoint of one side.) But we cannot pair two trees with their spares in the middle of one side because this would leave us with either a buried spare that is difficult to use when forming the next larger tree, or a spare on the perimeter at a site inappropriate for the embedding of the next larger tree (Figure 7).

The solution is to pair one subtree with a spare located at the middle of side with a subtree whose spare is at the corner. The spare in the middle becomes the root of the new tree, and the corner spare can be located (using reflection) to become either a middle spare or a corner spare of the new tree, depending on which is needed for the next inductive step. Thus, at each step in the induction we must use—and we can create—two types of embeddings: middles and corners (Figure 8). Notice that the basis tree, embedded in a 2×2 portion of the lattice, actually serves as both types.

Trees, of course, are planar; that is, they can be embedded in the plane without crossovers. But following the preceding algorithm with the lattice in Figure 2a makes it appear as though crossovers are required, at least during

the early stages of the embedding. It is possible, using basis elements of fifteen-node trees embedded in 4×4 square regions of the lattice, to achieve a completely planar embedding. A solution[12] is shown in Figure 9.

Solving a system of linear equations

In order to illustrate how the CHiP processor can be used to compose algorithms, we pose the problem of solving a system of linear equations, i.e., to solve $Ax=b$ for an $n \times n$ coefficient matrix A of bandwidth p and n vector b. We shall use two algorithmically specialized processors due to H. T. Kung and C. E. Leiserson as described in Mead and Conway.[1] The first is an LU-decomposition systolic array processor that factors A into lower and upper triangular matrices L and U.

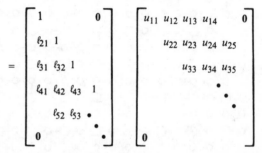

The second systolic processor solves a lower triangular linear system $Ly=b$ where L is the output from the decomposition step. (We call this the LTS solver.) The final result vector x can be found by solving $Ux=y$ where U is the upper triangular matrix from the first step and y is the vector output of the second step. By rewriting U as a lower triangular system, we can use another instance of the LTS solver. Our approach will be to compose these pieces into a harmonious process to solve the entire problem.

The first problem we must solve is the embedding of the Kung-Leiserson systolic processors. These algorithmically specialized processors are defined for $n \times n$ arrays of bandwidth p. (Figure 10 shows the LU-decompositon processor for a $p=7$ system. Figure 11 shows a suitable lower triangular system solver processor.) Since the LU-decomposition processor is hexagonally connected, it will be convenient to embed the processors into the lattice shown in Figure 2b. The obvious strategy is to connect the processors in such a way that the lower triangular output L of the decomposition step connects directly to the input of the lower triangular system solver. It is also obvious that these embeddings should be placed at the perimeter of the CHiP lattice so that matrix A and vector b can be

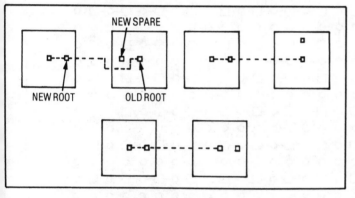

Figure 7. Paring subtrees using spares located at the midpoint of one side.

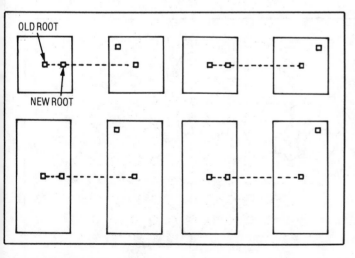

Figure 8. The formation of middle and corner embeddings using a middle and corner pair.

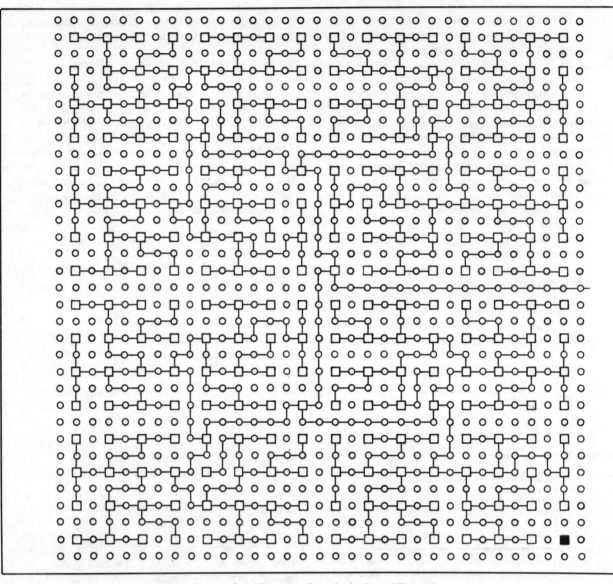

Figure 9. Planar embedding of a 255-node complete binary tree into the lattice of Figure 2a.

received from external storage. Figure 12 shows such an embedding where the PE labelings correspond to those given in Figures 10 and 11.

Several simple transformations have been employed to accomplish the embedding. The most noticeable is that the hexagonal structure has been slightly deformed to accommodate the rectangular CHiP lattice, and the LU-decomposition processor has been rotated clockwise 120 degrees. The constant inputs (0's and −1) that appear on the perimeter of the systolic array have been suppressed, since they can be generated internally to the PEs. The output wires carrying the L matrix result have been assigned to one of the available ports and routed to the inputs of the LTS solver. Finally, to embed the double channel between PEs of the LTS solver, we have routed data diagonally out of the north-east port into the south-east port. Notice that since the diagonal elements of L are all 1, they are not explicitly produced.

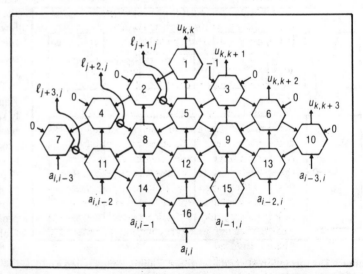

Figure 10. The Kung-Leiserson systolic array for LU-decomposition. Labelings indicate data paths. For timings, see Mead and Conway.[1]

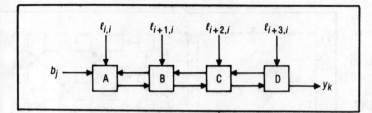

Figure 11. The Kung-Leiserson systolic LTS solver. Labelings indicate data paths for elements of L and b. For timings, see Mead and Conway.

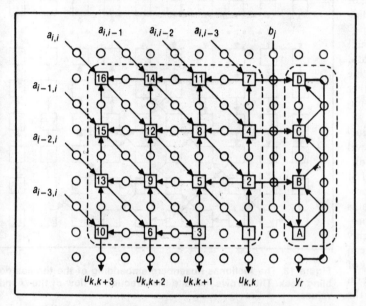

Figure 12. The embedding of the LU-decomposition processor and the LTS solver in the lattice of Figure 2b. Although the data paths are bidirectional, we have used arrows to emphasize the direction of data movement. PE labelings correspond to Figures 10 and 11.

The next problem is the rewriting of U as a lower triangular system suitable for input into another embedded LTS solver. We must wait until U has been entirely produced before performing this operation. So, rather than writing the elements of U to external storage as they are produced, we thread them through the lattice (assuming there is sufficient space to store them all). We also thread the y vector output from the LTS process along with U. Then, in the second phase of our algorithm, we can process the elements through another embedded LTS solver.

Perhaps the most elegant way to thread U and y through the lattice is to use the Aleliunas-Rosenberg graph embedding.[13] The scheme has the advantage of not requiring a large bundle of wires along the perimeter of the lattice when the threads double back. (Figure 13 illustrates the embedding required for doubling back.) As the U and y values are produced, they are passed from PE to PE. (They could be "concentrated" by storing several per PE.) When U and y are completely produced, the first phase is finished.

Between the first and second phases we make a minor reconfiguration. This reconfiguration would not have been necessary had the phase 1 configuration been

somewhat more clever, but as an example it would have been more confusing. The second configuration embeds the LTS solver into the fourth row of processors (Figure 14). The inputs to this group of processors come from reversing the flow direction of the threaded values from phase 1. Notice that this flow reversal has the effect of renumbering the matrix U in the lower triangular form appropriate for the LTS solver. The appropriate values of the y vector are also available at the proper locations. The outputs from the second phase emanate from the western port of processor$_{4,1}$. These are the values solving $Ax = b$.

To summarize, the system of linear equations $Ax = b$ is solved in two phases on the CHiP processor. In phase 1 an embedded LU-decomposition processor takes A as input and produces matrices L and U as output. The L output is immediately input to an LTS solver that also takes b as input and solves $Ly = b$. The vector y and the matrix U are threaded through the lattice. Phase 1 completes when A has been decomposed. In phase 2 another embedded LTS solver takes the threaded output from phase 1, by reversing its flow, and solves $Ux = y$.

Phase 2 makes scant use of parallelism; it runs in the same time as phase 1, and the data are already in the CHiP processor. The interphase reconfiguration is not essential, but there are algorithms to solve the phase 2 problem that employ configurability to make effective use of parallelism.[14] A complete development of the approach is not possible here, but the essential idea set forth by Chen, Kuck, and Sameh[15] is straightforward: A transformation on U enables us to decompose the matrix into blocks $B_1, \ldots, B_k$ whose product yields the result. Because the product operation is associative, the whole product can be formed by taking pairwise products in parallel, then pairwise products of the results, etc. By reconfiguring the threaded portion of the lattice using one of several rather complicated interconnection patterns that either implicitly or explicitly embed a tree, we can perform these pairwise products in parallel. The result is a faster parallel algorithm made possible by configurability.

Characteristics of our approach

The algorithmically specialized processors translate *mutatis mutandis* into programs for the CHiP computer. Thus, we have a ready supply of algorithms that can effectively use the parallel processor. Of course, all of these algorithms use one interconnection structure, and it is possible that improved algorithms might be found that exploit the availability of multiple interconnection structures.

Configurability provides both interphase and intraphase flexibility. This distinction, though not clearcut, tends to correlate with the use of pipelining. If a problem is solved by a sequence of phases where each completes before the next begins, we tend to use regular configurations that change at the completion of a phase (interphase). The whole lattice is in a mesh or tree pattern. For a series of pipelined algorithms that can be coupled together, we tend to form regions of the lattice dedicated to each algorithm with data paths interconnecting the regions. We refer to this as intraphase configurability because within one phase we interconnect several regular structures. Clearly, we need not change configurations to exploit the advantage of configurability.

Both types of configurability are useful in adapting to changes on problem size. For example, two separate small problems might operate concurrently on different regions of the CHiP processor using entirely different interconnection schemes. One pattern could change while the other remains fixed, by loading switches of the fixed region with two copies of the same configuration setting. Pipelined processors, whose size is usually a function of the input width, can be tailored to the right size at loading time.

Another consequence of configurability is its high fault tolerance. If an error is detected in a processor, data path, or switch, we can simply route around the offending device. For convenience, we might choose to leave other processors unused to square-up the lattice when it is important to have matching dimensions.

Perhaps the most intriguing consequence of configurability's fault tolerance is the possibility of wafer-level fabrication. That is, instead of dicing a wafer and discarding the faulty processor chips, we can leave a VLSI wafer whole and simply route around the unusable processors. (We could use the dicing corridors for data paths and switches.) For example, if a wafer contains 100 processor chips and yield characteristics indicate that roughly one third are faulty, then a wafer is acceptable if we can find an 8×8 sublattice that is functional. The mapping of the switches to host the 8×8 in the 100 could be done on the wafer by specially designed circuitry. Although the number of pins required for the wafer would be large, their number is proportional to the perimeter rather than the area. This actually reduces the total number of wires bonded.

By integrating programmable switches with the processing elements, the CHiP computer achieves a polymorphism of interconnection structure that also preserves locality. This enables us to compose algorithms that exploit different interconnection patterns. In addition to responding to problems of different sizes and characteristics, the flexibility of integrated switches provides substantial fault tolerance and permits wafer-level fabrication. ∎

References

1. Carver Mead and Lynn Conway, *Introduction to VLSI Systems,* Addison-Wesley, Reading, Mass., 1980.

2. H. T. Kung and C. E. Leiserson, "Systolic Arrays (for VLSI)," Technical Report CS-79-103, Carnegie-Mellon University, Pittsburg, Pa., Apr. 1979.

3. D. B. Gannon, "On Pipelining a Mesh-Connected Multiprocessor for Finite Element Problems by Nested Dissection," *Proc. Int'l Conf. Parallel Processing,* 1980, pp. 197-204.

4. Sally Browning, "The Tree Machine: A Highly Concurrent Programming Environment," PhD thesis, California Institute of Technology, Jan. 1980.

5. Jon L. Bentley and H. T. Kung, "A Tree Machine for Searching Problems," *Proc. Int'l Conf. Parallel Processing,* 1979, pp. 257-266.

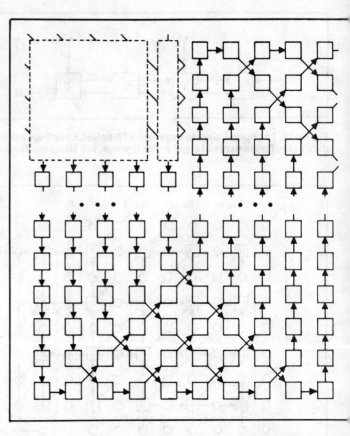

Figure 13. The Aleliunas-Rosenberg embedding of the threads doubling back. The arrows indicate the direction of flow of the U and values.

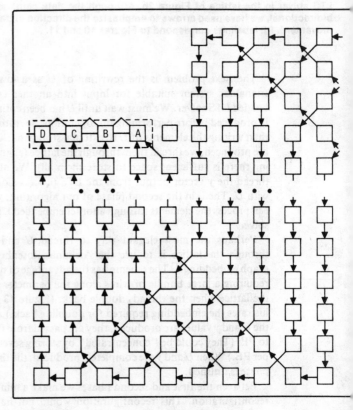

Figure 14. The simple phase 2 embedding.

6. L. Snyder, "Tree-Organized Processor Structure," Technical Report, Yale University, New Haven, Conn., Mar. 1980.

7. L. J. Guibas, H. T. Kung, and C. D. Thompson, "Direct VLSI Implementation of Combinatorial Algorithms," *Cal. Tech. Conf. VLSI*, Pasadena, Ca., Jan. 1979.

8. S. W. Song, "A Highly Concurrent Tree Machine for Data Base Applications," *Proc. Int'l Conf. Parallel Processing*, 1980, pp. 259-268.

9. L. G. Valiant, "University Considerations in VLSI Circuits," *IEEE Trans. Computers*, Vol. C-30, No. 2, Feb. 1981.

10. C. D. Thompson, "A Complexity Theory for VLSI," PhD thesis, Carnegie-Mellon University, Pittsburg, Pa., 1980.

11. L. Snyder, "Overview of the CHiP Computer," *VLSI 81*, John Gray (ed.), Academic Press, 1981, pp. 240-249.

12. L. Snyder, "Programming Processor Interconnection Structures," Department of Computer Sciences, TR-381, Purdue University, West Lafayette, Ind., 1981.

13. Romas Aleliunas and A. L. Rosenberg, "On Embedding Rectangular Grids into Square Grids," IBM Technical Report RC 8404, 1980.

14. D. B. Gannon and L. Snyder, "Linear Recurrence Algorithms for VLSI: The Configurable, Highly Parallel Approach," *Proc. Int'l Conf. Parallel Processing*, 1981, pp. 259-260.

15. S. C. Chen, D. J. Kuck, and H. H. Sameh, "Practical Parallel-Based Triangular System Solvers," *ACM TOMS*, Sept. 1978, pp. 270-277.

Acknowledgments

It is a great pleasure to thank Dennis Gannon for his encouragement and his assistance with the linear systems solving example. Janice Cuny's critical reading led to a simplification of the switch, and her insight is much appreciated. Thanks are due Paul McNabb who developed programs to produce the embedding of Figure 9. Finally, Robert Grafton, Leonard Haynes, and Richard Lau provided encouragement and support that is greatly appreciated.

The research described is part of the Blue CHiP Project. It is partially funded by the Office of Naval Research under Contract N00014-80-K-0816 and Contract N00014-81-K-0360, Special Research Opportunities Program Task SRO-100.

Lawrence Snyder is an associate professor of computer science at Purdue University. Formerly, he was associate professor of computer science at Yale and has been a visiting scholar at the University of Washington, Seattle, and visiting scientist at the IBM Watson Research Center, Yorktown Heights, NY. He has authored papers on process synchronization, data structures, parallel computation, VLSI, theory of graph embeddings, capability-based protection systems, and programming language semantics. In addition to serving on program committees for the Association for Computing Machinery's Symposium on the Theory of Computation, he has been guest editor and is now associate editor of the *Journal Computer and Systems Sciences*.

Snyder received the BA degree from the University of Iowa in mathematics and economics. In 1973 he received the PhD degree from Carnegie-Mellon University, Pittsburgh, Pa., in computer science.

The transputer

Colin Whitby-Strevens
INMOS Limited,
Whitefriars, Lewins Mead,
BRISTOL, BS1 2NP, UK

Abstract

The transputer is a programmable VLSI component with communication links for point-to-point connection to other transputers. Occam (*) is a language that enables a multi-transputer system to be described as a collection of processes that operate concurrently and communicate using message passing via named channels.

The INMOS transputer architecture is standardized at the level of the definition of occam (rather than at the level of the definition of an instruction set). The implementation of the first commercially available transputers is illustrated by describing the implementation of occam.

The paper concludes with outline examples of some applications.

1   Introduction

The transputer architecture has been developed to fulfil four main objectives:

> To create a commercial product range that sets new standards in ease of programming and ease of engineering.

> To provide the maximum performance to the user.

> To exploit future developments in VLSI technology within a compatible family.

> To create a programmable component that can be used to build systems with large numbers of concurrent computing elements.

VLSI currently permits 5-10 MIP processors to be manufactured in volume for low prices. There is therefore no economic barrier to the construction of very powerful computer systems containing many processing elements. The challenge is a technical one: how to engineer a system with, say, 1000 processors so as to make the inherent concurrency usable, and how to support the design of applications to take advantage of this amount of concurrency.

(*) occam is a trade mark of the INMOS Group of Companies

In the transputer architecture, the exploitation of a high degree of concurrency is made possible through a decentralized model of computation, in which local computation takes place on local data, and concurrent processes communicate by passing messages on point to point channels. The localized communications architecture also has substantial engineering advantages, described below.

An important design objective of occam and the transputer was to provide the same concurrent programming techniques both for a single transputer and for a network of transputers. Consequently, the features of occam were chosen to ensure an efficient distributed implementation on transputer systems. The concurrent processing mechanisms within the transputer were then designed to match.

The result is that a program ultimately intended for a network of transputers can be compiled and executed efficiently by a single computer used for program development. Once the logical behaviour of the program has been verified, the program may be configured for execution by a single transputer (low cost), or for execution by a network of transputers (high performance), or for a configuration representing a trade-off between these two extremes.

The choice of local processing and communications necessitates a significant change in programming concepts, and new algorithms need to be developed [4]. The study of various applications from this point of view is showing encouraging results ([15], [16], [17], [18], [19], [20], [21], [22]) and illustrative applications are given at the end of this paper.

2   Transputer architecture

2.1   Overview

The architecture of the transputer is defined by reference to occam. Occam provides the model of concurrency and communication for all transputer systems. Defining the architecture at this level leaves open the option of using different processor designs in different transputer products. This allows implementations which are optimized for different purposes. It also allows implementations to evolve with changes in technology, without compromising the standards established by the architecture.

A transputer contains memory, a processor and a number of standard point-to-point communication links which allow direct connection to other transputers. The processing capability may be general purpose, or may be optimized to a specific purpose. The on-chip memory may be extended off chip by a suitable interface.

A transputer may also have special purpose interfaces for connection to specific types of hardware. The separation of

Reprinted from *Proceedings of the 12th International Symposium on Computer Architecture*, 1985, pages 292-300. Copyright © 1985 by The Institute of Electrical and Electronics Engineers, Inc.

the transputer system interface from other interfaces (eg the memory interface) means that it is possible to optimize the various interfaces individually, simplifying their use and improving their performance.

A system is constructed from a collection of transputers which operate concurrently and communicate through the standard links. Occam formalizes the computational model. It enables such a system to be described as a collection of processes operating concurrently and communicating through named channels.

Transputers directly implement the occam model of a process. Internally, an individual transputer can behave like any occam process within its capability; in particular, it can implement internal concurrency by timesharing processes. Externally, a collection of processes may be configured for a network of transputers. Each transputer executes a component process, and occam channels are allocated to links, which directly implement occam message-passing.

2.2   Occam

Occam [1, 3, 4] enables a system to be described as a collection of concurrent processes, which communicate with each other and with peripheral devices through channels. Occam programs are built from three primitive processes:

```
v := e     assign expression e to variable v
c ! e      output expression e to channel c
c ? v      input from channel c to variable v
```

The primitive processes are combined to form constructs. Each construct is introduced by a keyword, followed by a list of the component processes:

```
SEQuential    components executed one after another
PARallel      components executed together
ALTernative   component first ready is executed
```

A construct is itself a process, and may be used as a component of another construct.

Conventional sequential programs can be expressed with variables and assignments, combined in sequential constructs. IF and WHILE constructs are also provided.

Concurrent programs can be expressed with channels, inputs and outputs, which are combined in parallel and alternative constructs.

Each occam channel provides a communication path between two concurrent processes. Communication is synchronized and takes place when both the inputting process and the outputting process are ready. The data to be output is then copied from the outputting process to the inputting process, and both processes continue.

An alternative process may be ready for input from any one of a number of channels. In this case, the input is taken from the channel which is first used for output by another process.

The choice of synchronized communication prevents the loss of data. The choice of unbuffered communication removes the need for any store to be associated with the channel. Copying data from the outputting process to the inputting process is clearly essential for communication between transputers, and it is easy to make copying within a machine fast by use of microcode.

2.2.1   Design correctness

It is necessary to ensure that systems built from transputers, possibly involving hundreds or thousands of concurrent devices, can be designed and programmed effectively.

The design of occam and the transputer architecture has followed two principles to help the designer increase his confidence that his design is correct: simplicity and formality.

Occam has been kept simple, with the aim of making it easy to learn, and easy to use [3].

Formal techniques become much more important when concurrency is involved, as techniques based on exhaustive testing are impracticable. Occam has been designed to have a formal semantics. The way that this was achieved was to define a set of formal properties that the language should possess. These take the form of a number of behaviour-preserving transformations that should be applicable to any occam program [12]. Many semantic issues in the design and development of the language were resolved by reference to this set of properties. Enforcing this discipline has enabled a formal semantics for the language to be developed [13], and has laid the basis for software engineering tools ranging from formal validation to program transformation.

Practical and immediate benefits have been that the language is very self-consistent (which makes life easier for the compiler writer and user alike), that the equivalence of concurrent algorithms can be studied, and that programs can be transformed to have greater or less decentralisation without changing their logical behaviour[4].

2.2.2   Real time

On an individual transputer, a parallel construct may be configured to prioritize its components, and an alternative construct may be configured to prioritize its inputs. A higher priority process always proceeds in preference to a lower priority one.

The equivalent of an interrupt (a high priority process being scheduled in order to respond to an external stimulus) is designed entirely in occam, as all input and output is formalized as channel communication. A high priority process may wait for the first of several different inputs to become ready by using the ALT construct.

A high priority process proceeds until it terminates or has to wait for a communication. A system can thus be designed to meet real-time constrains by designing each high priority process so that the amount of processor time it requires over a given period is bounded, thus placing a bound on the total time that a high priority process may have to wait for the cpu. In many cases, it may be possible to reason that two or more high priority processes will never conflict, and that the latency reduces to the time required to switch from a low priority process to a hgh priority process. Each transputer implementation places a bound on this time.

A global synchronized sense of time is not practicable, and not representative of real-world situations. There is therefore a local concept of time, each timer being implemented as an incrementing clock.

Logically, access to a timer is treated as an input. A delayed input may be used, which waits until the value of the clock reaches an appropriate value. A timer input may be used in an alternative construct. This can be used to provide timeout on a communication.

2.3 Inter-transputer links

A link between two transputers provides a pair of occam channels, one in each direction. A link between two transputers is implemented by connecting a link interface on one transputer to a link interface on the other transputer by two one-directional signal lines. Each signal line carries data and control information.

Communication through a link involves a simple protocol, which provides the synchronized communication of occam. The protocol provides for the transmission of an arbitrary sequence of bytes, which allows transputers of different wordlength to be connected.

Each message is transmitted as a sequence of single byte communications, requiring only the presence of a single byte buffer in the receiving transputer to ensure that no information is lost.

Each byte is transmitted as a start bit followed by a one bit followed by the eight data bits followed by a stop bit. After transmitting a data byte, the sender waits until an acknowledge is received; this consists of a start bit followed by a zero bit. The acknowledge signifies both that a process was able to receive the acknowledged byte, and that the receiving link is able to receive another byte. The sending process may proceed only after the acknowledge for the final byte of the message has been received.

Figure 1 Link protocol

Data packet

```
      0 1 2 3 4 5 6 7
┌───┬───┬─────────┬───┐
│ 1 │ 1 │ Data    │ 0 │
└───┴───┴─────────┴───┘
```

Acknowledge packet

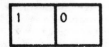

Data bytes and acknowledges are multiplexed down each signal line. An acknowledge is transmitted as soon as reception of a data byte starts (if there is a process waiting for it, and if there is room to buffer another one). Consequently transmission may be continuous, with no delays between data bytes.

Using point to point serial communications, rather than busses has a number of advantages:

> Board layout is much simplified.

> Communications bandwidth is increased, as many links in a system can operate concurrently.

> Devices of different word lengths and performance can be easily interconnected.

Transputers with different word lengths and performance will all interwork together, as will all future products, ensuring that systems can be readily upgraded as the technology advances. It is not necessary to downgrade the performance of a connected set of components to that of the slowest.

2.3.1 Electrical properties of links

The signals are TTL compatible and their range can be extended by inserting industry standard line drivers and receivers. The standard transmission rate is 10MHz, providing a maximum performance of about 1MByte/sec in each direction on each link.

The links are designed to make the engineering of transputer systems as easy as possible. Irrespective of internal performance, all transputers use a reference clock of 5MHz, and this is required only for approximate frequency information and not for phase. All future transputers will also use this same frequency. The low frequency was chosen to simplify the distribution of the clock in a large system and it is not neccesary for all transputers to be on the same clock, enabling interworking between independently designed systems. Thus, transputers can be interconnected just as easily as TTL gates - indeed, the constraint on the designer is just the same - he must not exceed the maximum capacitance.

3 Implementation

3.1 Instruction set requirements and overview

The first transputer product is the T424, a general purpose 32 bit machine with 4K bytes of on-chip memory (which can be extended with off chip memory) and four bi-directional communications links, which provide a total of 8Mbytes per second of communications bandwidth. This will shortly be followed by the T222, a 16 bit machine providing similar facilities.

The design objectives of the I1 instruction set and the processor for these first transputers were as follows:-

> To provide an efficient implementation of occam, so that the use of high level languages results in efficient use of silicon capability, and that highly concurrent programs execute with minimum overheads.

> To provide a simple and direct implementation of occam so that programs can be compiled simply and straightforwardly, and to ensure that there is no need to consider programming at a lower level than that defined architecturally.

> To provide word length independence, so that a program can be executed using processors of different word lengths without recompilation.

> To provide position independence, so that program and workspaces may be allocated anywhere in memory after compilation.

> To provide low latency response to communications with external devices.

The lowest level of programming transputers is to use occam (occam is equivalent in effectiveness to a conventional microprocessor's assembler). The instruction set, and the use of occam as its programming language, is therefore illustrated by describing the main usage of the various registers in the machine, and by giving typical instruction sequences for simple occam constructs. Note that it is not common practice to abbreviate the names of the instructions, or to use mnemonics. Transputer system designers have no general need to write down instruction sequences, and using full names aids readability of the examples.

3.2 The I1 instruction set

3.2.1 Performance note

Two important performance measures are the number of bytes to hold the program, and the speed of execution provided by an implementation. It should be realized that the speed of execution of individual instructions is less important than the speed with which key system functions are performed, bearing in mind the intended uses of the machine.

The I1 instruction set is designed specifically with a view to efficient and fast VLSI implementation, although various trade-offs of performance versus silicon area are still possible. On the first transputers, each instruction is executed in one or more processor cycles using one level microcode. The figures given in this paper assume that program and data are stored on chip. Extra cycles may be required if program and/or data are stored off chip, though the significance of this can be reduced to a low level with careful organisation of the application. Full details are given in [14].

It should be noted that although all transputers have an external clock cycling at 5 MHz, the internal speed is set as part of the manufacturing process. It is expected that the range of speeds of the first transputers will provide internal processor cycle rates of up to 20MHz.

The design of the first transputers carefully balances the costs of memory access and alu operation, and contains sufficient overlap to ensure a high degree of efficiency. Many of the instructions execute in a single cycle, and typical sequences of commonly used instructions can deliver a 15 MIPS execution rate.

3.2.2 Memory organization

The memory address space comprises a signed linear address space. The instruction architecture does not differentiate between on-chip and off-chip memory. This allows the application designer to have complete control over the placement of code and data to take advantage of the performance benefits of on-chip memory.

A byte in memory is identified by a single word value called a pointer. A pointer consists of two parts: a word address and a byte selector. The byte selector contains as many bits as are needed to identify a single byte within a word and occupies the least significant bits of the pointer. For example, in a 24 bit transputer the word address would occupy the 22 most significant bits and the byte selector the 2 least significant bits.

Special instructions, such as *load local pointer* and *word subscript*, are provided to construct and manipulate pointers. Pointer values are treated as signed integers, starting from the most negative integer and continuing, through zero, to the most positive integer. This enables the standard comparison functions to be used on pointer values in the same way that they are used on numerical values.

The addressing instructions provide access to items in data structures, using short sequences of single byte instructions, allowing the representation of data structure access to be independent of the word length of the processor.

3.2.3 Registers

The design of the transputer processor exploits the availability of fast on-chip memory by having only a small number of registers; six registers are used in the execution of a sequential process. In the internal organization of the processor, all internal registers and data paths are the wordlength number of bits wide. The small number of registers, together with the simplicity of the instruction set, enables the processor to have relatively simple (and fast) data paths and control logic.

The six registers are:

> The workspace pointer which points to an area of store where local variables are kept.

> The instruction pointer which points to the next instruction to be executed.

> The operand register which is used in the formation of instruction operands.

> The A, B and C registers which form an evaluation stack. The evaluation stack is used for expression evaluation, to hold the operands of scheduling and communication instructions, and to hold parameters of procedure calls.

Figure 2 Registers for sequential programming

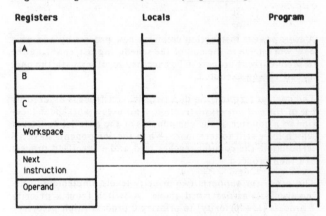

The evaluation stack removes the need for instructions to specify registers explicitly. Consequently, most of the executed operations (typically 80%) are encoded in a single byte. The I1 instruction set saves on time and area through not having to decode secondary control fields or register fields.

3.2.4 Support for concurrency

The processor provides efficient support for the occam model of concurrency and communication. It has a scheduler which enables any number of concurrent processes to be executed together, sharing the processor time. This removes the need for a software kernel. The processor does not need to support the dynamic allocation of storage as the occam compiler is able to perform the allocation of space to concurrent processes. There is also no need for the hardware to perform access checking on every memory reference, resulting in an overall improvement in performance.

At any time, a concurrent process may be

active   - being executed
           - on a list awaiting execution

inactive   - ready to input
           - ready to output
           - waiting until a specified time

The active processes waiting to be executed are held on a list. This is a linked list of process workspaces, implemented using two registers, one of which points to the first process on the list, the other to the last.

Figure 3 Concurrent processes

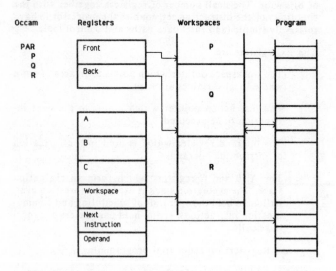

A *start process* instruction creates a new process by adding a new workspace to the end of the scheduling list, enabling the new concurrent process to be executed together with the ones already being executed.

The correct termination of a parallel construct is assured by use of the *end process* instruction. This uses a workspace location as a counter of the components of the parallel construct which have still to terminate. When the components have all terminated, the counter reaches zero, and a specified process can then proceed.

The processor supports two priority levels, implemented using two lists as described above. A switch from a priority 1 process (low priority) to priority 0 process (high priority), or vice versa, may occur when a process stops, when a channel becomes ready, or when a communication completes and causes a priority 0 process to become ready.

To allow a maximum latency figure to be calculated, the instructions which may take a long time to execute have been implemented to allow a switch during execution. Consequently, the maximum time taken to switch from priority 1 to priority 0 is 58 cycles (less than three microseconds with a 50ns processor cycle time). The switch from priority 0 to priority 1 only takes place when there is no priority 0 work available. The time taken for the switch is 17 cycles.

A context switch between processes, both executing at priority 1, occurs only at times when the evaluation stack has no useful contents, and therefore affects only the instruction pointer and the workspace pointer. With the need to save and restore registers at a minimum, the implementation of concurrency is very efficient.

3.2.5 Instruction format

All instructions have the same format. Each is one byte long, and is divided into two 4 bit parts. The four most significant bits of the byte are a function code, and the four least significant bits are a data value.

Figure 4 Instruction format

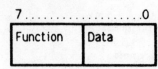

The use of a single instruction format requires only a simple decode mechanism in the processor, which reduces area and increases speed. The use of single byte instructions decouples the instruction format from the wordlength of the machine. In particular it avoids the commonly found problems concerned with aligning instructions on word boundaries.

Short instructions also improve the effectiveness of the instruction fetch mechanism, which in turn improves processor performance. The processor uses otherwise spare memory cycles to fetch instructions. As memory is word accessed, a 32 bit transputer will receive four instructions for every fetch. There are two words of instruction fetch buffer so that the processor rarely has to wait for an instruction fetch before proceeding (only on transfers of control if on-chip memory is used). Since the buffer is short, there is little time penalty when a jump instruction causes the buffer contents to be filled.

There is no instruction cache, as only rarely would such a cache reduce the number of processor cycles required. An on-chip cache incurs a significant cost in terms of chip area, as a cache requires several times the area of a simple memory to store the same amount of information. An off-chip cache complicates the external interface. Both require extra logic, even when aided by software (as in the IBM 801 [7]), which would be likely to slow down the overall speed of operation and use up even more chip area. The view is taken that the chip area is better spent on providing memory for the application.

3.2.6 Direct functions

The representation provides for sixteen functions, each encoded as a value in the range 0 to 15. Thirteen of these values are used to encode the most important functions performed by any computer. These include:

load constant	*load non local*
add constant	*store non local*
load local	*jump*
store local	*conditional jump*
load local pointer	
	call

The most common operations in a program are the loading of small literal values, and the loading and storing of one of a small number of variables. The *load constant* instruction enables values between 0 and 15 to be loaded onto the evaluation stack with a single byte instruction. The *load local* and *store local* instructions access locations in memory relative to the workspace pointer. The first 16 locations can be accessed using a single byte instruction.

The *load non local* and *store non local* instructions behave similarly, except that they access locations in memory relative to the A register. Compact sequences of these instructions allow efficient access to data structures, and provide for simple implementations of the static links or displays used in the implementation of block structured programming languages. This eliminates the need for complicated and difficult-to-use addressing modes.

In the following examples, **x** and **y** are assumed to be local variables allocated to offsets *x* and *y* respectively in the first sixteen words of workspace.

occam	instruction sequence	bytes	cycles
x := 0	*load constant 0*	1	1
	store local x	1	1
x := y	*load local y*	1	2
	store local x	1	1

In this example, **z** is assumed to have been declared externally to the **PROC** which contains this assignment statement. The compiler allocates a local workspace location, at offset *staticlink*, to hold the address of the workspace that contains the variable **z**.

occam	instruction sequence	bytes	cycles
z := 1	*load constant 1*	1	1
	load local staticlink	1	2
	store non local z	1	2

3.2.7 Prefixing functions

Two more of the function codes, prefix and negative prefix, are used to allow the operand of any instruction to be extended in length.

All instructions are executed by loading the four data bits into the least significant four bits of the operand register, which is then used as the the instruction's operand. All instructions except the prefixing instructions end by clearing the operand register, ready for the next instruction.

Figure 5 Use of operand register

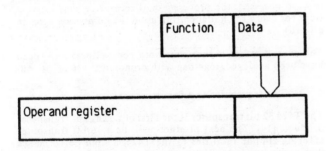

The *prefix* instruction loads its four data bits into the operand register, and then shifts the operand register up four places. The *negative prefix* instruction is similar, except that it complements the operand register before shifting it up. Consequently operands can be extended to any length up to the length of the operand register by a sequence of prefixing instructions. In particular, operands in the range -256 to 255 can be represented using one prefixing instruction.

The following example shows the instruction sequence for loading the hexadecimal constant #754 into the A register, and gives the contents of the O register and the A register after executing each instruction

	O register	A register
prefix #7	#7	?
prefix #5	#75	?
load constant #4	0	#754

The use of prefixing instructions has certain beneficial consequences. Firstly, they are decoded and executed in the same way as every other instruction, which simplifies and speeds instruction decoding. Secondly, they simplify language compilation, by providing a completely uniform way of allowing any instruction to take an operand of any size. Thirdly, they allow operands to be represented in a form which is independent of the processor wordlength.

Each prefixing instruction occupies one byte and takes one cycle to execute.

3.2.8 Indirect functions

The remaining function code, *operate*, causes its operand to be interpreted as an operation on the values held in the evaluation stack. For example, the plus operation adds the values of the A and B registers. The result is left in the A register, and C is copied into the B register.

The *operate* instruction allows up to 16 such operations to be encoded in a single byte instruction. However, the prefixing instructions can be used to extend the operand of an operate instruction just like any other.

The encoding of the indirect functions is chosen so that the most frequently occurring operations are represented without the use of a prefixing instruction. These include arithmetic, logical and comparison operations, together with the most frequently used control functions and register manipulation functions.

Less frequently occuring operations have encodings which require a single prefixing operation (the transputer instruction set is not large enough to require more than 512 operations to be encoded!).

3.2.9 Expression evaluation

Loading a value onto the evaluation stack pushes B into C, and A into B, before loading A. Storing a value from A, pops B into A and C into B.

The A, B and C registers are the sources and destinations for arithmetic and logical operations. For example, the *add* instruction adds the A and B registers, places the result in the A register, and copies C into B.

If there is insufficient room to evaluate an expression on the stack, then the compiler introduces the necessary temporary variables in the local workspace. However, expressions of such complexity are, in practice, rarely encountered. Three registers provide a good balance between code compactness and implementation complexity.

Single length signed and single length modulo arithmetic is directly supported. In addition, a quick unchecked multiply is provided, in which the time taken is proportional to the logarithm of the second operand. The performance of these instruction sequences compares favourably, in both space and time, to that achieved by more complex instruction sets. Where a more complex instruction set cannot achieve the same effect in a single instruction, the performance gain is significant.

occam	instruction sequence	bytes	cycles
x + 2	*load local x*	1	2
	add constant 2	1	1
(v + w)	* (y + z)		
	load local v	1	2
	load local w	1	2
	add	1	1
	load local y	1	2
	load local z	1	2
	add	1	1
	multiply	2	7+wordlength

3.2.10 Input and output

A channel provides a communication path between two processes. Channels between processes executing on the same transputer are implemented by single words in memory (internal channels); channels between processes executing on different transputers are implemented by point-to-point links (external channels).

As in the occam model, communication takes place when both the inputting and outputting processes are ready. Consequently, the process which first becomes ready must wait until the second one is also ready.

A process prepares for an input or an output by loading the evaluation stack with a pointer to a buffer, the identity of the channel, and the count of the number of bytes to be transferred. It then executes an *input message* or an *output message* instruction as appropriate.

The *input message* and *output message* instructions use the address of a channel to determine whether the channel is internal or external. This means that the same instruction sequence can be used for both internal and external channels, allowing a process to be written and compiled without knowledge of where its channels are connected. In particular, either an internal or an external channel can be used as the actual parameter for a channel parameter of a named process.

A communication primitive communicating a block of size n bytes requires only one byte of program, and on average the maximum of (24, 21+(8*n/wordlength)) cycles (including the scheduling overhead).

Instructions for enabling and disabling channels provide support for an implementation of alternative input without the use of polling.

3.3 Discussion

The requirements of the transputer indicate that a transputer processor should have a simple design. A transputer has a substantial amount of area given over to memory and communications, indeed a transputer can be thought of as a memory chip with a processor in one corner. In fact, the processor on the first transputers occupies about 25% of the available area.

It was clear that a simple processor could be constructed which would leave the majority of a chip area available for other purposes. The early RISC experiences [6, 7, 8, 9] lent further support to the evaluation that performance resulting from using a simple processor need not suffer.

Various projects, for example the IBM 801 [7] and MIPS [8], are willing to pay a price of software complexity in order to achieve implementation efficiency. However, the evidence of interpretive schemes for high level languages was that a simple instruction set could be designed which would lead to a better hardware/software relationship, and hence simplify the software as well. This would probably mean rejecting the strategy of compiling to a level best considered as microcode.

The justification for the use of multiple cycle instructions must be that the instructions well match the software requirements. In the transputer processor for the I1, repetitive operations, such as multiply, and block move, are implemented by microcode (with hardware assistance). The alternative RISC implementation [9] is to provide, for example, a single cycle multiply step, and for the software to compile the appropriate loop. The efficiency, in both code space and execution speed, resulting from the microcoded solution outweighs the cost of area and capacitance in the microcode ROM.

The I1 instruction set achieves word length independence, in that a program which manipulates bytes, words and truth values can be translated into an instruction sequence which behaves identically whatever the wordlength of the processor executing it (apart from overflow conditions resulting from word length dependencies). This results from the fact that the instruction size is independent of wordlength, the method of representing long operands as a sequence of prefixing instructions, and the memory addressing structure.

Workspaces are held in addressable memory, which the designer can choose to allocate on chip or off chip. Holding workspaces on chip forms a very effective alternative to the use of cache memory [11], the cost of which has already been discussed. A further advantage is that, unlike cache memory, rarely accessed data need not be brought on chip.

In general, a program needs much less store to hold it than an equivalent program in a conventional microprocessor. Since a program requires less store to represent it, less of the memory bandwidth is taken up with fetching instructions. As memory is word accessed, the processor will receive several instructions for every fetch (depending upon the number of bytes in a word).

The overall effect is thus that both compactness and speed have been achieved, together with economical use of silicon.

4   The transputer as a family

The T424 32 bit transputer is the first of a range of transputer products [14]. The next products will be a 16 bit transputer offering similar facilities to the T424, a high performance disk controller and a high performance graphics controller.

A transputer family device controller has the same organisation as a transputer, with the addition of special high speed control logic and interfaces. Device controllers are programmable, in occam, in the same way as transputers. This allows a designer to tailor the controller's function to his particular application.

4.1   A personal workstation

This section explores the design possibilities provided by the transputer architecture. The first step is the outline design of a personal workstation, which can be designed and built using functionally distributed transputers. One transputer, the applications processor, accepts the user's commands and carries out the appropriate processing, calling on two other transputers, which look after a disk system and a graphics display system respectively. Each of the latter two transputers and associated hardware can be replaced by transputer based device controllers as they become available.

Figure 6 Personal computer workstation

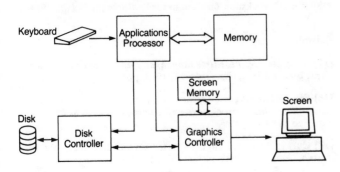

The transputers are connected together using the standard transputer communications links. The resulting system can be engineered onto a single card.

The architecture permits a number of variations on the implementation of the workstation to be made without major redesign.

For example, the disk controller can double as the applications processor, and the applications transputer removed completely. Alternatively, more processors can be added, and the occam processes redistributed to take advantage of the additional concurrency. Vastly more than 1 Mbyte of memory could be attached.

4.2 Transputer without external memory

This second example explores the design and use of a large amount of processing power based on a transputer with only link interfaces in, say, a 28 pin chip carrier.

Figure 7 Single board transputer system

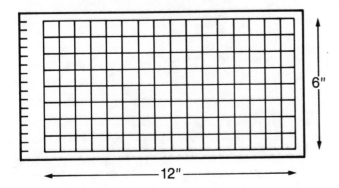

Figure 7 shows 128 transputers on a single printed circuit board. The board has 1/2Mbyte of fast static RAM and up to 1 GIPS (Giga Instruction Per Second) of processing power.

In this application, the board is used to provide high performance database searching. We assume that the database is partitioned, so that the most commonly accessed parts of a database can be placed in the transputer array.

The concept is shown in a simplified form in figure 8.

Figure 8 Concurrent database search

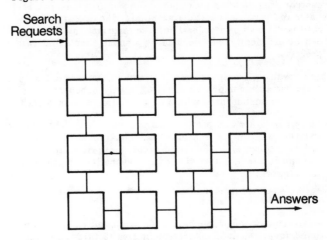

Here 16 transputers are connected into a square array with search requests input at one corner of the array, and answers being output from the other corner. Each transputer keeps a small part of the database in its local memory.

A small program in each transputer does the search. It can receive two sorts of input. A search request is forwarded to any connected transputer which has not yet received the request and simultaneously a search is made through the local data. The other sort of input is an answer from a transputer which has just searched its own local memory. This answer is merged with the answer generated from the local data and forwarded.

A simple performance analysis indicates the latency and throughput of this application on the 128 transputer board. Assume that each record is 16 bytes long, and that a search key is four bytes long. Each transputer can hold 200 records and the whole system can hold 25,000 records. For each transputer to search its own records against a request will take less than a millisecond.

The time taken to transmit a search request to each transputer in the array is proportional to the longest path across the system, in this case 24 links.

It takes about 6 microseconds to send a 4 byte message from one transputer to another. It will thus take about 150 microseconds to transmit a search request to the whole array, and about another 150 microseconds to transmit the answer. The whole search of 25,000 records will take less than 1.3 milliseconds.

However just as an individual transputer can be performing input, output and processing at the same time, so can the array. Requests can be pipelined through the system with a further request being input before the previous one has come out.

The size of the database partition can be increased by adding more boards. The search throughput is not adversely affected by this.

5 Conclusions

By taking an integrated approach to the design of a VLSI computer and a concurrent programming language it is possible to produce a new level of system building block which provides a very efficient implementation of the corresponding design formalism.

In particular, it is possible to support the use of the same concurrent programming techniques both within a single transputer and for a network of transputers. The concurrent processing features of a general purpose programming language can be efficiently implemented by a small, simple and fast processor.

The resulting transputer provides the unique concept of a programmable component enabling highly concurrent systems to be implemented within a formal design framework.

The architecture also provides a straight forward technology upgrade path. Future transputers can integrate more memory and more processors. The system architecture means that current and future products will be fully compatible and capable of interworking.

6   Acknowledgements

A large number of people have made invaluable contributions to the development of the transputer architecture and family of products, and these contributions are hereby collectively acknowledged. In particular, the original concept, and the drive to give it commercial reality, comes from Iann Barron, one of the founders of INMOS. David May designed occam, and led the team which developed the instruction set of the first products. Prof Tony Hoare, of Oxford University, has advised INMOS both generally on architecture and particularly on the basis for providing occam with a formal semantics.

7   References

[1] INMOS Limited, *Occam Programming Manual*, Prentice-Hall International, London, 1984.

[2] Barron, I.M. et al., *The Transputer*, Electronics, 17th Nov 1983, p 109.

[3] May, M.D., *OCCAM*, ACM SIGPLAN Notices vol 18-4 (Apr 1983) pp69-79.

[4] May, M.D. and Taylor, R.J.B., *OCCAM*, Microprocessors and Microsystems vol 8-2 (Mar/Apr 1984)

[5] May, M.D. and Shepherd, R, *Occam and the transputer*, IFIP WG10.3 workshop on Hardware Implementation of Concurrent Languages and Distributed Systems, North Holland (1984)

[6] Patterson, D.A and Sequin, C.H., *RISC I: A Reduced Instruction Set VLSI Computer*, Proc 8th International Symposium on Computer Architecture.

[7] Radin, G, *The 801 Minicomputer*, IBM Journal of Research and Development, Vol 27, No 3, pp237-246 (May 1983)

[8] Hennessy, J et al, *The MIPS machine*, Proceedings CompCon Spring 1982, IEEE, (February 1982)

[9] Colwell, R.P. et al, *Peering Through the RISC/CISC Fog: An Outline of Research*, Computer Architecture News, Vol 11, No 1 (March 1983)

[10] Patterson, D.A., *RISC Watch*, Computer Architecture News, Vol 12, No 1 (March 1984)

[11] Patterson, D.A. et al, *Architecture of a VLSI Instruction Cache for a RISC*, Proc 10th International Symposium on Computer Architecture, pp108-116, ACM (1983)

[12] Hoare, C.A.R. and Roscoe, A.W., *Programs as Executable Predicates*, Proc 1st Intl Conf on Fifth Generation Computer Systems, ICOT, 1984

[13] Roscoe, A.W., *Denotational Semantics for occam*, Proc NSF/SERC Workshop on Concurrency, Springer LNCS, 1984

[14] -, *IMS T424 transputer* data sheet,   INMOS Limited, Bristol, England

[15] Schindler, M. *Real-time languages speak to control applications*, Electronic design, July 21, 1983, pp105-120.

[16] Fay, D. *Working with occam: a program for generating display images*, Microprocessors and Microsystems, Vol 8. No 1, Jan/Feb 1984

[17] Curry, B. Jane, *Language based architecture eases system design*, Computer Design, jan 1984, pp127-136

[18] Taylor, R., *Graphics with the transputer*, Computer Graphics 84, 1984

[19] Pountain, R., *The transputer and its special language, occam*, Byte, Vol 9, No 8, Aug 1984

[20] Kerridge, J.M. and Simpson, D., *Three solutions for a robot arm controller using Pascal-Plus, occam, and Edison*, Software Practice and Experience, Vol 14, No 1, Jan 1984

[21] Harp, J.G. et al, *Signal processing with transputers (traps)*, Computer Physics Communications (in press)

[22] Broomhead, D.S. et al, *A practical comparison of the systolic and wavefront array processing architectures*, 2nd Proc IEEE Conf on Acoustics, Speech and Signal Processing (March 1985).

DICTIONARY MACHINES WITH A SMALL NUMBER OF PROCESSORS

Allan L. Fisher

Department of Computer Science
Carnegie-Mellon University
Pittsburgh, Pennsylvania 15213

Abstract

A number of tree-structured multiprocessor designs have been proposed for performing a group of dictionary operations (INSERT, DELETE, EXTRACTMIN, NEAR, etc.) on a set of keys. These designs typically use one processor for each key stored and operate with constant throughput, assuming unit time to communicate and compare keys. This assumption breaks down in applications with long keys. This paper describes a machine which uses a number of processors proportional to the maximum length of a key to achieve constant throughput, regardless of key length. This design has important practical advantages over the family of tree-structured machines, and demonstrates that processor-intensive VLSI structures are not always the best route to a high-performance system.

1. Introduction

The dictionary task can be loosely defined as the problem of maintaining a set of keys drawn from some ordered domain; often some indivisible piece of information, a record or pointer to a record, is associated with each key. Maintaining the key database consists of performing a series of update and query operations on its contents. A typical set of operations includes some subset of the following:

- INSERT: add a key to the database.

- DELETE: remove a key.

- FIND: determine whether a key belongs to the database (and return its associated information).

- EXTRACTMIN: remove and report the lowest key in the database.

- EXTRACTMAX: remove and report the highest key in the database. (Some data structures can support EXTRACTMIN or EXTRACTMAX, but not both simultaneously.)

- NEAR: report the stored key closest in the domain ordering to a specified query key.

The INSERT and DELETE operations come in two flavors: redundant and nonredundant. An insertion is redundant when the key being inserted already exists in the database; a deletion is redundant when the key being deleted does *not* exist. Allowing redundant operations is more natural in some applications than forbidding them (for example, a user might wish to insert a key without knowing or checking whether it already exists), but can cause difficulty in pipelined implementations.

A great number of useful computations can be cast in terms of the dictionary task. The simplest example is a symbol table (or dictionary), where only the INSERT, DELETE, and FIND operations are used. Another example is priority queues, which use INSERT and EXTRACTMIN (and EXTRACTMAX, if the queue is actually a deque). A median filtering algorithm could use INSERT,

DELETE, and "EXTRACTMIDDLE", which can be implemented by using the other EXTRACT operations on a bisected database. Pattern matching systems might use INSERT, DELETE, and NEAR.

In general, the best implementation of the dictionary operations for a particular application will depend on the number and size of the keys to be stored, on the particular set of operations to be performed, and on the cost/performance goals of the system. This paper first reviews a few serial algorithms for some versions of the dictionary problem. It then surveys a family of tree-structured algorithmic machines[1, 4, 7, 9] which have been proposed as high-performance solutions, along with a tree algorithm which runs on a linear array of processors[2]. Finally, it proposes a new parallel algorithm, based on a linear array of a small number of processors with large memories, which has important advantages over the tree architectures and is preferable to the previous linear architecture in many cases.

A note on notation: Following Ottmann *et al.*[7], the variable n is used to denote the number of keys stored in the database at a particular time, and N to denote the maximum number of keys that may be stored. Two types of time complexity are considered: *latency*, the time elapsed between the initiation and completion of a query, and *pipeline period*, the minimum time between the initiation of two separate operations. The pipeline period of an algorithm is inversely proportional to its throughput. We will also distinguish, in complexity expressions, between *key* complexity (storing or operating on entire keys) and *symbol* complexity (dealing with symbols drawn from a finite alphabet). This distinction is needed to compare algorithms which treat keys as unit objects with those that treat keys as strings of symbols. Complexity functions in each case are written $O_k(f)$ and $O_s(f)$, respectively. The function "log" represents the base 2 logarithm.

2. Previous solutions

This section briefly reviews two types of realizations of the dictionary task: serial algorithms and parallel algorithmic architectures. Four serial algorithms are illustrative in this context. Each is informally summarized here; details can be found in Knuth[3]. Also briefly surveyed are a family of tree-structured parallel architectures and a linearly structured architecture; more details on the tree machines are given in Appendix I.

Hashing

Hashing algorithms store keys in a table, with indices derived from the keys by a random or pseudorandom hash function. Collisions are resolved by one of a number of methods. Assuming a uniform distribution of hash values and a table that is not too full, the expected time to perform INSERT, DELETE, or FIND is $O_k(1)$, though this grows in the worst case to $O_k(n)$. The algorithm uses $O_k(N)$ space, though this can be reduced to $O_k(n)$ at the cost of

Reprinted from *Proceedings of the 11th International Symposium on Computer Architecture*, 1984, pages 151-156. Copyright © 1984 by The Institute of Electrical and Electronics Engineers, Inc.

occasional reorganization by doubling the size of the table and rehashing each key when the table grows too full.

Heaps

A heap is a binary tree of keys organized so that all of a key's descendants have higher values. The worst case time to execute INSERT or EXTRACTMIN is $O_k(\log n)$, and the algorithm uses $O_k(n)$ space. Because of the weak ordering conditions, the tree is always balanced and can be implemented without pointers.

Balanced trees

In this scheme, a binary tree of keys is maintained so that all of a key's left-hand descendants have smaller values while all of its right-hand descendants have larger values. The tree is kept balanced by rotation operations. All of the dictionary operations can be performed in $O_k(\log n)$ time. Two auxiliary pointers are associated with each key.

Tries [radix trees]

The name "trie" is derived from "information re*trie*val"; because its pronunciation either sounds like "tree" or is nonintuitive, the term "radix tree" is used here instead. Nodes in a radix tree represent prefixes of keys in the database, represented as strings over some alphabet Σ. The root of the tree is the null string, and a node representing substring α has a descendant corresponding to $s \in \Sigma$ if αs is also a substring of a key in the database. Figure 1 shows a small radix tree storing six words. All of the dictionary operations can be performed in $O_s(l)$ time, where l is the length of the key specified or retrieved.

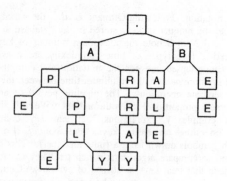

Figure 1: Radix tree

Since its speed is independent of the size of the database, this method is faster than balanced trees for large collections of keys. On the other hand, radix trees require much more space for pointers; one pointer is needed for each prefix, and a factor of $|\Sigma|$ may be wasted in the worst case if nodes are represented as tables. This space penalty is ameliorated by prefix sharing, since each prefix in the database occurs just once. Nodes in the tree where there is no branching offer additional opportunities for compression. Knuth mentions a few transformations that can be applied to reduce memory requirements, and many more can be imagined.

Tree architectures

At least four different papers in the literature[1, 4, 7, 9] propose tree-structured architectures for the implementation of dictionary operations. While they differ in detail, they all share some basic principles. A machine is a rooted, balanced binary tree of processors, each processor holding one or a few keys. Dictionary operations are broadcast from the root, and are pipelined along the depth of the tree. Because of this pipelining, the tree structures have pipeline period $O_k(1)$, independent of n.

All of these architectures are processor-profligate in the sense that they use $\Theta(N)$ processors to achieve only an $O(\log n)$ throughput improvement over the serial balanced tree algorithm. Asymptotically, this is an improvement, at least where n is not too much smaller than N; the algorithm runs faster, and the hardware cost differs only by the constant factor of one processor for every one to three keys. In the real world, though, if n keys fit in primary storage, $\log n$ is not likely to be much larger than 25 or 30, and a processor takes many more transistors to build than a few bits of memory. Another issue is that for applications where duplicate keys are not allowed or are stored as one key with a count, the length of a key in bits is at least $\log n$, and in most cases is several times larger. Thus it may be possible to break up the processing of a key over several processors, and achieve a factor of at least $\log n$ in parallelism along the length of a key.

In defense of the tree architectures, it should be noted that they offer capabilities which go beyond dictionary operations, and which require $O_k(n)$ time on a uniprocessor. These capabilities include parallel modifications of stored keys and NEAR-style searches where the distance measure is not constrained by the key ordering. Although most of the papers cited do not mention the possibility of using their designs for anything other than dictionary tasks, they are more likely to be useful in solving more difficult problems.

An $O(\log N)$-processor architecture

The many processor − small speedup problem of the tree architectures has been previously addressed by Carey and Thompson[2] They propose a linear array of $O(\log N)$ processors, each of which stores one level of a special type of B-tree. Keys are stored at the leaves of the tree, and interior nodes hold keys which direct a search to one of two, three, or four descendants. The tree is balanced by splitting full nodes and merging nearly empty nodes. The algorithms for all of the dictionary operations can be pipelined with period $O_k(1)$.

3. A level-parallel radix tree algorithm

We have noted two undesirable features of the tree machine designs. The first is that they use $O(N)$ processors to achieve an $O(\log n)$ speedup over uniprocessors. The second is that, by treating keys as indivisible units, they do not do as good a job as possible on long keys. Carey and Thompson's design is also subject to the second criticism. This section proposes a parallel implementation of radix trees that addresses these problems. It first describes a basic version of the algorithm, along with a "radix machine" on which it runs, and then indicates some cost-performance tradeoffs and efficiency tunings. This is followed by a comparison with previous designs.

3.1. The algorithm and the radix machine

The central idea of the parallel radix tree algorithm is to attach a processor to each level of the tree, starting with the children of the root (i. e., the first symbols of the keys). A machine to execute the algorithm has L processors, where L is the length of the longest key. Radix tree nodes representing prefixes of length k are stored in a local memory attached to processor k. The processors are connected in a linear array in consecutive order. The symbols of each input key arrive at the appropriate processors from the side of the array, skewed one cycle apart so that the processing of a key is pipelined along the array. Output keys are produced in a similar fashion. This organization is sketched in Figure 2, which shows several input keys (read diagonally) approaching from the right. Input symbols which are vertically aligned will enter their respective processors at the same time.

The data structure is just as specified above for the serial algorithm, except that a descendant count, the number of keys beginning with a particular prefix, is added to each node. This count is

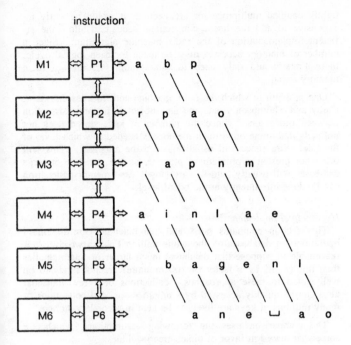

instruction

Figure 2: Structure of a radix machine

updated along the length of each string that is inserted, deleted, or extracted. The count is used to allow pipelining of operations that remove keys from the database.

The procedures for carrying out each of the operations are similar to the serial case, except for some changes that must be made to accommodate pipelining. If redundant INSERTs or DELETEs are not allowed, then every operation proceeds from root to leaf. DELETEs and EXTRACTs free nodes as they become empty, and INSERTs allocate new nodes as necessary.

If redundant operations are allowed, a scheme similar to that used by Atallah and Kosaraju is employed. In this approach, insertions are performed as if nonredundant, and if necessary a correction pass is performed from the bottom to the top of the tree to decrement spuriously incremented counters. Deletions are assumed to be redundant, and no action is taken on the trip down the tree. If the deletion turns out to be valid, an upward pass is taken which performs the appropriate decrementing of counters and freeing of nodes. Upward passes which begin in processors other than the last are delayed so that a "round trip" always takes $2L$ cycles; thus at most one upward pass is active in a single processor at any time. Note that the information necessary for upward trips, except for a single bit traveling upward indicating redundancy or nonredundancy, can be stored in a small ring buffer at each processor.

This scheme limits the pipelining of operations in the following way. An EXTRACT or a NEAR following within $2L$ cycles of a redundant INSERT or nonredundant DELETE can be "fooled" down the wrong path by counts which are erroneously high. An EXTRACT is on the wrong path if it is at a node with only one possible suffix, and that suffix is about to be deleted by a correction pass which is delayed or moving upward. If that is the case, the EXTRACT operation will delete nodes as it moves downward, and the correction pass will delete nodes as it moves upward. When they meet, the correction pass will stop, since the EXTRACT has already done its work higher up in the tree, and the EXTRACT will report an error. In the case of a NEAR operation, the correction phase will proceed undisturbed, and the NEAR will report failure. Thus redundant operations, while restricting pipelining in this sense, will not destroy any information in the database. It should also be noted that, especially in large databases, the probability of a failed EXTRACT or NEAR will usually be very low.

In summary: a radix machine uses L processors, each with memory capacity for at most N radix tree nodes. It accepts one operation per cycle, and has a latency of L cycles for all operations returning an answer. This constitutes linear speedup over the serial algorithm. Redundant operations can be performed, with the restriction mentioned above.

3.2. Tradeoffs and tuning

This basic algorithm admits a large number of modifications in the interest of memory savings or speed enhancements. Some of the variations on the serial algorithm can be used, such as the choice between implementing nodes as tables or linked lists, or the possibility of storing keys with their component symbols reversed. This section mentions a few other possibilities; many more are possible, especially given some knowledge of the statistics of the keys to be used.

A fundamental tradeoff is based on the size of the alphabet. If the keys are expressed in binary, more processors will be used than if the alphabet is larger, and more pointers will be used per key. On the other hand, this approach speeds the EXTRACT and NEAR operations, and will cut down on the average number of empty pointers in a node, possibly resulting in a net savings in hardware. In general, the radix can be tuned according to key statistics and implementation technology.

More tuning can be done by small specializations of the data structure. For example, special types of nodes can be used where there is only one descendant, saving on unused pointer space while keeping an efficient table structure for nodes with multiple descendants. In addition, only the first single-descendant node in a chain needs to keep a count, if interprocessor bandwidth is sufficient to carry a count downwards. An example of the power of these techniques is their application to large databases of English words, where they typically achieve a factor of four to five in memory compression (see Appendix II).

Another opportunity for speed improvement is related to bandwidth between processors and their local memories, which will probably be the speed bottleneck for large databases. Memory transfers to and from the processor can be avoided by on-memory-board intelligence. In the case where nodes are implemented as linked lists, a list-searching unit might be added. Where nodes are implemented as tables, a "find first one-bit" device similar to a priority encoder could be used along with a small, specialized occupancy memory to quickly find the appropriate child in EXTRACT or NEAR searches.

3.3. Comparison with previous architectures

This section argues that, for most dictionary tasks of practical interest, the radix machines described above are more appropriate than tree machines. In many cases, they are also superior to the design of Carey and Thompson. The first part of this argument is given in terms of trends and rough comparisons of cost and performance. The second part consists of a description of hypothetical implementations of the radix machine and a tree machine. Carey and Thompson's scheme is omitted from this comparison, as its difference in cost and performance from the radix machine is very sensitive to the assumptions made, and a specific comparison made at this level of detail cannot be very informative. An asymptotic counterpart of this comparison is given in Appendix III.

Comparisons

The different possibilities for the implementation of dictionary operations can be compared in terms of hardware cost and execution speed. The radix machine and the Carey-Thompson machine have roughly similar hardware costs; they use a small number of processors and a large amount of memory. The radix machine may tend to use more memory, depending on node packing density, alphabet size, and key length; on the other hand, prefix sharing will tend to reduce memory requirements. Which system uses less hardware will depend on the characteristics of the keys to be stored.

On the other hand, the hardware cost comparison with tree machines boils down to one between a 1) single processor and $O(N)$ nodes in memory, each holding some number of pointers, and 2) $\Theta(N)$ small processors, each holding a few keys. Assuming a reasonable degree of complexity in a processor, and given current relative densities for memory and processing in, for example, MOS technology, there are very few cases where a radix machine is not significantly cheaper to build than a tree machine. The discussion below describes a pair of hypothetical implementations which support this point.

A comparison of the speeds of the different approaches hinges on the length of a key. If keys are small enough to be handled in a primitive operation of the machine in question, radix machines and Carey-Thompson machines should have roughly comparable performance. Tree machines may have a performance edge, since they will not need to access large memories and they have slightly simpler data structures. They will also have long wires, though (see Appendix III), so interprocessor communication delays may dull that edge in large machines.

The picture changes, however, when keys are significantly longer than the native word size of the machine. While a radix machine approach can maintain constant throughput by using more processors for longer keys, the other types of machines must simply serialize the communication and handling of keys. Their performance will therefore degrade in proportion to the length of the keys stored. This effect may, in fact, reduce the speedup that these approaches gain over a uniprocessor balanced tree algorithm. If the number of keys is small compared to the number of possible keys, a search will usually examine only a few symbols at each node until it reaches the bottom of the tree, since it will usually find a mismatch very quickly. Thus the time for a serial implementation to perform an operation may not increase in strict proportion to L. The tree machines and the Carey-Thompson machine, on the other hand, are limited by the need to transfer entire keys between processors and by the need to perform a full-length comparison in at least one node in the tree for each search. Because of this effect, it is even possible that a sparse set of keys could cause the Carey-Thompson and tree machines to run slower than a serial algorithm with a simpler inner loop.

Beyond the sheer cost of hardware and the long-key issue, the radix machine has several other advantages, which are shared by the Carey-Thompson machine. First, off-the-shelf memory chips and bit-slice processor components can be used instead of custom chips. Besides avoiding the cost of custom LSI design, this allows the use of technologies which have been highly optimized for different goals: the memory technology for density, and the processor technology for speed. Custom tree processors are unlikely to be simultaneously dense and fast.

Second, because each processor can be more expensive than when a million of them are used, processors can be much more flexible and powerful. Most of the tradeoffs and performance tunings mentioned in the previous section can be made without hardware modification. The dictionary operations can be modified and subtle variations introduced. None of this is feasible with a tree processor whose control circuitry needs to be as simple as possible.

Finally, a radix machine is not as "single-purpose" as a binary tree dictionary machine. Since the processors can be fairly complex, the machine could actually be a general-purpose linearly connected multiprocessor. Such a machine could be extremely useful in the performance of many regular-structured computations, especially systolic algorithms. Conversely, given any general-purpose,

tightly coupled multiprocessor architecture, it would be fairly inexpensive to add the linear connections needed to allow the efficient implementation of the radix machine algorithm. Since a number of memory accesses must be made for each logical cycle, these links would only need to run at some fraction of local memory speed.

One problem to which the radix machine and, to a lesser extent, Carey and Thompson's machine are subject is memory allocation between processors. Since the number of keys stored does not uniquely determine how much memory is needed at which level of the tree, extra space will usually need to be allocated. This will often not present a problem in practice, as the statistics of large databases will usually tend to vary slowly, and memory allocation can be done infrequently at the board level.

Hypothetical implementations

This section compares radix and tree machines for dictionary operations on databases of about one million English words. It is reasonable to suppose that databases much larger or much smaller than this (*i. e.*, by a factor of 100 or more) are not likely to be well suited to these approaches: collections of a few thousand keys can be quickly accessed by a uniprocessor, and collections of many millions of keys are likely to be kept in secondary storage.

The comparison uses the following assumptions, which are somewhat biased in favor of binary tree machines:

- Keys are represented as strings of six-bit bytes. This is well-suited to alphabetic data, and will help the tree machine to be decomposed onto low-pinout chips. The maximum key length allowed is 16 bytes.

- The tree machine considered is Somani and Agarwal's, which requires the smallest amount of internode I/O among the pure binary tree machines and wastes the fewest processors among the machines performing redundant operations. Since COMPRESS operations need not, in fact, be done in every cycle, they are not counted here. If Somani and Agarwal's scheme were followed exactly, the implementation described here would run twice as slow.

- A tree processor (containing key registers, three bidirectional ports, an ALU, and a relatively complex controller) occupies one mm^2 of chip area. A single chip, organized according to a tree decomposition scheme proposed by Leiserson[5], holds 32 processors and four off-chip ports and fits in a 28-pin DIP. (This density is several years from feasibility, and it is questionable whether the four pins left will suffice for power, synchronization, and control.)

- Circuit boards for both machines hold 100 28-pin DIPS.

- The radix machine is built using 256K-bit memory chips. Memory boards use 25 chips for peripheral circuitry. A memory board thus holds 75 × 256K % 6 bytes, more than 3 MB. For simplicity, 3 MB is assumed.

- A processor board holds a processor and .5 MB of memory.

- The memory cycle time for the radix machine is 500 ns.

- Cycle time for the tree machine, dominated by the time to drive signals between boards, is 250ns.

Given these assumptions, the binary tree machine needs about 30,000 chips and hence 300 boards. Since each key step potentially requires transmitting a key to and from the parent node, at least 32 machine cycles, or 8 μs, are needed per operation. Based on statistics gathered from several large dictionaries of English words (see Appendix II), the radix machine (using a special representation for nodes with only one successor) would need 16 processor boards and 26 extra memory boards, for a total of 42. Especially since 25 chips on the memory boards is enough to build in some intelligence, it is reasonable to assume that one logical cycle can be carried out within 16 memory cycles, or 8 μs, thus achieving the same performance as the tree machine with about 14% of the hardware cost. Appendix II further indicates that a tree machine with *any* set of one million 16-byte keys will require less than 40% as much hardware as a million-node tree machine.

4. Conclusions

The discussions above show that, in most practical cases, a radix machine with a small number of processors is preferable to a tree machine for rapid execution of dictionary tasks. In addition to lower hardware cost and higher speed for longer keys, the radix machine has practical advantages of implementability, flexibility, and generality. Where keys are relatively short and their statistics cause poor utilization of a radix machine's memory, Carey and Thompson's design may be preferable. Tree machines can be expected to be of more value in applications where a query or update requires $O_k(n)$ time on a uniprocessor.

More generally, this example serves to show that VLSI architectures with large numbers of processors are not always the best approach to constructing high-performance systems. Especially where asymptotic performance gains are small and the asymptotic growth in processor count is large, architectures with fewer processors and more memory may be preferable.

Acknowledgments

I thank H.T. Kung for insightful criticism of the presentation.

This research was supported in part by the Defense Advanced Research Projects Agency (DoD), ARPA Order No. 3597, monitored by the Air Force Avionics Laboratory under Contract F33615-81-K-1539, and in part by an IBM graduate fellowship.

Appendix I. Tree machines

A very straightforward architecture implementing some of the dictionary operations is Kung and Leiserson's systolic priority queue[4], which uses a linear array of N processors, each storing one key, to perform INSERT and EXTRACTMIN operations. Each of these operations is performed with $O_k(1)$ period and latency. Leiserson notes that this scheme can be extended (by folding the array in half) to include the EXTRACTMAX operation, maintaining the same performance. In fact, the DELETE, FIND, and NEAR operations can also be added, although the latter two have $O_k(n)$ response time. Insertions and deletions may be redundant.

In the same paper, Leiserson also gives a binary tree architecture (again, designed only as a priority queue) that can support all of the dictionary operations, barring redundancy, with $O_k(1)$ pipeline period. The EXTRACTMIN operation has latency $O_k(1)$, and the other value-returning operations have latency $O_k(\log N)$. If a DELETE is redundant, a valid key can be destroyed; if an INSERT is redundant, a hole in the data structure is created which wastes a processor. It might be noted that the folding trick mentioned above can bring the latency for EXTRACTMAX down to $O_k(1)$.

Ottman et al.[7] give a tree machine design whose topology is actually an X-tree, where all of the nodes on one level of the tree are strung together in a row. This feature makes implementation less convenient. Their design cuts Leiserson's $\log N$ latencies down to $\log n$. This design also supports redundant insertions and deletions with the use of COMPRESS operations which eliminate holes in the data structure. The cost of this flexibility is that $O(n)$ holes may

exist at any time, wasting that many processors.

Atallah and Kosaraju[1] describe an improved design that has all of the properties of the previous one except that it supports EXTRACTMIN with $O_k(1)$ latency and has a pure binary tree structure. This design still suffers from the wasted processor problem.

Most recently, Somani and Agarwal[9] have proposed a tree-structured machine in which the keys are unordered, which simplifies the algorithm in some respects. It also allows a scheme for handling redundant operations in which only $\log n$ processors can be wasted. Their method of keeping the tree balanced, however, does not lend itself to modular implementation. Inserted keys are added at the bottom of the tree across its breadth, rather than on one side, as in some of the other machines. As a result, the machine can be conveniently enlarged only by factors of two. The other machines can have all of the leaves at the deepest level arranged on one side of the tree. Such trees, if decomposed onto chips according to Leiserson's scheme[5], may have any number of processors in the bottom level of the tree which is a multiple of the number of leaf cells on a chip.

Table 1 summarizes the latencies and some other properties of these machines. XMIN and XMAX abbreviate EXTRACTMIN and EXTRACTMAX, and the machines are listed by first author.

Table 1: Tree machine latencies

machine	FIND	XMIN	XMAX	*comments*
Leiserson	$\log N$	1	$\log N$	redundant INSERT/DELETE corrupts database.
Ottmann	$\log n$	1	$\log n$	redundant operations OK. up to n wasted processors. X-tree topology.
Atallah	$\log n$	1	1	redundant operations OK. up to n wasted processors.
Somani	$\log n$	$\log n$	$\log n$	redundant operations OK. up to $\log n$ wasted processors. not modular.

Appendix II. A radix machine size estimate

The English language statistics used here are drawn from an on-line copy of Webster's Second International dictionary, containing 235,405 words. Several smaller wordlists were also consulted, with similar results. Memory requirements for one million words were extrapolated from dictionary measurements by scaling by a factor of 4.5, thereby adding a 5% margin of extra capacity.

Radix tree nodes are represented as tables with twenty-six entries, with one specialization. Nodes with fewer than two children are coded in nine bytes: one for a character, four for an address, and four for a count. The space required for these nodes could be reduced further by eliminating all but the first count in a string of such nodes (most nodes would then require just four bytes), but that option is not taken here to avoid the proliferation of node types. Nodes with more than one child are allocated 108 bytes, four for each descendant address and four for a count.

Of about 3.4 million nodes required, about 87% have no more than one child. This allows a reduction in node space by a factor of slightly less than five. The number of boards required per processor is as follows, for a total of 42:

```
P:  1  2  3  4  5  6  7  8  9  10 11 12 13 14 15 16
#:  1  1  2  3  4  5  5  4  4  3  2  2  2  2  1  1
```

It is also interesting to consider the worst-case memory requirements, where every word is sixteen characters long and nodes are used as inefficiently as possible. An exact calculation of the worst case is difficult, since the tradeoff between sharing and node efficiency is complex. As a crude upper bound, however, note that at most one million large nodes can be used to produce one million leaves. Furthermore, at most 16 million small nodes can be used, one per key per processor. The small nodes account for 3 memory boards per processor. The large nodes require 108 Mbytes, or 36 boards' worth; disregarding memory on processor boards and assuming the worst possible distribution of nodes over processors, at most 16 extra boards are needed, for a total of 52. Taking this figure, adding both (incompatible) worst cases together, and including processor boards yields a total board count of 116, still significantly fewer than needed for a tree machine.

Appendix III. Theoretical comparisons

This appendix compares the asymptotic time and hardware complexities of the two types of schemes, and gives some observations on how these results should be interpreted. The main difficulty with asymptotic measures in this case is that many of the interesting comparisons to be made hinge on factors of $\log N$, which cannot in practice be very large; in fact, the "constant factors" which are disregarded in such analyses are often of equal importance. Nonetheless, an asymptotic point of view provides a framework within which very different structures can be compared.

In assessing time and hardware requirements, we will in fact discuss three quantities: hardware area, pipeline period in basic machine cycles, and the amount of time needed to perform a machine cycle. The product of the latter two quantities gives the actual period. Machine cycle time will depend on maximum wire lengths in the machine, which are in turn derived from the hardware area.

One extra complication arises in comparing quantities of $O_k()$ and $O_s()$. In what follows, L, the bit length of the longest possible key, is taken to be $\Theta(\log N)$.

Hardware area

A binary tree machine has N processors, each of which stores $L = \Theta(\log N)$ bits of data. Hence its total area is $\Omega(N \log N)$. A radix machine has $L = \Theta(\log N)$ processors, each with a memory holding, in the worst case, N nodes containing $\log N$-bit pointers. The total hardware complexity of this machine, then, is $O(N \log^2 N)$. In practice, the factors of $\log N$ are of questionable import, since the major comparison to make is between one processor per word and some small multiple of $\log N$ bits of memory per word.

Machine cycles

A pipeline period for the radix machine takes $O(1)$ cycles, independent of the size of the keys or of the size of the database. The pipeline period for a tree machine depends on whether keys are handled serially or in parallel. If they are handled serially, $L = \Theta(\log N)$ cycles are needed. If they are handled in parallel only $O(1)$ cycles are necessary, but this will typically be a very costly option.

Cycle time

Following the method of Paterson, et al.[8], it is easy to show that the smallest possible maximum wire length for a binary tree machine is $\Omega(\sqrt{N} \log N / \log N)$, or $\Omega(\sqrt{N}/\log N)$. The longest wire in a radix machine processor memory will be on the order of the diameter of a single memory array, or $O(\sqrt{N} \log N)$.

The question of how to derive delays from wire lengths is complex. A simple asymptotic lower bound, $delay = \Omega(wirelength)$, is given by the speed of light. Depending on conditions, models ranging from $\Theta(1)$ to $\Theta(wirelength^2)$ may be appropriate[6]. In practical cases, where most of the wire length is off-chip and systems are physically small enough that other effects dominate the speed of light, delays are less than linear in wire length. Thus the $\log N$ difference in longest wire length in this case is probably insignificant.

Results

The two schemes are roughly comparable in asymptotic complexity, with the tree machines having a $\log N$ advantage in area and wire length, and the radix machine having a $\log N$ advantage in cycles needed for a pipeline stage over a serialized tree machine. As the example in Section 3.3 shows, the two complexity factors that are most telling in practice are the (constant) difference in cost between a processor and a small amount of memory, and the time cost of having a byte-serial machine.

References

1. Mikhail J. Atallah and S. Rao Kosaraju, "A generalized dictionary machine for VLSI," Tech. report JHU 81-17, Johns Hopkins University, Department of Electrical Engineering and Computer Science, 1981.

2. Michael J. Carey and Clark D. Thompson, "An efficient implementation of search trees on $O(\log N)$ processors," Tech. report UCB/CSD 82/101, University of California at Berkeley, Computer Science Division (EECS), April 1982.

3. Donald E. Knuth, *Sorting and Searching*, Addison-Wesley, The Art of Computer Programming, Vol. 3, 1973.

4. Charles E. Leiserson, "Systolic priority queues," Tech. report CMU-CS-79-115, Carnegie-Mellon University, Computer Science Department, April 1979.

5. Charles E. Leiserson, *Area-Efficient VLSI Computation*, PhD dissertation, Carnegie-Mellon University, Computer Science Department, October 1981.

6. Carver A. Mead and Lynn A. Conway, *Introduction to VLSI Systems*, Addison-Wesley, Reading, Mass., 1980.

7. Thomas A. Ottmann, Arnold L. Rosenberg, and Larry J. Stockmeyer, "A dictionary machine (for VLSI)," *IEEE Transactions on Computers*, Vol. C-31, No. 9, September 1982, pp. 892-897.

8. M. S. Paterson, W. L. Ruzzo, and L. Snyder, "Bounds on minimax edge length for complete binary trees," *Proceedings of the Thirteenth Annual ACM Symposium on Theory of Computing*, ACM SIGACT, May 1981, pp. 293-299.

9. Arun K. Somani and Vinod K. Agarwal, "An unsorted dictionary machine for VLSI," Tech. report, McGill University, VLSI Design Laboratory, 1983.

Chapter 10: Application-Directed Architecture

In earlier computers, the architecture was greatly influenced by cost considerations. With advances in semiconductor technology, however, this is no longer true. Application specifications and requirements have always played an important role in defining the architecture. Of course, different criteria are used in designing special purpose architecture as opposed to a general purpose architecture.

Signal processing has been an important application area wherein a very high throughput is desired and similar operations are performed on a set of data and where it is relatively easier to design a regular structure. Several schemes based on data flow and cellular arrays have been designed for various signal-processing primitives ranging from a general image processing to specific operations of satellite imagery, fast fourier transform, medical imaging, and numerical calculations in the literature[1-32]. Each one of these has its own advantages, and preference of one scheme over another depends on various factors, including the cost and the performance. These primitive functions are employed as basic operations in real-life applications. A systematic processing of pictorial information is considered to be fairly complex[34]. Some distinct steps in identifying moving objects include labeling, segmentation, lexical processing, and motion analysis. Architectures based on the processing and communication requirements for these steps are reviewed[35-41].

Several multicomputer systems proposed for other applications[42-48] include pyramid network-based architecture, generalized architecture[49-50], and architecture[51-57] or database management. Emphasis is also given to the definition of architecture for branch and bound applications[58-59] and for LISP and task-oriented schemes[60-62], which have gained added importance because of increased use of pattern matching strategies[63-67]. Iterative techniques, vector processing, finite-element analysis, and acoustic processing are applicable to many applications, and several such architectures have been given in[68-80].

Four papers are included in this chapter to illustrate strategies for application-directed architecture.

References

1 P.S. Sawkar, T.J. Forquer, and R.P. Perry, "Programmable Modular Signal Processor-A Data Flow Computer System for Real-Time Signal Processing," *Proc. 1983 Int'l. Conf. Parallel Processing,* IEEE Computer Society, Washington, D.C., 1983, pp. 344-349.

2 E.B. Hogenauer, R.F. Newbold, and Y.J. Inn, "DDSP-A Data Flow Computer for Signal Processing," *Proc. Int'l. Conf. Parallel Processing,* IEEE Computer Society, Washington, D.C., pp. 126-133.

3 A. Rosenfeld, "Parallel Image Processing Using Cellular Arrays," *Computer,* Vol. 16, No. 1, Jan. 1983, pp. 14-21.

4 R.W. Priester et al., "Signal Processing with Systolic Arrays," *Proc. 1981 Int'l. Conf. Parallel Processing,* IEEE Computer Society, Washington, D.C, 1981, pp. 207-215.

5 T.N. Mudge and T.A. Rahman, "Efficiency of Feature Dependent Algorithms for the Parallel Processing of Images," *Proc. 1983 Int'l. Conf. Parallel Processing,* IEEE Computer Society, Washington, D.C., 1983, pp. 369-373.

6 H.M. Ahmed, J.-M Delosme, and M. Morf, "Highly Concurrent Computing Structures for Matrix Arithmetic and Signal Processing," *Computer,* Vol. 15, No. 1, Jan. 1982, pp. 65-86.

7 A. Borodin, J.V. Gathen, and J. Hopcroft, "Fast Parallel Matrix and GCD Computations," *Information and Control,* Vol. 52, No. 3, pp. 241-256.

8 C.P. Arnold, M.I. Parr, and M.B. Bewe, "An Efficient Parallel Algorithm for the Solution of Large Sparse Linear Matrix Equations," *IEEE Trans. Computers,* Vol. C-32, No. 3, March 1983, pp. 265-272.

9 G. Gaillat, "The Design of a Parallel Processor for Image Processing On-Board Satellites: An Application Oriented Approach," *Proc. of 10th Ann. Symp. Computer Architecture,* IEEE Computer Society, Washington, D.C., 1983, pp. 379-386.

10 K. Hwang and S.P. Su, "VLSI Architectures for Feature Extraction and Pattern Classification," *Computer Vision, Graphics, and Image Processing,* Vol. 24, Nov. 1983, pp. 215-228.

11 M. Kidode, "Image Processing Machines in Japan," *Computer,* Vol. 16, No. 1, Jan. 1983, pp. 68-80.

12 P.E. Danielsson, "Serial/Parallel Convolvers," *IEEE Trans. Computers,* Vol. C-33, No. 7, July 1984, pp. 652-667.

13 T.K. Truong, K.Y. Liu, and I.S. Reed, "A Parallel Pipeline Architecture of the Fast Polynomial Transform for Computing a Two-Dimensional Cyclic Convolution," *IEEE Trans. Computers,* Vol. C-32, No. 3, March 1983, pp. 301-306.

14 J.L. Potter, "Image Processing on the Massively Parallel Processor," *Computer,* Vol. 16, No. 1, Jan. 1983, pp. 62-67.

15 K.Y. Liu, "A Pipelined Digital Architecture for Computing a Multi-Dimensional Convolution," *Proc. 1981 Int'l. Conf. Parallel Processing,* IEEE Computer Society, Washington, D.C., 1981, pp. 109-111.

16 H. Li, "A VLSI Modular Architecture Methodology for Real-Time Signal Processing Applications," *Proc. 1983 Int'l. Conf. Parallel Processing*, IEEE Computer Society, Washington, D.C., 1983, pp. 319-324.

17 L.M. Chen and J. Sklansky, "A Parallel Multimicroprocessor Architecture for Image Processing," *Proc. 1984 Int'l. Conf. Parallel Processing*, IEEE Computer Society. Washington, D.C., 1984, pp. 185-192.

18 M. Yasrebo and G.J. Lipovski, "A State-of-the-Art SIMD Two-Dimensional FFT Array processor," *Proc. 11th Ann. Int'l. Symp. Computer Architecture*, IEEE Computer Society, Washington, D.C., 1984, pp. 21-29.

19 E.H. Wolf and A.M. Despain, "Pipeline and Parallel-Pipeline FFT Processors for VLSI Implementations," *IEEE Trans. Computers*, Vol. C-33, No. 5, May 1984, pp. 414-426.

20 W. Crowther et al., "Performance Measurements on a 128-Node Butterfly Parallel Processor," *Proc. 1985 Int'l. Conf. Parallel Processing*, IEEE Computer Society, Washington, D.C., 1985, pp. 531-540.

21 H.J. Siegel, L.J. Siegel, F.C. Kemmerer, P.T. Mueller, H.E. Smalley, and S.0. Smith, "PASM: A Reconfigurable SIMD/MIMD System for Image Processing and Pattern Recognition," *IEEE Trans. Computers*, Vol. C-30, No. 12, Dec. 1981, pp. 934-947.

22 C.L. Wu, T.Y. Feng, and M.C. Lin, "Star: A Local Network System for Real-Time Management of Imagery Data, *IEEE Trans. Computers*, Vol. C-31, No. 10, October 1982, pp. 923-933.

23 T. Ericsson and P.E. Danielson, "LIPP-A SIMD Multiprocessor Architecture for Image Processing," *Proc. 10th Ann. Symp. Computer Architecture*, IEEE Computer Society, Washington, D.C., 1983, pp. 395-401.

24 K. Kawakami and S. Shimazaki, "A Special Purpose LSI Processor Using the ODA Algorithm for Image Transformation," *Proc. 11th Ann. Int'l. Symp. Computer Architecture*, IEEE Computer Society, Washington, D.C., 1984, pp. 48-54.

25 K. Preston, M.J.B. Duff, D.S. Levialdi, P.E. Norgren, and J-i Toriwaki, "Basics of Cellular Logic with Some Applications in Medical Image Processing," *Proc. IEEE*, Vol. 67, No. 5, May 1979, pp. 826-856.

26 P. Alexander, "Array Processors in Medical Imaging," *Computer*, Vol. 16, No. 6, June 1983, pp. 17-31.

27 S.R. Sternberg, "Biomedical Image Processing," *Computer*, Vol. 16, No. 1, Jan. 1983, pp. 22-34.

28 H. Amano, T. Yoshida, and H. Aiso, "(SM): Sparse Matrix Solving Machine," *Proc. 10th Ann. Symp. on Computer Architecture*, IEEE Computer Society, Washington, D.C., 1983, pp. 213-221.

29 S.M. Jacobs, L.V. Johnson, and O. Khedr, "A Technique for Systems Architecture Analysis and Design Applied to the Satellite Ground System," *Proc. 4th Int'l. Conf. Distributed Computer Systems*, IEEE Computer Society, Washington, D.C., 1984, pp. 131-140.

30 R. Kober and C. Kuznia, "SMS-A Multiprocessor Architecture for High-Speed Numerical Calculations," *Proc. 1983 Int'l. Conf. Parallel Processing*, IEEE Computer Society, Washington, D.C., 1983, pp. 18-23.

31 C.G. Davis and R.L. Crouch, "Ballistic Missile Defense: A Supercomputer Challenge," *Computer*, Vol. 13, No. 11, November 1980, pp. 37-46.

32 B. Awerbuch and Y. Shiloach, "New Connectivity and MSF Algorithms for Ultracomputer and PRAM," *Proc. 1983 Int'l. Conf. Parallel Processing*, IEEE Computer Society, Washington, D.C., 1983, pp. 175-179.

33 P.E. Danielsson and S. Levialdi, "Computer Architectures for Pictorial Information Systems," *Computer*, Vol. 14, No. 11, Nov. 1981, pp. 53-67.

34 B. Ackland, N. Weste, and D.J. Burr, "An Integrated Multiprocessing Array for Time Warp Pattern Matching," *Proc. 8th Ann. Symp. Computer Architecture*, IEEE Computer Society, Washington, D.C., 1981, pp. 197-216.

35 D.P. Agrawal and R. Jain, "A Pipelined Pseudoparallel System Architecture for Real-Time Dynamic Scene Analysis," *IEEE Trans. Computers*, Vol. C-31, No. 10, Oct. 1982, pp. 952-962.

36 E.C. Bronson and L.J. Siegel, "A Parallel Architecture for Labeling, Segmentation and Lexical Processing in Speech Understanding," *Proc. 1983 Int'l. Conf. Parallel Processing*, IEEE Computer Society, Washington, D.C., 1983, pp. 275-280.

37 S.M. Goldwasser and R.A. Reynolds, "An Architecture for the Real-Time Display and Manipulation of Three-Dimensional Objects," *Proc. 1983 Int'l. Conf. Parallel Processing*, IEEE Computer Society, Washington, D.C., 1983, pp. 269-274.

38 G. Demos, M.D. Brown, and R.A. Weinberg, "Digital Scene Simulation: The Synergy of Computer Technology and Human Creativity," *Proc. IEEE*, Vol. 72, No. 1, Jan. 1984, pp. 22-31.

39 S.M. Goldwasser, "A Generalized Object Display Processor Architecture," *Proc. 11th Ann. Int'l. Symp. Computer Architecture*, IEEE Computer Society, Washington, D.C., 1984, pp. 38-47.

40 Y.W. Ma and R. Krishnamurthi, "The Architecture of REPLICA-A Special Purpose Computer System for Active Multi-Sensory Perception of 3-Dimensional Objects," *Proc. 11th Ann. Int'l. Symp. Computer Architecture*, IEEE Computer Society, Washington, D.C., 1984, pp. 30-37.

41 J.T. Schwartz, "Ultra-Computers," *ACM Trans. Programming Languages and Systems*, Vol. 2, No 4, Oct. 1980, pp. 484-521.

42 D.H. Shafer, "Spatially Parallel Architectures: An Overview," *Computer Design*, Vol. 21, No. 8, Aug. 1982, pp. 117-124.

43 T. Kushner, A.Y. Wu, and A. Rosenfeld, "Image Processing on ZMOB," *IEEE Trans. Computers*, Vol. C-31, No. 10, Oct. 1982, pp. 943-951.

44 F.A. Briggs, K.S. Fu, K. Hwang, and B. Wah, "PUMPS Architecture for Pattern Analysis and Image Database Management," *IEEE Trans. Computers*, Vol. C-31, No. 10, October 1982, pp. 969-982.

45 S.L. Tanimoto, "A Pyramidal Approach to Parallel Processing" *Proc. 10th Ann. Symp. Computer Architecture*, IEEE Computer Society, Washington, D.C., 1983, pp. 372-378.

46 H.M. Levy, *Capability Based Computer Systems*, Digital Press, Bedford, Mass., 1983.

47 H. Nishimura et al., "LINKS-1: A Parallel Pipelined Multimicrocomputer System for Image Creation," *Proc. 10th Ann. Symp. Computer Architecture*, IEEE Computer Society, Washington, D.C., 1983, pp. 387-394.

48 S.L. Tanimoto, "A Pyramidal Approach to Parallel Processing," *Proc. 10th Ann. Int'l. Symp. Computer Architecture*, IEEE Computer Society, Washington, D.C., 1983, pp. 372-378.

49 G. Fritsch, W. Kleinoeder, C.U. Linster, and J. Volkert, "EMSY85-The Erlangen Multi-Processor System for a Broad Spectrum of Applications," *Proc. 1983 Int'l. Conf. Parallel Processing*, IEEE Computer Society, Washington, D.C., 1983, p. 325-330.

50 D.P. Agrawal and W.E. Alexander, "B-HIVE: A Heterogeneous Interconnected Versatile and Expandable Multicomputer System," *IEEE-CS Computer Architecture Technical Committee Newsletter*, IEEE Computer Society, Washington, D.C., Sept. 1984, pp. 19-25.

51 M. Kitsuregawa, H. Tanaka, and T. Moto-Oka, "Architecture and Performance of Relational Algebra Machine GRACE," *Proc. 1984 Int'l. Conf. Parallel Processing*, IEEE Computer Society, Washington, D.C., 1984, pp. 241-250.

52 S.C. Lchen, J. Dongarra, and C.C. Hsiung, Multiprocessing for Linear Algebra Algorithms on the Cray X-MP-2: Experience with Small Granularity," *Journal of Parallel and Distributed Computing*, Vol. 1, No. 1, Aug. 1984, pp. 22-31.

53 P.B. Berra and E. Oliver, "The Role and Associative Array Processors in Database Machine Architecture," *Computer*, Vol. 12, No. 3, March 1979, pp. 53-61.

54 Y. Dohi, A. Suzuki, and N. Matsui, "Hardware Sorter and Its Application to Data Base Machine," *Proc. of 9th Ann. Symp. Computer Architecture*, IEEE Computer Society, Washington, D.C., 1982, pp. 218-228.

55 K. Murakami et al., "A Relational Data Base Machine: First Step to Knowledge Base Machine," *Proc. 10th Ann. Symp. Computer Architecture*, IEEE Computer Society, Washington, D.C., 1983, pp. 423-425.

56 S. Kamiya et al., "A Hardware Pipeline Algorithm for Relational Database Operation and Its Implementation Using Dedicated Hardware," *Proc. 12th Int'l. Symp. Computer Architecture*, IEEE Computer Society, Washington, D.C., 1985, pp. 250-257.

57 D. Gajski, W. Kim, and S. Fushimi, "A Parallel Pipe lined Relational Query Processor: An Architectural Overview," *Proc. 11th Ann. Int'l. Symp. Computer Architecture*, IEEE Computer Society, Washington, D.C., 1984, pp. 134-141.

58 B.W. Wah and Y.W.E. Ma, "MANIP-A Multicomputer Architecture for Solving Combinational Extremum-Search Problems," *IEEE Trans. Computers*, Vol. C-33, No. 5, May 1984, pp. 377-390,

59 G.J. Li and B.W. Wah, "MANIP-Z: A Multicomputer Architecture for Evaluating Logic Programs," *Proc. 1985 Int'l. Conf. Parallel Processing*, IEEE Computer Society, Washington, D.C., 1985, pp. 123-130.

60 S. Sugimoto, K. Agusa, K. Tabata, and Y. Ohno, "A Multi-Microprocessor System for Concurrent LISP," *Proc. 1983 Int'l. Parallel Processing*, IEEE Computer Society, Washington, D.C., 1983, pp. 135-143.

61 D.A. Moon, "Architecture of the Symbolics 3600," *Proc. 12th Int'l. Symp. Computer Architecture*, IEEE Computer Society, Washington, D.C., 1985, pp. 76-83.

62 H. Hayashi, A. Hattori, and H. Akimoto, "ALPHA: A High-Performance LISP Machine Equipped with a New Stack Structure and Garbage Collection System," *Proc. 10th Ann. Int'l. Symp. Computer Architecture*, IEEE Computer Society, Washington, D.C., 1983, pp. 342-348.

63 R. Bisiani, H. Mauersberg, and R. Reddy, "Task-Oriented Architecture," *Proc. IEEE*, Vol. 71, No. 7, July 1983, pp. 885-898.

64 S. Uchida, "Inference Machine," *Proc. 10th Ann. Symp. Computer Architecture*, IEEE Computer Society, Washington, D.C. 1983, pp. 410-416.

65 Y. Ishikawa and M. Tokoro, "The Design of an Object Oriented Architecture," *Proc. 11th Ann. Int'l. Symp. Computer Architecture*, IEEE Computer Society, Washington, D.C., 1984, pp. 178-187.

66 C. Ebeling and A. Palay, "The Design and Implementation of a VLSI Chess Move Generator," *Proc. 11th Ann. Int'l. Symp. Computer Architecture*, IEEE Computer Society, Washington, D.C., 1984, pp. 74-80.

67 S.J. Stolfo and D.P. Miranker, "DADO: A Parallel Processor for Expert Systems," *Proc. 1984 Int'l. Conf. Parallel Processing*, IEEE Computer Society, Washington, D.C., 1984, pp. 74-82.

68 V. Conrad and Wallach, "Iterative Solution of Linear Equations on a Parallel Processor System," *IEEE Trans. Computers*, Vol. C-26, No. 9, Sept. 1977, pp. 838-847.

69 L.G. Valiant et al., "Fast Parallel Computation of Polynomials Using Few Processors," *SIAM Journal Computers*, Vol. 12, No. 4, Nov. 1983, pp. 641-644.

70 M. Vajtersic, "Parallel Poisson and Biharmonic Solvers Implemented on the EGPA Multiprocessor," *Proc. 1982*

Int'l. Conf. Parallel Processing, IEEE Computer Society, Washington, D.C., 1982, pp. 72-81.

71 J.S. Nolen, D.W. Kuba, and M.J. Kascic, Jr., "Application of Vector Processors to the Solution of Finite Difference Equations," *AIME Fifth Symp. Reservoir Simulation,* 1979, pp. 37-44.

72 K.H. Chu and K.S. Fu, "VLSI Architectures for High-Speed Recognition of Context-Free Languages and Finite State Languages," *Proc. 9th Ann. Conf. Computer Architecture,* IEEE Computer Society, Washington, D.C., 1982, pp. 43-49.

73 K.S. Forsstrom, "Array Processors in Real-Time Flight Simulation," *Computer,* Vol. 16, No. 6, June 1983, pp. 62-72.

74 P. Berger, P. Brouaye, and J.C. Syre, "A Mesh Coloring Method for Efficient MIMD Processing in Finite Element Problems," *Proc. 1982 Int'l. Conf. Parallel Processing,* IEEE Computer Society, Washington, D.C., pp. 41-46.

75 J.A. Swanson, G.R. Cameron, and J.C. Haberland, "Adapting the Ansys Finite-Element Analysis Program to an Attached Processor," *Computer,* Vol. 16, No. 6, June 1983, pp. 85-94.

76 J.F. Gloudeman, "The Anticipated Impact of Super-computers on Finite Element Analysis," *Proc. IEEE,* Vol. 72, No. 1, Jan. 1984, pp. 80-84.

77 E.C. Bronson and L.J. Siegel, "A Parallel Architecture for Acoustic Processing in Speech Understanding," *Proc. 1982 Int'l. Conf. Parallel Processing,* IEEE Computer Society, Washington, D.C., 1982, pp. 307-312.

78 V. Milutinovic, B. Furht, K. Hwang, N. Lopez-Benitez, and K. Waldschmidt, "The VM-Architecture: A HLL-Microprocessor Architecture for Dedicated Real-Time Applications," *Proc. Int'l. Workshop on High-Level Computer Architecture,* University of Maryland, College Park, Md., 1984, pp. 7.20-7.27.

79 J.B. Dennis, G.R. Rao, and K.W. Todd, "Modeling the Weather with a Data Flow Computer," *IEEE Trans. Computers,* Vol. C-33, No. , July 1984, pp. 592-603,

80 V.L. Peterson, "Impact of Computers on Aerodynamics Research and Development," *Proc. IEEE,* Vol. 72, No. 1, Jan. 1984, pp. 68-79.

PASM: A Partitionable SIMD/MIMD System for Image Processing and Pattern Recognition

HOWARD JAY SIEGEL, MEMBER, IEEE, LEAH J. SIEGEL, MEMBER, IEEE,
FREDERICK C. KEMMERER, MEMBER, IEEE, PHILIP T. MUELLER, JR., MEMBER, IEEE,
HAROLD E. SMALLEY, JR., MEMBER, IEEE, AND S. DIANE SMITH, MEMBER, IEEE

Abstract—PASM, a large-scale multimicroprocessor system being designed at Purdue University for image processing and pattern recognition, is described. This system can be dynamically reconfigured to operate as one or more independent SIMD and/or MIMD machines. PASM consists of a parallel computation unit, which contains N processors, N memories, and an interconnection network; Q microcontrollers, each of which controls N/Q processors; N/Q parallel secondary storage devices; a distributed memory management system; and a system control unit, to coordinate the other system components. Possible values for N and Q are 1024 and 16, respectively. The control schemes and memory management in PASM are explored. Examples of how PASM can be used to perform image processing tasks are given.

Index Terms—Image processing, memory management, MIMD machines, multimicroprocessor systems, multiple-SIMD machines, parallel processing, partitionable computer systems, PASM, reconfigurable computer systems, SIMD machines.

I. INTRODUCTION

AS a result of the microprocessor revolution, it is now feasible to build multimicroprocessor systems capable of performing image processing tasks more rapidly than previously possible. There are many image processing tasks which can be performed on a parallel processing system, but are prohibitively expensive to perform on a conventional computer system due to the large amount of time required to do the tasks [37]. In addition, a multimicroprocessor system can use parallelism to perform the real-time image processing required

for such applications as robot (machine) vision, automatic guidance of air and spacecraft, and air traffic control.

There are several types of parallel processing systems. An *SIMD (single instruction stream-multiple data stream) machine* [18] typically consists of a set of N processors, N memories, an interconnection network, and a control unit (e.g., Illiac IV [10]). The control unit broadcasts instructions to the processors and all active ("turned on") processors execute the same instruction at the same time. Each processor executes instructions using data taken from a memory with which only it is associated. The interconnection network allows interprocessor communication. An *MSIMD (multiple-SIMD) system* is a parallel processing system which can be structured as one or more independent SIMD machines (e.g., MAP [31], [32]). The Illiac IV was originally designed as an MSIMD system [3]. An *MIMD (multiple instruction stream-multiple data stream) machine* [18] typically consists of N processors and N memories, where each processor can follow an independent instruction stream (e.g., C.mmp [60]). As with SIMD architectures, there is a multiple data stream and an interconnection network. A *partitionable SIMD/MIMD system* is a parallel processing system which can be structured as one or more independent SIMD and/or MIMD machines. In this paper PASM [47], [48], a partitionable SIMD/MIMD system being designed at Purdue University for image processing and pattern recognition, is described.

Many designers have discussed the possibilities of building large-scale parallel processing systems, employing 2^{14} to 2^{16} microprocessors, in SIMD (e.g., binary n-cube array [34]) and MIMD (e.g., CHoPP [54], [55]) configurations. Without the presence of such a large number of processors, the concept of partitioning the system into smaller machines which can operate as SIMD or MIMD machines was unnecessary. Nutt [31] has suggested a machine which is a multiple-SIMD system. Lipovski and Tripathi [27] have considered the idea of combining the SIMD and MIMD modes of operation in one system. In addition, developments in recent years have shown the importance of parallelism to image processing, using both cellular logic arrays (e.g., CLIP [50], BASE 8 [35]) and SIMD systems (e.g., STARAN [36]). A variety of such systems are discussed in [19]. Thus, the time seems right to investigate how to construct a computer system such as PASM: a machine which can be dynamically reconfigured as one or more SIMD and/or MIMD machines, optimized for a variety of important image processing and pattern recognition tasks.

Manuscript received September 11, 1979; revised May 8, 1980 and March 4, 1981. This work was supported by the Air Force Office of Scientific Research, Air Force Systems Command, USAF, under Grant AFOSR-78-3581, and the Defense Mapping Agency, monitored by the US Air Force Rome Air Development Center Information Sciences Division, under Contract F30602-78-C-0025 through the University of Michigan.

H. J. Siegel and L. J. Siegel are with the School of Electrical Engineering, Purdue University, West Lafayette, IN 47907.

F. C. Kemmerer was with the School of Electrical Engineering, Purdue University, West Lafayette, IN 47907. He is now with Bell Laboratories, Whippany, NJ 07981.

P. T. Mueller, Jr. was with the School of Electrical Engineering, Purdue University, West Lafayette, IN 47907. He is now with Geophysical Services, Inc., Dallas, TX 75265.

H. E. Smalley, Jr. was with the School of Electrical Engineering, Purdue University, West Lafayette, IN 47907. He is now with Hitachi America, Ltd., Atlanta, GA 30360.

S. D. Smith was with the School of Electrical Engineering, Purdue University, West Lafayette, IN 47907. She is now with the Department of Electrical and Computer Engineering, University of Wisconsin, Madison, WI 53706.

Reprinted from *IEEE Transactions on Computers*, Volume C-30, Number 12, December 1981, pages 934-947. Copyright © 1981 by The Institute of Electrical and Electronics Engineers, Inc.

The use of parallel processing in image processing has been limited in the past due to cost constraints. Most systems used small numbers of processors (e.g., Illiac IV [10]), processors of limited capabilities (e.g., STARAN [36]), or specialized logic modules (e.g., PPM [24]). With the development of microprocessors and related technologies it is reasonable to consider parallel systems using a large number of complete processors.

SIMD machines can be used for "local" processing of segments of images in parallel. For example, the image can be segmented and each processor assigned a segment. Then following the same set of instructions, such tasks as line thinning, threshold dependent operations, and gap filling can be done in parallel for all segments of the image simultaneously. Also in SIMD mode, matrix arithmetic used for such tasks as statistical pattern recognition can be done efficiently. MIMD machines can be used to perform different "global" pattern recognition tasks in parallel, using multiple copies of the image or one or more shared copies. For example, in cases where the goal is to locate two or more distinct objects in an image, each object can be assigned a processor or set of processors to search for it. An SIMD/MIMD application might involve using the same set of microprocessors for preprocessing an image in SIMD mode and then doing a pattern recognition task in MIMD mode.

PASM, a *p*artitionable *S*IMD/*M*IMD machine, is a large-scale dynamically reconfigurable multimicroprocessor system [43], [46]–[48]. It is a special purpose system being designed to exploit the parallelism of image processing and pattern recognition tasks. It can also be applied to related areas such as speech processing and biomedical signal processing. In this paper the architecture of PASM is presented and examples of its use in performing image processing tasks are given.

Computer system designers have been considering various multimicrocomputer architectures, such as [9], [11], [23], [26], [27], [34], [54], [58], and [59]. PASM combines the following features:

1) it can be partitioned to operate as many independent SIMD and/or MIMD machines of varying sizes, and

2) it is being developed using a variety of problems in image processing and pattern recognition to guide the design choices.

The purpose of PASM is to serve as a vehicle for experimenting with parallel image processing and pattern recognition. It is not meant to be a production-line machine, but rather a research tool. The design attempts to incorporate the needed flexibility for studying large-scale SIMD and MIMD parallelism, while keeping system costs "reasonable."

In this paper the overall organization of PASM is presented. In particular, the control structure and secondary storage systems are described, and some application examples are given. The purpose here is to present design concepts that will allow a system to exploit the parallelism that, for example, 1024 processors can provide. Implementation details are currently under study and are beyond the scope and length of this paper.

Fig. 1 is a block diagram of the basic components of PASM. The *parallel computation unit* (*PCU*) contains $N = 2^n$ pro-

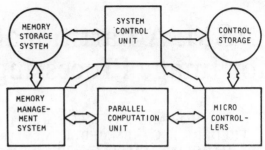

Fig. 1. Block diagram overview of PASM.

cesors, N memory modules, and an interconnection network. The *PCU processors* are microprocessors that perform the actual SIMD and MIMD computations. The *PCU memory modules* are used by the PCU processors for data storage in SIMD mode and both data and instruction storage in MIMD mode. The *interconnection network* provides a means of communication among the PCU processors and memory modules. Two possible ways to organize the PCU and different types of partitionable networks which can be used are described in Section II.

The *microcontrollers* (*MC's*) are a set of microprocessors which act as the control units for the PCU processors in SIMD mode and orchestrate the activities of the PCU processors in MIMD mode. There are $Q = 2^q$ MC's. Each MC controls N/Q PCU processors. A virtual SIMD machine (partition) of size RN/Q, where $R = 2^r$ and $0 \le r \le q$, is obtained by loading R MC memory modules with the same instructions simultaneously. Similarly, a virtual MIMD machine of size RN/Q is obtained by combining the efforts of the PCU processors of R MC's. Q is therefore the maximum number of partitions allowable, and N/Q is the size of the smallest partition. Possible values for N and Q are 1024 and 16, respectively. *Control storage* contains the programs for the MC's. The MC's are discussed in more detail in Section III.

The *memory storage system* provides secondary storage space for the data files in SIMD mode, and for the data and program files in MIMD mode. The *memory management system* controls the transferring of files between the memory storage system and the PCU memory modules. It employs a set of cooperating dedicated microprocessors. Multiple storage devices are used in the memory storage system to allow parallel data transfers. The secondary memory system is described in Section IV.

The *system control unit* is a conventional machine, such as a PDP-11, and is responsible for the overall coordination of the activities of the other components of PASM. Examples of the tasks the system control unit will perform include program development, job scheduling, and coordination of the loading of the PCU memory modules from the memory storage system with the loading of the MC memory modules from control storage. By carefully choosing which tasks should be assigned to the system control unit and which should be assigned to other system components, the system control unit can work effectively and not become a bottleneck. Examples of this include using the MC's to act as the control units for virtual SIMD machines, controlling the interconnection network with routing tags generated by each PCU processor, and having the memory management system supervise primary/secondary memory transfers.

Together, Sections II, III, and IV present the overall architecture of PASM. Particular attention is paid to the ways in which the control structure and secondary memory scheme allow PASM to be efficiently partitioned into independent virtual machines. Variations in the design of PASM's PCU which still support these control and secondary memory ideas are examined. This examination demonstrates how the concepts underlying PASM can be used in the design of different systems.

In Section V image processing algorithms using PASM are presented. In particular, smoothing and histogram calculations are examined. Using these examples, the potential improvement a system such as PASM can provide over serial machines is demonstrated.

II. PARALLEL COMPUTATION UNIT

A. PCU Organization

The parallel computation unit (PCU) contains processors, memories, and an interconnection network. One configuration of these components is to connect a memory module to each processor to form a processor–memory pair called a *processing element* (*PE*) (e.g., Illiac IV [10]). The interconnection network is used for communications among PE's. This "*PE-to-PE*" configuration is shown in Fig. 2. A pair of memory units is used for each memory module. This double-buffering scheme allows data to be moved between one memory unit and secondary storage (the memory storage system) while the processor operates on data in the other memory unit. In the PE-to-PE configuration, "local" memory references are relatively fast, however, the transfer of large blocks of data from PE to PE is delayed by the memory fetching and storing which must be done.

The "*P-to-M*" (processor-to-memory) configuration, shown in Fig. 3, uses the interconnection network to connect the processors to the memory modules. Again, double-buffering is employed. There is no "local" memory. To fetch an operand from memory, the processor must first send the address of the operand through the interconnection network to a memory. Then the processor receives the operand from the memory via the interconnection network. Advantages of the P-to-M configuration are that a memory connected to a processor can be reconnected to another processor, effectively transferring the entire contents of the memory from one processor to another, and that the number of memories does not have to be equal to the number of processors (e.g., BSP [12]). A disadvantage is that all memory references must go through the interconnection network.

A more detailed analysis reveals some of the tradeoffs involved in these two configurations. If T_{mr} is the time required for a memory access (either a read or a write), and T_{in} is the time to send a data item through the interconnection network, then the time required for a memory reference in the P-to-M configuration, T_{P-M}, is given by

$$T_{P-M} = T_{in} + T_{mr} + T_{in}. \tag{1}$$

T_{in} must be included twice, once for the processor to send the

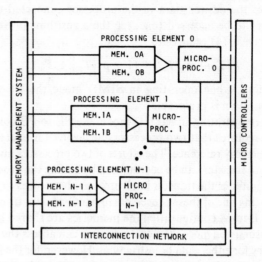

Fig. 2. PE-to-PE configuration of the parallel computation unit.

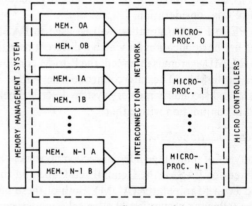

Fig. 3. Processor-to-memory configuration of the parallel computation unit.

address to the memory and once for transferring the data. (The time required for controlling the network is omitted since control methods vary.)

For the PE-to-PE configuration the time required for a memory reference, T_{PE}, depends on the location of the memory which is to be used. If the memory is local, then

$$T_{PE} = T_{mr}. \tag{2}$$

If the memory is connected to some other processor, then

$$T_{PE} = T_{in} + T'_{mr} + T_{in}. \tag{3}$$

T'_{mr} represents the time required for the PE which has the data item to recognize and service the data request. This may require a significantly longer delay than T_{mr}. If p is the probability of a local memory reference, then (2) and (3) can be combined to give the expected memory reference time

$$E[T_{PE}] = pT_{mr} + (1 - p)(T_{in} + T'_{mr} + T_{in}). \tag{4}$$

Comparing (1) and (4)

$$T_{P-M} \geq E[T_{PE}] \tag{5}$$

for p sufficiently large. Thus, the "best" configuration is task dependent.

When operating in SIMD mode with the PE-to-PE configuration, it is often possible to omit one occurrence of T_{in} in (3) and reduce T'_{mr} to T_{mr}. This is done by computing the address of the desired data in the processor connected to the memory to be accessed (e.g., see the algorithms in Section V-B). Thus, (4) reduces to

$$E[T_{\text{PE}}] = pT_{\text{mr}} + (1 - p)(T_{\text{mr}} + T_{\text{in}}). \qquad (6)$$

Therefore, when operating in SIMD mode the PE-to-PE configuration is preferable.

When operating in MIMD mode, the PE-to-PE configuration requires that two processors be involved in every non-local memory reference. The efforts of two processors involved in a data transfer can be coordinated by having the processor which initiates the transfer interrupt the other processor or by dedicating one of these processors to handling data transfers. In the P-to-M configuration the memories are shared by the processors, i.e., more than one processor can access the same memory for either data or instructions. However, for the image processing tasks that have been examined, most data and instructions can be stored in the local memory, reducing the impact of this consideration.

The PE-to-PE configuration will be used in PASM. Depending on the application for which a different partitionable SIMD/MIMD system is intended, the P-to-M configuration may be preferable. The interconnection networks, control structure, and secondary memory system described below can be used in conjunction with either.

B. Interconnection Networks

Two types of multistage interconnection networks are being considered for PASM: the Generalized Cube and the Augmented Data Manipulator (ADM). Both of these networks have the following properties: 1) a logical structure consisting of n stages of $N/2$ (Cube) or N (ADM) switches [49]; 2) distributed control by routing tags generated by each processor [25], [28]; 3) the ability to operate in SIMD mode (N simultaneous transfers) and MIMD mode [44], [45]; and 4) the ability to be partitioned into independent subnetworks [42]. As discussed in [49], the Cube network is equivalent or directly related to other networks in the literature (e.g., [5], [6], [25], [33], and [34]). The ADM is an extension of the data manipulator [16].

Both the Cube and ADM networks can be implemented as single stage networks [38], [40], [41] instead of as multistage networks. These single stage implementations can also be partitioned [42], are compatible with the PASM control and memory management schemes, and may be appropriate for MSIMD systems, depending on the intended applications. However, since there is only a single stage of switches, for the MIMD mode of operation intermediate processors may have to be interrupted to transfer data. (See [40] for more information.) Thus, single stage networks are not appropriate for PASM, but might be for an MSIMD system based on the design concepts of PASM.

The tradeoffs between the Cube and ADM multistage networks for PASM are currently under study. The ADM network is more flexible and fault tolerant [40], [44], but is more complex. The Cube may be more cost effective and sufficient for the system's needs. In the following sections it will be assumed that the processors will be partitioned such that the addresses of all of the processors in a partition agree in their low-order bit positions. This constraint will allow either the Cube or ADM network to be used as the partitionable interconnection network in PASM. Details of these networks are beyond the scope of this paper, and readers are referred to the references indicated.

C. PCU Processors

The PCU processors will be specially designed for parallel image processing. Simulation studies are currently being conducted to aid in determining an efficient instruction set. A PASM prototype will most likely be based on user microprogrammable components to obtain needed flexibility, while the final system will employ custom VLSI processors.

III. MICROCONTROLLERS

A. Introduction

In this section the microcontrollers (MC's) are discussed. It is the MC's that enable PASM to operate as an MSIMD system.

In general, the possible advantages of an MSIMD system over an SIMD system with a similar number of PE's include the following.

1) Fault Detection: For situations where high reliability is needed, three partitions can run the same program on the same data and compare results.

2) Fault Tolerance: If a single PE fails, only those logical SIMD machines (partitions) which must include the failed PE need to be disabled. The rest of the system can continue to function.

3) Multiple Simultaneous Users: Since there can be multiple independent virtual SIMD machines, there can be multiple simultaneous users of the system, each executing a different SIMD program.

4) Program Development: Rather than trying to debug an SIMD program on, for example, 1024 PE's, it can be debugged on a smaller size virtual SIMD machine of 32 or 64 PE's.

5) Variable Machine Size for Efficiency: If a task requires only $N/2$ of N available PE's, the other $N/2$ can be used for another task.

6) Subtask Parallelism: Two independent SIMD subtasks that are part of the same job can be executed in parallel, sharing results if necessary.

For PASM's intended application as a tool for experimenting with the use of parallelism in image processing and pattern recognition, points 2)–6) above will be significant.

B. Microcontroller Organization and Addressing Conventions

In order to have a partitionable system, some form of multiple control units must be provided. In PASM this is done by having $Q = 2^q$ MC's, physically addressed (numbered) from 0 to $Q - 1$. Each MC controls N/Q PCU processors, as shown in Fig. 4.

An MC is a microprocessor which is attached to a memory module. Each memory module consists of a pair of memory units so that memory loading and computations can be overlapped. This double-buffering reduces the likelihood of MC's

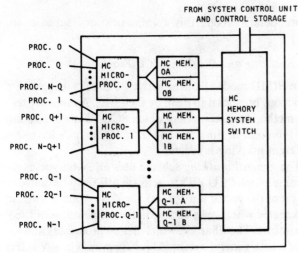

Fig. 4. PASM microcontrollers (MC's).

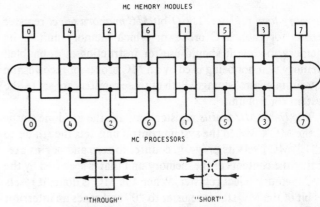

Fig. 5. Reconfigurable shared bus scheme for interconnecting microcontroller (MC) processors and MC memory modules, for $Q = 8$. Each box can be set to "through" or "short."

being idle while waiting for a program to be loaded. In SIMD mode, each MC fetches instructions from its memory module, executing the control flow instructions (e.g., branches) and broadcasting the data processing instructions to its PCU processors. The physical addresses of the N/Q processors which are connected to an MC must all have the same low-order q bits so that the network can be partitioned. The value of these low-order q bits is the physical address of the MC. A virtual SIMD machine of size RN/Q, where $R = 2^r$ and $0 \leq r \leq q$, is obtained by loading R MC's with the same instructions and synchronizing the MC's. The physical addresses of these MC's must have the same low-order $q - r$ bits so that all of the PCU processors in the partition have the same low-order $q - r$ physical address bits. Similarly, a virtual MIMD machine of size RN/Q is obtained by combining the efforts of the PCU PE's associated with R MC's which have the same low-order $q - r$ physical address bits. In MIMD mode the MC's may be used to help coordinate the activities of their PCU PE's.

The approach of permanently assigning a fixed number of PCU PE's to each MC has several advantages over allowing a varying assignment, such as in [11] and [31]. One advantage is that the operating system need only schedule (and monitor the "busy" status of) Q MC's, rather than N PCU PE's. When $Q = 16$ (or even 32) and $N = 1024$, this is a substantial savings. Another advantage is that no crossbar switch is needed for connecting processors and control units (as proposed in [11] and [31]). Also, this fixed connection scheme allows the efficient use of multiple secondary storage devices, as is discussed in Section IV-B. The main disadvantage of this approach is that each virtual machine size must be a power of two, with a minimum value of N/Q. However, for PASM's intended experimental environment, flexibility at reasonable cost is the goal, not maximum processor utilization.

This basic MC organization can be enhanced to allow the sharing of memory modules by the MC's in a partition. The MC's can be connected by a shared reconfigurable ("shortable") bus such as described in [2], as shown in Fig. 5. The MC's must be ordered on the bus in terms of the bit reverse of their addresses due to the partitioning rules. (The sharing of

memories using a reconfigurable bus is employed in [22].) This enhanced MC connection scheme would provide more program space for jobs using multiple MC's and would also provide a degree of fault tolerance, since known-faulty MC memory modules could be ignored. These advantages come at the expense of additional system complexity, and the inclusion of the enhanced scheme in PASM will depend on cost constraints at implementation time.

In each partition the PCU processors and memory modules are assigned *logical addresses*. Given a virtual machine of size RN/Q, the processors and memory modules for this partition have logical addresses (numbers) 0 to $(RN/Q) - 1$, $R = 2^r$, $0 \leq r \leq q$. Assuming that the MC's have been assigned as described above, then the logical number of a processor or memory module is the high-order $r + n - q$ bits of the physical number. Similarly, the MC's assigned to the partition are logically numbered (addressed) from 0 to $R - 1$. For $R > 1$, the logical number of an MC is the high-order r bits of its physical number. The PASM language compilers and operating system will be used to convert from logical to physical addresses, so a system user will deal only with logical addresses.

C. Communications with the System Control Unit

SIMD programs are stored in control storage (see Fig. 1), which is the secondary storage for the MC's. The loading of these programs from control storage into the MC memory units is controlled by the system control unit. When large SIMD jobs are run, that is, jobs which require more than N/Q processors, more than one MC executes the same set of instructions. With the basic scheme in the previous section, each MC has its own memory, so if more than one MC is to be used, then several memories must be loaded with the same set of instructions.

The fastest way to load several MC memories with the same set of instructions is to load all of the memories at the same time. This can be accomplished by connecting the control storage to all of the MC memory modules via a bus. Each memory module is either enabled or disabled for loading from control storage, depending on the contents of the Q-bit *MC memory load* register. The Q-bit *MC memory select* register selects for each MC processor which memory unit of its memory module it should use for instructions. An enabled memory unit not being used by an MC processor receives the data from control storage. Both of these registers are set by the system control unit.

The Q-bit *MC status* register contains the go/done status of the MC's. When the system control unit sets the ith bit to a "1," MC i sets its program counter to zero and begins executing the contents of the memory unit that is specified by the MC memory select register. When the MC is done, it resets its bit of the MC status register to "0" and sends an interrupt to the system control unit to inform it that an MC has finished.

Further details about the communications between the MC's and the system control unit are in [47].

D. Communications Among Microcontrollers

Instructions which examine the collective status of all of the PE's of a virtual SIMD machine include "if any," "if all," and "if none." These instructions change the flow of control of the program at execution time depending on whether any or all processors in the SIMD machine satisfy some condition. For example, if each PE is processing data from a different radar unit, but all PE's are looking for enemy planes, it is desirable for the control unit to know "if any" of the PE's has discovered a possible attack.

The task of computing an "if any" type of statement that involves several MC's can be handled using the existing hardware. This can be accomplished by having the PCU processors associated with these MC's use a recursive doubling [53] type of algorithm.

Specialized hardware to handle this task can be added inexpensively and will result in a faster solution than the software approach. Each MC will have a $q + 1$ bit *job identification number* (*ID*) for the job it is running (there can be at most one job in each of the $2Q$ memory units). The MC's will share an *MC communication bus*, consisting of an ID bus and a data bus. When an "if any" type instruction is encountered, each MC associated with the job determines the result of the "if any" type of statement for its N/Q PE's and sends a request to use the communication bus. When an MC receives permission to use the bus, it broadcasts its job ID to all of the MC's (including itself) via the ID bus. If an MC is running the job with the ID which is on the ID bus it then puts its local results onto the data bus. The data bus is one bit wide and will be constructed as a Q input "wired and" gate. This allows all of the MC's associated with a job to put their data on the bus simultaneously and read the result. Each MC serviced removes itself from the queue. The MC's will then execute the conditional branch in the common instruction stream. All MC's in a partition will be synchronized, executing the "if any" type of instruction at the same time. None of the MC's will continue past that instruction until after its job ID has appeared on the ID bus.

The system control unit is not burdened under this method.

More details about this communications scheme are in [47].

E. Enabling and Disabling PCU Processors

In SIMD mode all of the active PCU PE's will execute instructions broadcast to them by their MC. A *masking scheme* is a method for determining which PCU PE's will be active at a given point in time. An SIMD machine may have several different masking schemes.

The *general masking* scheme uses an N-bit vector to determine which PCU PE's to activate. PE i will be active if the ith bit of the vector is a 1, for $0 \leq i < N$. A mask instruction is executed whenever a change in the active status of the PE's is required. The Illiac IV, which has 64 processors and 64-bit words, uses general masks [51]. However, when N is larger, say 1024, a scheme such as this becomes less appealing.

The *PE address masking* scheme [38] uses an n-position mask to specify which of the N PCU PE's are to be activated. Each position of the mask corresponds to a bit position in the addresses of the PE's. Each position of the mask will contain either a 0, 1, or X (DON'T CARE) and the only PE's that will be active are those whose address matches the mask: 0 matches 0, 1 matches 1, and either 0 or 1 matches X. Square brackets denote a mask. Superscripts are used as repetition factors. For example, MASK $[X^{n-1}0]$ activates all even numbered PE's; MASK $[0^{n-i}X^i]$ activates PE's 0 to $2^i - 1$.

A *negative PE address mask* [39] is similar to a regular PE address mask, except that it activates all those PE's which do not match the mask. Negative PE address masks are prefixed with a minus sign to distinguish them from regular PE address masks. For example, for $N = 8$, MASK $[-00X]$ activates all PE's except 0 and 1. This type of mask can activate sets of PE's a single regular PE address mask cannot.

Like general masks, PE address masks are specified in the SIMD program. PE address masks are more restictive than general masks, in that a general mask can activate any arbitrary set of PE's and a PE address mask cannot. However, for $N \gg 64$, general masks are impractical in terms of storage requirements and ease of programming, and so system architects must consider alternatives. Together, regular and negative PE address masks provide enough flexibility to allow the easy programming of a variety of image processing tasks.

For ease of encoding and decoding, two bits are used to represent each PE address mask position and one bit for the sign, as shown in Fig. 6. The $2(n - q)$ high-order bits pertain to the PCU PE's in an MC group, while the low-order $2q$ bits pertain to the MC addresses. The entire mask word is a *physical mask* and is used with the physical addresses of the PCU PE's and the MC's. For a partition of size 2^p, the p position *logical mask* forms the p high-order positions of the physical mask and "X"'s are used in the low-order $n-p$ positions. Each MC contains a *mask decoder*, as shown in Fig. 7, which transforms the $2n + 1$ bit physical mask into an N/Q bit general mask vector for PE's connected to that MC. This is all that is required to translate a logical mask into enable signals.

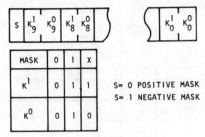

MASK	0	1	X
K^1	0	1	1
K^0	0	1	0

S = 0 POSITIVE MASK
S = 1 NEGATIVE MASK

Fig. 6.   PE address mask binary encoding for $N = 1024$.

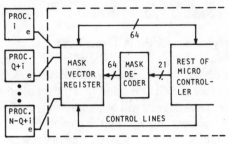

Fig. 8.   Masking portion of microcontroller i, for $N = 1024$ and $Q = 16$. "e" is PCU processor enable bit.

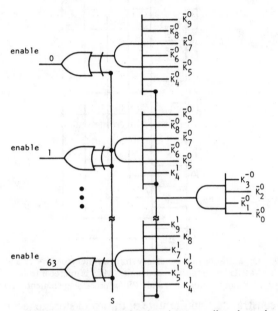

Fig. 7.   PE address mask decoder for the microcontroller whose physical address is 0, for $N = 1024$ and $Q = 16$.

The system of Fig. 8 allows an arbitrary general mask vector or the output of the PE address mask decoder to be sent to the *mask vector register* of each MC. If the general masking scheme were implemented on PASM, a reformatting operation would be needed. Assume that the mask is being used in a partition of size RN/Q. The system compiler can rearrange the programmer's *logical general mask* to form a *physical general mask*. The PCU PE whose logical address is $(R * j) + i$ will be the jth PE controlled by the ith logical MC, $0 \le i < R$, $0 \le j < N/Q$. The logical mask bit $(R * j) + i$ is moved to the physical mask position $(N/Q)i + j$. Then the MC whose logical address is i will load its N/Q-bit mask register with bits $i * N/Q$ through $((i + 1) * N/Q) - 1$ of the physical mask. (The translation of logical MC addresses to physical addresses was described in Section III-B.) This method of loading will send the ith bit of the logical general mask to the ith logical PCU PE.

Based on the intended size and applications of PASM, general mask vectors will not be used. However, the previous paragraph shows how they can be used on a PASM-type system designed for a different size and/or application domain.

As a compromise between the flexibility of general mask vectors and the conciseness of PE address masks, the MC is allowed to fetch the N/Q-bit vector from the mask vector register, perform various logical operations on the vector, and then reload it. A logical OR of two (or more) vectors generated by PE address masks is equivalent to taking the union of the sets of processors activated by the masks. A logical AND is equivalent to the intersection. The complement operation can be used to implement negative PE address masks instead of using the EXCLUSIVE-OR gates shown in Fig. 7. This is the way in which the PE address masking scheme will be implemented on PASM. This same scheme could be used in any SIMD or MSIMD system.

Thus, PE address masks are concise, easily converted from logical to physical masks, and can be combined using Boolean functions for additional flexibility. Examples of how PE address masks can be used in algorithms for image processing tasks are presented in Section V. More information about these masks and their use is in [38], [39], and [41].

Both general mask vectors and PE address masks are set at compile time. Data conditional masks will be implemented in PASM for use when the decision to enable and disable PE's is made at execution time.

Data conditional masks are the implicit result of performing a conditional branch dependent on local data in an SIMD machine environment, where the result of different PE's evaluations may differ. As a result of a conditional *where statement* of the form

$$where \ \langle data\ condition \rangle \ do \cdots elsewhere$$

each PE will set its own internal flag to activate itself for either the "do" or the "elsewhere," but not both. The execution of the "elsewhere" statements must follow the "do" statements, i.e., the "do" and "elsewhere" statements cannot be executed simultaneously. For example, as a result of executing the statement

$$where \ A > B \ do \ C \leftarrow A \ elsewhere \ C \leftarrow B$$

each PE will load its C register with the maximum of its A and B registers, i.e., some PE's will execute "$C \leftarrow A$," and then the rest will execute "$C \leftarrow B$." This type of masking is used in such machines as the Illiac IV [3] and PEPE [13]. "Where" statements can be nested using a run-time control stack, as discussed in [46].

IV. SECONDARY MEMORY SYSTEM

A. Introduction

The memory management system in PASM will have its own intelligence and will use the parallel secondary storage devices of the memory storage system. Giving the memory management system its own intelligence will help prevent the system control unit from being overburdened. The parallel secondary storage devices will allow fast loading and unloading of the N double-buffered PCU memory modules and will provide storage for system image data and MIMD programs.

B. Memory Storage System

Secondary storage for the PCU memory modules is provided by the memory storage system. The memory storage system will consist of N/Q independent *memory storage units*, where N is the number of PCU PE's and Q is the number of MC's. The memory storage units will be numbered from 0 to $(N/Q) - 1$. Each memory storage unit is connected to Q PCU memory modules. For $0 \leq i < N/Q$, memory storage unit i is connected to those memory modules whose physical addresses are of the form $(Q * i) + k$, $0 \leq k < Q$. Recall that for $0 \leq k < Q$, MC k is connected to those PE's whose physical addresses are of the form $(Q * i) + k$, $0 \leq i < N/Q$. This is shown for $N = 32$ and $Q = 4$ in Fig. 9.

The two main advantages of this approach for a partition of size N/Q are that: 1) all of the memory modules can be loaded in parallel, and 2) the data is directly available no matter which partition (MC group) is chosen. This is done by storing in memory storage unit i the data for a task which is to be loaded into the ith logical memory module of the virtual machine of size N/Q, $0 \leq i < N/Q$. Memory storage unit i is connected to the ith memory module in each MC group so that no matter which MC group of N/Q processors is chosen, the data from the ith memory storage unit can be loaded into the ith logical memory module, $0 \leq i < N/Q$, simultaneously.

Thus, for virtual machines of size N/Q, this secondary storage scheme allows all N/Q memory modules to be loaded in one parallel block transfer. This same approach can be taken if only $(N/Q)/2^d$ distinct memory storage units are available, where $0 \leq d \leq n - q$. In this case, however, 2^d parallel block loads will be required instead of just one.

Consider the situation where a virtual machine of size RN/Q is desired, $1 \leq R \leq Q$, and there are N/Q memory storage units. In general, a task needing RN/Q PE's, logically numbered 0 to $RN/Q - 1$, will require R parallel block loads if the data for the memory module whose high-order $n - q$ logical address bits equal i is loaded into memory storage unit i. This is true no matter which group of R MC's (which agree in their low-order $q - r$ address bits) is chosen.

For example, consider Fig. 9, and assume that a virtual machine of size 16 is desired. The data for the memory modules whose logical addresses are 0 and 1 is loaded into memory storage unit 0, for memory modules 2 and 3 into unit 1, etc. Assume that the partition of size 16 is chosen to consist of the processors connected to MC's 0 and 2. Given this assignment of MC's, the PCU memory module whose physical address is $2 * i$ has logical address i, $0 \leq i < 16$. The memory storage units first load memory modules physically addressed 0, 4, 8, 12, 16, 20, 24, and 28 (simultaneously), and then load memory modules 2, 6, 10, 14, 18, 22, 26, and 30 (simultaneously). No matter which pair of MC's is chosen, only two parallel block loads are needed.

Thus, for a virtual machine of size RN/Q, this secondary storage scheme allows all RN/G memory modules to be loaded in R parallel block transfers, $1 \leq R \leq Q$. If only $(N/Q)/2^d$ distinct memory storage units are available, $0 \leq d \leq n - q$, then $R * 2^d$ parallel block loads will be required instead of just R.

The actual devices that will be used as memory storage units will depend upon the speed requirements of the rest of PASM,

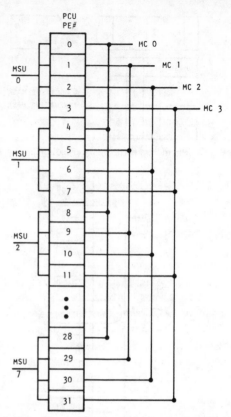

Fig. 9. Organization of the memory storage system for $N = 32$ and $Q = 4$, where "MSU" is memory storage unit, "MC" is microcontroller, "PCU" is parallel computation unit, and "PE" is processing element.

cost constraints, and the state of the art of storage technology at implementation time. This memory organization concept could be employed in any SIMD, MSIMD, MIMD, or partitionable SIMD/MIMD system that uses the PASM (or similar) addressing conventions for partitioning.

C. Handling Large Data Sets

The memory management system makes use of the double-buffered arrangement of the memory modules to enhance system throughput. The scheduler, using information from the system control unit such as the number of PCU PE's needed and maximum allowable run time, will sequence tasks waiting to execute [48]. Typically, all of the data for a task will be loaded into the appropriate memory units before execution begins. Then while a processor is using one of its memory units, the memory management system can be unloading the other unit and then loading it for the next task. When the task currently being executed is completed, the PCU processor can switch to its other memory unit to begin the next task.

There may be some cases where all of the data will not fit into the PCU memory space allocated. Assume that a *memory frame* is the amount of space used in the PCU memory units for the storage of data from secondary storage for a particular task. There are tasks where many memory frames are to be processed by the same program (e.g., maximum likelihood classification of satellite data [57]). The double-buffered memory modules can be used so that as soon as the data in one memory unit are processed, the processor can switch to the other unit and continue executing the same program. When the processor is ready to switch memory units, it signals the memory management system that it has finished using the data in the memory unit to which they are currently connected.

Hardware to provide this signaling capability can be provided in different ways, such as using interrupt lines from the processors or by using logic to check the address lines between the processor and its memory modules for a special address code. The processor switches memory units, assuming that the data is present, and then checks a data identification tag to ensure that the new memory frame is available. The memory management system can then unload the "processed" memory unit and load it with the next memory frame or next task. Such a scheme, however, requires some mechanism which can make variable length portions of programs or data sets (its *local data*) stored in one unit of a memory module available to the other unit when the associated processor switches to access the next memory frame.

One method to do this maintains a copy of local data in both memory units associated with a given processor so that switching memory units does not alter the local variable storage associated with the processor. A possible hardware arrangement to implement this makes use of two characteristics of the PASM memory access requirements: 1) secondary memory will not be able to load a given memory unit at the maximum rate it can accept data, and 2) PCU processors will not often be able (or desire) to write to memory on successive memory cycles. (An exception to the second characteristic is multiple precision data, but this can be handled by a simple buffering scheme.) Because of these two characteristics, processor stores to local variable storage locations in an active memory unit can be trapped by a bus interface register and stored in the inactive memory unit by stealing an access cycle from the secondary memory bus. In essence, this technique makes use of the conventional store-through concept as described in [21]. This scheme would be used only when multiple memory frames are to be processed.

The method described is applicable to any system which allows its processing tasks to utilize several separate memories and which requires that identical copies of variable amounts of certain data be maintained in all memories so used. Further information about this scheme and a discussion of other possible methods for providing local data storage are presented in [43].

D. Altering Loading Sequences

A task may alter the sequence of data processed by it during execution. As an example, consider a task which is attempting to identify certain features in a series of images. The task might examine a visible spectrum copy of an image and, based on features identified in the image, choose to examine an infrared spectrum copy of the same image. Rather than burden the system control unit to perform data loading sequence alterations, the task is allowed to communicate directly with the memory management system.

For SIMD mode this can be handled by allowing each MC to interrupt and pass the necessary information to the memory management system. Alternatively, a PE (e.g., logical PE 0) can signal the memory management system (as mentioned in Section IV-C), which would read the loading sequence information stored in the PE's memory module. More details about this are in [43].

The same hardware arrangement described for SIMD tasks is used for MIMD tasks. With each group of N/Q MIMD PE's, there is associated a memory supervisor which is logical PE 0 within the group. This is less costly than providing hardware for each PE to communicate with the memory management system. All PE's associated with a given memory supervisor make requests for loading sequence changes through the memory supervisor, without involving the MC(s) or system control unit. This reduces system control unit contention problems and helps prevent the MC(s), possibly busy orchestrating the activities of the virtual MIMD machine, from becoming overburdened.

E. Memory Management System

A set of microprocessors is dedicated to performing the memory management system tasks in a distributed fashion, i.e., one processor handles memory storage system bus control, one handles the peripheral device I/O, etc. This distributed processing approach is chosen in order to provide the memory management system with a large amount of processing power at low cost. Requests coming from different devices (e.g., system control unit, PCU PE) can be handled simultaneously. In addition, dedicating specific microprocessors to certain tasks simplifies both the hardware and software required to perform each task.

The division of tasks chosen is based on the main functions which the memory management system must perform, including: 1) generating tasks based on PCU memory module load/unload requests from the system control unit, 2) interrupt handling and generating tasks for data loading sequence changes, 3) scheduling of memory storage system data transfers, 4) control of input/output operations involving peripheral devices and the memory storage system, 5) maintenance of the memory management system file directory information, and 6) control of the memory storage system bus system. These are all tasks with which the system control unit might otherwise be burdened. Further details are in [43].

V. Image Processing on PASM

A. Introduction

In this section an example of how PASM can be used to expedite image processing tasks is presented. A high level language algorithm to smooth an image and build a histogram demonstrates some of the features of a programming language for PASM. Implementation of this algorithm demonstrates the ways in which PASM's parallelism may be used to obtain significant reductions of execution time on computationally intensive tasks.

Ideally, a high level language for image processing will allow algorithms for image processing tasks to be expressed easily. The language being designed for PASM is a procedure based structured language which allows the use of index sets similar to those in TRANQUIL [1]. The characteristics of the image processing problem domain are being used to facilitate compiling. Analyses of image processing tasks (e.g., [15], [30], and [56]) are being employed to identify efficient techniques for performing common tasks and to define storage allocation strategies.

B. Smoothing and Histogram Algorithms

An $M \times M$ image is represented by an array of M^2 pixels (picture elements), where the value of each pixel is assumed to be an eight bit unsigned integer representing one of 256 possible gray levels. In image smoothing each pixel is assigned a gray level equal to the average of the gray levels of the pixel and its eight nearest neighbors in the unsmoothed image. This operation is performed for each pixel in the image, with the possible exception of the edge pixels. The 256-bin histogram of the image contains a j in bin i if exactly j of the pixels have a gray level of i, $0 \leq i < 256$.

The high level language algorithm "picture," shown in Fig. 10, performs smoothing on a 512×512 image, and also produces a 256-bin histogram, "hist," of the smoothed image. The language constructs used are described in [29].

To implement image smoothing on PASM, assume $N = s^2$ and that the PE's are logically configured as an $s \times s$ grid, on which an $M \times M$ image is superimposed, i.e., each processor holds a $M/s \times M/s$ subimage. This is shown in Fig. 11(a). For $N = 1024$ and $M = 512$, each PE stores a 16×16 block of the image. Let each PE consider its 16×16 block as a matrix m with elements $m(i, j)$, $0 \leq i, j < 16$. Also, let the subscripts of $m(i, j)$ extend to -1 and 16, in order to aid in calculations across boundaries of two adjacent blocks in different PE's. For example, the pixel to the left of $m(0, 0)$ is $m(0, -1)$, and the pixel below $m(15, 15)$ is $m(16, 15)$. Therefore, $-1 \leq i, j \leq 16$.

In the 1024-PE SIMD algorithm, smoothing will be performed on the 1024 subimages in parallel. At the boundaries of each 16×16 array, data must be transmitted between PE's, as shown in Fig. 11(b), in order to calculate the smoothed value ms. For example, $m(i, 16)$, $0 \leq i < 16$, must be transferred from the PE "to the right of" the local PE, except for PE's 31, 63, 95, $\cdots$, 1023, those at the "right edge" of the logical array of PE's.

The compiler generated code to transfer data from PE $k + 1$ to PE k can be expressed as follows.

SET ICN to PE $- 1$;

DTRin $\leftarrow m(0 \rightarrow 15, 0)$;

TRANSFER;

MASK $[-X^5 1^5]$ $m(0 \rightarrow 15, 16) \leftarrow$ DTRout;

"Set ICN to PE $\pm d$" sets the *inter*connection *n*etwork so that PE P sends data to PE $P \pm d$ mod N, $0 \leq P < N$. PE's transfer data through *d*ata *t*ransfer *r*egisters. First, the data are loaded into the *DTRin* of each PE, then the TRANSFER command moves the data through the network, and finally the data are retrieved from *DTRout*. The notation "$l \rightarrow u$" denotes that the operation is performed for each subscript value i in the range $l \leq i \leq u$. The set of three statements "DTRin $\leftarrow m(0 \rightarrow 15, 0)$, TRANSFER, $m(0 \rightarrow 15, 16) \leftarrow$ DTRout" will cause a block transfer of 16 elements, using the current network setting. This may occur one word at a time, depending upon the network implementation. The command *MASK* [*address set*] is a PE address mask that determines which PE's will execute the instructions that follow. The absence of a mask

```
PROCEDURE picture

    /* define pixin and pixout to be 512x512
       arrays of unsigned eight bit integers */

    UNSIGNED BYTE pixin[512][512], pixout[512][512];

    /* define hist to be a 256 word array of integers */

    INTEGER hist[256];

    /* define x and y to be index sets */

    INDEX x, y;

    /* declare pixin to be loaded by input data and
       pixout and hist to be unloaded as output data */

    DATA INPUT pixin;
    DATA OUTPUT pixout, hist;

    /* define the sets of indices which x and y represent, i.e.,
       x and y represent the integers between 1 and 510 inclusive */

    x = y = {1 + 510};

    /* compute average of each point and its eight
       nearest neighbors (simultaneously if possible) */

    pixout[x][y] = (pixin[x-1][y-1]+pixin[x-1][y]+pixin[x-1][y+1]+
                    pixin[x][y-1]+pixin[x][y]+pixin[x][y+1]+
                    pixin[x+1][y-1]+pixin[x+1][y]+pixin[x+1][y+1])/9;

    /* initialize each bin to zero */

    hist[0 + 255] = 0;

    /* compute histogram */

    hist[pixout[x][y]] = hist[pixout[x][y]] + 1;

END picture
```

Fig. 10. High level language algorithm for smoothing and computing histogram. Keywords are in upper case for ease of identification; however, in actual use they need not be.

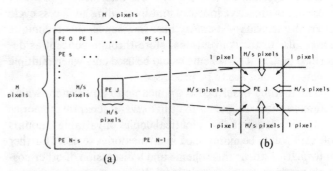

Fig. 11. (a) Data allocation for smoothing an $M \times M$ image using N PE's, where $N = s^2$. (b) Data transfers needed to smooth edge pixels in each PE.

implies that all PE's are active. The mask $[-X^5 1^5]$ deactivates the PE's on the right side of the image, i.e., PE's 31, 63, $\cdots$, 1023.

The transfers of data for the remaining three sides of the array m, i.e., from PE's $k - 1$, $k + 32$, and $k - 32$, are accomplished in a similar manner. Smoothing of the four points $m(0, 0)$, $m(0, 15)$, $M(15, 0)$, and $m(15, 15)$ requires data transfers from PE's $k - 33$, $k - 31$, $k + 31$, and $k + 33$, respectively. Both the multistage Cube and ADM networks can perform each of these connections in a single pass.

In order to perform a smoothing operation on a 512×512 image by the parallel smoothing of blocks of size 16×16, the total number of parallel word transfers is $(4 * 16) + 4 = 68$. The corresponding sequential algorithm needs no data transfers between PE's, but calculates ms for $512 * 512 = 262,144$ points. If no data transfers were needed, the parallel algorithm would be faster than the sequential algorithm by a factor of

348

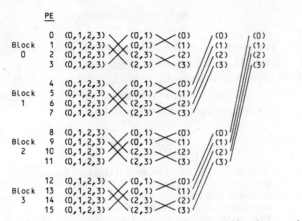

Fig. 12. Histogram calculation for $N = 16$ PE's, $B = 4$ bins. $(w, \cdots, z)$ denotes that bins w through z of the partial histogram are in the PE.

```
/*algorithm to combine "local" histograms. b' = (log₂B)-1; n = log₂N;

    keep is the index of the first bin which to be kept.
    send is the index of the first bin which is to be sent to another PE */

keep ← 0;
/*form histogram for each group of B PEs */
for i ← 0 to b' do
        /*group of PEs with higher addresses prepares to send first half
          of remaining bins to group of PEs with lower addresses */

        MASK [Xⁿ⁻⁽ᵇ'⁻ⁱ⁾⁻¹1Xᵇ'⁻ⁱ]
            send ← keep;

            keep ← send + 2ᵇ'⁻ⁱ;

            SET ICN to PE - 2ᵇ'⁻ⁱ;

        /*group of PEs with lower addresses prepares to send second half
          of remaining bins to group of PEs with higher addresses. */

        MASK [Xⁿ⁻⁽ᵇ'⁻ⁱ⁾⁻¹0Xᵇ'⁻ⁱ]

            send ← keep + 2ᵇ'⁻ⁱ;

            SET ICN to PE + 2ᵇ'⁻ⁱ;

        /*transfer 2ᵇ'⁻ⁱ bins, add received data to kept data */

        MASK [Xⁿ]

            DTRin ← hist[send ← send + 2ᵇ'⁻ⁱ⁻1];

            TRANSFER;

            hist[keep ← keep + 2ᵇ'⁻ⁱ⁻1]

                ← hist[keep ← keep + 2ᵇ'⁻ⁱ⁻1] + DTRout;

/*Combine N/B partial histograms to form histogram of entire image. */

for i ← 0 to log₂(N/B)-1

        MASK [Xⁿ⁻ᵇ'⁻ⁱ1Xᵇ'⁺1⁺ⁱ]

            SET ICN to PE + 2ᵇ'⁺1⁺ⁱ;
            DTRin ← hist[keep];
            TRANSFER;

        MASK [Xⁿ⁻ᵇ'⁻ⁱ0Xᵇ'⁺1⁺ⁱ]
            hist[keep] ← hist[keep] + DTRout
```

Fig. 13. Algorithm to perform the B-bin histogram calculation for image distributed over N PE's.

$262,144/(16 * 16) = 1024$. If it is assumed that each parallel data transfer requires at most as much time as one smoothing operation, then the time factor is $262,144/324 = 809$. That is, the parallel algorithm is about three orders of magnitude faster than the sequential algorithm executed on a single PCU PE. The approximation is a conservative one, since calculating the addresses of the nine pixels involves nine multiplications using the subscripts [20].

Now consider implementing the histogram calculation. Since the image ms is distributed over 1024 PE's, each PE will calculate a 256-bin histogram based on its 16×16 segment of the image. Then these "local" histograms will be combined using the algorithm described below. This algorithm is demonstrated for $N = 16$ and $B = 4$ bins, instead of $N = 1024$ and $B = 256$ bins, in Fig. 12. Both the Cube and ADM multistage networks can perform each of the needed transfers in a single pass.

In the first $b = \log_2 B$ steps, each block of B PE's performs B simultaneous recursive doublings [53] to compute the histogram for the portion of the image contained in the block. At the end of the b steps, each PE has one bin of this partial histogram. This is accomplished by first dividing the B PE's of a block into two groups. Each group accumulates the sums for half of the bins, and sends the bins it is not accumulating to the group which is accumulating those bins. At each step of the algorithm, each group of PE's is divided in half such that the PE's with the lower addresses form one group, and the PE's with the higher addresses form another. The accumulated sums are similarly divided in half based on their indices in the histogram. The groups then exchange sums, so that each PE contains only sum terms which it is accumulating. The newly received sums are added to the sums already in the PE. After b steps, each PE has the total value for one bin from the portion of the image contained in the B PE's in its block.

The next $n - b$ steps combine the results of these blocks to yield the histogram of the entire image distributed over B PE's, with the sum for bin i in PE i, $0 \leq i < B$. This is done by performing $n - b$ steps of a recursive doubling algorithm to sum the partial histograms from the N/B blocks, shown by the last two steps of Fig. 12. A general algorithm to compute the B-bin histogram for an image distributed over N PE's is shown in Fig. 13.

A sequential algorithm to compute the histogram of an $M \times M$ image requires M^2 additions. The SIMD algorithm uses M^2/N additions for each PE to compute its local histogram. At step i in the merging of the partial histograms, $0 \leq i < b$, the number of data transfers and additions required is $B/2^{i+1}$. A total of $B - 1$ transfers are therefore performed in the first b steps of the algorithm. $n - b$ parallel transfers and additions are needed to combine the block histograms. This technique therefore requires $B - 1 + n - b$ parallel transfer/add operations, plus the M^2/N additions needed to compute the local PE histograms. For the example considered, the sequential algorithm would require 262144 additions; the parallel algorithm uses 256 addition steps plus 257 transfer/add steps. The result of the algorithm, i.e., the histogram, is distributed over the first B PE's. This distribution may be efficient for further processing on the histogram, e.g., finding the maximum or minimum, or for smoothing the histogram. If it is necessary for the entire histogram to be in a single PE, $B - 1$ additional parallel data transfers are required.

VI. CONCLUSIONS

PASM, a large-scale partitionable SIMD/MIMD multimicroprocessor system for image processing and pattern recognition, has been presented. Its overall architecture was described and examples of how PASM can realize significant computational improvements over conventional systems was demonstrated.

PASM differs from other large-scale parallel processing systems whose capabilities include the ability to operate in SIMD mode in terms of its balance of flexibility and complexity. PASM is more complex than the CLIP4 [14], DAP [17], MPP [8], and BASE 8 processsors [35] in the sense that these systems use bit-serial processors connected in a four or eight nearest neighbor pattern. The PASM design is more flexible than the STARAN [4], [7], which uses bit serial processors and can only operate in the SIMD mode. The interconnection network in STARAN is a multistage Cube network, but it differs from the networks proposed for PASM in that it has a limited control scheme [5]. PASM is also more flexible than the Illiac IV [10], which has a four nearest neighbor interconnection network, and can only operate in SIMD mode. (The original Illiac design had four control units and could operate in MSIMD mode [3].) PASM differs from the BSP organization [52] in that the BSP uses 16 processors (a smaller scale of parallelism) and is limited to just the SIMD mode of operation. The MAP [31] system is an MSIMD machine design in which the control units are connected to groups of processors via a crossbar switch, making its control unit to processor connection abilities more flexible than PASM's. However, the processors in MAP communicate with each other via a bus system, so all processors cannot send data in parallel, and there are no provisions for the system to operate in MIMD mode.

Two other microprocessor based systems capable of both MSIMD and MIMD modes are the Reconfigurable Varistructure Array Processor [27] (now called TRAC) and PM4 [11]. TRAC does not have any explicit control units; SIMD processing is achieved by having more than one processor fetch instructions from the same memory. In addition, TRAC can combine the effects of processors to vary its machine word size. In PM4, the control units are connected to the processors via a crossbar type of switch, so any processor can be driven by any control unit. Also, in addition to a network for interprocessor communications, there is a different multistage network between the processors and shared memory. Another system capable of operating in the MSIMD and MIMD modes is the dc group system [22]. This is a dynamically reconfigurable system, capable of creating virtual machines of different word sizes. PASM is, in general, less complex and less flexible than each of these three systems. However, for the image processing tasks studied thus far, the PASM design has had sufficient flexibility.

In summary, the objective of the PASM design is to achieve a system which attains a compromise between flexibility and cost-effectiveness for a specific problem domain. Future work on PASM includes choosing a microprocessor architecture suitable for PASM, investigating system reliability and fault tolerance, designing an "intelligent" compiler for a high level parallel image processing language, specifying the hardware design details, and developing the operating system and programming languages for a prototype system. A dynamically reconfigurable system such as PASM should be a valuable tool for both image processing/pattern recognition and parallel processing research.

ACKNOWLEDGMENT

The authors would like to thank R. J. McMillen, G. B. Adams, III, P. A. England, J. Bogdanowicz, and M. Washburn for their contributions to the design of PASM, and L. Wittie for many useful conversations. They also gratefully acknowledge the comments of the referees.

REFERENCES

[1] N. E. Abel et al., "TRANQUIL: A language for an array processing computer," in Proc. AFIPS 1969 SJCC, May 1969, pp. 57-68.
[2] R. Arnold and E. Page, "A hierarchical, restructurable multimicroprocessor architecture," in Proc. 3rd Annu. Symp Comput. Arch., Jan. 1976, pp. 40-45.
[3] G. Barnes et al., "The Illiac IV computer," IEEE Trans. Comput., vol. C-17, pp. 746-757, Aug. 1968.
[4] K. E. Batcher, "STARAN parallel processor system hardware," in Proc. AFIPS 1974 Nat. Comput. Conf., vol. 43, May 1974, pp. 405-410.
[5] ——, "The flip network in STARAN," in Proc. 1976 Int. Conf. Parallel Processing, Aug. 1976, pp. 65-71.
[6] ——, "The multidimensional access memory in STARAN," IEEE Trans. Comput., vol. C-26, pp. 174-177, Feb. 1977.
[7] ——, "STARAN series E," in Proc. 1977 Int. Conf. Parallel Processing, Aug. 1977, pp. 140-152.
[8] ——, "MPP—A massively parallel processor," in Proc. 1979 Int. Conf. Parallel Processing, Aug. 1979, p. 249.
[9] J. Bogdanowicz and H. J. Siegel, "A partitionable multi-microprogrammable-microprocessor system for image processing," in Proc. IEEE Comput. Soc. Workshop Pattern Recog. Artificial Intell., Apr. 1978, pp. 141-144.
[10] W. J. Bouknight et al., "The Illiac IV system," Proc. IEEE, vol. 60, pp. 369-388, Apr. 1972.
[11] F. Briggs, K. S. Fu, K. Hwang, and J. Patel, "PM4—A reconfigurable multimicroprocessor system for pattern recognition and image processing," in Proc. AFIPS 1979 Nat. Comput. Conf., vol. 48, June 1979, pp. 255-265.
[12] Burroughs, BSP—Burroughs Scientific Processor, Burroughs Corp., June 1977.
[13] B. A. Crane et al., "PEPE computer architecure," in Proc. COMPCON 1972, IEEE Comput. Soc. Conf., Sept. 1972, pp. 57-60.
[14] M. J. B. Duff, "CLIP 4: A large scale integrated circuit array parallel processor," in Proc. 3rd Int. Joint Conf. Pattern Recog., 1976, pp. 728-732.
[15] A. E. Feather, L. J. Siegel, and H. J. Siegel, "Image correlation using parallel processing," in Proc. 5th Int. Conf. Pattern Recog., Dec. 1980, pp. 503-507.
[16] T. Feng, "Data manipulating functions in parallel processors and their implementations," IEEE Trans. Comput., vol. C-23, pp. 309-318, Mar. 1974.
[17] P. M. Flanders et al., "Efficient high speed computing with the distributed array processor," in Proc. Symp. High Speed Comput. Algorithm Organization, Apr. 1977, pp. 113-128.
[18] M. J. Flynn, "Very high-speed computing systems," Proc. IEEE, vol. 54, pp. 1901-1909, Dec. 1966.
[19] K. S. Fu, "Special computer architectures for pattern recognition and image processing—An overview," in Proc. AFIPS 1978 Nat. Comput. Conf., vol. 47, June 1978, pp. 1003-1013.
[20] D. Gries, Compiler Construction for Digital Computers. New York: Wiley, 1971.
[21] J. Hayes, Computer Architecture and Organization. New York: McGraw-Hill, 1978.
[22] S. I. Kartashev and S. P. Kartashev, "A multicomputer system with dynamic architecture," IEEE Trans. Comput., vol. C-28, pp. 704-720, Oct. 1979.
[23] J. Keng and K. S. Fu, "A special computer architecture for image processing," in Proc. 1978 IEEE Comput. Soc. Conf. Pattern Recog. Image Processing, June 1978, pp. 287-290.
[24] B. Kruse, "A parallel picture processing machine," IEEE Trans. Comput., vol. C-22, pp. 1075-1087, Dec. 1973.
[25] D. H. Lawrie, "Access and alignment of data in array processor," IEEE Trans. Comput., vol. C-24, pp. 1145-1155, Dec. 1975.
[26] G. J. Lipovski, "On a varistructured array of microprocessors," IEEE Trans. Comput., vol. C-26, pp. 125-138, Feb. 1977.

[27] G. J. Lipovski and A. Tripathi, "A reconfigurable varistructure array processor," in *Proc. 1977 Int. Conf. Parallel Processing*, Aug. 1977, pp. 165–174.

[28] R. J. McMillen and H. J. Siegel, "MIMD machine communication using the augmented data manipulator network," in *Proc. 7th Annu. Symp. Comput. Arch.*, May 1980, pp. 51–58.

[29] P. T. Mueller, Jr., L. J. Siegel, and H. J. Siegel, "A parallel language for image and speech processing," in *Proc. COMPSAC 1980*, Oct. 1980, pp. 476–483.

[30] ——, "Parallel algorithms for the two-dimensional FFT," in *Proc. 5th Int. Conf. Pattern Recog.*, Dec. 1980, pp. 497–502.

[31] G. J. Nutt, "Microprocessor implementation of a parallel processor," in *Proc. 4th Annu. Symp. Comput. Arch.*, Mar. 1977, pp. 147–152.

[32] ——, "A parallel processor operating system comparison," *IEEE Trans. Software Eng.*, vol. SE-3, pp. 467–475, Nov. 1977.

[33] J. H. Patel, "Processor-memory interconnections for multiprocessors," in *Proc. 6th Annu. Symp. Comput. Arch.*, Apr. 1979, pp. 168–177.

[34] M. C. Pease, "The indirect binary *n*-cube microprocessor array," *IEEE Trans. Comput.*, vol. C-26, pp. 458–473, May 1977.

[35] A. P. Reeves and R. Rindfuss, "The BASE 8 binary array processor," in *Proc. 1979 IEEE Comput. Soc. Conf. Pattern Recog. Image Processing*, Aug. 1979, pp. 250–255.

[36] D. Rohrbacker and J. L. Potter, "Image processing with the Staran parallel computer," *Computer*, vol. 10, pp. 54–59, Aug. 1977.

[37] S. Ruben, R. Faiss, J. Lyon, and M.Quinn, "Application of a parallel processing computer in LACIE," in *Proc. 1976 Int. Conf. Parallel Processing*, Aug. 1976, pp. 24–32.

[38] H. J. Siegel, "Analysis techniques for SIMD machine interconnection networks and the effects of processor address masks," *IEEE Trans. Comput.*, vol. C-26, pp. 153–161, Feb. 1977.

[39] ——, "Controlling the active/inactive status of SIMD machine processors," in *Proc. 1977 Int. Conf. Parallel Processing*, Aug. 1977, p. 183.

[40] ——, "Interconnection networks for SIMD machines," *Computer*, vol. 12, pp. 57–65, June 1979.

[41] ——, "A model of SIMD machines and a comparison of various interconnection networks," *IEEE Trans. Comput.*, vol. C-28, pp. 907–917, Dec. 1979.

[42] ——, "The theory underlying the partitioning of permutation networks," *IEEE Trans. Comput.*, vol. C-29, pp. 791–801, Sept. 1980.

[43] H. J. Siegel, F. Kemmerer, and M. Washburn, "Parallel memory system for a partitionable SIMD/MIMD machine," in *Proc. 1979 Int. Conf. Parallel Processing*, Aug. 1979, pp. 212–221.

[44] H. J. Siegel and R. J. McMillen, "Using the augmented data manipulator network in PASM," *Computer*, vol. 14, pp. 25–33, Feb. 1981.

[45] ——, "The cube network as a distributed processing test bed switch," in *Proc. 2nd Int. Conf. Distributed Comput. Syst.*, Apr. 1981, pp. 377–387.

[46] H. J. Siegel and P. T. Mueller, Jr., "The organization and language design of microprocessors for an SIMD/MIMD system," in *Proc. 2nd Rocky Mt. Symp. Microcomput.*, Aug. 1978, pp. 311–340.

[47] H. J. Siegel, P. T. Mueller, Jr., and H. E. Smalley, Jr., "Control of a partitionable multimicroprocessor system," in *Proc. 1978 Int. Conf. Parallel Processing*, Aug. 1978, pp. 9–17.

[48] H. J. Siegel, L. J. Siegel, R. J. McMillen, P. T. Mueller, Jr., and S. D. Smith, "An SIMD/MIMD multimicroprocessor system for image processing and pattern recognition," in *Proc. 1979 IEEE Comput. Soc. Conf. Pattern Recog. Image Processing*, Aug. 1979, pp. 214–224.

[49] H. J. Siegel and S. D. Smith, "Study of multistage SIMD interconnection networks," in *Proc. 5th Annu. Symp. Comput. Arch.*, Apr. 1978, pp. 223–229.

[50] C. D. Stamopoulous, "Parallel algorithms for joining two points by a straight line segment," *IEEE Trans. Comput.*, vol. C-23, pp. 642–646, June 1974.

[51] K. G. Stevens, Jr., "CFD—A Fortran-like language for the Illiac IV," in *Proc. ACM Conf. Programming Lang. Compilers for Parallel and Vector Mach.*, Mar. 1975, pp. 72–76.

[52] R. A. Stokes, "Burroughs scientific processor," in *Proc. Symp. High Speed Comput. Algorithm Organization*, Apr. 1977, pp. 71–75.

[53] H. S. Stone, "Parallel computers," in *Introduction to Computer Architecture*, H. S. Stone, Ed. Chicago, IL: SRA, Inc., 1975, pp. 318–374.

[54] H. Sullivan, T. R. Bashkow, and K. Klappholz, "A large scale homogeneous, fully distributed parallel machine," in *Proc. 4th Annu. Symp. Comput. Arch.*, Mar. 1977, pp. 105–124.

[55] H. Sullivan *et al.*, "The node kernel: Resource management in a self-organizing parallel processor," in *Proc. 1977 Int. Conf. Parallel Processing*, Aug. 1977, pp. 157–162.

[56] P. H. Swain, H. J. Siegel, and J. El-Achkar, "Multiprocessor implementation of image pattern recognition: A general approach," in *Proc. 5th Int. Conf. Pattern Recog.*, Dec. 1980, pp. 309–317.

[57] P. H. Swain, H. J. Siegel, and B. W. Smith, "Contextual classification of multispectral remote sensing data using a multiprocessor system," *IEEE Trans. Geosci. Remote Sensing*, vol. GE-18, pp. 197–203, Apr. 1980.

[58] R. J. Swan, S. H. Fuller, and D. P. Siewiorek, "Cm*: A modular, multi-microprocessor," in *Proc. AFIPS 1977 Nat. Comput. Conf.*, June 1977, pp. 637–644.

[59] R. J. Swan *et al.*, "The implementation of the Cm* multi-microprocessor," in *Proc. AFIPS 1977 Nat. Comput. Conf.*, June 1977, pp. 645–655.

[60] W. A. Wulf and C.G. Bell, "C.mmp—A multi-miniprocessor," in *Proc. AFIPS 1972 Fall Joint Comput. Conf.*, Dec. 1972, pp. 765–777.

Howard Jay Siegel (M'77) was born in New Jersey on January 16, 1950. He received the S.B. degree in electrical engineering and the S.B. degree in management from the Massachusetts Institute of Technology, Cambridge, in 1972, the M.A. and M.S.E. degrees in 1974, and the Ph.D. degree in 1977, all in electrical engineering and computer science from Princeton University, Princeton, NJ.

In 1976 he joined the School of Electrical Engineering, Purdue University, West Lafayette, IN, where he is currently an Associate Professor. Since January 1979 he has also been affiliated with Purdue's Laboratory for Applications of Remote Sensing. His research interests include parallel/distributed processing, multimicroprocessor systems, image processing, and speech processing.

Dr. Siegel was Chairman of the Workshop on Interconnection Networks for Parallel and Distributed Processing held in April 1980, which was co-sponsored by the IEEE Computer Society and the Association for Computing Machinery. He is currently a Vice Chairman of both the IEEE Computer Society TCCA (Technical Committee on Computer Architecture) and TCDP (Technical Committee on Distributed Processing), the Vice Chairman of ACM SIGARCH (Special Interest Group on Computer Architecture), an IEEE Computer Society Distinguished Visitor, and the General Chairman of the Third International Conference on Distributed Computing Systems, to be held in October 1982. He is a member of Eta Kappa Nu and Sigma Xi.

Leah J. Siegel (S'75-M'77) was born in Trenton, NJ, on August 27, 1949. She received the S.B. degree in mathematics in 1972 from the Massachusetts Institute of Technology, Cambridge, the M.A. and M.S.E. degrees in 1974, and the Ph.D. degree in 1977, all in electrical engineering and computer science, from Princeton University, Princeton, NJ.

Since 1976 she has been an Assistant Professor in the School of Electrical Engineering, Purdue University, West Lafayette, IN. Her research interests include speech analysis and recognition, and the design of parallel processing algorithms for digital speech, signal, and image processing. At Purdue she has been involved in the development of the Laboratory for One-Dimensional Signal Processing.

Dr. Siegel is a member of the Administrative Committee of the IEEE Acoustics, Speech, and Signal Processing Society. She is also a member of the Association for Computing Machinery, Eta Kappa Nu, and Sigma Xi.

Frederick C. Kemmerer (S'78-M'79) was born in Allentown, PA, on July 21, 1956. He received the B.S. degree in electrical engineering from the Pennsylvania State University, University Park, in 1978 and the M.S. degree in electrical engineering from Purdue University, West Lafayette, IN, in 1979.

In 1978 he joined Bell Laboratories, Whippany, NJ, where he is currently a member of the Technical Staff. His research interests include parallel processing, distributed processing, operating systems, and distributed computer architecture.

Mr. Kemmerer is a member of Phi Kappa Phi.

Philip T. Mueller, Jr. (S'79–M'80) was born in St. Louis, MO, on August 31, 1956. He received the B.S. degree in electrical engineering in 1977 and the M.S. degree in electrical engineering in 1979, both from Purdue University, West Lafayette, IN.

Currently, he is pursuing a Ph.D. degree in electrical engineering from Purdue University, while working for Geophysical Services, Inc., Dallas, TX. His research interests include parallel/distributed processing, multimicroprocessor systems, and artificial intelligence.

Harold E. Smalley, Jr. (S'75–M'78) was born in Willimantic, CT, in 1953. He received the B.E.E. degree from Auburn University, Auburn, AL, in 1975 and the M.S.E.E. degree from Purdue University, West Lafayette, IN, in 1978.

From 1978 to 1980 he was a member of the Technical Staff of Bell Laboratories, Holmdel, NJ. From 1980 to 1981 he worked at the Georgia Institute of Technology, Atlanta, as a Research Engineer. Presently, he is with Hitachi America Ltd., Atlanta, GA, in the Telecommunications Research and Development Division. His interests include distributed processing, parallel processing, and interprocess communication.

Mr. Smalley is a member of Tau Beta Pi and Eta Kappa Nu.

S. Diane Smith (S'73–M'79) was born in Danville, IL, on June 19, 1952. She received the B.S. degree in computer engineering in 1973 and the M.S. degree in electrical engineering in 1974 from the University of Illinois, Urbana-Champaign, and the Ph.D. degree in electrical engineering from Purdue University, West Lafayette, IN, in 1979.

In 1979 she joined the Department of Electrical and Computer Engineering at the University of Wisconsin, Madison as an Assistant Professor. Her research interests include parallel and distributed processing and computer architecture.

Dr. Smith is a Past President of the Alpha Chapter of Eta Kappa Nu and a member of the Association for Computing Machinery.

Reprinted from *IEEE Transactions on Computers,* Volume C-31, Number 10, October 1982, pages 952-962. Copyright © 1982 by The Institute of Electrical and Electronics Engineers, Inc.

A Pipelined Pseudoparallel System Architecture for Real-Time Dynamic Scene Analysis

DHARMA P. AGRAWAL, SENIOR MEMBER, IEEE, AND RAMESH JAIN, MEMBER, IEEE

Abstract—In this paper we introduce the concept of pseudoparallelism, in which the serial algorithm is partitioned into several noninteractive independent subtasks so that parallelism can be used within each subtask level. This approach is illustrated by applying it to a real-time dynamic scene analysis. Complete details of such a pseudoparallel architecture with an emphasis to avoid interprocessor communications have been worked out. Problems encountered in the course of designing such a system with a distributed operating system (no master control) have been outlined and necessary justifications have been provided. A scheme indicating various memory modules, processing elements, and their data-path requirements is included and ways to provide continuous flow of partitioned information in the form of a synchronized pipeline are described.

Index Terms—Algorithmic steps, distributed control, dynamic scene analysis, interconnection networks, interprocessor communication, pipelining, problem partitioning, pseudoparallelism, real-time computation, SIMD and MIMD.

I. INTRODUCTION

COMPUTER vision and digital image processing require a large amount of computation. A complete vision system requires many number-crunching operations at the lowest level and sophisticated decision making at the highest level. The advances in LSI and VLSI circuits have influenced researchers in computer vision and digital image processing. Many approaches for fast image processing using a network of processors have been presented [1]–[20]. However, parallelism has been applied mostly to those problems that are well defined or where use of partitioning is obvious. For example, various types of multiple processor-memory organizations described in the literature for different applications [1]–[7], are direct extensions or variations of four system types defined by Flynn [21]. These systems lack the ability to handle complex decision making, which is vital in a complete Computer Vision System. In fact, only PICAP and GOP systems [17], [20] have included features which may allow its application to solve intermediate and high level problems. With the in-

Manuscript received December 21, 1981; revised July 2, 1982. An earlier version of this work was presented at the 1981 IEEE Computer Society Workshop on Computer Architecture for Pattern Analysis and Image Database Management, November 11–13, 1981.

D. P. Agrawal was with the Department of Electrical and Computer Engineering, Wayne State University, Detroit, MI 48202. He is now with the Department of Electrical Engineering, North Carolina State University, Raleigh, NC 27650.

R. Jain was with the Intelligence Systems Laboratory, Department of Computer Science, Wayne State University, Detroit, MI 48202. He is now with the Department of Electrical and Computer Engineering, University of Michigan, Ann Arbor, MI 48109.

creasing applications of computer vision systems in robotics and other high technology areas, the need for real-time systems for image understanding has become extremely important.

In parallel processor systems, only single instruction multiple data (SIMD) and multiple instruction multiple data (MIMD) [21] characteristics are useful in providing parallelism. While outlining the general architecture of such a system, two functional modules (processing element and memory blocks) are first separately identified, and then their data path requirements are established. Most existing and proposed systems are modeled in two ways [Fig. 1(a) and (b)] [22]. In the first system of Fig. 1(a), each processing element has its own private memory, and the communication link between various processors is established through the network. Placing the network between the two types of modules provides a shared memory system [Fig. 1(b)]. The first type of system can be classified as a loosely coupled system while organizations in Fig. 1(b) are tightly coupled. Real-world problems usually require both private and shared memories and this leads to a more complex organization (Fig. 2). The private memory is used to store the necessary instructions while the large memory contains the data to be shared by various processors. This generalized architecture can support several concurrent but independent SIMD computation modes.

One of the oldest and most frequently referred to parallel systems is ILLIAC IV. Its usefulness in solving some matrix problems is well known, but it is not suitable for other complex applications in which relatively versatile intercommunication is a major concern. In fact, the memory contention problem or the interprocessor communication is considered to be a bottleneck affecting the performance of a multiple processor system and is at least as important as parallel computation [23]. As the cost of the hardware is no longer prohibitive, it is now time to identify the basic strategies in defining suitable architecture for a parallel computing system so that a given practical problem can be solved as effectively as possible. Such tuning of the system design is expected to lead to an improved throughput.

This paper is the result of an ongoing project at Wayne State University [24], [25], outlined in Section II. In Section III, we briefly review some existing/proposed machines for image processing and discuss their efficiency for real-time dynamic scene analysis. Since our aim in this paper is to study the special requirements of a real-time dynamic scene analysis system pertinent to the architecture design, we discuss an algorithm for the extraction of moving images in Section IV. This algo-

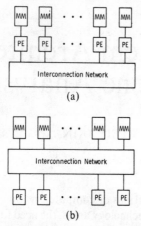

(a)

(b)

Fig. 1. (a) Memory blocks and processing elements in parallel computers. (b) Alternative organization.

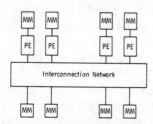

Fig. 2. Generalized architecture.

rithm is selected for the discussion due to its familiarity by one of the authors [26]; no claim is made about the efficiency or efficacy of the algorithm in this paper. Some problems in the implementation of this algorithm on the existing/proposed architectures are discussed in the Section V, where we propose a pseudoparallel pipeline implementation of the system. The performance evaluation of the proposed system is presented in Section VI and the conclusion is included in Section VII.

II. A DYNAMIC SCENE ANALYSIS SYSTEM

Dynamic scene analysis is concerned with the analysis of a frame sequence describing a scene. The camera may be stationary or nonstationary and objects in the scene may be moving. The time lapse between two contiguous frames of the sequence is assumed small so that radical changes in the shape of objects do not take place. In our current research project, it is assumed that the illumination in the scene remains unchanged.

Our long term goal is to design and implement a system capable of recognizing moving objects and their motion characteristics. This system, as shown in Fig. 3, has three distinct phases: peripheral, attentive, and cognitive. The peripheral phase identifies areas in the field of view with persistent changes and extracts gross information about the moving objects and their motion characteristics [27]. The attentive phase focuses attention on the "active" image areas in order to investigate them in more details. The attentive phase will generate symbolic/iconic structures which allow semantic interpretation of segments or images. As shown in the Fig. 3, the processes in the attentive phase will use some general knowledge sources and will be influenced by the requirements

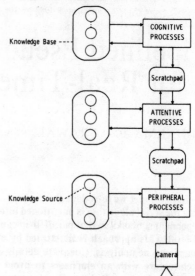

Fig. 3. Dynamic scene understanding system.

of the cognitive phase. The cognitive phase relates the observations derived from the frame sequence to the real world through a knowledge base containing information, arranged in many independent domain knowledge sources, about objects and their motion characteristics.

The peripheral phase of this system requires low level processing; most operations are local and can be implemented using SIMD type architectures. The cognitive phase is one of the least understood phase of the systems. We are investigating methods for the representation of object and domain knowledge. The attentive phase comprises image understanding problems; segmentation being the main task.

Currently, we are in the design phase of the system. Some of the important factors influencing our design are loose coupling of various blocks, independence of knowledge sources, distributed problem solving to combine information from different sources, and application of distributed/parallel processing wherever appropriate. In fact, our system design is very much influenced by the following four principles for large symbolic programs, outlined by Marr [28]:

1) Principle of Explicit Naming;
2) Principle of Modularity;
3) Principle of Least Commitment;
4) Principle of Graceful Degradation.

Our design philosophy as outlined in [29], employs these principles extensively. In this paper we consider an algorithm for segmentation of a dynamic scene and discuss our approach for designing suitable architecture for the real-time implementation of the algorithm. This algorithm is mainly concerned with the peripheral and attentive phases of the dynamic scene analysis system and has limited applicability in a general scene. We consider this algorithm in our study, mainly due to our good understanding of the algorithm, and the fact that this algorithm clearly demonstrates the type of problems one faces in a dynamic scene analysis system. The algorithm discussed in this paper assumes a stationary camera and uniform illumination. Since this algorithm extracts images of moving objects, in the following we use "motion analysis" to describe the task of the algorithm.

III. Multiple Processor Systems for Motion Analysis and Pseudoparallelism

Architectures for several systems have been proposed for picture processing and image analysis. If communication is needed only between the neighboring processors, several of these parallel systems [7], [12]–[14] can provide the speedup needed for real-time computation. The massively parallel processor system [12], [30] currently being built for NASA employs 16 384 processors to be assembled in a grid organization of 128×128 units and an SIMD type of computation is to be utilized. As a large number of processors is to be designed using VLSI chips, the computation is bit serial in nature. Moreover, as each processor is connected to only four of its neighbors, data transfer between nonadjacent processors is time consuming, making it suitable for only local image processing operations. The CLIP-4 system [3], [13] also provides serial data processing capabilities and allows only intraneighborhood communication. Further advancement has been proposed in CLIP-6 [14] system where serial processing of the gray-coded pixels are provided but a provision for the parallel transfer of data between the processors has been included. The system is suitable for SIMD type operations and the sharing of data by all the processors is not practical.

The multilayered pyramid of arrays [2], [15] is excellent for reduction and convergence of data in successive stacks that involve near-neighbor processing. This well-structured pipeline system is well suited for pattern recognition and matrix manipulation applications. Retention and sharing of data between various layers and data transfer between processors at the same layer is time-consuming and is not suitable for computer vision. Another noteworthy system currently being built at the University of Maryland [6], [16] will consist of 256 Z80A microcomputers to be controlled by a VAX system. This system, called ZMOB, is useful for various image processing operations including point and local operations, discrete transforms, geometric operations, and computation of image statistics. The micros process the disjoint parts of the information in parallel and the amount of data exchange depends on the information contents. The communication in this 100 million instructions/s system is achieved by 257 bins connected in the form of a high-speed ring. One way to reduce the amount of data transfer is to distribute the data to the micros in an overlapped fashion. But, in general, the computer vision tasks might require data for the complete frame and any effective speedup may not be achieved from the ZMOB system.

The architecture proposed by Siegel et al. [8], [18] can be dynamically configured as one or more independent SIMD and/or MIND machines. The partitioning is achieved through proper selection of the control signals in the interconnection networks and is based on the ideal concept of "any processor can have access to any memory module." This is attractive theoretically, but is neither feasible with a large number of functional modules nor is required in a pipeline system in which communication is needed between a group of modules. A generalized and more complex system (PUMPS) currently being developed at Purdue [1], [19] can also provide SIMD and MIMD modes, and resources could be distributed by the arbitration network to suit the computation requirements of the active processes. A distributed operating system is supposed to run on this reconfigurable system. Various applicative domains have also been indicated. The system implementation requires a lot of manpower and the initial investment seems to be too excessive. Moreover, it is not clear as to how intelligence will be provided in the operating system to distribute an AI problem and optimize the use of its resources. In addition, computer vision requires interaction of information contents in various parts of the system. In brief, any measure indicating the suitability of PUMPS for computer vision cannot be predicted.

The PICAP [17] and GOP [20] systems, currently being developed in Sweden, are capable of providing parallelism at both global and local levels and show a potential for use in computer vision. The PICAP system utilizes a large shared memory using a time-shared bus which eliminates any needs for data transfer. On the other hand, the memory contention problem may not provide the parallel processing and speed up needed for a real-time application. The GOP system is divided into two individually microprogrammable parts. Part I combines mask and image data in four reconfigurable arithmetic parallel pipelines and part II is a serial special purpose processor with a high degree of flexibility. One of the advantages of the GOP system can be said to be the unique representation of the image data at various levels so that computation can be continued without any data transfer. The lack of architectural details makes it difficult to categorize its effectiveness for computer vision and other real-time applications.

In motion analysis, an interaction between data pertaining to various parts of a picture frame is needed and a direct use of parallelism is not possible. This makes the existing systems unsuitable for motion analysis, and a new direction or basic strategy should be sought to introduce parallelism in such a complex sequential problem. Flynn and Hennessy [31] have emphasized the concurrency determination for using any distributed system effectively. Their main concern has been the use of a proper functional language. Kieburz [32] has advocated using decomposition for problem solving. He has considered a general case using an acyclic dependence graph that determines parallelism at the subtask level. The degree of parallelism provided by such a scheme is algorithm dependent, and in the worst case of totally sequential problems like motion analysis, it may not provide any speedup. Recently, data-driven and demand-driven parallel organizations with decentralized control have been proposed which possess a promising potential for utilizing natural parallelism in a given algorithm. Although few prototype data-flow machines with up to four processors have been built [33], a number of key questions are yet to be answered and various proposed alternatives are still controversial [34]. Hence, a lot of effort is needed and it will be some time before it will be feasible to implement such a large system with minimum desirable capabilities.

To overcome this situation, we propose using parallelism within each subtask so that the interprocessor coordination or synchronization can be achieved very easily. We divide the algorithm into several sequential steps and use the appropriate degree of parallelism within each step. The computation is still sequential in terms of subtasks or steps, so we call our approach "pseudoparallel" [24], [25]. Our basic strategy of tuning the architecture to a partitioned algorithm will provide effective speedup for most sequential problems as long as the interaction or forward/backward branching is required within each partitioned step. The "pseudoparallel" algorithm thus converts the serial algorithms into a form suitable for running in a distributed operating system environment [35], [36] and the system throughput can be increased considerably by using the system in a pipelined manner.

A brief description of the algorithmic steps required in a motion analysis system is included in the next section.

IV. Algorithm for Motion Analysis

In this section we describe some modules of an algorithm for extracting images of moving objects. We also indicate briefly the necessary information flow between the modules. Our aim is not to describe the algorithm in detail, but to bring out some problems associated with parallel problem solving as applied to a real-time system for motion analysis. The details of the algorithm are given in Jain *et al.* [26].

A. Condensed Frame Generator

The input frames are usually obtained using a television camera. These frames have 570×512 pixels; each pixel represents the gray level at a point in the frame. The gray level is quantized in 256 levels. The input frames are condensed to a 95×128 picture obtained by grouping together four consecutive columns and six consecutive rows of the original frame. Each element of the condensed frame contains the mean and the variance of the intensities of the corresponding pixels of the raw fame. (The term frame is used for condensed frame and the term pixel is used for an element of the condensed frame.)

B. Difference Picture Generator

A difference picture (DP) is a binary picture generated by comparing two frames. The DP is generated by placing a "1" in each pixel for which the corresponding pixels in the two frames being compared have an appreciable difference in gray level characteristics. The difference picture for motion analysis is prepared by comparing two continuous frames of the sequence. For determining whether or not the corresponding pixels of the frames, called the previous and current frames, may be considered different, we compute

$$R = ((S_p + S_c)/2 + ((M_p - M_c)/2))**2/(S_p*S_c) \quad (1)$$

in which M and S denote the mean and variance values contained at a pixel of the condensed frame, and subscripts p and c indicate that the mean and variance is taken from the previous and current frames, respectively. If the ratio R is greater than a preset threshold, then the gray levels for this location in the previous and current frames are taken to be from different gray level distributions.

C. Labeling

A labeled picture is obtained by applying the algorithm

```
If    DP (I,J) = 1   THEN
    IF E (DP(I,J))    THEN
      BEGIN
        DP (I,J) = 2;
        IF SOB (PREV(I,J))    THEN DP(I,J) = 3;
        IF SOB (CURR(I,J))    THEN DP(I,J) = DP(I,J) +2
      END;
```

Fig. 4.   Labeling algorithm.

given in Fig. 4 to every point (I, J) of the DP and the previous and current frames. In this algorithm DP, PREV, and CURR are the difference picture, previous frame, and current frame respectively; $E(P(I, J))$ and SOB $(P(I, J))$ are Boolean operators determining whether or not $P(I, J)$ is an edge point in a binary and gray picture, respectively.

Edges in the DP, the previous frame, and the current frame are denoted by ED, EP, and EC, respectively. The labels 1, 2, 3, 4, and 5 in the labeled difference picture are 1 points of DP, which are $(\overline{ED}, \overline{EP}, \overline{EC})$, $(ED, \overline{EP}, \overline{EC})$, $(ED, EP, \overline{EC})$, $(ED, \overline{EP}, EC)$, and (ED, EP, EC), respectively. Note that the labeled difference picture displays edginess of points through different pictures; that is the DP, previous frame, and current frame.

D. Motion Detector

The difference picture contains intensity dissimilarity (change) information for the corresponding points in two frames. The dissimilarities may be caused by the lighting changes, camera noise, or motion. We consider the isolated dissimilarities caused by the noise and assume that lighting remains constant. Based on these assumptions, a simple filtering scheme is used to filter entries in the DP caused by motion. All connected components that contain more than N elements (say 10) are considered the result of motion, and the "1" entries that do not belong to such a component are discarded as noise. There are several algorithms for component labeling in a picture. A component of size greater than N is called an active region.

E. Region Classifier

It has been shown that regions in a difference picture are formed due to occlusion or disocclusion (or both) of the background by a moving object. In many cases it is possible to determine whether a DP region is the result of occlusion or disocclusion, or both. These three types of regions are denoted as type O, B, and X regions. For a given region the type can be found by computing a ratio called CURPRE which equals the number as defined

$$\text{CURPRE} = \frac{\text{\# of points labeled 4 in the region}}{\text{\# of points labeled 3 in the region}} \quad (2)$$

The CURPRE is much less than 1 for type B regions, much greater than 1 for type O regions, and near 1 for type X regions.

F. Object Extractor

We use region growing for O and B type regions to obtain the masks in the previous and current frames. A region is grown by taking each nonregion pixel that has a horizontal

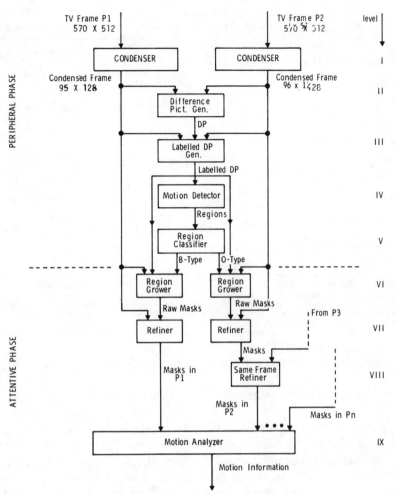

PERIPHERAL PHASE

CONDENSER

CONDENSER

I

Condensed Frame
95 X 128

Condensed Frame
96 x 128

II

Difference
Pict. Gen.

DP

Labelled DP
Gen.

III

Labelled DP

Motion Detector

IV

Regions

Region
Classifier

V

B-Type   O-Type

ATTENTIVE PHASE

Region
Grower

Region
Grower

VI

Raw Masks   Raw Masks

From P3

Refiner

Refiner

VII

Masks

Masks in
P1

Same Frame
Refiner

VIII

Masks in
P2

Masks in Pn

Motion Analyzer

IX

Motion Information

Fig. 5.   Sequential data flow and motion analyzer.

neighbor within the region and comparing its gray level with that of an adjacent region pixel. If the gray levels are similar, then the nonregion pixel is added to the region. The gray levels are taken from the previous frame for the DP regions of type B and from the current frame for the DP region of type O. A similar process is applied to the nonregion pixels that have vertical neighbors within the region. These processes are iterated until no new pixels are added to the region. The region obtained represents the previous frame object mask when grown from a type B region and the current frame object mask when grown from a type O region.

The masks obtained in this way are improved by using the following refinement processes:

1) same object refinement;
2) termination refinement;
3) gap filling;
4) same frame refinement.

The first three refinement steps are applied to the data stream based only on one difference picture. The same frame refinement exploits the fact that the frame F_i participates in two difference pictures, namely those obtained by comparing pairs (F_{i-1}, F_i) and (F_i, F_{i+1}) and thus two images of a moving object in the frame F_i are obtained. These images should be the same.

G. Motion Analyzer

The outputs of the object extractor are the images of the moving objects in continuous frames. Some motion characteristics such as velocity and acceleration are easily obtained from the displacement of the image. Note that there is no need to save masks for all pairs of frames, and a single updated and overall mask can take care of information contained in all successive masks.

Fig. 5 shows the sequential data flow diagram for the algorithm comprising the preceding blocks; Table I indicates the approximate time taken by each block. The outputs of condenser, difference picture generator, labeled difference picture generator, region grower, refiner, and same frame refiner are alphanumeric. It is clear from the problem that it is impossible to use parallelism for the overall execution of the algorithm. However, parallelism can be introduced within each step, and depending on the time required for a particular step, an adequate number of processors can be assigned so that each step can effectively complete the computation in one unit of time, and pipelining achieved with synchronous transfer of information between steps. A problem in the pipelining process is created due to the fact that several blocks require data from the immediate preceding blocks as well as outputs from several earlier blocks.

TABLE I
CHARACTERISTICS OF VARIOUS FUNCTIONAL BLOCKS FOR MOTION ANALYSIS

Level No.	Functional Block	Required Processing Time*	No. of Processors Allocated for the Block	Data Needed Through Level Numbers	Computation Mode	Computation Time With Distributed Processing
I	Condenser	20	20	I - VII	SIMD	1
II	Difference Picture Generator	10	10	II - III	SIMD	1
III	Labelled Difference Picture	5	5	III - VI	SIMD	1
IV	Motion Detector	5	5	IV - V	MIMD	1
V	Region Classifier	0.5	1	V - VI	SISD	0.5
VI	Region Growing	3	1@	VI - VII	SISD	1
VII	Refinement	3	1@	VII - VIII	SISD	1
VIII	Same Frame Reference	1	1	VIII - IX	SISD	1
IX	Motion Analyzer	1	1	IX	SISD	1
	Total no. when not Pipelined	48.5 for uniprocessor	20		SISD/SIMD/MIMD	8.5
	Total no. when Pipelined	48.5 for uniprocessor	45		SISD/SIMD/MIMD	1

* Integer indicate their relative values
@ Only one region to the processed for a frame pair.

V. PSEUDOPARALLEL SYSTEM ARCHITECTURE FOR MOTION ANALYSIS

Since our objective is to design a pipelined distributed system, we should use enough processors and memory modules for each functional block such that there is an uninterrupted flow of information throughout the system. If we assume that one unit time period is the desired processing time for each block, the number of processors for individual blocks should be large enough so that the effective time delay can be matched with its sequential processing time. Thus, the number of parallel processors required to make the computation time equal to one unit time can easily be obtained (Table I). It is assumed that for every step of the algorithm, there is no restriction on the number of memory modules, and that each module is large enough to store the data. Another assumption is that parallel algorithms, where applicable, are available to compute the task in the required time.

In regard to the operating mode of each block, the first three blocks of Fig. 5 (condenser, DPG, and LDP) can be computed in SIMD mode by sectionalizing the frame. In the beginning, a frame is divided into 20 sections, and each section is stored in 20 different memory modules so that 20 processing elements can work in parallel on such distributed data. In the second level, the generation of the difference picture requires only 10 processors and hence, data must be distributed over only 10 memory blocks. This necessitates movement of data and can be avoided by considering two logically adjacent memory modules of level I as a large single "macro memory" block. The resultant data of level I is stored in only 10 different memory blocks of level II, and multiple-port memory blocks [37] for such compact generation of data may be useful. This would require an appropriate procedure for memory mapping such that the macro module would contain information corre-

sponding to sections of the picture physically adjacent to each other. Similar assumptions are made as the step moves to level III of labeled difference picture generation.

Note that three time unit delays are required for the region growing and refinement steps. But still, only one processor is allocated to these steps. This is done primarily because these steps may require data corresponding to a complete frame, and if three processors are to work in parallel, one copy of data is to be supplied to each processor, which imposes generation of multiple copies of data. Moreover, in motion analysis, a large volume of data is to be processed and a large portion of data is redundant. It is not always necessary to analyze all regions of each frame. For example, in the first frame, the most important region could be considered by the two blocks, and for successive frames, other regions could be analyzed.

The computation mode and required time are also shown in Table I. A memory module allocated to a particular level is needed at two instances: when it is generated, and when it is used to compute data for the next level. This is strictly true for levels II, and IV–IX. The memory space for the condenser is needed when it is generated and also in phases II, VI, and VII. Similarly, the labeled DP is required for levels IV and VI. This enables us to calculate the minimum number of memory blocks required for a pipelined distributed system (Table I). The effective time delay of one unit could be achieved with 162 shared memory modules and 45 processors with their own private memories.

The next thing to be considered is the internal structure of the system. The interconnection of various functional modules should be such that an optimum performance can be achieved by proper reconfiguration of the system. This makes the dynamic data path requirements clear and system architecture for such a scheme can be obtained (Fig. 6). The interconnec-

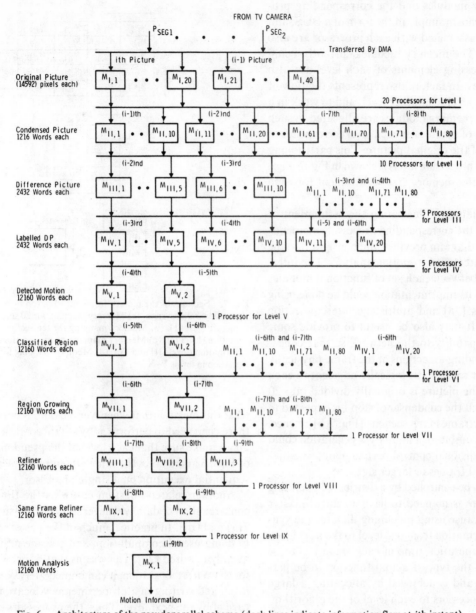

Fig. 6. Architecture of the pseudoparallel scheme (dark lines indicate information flow at ith instant).

TABLE II
INFORMATION CONTENTS OF VARIOUS MEMORY BLOCKS IN THE PROPOSED PIPELINED PSEUDOPARALLEL SYSTEM FOR FRAME SIZE OF 570×512 (AT THE ith INSTANT)

Storage Step	Total No. of Memory Modules	Size of Each Memory Module in Words	Number of Memory Modules for Frame Number									
			i	(i-1)	(i-2)	(i-3)	(i-4)	(i-5)	(i-6)	(i-7)	(i-8)	(i-9)
Original Picture	40	14592	20	20								
Condensed Picture	80	1216		10	10	10	10	10	10	10	10	
Difference P.G.	10	2432			5	5						
Labelled D.P.	20	12160				5	5	5	5			
Motion Detector	2	12160					1	1				
Region Classifier	2	12160						1	1			
Region Growing	2	12160							1	1		
Refinement	3	12160								1	1	1
Same Frame Refinement	2	12160									1	1
Motion Analyzer	1	12160										1
TOTAL	162											

tion between memory modules and the corresponding processing elements are shown simply in the form of a BUS, and the private memories associated with each processor are also omitted from Fig. 6. The memory modules currently being accessed by the processing elements of each level are also identified by dark lines. In fact, it also represents the flow of information from one level to another level, and to work in a pipelined fashion, the memory modules are allocated in such a way that each group of modules at each level corresponds to one complete frame of the original picture. This partitioning of the frame at various processing levels is shown in Fig. 7. Figs. 6 and 7 also provide the memory size requirement for each stage.

A more detailed diagram, illustrating the assignment of memory modules and the corresponding processing elements, is given in Fig. 8. The diagram provides much insight into the complex system architecture for motion analysis. The interconnection structure between each set of functional modules has been omitted, and its implementation could be done using a pair of generalizers [38] and multistage interconnection networks [38]-[44]. It may also be useful to provide some additional control capability to the network so that concatenated data corresponding to sections of the frame physically adjacent to each other can also be logically adjacent to each other. For example, the picture is originally divided into 20 sections [Fig. 7(a)] and the condenser of step I is expected to provide the condensed frame in ten sections [Fig. 7(b)]; hence, two sections are to be combined. The address generation could be assigned to the additional control part to maintain adjacency for sectionalized frames of larger size.

The system can also be controlled by a distributed operating system, and then there is no need to have a central master controller. This is because using pipelining dictates the synchronous flow of information from one level to the next level, and the effective computation time of each stage has to be made independent of the type of actual function to be performed by the stage and is achieved by allocating a large enough number of processors to each level of the algorithm. Thus, there is no need to have a central controller for monitoring and guiding the sequency of the processes, as this has already been tailored in the system architecture.

VI. Performance Evaluation

The "pseudoparallel" implementation of motion analysis presented in earlier sections provides a general design strategy for implementing a system for any other specific application. But, it also poses some interesting questions.

The first question is the degree of parallelism allowed in each step. This has been done on the basis of the data reported in an earlier work [26], and if advances made in this direction would modify the algorithm or change the time required for any level of Fig. 5, then similar alternations in Fig. 6 could be done very easily.

The other important question is the data generation time in the proposed pseudoparallel scheme. In the sequential process of Fig. 5, while moving from one level to another, a new data file is not always created, and the desired operations are performed on the old data area. Still going to the machine level,

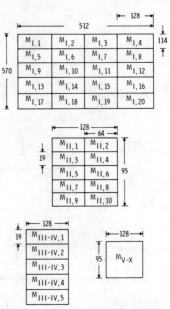

Fig. 7. Sections of the picture frame information in various levels of the pseudoparallel system. (a) Memory mapping for 20 sections of the original picture (level I). (b) Memory mapping for ten sections of the condensed picture (level II). (c) Memory mapping for five sections of the picture information (levels III and IV). (d) Memory mapping for the picture information in levels V-X.

what this means is that whenever old data is not to be modified, there is no need to perform a "WRITE" operation. Hence, how do we make sure that each level of the pseudoparallel scheme of Figs. 6 and 8 takes the same amount of time as taken by the sequential execution on a single processor.

Another related question concerns the time required for concatenation of data whenever it is needed [such as from Fig. 7(a) and (b)]. In practice, much of the processor time is spent in doing useful computation, and storage of data is less frequently required [26]. This means that whenever data is ready for the WRITE operation, it can immediately be sent to the next level, and writing in a proper memory location can be taken care of by the next level. Thus, the processors can keep themselves busy just doing useful computations.

A similar argument can be given for concatenation, and either multiple port memory or simple memory with multiplexed inputs can be used. This should also not create any problem because the rate of data transfer from each processor is small in relation to the computation time [26].

The design of data paths that can be restructured is itself a problem and has been widely addressed in the literature [39]-[44]. This could introduce some additional time delay. Besides parallelism, one advantage of the proposed system can be mentioned. The processors assigned to each level have to do a very specific job, and the associated private memory should store the program needed for that part only. As the private memory will be considerably smaller than the memory required in a sequential process, another advantage of the proposed system is the absence of any synchronization problems which have been commonly observed in most distributed data base management systems. In fact, the proposed system is a perfect candidate for the distributed operating system with no central master control.

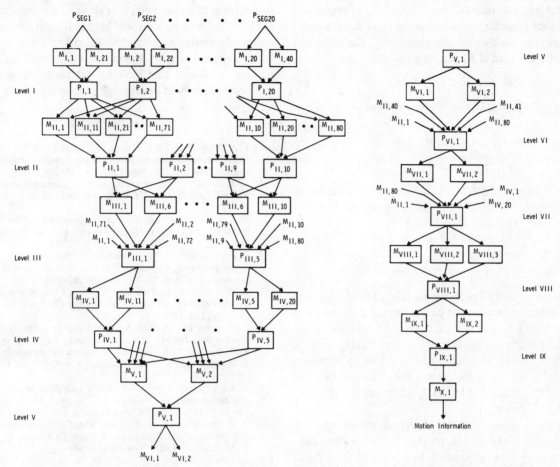

Fig. 8. Illustration of memory-processor interconnection for the pseudoparallel scheme.

To evaluate the performance of a general pseudoparallel scheme, let us assume the following:

$m \equiv$ total number of levels or stages in a sequential problem
$t_i \equiv$ time taken by the ith stage in a sequential problem, for $1 \leqq i \leqq m$.

A. Sequential Implementation

In regard to the assumptions just mentioned the total time taken in a sequential processing scheme will be

$$T_{\text{seq}} = \sum_{i=1}^{m} t_i. \tag{3}$$

B. Pseudoparallel Implementation

In this scheme, there may be overhead from switching for dynamic path establishment and memory mapping. Let this be denoted by α_i such that:

$\alpha_i \equiv$ total overhead in ith level of pseudoparallel implementation.

Then, the time taken by the ith stage can be given as

$$t'_i = (t_i + \alpha) = (1 + \beta_i)\, t_i \tag{4}$$
$$\text{in which } \beta_i = \alpha_i/t_i.$$

Let K_i processors be assigned to ith stage of pseudoparallel implementation. It may be noted that the value of K_i should be such that it is feasible to use parallelism in ith stage with K_i processors working in parallel. The time needed to complete ith stage evaluation can be given as

$$t_{pi} = t'_i/K_i \qquad \text{for } l \leqq i \leqq m. \tag{5}$$

The total time needed for psuedoparallel implementation can be obtained as

$$T_{pp} = \sum_{i=1}^{m} t_{pi}. \tag{6}$$

C. Pseudoparallel Pipelined Implementation

If the overall scheme is to operate as a pipeline, then the data from each level must be moved to the next level within a fixed amount of time. This means that the effective time taken by each step should be constant, say "U." Then the effective time taken by such a system can be given by

$$T_{ppp} = U. \tag{7}$$

For the pipeline to operate synchronously, we have to put additional constraints on relation (6). The number of processors allocated to each stage should be large enough so that the result of each stage is available in at most time "U." The condition for the minimum value of K_i can be given as

$$(K_i - 1)U < t_i' \leq K_i U. \qquad (8)$$

Now, the speed up ratio can be easily obtained

$$\frac{T_{seq}}{T_{pp}} = \frac{\sum\limits_{i=1}^{m} t_i}{\sum\limits_{i=1}^{m} t_{pi}} \qquad (9)$$

and

$$\frac{T_{seq}}{T_{ppp}} = \frac{\sum\limits_{i=1}^{m} t_i}{U}. \qquad (10)$$

It may be noted that 50 memory modules of level II used to store the condensed picture can be eliminated if six modules are added at level III, such that each can store the information corresponding to one complete frame-pair currently saved in ten modules of level II. This could be easily done by providing one additional processor to concatenate data from ten modules of level II (to one module of level III) whenever it is not used by the next level processor.

It is also worth mentioning that if several regions are to be concurrently examined at the motion analyzer step, then multiple copies of data could easily be generated. This could be achieved by sending and storing the information from same frame refinement step to several memory modules of the motion analyzer step. The system can also be made robust by providing various degrees of hardware redundancy at all the levels of the system. This might include additional processors memory blocks and alternate data paths between these functional modules.

VII. Conclusion

Tuning of the proposed architecture to the pseudoparallel algorithmic steps of motion analysis enables us to use parallelism in the best way possible. In fact, it can be conjectured that this is the only way parallelism can be introduced to the problem of real-time motion analysis in particular, and to real time computer vision systems in general. Moreover, pipelining technique provides increased effective speed of the system, and makes the using of a distributed operating system without any central controller feasible.

The main advantage of the proposed pseudoparallel scheme is the generality of the procedure. A suitable architecture for other specific applications that are basically sequential in nature can be designed using the proposed approach. This will require a thorough knowledge of the algorithmetic steps, the time required in solving each step of the problem, and the desired degree of speedup for balancing the computational requirements of each step. The basic philosophy can be easily

used for other unexplored problems if the algorithm is modeled in the form of either Petri nets or abstract process networks [45]–[47]. These models will help to identify noninteractive independent subtasks within the algorithm. Thus, the proposed pseudoparallel scheme shows great potential for its use in complex problems that have not yet been touched by other existing parallel and distributed processing systems.

References

[1] F. A. Briggs, K. S. Fu, K. Hwang, and J. Patel, "PM⁴: A reconfigurable multiprocessor system for pattern recognition and image processing," in *Proc. NCC, AFIPS*, June 1979, pp. 255–266.

[2] L. S. Davis, "Computer architecture for image processing," in *Proc. Picture Data Descrip. Management Conf.*, Aug. 27–28, 1980, pp. 249–254.

[3] M. J. B. Duff, "Future trends in cellular logic image processing," in *Proc. Picture Data Descrip. Management Conf.*, Aug. 27–28, 1980, pp. 294–297.

[4] B. Parvin and K. S. Fu, "A microprogrammable vector processor for image processing application," in *Proc. Picture Data Descrip. Management Conf.* Aug. 27–28, 1980, pp. 287–292.

[5] A. P. Reeves and R. Rindfuss, "The base 8 binary array processors," in *Proc. Pattern Recogn. Image Process. Conf.*, Chicago, Aug. 6–8, 1979, pp. 250–255.

[6] C. Rieger *et al.*, "ZMOB: A highly parallel multiprocessor," in *Proc. Picture Data Descrip. Management Conf.*, Aug. 1980, pp. 298–304.

[7] R. P. Roesser, "Two-dimensional microprocessor pipelines for image processing," *IEEE Trans. Comput.*, vol. C-27, pp. 144–156, Feb. 1979.

[8] H. J. Siegel *et al.*, "An SIMD/MIMD multiprocessor system for image processing and pattern recognition," in *Proc. 1979 Pattern Recogn. Image Process. Conf.*, Chicago, IL, Aug. 6–8, pp. 214–220.

[9] A. R. Hanson and E. M. Riseman, "VISIONS: A computer system for interpreting scenes," in *Computer Vision Systems*, A. R. Hanson and E. M. Riseman, Eds. New York: Academic, 1978.

[10] B. Kruse, "System architecture for image analysis," in *Structured Computer Vision*, S. Taninoto and A. Klinger, Eds. New York: Academic, 1980.

[11] P. Narendra "VLSI architectures for real-time image processing," in *Proc. Spring 1981, COMPCON*, pp. 303–306.

[12] J. L. Potter, "Continuous image processing on the MPP," in *Proc. 1981 IEEE Comput. Soc. Workshop Comput. Arch. Pattern Anal. Image Database Management*, Nov. 11–13, pp. 51–56.

[13] M. J. B. Duff, "CLIP 4: A large scale integrated circuit array parallel processor," in *Proc. 3rd Int. Conf. Pattern Recogn.*, 1976, pp. 728–733.

[14] T. J. Fountain, "Towards CLIP 6—An extra dimension," in *Proc. 1981 IEEE Comput. Soc. Workshop Comput. Arch. Pattern Anal. Image Database Management*, Nov. 11–13, pp. 25–30.

[15] L. Uhr, "Converging pyramids of arrays," in *Proc. 1981 IEEE Comput. Soc. Workshop Comput. Arch. Pattern Anal. Image Database Management*, Nov. 11–13, pp. 31–34.

[16] C. Rieger, "ZMOB: Doing it in parallel," in *Proc. 1981 IEEE Comput. Soc. Workshop Comput. Arch. Pattern Anal. Image Database Management*, Nov. 11–13, pp. 119–124.

[17] D. Antonsson *et al.*, "PICAP—A system approach to image processing," in *Proc. 1981 IEEE Comput. Soc. Workshop Comput. Arch. Pattern Anal. Image Database Management*, Nov. 11–13, pp. 35–42.

[18] H. J. Siegel *et al.*, "PASM: A partitionable SIMD/MIMD system for image processing and pattern recognition," *IEEE Trans. Comput.*, vol. C-30, pp. 934–947, Dec. 1981.

[19] F. A. Briggs et al., "PUMPS architecture for pattern analysis and image database management," in *Proc. 1981 IEEE Comput. Soc. Workshop Comput. Arch. Pattern Anal. Image Database Management*, Nov. 11–13, pp. 51–56.

[20] G. H. Granlund *et al.*, "The GOP image processor," in *Proc. 1981 IEEE Comput. Soc. Workshop Comput, Arch. Pattern Anal. Image Database Management*, Nov. 11–13, pp. 195–200.

[21] M. J. Flynn, "Some computer organizations and the effectiveness," *IEEE Trans. Comput.* vol. C-21, pp. 1901–1909, Sept. 1972.

[22] D. P. Agrawal and T. Y. Feng, "A study of communication processor systems," Rome Air Development Center Rep. RADC-TR-310, pp. 1–179, Dec. 1979.

[23] B. Lint and T. Agerwala, "Communication issues in the design and analysis of parallel algorithms," *IEEE Trans. Software Eng.*, vol. SE-7, pp. 174–188, Mar. 1981.

[24] D. P. Agrawal and R. Jain, "Computer analysis of motion using a network of processors," in *Proc. 5th Int. Conf. Pattern Recogn.*, Miami, FL, Dec. 1–4, 1980, pp. 305–308.

[25] D. P. Agrawal, "A pipelined pseudoparallel system architecture for motion analysis," in *Proc. 8th Int. Symp. Comput. Arch.*, May 12–14, 1981, pp. 21–35.

[26] R. Jain, W. Martin and J. K. Agrawal, "Segmentation through the detection of change due to motion," *Comput. Graphics Image Process.*, vol. 11, 1979. pp. 13–34.

[27] R. Jain, "Extraction of motion information from peripheral processes," *IEEE Trans. Pattern Anal. Machine Intell.*, vol. PAM-3, pp. 489–503, Sept. 1981.

[28] D. Marr, "Early processing of visual information," AI Memo 340, Massachusetts Inst. Technol., Cambridge, MA, Dec. 1975.

[29] R. Jain and S. Haynes, "Imprecision in computer vision," *IEEE Computer*, vol. 15, July 1982.

[30] K. Batcher, "MPP—A massively parallel processor," in *Proc. 1979 Int. Conf. Parallel Process.*, Aug. 21–24, p. 249; also in *IEEE Trans. Comput.*, vol. C-29, pp. 836–840, Sept. 1980.

[31] M. J. Flynn and J. L. Hennessy, "Parallelism and representation problems in distributed systems," in *Proc. 1st Int. Conf. Distributed Computing Syst.*, Alabama, Oct. 1–5, 1979, pp. 124–130.

[32] R. B. Kieburtz, "A hierarchical multicomputer for problem-solving by decomposition," in *Proc. 1st Int. Conf. Distributed Computing Syst.*, Alabama, Oct. 1–5, 1979, p. 63–71.

[33] P. C. Treleaven *et al.*, "Data-driven and demand-driven computer architecture," *ACM Comput. Surveys*, vol. 14, pp. 93–143, Mar. 1982.

[34] D. D. Gajski *et al.*, "A second opinion on data flow machines and languages," *IEEE Computer*, vol. 15, pp. 58–69, Feb. 1982.

[35] R. Y. Kain *et al.*, "Multiple processor scheduling policies," in *Proc. 1st Int. Conf. Distributed Computing Syst.*, Oct. 1–5, 1979, pp. 660–668.

[36] L. D. Wittie, "A distributed operating system for a reconfigurable network computer," in *Proc. 1st Int. Conf. Distributed Computing Syst.*, Oct. 1–5, 1979, pp. 669–679.

[37] S. M. Ornstein *et al.*, "Pluribus—A reliable multiprocessor," in *Proc. AFIPS 1975 Nat. Comput. Conf.*, pp. 551–559.

[38] K. M. Chung and C. K. Wong, "Construction of a generalized connector with $5 \cdot 8n \log_2$ edges," *IEEE Trans. Comput.*, vol. C-29, pp. 1029–1032, Nov. 1980.

[39] M. A. Abidi and D. P. Agrawal," On conflict-free permutations in multi-stage interconnection networks," in *Proc. 1979 Int. Conf. Parallel Process.*, Aug. 1979; also in *J. Digital Syst.*, vol. 4, no. 2, pp. 115–134, Summer 1980.

[40] M. A. Abidi, D. P. Agrawal, and J. J. Metzner, "Two single-pass permutations in multistage interconnection networks," in *Proc. 14th Annu. Conf. Inform. Sci. Syst.*, Princeton Univ., Mar. 26–28, 1980, pp. 516–522.

[41] T. Y. Feng, C. L. Wu, and D. P. Agrawal, "A microprocessor controlled asynchronous circuit switching network," in *Proc. 6th Annu. Symp. Comput. Arch.*, Philadelphia, PA, Apr. 23–25, 1979, pp. 202–215.

[42] D. P. Agrawal and S. C. Kim, "On nonequivalent multistage interconnection networks," in *Proc. 10th Int. Conf. Parallel Process.*, Aug. 25–28, 1981, pp. 234–237.

[43] D. P. Agrawal, "On graph theoretic approach to n- and $(2n-1)$ stage interconnection networks," in *Proc. 19th Annu. Allerton Conf. Commun. Contr.*, *Comput.*, Sept. 30–Oct. 2, 1981, pp. 559–568.

[44] L. Bhuyan and D. P. Agrawal, "Design and performance of a general class of interconnection networks," in *Proc. 1982 Int. Conf. Parallel Process.*, Aug. 24–27, 1982.

[45] C. V. Ramamoorthy and G. S. Ho, "Performance evaluation of asynchronons concurrent systems using Petri Nets," *IEEE Trans. Software Eng.*, vol. SE-6, pp. 440–449, Sept. 1980.

[46] L. J. Mekly and S. S. Yau, "Software design representation using abstract process networks, *IEEE Trans. Software Eng.*, vol. SE-6, pp. 420–435, Sept. 1980.

[47] T. McKelvey and D. P. Agrawal, "Design of software for distributed/multiprocessor systems," in *Proc. 1982 Nat. Comput. Conf.*, AFIPS, vol. 51, June 7–10, 1982, pp. 239–249.

Dharma P. Agrawal (M'74–SM'79) was born in Balod, India, on April 12, 1945. He received the B.E. degree in electrical engineering from the Ravishankar University, Raipur, India, in 1966, the M.E. degree (with honors) in electronics and communication engineering from the University of Roorkee, Roorkee, India, in 1968, and the D.Sc.Tech. degree in electrical engineering from the Ecole Polytechnique Federale de Lausanne, Switzerland, in 1975.

He has been a member of faculty in the M.N. Regional Engineering College, Allahabad, India; the University of Roorkee, Roorkee, India; the Federal Institute of Technology, Lausanne, Switzerland; the University of Technology, Baghdad, Iraq; the Southern Methodist University, Dallas, TX; and Wayne State University, Detroit, MI. Currently he is at North Carolina State University, Raleigh, NC, as an Associate Professor in the Department of Electrical Engineering. His research interests include parallel/distributed processing, computer architecture, fault-tolerance, and information retrieval.

He has served as a referee for various reputable journals and international conferences. He was a member of Program Committees for the COMPCON Fall of 1979 and the Sixth IEEE Symposium on Computer Arithmetic. Currently, he is a member and the Secretary of the Publications Board, IEEE Computer Society. He is also serving as a Co-Guest Editor for the Special Issue of IEEE TRANSACTIONS ON COMPUTERS in the area of Computer Arithmetic. He is listed in Who's Who in the Midwest, the 1981 Outstanding Young Men of America, and the Directory of World Researchers' 1980's subjects published by the International Technical Information Institute, Tokyo, Japan.

Dr. Agrawal is a member of the Association for Computing Machinery and Sigma Xi.

Ramesh Jain (M'79) received the Ph.D. degree in electronics and electrical communication from the Indian Institute of Technology, Kharagpur, India, in 1975.

He has worked at the Indian Institute of Technology, Kharagpur, India; the University of Hamburg, Hamburg, Germany; the University of Texas, Austin; Wayne State University, Detroit, MI; and at General Motors Research Lab. Currently, he is an Associate Professor with the Department of Electrical and Computer Engineering, University of Michigan, Ann Arbor. His research interests include artificial intelligence, computer vision, and computer graphics.

Dr. Jain is a member of the Association for Computing Machinery, the Pattern Recognition Society, and the AAAI.

DADO: A Parallel Processor for Expert Systems*

Salvatore J. Stolfo
and
Daniel P. Miranker
Department of Computer Science
Columbia University
New York City, N. Y. 10027

Abstract -- DADO is a parallel, tree-structured machine designed to provide significant performance improvements in the execution of large expert systems implemented in production system form. A full-scale version of the DADO machine would comprise a large (on the order of a hundred thousand) set of processing elements (PE's), each containing its own processor, a small amount (16K bytes, in the current prototype design) of local random access memory, and a specialized I/O switch. The PE's are interconnected to form a complete binary tree.

This paper describes the application domain of the DADO machine and the rationale for its design. We then focus on the machine architecture and detail the hardware design of a moderately large prototype comprising 1023 microprocessors currently under development at Columbia University. We conclude with very encouraging performance statistics recently calculated from an analysis of extensive simulations of the system.

Introduction

Due to the dramatic increase in computing power and the concomitant decrease in computing cost occurring over the last decade, many researchers are attempting to design computing systems to solve complicated problems or execute tasks which have in the past been performed by human experts. The focus of *Knowledge Engineering* is the construction of such complex, knowledge-based expert computing systems.

In general, knowledge-based expert systems are Artificial Intelligence (AI) problem-solving programs designed to operate in narrow "real-world" domains, performing tasks with the same competence as a skilled human expert. Illucidation of unknown chemical compounds [3], medical diagnosis [23], mineral exploration [4] and telephone cable maintenance [30] are just a few examples. The heart of these systems is a *knowledge base*, a large collection of facts, definitions, procedures and heuristic "rules of thumb", *acquired directly from a human expert*. The knowledge engineer is an intermediary between the expert and the system who extracts, formalizes, represents, and tests the relevant knowledge within a computer program.

*This research has been supported by the Defense Advanced Research Projects Agency through contract N00039-82-C-0427, as well as grants from Intel, Digital Equipment, Hewlett-Packard, Valid Logic Systems, AT&T Bell Laboratories and IBM Corporations and the New York State Science and Technology Foundation. We gratefully acknowledge their support.

Just as robotics and CAD/CAM technologies offer the potential for higher productivity in the "blue-collar" work force, it appears that AI expert systems will offer the same productivity increase in the "white-collar" work force. As a result, Knowledge Engineering has attracted considerable attention from government and industry for research and development of this emerging technology. However, as knowledge-based systems begin to grow in size and scope, they will begin to push conventional computing systems to their limits of operation. Even for experimental systems, many researchers reportedly experience frustration based on the length of time required for their operation. Much of the research in AI has focused on the problem of representing and organizing knowledge, but little attention has been paid to specialized machine architectures supporting problem-solving programs.

DADO is a large-scale parallel machine designed to support the rapid execution of expert systems, as well as multiple, independent systems. In the following sections we present an overview of DADO's application domain as well as the rationale for its design. We then detail the hardware design of the *DADO2* prototype, currently under construction at Columbia University, consisting of *1023 microprocessors*. We conclude with a presentation of performance statistics recently calculated from extensive simulations of the system, and an overview of the software systems implemented to date. Based on our studies, a full scale version of *DADO* comprising many thousands of processing elements will, in our opinion, be technically and economically feasible in the near future.

Expert Systems

Current Technology. Knowledge-based expert systems have been constructed, typically, from two loosely coupled modules, collectively forming the *problem-solving engine* (see Figure 1). The *knowledge base* contains all of the relevant domain-specific information permitting the program to behave as a specialized, intelligent problem-solver. Expert systems contrast greatly with the earlier general-purpose AI problem-solvers which were typically implemented without a specific application in mind. One of the key differences is the large amounts of problem-specific knowledge encoded within present-day systems.

Much of the research in AI has concentrated on effective methods for representing and operationalizing human experiential domain knowledge. The representations that have been proposed have taken a variety of forms including purely declarative-based logical formalisms, "highly-stylized" rules or productions, and

Reprinted from *Proceedings of the 1984 International Conference on Parallel Processing*, 1984, pages 74-82. Copyright © 1984 by The Institute of Electrical and Electronics Engineers, Inc.

structured generalization hierarchies commonly referred to as semantic nets and frames. Many knowledge bases have been implemented in rule form, to be detailed shortly.

Figure 1: Organization of a Problem-Solving Engine.

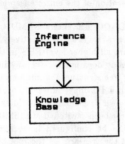

The *inference engine* is that component of the system which *controls* the deductive process: it implements the most appropriate strategy, or *reasoning* process for the problem at hand. The earliest AI problem-solvers were implemented with an iterative branching technique searching a large combinatorial space of problem states. Heuristic knowledge, applied within a static control structure, was introduced to limit the search process while attempting to guarantee the successful formation of solutions. In contrast, state-of-the-art expert systems separate the control strategy from an inflexible program, and deposit it in the knowledge base along with the rest of the domain-specific knowledge. Thus, the problem-solving strategy becomes domain-dependent, and is responsible to a large extent for the good performance exhibited by today's systems. However, a great deal of this kind of knowledge is necessary to achieve highly competent performance.

Within a great number of existing expert system programs, the corpus of knowledge about the problem domain is embodied by a *Production System* program. As has been reported by several researchers, production system representation schemes appear well suited to the organization and implementation of knowledge-based software. Rule-based systems provide a convenient means for human experts to explicate their knowledge, and are easily implemented and readily modified and extended. Thus, it is the ease with which rules can be acquired and explained that makes production systems so attractive.

Production Systems. In general, a *Production System* [6, 17, 18, and 19] is defined by a set of rules, or *productions*, which form the *Production Memory*(PM), together with a database of assertions, called the *Working Memory*(WM). Each production consists of a conjunction of *pattern elements*, called the *left-hand side* (LHS) of the rule, along with a set of actions called the *right-hand side* (RHS). The RHS specifies information that is to be added to (asserted) or removed from WM when the LHS successfully matches against the contents of WM. An example production, borrowed from the blocks world, is illustrated in Figure 2.

In operation, the production system repeatedly executes the following cycle of operations:

1. *Match*: For each rule, determine whether the LHS

Figure 2: An Example Production.

```
(Goal (Clear-top-of Block))
(Isa =x Block)
(On-top-of =y =x)
(Isa =y Block)   -->
            delete(On-top-of =y =x)
            assert(On-top-of =y Table)
```

If the goal is to clear the top of a block,
   and there is a block (=x)
   covered by something (=y)
   which is also a block,
            then
         remove the fact that =y is on =x
         and assert that =y is on top of the table.

– – – – – – – – – –

matches the current environment of WM. All matching instances of the rules are collected in the *conflict set of rules*.

2. *Select*: Choose exactly one of the matching rules according to some predefined criterion.

3. *Act*: Add to or delete from WM all assertions specified in the RHS of the selected rule or perform some operation.

During the selection phase of production system execution, a typical interpreter provides *conflict resolution strategies* based on the *recency* of matched data in WM, as well as syntactic discrimination. Rules matching data elements that were more recently inserted in WM are preferred, with ties decided in favor of rules that are more specific (i.e., have more constants) than others.

Why a specialized PS architecture? One problem facing expert systems technology is efficiency. It should be evident from the above description that large PS programs would spend most of their time executing the match phase requiring an enormous number of primitive symbol manipulation tasks. (Indeed, Forgy [6] notes that some PS interpreters spend 90% of their time in the match phase.) Hence, as this technology is ambitiously applied to larger and more complex problems, the size and concomitant slow speed of execution of production system programs, *with large rule bases*, on conventional machines will most likely doom such attempts to failure. The *R1* program [13], designed to configure Digital Equipment Corporation VAX computers, provides a convincing illustration.

In its current form, *R1* contains approximately 2500 rules operating on a WM containing several hundred data items, describing a partially configured VAX. Running on a DEC VAX 11/780 computer and implemented in OPS5 [8], a highly efficient production system language, *R1* executes from 2 to 600 production system cycles per minute. Configuring an entire VAX system requires a considerable amount of computing time on a moderately large and expensive computer. The performance of such systems will quickly worsen as experts are designed with not only one to two thousand rules, but perhaps with *tens of thousands* of rules. Indeed, several such large-scale systems are currently under development at various research centers. Statistics are difficult to calculate in the absence of specific empirical data, but it is conceivable that such large systems may require an unacceptable amount of computing time for a medium size conventional computer to execute a single cycle of production system execution! Thus, we consider the design and implementation of a specialized *production system machine* to warrant serious attention by parallel architects and VLSI designers.

Much of the experimental research conducted to date on specialized hardware for AI applications has focused on the realization of high-performance, cleverly designed, but for the most part, architecturally conventional machines. (MIT's LISP Machine exemplifies this approach.) Such machines, while quite possibly of great practical interest to the research community, make no attempt to employ hardware parallelism on the massive scale characteristic of our own work.

Thus, simply stated, the goal of the DADO machine project is the design and implementation of a *cost effective* high performance *rule processor*, based on large-scale parallel processing, capable of rapidly executing a production system cycle for very large rule bases. The essence of our approach is to execute a very large number of pattern matching operations on concurrent hardware, thus substantially accelerating the match phase. Our goals do not include the design of a high-speed parallel processor capable of a fruitless parallel search through a combinatorial solution space.

A small (15 processor) prototype of the machine, constructed at Columbia University from components supplied by Intel Corporation, has been operational since April 1983. Based on our experiences with constructing this small prototype, we believe a larger DADO prototype, comprising 1023 processors, to be technically and economically feasible for implementation using current technology. We believe that this larger experimental device will provide us with the vehicle for evaluating the performance, as well as the hardware design, of a full-scale version of DADO implemented entirely with custom VLSI circuits.

The DADO Machine

The System Architecture. DADO is a fine-grain, parallel machine where processing and memory are extensively intermingled. A full-scale production version of the DADO machine would comprise a very large (on the order of a hundred thousand) set of *processing elements* (PE's), each containing its own processor, a small amount (16K bytes, in the current design of the prototype version) of local random access memory (RAM), and a specialized I/O switch. The PE's are interconnected to form a *complete binary tree* (see Figure 3).

Within the DADO machine, each PE is capable of executing in either of two modes under the control of run-time software. In the first, which we will call *SIMD mode* (for single instruction stream, multiple data stream [5]), the PE executes instructions broadcast by some ancestor PE within the tree. (SIMD typically refers to a single stream of "machine-level" instructions. Within DADO, on the other hand, SIMD is generalized to mean a single stream of remote procedure invocation instructions. Thus, DADO makes more effective use of its communication bus by broadcasting

more "meaningful" instructions.) In the second, which will be referred to as *MIMD* mode (for multiple instruction stream, multiple data stream), each PE executes instructions stored in its own local RAM, independently of the other PE's. A single conventional coprocessor, adjacent to the root of the DADO tree, controls the operation of the entire ensemble of PE's.

When a DADO PE enters MIMD mode, its logical state is changed in such a way as to effectively "disconnect" it and its descendants from all higher-level PE's in the tree. In particular, a PE in MIMD mode does not receive any instructions that might be placed on the tree-structured communication bus by one of its ancestors. Such a PE may, however, broadcast instructions to be executed by its own descendants, providing all of these descendants have themselves been switched to SIMD mode. The DADO machine can thus be configured in such a way that an arbitrary internal node in the tree acts as the root of a tree-structured SIMD device in which all PE's execute a single instruction (on different data) at a given point in time. This flexible architectural design supports *multiple-SIMD* execution (MSIMD), as, for example, [24], but on a much larger scale. Thus, the machine may be logically divided into distinct partitions, each executing a distinct task, and is the primary source of DADO's speed in executing a large number of primitive pattern matching operations concurrently.

The DADO I/O switch, which will be implemented in semi-custom gate array technology and incorporated within the 1023 processing element version of the machine, has been designed to support rapid global communication. In addition, a specialized combinational circuit incorporated within the I/O switch will allow for the very rapid selection of a single distinguished PE from a set of candidate PE's in the tree, a process we call resolving. Currently, the 15 processing element version of DADO performs these operations in firmware embodied in its off-the-shelf components.

The Binary Tree Topology. In our initial work, several alternative parallel machine architectures were studied to determine a suitable organization of a special-purpose production system machine. High-speed algorithms for the parallel execution of production system programs were developed for the perfect shuffle [21] and binary tree machine architectures [1]. Forgy [7] proposed an interesting use of the mesh-connected ILLIAC IV machine [12] for the parallel execution of production systems, but recognized that his approach failed to find all matching rules in certain circumstances. Of these architectures, the binary tree organization was chosen for implementation. For the present paper we summarize these reasons as follows:

- Binary trees are efficiently implemented in VLSI technology:

    * Using the well known "Hyper-H" embedding (see [2]), binary trees can be embedded in the plane in an amount of area proportional to the number of processors. Thus, as VLSI continues scaling downward, higher processor densities can be achieved.

    * A design for a single chip type, first reported by Leiserson [11], embeds both a complete binary subtree and one additional PE, which can be used to implement an arbitrarily large binary tree. Thus, binary tree machines have a very low number of distinct integrated parts.

* Pin-out on the Leiserson chip remains constant for any number of embedded PE's.

* The Leiserson chip used with a simple recursive construction scheme produces printed circuit board designs that make optimal use of available area. This single printed circuit board design is suitable for implementing an arbitrarily large binary tree.

- Broadcasting data to a large number of recipients is handled efficiently by tree structures.

- Most importantly, the binary tree topology is a natural fit for production system programs.

We note that binary trees do have certain limitations of practical importance. Although broadcasting a small amount of information to a large number of recipients is efficiently handled by binary trees, the converse is, in general, unfortunately not true. That is, for certain computational tasks (permutation of data within the tree, for example) the effective bandwidth of communication is restricted by the top of the tree. Fortunately, as we shall see shortly, this "binary tree bottleneck" does not arise in the execution of production systems.

Production System execution. In our earlier work, extensive theoretical analyses and software simulations of a high-speed algorithm for production system execution on *DADO* was completed and reported in [25]. In its *simplest* form, the algorithm operates in the following way:

1. By assigning a single rule to each PE, executing in MIMD mode, at a (logically) fixed level within the tree, each rule in PM is matched concurrently. (This fixed level within the tree is referred to as the PM-level, see Figure 3.) Thus, the time to calculate the conflict set of rules on each cycle is independent of the number of productions in the system. Variations of this approach allow for multiple rules to be located at a PM-level PE, thus increasing the time to match a modest degree.

2. By assigning a data item in WM to a single PE executing in SIMD mode, lying below the PM-level, WM is implemented as a true hardware *content-addressable memory*. Thus, the time required to match a single pattern element in the LHS of a rule is independent of the number of facts in WM. (In a manner similar to production storage, more effective use of the WM PE's is made by allowing several WM elements to be present. The WM elements stored at a single PE, however, are "disjoint" in the sense that they may match different condition elements in the LHS of a rule.)

3. The selection of a single rule for execution from the conflict set is also performed in parallel by a logarithmic time binary tree selection executed above the PM-level. Thus, the logarithmic time lower bound of comparing and selecting a single item from a collection of items is achievable on *DADO* as well.

4. Lastly, the RHS actions specified by the selected rule

are broadcast to all PM-level PE's which update their respective WM-subtrees in parallel.

Figure 3: Functional Division of the DADO Tree.

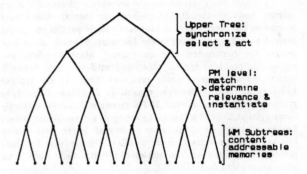

A comparative evaluation of this algorithm with various allocation schemes has been reported elsewhere (see [10, 15, 25, 27, and 28]). It should be noted that although the running time of the basic algorithm is shown to be insensitive to the size of PM and WM, in practice a fixed size machine may not, in general, attain these lower bound results. Thus, in situations where WM and PM are too large to be conveniently distributed in the manner discussed above for a machine of fixed size, some performance degradation will result.

For example, the second DADO prototype will consist of 1023 PE's and is expected to be logically divided with a PM-level consisting of 32 PE's, each rooting a WM-subtree with 31 PE's. To execute a 2500 rule system such as R1 will require partitioning ~75 rules to each PM-level PE. It would appear that the time to match would depend on 75 rules rather than 2500 for this example. However, recent statistics reported indicate that never more than ~30 rules are active on each cycle of execution of R1. Hence, with a suitable partitioning of rules, no more than 1 rule would be processed by each PM-level PE in our example configuration, thus attaining a match time independent of 2500 rules. Note, though, that each PM-level PE can access 31 WM elements in parallel. Thus, in total, 32 X 31 or ~1000 WM elements would be accessed at any one point in time. In the case where a single rule might require access to more than 31 WM elements at a time, performance will degrade gracefully. Hence, 31 elements can be accessed by a single PM-level PE in one time unit, 62 in two time units, 93 in three, etc.

Recently, we have completed a number of reports which detail five related algorithms for the parallel execution of PS programs to account for various differences in PS programs. As noted, some PS programs, (R1, for example) may not have a high degree of "production-level parallelism". That is, on each cycle only a relatively small number of productions may have satisfied LHS's. Other PS programs may have a high degree of production-level parallelism. Many other variations are possible which lead to a variety of related algorithms which attempt to maximize system performance by integrating various rule partitioning schemes with clever "state saving" schemes. The details of the various methods are beyond the scope of this paper, and thus the reader is encouraged to see [15] and [28]. Studies of such situations have been made and the projections of possible performance degradation are summarized in a later section of this paper.

Although analytical studies and software implementations are primary tasks of the *DADO* project, our current efforts have focused on the construction of hardware. Many parallel computing devices have been proposed in the literature, however, often such devices are constructed only on paper. Many scientific and engineering problems remain undetected until an actual device is constructed and experimentally evaluated. Thus, we are actively building a large prototype consisting of 1023 Intel 8751 microcomputer chips. A small 15 PE version of *DADO* is currently operational at Columbia University acting as a development system for the software base of the larger prototype. In the remainder of this paper we concentrate on the details of the hardware for these prototypes as well as the software systems that have been implemented thus far.

The DADO Prototypes

Physical Characteristics. A 15-element *DADO1* prototype, constructed from (partially) donated parts supplied by Intel Corporation, has been operational since April 25, 1983. The two wire-wrap board system, housed in a chassis roughly the size of an IBM PC, is clocked at 3.5 megahertz producing 4 million instructions per second (MIPS)[16]. (The effective usable MIPS is considerably less due to the significant overhead incurred in interprocessor communication. For each byte quantity communicated through the system, 12 machine instructions are consumed at each level in the tree while executing an asynchronous, 4-cycle handshake protocol.) DADO1 contains 124K bytes of user random access storage and 60K bytes of read only memory. A much larger version, *DADO2*, is currently under construction which will incorporate 1023 PE's constructed from two commercially available Intel chips and one semi-custom gate array chip (to be fabricated by LSI Logic). DADO1 does not provide enormous computational resources. Rather, it is viewed as the development system for the software base of DADO2, and is not expected to demonstrate a significant improvement in the speed of execution of a production system application.

DADO2 will be implemented with 32 printed circuit boards housed in an IBM Series I cabinet (donated by IBM Corporation). A DEC VAX 11/750 (partially donated by DEC Corporation) serves as DADO2's coprocessor (although an HP 9836 workstation may be used as well) and is the only device a user of DADO2 will see. Thus, DADO2 is considered a transparent back-end processor to the VAX 11/750.

The DADO2 system will have roughly the same hardware complexity as a VAX 11/750 system, and if amortized over 12 units will cost in the range of 70 to 90 thousand dollars to construct considering 1982 market retail costs. The DADO2 semi-custom I/O chip is planned for implementation in gate array technology and will allow DADO2 to be clocked at 12 megahertz, the full speed of the Intel chips. The average machine instruction cycle time is 1.8

microseconds, producing a system with a raw computational throughput of roughly 570 million instructions per second. We note that little of this computational resource is wasted in communication overhead as in the DADO1 machine.

The Prototype Processing Element. Each PE in the 15-element DADO1 prototype system incorporates an Intel 8751 microcomputer chip, serving as the processor, and an 8K X 8 Intel 2186 RAM chip, serving as the local memory. DADO2 will incorporate a slightly modified PE. The Intel 2187, which is fully compatible with but faster than an Intel 2186, replaces the DADO1 RAM chip allowing the processor to be clocked at its fastest speed. Two such chips will be used (with a 16K X 1 chip for parity), increasing the PE storage capacity to 16K bytes. Further, the custom I/O chip will contain memory support circuitry and thus also replaces several additional gates employed in DADO1.

Although the original version of DADO had been designed to incorporate a 2K byte RAM within each PE, a 16K byte RAM was chosen for the prototype PE to allow a modest degree of flexibility in designing and implementing the software base for the full version of the machine. In addition, this extra "breathing room" within each PE allows for experimentation with various special operations that may be incorporated in the full version of the machine in combinational circuitry, as well as affording the opportunity to critically evaluate other proposed (tree-structured) parallel architectures through software simulation.

It is worth noting though that the proper choice of "grain size" is an interesting open question. That is, through experimental evaluation we hope to determine the size of RAM for each PE, chosen against the number of such elements for a fixed hardware complexity, appropriate for the widest range of production system applications. Thus, future versions of DADO may consist of a number of PE's each containing an amount of RAM significantly larger or smaller than implemented in the current prototype systems.

The Intel 8751 is a moderately powerful 8-bit microcomputer incorporating a 4K erasable programmable read only memory (EPROM), and a 256-byte RAM on a single silicon chip. One of the key characteristics of the 8751 processor is its I/O capability. The 4 parallel, 8-bit ports provided in a 40 pin package has contributed substantially to the ease of implementing a binary tree interconnection between processors. Indeed, DADO1 was implemented within 4 months of delivery of the hardware components. Figure 4 illustrates the DADO1 prototype PE, while figure 5 illustrates DADO2's PE.

Note that the same processor connections exist in the DADO2 PE design as those appearing in the DADO1 design. If in the unlikely event that the planned I/O chip does not function properly, DADO2 will thus remain operational, but will not run as fast as envisaged. Since the DADO1 hardware to date has remained operable, we are convinced that the fully upward compatible DADO2 PE design ensures the successful operation of a 1023 PE version of the machine.

In DADO1 the communication primitives and execution modes of a DADO PE are implemented by a small *kernel system* resident within each processor EPROM. The specialized I/O switch envisaged for the larger version of the machine is simulated in the

Figure 4: The DADO1 Prototype Processing Element.

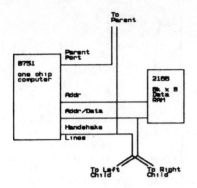

Figure 5: The DADO2 Prototype Processing Element.

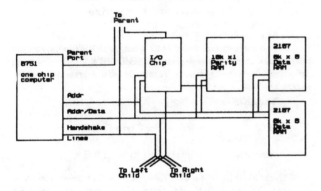

smaller version by a short sequential computation. As noted, the 1023 element prototype would be capable of executing in excess of 570 MIPS. Although pipelined communication is employed in the DADO1 kernel design, it is expected that fewer MIPS would be achieved on DADO2 without the I/O chip, as detailed in the following section. Thus, the design and implementation of a custom I/O chip forms a major part of our current hardware research activities.

It should be noted that, in keeping with our principles of "low-cost performance," we have selected a processor technology one generation behind existing available microcomputer technology. For example, DADO2 could have been designed with 1023 Motorola 68000 processors or Intel 80286 chips. Instead, we have chosen a relatively slow technology to limit the number of chips for each PE, as well as to demonstrate our most important architectural principals in a cost effective manner.

Furthermore, since the Intel 8751 does not press current VLSI technology to its limits, it is surely within the realm of feasibility to implement a DADO2 PE on a single silicon chip. Thus, although

DADO2 may appear impressive (an inexpensive, compact system with a thousand computers executing roughly 600 million instructions per second) its design is very conservative and probably at least an order of magnitude less powerful than a similar device using faster technology. It is our conjecture though that the machine will be practical and useful and many of its limitations will be ameliorated as VLSI continues its downward trend in scaling. (DADO3 may serve to prove this conjecture.)

Performance Evaluation of DADO2.

Design Alternatives. Much of the available computing power in the *DADO1* prototype is consumed by firmware executing a four cycle handshake communication protocol. For this reason we investigated the tradeoffs involved with adding a specialized I/O circuit to each PE to handle global communication in *DADO2*. The current I/O circuit design provides the means to broadcast a byte to all PE's in the tree in less than one Intel 8751 instruction cycle. This efficiency gain does not come free. The I/O circuit increases a PE's component count as well as the total area on a printed circuit board for the system. To decide this issue, we investigated the relative performance of a machine design incorporating the I/O circuit and a design without the I/O circuit, using the available area for additional PE's.

A second but orthogonal issue for the machine design is whether or not it is worthwhile to buffer the instruction stream broadcast to PE's executing in SIMD mode. In a typical SIMD machine a control processor issues a stream of machine level instructions that are executed synchronously in lock step by all of the slave processors in the array. *DADO* is different. Since each PE of *DADO* is a fully capable computer, and communication between PE's is generally expensive, we wish to make an instruction as "meaningful" as possible. What is communicated as an instruction in *DADO* is usually a pointer to a procedure, stored locally in each slave PE. Primitive SIMD *DADO* instructions are in fact parallel procedure calls and may be viewed as macro instructions.

For example, a common instruction that will be executed by a *DADO* PE is "MATCH(pattern)", where MATCH is a generalized pattern matching routine local to each processor.

Transmitting pointers to procedures makes effective use of communication links but introduces a difficult problem. A procedure may behave differently depending on the local data. Thus, the same macro instruction may require different amounts of processing time in each PE. In such a device either the PE's must synchronize on every instruction, and therefore potentially lay idle while the slowest PE finishes, or the PE's must be able to buffer the instruction stream to possibly achieve better utilization. However, buffering the instructions requires overhead and may in fact decrease the overall performance.

Evaluation Method. To resolve these two design issues the *DADO* instruction stream was characterized by studying the code implementing the match phase of the *DADO* production system algorithm, (roughly 10 pages of PPL/M, detailed in the following section). Queuing models were developed for each configuration representing the 4 possible combinations: a DADO PE with and without the I/O circuit, and with and without buffering. The four models were simulated using the IBM Research Queuing Network Simulation package, RESQ2, [20]. The package has a number of very powerful simulation primitives including generation of job streams with a variety of distributions times, active queues with a variety of queueing service disciplines as well as mechanisms to provide flow control. Complete details of this study can be found in [14].

Evaluation Results. Figure 6 summarizes the relative throughput of the four configurations working on a problem typical of the size we expect a 1023 node *DADO* to handle: 1000 productions and 1000 working memory elements (although for certain PS programs, R1, for example, we will be able to implement nearly 2500 production rules). The simulations show that the I/O circuit can be expected to nearly double the performance of the *DADO* machine. However, the overhead associated with buffering causes a decrease in performance of 27 and 20 percent in configurations with and without the I/O circuit, respectively.

Figure 6: Relative Performance of Four PE Configurations.

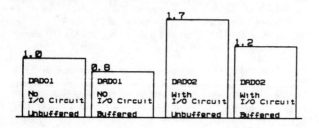

Figure 7 is a comparison of a 5 level *DADO* subtree (comprising 31 PE's) without the I/O circuit, and a 4 level *DADO* subtree, (comprising 15 PE's) with the I/O circuit. The x-axis represents a rough approximation of the number of WM data elements in the system. The graph shows that for a typical size problem a 9 level deep *DADO2* with the I/O circuit will outperform a 10 level deep *DADO1* without the I/O circuit by roughly 15 percent. However, the smaller machine's performance degrades faster than that of the larger machine. The simulations indicate for problems larger than those we anticipate it is worthwhile to dispense with the I/O circuit in favor of additional PE's.

Programming DADO

PL/M [9] is a high-level language designed by Intel Corporation as the host programming environment for applications using the full range of Intel microcomputer and microcontroller chips. A superset of *PL/M*, which we call *PPL/M*, has been implemented as the system-level language for the *DADO* prototypes. *PPL/M* provides a set of facilities to specify operations to be performed by independent PE's in parallel.

Intel's *PL/M* language is a conventional block-oriented language providing a full range of data structures and high-level statements. The following two syntactic conventions have been added to *PL/M* for programming the SIMD mode of operation of *DADO*. The design of these constructs was influenced by the methods employed in specifying parallel computation in the *GLYPNIR* language [12] designed for the *ILLIAC IV* parallel processor. The *SLICE* attribute defines variables and procedures

Figure 7: Performance Comparison of DADO1 and DADO2 on Variable Size Working Memory.

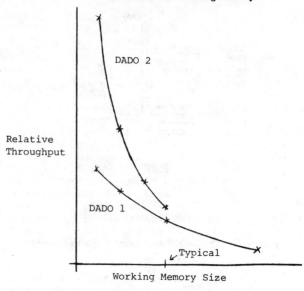

Figure 7: Performance Comparison of DADO1 and DADO2 on Variable Size Working Memory.

that are resident within each PE. The second addition is a syntactic construct, the *DO SIMD block*, which delimits *PPL/M* instructions broadcast to descendant SIMD PE's. (In the following definitions, optional syntactic constructs are represented within square brackets.)

The SLICE attribute:

DECLARE variable[(dimension)] type SLICE;

name: PROCEDURE[(params)] [type] SLICE;

Each declaration of a SLICEd variable will cause an allocation of space for the variable to occur within each PE. SLICEd procedures are automatically loaded within the RAM of each PE by an operating system executive resident in *DADO*'s coprocessor.

Within a *PPL/M* program, an assignment of a value to a SLICEd variable will cause the transfer to occur within each enabled SIMD PE concurrently. A constant appearing in the right hand side will be automatically broadcast to all enabled PE's. Thus, the statement

X=5;

where X is of type BYTE SLICE, will assign the value 5 to each occurrence of X in each enabled SIMD PE. (Thus, at times it is convenient to think of SLICEd variables as vectors which may be operated upon, in whole or in part, in parallel.) However, statements which operate upon SLICEd variables can only be specified within the bounds of a DO SIMD block.

DO SIMD block:

```
DO SIMD;
    r-statement_0;
    ...
    r-statement_n;
END;
```

The r-statement is restricted to be any *PL/M* statement *incorporating only SLICEd variables and constants.*

In addition to the full range of instructions available in *PPL/M*, a *DADO* PE in MIMD mode will have available to it a set of built-in functions to perform the basic tree communication operations, in addition to functions controlling the various modes of execution.

Direct hardware support is provided by the semi-custom I/O chip for each of the global communication functions: BROADCAST, REPORT and RESOLVE, other communication primitives are implemented by firmware embedded in the processor EPROM. The interested reader is referred to [26] for the details of these primitives, as well as a complete specification of the *PPL/M* language.

The RESOLVE instruction recently redesigned from studying DADO1's behavior deserves special mention here. The RESOLVE instruction is used in practice to disable all but a single PE, chosen from among a specified set of PE's. In DADO1, first a SLICEd variable is set to one in all PE's to be included in the candidate set. The RESOLVE instruction is then issued by a PE executing in MIMD mode, causing all but one of the flags in descendant PE's, executing in SIMD mode, to be changed to zero. (Upon executing a RESOLVE instruction, one of the inputs to the MIMD PE will become high if at least one candidate was found in the tree, and low if the candidate set was found to be empty. This condition code is stored in a SLICEd variable, which exists within the MIMD PE.) By issuing an assignment statement, all but the single, chosen PE may be disabled, and a sequence of instructions may be executed on the chosen PE alone. In particular, data from the chosen PE may be communicated to the MIMD PE through a sequence of REPORT commands.

In DADO1, the RESOLVE function is implemented using special sequential code, embedded within the EPROM, that propagates a series of "kill" signals in parallel from all candidate PE's to all (higher-numbered) PE's in the tree. In DADO2, the RESOLVE operation has been generalized to operate on 8-bit data, producing the *maximum* value stored in some candidate PE. Repeated use of this max-RESOLVE function allows for the very rapid selection of multiple byte data. This circuit has proven very useful for a number of DADO algorithms which made use of the tree neighbor communication instructions primarily for ordering data within the tree. The use of the high-speed max-RESOLVE often obviates the need for such communication instructions. Consequently, the view of DADO as a binary tree architecture has become, fortuitously, nearly transparent in most of the algorithms written for DADO thus far.

Conclusion

The largest share of our software effort has concentrated on parallel implementations of various AI applications. The most important of these is an interpreter for the parallel execution of production system programs. A restricted model of production systems has been implemented in *PPL/M* and is currently being tested. Our plans include the completion of an interpreter for a more general version of production systems in the coming months.

We have also become very interested recently in *PROLOG*. Since *PROLOG* may be considered as a special case of production systems, it is our belief that *DADO* can quite naturally support performance improvements of *PROLOG* programs over conventional implementations. Some interesting work in this direction has been reported in [31].

Lastly, we note the relationship of *LISP* to *DADO*. Part of our work has concentrated on providing *LISP* with additional parallel processing primitives akin to those employed in *PPL/M*. We have come to use PSL LISP this purpose due to its relative ease in porting to a new processor.

By way of summary, it is our belief that *DADO* can in fact support the high-speed execution of a very large class of AI applications specifically expert systems implemented in rule form. Coupled with an efficient implementation in VLSI technology, the large-scale parallelism achievable on *DADO* will indeed provide significant performance improvements over von Neumann machines. Indeed, our preliminary statistics suggest that the 1023 PE version of *DADO* is expected to execute *R1*, for example, at an average rate in excess of *85 production system cycles per second!* Present statistics for a reimplementation of R1 on a VAX 11/780 project a performance of 30-50 cycles per second. It is interesting to note further that the DADO2 prototype will be comparable in hardware complexity to the DEC VAX 11/750, a smaller, slower and much less expensive version of the VAX 780 used presently to execute *R1*. Hence, DADO2's parallelism achieves a 50% performance improvement over a machine roughly six times its size.

References

[1] Browning, S., "Hierarchically organized machines," In Mead and Conway (Eds.), *Introduction to VLSI Systems*, 1978.

[2] Browning, S., *The Tree Machine: A Highly Concurrent Computing Environment*, Ph.D. Thesis, California Institute of Technology, 1980.

[3] Buchanan, B. G. and Feigenbaum, E. A., "DENDRAL and Meta-DENDRAL: Their applications dimension," *Artificial Intelligence*, 11:5-24, 1978.

[4] Duda, R., Gashnig, J. and Hart, P.E., "Model design in the PROSPECTOR consultant system for mineral exploration," In D. Michie (Ed.), *Expert Systems in the Micro-Electronic Age*, Edinburgh University Press, 1979.

[5] Flynn, M. J., "Some computer organizations and their effectiveness," *IEEE Transactions on Computers*, 1972.

[6] Forgy, C. L., *On the Efficient Implementation of Production Systems*, Ph.D. Thesis, Carnegie-Mellon University, 1979.

[7] Forgy, C. L., "A note on production systems and ILLIAC IV," Technical Report 130, Department of Computer Science,

Carnegie-Mellon University, 1980.

[8] Forgy, C. L., "RETE: A fast algorithm for the many pattern/many object pattern problem," *Artificial Intelligence Journal*, 1982.

[9] Intel Corporation, *PL/M-51 Users's Guide for the 8051 Based Development System*, Order Number 121966, 1982.

[10] Ishida, T. and S. J. Stolfo, "Simultaneous firing of production rules on tree-structured machines," Technical Report, Department of Computer Science, Columbia University, 1984. (Submitted to *Int. Conf. Fifth Generation Computer Systems*.)

[11] Leiserson, C. E., *Area-Efficient VLSI Computation*, Ph.D. Thesis, Department of Computer Science, Carnegie-Mellon University, 1981.

[12] Lowrie, D. D., T. Layman, D. Daer and J. M. Randal, "GLYPNIR-A programming language for ILLIAC IV," *Comm. ACM*, 18-3, 1975.

[13] McDermott, J., "R1: The formative years," *AI Magazine* 2:21-29, 1981.

[14] Miranker, D. P., "The performance analysis of four competing DADO PE configurations," Technical Report, Department of Computer Science, Columbia University, 1983.

[15] Miranker, D. P., "Performance estimates for the DADO machine: A comparison of TREAT and RETE," Technical Report, Department of Computer Science, Columbia University, 1984. (Submitted to *Int. Conf. on Fifth Generation Computer Systems*.)

[16] Miranker, D. P., "The system-level design of the DADO1 prototype," (in preparation).

[17] Newell, A., "Production systems: models of control structures," In W. Chase (editor), *Visual Information Processing*, Academic Press, 1973.

[18] Nilsson, N., *Fundamental Principles of Artificial Intelligence*, Tioga Press, Menlo Park, California, 1980.

[19] Rychener, M., *Production Systems as a Programming Language for Artificial Intelligence Research*, Ph.D. Thesis, Department of Computer Science, Carnegie-Mellon University, 1976

[20] Sauer, Charles H., Macnair, Edward A., Kurose, James F. "The research queueing package, CMS User's Guide," Technical Report RA 139 #41127, IBM Research Division, 1982.

[21] Schwartz, J. T., "Ultracomputers," *ACM Transactions on Programming Languages and Systems* 3(1), 1980.

[22] Shaw, D. E., "The NON-VON supercomputer," Technical Report, Department of Computer Science, Columbia University, 1982.

[23] Shortliffe, E. H., *Computer-Based Medical Consultations: MYCIN*, New York: American Elsevier, 1976.

[24] Siegel, H. J., L. J. Siegel, F. C. Kemmerer, P. T. Mueller, H. E. Smolky and D. S. Smith, "PASM: A partitionable SIMD/MIMD system for image processing and pattern recognition," *IEEE Transactions on Computers*, 1981.

[25] Stolfo, S. J. and D. E. Shaw, "DADO: A tree-structured machine architecture for production systems," *Proc. National Conference on Artificial Intelligence*, Carnegie-Mellon University and University of Pittsburgh, 1982.

[26] Stolfo, S. J., D. Miranker and M. Lerner, "PPL/M: The system level language for programming the DADO machine," Technical Report, Department of Computer Science, Columbia University, 1982. (Submitted to *ACM TOPLAS*.)

[27] Stolfo, S. J., "The DADO parallel computer," Technical Report Department of Computer Science, Columbia University, 1983. (Submitted to *AI Journal*.)

[28] Stolfo, S. J., "Five algorithms for PS execution on the DADO machine," Technical Report, Department of Computer Science, Columbia University, 1984. (Submitted to *AAAI 84*.)

[29] Stolfo, S. J., "On the design of parallel production system machines: What's in a LIP?," Technical Report, Department of Computer Science, Columbia University, 1984. (Submitted to *Int. Conf. on Fifth Generation Computer Systems*.)

[30] Stolfo, S. J., Vesonder, G. T., "ACE: An expert system supporting analysis and management decision making," *Bell System Technical Journal*, (To appear 1984).

[31] Taylor, S., C. Maio, S. J. Stolfo and D. E. Shaw, "PROLOG on the DADO machine: A parallel system for high-speed logic programming," *Proc. Third International Phoenix Conference on Computers and Communication*, 1984.

PERFORMANCE STUDIES of a
PROLOG MACHINE ARCHITECTURE

T. P. Dobry
A. M. Despain
Y. N. Patt

Computer Science Division
University of California,Berkeley
Berkeley, California 94720

Abstract

The PLM is a co-processor architecture designed for efficient execution of Prolog programs. It is the first prototype of a logic processor for our Aquarius heterogeneous MIMD machine. Currently, it is attached to an NCR/32 system which provides the memory and I/O subsystems as well as processing power for other operations not suited to the functional unit of the PLM (e.g. floating point operations). This paper describes the architecture of the PLM and some aspects of its implementation. We conclude with an analysis of some performance data obtained from a simulation of the design.

1. Introduction

This paper describes a special purpose processor, the PLM, which we have designed for high performance execution of Prolog programs. It is part of Aquarius [4], a high , performance heterogeneous MIMD multiprocessor being designed at Berkeley. Figure 1 is an overall block diagram of Aquarius.

The goal of the Aquarius Project is to understand the principles by which a machine can be organized from diverse functional units such that it will concurrently execute both symbolic and numeric operations. The approach is to support logic-programming at the control level and array operations at the functional level.

It is envisioned that the machine will employ a variety of autonomous VLSI components; each with considerable, if specialized, computation capability. The control language is adapted to its source language and can best be thought of as an intermediate form of PROLOG [3,8], much as P-code is thought of as an intermediate form of PASCAL. It is compiled prior to execution from PROLOG or other high-level, logic-programming languages. In this paper, we focus on the performance of a processor architecture, specialized for the execution of the control language.

The Aquarius group has recently designed a special co--processor, the Programmed Logic Machine (PLM), as the first experimental processor of the new system. We have simulated it at several levels of detail during its design, and have now constructed it in TTL logic. It is composed of about 500 chips, ranging from simple gates to LSI circuits (e.g. PAL's). At the time of this writing, the TTL version of the processor is being debugged, so at the moment, we can only report on our simulated results. The purpose of this paper is to report on the improvement in performance that can be achieved by a specialized architecture.

2. The Architecture

This section describes the overall architecture of the Aquarius-I system as shown in Figure 2. The processor is attached to the PM Bus of the host NCR/32 system. Also attached to the bus are the host central processor, I/O co-processor, and floating point co-processor, as well as the main memory unit and its associated address translation unit. Further details of the NCR/32 system can be found in [1]. Section 2.1 describes the abstract execution model and Instruction Set Architecture (ISA) of the PLM. Section 2.2 describes the PLM interface to the PM bus, the PLM Memory Interface unit (PMI). Section 2.3 describes the Prolog engine.

2.1. Abstract Model and ISA

2.1.1. Abstract Model. As seen in Figure 3, a Prolog [3] program is a collection of procedures. Each procedure is a collection of clauses. A clause has a head (or goal) and a body consisting of procedure calls (sub-goals). If the body is empty, the clause becomes a "fact". The head has a predicate (or functor) and a collection of arguments (which can be empty).

Execution proceeds as follows: [†] Given a goal (query) (with the format of a head):

(1) Find the first clause in the program which has a matching predicate and whose arguments will "unify" [7] with the goal. Unification is a matching process which will generally bind some variables.

(2) Invoke each sub-goal, of the body of the clause, as a goal.

-If all sub-goals succeed, then the clause succeeds and all variable bindings are valid.

-If a sub-goal fails, backtrack to the most recent subgoal visited during the execution at which a further choice exists (indicated by a "choice-point").

-If all. the choices within a clause's sub-goals are exhausted (return failure), then give up on the current clause and try to unify the goal with the next clause in the procedure.

-If there are no further matching clauses, return failure.

The design of the PLM is based on an abstract model for Prolog execution and instruction set architecture (ISA) originally described by Warren [12] and modified by Dobry, Patt and Despain [6]. Under this model, the address space of the PLM is divided into two separate and distinct areas, the Code Space and the Data Space. The Code Space is a pseudo-static

---

[†] An excellent tutorial on Prolog is in the text by Clocksin and Mellish [2].

Reprinted from *Proceedings of the 12th International Symposium on Computer Architecture*, 1985, pages 180-190. Copyright © 1985 by The Institute of Electrical and Electronics Engineers, Inc.

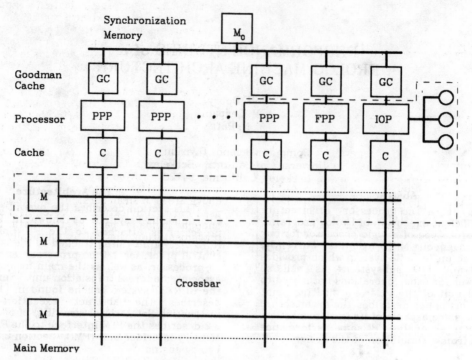

Figure 1: Aquarius Architecture

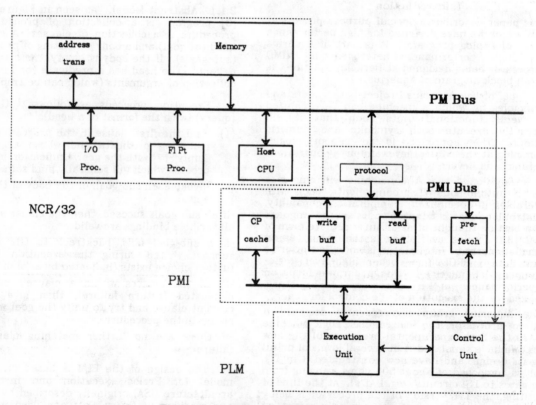

Figure 2: Aquarius-I System Architecture

area (pseudo-static due to the Prolog predicates **assert** and **retract**). It contains the code constituting the Prolog program and other information used to describe atoms (akin to the property lists of LISP). Items in the Code Space have variable length and addressing is at the byte level. The instruction prefetch unit and some built-in functions have access to the Code Space. The Instruction set is described below.

Prolog Program

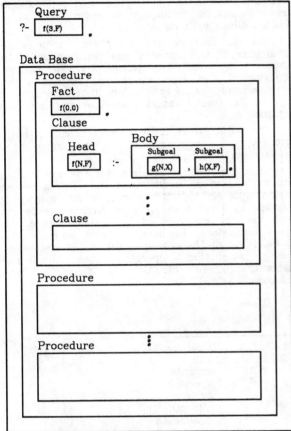

Figure 3 : Prolog Program structure.

The Data Space contains tagged 32-bit words representing all data items and state information for a running Prolog program. It is addressed as 32-bit words. For data items, of the 32 bits, as few as 4 and as many as 6 bits are used for tags depending on the type of the data item. Four data types are distinguishable by the processor via two primary tag bits as seen in Figure 4. They are **reference** representing Prolog variables, both bound and unbound; **constant** representing various types of constant data; and two forms of compound data, **list** and **structure**. In addition, each data item has a *cdr*-bit in its tag field to support a *cdr*-coded representation of compound data, and a garbage collection bit used by a garbage collection mechanism (via a built-in function). Secondary tag bits (and in the case of constants, possibly terciary tag bits in the identifier field) may further refine the data types, but these are generally not recognized by the instruction set and are used only by built-in functions.

The Data Space is further divided into three main areas: the Heap, the Stack and the Trail. The Heap contains all of the compound data items generated by the program and possibly global variables (as well as an area for "side-effect" variables used by some built-in functions). It is allocated as a LIFO and only deallocated upon backtracking. It is the area which participates in garbage collection. The Stack contains two forms of frames, environments and choice points. An environment, allocated for an individual clause, contains a small amount of state information associated with the clause and space for all permanent variables (variables not residing in registers) used by the clause. A choice point contains sufficient state information to restore the state of the processor in the event of failure and subsequent backtracking. Environments and choice points are created and removed by explicit instructions in the instruction set. The Stack is allocated and deallocated as a LIFO and is not garbage collected. The Trail contains pointers to the variables in the Stack and Heap which have been bound and must be unbound upon backtracking. It is allocated and deallocated as a LIFO. In addition to the above areas, a small scratchpad area called the PDL is used during unification of nested lists and structures. Though logically part of the Data Space, in our implementation the PDL is physically located in the execution unit.

2.1.2. The ISA. The instruction set of the PLM is designed to implement the above algorithm. In general, a Prolog program is compiled into the instruction set with each symbol mapping into approximately one instruction plus some "glue" to hold them all together. The instructions may be divided into six groups; Procedure Control, Indexing, Clause Control, Get, Put, and Unify

Reference

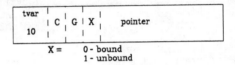

Constant

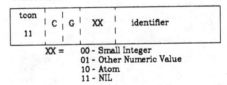

Structure

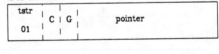

List

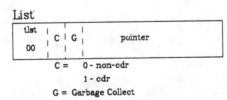

Figure 4: Data Types

instructions. Each group is briefly described below. The complete instruction set is shown in Table 1.

The Procedure Control group consists of instructions for managing the choice point for a procedure. They include instructions to create the choice point (**try**, **try_me_else**), modify the choice point (**retry**, **retry_me_else**), and discard the choice point (**trust**, **trust_me_else**). These instructions identify the block of code corresponding to the clause to be attempted. Two additional instructions (**cut**, **cutd**) are provided to discard choice points in support of the **cut** operation of Prolog.

The Indexing group of instructions works in conjunction with the Procedure Control instructions to provide a more efficient selection of clauses within a procedure for which unification should be attempted. They have the effect of filtering out those clauses which can be identified at compile time that will not unify with the invoking goal. The **switch_on_term** instruction uses the *type* of the first argument of the invoking goal to filter clauses. The **switch_on_constant** (**switch_on_structure**) instruction is used when the type of the first argument has been identified as a constant (structure). It hashes the constant (functor of the structure) to further filter the clauses.

The Procedure Control and Indexing instructions are used to generate the code for a procedure. Figure 5 shows a generic block of procedure code for a general procedure.

The Clause Control group includes instructions for sequencing the invocation of subgoals (**call**, **execute**, **proceed**) and for managing the environment of the clause (**allocate**, **deallocate**).

The Get instructions are used to unify the arguments of the invoking goal with those of the clause being tried. The general pattern matching behavior of the unify operation provides a dual purpose functionality for the Get instructions; either as a verifier (match) or as a constructor (binding) of arguments.

The Put instructions are data transfer instructions to set up the argument registers in preparation for subgoal invocation.

Unify instructions are used for the construction and unification of compound data. Such a process begins with an appropriate get or put instruction followed by a series of unify instructions to process each element/argument of the list/structure. The operation performed is determined by the mode (read or write) set by the preceding get or put instruction. Each instruction operates on the next element/argument of the list/structure being processed.

Procedure Control		Indexing		Clause Control	
try	L	switch_on_term	Lc,Ll,Ls	call	P,n
retry	L	switch_on_constant	n,ff	execute	P
trust	L	switch_on_structure	n,ff	proceed	
try_me_else	L			escape	BI
retry_me_else	L			allocate	
trust_me_else	fail			deallocate	
cut					
cutd	L				
fail					
Get		**Put**		**Unify**	
get_variable	Vi,Ai	put_variable	Vi,Ai	unify_variable	Vi
get_value	Vi,Ai	put_value	Vi,Ai	unify_value	Vi
		put_unsafe_value	Yi,Ai	unify_unsafe_value	Yi
get_constant	C,Ai	put_constant	C,Ai	unify_constant	C
get_list	Ai	put_list	Ai		
get_structure	F,Ai	put_structure	F,Ai	unify_cdr	Vi
get_nil	Ai	put_nil	Ai	unify_nil	
				unify_void	N

Table 1 : PLM Instruction Set

```
      procedure   a

        switch_on_term      Lc,Ll,Ls
Lv:     try                 Cx
        retry               Cy
        ...
        trust               Cn
Lc:     switch_on_constant  N,ff
          hash table
        ...
Ll:     try                 Cz
        ...
        trust               Cm
Ls:     switch_on_structure
          hash table
        ...
```

Figure 5: Procedure Code

```
Ci:    allocate
       get instructions
       put instructions
       call              SG1
       put instructions
       call              SG2
       ...
       put instructions
       deallocate
       execute           SGn
```

Figure 6: Clause Code

The Clause Control, Get, Put, and Unify instructions are used to construct the clause code blocks for each clause in the program. Figure 6 shows a typical format for clause code.

In addition to the explicit PLM instructions, the Prolog Engine must provide several fundamental operations in support of Prolog. They are:

dereference: used to follow chains of reference pointers which arise due to binding of variables to other variables during unification.

decdr: used while unifying lists and structures to follow *cdr* pointers.

fail: used for backtracking when a failure condition arises during unification. **fail** restores the machine state, including the failure address, from the current choice point. Restoration of the necessary trailed variables to unbound also occurs.

unify: used to unify arbitrary Prolog data items binding variables as required. **unify** uses the PDL as a scratch pad for nested lists and structures. Such unifications occur depth first.

bind: used to perform the binding of values to variables.

trail: used to manage the trail during binding. **trail** determines if a particular variable must be trailed.

2.2. The PMI

The PMI is responsible for all interface operations between the Prolog engine and the system bus. This includes logic for meeting the bus protocol and several modules buffering memory accesses to both the Code Space and the Data Space, as well as the logic for prioritizing and sequencing these memory accesses on the bus.

The need for the Data Space access buffering arises from the difference in cycle times between the Prolog engine (100 ns) and the NCR system (150 ns). The primary buffer is the write buffer. All memory write operations initiated by the PLM are queued in the write buffer awaiting bus access to be sent to the memory subsystem. This allows the processor to continue execution seeing an effective write access time of one cycle. A memory read request by the PLM is also buffered awaiting access to the bus. In this case, the PLM processor must wait for the read to be serviced. A simple scheme to avoid memory data consistency problems is implemented; read request servicing is delayed until all of the pending write requests have been serviced.

In addition to read and write buffering, a special choice point (CP) cache is provided by the PMI. Only the current choice point is cached. The CP cache is maintained using a write-through paradigm and is invalidated any time the current choice point is discarded. Revalidation of the CP cache takes place only as a side effect of a subsequent choice point access from memory at the next fail operation. This eliminates excess bus cycles for revalidation of the cache. With a valid CP cache, the processor sees an effective CP access time of one cycle.

In addition to Data Space buffering, the PMI provides Code Space buffering and partial instruction decode with its Prefetch Unit. A small instruction buffer, holding up to four instructions, is included. Since the PLM instructions are variable length, the Prefetch Unit uses information in the opcodes to align the instructions and operand specifiers before buffering. Thus instructions are provided to the PLM control unit in a uniform, ready to use format. In addition, the Prefetch Unit recognizes all control flow change instructions as they are fetched. Due to the simplicity of most of these instructions, the Prefetch Unit can continue fetching through many branches in control flow. Only a few of the instructions require the Prefetch Unit to wait for the Execution Unit to catch up and decide on the direction of control flow. One additional source of control flow change is the fail operation. This causes the Prefetch Unit to flush the instruction buffer and begin fetching again at the backtrack point.

Finally, the PMI controller must coordinate the efforts of the various buffers and units of the PMI. This is done by imposing a priority scheme on accesses to the PMI bus. Instruction fetch access has the lowest priority for the bus unless the instruction buffer becomes empty, in which case it has highest priority. Thus prefetch takes place as time permits as long as there is at least one instruction ready to execute. At a priority just above the low priority instruction fetch are memory read requests; followed at the next higher priority by memory write requests. This ensures that the read requests are held until the write buffer clears.

An analysis of the effects on performance of the various buffers and units of the PMI can be found in Section 4. Further details on the PMI can be found in Williams [13].

2.3. The Prolog Engine

The Prolog engine consists of two units as seen in Figure 2, the Execution Unit and the Control Unit. The Control Unit consists of a control store containing wide horizontal microcode and a microsequencer for executing the microcode. The Control Unit is primarily responsible for directing the actions of the Execution Unit under its own command as well as communicating with the PMI controller. However, facilities are also provided for control input from the NCR/32 system to allow the host processor to act as the "front panel" for the PLM for debugging and testing.

Figure 7 shows the overall organization of the Execution Unit. It consists of two major units, a register file and an ALU, together with the bus and stage register interconnections. Six major busses are provided organized in three bus pairs. The register file contains all of the processor registers supporting the instruction set. These are:

P   - Program Pointer. This register contains the Code Space address of the next instruction to be executed. This is the PC of a conventional processor.

CP   - Continuation Pointer. This register contains the Codes Space address of the next instruction to be executed upon successful completion of the current clause. This is analogous to a return pointer.

E   - Environment Register. This register contains a Data Space address pointing to the current environment frame on the Stack.

N   - Environment Size. This register contains the size of the last allocated environment frame on the Stack.

B   - Backtracking Register. This register contains a Data Space address pointing to the active choice point frame on the Stack. It is used for backtracking.

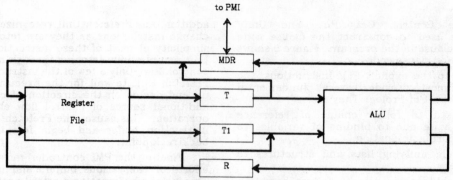

to PMI

Figure 7: Execution Unit

H   - Heap Pointer. This register contains a Data Space address pointing to the current top of the Heap.

HB   - Heap Backtrack Pointer. This register contains a Data Space address pointing to the top of the Heap at the last backtracking point (choice point). It is used to reclaim Heap space upon backtracking.

S   - Structure Pointer. This register contains a Data Space address pointing into the Heap. It represents the location of the next item of an existing list or structure currently being processed. The S register may also contain the constant **NIL**.

TR   - Trail Pointer. This register contains a Data Space address indicating the current top of the Trail.

In addition the processor includes the argument registers and the PDL. The ALU performs the arithmetic and comparison operations in support of the instruction set including address computation for operand memory accesses as well as providing the facilities for some built-in functions.

The execution of a PLM instruction is patterned on the three stage model described by Tick and Warren [10]. The T, T1, R,and MDR registers as well as the registers in the register file separate the stages of operation. (Note that the ALU does not contain registers and therefore does not divide a stage). In addition, bypass paths are provided around stages for efficiency. The three stages are:

C stage -
Access registers. In this stage, data is accessed from the register file and placed in the T and T1 registers.

E stage -
ALU operation. In this stage the T and T1 register contents are used as data for ALU operations with results going to the R and MDR registers. Memory operations may also be considered to take place during this stage.

P stage -
Put away results to registers. In this stage, the data in the R and MDR registers are put away into the register file.

Access to memory takes place in parallel through the MDR register and its associated MAR. The microcode controlling the Execution Unit is written to utilize the stages in parallel as much as possible within each macroinstruction. A typical microroutine may involve one C stage operation, several E stage

operations, and then a P stage operation.

A static analysis of the microcode for the PLM shows that the percentage of states utilizing zero,one,two, or three bus pairs is as follows:

no bus pairs	13.9
one bus pair	53.7
two bus pairs	26.8
three bus pairs	5.6

States which use no busses are those that perform microbranches based on ALU operations performed in the previous cycle. Relatively few states are able to make use of all three stages of the Execution Unit simultaneously.

It is also possible to overlap the execution of microinstructions across the PLM macroinstruction boundary; however, data dependencies between the macroinstructions reduces the availability of overlap. Simulation results on the current benchmark set show that while 30% of the instructions executed could be overlapped by one cycle with the next instruction, this would result in only a 3.6% speedup in execution time. At present, overlap between macroinstructions is not supported.

A more detailed discussion of the design trade-offs can be found in our previous paper [6].

3. Simulators and Benchmarks

At present, the PLM architecture has been simulated at two levels of detail. The Level 1 simulator models at the ISA level and the Level 2 simulator models at the microarchitecture level. In addition to providing execution of PLM assembly code, the simulators provide a debugging facility for monitoring and debugging the execution of compiled Prolog programs and an instrumentation package for measuring the performance and behavior patterns of the design. The simulators are written in the C language and run on a VAX11/750 under Berkeley (4.2 BSD) Unix†. Details of the features available from the simulators can be found in Dobry [5].

The Level 1 simulator models the PLM at the ISA level. Each PLM macroinstruction is modeled by a C routine. This level of simulation is useful for debugging and observing execution of a compiled Prolog program. Its instrumentation package provides frequency measurements of instructions and fundamental operations as well as statistics on Data Space area usage and memory reference counts.

† Unix is a Trademark of Bell Laboratories.

The Level 2 simulator models the PLM at the microarchitecture level with each microinstruction implemented as a C routine. This level of simulation is useful for measuring the performance of the design and for observing how changes to the design affect the performance. The instrumentation package of the Level 2 simulator provides those features of Level 1 as well as such timing information as total clock ticks, idle time for memory access, Prolog engine bus utilization, and prefetch behavior.

The base model in the level 2 simulator makes several simplifying assumptions. For example, memory accesses are assumed to take a single clock cycle and instruction prefetch is assumed to be perfect (i.e. no wait is ever required for instruction fetch). Built-in functions implemented via the escape mechanism are also not accurately timed; a standard three cycles is allotted for these operations (the current benchmark set uses only very simple built-in functions so this assumption is not unreasonable). The operations performed by the PMI are not simulated directly by the Level 2 simulator but their effects may be measured via switches which activate models of these operations to act on the clock counter of the simulator. For example, the Prefetch Unit is modeled to include processor stalls due to jump instructions. A more realistic memory access time of three cycles, corresponding to the access time of the NCR/32, may be selected as well as separate switches to enable models for the Write Buffer (and associated processor stalls for data reads) and the CP Cache to measure the effect on performance of the system. The measurements obtained from the Level 2 simulator are discussed in Section 4.

A set of benchmark programs has been used to verify the correctness and measure the performance of the PLM. They are shown in Table 2 together with their static size in lines of PLM code. The programs in the left column are the benchmarks provided by Warren [11] which allowed us to compare the performance of the PLM with Warren's results. They include a naive reverse of a list of 30 numbers (nrev1), a quicksort program of 50 numbers (qs4), a structure oriented sorting problem (serialize), a symbolic differentiation program with four examples (times10,divide10,log10,ops8), and a data base query problem (query). The right column of Table 2 lists seven additional more complicated programs from various sources which we also analyzed. Two simple list concatenation examples are included on lists of five elements, one determinate (con1) and the other non-determinate (con6) providing all solutions. In addition, the benchmarks include a solution to the Tower of Hanoi problem with 8 disks (hanoi), a solution to the queens on a chess board problem for a 4x4 board (queens), the proof of the theorem "muiiu" in Hofstadter's mu math system (mutest), the sieve of Eritosthenes algorithm for finding prime numbers less than 100 (pri2), and a branch and bound circuit design problem using NAND gates to design a 2 to 1 MUX (ckt2).

The benchmarks were hand compiled from the original Prolog statements. When a compiler was later available, many of these programs were compiled and also run for comparison. The results are described in Section 4.

4. Measurements

This section describes the results obtained for the benchmark programs executed on the simulators. First, a discussion of instruction use frequency and cost is given. Then performance of the PLM is discussed under various assumptions about memory access time.

4.1. Instruction Frequencies and Timing

Table 3 shows the instruction set of the PLM sorted by average frequency of usage for the benchmark set. Also included in the Table is a measure of the time required for each instruction, in cycles. Since the behavior of many instructions is dependent on the data it is operating on (i.e. is dereferencing or decdring required?) and the machine state (read or write mode), as well as the form of the instruction being used (X or Y register form), the timing data must include variable parameters. Some typical values for these parameters are:

a - is the time to find the top of the stack. (a = 3)

c - is the time for a decdr operation. (c = 3)

d - is the time for a dereference operation. (d = 5)

t - is the time for a trail operation. (t = 4)

u - is the time for a unify operation. (u = 4)

l - is the number of loop iterations.

These are only rough estimates as many of them are very data dependent. For example, unification time may be much longer for nested lists and structures than for a constant or variable. Dereference and decdr operations take zero time if no action is needed. These rough figures may be used to generate some "average" time for each instruction, which when multiplied by the frequency produces the Weight column of Table 3.

The data provided in Table 3 was instrumental in fine tuning the data path and microcode in the PLM design. Attempts were made to optimize frequently used or costly instructions.

Warren Benchmarks			Additional Benchmarks	
Program	**Lines**		**Program**	**Lines**
nrev1	73		concat	
qs4	125		con1	29
serialize			con6	33
palin25	187		hanoi	55
differen			queens	267
times10	222		mutest	142
divide10	222		pri2	141
log10	216		ckt2	601
ops8	214			
query	340			

Table 2: Benchmark Programs

4.2. Performance Measurements

Table 4 summarizes the performance results obtained from the Level 2 simulated execution of the benchmark set. Measurements are provided in KLIPS (Kilo Logical Inferences Per Second). A logical inference is taken to be the invocation of a goal and is counted as the number of **call**, **execute**, and **escape** instructions executed for these results. The table includes the number of inferences counted for each

Instruction	Frequency (%)	Time (cycles)	Weight
put_value	10.7		32.1
X		2	
Y		4	
unify_variable	8.8		41.4
read			
X		5	
Y		6	
write		3	
get_list	7.27		72.7
bound		3+d	
unbound		3+t+d	
unify_cdr	6.88		34.4
read		6	
write		4	
unify_value	4.96		71.9
read			
X		6+2d+c+u	
Y		9+2d+c+u	
write			
X		3	
Y		6	
escapes	4.9	variable	
switch_on_term	4.87	5+1	29.2
unify_nil	4.86		19.5
read		6	
write		2	
get_structure	4.11		53.4
bound		6+d	
unbound		4+t+d	
execute	4.01	1	4.0
allocate	3.47	8+a	38.2

Instruction	Frequency (%)	Time (cycles)	Weight
get_variable	3.44		8.6
X		2	
Y		3	
unify_constant	3.33		26.6
read		6+d+c	
write		2	
deallocate	2.87	6	17.2
put_constant	2.71	2	5.4
proceed	2.65	1	2.7
try_me_else	2.45	17+a	49.0
call	2	1	2.0
cut	1.85	10	18.5
get_constant	1.83	2+u+d	20.1
put_variable	1.79		6.3
X		4	
Y		3	
get_value	1.44		18.7
X		3+u+d	
Y		5+u+d	
trust_me_else	1.32	5	6.6
get_nil	1.29	2+u+d	12.9
put_unsafe_value	1.24	6,9,10+d	11.2
retry_me_else	0.88	2	1.8
switch_on_structure	0.866	8+d	11.3
put_list	0.769	3	2.3
try	0.711	17+a	14.2
fails	0.564	19+4l	13.0
trust	0.35	5	1.8
unify_void	0.324	1+5l	1.9
switch_on_constant	0.201	5+d	2.0
retry	0.0593	2	0.1
put_structure	0.052	4	0.3
unify_unsafe_value	0.0127	6,9+d 10+2d+c+u	0.1
put_nil	0.00267	2	0.005

where :

a - is the time to find the top of the stack.
c - is the time for a decdr operation.
d - is the time for a dereference operation.
t - is the time for a trail operation.
u - is the time for a unify operation.
l - is the number of loop iterations.

Table 3: Instruction Frequency and Timing

benchmark.

Five sets of data are shown in Table 4. Column 1 shows the base performance of the PLM under the simplifying assumptions mentioned in Section 3, (single cycle memory reference and perfect instruction prefetch). Column 2 adds a more realistic instruction fetch model which includes the prefetch scheme implemented by the PMI. The resulting 6% slowdown is a result of processor stalls due to jump instructions which suspend the prefetching activity. Column 3 adds the realistic three cycle memory access requirements for all accesses of the current implementation. The result is a 41% slowdown from the ideal basic model.

The PLM design incorporates several features to enhance performance. Column 4 of Table 4 shows the resulting performance data when the write buffer is incorporated in the model, i.e. memory write accesses require one cycle, while memory read accesses require at least 3 cycles (longer if the write buffer is not empty at the time of the read). The result is a 7% gain over column 3 to 66% of base performance. Finally, Column 5 includes the choice point cache to complete the modeling of the PLM design. The resulting data shows the expected performance of the PLM on the

benchmark set. A peak speed of 482 KLIPS with an average of 206 KLIPS for these benchmarks represents a performance improvement of 27.6% over the realistic measurement of column 3 and a realization of 75.6% of the ideal base model.

In Table 5 the benchmark program measurements are compared for hand coded vs compiler generated [9] PLM code. The table shows that the compiler produces code comparable to hand coding in most cases and even out-performs hand coding in three cases (*palin25*, *qs4*, and *query*). Two exceptions are notable, *pri2* and *queens*. In these instances, the compiler coded performance data is worse than hand coded when measured in KLIPS, but when actual running time in microseconds is compared, the compiled code is faster. In particular for *queens*, the hand coded version appears to be more than twice as fast in terms of KLIPS, yet the compiler version is actually slightly faster in elapsed time. These anomalies are due to the fact that the compiler uses

Bench Marks	# of Inferences	Base (1)	Prefetch (2)	Memory Data (3)	Write Buffer (4)	CP Cache (5)
Warren						
nrev1	500	238	216	169	188	188
qs4	843	213	203	125	141	153
palin25	421	183	176	111	121	132
times10	23	104	97	61	69	70
divide10	23	89	83	52	60	60
log10	15	183	164	118	137	137
ops8	25	166	155	96	107	117
query	5904	452	411	278	306	336
Average		204	188	126	141	149
Other						
con1	8	426	383	300	346	346
con6	66	658	624	386	420	482
hanoi	2297	375	363	190	213	314
queens	1357	421	409	222	246	314
mutest	1285	142	135	82	91	104
pri2	2728	293	287	151	166	227
ckt2	6868	141	139	81	93	106
Average		351	334	202	225	270
Overall Avg		272	256	161	180	206

Table 4: Performance Results (in Klips).

Compiler	Klips	µs	Hand	Klips	µs
Ccon1	305	26.2	con1	346	23.1
Ccon6	465	142	con6	482	137
Cdivide10	55	433	divide10	60	380
Chanoi	310	9063	hanoi	314	7323
Clog10	79	202	log10	137	109
Cmutest	89	14852	mutest	104	12407
Cnrev1	115	4362	nrev1	188	2657
Cops8	106	246	ops8	117	214
Cpalin25	134	3152	palin25	132	3186
Cpri2	191	10001	pri2	227	12004
Cqs3	174	4854	qs4	153	5509
Cqueens	148	4223	queens	314	4321
Cquery	367	17342	query	336	17571
Ctimes10	63	382	times10	70	330

Table 5: Compiler Results

fewer "call" operations by compiling more built-in operations in-line for subgoal resolution. This result identifies a weakness in the KLIPS measurements which remains to be resolved.

5 Conclusions

It is interesting to compare the expected performance of PLM to other computer systems executing Prolog programs. A comparison of running time for the Warren benchmark set is shown in Table 6. The first two columns are due to Warren [11].

Benchmark	Prolog-10I Interpreter	Prolog-10 Compiler	PLM Machine
nrev1	1160	53.7	2.66
qs4 serialize	1344	75.0	5.50
palin25 differen	602	40.2	3.19
times10	76.2	3.00	0.329
divide10	84.4	2.94	0.380
log10	49.2	1.92	0.109
ops8	63.7	2.24	0.213
query	8888	185	17.57

Table 6: Comparison with Warren's Results (in ms).

Column 1 represents the timing in milliseconds for the benchmarks as interpreted by DEC-10 Prolog. Column 2 represents the timing for the benchmarks as compiled running on the DEC-10. The right hand column shows the simulated performance of the PLM processor taken from our measurements. It can be seen that compilation to an optimized instruction set for Prolog can gain factors of 20 over interpretation. It can also be seen that a specialized PLM architecture can produce an additional gain of a factor of 10.

Table 7 illustrates all the estimates known to us that have been made of Prolog execution systems. With Prolog being a relatively new language and specialized Prolog architectures just now appearing on the scene, detailed comparisons among such machines are not readily available. We can, howver, compare the PLM and the PSI machine of the Japanese Fifth Generation Project. Both were explicitly designed to execute Prolog. Both employ microcode. Both are about the same physical size.

The primary conclusion of this work is that a specialized architecture can greatly improve performance for compiled Prolog over general purpose processors. Our architecture for the PLM, while adhering to the general Von Neumann model, provides several distinguishing features directed at the execution model of Prolog. First, a specialized instruction set aimed at those operations required by Prolog both simplifies the compilation task and enhances the performance of the machine at Prolog tasks. The tagged architecture to support Prolog data types, and a hardware hashing operation for efficient filtering of clauses to be attempted are two features which support this instruction set. In addition, the PLM implements four stack areas, the usual environment stack (Stack), the Heap for Prolog compound data items, the PDL used for unification, and the Trail. The Trail stack is particularly unique to Prolog in that its purpose is to identify variables which must be unbound during backtracking. Specialized registers are provided in the architecture to support these four stacks. At the microarchitecture level, the PDL is maintained entirely within the processor to enhance unification. In the design of the processor, the tuning of the data path and control unit allow both parallelism and cycle reduction within the microcode implementing the instruction set. Finally, the addition of a specialized cache directed at the Prolog model (the CP cache), as well as more conventional buffering techniques (the write buffer and prefetch unit) allow us to realized further performance gains. In our heterogeneous multiple co-processor system, Aquarius-I, we will employ the PLM along with other specialized co-processors, e.g. floating point and I/O processors. We expect the result to be high performance execution of a wide spectrum of programs that include symbolic, logic and numeric calculations.

ACKNOWLEDGEMENTS

The Aquarius Project, of which this work is a part, is a group effort. The authors wish to express their gratitude to the other members of the group: Barry Fagin, Philip Bitar, Jung-Herng Chang, Carl Ponder, Wen-Mei Hwu, Steve Melvin, Michael Shebanow, Vason Srini, Peter Van Roy, Wayne Citrin, Robert Williams, Michael Kates, Rick McGeer, and Robert Yung.

This work was partially sponsored by Defense Advance Research Projects Agency (DOD) and monitored by Naval Electronic System Command under Contract No. N00039-84-C-0089 and Contract No. N0039-83-C-0107. Support from the Advanced Computer Architecture Laboratory of the Lawrence Berkeley Laboratory is gratefully acknowledged. Part of the work was sponsored by the California MICRO program. Thanks are also due to the NCR Corporation for their generous contribution of equipment, and for funding part of the work done under the project.

PERFORMANCE ESTIMATES FOR LOGIC-PROGRAMMING SYSTEMS			
DETERMINISTIC CONCATENATE (ONLY).			
Machine	System	Performance	Reference
Berkeley PLM	(TTL)/Compiled	425,000 LIPS	Simul(no wait)
TICK & WARREN	VLSI	415,000 LIPS	Est: Tick&Warren
Aquarius I	(TTL)/Compiler	305,000	Simul(NCR bus)
SYMBOLICS3600	Microcoded	110,000 LIPS	Est: Tick&Warren
DEC 2060	Warren Compiled	43,000 LIPS	Warren
J. 5th Gen PSI	Microcoded	30,000 LIPS	Est: PSI paper
IBM 3033	Waterloo	27,000 LIPS	Warren
VAX-780	Macrocoded	15,000 LIPS	Est: Tick&Warren
SUN-2	Quintus Comp.	14,000 LIPS	Warren
LMI/LAMBDA	Uppsala	8,000 LIPS	Warren
VAX-780	POPLOG	2,000 LIPS	Warren
VAX-780	M-PROLOG	2,000 LIPS	Warren
VAX-780	C-PROLOG	1,500 LIPS	Warren
SYMBOLICS3600	Interpreter	1,500 LIPS	Warren
PDP 11/70	Interpreter	1,000 LIPS	Warren
Z-80	MicroProlog	120 LIPS	Warren
Apple-II	Interpreter	8 LIPS	Warren
PERFORMANCE ON GENERAL BENCHMARK PROGRAMS			
Machine	System	Performance	Reference
Berkeley PLM	(TTL)/Compiled	205,000 LIPS	Simulator result
LMI/LAMBDA	Micro/Compiled	12,400 LIPS	LMI Corp.
J. 5th Gen PPC	Microcoded	10,000 LIPS(est)	NTIS (#N83-31379)
LM-2	Microcoded	9,500 LIPS	Prolog Digest v2.20
LMI/LAMBDA	Macro/Compiled	6,200 LIPS	LMI Corp.
SYMBOLICS 3600	Microcoded	5,000 LIPS	Prolog Digest v2.20
LMI/LAMBDA	Micro/Interpreter	3,400 LIPS	LMI Corp.
LMI/LAMBDA	Macro/Interpreter	1,700 LIPS	LMI Corp.
Apple-II	PASCAL-Interpreter	10 LIPS	Colmerauer
PERFORMANCE ON THE WARREN BENCHMARK			
(list30 list50 times10 divide10 log10 ops8 palin25 query)			
Machine	System	Performance	Reference
Berkeley PLM	(TTL)/Compiled	149,216 LIPS	Simulator result
LMI/LAMBDA	Micro/Compiled	12,400 LIPS	LMI Corp.
DEC 2060	Warren Compiled	12,175 LIPS	Warren Thesis

Table 7: Performance Comparison Among Logic Programming Systems

6. References

1. , *NCR/32 General Information*, NCR Corp., Dayton, Ohio (1983).

2. W. F. Clocksin and C. S. Mellish, *Programming in Prolog*, Springer-Verlag, New York (1981).

3. A. Colmerauer, H. Kanoui, and M. van Caneghem, *Etude et Realization d'un System Prolog*, Groupe de Researche en Intelligence Artificielle, Univ. d'Aix-Marseille, Luminy (1979).

4. A. M. Despain and Y. N. Patt, "The Aquarius Project," *Digest of Papers, COMPCON Spring 1984*, pp. 364-367 IEEE Press, (Spring 1984).

5. Tep Dobry, "PLM Simulator Reference Manual," Technical Note, Computer Science Division, UCB (July 1984).

6. T.P. Dobry, Y.N. Patt, and A.M. Despain, "Design Decisions Influencing the Microarchitecture For A Prolog Machine," *MICRO 17 Proceedings*, (Oct. 1984).

7. J. A. Robinson, "A Machine Oriented Logic Based on the Resolution Principle," *J. ACM* **12**(1) pp. 23-41 (Jan.1965).

8. P. Roussel, *Prolog: Manuel de Reference et d'Utilisation*, Groupe de Researche en Intelligence Artificielle, Univ. d'Aix-Marseille, Luminy (1975).

9. Peter Van Roy, "A Prolog Compiler for the PLM," *Masters Report*, Computer Science, University of California, (August 1984).

10. Evan Tick and David Warren, "Towards a Pipelined Processor," Tech. Report, SRI A.I. Center, Menlo Park, Ca. (Aug. 1983).

11. D. H. D. Warren, "Applied Logic - Its Use and Implementation as Programming Tool," Ph.D. Thesis, Univ. Edinburgh, Scotland (1977). Available as Tech. Note 290, AI Center, SRI International

12. D. H. D. Warren, *An Abstract Prolog Instruction Set*, AI Center, SRI International, Menlo Park, CA 94025 (1983).

13. Robert L. Williams, "A Prolog Machine Memory Interface For A NCR/32 Microcomputer," *Masters Report*, Computer Science, University of California, (July 1984).